A TIME FOR ANGELS

A TIME
FOR ANGELS

THE TRAGICOMIC
HISTORY OF THE
LEAGUE OF NATIONS
by ELMER BENDINER

 ALFRED A. KNOPF

New York, 1 9 7 5

This is a Borzoi Book
Published by Alfred A. Knopf, Inc.
Copyright © 1975 by Elmer Bendiner.
All rights reserved under International and Pan-American
Copyright Conventions. Published in the United States by
Alfred A. Knopf, Inc., New York, and simultaneously in
Canada by Random House of Canada Limited, Toronto.
Distributed by Random House, Inc., New York

Library of Congress Cataloging in Publication Data:
Bendiner, Elmer.   A time for angels.
Bibliography: p.   Includes index.
1. League of Nations—History. I. Title.
JX1975.B3644   341.22   74–21279
ISBN 0–394–48183–6

Manufactured in the United States of America
First Edition

To Esther, Jessica,
Winnie, and Paul

The draft of the League of Peace is almost as simple as one of the Parables of Jesus and almost as illuminating and as uplifting. It is a time for church bells to peal, for preachers to fall upon their knees, for statesmen to rejoice, and for the angels to sing, "Glory to God in the Highest!"

Secretary of the Navy Josephus Daniels, greeting the publication of the Draft Covenant of the League of Nations, February 14, 1919

CONTENTS

ILLUSTRATIONS

ACKNOWLEDGMENTS

Geneva, that misty town of nervous neutrality and self-conscious rectitude, in the very eye of Europe's storms, was a vantage point from which
to observe the high comedy and underlying tragedy of diplomacy during
the lull in the two world wars that were in fact one war. This decorous,
mountain-ringed city of triumphant powerlessness was a most fitting setting for what Ivy Lee Litvinov has called—in a postcard to the writer—
"that absurd organization, the League of Nations."

If it was indeed absurd it was also the repository—at times it seemed
the tomb—of lofty hopes, and the arena in which serious, witty, wise, and
foolish men articulated the history of their times and evolved their
stratagems for peace and war.

Much of the documentation of that richly ironic episode of history lies
in the League of Nations Archives in the Geneva headquarters of the
United Nations. The lid is only now being lifted on some of the letters,
memoranda and scribbled notes of conversations that hitherto have lain
under the classification of "secret."

To explore those archives was a labor made possible by the help of
many people. Mr. Sven Welander, archivist of the League of Nations
Archives, generously gave his time and his guidance. He also read the
manuscript of this book with a most knowledgeable, discerning eye. Mr.
Basil I. Ross, law librarian at the United Nations Library, also lent his
expert, gracious assistance.

Mrs. Ann Lester Gorski and Mr. Christophe Gorski merit my special gratitude for making available the extraordinary unpublished diary of Mrs. Gorski's father, Sean Lester, the last Secretary-General of the League. Both Mr. and Mrs. Gorski were also invaluable in recalling incidents and personal details of the career of Mr. Lester. They added to the pleasures of writing this book by their enthusiasm and their familiarity with the period, which they shared generously and charmingly.

Mr. Thanassis Aghnides, a distinguished statesman who figured largely in the history of the League, generously gave me the benefit of his prodigious memory and his intimate knowledge of the background of many of the events described.

Mr. Ernest Schelling added his reminiscences of the troubled latter days of the League, when he served as concierge and guide at the beleaguered Secretariat.

The work had the benefit of constructive comments and encouragement by Mrs. Réhane Répond and Mr. and Mrs. Peter DuBerg, who read the manuscript.

My gratitude goes to all these people and to the numerous librarians and archivists in Geneva, London, and Paris who cheerfully and patiently guided me to what I sought. But to no one am I more indebted than to my wife, Esther, who systematized the research and in even more important ways shared, as a full collaborator, in the joys and difficulties of this work, giving it the touch of her enthusiasm and intelligence.

Credit for whatever value, interest, or enjoyment this book may offer is thus widely distributed, but responsibility for its defects must remain exclusively the author's.

Elmer Bendiner

July 1974

A TIME FOR ANGELS

One

THE AMERICAN CONSPIRACY
AGAINST SIN

On the night of October 16, 1918, Edward Mandell House said farewell to the President of the United States and confided to his diary: "I am going on one of the most important missions anyone ever undertook, and yet there is no word of direction, advice or discussion between us."

It was the sixth year of the Wilson era, the fourth year of the only total war the world had known, which was decimating not armies alone but peoples, and devastating not battlefields alone but whole continents. It was the year when the 100,000th American died on a battlefield in France, a year when empires were in dissolution and when the world's machinery for war or peace could no longer turn without the help of the United States of America. Nineteen-eighteen was also the year and October was the month when peace seemed possible.

When President Wilson had handed the frail, sixty-year-old Colonel House credentials presenting him to the statesmen of Europe as the "Special Representative of the Government of the United States of America," the two men stood in awkward silence. Then Wilson added: "I have not given you any instructions because I feel you will know what to do."

In essence House's mission was to bring the world to peace on Wilson's terms: not peace for a time but the millennial peace for all time, not an alliance of victors but an organization of nations based on honor, rectitude, and law. He was to carry America's light into the dark world.

Earlier, in 1914, when the United States was still above the squabble that had broken out in Europe, Wilson had called upon the world to see that light when he said: "The United States have not the distinction of being masters of the world but the distinction of carrying certain lights for the world that the world has never so distinctly seen before, certain guiding lights of liberty and principle and justice."

It was a vision rather than a policy, and for four years Woodrow Wilson had to wait and work in mysterious ways to perform this wonder. Like a canny missionary planning a strategy to bring the wayward to virtue despite themselves, Wilson wrote to House on July 21, 1917: "England and France have not the same views with respect to peace that we have by any means. When the war is over we can force them to our way of thinking because by that time they will, among other things, be financially in our hands . . ."

Now that time had come, for England and France had neither the money nor the credit to buy the food, machinery, and oil to keep the war going, and Germany had realized that it could no longer hope to win against armies backed by the massive reserves of dollars, manpower, and the fully mobilized, and highly regimented, industries of the United States. The economist John Maynard Keynes wrote of Wilson in that time: "Never had a philosopher held such weapons with which to bind the princes of the world."

The future course of this grandiose conspiracy against the sins of the world becomes understandable only if one traces its origins in the personality of Wilson and House, for this was, in some respects at least, a personal plot, hatched by two Americans spinning a particularly American brand of idealism. Although not a single idea contained in the Covenant establishing the League of Nations or in the peace that took shape at Versailles originated in the United States, the force, the passion, and the rhetoric were uniquely American and Wilsonian.

By 1918 the nation and the world had grown accustomed to the partnership of Wilson and House. The Colonel held no post in government and coveted none. He bore only one title—that of friend of the President—and it had been enough. That magic credential opened the doors of Kaiser, Pope, and Prime Minister. Ambassadors often came to House's apartment at Park Avenue and Fifty-third Street or to his summer home at Magnolia, Massachusetts, and the State Department was largely confined to matters of protocol. In both places direct telephone lines linked House at all times to the President's study. And when in Washington, he stayed at the White House, where two rooms were specially set aside for him in the North Wing.

When Wilson was asked by a politician whether Colonel House accurately reflected his thinking, the President replied: "Mr. House is my second personality. He is my independent self. His thoughts and mine are one." There were certain similarities in the backgrounds of these two men, as well as differences that complemented rather than clashed. Thomas Woodrow Wilson grew up in Virginia, Georgia, and the Carolinas, in the shadow of an adored father who from his Presbyterian pulpit thundered sermons, some of which justified slavery and secession. Edward Mandell House was raised on a Texas frontier in a family that enshrined the touchy honor and trigger finger of the gallant "bad men" of Texas. He, too, had a Confederate father and a fondly remembered brother who joyfully led a gang in bashing carpetbaggers and blacks who had gotten out of hand.

The politics of their families in the Civil War and Reconstruction periods clung to neither man in later life, but the romance of those days glossed the memories of slavery and Confederate defeat and became a fixed part of their temperaments.

Both, too, were frail as boys and experienced difficulties at school. And both were seized early with a passion for politics—not ideological politics, but politics in the American tradition, politics for the fun and glory of it.

In Edward Mandell House ambition grew simultaneously with a taste for the shadows beyond the limelight. He confided some years later: "I have been thought without ambition. That, I think, is not quite true. My ambition has been so great that it has never seemed to me worth while to strive to satisfy it." He told George Sylvester Viereck in a revealing interview: "I do not like to make speeches. I abhor routine. I prefer the vicarious thrill which comes to me through others. . . . I want to be a myth."

Wilson's ambition in a way surmounted House's and it stemmed from the deeply felt, literal, demanding Presbyterianism he inherited from his father. Throughout his life Wilson prayed on his knees every morning and evening and read passages from the Bible to his family before retiring. It was self-evident to Woodrow Wilson, as it was to his preacher father, that, inasmuch as he was so emphatically on God's side, God must inevitably be on his side. That faith made even the most devious political stratagem a means toward a Divine end.

House as a young man wrote a utopian novel interlarded with romantic revolution that gave a clue to his thinking—a thinking which in general was to win Wilson's eager approval. *Philip Dru, Administrator* tells of a West Point cadet who, in an unlikely dialogue with his bride, declares:

"Nowhere in the world is wealth more defiant and monopoly more insistent than in this mighty republic, and it is here that the next great battle for human emancipation will be fought and won."

Dru then goes out to fight and win that battle and in so doing spells out much of House's and Wilson's version of a restored American democracy. After a bloody revolution, Dru forces the giant corporations to share their profits with their workers and allow them representation on the boards of directors. A Federal Reserve System is established (as Wilson was later to do) and women are emancipated, or at least given the vote. A tax is put on idle land in the manner of the Henry George proposals, and the Constitution is rewritten to allow a parliamentary system. (House, like Wilson, was an Anglophile.) Canada and Mexico freely request admission to the Union. The United States joins Britain in ruling the seas and effects a friendly alliance with Germany and Japan, thus preserving the world's peace under an Anglo-American hegemony. Administrator Dru then takes his Gloria and disappears into self-exile, mission accomplished.

Almost as a hobby, House began to manage political material that was likely to bring the callow politics of Dru to fruition. In 1892 he backed Governor Hogg of Texas largely because the big trusts opposed him. House ran Hogg's campaign so skillfully that the victorious governor conferred upon him his one and only title—that of Colonel in the Texas reserves. With it went an elegant uniform, which House promptly bestowed upon his butler, who wore it thereafter at lodge meetings and funerals. The title, however, stuck and gave House a specious military reputation in circles unfamiliar with the limitations of a Texas colonel.

While the Colonel was becoming a celebrated "kingmaker" and wirepuller in Texas and within the local Democratic party, Wilson had risen in his academic career to the presidency of Princeton, where he made a considerable stir in a valiant crusade to rid the campus of snobbish student clubs. New Jersey businessmen seized on this scholarly, Biblequoting crusader as a likely candidate in the governorship race of 1910. One of his backers was quoted at the time as saying: "How the hell do I know whether he'll make a good governor? He'll make a good candidate, and that is the only thing that interests me."

Actually Wilson did both. Once in office he turned his back on the machine in which he rode to power. New Jersey's Boss Jim Nugent voiced his disappointment in a toast at a gathering of party notables: "Gentlemen, I give you the Governor of New Jersey . . . a liar and an ingrate."

Deep divisions within the Republican party in those years seemed to provide a Democratic opportunity, and House, broadening his sights beyond the Texas borders, went shopping for a man he could support for the presidency. He had read Wilson's speeches and perhaps was prompted by the echoes of Philip Dru he heard in them. Certainly he was impressed by the professor's eminently articulate style.

House let the word go around that he was interested, and Wilson, hearing this word, went to meet him on the afternoon of November 24, 1911, in a room at New York's Hotel Gotham, off Fifth Avenue. Wilson had scarcely known of House but was interested in any political figure who was interested in him. The encounter was an instantaneous success. House promptly reported his reaction to his friend Dr. Sidney E. Mezes, then president of the University of Texas: ". . . we had a perfectly bully time. . . . He is not the biggest man I have ever met, but he is one of the pleasantest and I would rather play with him than any prospective candidate I have seen." House later explained the mutual attraction this way: "It was my desire to see him President. He very much wanted to be President. There, from the start, was our common goal."

So began the strange partnership that was not only to guide the policy of the United States but to set its stamp upon the world for the next half-century.

Wilson was fifty-six years old then, House was fifty-four. Both were married and had children. (House was actually a grandfather). Both were moved by a sense of mission and high adventure. Both were steeped in one or another aspect of an American romantic tradition that gilded the harshest aspects of history with the glow of New World mythology. Wilson craved the glories of the platform, and House desired the unseen, unsung power of the wirepuller. Both saw in their association a means to make the world safe for a genteel society, run on their concepts of British fair play and American freedom.

As House anticipated, Taft and Theodore Roosevelt did indeed tear apart the Republican party in 1912, opening the White House to Wilson and the Capitol to a Democratic majority. House had masterminded the campaign.

While Wilson, with House's advice and consent, piloted through Congress a series of domestic reforms collectively labeled "the New Freedom," it was plain that the Administration would not and probably could not keep such a tantalizingly American conception for domestic consumption only.

In 1913 the very heart of what Wilson and House understood to be

civilization seemed threatened. Germany was clamoring for a share of the
trade and colonies of the world and, what was more, was building a
formidable navy, an action which was in itself an affront to Britain.

On April 23, 1913, House recorded in his diary that he had received a
letter from a friend asking him to lunch downtown so that he could be
introduced to the German ambassador, Count von Bernstorff, who had
expressed a wish to meet the celebrated friend of the President. "I never
go downtown," House said, and declined. Two days later a lunch was
arranged uptown, at Delmonico's. Afterward the Colonel and the Ambassador strolled along Fifth Avenue. "I suggested," the Colonel later recalled, "that it would be a great thing if there was a sympathetic understanding between England, Germany, Japan, and the United States.
Together, I thought, they would be able to wield an influence for good
throughout the world. They could ensure peace and the proper development of the waste places, besides maintaining an open door and equal
opportunity to everyone, everywhere." It was a splendid prospect, and
Count von Bernstorff was delighted with it. He proposed China as "a
most promising field for concerted action, for the United States could
work there with Germany and England."

Eager to implement such starry visions with the tools of politics, the
Colonel thought that perhaps he ought to go and see the Kaiser, who, he
had been told, was rather a Prussian Theodore Roosevelt, equally impulsive but more deeply religious and with somewhat more polished
manners than his American counterpart. (Roosevelt himself had noted
the resemblance when the two met in 1910 and flatteringly told the
Kaiser: "In America you would have your ward behind you and would
lead your delegation at your party's national convention.")

House thought he might persuade the Rooseveltian Hohenzollern to
join in a disarmament scheme. Wilson was enthusiastic about the idea and
readily agreed that, as the price of peace, Germany be offered a zone of
influence in the Middle East and Persia and a freer commercial entrée into
the markets of Central and South America. He dubbed House's errand
"the Great Adventure," said "it was too important to neglect," and sent
him off with credentials identifying him to the crowned heads of Europe
as the "friend of the President of the United States."

House found that he had no need for credentials of any kind. The
chancelleries were opened to him, but, before an interview with the
Kaiser could be arranged, he had formed an alarming impression of Germany on the eve of war. From the American Embassy in Berlin he
reported to Wilson: "The situation is extraordinary. It is militarism run
stark mad. Unless someone acting for you can bring about a different

understanding, there is some day to be an awful cataclysm. No one in Europe can do it. There is too much hatred, too many jealousies. Whenever England consents, France and Russia will close in on Germany and Austria. England does not want Germany wholly crushed, for she would then have to reckon alone with her ancient enemy, Russia; but if Germany insists upon an ever-increasing navy, then England will have no choice.

"The best chance for Peace is an understanding between England and Germany in regard to naval armaments, and yet there is some disadvantage to us by these two getting too close." But there was opportunity too. "It is an absorbing problem," House noted, "and one of tremendous consequences. I wish it might be solved, and to the everlasting glory of your Administration and our American civilization."

On Whitmonday of every year the Prussian High Command made its ceremonial nod to the humble enlisted man in what was known as the *Schrippenfest,* the feast of white rolls. One battalion was selected for its soldierly virtues, summoned to Potsdam, and given the unusual luxuries of white rolls, meat, stewed prunes, and wine. What is more, the Kaiser himself sat down with the troops, shared their *Schrippen,* and, in brotherly disregard for hygiene, drank wine from a glass already used by a simple soldier.

The entire imperial family and, in some years, foreign dignitaries were invited to watch this act of German *noblesse oblige.* At the 1914 *Schrippenfest,* Colonel House and the American Ambassador Gerard were the only foreigners invited. They sat through the religious exercises, the parade, the award of decorations, and a dinner which produced some mild complications stemming from an inability of the German military mind to understand the insignificance of the rank of a Texas colonel.

With an eye to putting kindred spirits together, the German Chief of Protocol had seated Colonel House between two generals who insisted on discussing military techniques. In vain House tried to explain his utter ignorance of such matters, the totally honorary nature of his title, and how he, an incorrigible civilian, had been granted it. The incredible tale did no good, he later reported, and the generals went on talking incomprehensible shop as if with a semi-equal.

Then Colonel House stood in the drawing room chatting with the Kaiserin about springtime in Germany until an aide-de-camp informed him that the Kaiser was waiting on the terrace. To House the Kaiser seemed less warlike than his advisers. He spoke kindly of England and the United States and declared that with Germany these three formed a bulwark of Christian civilization. It was the sheerest folly, the Kaiser

pointed out, to form alliances with "shifty and unreliable" Latins or
Slavs. House readily agreed that Russia was "the greatest menace to
England" and that Germany was indeed the barrier between Europe and
the Slavs. He commented dryly to his diary: "I found no difficulty in
getting [the Kaiser] to admit this." As for the German naval program,
however, there was less agreement. A strong German navy, the Emperor
insisted, was necessary to defend the Fatherland against France and
Russia.

House asked when the German naval building program would be
completed. The Kaiser's response was ambiguous. According to House's
notes, the Kaiser said "this was well known, since they had formulated a
policy for building, and when that was completed, there would be an
end." His Majesty did, however, express his personal friendship for
England and enthusiastically endorsed the proposal that House go on to
London to act as a broker in arranging a possible peace.

Shortly thereafter the Kaiser embarked on his yacht for his annual
North Sea cruise and House went off cheerily to Paris. France, however,
would not be distracted from the unfolding romantic and political scandal
concerning the wife of the Minister of Finance, who had shot and killed
the editor of *Figaro*. That murder seemed vastly more exciting than
another assassination which occurred in the Bosnian capital of Sarajevo on
June 28. The heir apparent to the throne of Austria-Hungary had been
killed by Serbian patriots.

The news scarcely stirred a ripple outside the Balkans until the German
Foreign Office encouraged the Austrians to make utterly impossible
demands for reparations on Serbia. This little Slavic kingdom turned for
protection to the grandfather of all Slavs, the Czar of Russia, who
ordered immediate mobilization.

On July 28, 1914, Austria-Hungary declared war on Serbia. On August
1, Germany declared war on Russia and marched its armies not east but
westward against the Czar's allies. The Kaiser's troops quickly overran
Belgium, whose neutrality all powers had solemnly agreed to respect.

More decisive than the violation of gallant little Belgium was the fact
that Germany seemed to be threatening the Channel ports. There had
been no written treaty binding Britain to come to France's aid and British
leaders might have hesitated. But England's historic continental policy
was based on fear of three bugaboos: a power that might dominate
Europe; a power that could challenge Britain's naval supremacy; a power
that could sit astride the Channel ports and close the gates of Europe to
British commerce. Now Germany emerged as all three bugaboos rolled
into one.

By the end of October the world found itself at war in all of Europe, the Middle East, and in those parts of Asia and Africa where Europeans had planted their flags.

The Archduke Ferdinand was quickly forgotten; more potent stuff would be found for banners. Europe rallied to war cries calling for the defense of liberty against the Hun who had raped Belgium. Across the Atlantic the European horrors bred a serene sense of superiority. Wilson's Fourth of July address in 1914, on the eve of war, bespoke the nation's pride and sense of mission. In it he glossed over the flaws of American life and the sometimes tarnished glories of American arms to describe the Messianic vision of America the Redeemer:

"My dream is that as the years go on and the world knows more and more of America it will also drink at these fountains of youth and renewal . . . that the world will never fear America unless [the world] feels that it is engaged in some enterprise which is inconsistent with the rights of humanity. . . . To what other nation in the world can all eyes look for an instant sympathy that thrills the whole body politic when men anywhere are fighting for their rights? I do not know that there will ever be a declaration of independence and of grievances for mankind, but I believe that if such a document is ever drawn it will be drawn in the spirit of the American Declaration of Independence."

The hazy but glorious outlines of an American-inspired peace to come took shape in letters, memoranda, and speeches.

On November 14, 1914, the President was relaxing at the Colonel's cottage in Magnolia, Massachusetts, when the Colonel urged him to concentrate for the next two years on foreign policy and suggested that if Europe for the moment was in no position to heed American counsel, a start might be made in the Americas. "I thought the time had arrived," House noted, "to show the world that friendship, justice and kindliness were more potent than the mailed fist." House persuaded the President that a loose federation of American nations with mutual guarantees against aggression and the machinery for peaceful settlement of disputes would "serve as a model for the European nations when peace is at last brought about."

This scheme for a Pan-American Union was in many ways a dry run for the eventual League of Nations, not only in some of the ideas involved but in its propensity to ignore unpleasant realities that might interfere with the rhetoric. It was surely apparent to the most casual observer that only one power could actually guarantee the peace and territorial integrity of the Americas and that was the United States. It was equally apparent that the role of Paraguay, for example, in preserving the integrity of the United States, should it ever be threatened, would be minuscule. Moreover, the United States had itself been the principal offender in intervening in the domestic affairs and territorial integrity of states in the hemisphere.

The Pan-American Union did not get off the ground because it collided with economic and political realities. Still, Wilson and House persisted in trying to find a moral foreign policy with which to confront the war and Europe. In many respects Europe was a far better setting for a moral approach inasmuch as the United States had no particular economic or territorial interest there. It could, in short, afford to be generous.

The United States up to that time could not rightly be said to have had a foreign policy with regard to Europe. In practical terms, as George F. Kennan has written, the United States had come to feel secure, sheltered by the Atlantic Ocean, the British fleet, and British diplomacy, which was dedicated to keeping Europe safely divided and hence harmless. Foreign policy, in fact, had always been a distasteful backwater of American officialdom, and the State Department, except for crises in the Americas, basked in gentle somnolence. Now, with much of the world at war, the passionate idealism of Wilson and House, like that of the fictional Philip Dru, had to develop an attitude more far-reaching than a pious reiteration of George Washington's warning against foreign entanglements.

House began to sound out men in Britain and France and at home. The feeling that the European war must end in a reordering of the world for peace was becoming very nearly universal. In France the statesman Léon Bourgeois had coined the phrase "Société des Nations" and in 1908 used it as the title of a book setting forth the principles of a world of international, if not supranational law. In England the idea was advanced in books such as Norman Angell's *The Great Illusion* and Leonard Woolf's *International Government*, which formed the basis of a utopian proposal by the Fabian Society.

Both the French and the British organized commissions to gather data on the coming dawn of the world rule of law. Lord Cecil had prevailed upon the less than enthusiastic Foreign Office to establish a committee of experts under Lord Phillimore, and Léon Bourgeois gathered around him a similar group in Paris.

At The Hague an antiwar council had been functioning since 1915 as a clearinghouse for organized efforts to secure a durable peace. Socialists and conservatives, labor unions and industrialists were all talking—some in simple piety, others in detailed specifics—of the new kind of peace that was to come.

While the armies continued to slaughter each other for every square yard on the Western front and civilian populations wandered over the face of Europe in flight from burning towns, the spirit of the as yet unborn League crisscrossed the battle lines like a cheeky sparrow, lighting even in Berlin. There in the spring of 1916 the German Chancellor Bethmann-Hollweg acknowledged the spirit of the times by pledging Germany to collaborate at the war's end in all efforts to prevent another like it. He added only a mild reservation to the effect that he personally doubted that peace would ever be maintained by an international organization, a doubt which at the time seemed ascribable only to Prussian nationalist arrogance.

In the United States, Theodore Roosevelt had not yet moved from the position he took in 1910 when on receiving the Nobel Peace Prize he declared: "Finally, it would be a masterstroke if those great powers honestly bent on peace would form a league of peace, not only to keep the peace but to prevent, by force if necessary, its being broken by others." And Taft, taking up what was then a Republican idea, had formed the League to Enforce the Peace at a Washington mass meeting which counted among the speakers Wilson and Henry Cabot Lodge, who later was to become an inveterate opponent of both Wilson and the League. The League idea was thus noncontroversial, and therein lay its strength and its weakness. It was so airy that no one could attack it, unchallengeable simply because as yet it presented no challenge.

On December 30, 1916, the Allies had added a formal commitment to their aspirations by declaring: "No peace is possible until . . . the principles of nationality and of freedom of small states will be recognized and that some settlement definitely eliminating the causes that have so long menaced the nations, establishes the only effective guarantee for the world's safety." Such declarations were robbed of much of their effectiveness, however, by the fact that the nations to be freed were exclusively those oppressed by the enemy.

In the winter of 1915–16 the Colonel traveled once again to Europe, where he found German Chancellor Bethmann-Hollweg much too fond of his beer. ("Into such hands are the destinies of the people placed," he noted primly in his diary.) He also listened to the rumor that the Kaiser was behaving oddly, giving himself over to prayer and the study of Hebrew. In London he nodded appreciatively when Lloyd George told him that only Wilson could win the war. He returned convinced that European statesmanship was incompetent and "selfish" and that only America could bring the world to a sense of honor.

Whatever might have been House's—and Wilson's—thoughts about

America's mission to the world, the election campaign of 1916 was fought on the Administration's policy of steering clear of the war. This brought upon the President's head Theodore Roosevelt's choicest epithet—"flap-doodle pacifist."

To avoid handicapping the country with a lame-duck administration, Wilson was fully prepared to resign at once in the quite likely event that his Republican opponent, Charles Evans Hughes, should win. However, Wilson was returned by the narrowest of margins, and again he could think of the peace he would fashion for the world.

In the months that followed, the President called on all belligerents to state their war aims, hoping by some semantic magic to reconcile them. This was not difficult if one took at face value the grandiloquent phrase-ology used to gild conflicting territorial ambitions. Wilson observed this phenomenon and, in a note to all warring powers, remarked that the objectives on both sides were "virtually the same, as stated in general terms to their own people and to the world."

The note shocked London, and the American ambassador, Walter H. Page, bore the brunt of British resentment. The influential press baron Lord Northcliffe told him to tell Wilson that "everybody is as angry as hell." Wilson continued, however, to call for "peace without victory," a slogan and a concept that did not appeal to the Allies, who were then panting for victory even more than for peace. Lord Balfour wistfully recalled that only a year earlier he had received a letter from Theodore Roosevelt in which he said: "You do not need to be told that if I had had control of the government we would have acted in decisive fashion long ago."

While the dialogue went on, the war did likewise, and the mood of America was changing. American ships were being sunk by German U-boats and American lives were being lost while Washington answered with notes. It was becoming clear that sooner or later words would not suffice: either the United States would have to hole up for the duration, forgo all trade with the Allies, and see its influence wane in the world, or it would be swept into war.

Wilson had threatened and pleaded in elegant diction and had armed American freighters, but they nevertheless were sunk. House, along with much of the press, chafed at Wilson's reluctance to take the step of open alliance with Britain and France to win the war that otherwise seemed doomed to bloody and exhausting stalemate.

In evident anguish, the President beheld the inevitable, but still he hesitated. On March 25, 1917, House wrote him a quick note: "Dear Governor: If it is convenient to you I will come down Tuesday for there are some things I would like to talk over with you . . ." Then, without waiting for an answer, he took the 11:08 train from New York to Washington, arriving at the White House after the afternoon cabinet meeting. The President had a headache but the two went into the study to discuss the President's decision. The question was no longer whether to go to war, but how. Congress was to convene in special session on April 2. House advised the President not to call for a declaration of war because this might stir a divisive debate, but rather to declare that a state of war existed and ask Congress for the means to wage it.

Wilson said he doubted that he was the man to lead the nation in war, and House agreed, but in terms so sweetly critical that it was balm to Wilson's tortured spirit. "I thought he was too refined, too civilized, too intellectual, too cultivated not to see the incongruity and absurdity of war," House recalled. "It needs a man of coarser fiber and one less a philosopher than the President to conduct a brutal, vigorous and successful war."

Then House turned the conversation to Wilson's past achievements in persuading a "more or less ignorant, disorganized party in Congress" to pass the Federal Reserve Act and the rest of the New Freedom legislation. Surely, leading the nation in war would present no greater challenge, he argued.

Wilson disputed the question, but softly, and later Edith Bolling Wilson, no admirer of the Colonel's, told him he had bolstered her husband's wavering self-confidence.

When Congress, at the end of a four-day debate, voted the war resolution on April 16, 1917, the President was no longer above the battle. He was in it, holding the key to victory and to the peace that would come afterward. From the start the peace preoccupied Wilson; the war was left largely to the technicians.

The Allies lost no time in dispatching emissaries to Washington, but whereas the French delegations were largely ceremonial, the British Foreign Secretary himself arrived, with authority and ability to deal with the center of power. Arthur James Balfour was described by John Maynard Keynes as "the most extraordinary *objet d'art* our society has produced." By 1917 he had been an elegant fixture of Tory politics for close to half a century. A Scot of venerable lineage, Balfour cultivated a pose of aristocratic languor that delighted caricaturists, who pictured him as an enervated "Prince Arthur." His habits confirmed the image. For example, he would rarely rise before noon, though he was known to study state papers in bed.

He was a conservative by philosophical conviction as well as inherited party affiliation. Noting the changing times, he once remarked: "Everything is now permissible—even orthodoxy."

In April 1917, he and a party of thirty-three British experts in a variety of fields landed in Halifax and took the train south, arriving at Pennsylvania Station in New York at nine in the morning of April 22. When, on being shown the sprouting skyscrapers of New York, and assured that each of the new, efficient, but graceless buildings was fireproofed from roof to cellar, he murmured: "What a pity!" Colonel House, for whom Balfour had great respect and affection, came on board for a welcoming chat before the brass band and cavalry parade that was to officially greet the ally.

The conversations that ensued over the following days in New York and Washington so plainly revealed the terrible gap between the ideal and the reality that in the end Wilson could proceed only by resolutely shutting the disparity from his mind. House saw the trouble looming and tried to side-step it. He already had intimations of the price paid for the allegiance of various nations in the war of democracy against autocracy. In his talks with the Germans before the war, he and Wilson had seen nothing wrong with parceling off bits of Africa and Asia to Germany to prevent the war, but these proposals never involved the bartering of European lands and peoples. It was this that disturbed the conscience. For liberalism, in the days before the war and up to the peace, offered a principled respect for white people and a benevolent sympathy for the rest of humanity. House therefore deplored the "secret treaties" that bargained away whole European nations, and expressed his high-minded irritation to Balfour, who agreed that it was most unfortunate, however necessary it had seemed in the crass pre-Wilson era.

House suggested to Balfour that he not press the matter of war aims at this point. To Wilson, House wrote: "I hope you will agree with me that the best policy now is to avoid a discussion of peace settlements. Balfour concurs in this. If the Allies begin to discuss terms among themselves, they will soon hate one another worse than they do Germany . . ."

Wilson, on the other hand, was eager to formulate Allied war aims with crystal clarity, for it was difficult enough for a pacifist to make war but, at least, his banner should be unsullied and plainly legible in the eyes of the world. It was therefore not surprising that after a few days of ceremonial demonstrations of solidarity in Washington, Wilson wrote to House: "My conversation with Balfour was not satisfactory. How would it be to invite him to a family dinner, you being present, and go into a conference afterwards?"

Around the table at the White House were the President and Mrs.

Wilson, Balfour, House, and Wilson's cousin, Helen Bones. Wilson was in good conversational form, delighting his British visitor with stories of Lincoln and agreeing with him that the literary flavor of Lincoln's speeches was remarkable in view of his "antecedents and limited opportunities."

Over coffee in the Oval Room, Balfour produced maps on which the promised boundaries of the new Europe took shape according to the "secret treaties": Alsace-Lorraine was to go to France; Poland was to get a corridor to Danzig, its outlet to the sea; Serbia was to get Bosnia and Herzegovina but give up Macedonia to Bulgaria; Rumania was promised parts of Hungary and Russia; and Italy was to have the singularly un-Italian coast of Dalmatia.

It was "all bad," said House, who saw the promises and bargains as "the breeding grounds of future wars." Balfour admitted that they were "dividing the bearskin before the bear was killed."

The session in the Oval Room broke up after two and a half hours because Wilson and Balfour were due at a reception. Wilson later told House how "delighted" he was at the results of the evening, but the delight paled on sober reflection, and Wilson, months afterward, expressed misgivings. When these were reported to London, Balfour wrote Wilson a letter:

"My dear Mr. President:

"I gather . . . that you would like to know my thoughts on the Italian territorial claims under the Treaty of London concluded in 1915.

"That Treaty (arranged of course long before I was at the Foreign Office) bears on the face of it evident proof of the anxiety of the Allies to get Italy into the war, and of the use to which that anxiety was put by the Italian negotiators. But a treaty is a treaty; and we—I mean England and France (of Russia I say nothing)—are bound to uphold it in letter and in spirit. The objections to it indeed are obvious enough: It assigns to Italy territories on the Adriatic which are not Italian but Slav; and the arrangement is justified not on grounds of nationality but on grounds of strategy.

"Now I do not suggest that we should rule out such arguments with a pedantic consistency. Strong frontiers make for peace; and though great crimes against the principle of nationality have been committed in the name of 'strategic necessity,' still if a particular boundary adds to the stability of international relations, and if the populations concerned be numerically insignificant, I would not reject it in deference to some *a priori* principle. Each case must be considered on its merits. . . ."

Although Balfour seems to have made a clean breast of the deals entered into for the support of Italy and Rumania, there is no evidence that at this point he informed his American allies of other war aims that resembled land grabs more than a crusade for freedom: for example, the partition of the Ottoman Empire under which Britain was to have Mesopotamia; Syria was to go to France; Armenia and Kurdistan were awarded to Russia; and an Arab Empire was to be established with carefully demarcated zones of French and British influence. Nor was Wilson informed in the spring of 1917 of the deal in the Pacific under which Japan was to be granted rights in China and be given the German islands in the Pacific north of the equator.

What Wilson was told concerning the secret treaties he seemed unaccountably to forget. In a most curious lapse, Wilson was later to deny that he had heard of any of these matters and House was to be accused of keeping the secrets from him. When asked to explain this odd forgetfulness on Wilson's part, House later said: "Mr. Wilson's denial was based on a misunderstanding or some confusion." That misunderstanding was to haunt Wilson, the League, and the Peace.

Some unmistakably clear understandings, however, were reached in the conversations with the Balfour mission. It was made plain to Wilson and House that the Allied cause was completely dependent on the United States. The Kerensky regime, which had succeeded the Czar, was threatening to withdraw from the war and in any case the Eastern Front was not likely to worry the Germans much longer. French morale was near the breaking point and England's finances were close to calamity.

The missions of the Allies to Washington that spring served to open the eyes of Wilson and House to the uneasy nature of wartime alliances. It was as if they saw their prejudices in a mirror and could foretell the future but do nothing to amend it.

House wrote in his diary on April 30, 1917: "I can see more and more clearly the danger of friction between the Allies. Distrust lies close beneath the surface, and a little difference between them would bring it from under cover. This danger is not being well guarded. The Japanese, Russians and Italians are being left out of English, French and American calculations. As far as one can see, they do not appear at any of the functions in Washington except the larger ones, and there is a lack of Russian, Japanese and Italian flags which might easily hurt sensibilities. The British and ourselves are not unlike the Germans in that our manner indicates that other nations do not much matter."

Regretfully, Wilson, who a little while earlier had dismissed the idea of a team of experts to plan postwar policy as a project for "wool gatherers," now felt that his and House's partnership in idealism would shortly need wool to compete with the English and French, who were busily weaving their own fabric for the world to come. House therefore put together a group of some 150 geographers, ethnologists, statisticians, map makers, historians, economists, and international lawyers thereafter called the Inquiry. He scouted university faculties for experts on the Balkans, Poland, Italy, Northern Europe, Eastern Europe, and the colonial world.

Though in the aggregate this was a distinguished body of scholars who compiled an astonishing collection of information, some of the appointments bore the stamp of the Colonel's flair for improvisation. For example, the man assigned to propose plans for the future of the Baltic lands, Professor Samuel Eliot Morison, although he went on to be a most prolific and scintillating historian, freely confessed at the time that he could speak no Baltic language. And at the head of the team the Colonel placed Professor Sidney Mezes, whose experience as a Texas professor of the philosophy of religion would scarcely have qualified him had he not also been House's brother-in-law.

For secretary, House chose a promising young staff member of *The New Republic*, Walter Lippmann, a brilliant, crusading liberal who proceeded almost at once to antagonize his colleagues to the point of desperation. When Inquiry staff members complained, the Colonel explained the political necessity to involve the nation's liberals and pointed out that, at least, Lippmann was "the least vocal of that crowd."

The group met at first in a room at the New York Public Library on Fifth Avenue in an air of great secrecy. The secrecy was meant to conceal the deliberations of these scholars not from the enemy, but from the State Department, which was eager to stake a claim in foreign policy expertise. After news of the Inquiry leaked out, the State Department allegedly sent scholar-agents to bore from within the Colonel's team. In time the Inquiry headquarters was moved to the cool, quiet, and out-of-the-way offices of the National Geographic Society in upper Manhattan, a retreat surrounded by sedate neoclassic museums and a woodsy cemetery that stretched down to the shores of the Hudson. In addition to the sense of detachment provided by that cloistered setting, the choice of headquarters gave the team the services of the Society's director, Dr. Isaiah Bowman, who became the "Chief of Territorial Intelligence," in charge of redrawing the map of Europe with the objective of righting ancient wrongs and forestalling future grievances.

In their sanctuary on Washington Heights the Inquiry prepared some three thousand maps and great masses of documents, data, and propositions which, it was expected, would serve as the framework of a better world.

Peace balloons rose and fell in various parts of the world throughout that year of 1917. In August, the Pope had sent a round-robin to all belligerents, and Wilson composed a cool and firm answer in which he attempted to reach over the head of the Kaiser to the German people. It was the beginning of a tactic that was to have enormous influence on the course of the war and the armistice, stirring hopes from below and outrage from on high.

He wrote: "We cannot take the word of the present rulers of Germany as a guarantee of anything that is to endure unless explicitly supported by such conclusive evidence of the will and purpose of the German people themselves as the other peoples of the world would be justified in accepting."

By the end of the year Wilson could think of little else but the structure of the peace that was to be his monument. The war itself had become only an agony on the way to a divine mission. When he concluded his message to Congress on December 4, he turned from the ovation which his words had elicited and, with tears welling in his eyes, told Bullitt: "Wasn't it horrible? All those Congressmen and Senators applauding every wretched little warlike thing I had to say, ignoring all the things for which I really care. I hate this war! I hate all war and the only thing I care about on earth is the peace I am going to make at the end of it."

There seemed to be no doubt in Wilson's mind that indeed it was he who would make the peace and that the Allies would be God's instruments for the re-creation of the world. But ever since November a rival Gospel had been sounding in Russia, calling on the belligerents to end the war and join in a peace with "no annexations and no indemnities."

The British Foreign Office myopically saw the historic advent to power of the Bolsheviks in November as no more than a German maneuver. Even the customarily guileless Lord Cecil was convinced that both Lenin and Trotsky were German staff officers in a clever disguise—though presumably not clever enough to deceive the British. This fundamental misconception was to dog Allied diplomacy throughout the war and the troubled peace that followed. It was to drive Britain's own agents to distraction.

The inability to grasp the portent of the November revolution is frequently ascribed to the sheltered lives of British diplomats who evaluate all events only as they affect British interests. The nineteenth-century French historian Michelet once opened a lecture on English history this way: "Gentlemen, England is an island. That fact explains everything."

The Bolsheviks did their best to break through the British insulation. They did not content themselves with denouncing secret diplomacy; they

published the secret treaties which they found in the Czar's files for all
the world to see. The only ones omitted by *Izvestia* in that most massive
diplomatic leak were those giving Japan access to China and the German
colonies in the Pacific. It is possible that even the Czar had not been
informed of that particular deal.

Leon Trotsky, Commissar for Foreign Affairs, prefaced *Izvestia*'s disclosure with a declaration that "the people should have the documentary
truth about these plots which were hatched in secret by financiers and
industrialists, together with their parliamentary and diplomatic agents."

With few exceptions the Allied press ignored the revelations of common crassness on the side of the angels. In Britain the Manchester
Guardian published the treaties; and pamphlets were issued by labor
groups, detailing the various land grabs on maps and drawing pertinent
conclusions.

In Parliament, Balfour had difficulty in fielding the questions relentlessly posed by the opposition. To one questioner demanding to know
whether the "secret treaties" had been shown to the Americans, Balfour
declared: "The honorable member may rest assured that President Wilson is kept fully informed by the Allies."

Balfour was prepared to let Wilson in on the "secrets" but apparently
drew the line at members of the House of Commons. In Parliament he
came close to losing his celebrated aplomb in assailing those members
who, "without the least sense of the absurdity of what they are saying,
explain to the public that if only everything was said at Charing Cross
with the sound of a trumpet all diplomatic difficulty would vanish."

The difficulty for the astute but hidebound Foreign Minister was that
although ample precedent existed for secret diplomacy none at all could
be found for the "open diplomacy" championed in Washington and
Petrograd. "It is better," said Balfour, "to do something quite absurd for
which there is a precedent than to make oneself responsible for an unprecedented act of wisdom." Even in the United States, where the unprecedented encountered somewhat less prejudice, the secret-treaty revelations had little lasting impact. *The Nation* published them, then some
months later had second thoughts and declared that "their disclosure
weakened the morale and prestige of the Allies, and the treaties were
properly brushed aside by President Wilson."

It is possible that Wilson, habitually impatient with factual details
which might seem sordid, may not have known the provisions of those
treaties, as he later claimed, but they were becoming common knowledge
in the trenches and factories of Europe and upsetting the chancellories.

The Allied statesmen were upset for other reasons as well. The Italians had unexpectedly collapsed at Caporetto; the French and British forces were operating without a unified command; and Lloyd George was having difficulties at home, where labor was restive at the failure of the government to keep its agreements and plagued with doubts about the nature of the war.

Another House mission to Europe in 1917, ostensibly to coordinate the American supply effort but actually to find the statesmen most attuned to Wilsonian thought, was a bitter disappointment. The Colonel and Mrs. House much enjoyed walking in the gardens of Buckingham Palace with the King and the royal family, but the diplomatic conversations left the Colonel discouraged, for nowhere did he find place in the discussions for the thinking of Philip Dru, Administrator. Whatever could be snatched from the shambles of secret deals, whatever advantage could be won over the growing influence of the Bolsheviks would have to be the work of Wilson.

On his way home aboard the U.S.S. *Mount Vernon*, House drafted a report in which he told Wilson: "The Supreme War Council as at present constituted is almost a farce. It could be the efficient instrument to win the war, the United States could make it so, and I hope she will exercise her undisputed power to do it."

House wanted a "world-appealing policy" that would reach behind the German lines, he told Wilson, one that would rally the liberals of the world in answer to Lenin. Wilson asked him to gather material for such a speech, and House turned to his Inquiry team that had been quietly drawing its maps in the offices of the National Geographic Society. He took some of the data with him to Washington for his Christmas at the White House.

Wilson and House agreed that the speech would be given to a joint session of Congress and that it would have three purposes: It must be an eloquent answer to the Bolsheviks, rivaling their appeal in breadth and grandeur; it must be addressed to the German socialists and liberals over the heads of their military; it must warn the Allies that their war aims must be drastically revised—heavenward.

On Saturday, January 5, 1918, House arrived at the White House at 10:15 in the morning, after breakfasting with State Department officials. By 10:30 he and the President set to work with the maps and studies of the Inquiry team before them. By noon they had rearranged the world and outlined on paper a series of fourteen points that were to profoundly affect the war, the peace, the League, and the decades that followed.

The first five points amounted to a declaration of principles of international good behavior: "open covenants openly arrived at"; "absolute freedom of . . . the seas"; the lifting "so far as possible" of trade barriers; reduction of armaments "to the lowest point consistent with domestic safety"; an "adjustment of all colonial claims," giving equal weight to the interests of the colonized along with those of the colonizers.

Then followed points on specific territorial and political problems: Foreign troops were to evacuate Russia and that country was to be given "an unhampered and unembarrassed opportunity" to determine her own destiny. She was to be welcomed into "the society of free nations" and given "assistance of every kind." Wilson emphasized the importance of the point by declaring: "The treatment accorded Russia by her sister nations in the months to come will be the acid test of their good will, of their comprehension of her needs as distinguished from their own interests, and of their intelligent and unselfish sympathy."

The Russian point was designed in part at least to cut the ground from under Lenin and Trotsky rather than to woo them. House thought that section of the speech was Wilson's most adroit. Kerensky's ambassador, Boris V. Bakhmeteff, stranded in New York after the collapse of his government, advised House that a soft approach would serve to undercut the extremists and that a protest against the Bolshevik seizure of power would only "aggravate the situation." Tactically both Wilson and House felt that whatever was to be said about the Bolsheviks must serve to prevent, if possible, a separate German-Russian peace. To that end friendliness and aid were in order.

Belgium, of course, was to be evacuated and restored, and likewise France, which was also to be given Alsace-Lorraine. On Italy, Wilson and House fudged the entire secret treaty by promising to readjust her frontiers "along clearly recognizable lines of nationality."

The peoples of the Austro-Hungarian Empire were assured of "the freest opportunity of autonomous development."

Rumania, Serbia, and Montenegro were to be restored, with Serbia given access to the sea and the proverbial Balkan "powder keg" defused under international guarantees.

Turkish rule would henceforth be limited to Turks, and the subject peoples of the Ottoman Empire assured "an absolutely unmolested opportunity of autonomous development."

An independent Poland should be established and given access to the sea.

Last in the list of fourteen, because Wilson felt that this was the position of utmost importance, "a general association of nations must be formed under specific covenants for the purpose of affording mutual guarantees of political independence and territorial integrity to great and small states alike."

When they were through with the outline Wilson expressed regret that this most important document reshaping the world could not have been condensed from fourteen points into thirteen, a number which possessed a magical meaning for him, stemming, some thought, from the fact that the name Woodrow Wilson is inscribed in thirteen characters.

House looked at his and his President's handiwork, found it good, and noted in his diary: "Saturday was a remarkable day . . ."

The Colonel was convinced that advance publicity would alert the nation and the world to the importance of the declaration. But Wilson felt that the press would be instantly moved to speculate on what was to be said and that often these speculations took on a life of their own, outshining and outrunning the laggard truth.

Extraordinary precautions were thus taken to keep the text a secret. When, after days of working and reworking the speech, Wilson was prepared to let it go, he summoned the printer, handed him the script, and told him that he would be held responsible for any leaks. There were none.

Wilson and House had already experienced one major discomfiture, however. Three days before the scheduled date of the President's address, while the two were still at work on the text, some of Wilson's thoughts were expressed in public with such exactitude as to give the President pause.

On January 5, 1918, a cablegram arrived at the White House from Balfour, marked "private and secret" for the President alone: "Negotiations have been going for some time between the Prime Minister and the Trades Unions. The main point was the desire of the Government to be released from certain pledges which were made to the labour leaders earlier in the war. This release is absolutely indispensable from the military point of view for the development of manpower on the Western Front. Finally the negotiations arrived at a point at which their successful issue depended mainly on the immediate publication by the British Government of a statement setting forth their war aims. This statement has now been made by the Prime Minister. It is the result of consultations with the labour leaders as well as the leaders of the Parliamentary opposition.

"Under these circumstances there was no time to consult the Allies as to the terms of the statement agreed on by the Prime Minister and the above-mentioned persons. It will be found on examination to be in accordance with the declarations hitherto made by the President on this subject.

"Should the President himself make a statement of his own views which, in view of the appeal made to the peoples of the world by the Bolsheviks, might appear a desirable course, the Prime Minister is confident that such a statement would also be in general accordance with the lines of the President's previous speeches, which in England as well as in other countries have been so warmly received by public opinion. Such a further statement would naturally receive an equally warm welcome."

Lloyd George, driven by the goads of Lenin and Labour, had ascended to the upper reaches of political principle. On the night of January 5 he appeared before the Trades Union Congress in London and declared: "We can no longer submit the future of European civilization to the arbitrary decisions of a few negotiators striving to secure by chicanery or persuasion the interests of this or that dynasty or nation . . . government in the interests of the governed must be the basis of any territorial settlement in this hour."

He called for the restoration of Belgium, Serbia, Montenegro, and the occupied parts of France, Italy, and Rumania. He vowed to stand by France and her claim to Alsace-Lorraine "to the death."

He advocated an independent Poland and autonomy for the component parts of the Austro-Hungarian and Turkish empires and declared that the German colonies should be given the right of self-determination.

On the Bolsheviks, he declared: "We shall be proud to fight to the end side by side with the new democracy of Russia . . . But if the present rulers of Russia take action which is independent of their Allies [the specter of a separate peace] we have no means of intervening to avert the catastrophe which is assuredly befalling their country. Russia can only be saved by her own people."

The Prime Minister closed with what Wilson too had reserved for his dramatic finale: ". . . and lastly, we must seek by the creation of some international organization to limit the burden of armaments and diminish the possibility of war."

Wilson's first reaction to this untimely dawn of principle over the British Empire was bleak dismay. He considered abandoning his Fourteen Points, fearing that Lloyd George had stolen all the available thunder. Actually the British Prime Minister had not been nearly as specific as Wilson intended to be. House encouraged the President to go on as he had planned.

The timing was unfortunate but the coincidence was not phenomenal. In fact, many of the ideas embodied in the Fourteen Points had already been offered by the Allies. The territorial program in eight high-sounding if somewhat vague points had been presented as the war aims of the Allies by Aristide Briand of France a year earlier, in January 1917. And in June 1917 the French Chamber of Deputies had passed a resolution declaring: "Foreign to all thought of conquest or enslavement of foreign people, the Chamber trusts that the efforts of the Army of the Republic and her Allies will permit, after Prussian militarism is overthrown, the securing of lasting guarantees of peace and independence from great and small nations alike by association in a League of Nations, already in preparation."

Thus it was that when Wilson spoke to Congress on January 8, 1918, three days after Lloyd George had talked to the British Trades Unions, he had nothing startlingly new to offer, except for certain changes in emphasis and a style grand enough to match his concepts.

Nonetheless, the Fourteen Points created a stir, largely because they were uttered by Wilson, behind whose eloquence lay not only the power of America but its innocence as well. Principle in the mouth of any European statesman was suspect in the fourth year of that horrifying and dreary war, with its secret deals exposed for all to read. The rivalries and ambitions and land grabs of centuries had stained Europe's politicians. The United States, whatever its "manifest destiny" might be in the Americas or the Pacific, was known to have no part in the game of Europe. Wilson's words were thus taken not as pieties uttered by a sinner in trouble but as the principled doctrine of a messiah above reproach.

The effect was enhanced by the high-pressure tactics of George Creel, the ebullient and energetic director of the Committee on Public Information. The Fourteen Points, in appropriate translation, showered down behind the enemy lines from airplanes and balloons. They appeared on walls in all the neutral capitals.

At home the speech was acclaimed alike by socialists Morris Hillquit and Meyer London and jingoes such as Theodore Roosevelt. The New York *Tribune* declared: "In a very deep sense Mr. Wilson now pledges his country to fight for the liberation of the Belgian and the Pole, the Serb and the Rumanian. For the long-suffering populations of Alsace-Lorraine and the Italian Irredenta the words of the President of the United States are a promise of freedom after a slavery worse a thousand times than that of the negro."

The reception abroad was more restrained but still enthusiastic. The British objected, however, to the emphasis on "freedom of the seas," which challenged Britain's bulwark, its fleet, and *The Times* in London said: "Our chief criticism of the President's speech is that in its lofty flight of an ideal it seems not to take into account certain hard realities of the situation. We would all rejoice to see some such splendid vision as he beholds clothed in flesh and blood, and we are all working toward it according to our lights, but some of the proposals Mr. Wilson puts forward assume that the reign of righteousness on earth is already within our reach."

Italian comment was distinctly cool, reading into the message a clear warning that the bargain struck in London in 1915 was likely to be canceled out and Italy's bid for greatness frustrated. The call for Italian rule to be restricted to Italians would negate the claim to Dalmatia, for example. It seemed unfair that Italy should pay the price of principle when others could espouse it free of charge.

The German press was, of course, suspicious and even the socialist *Vorwärts* suspected that Wilson's purpose was to "deceive Russia about a general peace and move her once again into the morass of blood of the world war."

In Vienna the *Fremdenblatt,* organ of the Empire's Foreign Office, referred to Wilson's "cynical brutality" and likened the Fourteen Points to "a draconic police order or a dictated military reglement." The *Neue Freie Presse* called them "a scheme for the future distribution of the earth" and the *Neues Wiener Tageblatt* closed the matter by declaring that they constituted "demands which are insulting, impossible and incapable of discussion."

Wilson nevertheless repeated the exercise by offering his "four principles" on February 11. In a Fourth of July ceremony at Mount Vernon he added "the four objects" and in September the "five particulars."

In essence, these points, particulars, principles, and objects restated the fundamental ideas: that each item of settlement in the peace to come was to be based on justice, that people were never again to be bargained away or manipulated as "pawns," that within the League there were to be no economic or political blocs, no separate interests and no deals. Moreover, "every arbitrary power" capable of disturbing the world's peace was to be destroyed, but there were to be no vengeful reprisals against the vanquished. Empires on the Allied side were to lie down with their colonial subjects like allegoric lions with allegoric lambs.

As the year went on, the euphoria over the Fourteen Points faded and the American opposition grew ever more waspish. Theodore Roosevelt came to call the accumulating Wilsonian points "sheer nonsense" and declared: "The American people want Germany smashed." The chairman of the Republican National Committee, Will Hays, charged that

Wilson was devising a world "in unimpeded conformity with whatever Socialistic doctrines, whatever unlimited government-ownership notions, whatever hazy whims may happen to possess him at the time."

The enemy, however, took an increasingly enthusiastic view of Wilson as the fortunes of war worsened. Justice and high-mindedness is generally more attractive to an underdog than to a conqueror. And in the spring of 1918 there was a feeling among the Central Powers that, if defeat was not certain, it was at least eminently possible.

When the Bolsheviks issued their round-robin telegram to all belligerents calling upon them to make known "before their own people and before the whole world" whether they were ready to negotiate a "peace with honor through mutual accommodation" renouncing all land grabs, the Austrian Court, if not yet the Kaiser's General Staff, saw some hope amid the gloom. Emperor Karl thought the doctrine of self-determination might yet save his empire from Italian ambitions but dared not espouse it too loudly lest the Czechs and Slavs overhear him and take him at his word. Thus, when the peace negotiations between the Central Powers and the Soviet government opened at Brest-Litovsk in February 1918, Austria's Prime Minister, Count Ottokar Czernin, was hopefully dispatched to bring back "a peace of bread" for the hungry Empire.

The Russians came to Brest-Litovsk in high spirits. Karl Radek reached from his train window and scattered inflammatory leaflets at the German guards along the tracks. Adolf Joffe confided to Count Czernin: "I hope that we shall succeed in starting a revolution in your country also." The Count was unruffled.

When Leon Trotsky arrived, however, the playful dialogue ceased, and the German Foreign Minister, Richard von Kühlmann, complained: "He is putting them all into a convent." Trotsky issued flaming manifestoes that were meant not so much for the negotiators as for the world at large, and they found their mark in trenches and coffeehouses all over Europe.

When Trotsky realized that the Germans and Austrians were demanding not only Ukrainian wheat but seventeen provinces of Russia and the port of Riga, key to Petrograd's defenses, he stormed out of Brest-Litovsk. He did not accept the peace but announced only that "Russia is giving up the war." The war, however, did not give Russia up. The German army sped forward deep into Soviet territory.

Count Czernin was caught between German ambitions and Russian resistance, when all he wanted was Ukrainian wheat to keep the Austrian people from starvation and/or Bolshevism. Already Austrian sailors had raised the red flag in the Adriatic ports of Pola and Cattaro and had imprisoned their officers. Nationalists were quoting Wilson and workers were quoting Lenin. Manifestoes were already speaking "in the name of the Czech nation and of its enslaved and politically disfranchised Slovak branch in Hungary."

The Russians were in worse shape, however. After two days of the resumed German offensive Lenin declared: "Their knees are on our chest and our position is hopeless."

London still nurtured its dark suspicions that the Bolsheviks were being manipulated by the Kaiser, and its equally absurd hope that in any case they would disappear within a few weeks' time, despite all reports to the contrary from its man in Russia, R. H. Bruce Lockhart. Seeing no prospect of genuine help and recognition from the Allies or of immediate universal peace or of world revolution, the Russians returned to Brest-Litovsk and signed the devastating terms of peace with Germany. Lenin commented: "We must not deceive ourselves. We must have courage to face the unadorned, bitter truth. We must size it up in full, to the very bottom, the abyss of defeat, partition, enslavement, and humiliation into which we have been thrown. The more clearly we understand this, the firmer, the more hardened and inflexible will become our will for liberation, our desire to arise anew from enslavement to independence, our firm determination to see at all costs that Russia shall cease to be poor and weak, that she may become truly powerful and prosperous."

The growing desperation in Central Europe was only dimly perceived in Washington and New York, where Wilson and House and the Inquiry team were beginning to put together the shape of the world to come.

House, seeking ideas from everyone and everywhere, conferred at lunch with Senator Elihu Root, Dr. Mezes, and the Archbishop of York. He read to his guests a message from Wilson: "My own conviction, as you know, is that the administrative constitution of the League must grow and not be made; that we must begin with solemn covenants, covering mutual guarantees of political independence and territorial integrity (if the final territorial agreements of the peace conference are fair and satisfactory and ought to be perpetuated), but the method of carrying those mutual pledges out should be left to develop of itself, case by case. Any attempt to begin by putting executive authority in the hands of any particular group of powers would be to sow a harvest of jealousy and distrust which would spring up at once and choke the whole thing . . . The United States Senate would never ratify any treaty which put the force of the United States at the disposal of any such group or body. Why begin at the impossible end, when it is feasible to plant a system which will slowly but surely ripen into fruition."

Wilson's message to that luncheon party voiced the fears that were to haunt him for a year and in the end prove fatally well founded. House looked not so far ahead but was alert to other dangers of a political sort that might rob the President and the United States of history's laurels. He wrote to Wilson:

"The trouble that I see ahead is that the English, French or the groups here may hit upon some scheme that will appeal to people generally, and around it public opinion will crystallize to such an extent that it will be difficult to change the form at the Peace Conference. It is one of the things with which your name should be linked during the ages. The whole world looks upon you as the champion of the idea, but there is a feeling not only in this country but in England and France as well that you are reluctant to take the initiative."

In Britain, the Phillimore Commission—corresponding to the Inquiry— had already produced a Constitution for the coming League. It was time for an American document, however tentative or flexible it might have to be in order to meet Wilson's requirement of gentle ripening.

Discussions followed at Magnolia under the benign skies of a New England summer, where no bombs were falling and where the picnic baskets were full.

Sir William Wiseman, Britain's Chief of Intelligence in the United States, who conveniently lived in an apartment on the floor above the Colonel's Park Avenue residence and who made House the prime subject of his reports to the Foreign Office, chronicled the pastoral genesis of the League and the Peace that summer: "I remember one afternoon in particular," he wrote in his diary, "the President and Colonel House sat on the lawn in front of House's cottage with maps of Europe spread out before them discussing ways and means of organizing liberal opinion to break down the German military machine, and how the nations which had suffered from oppression might be safeguarded in the future."

In the course of that summer, House, assisted by David Hunter Miller of the Inquiry team, drafted the "Covenant"—a term full of prophetic associations so dear to Wilson. The President studied the document, discussed it repeatedly with House, edited it, modified it, and at last had it in shape. Words were to Wilson the ultimate reality, and with that document, gleaned from a Magnolia summer, the League of Nations had taken form out of the void.

He asked that the Phillimore papers and the French preliminary documents be kept under wraps, and so they were—in effect buried except for what inspiration the House draft had derived from them.

Throughout the spring and summer of 1918, Allied diplomats, lacking the entrée of Sir William Wiseman to the cottage at Magnolia, prowled the nearby beaches in hopes of picking up word of what was happening in the long afternoons when the presidential yacht *Mayflower* was anchored offshore. For the rumors of peace swarmed like flies that year.

On June 24, 1918, the German Foreign Minister von Kühlmann tossed a straw into the wind. He told the Reichstag that "an absolute end can hardly be expected through purely military decisions alone." This was gall to the military, and he continued, mingling pseudo-Wilsonian nobility with imperial self-congratulations: "We wish in the world for the German people, and the same applies *mutatis mutandi* to our Allies, a secure, free, strong, and independent life. We wish beyond the seas to have the possessions which correspond to our greatness, wealth, and proved colonial capacities. We wish to have the possibility and the freedom for carrying our trade on the free sea to all continents." It was a plea for peace, but on Germany's terms, and he insisted upon "the absolute integrity of the German Empire."

That last demand failed to soothe the ruffled pride of the generals and admirals, who did not forgive him for suggesting that German arms could not bring victory. Kühlmann was forced out and his successor, Admiral Paul von Hintze, put a question directly to General Ludendorff: Was he sure of winning the offensive then under way on the Western Front?

Ludendorff replied emphatically: "To that I answer positively, yes . . . yes."

The German people declined to echo the General's "yes" and, faced with a serious slump in morale, the Kaiser decreed: "Fiery speeches must be made by private persons of high position."

Fiery speeches, however, proved inadequate to turn the tide and, as the summer wore on, even the General's "yes" turned to "maybe" and in the early fall to a panicky "no." On the morning of October 1, at Spa, headquarters of the German High Command, the Kaiser was closeted with the Chancellor of the hour, Count Georg von Hertling (Chancellors came and went in rapid succession in those difficult days). In fact, they were discussing the next in line for the office, since Hertling was about to resign. During the conversation General Ludendorff barged in unannounced and excitedly demanded: "Has the new government not been formed yet?"

The Kaiser answered curtly: "I am not a wizard."

Ludendorff heatedly told his Majesty: "But the government must be formed immediately; the offer of peace must be made today."

"You ought to have told me that a fortnight ago," said the Emperor, and resumed his search for the likeliest man to preside over a defeat. His choice fell upon Prince Max of Baden, a liberal who might be acceptable to Wilson but who was still loyal to the monarchy. It was Prince Max who had coined that ingenious phrase "Ethical Imperialism" to characterize the lofty conservatism he espoused.

No sooner was the Prince appointed than an emissary arrived from army headquarters to tell him that he must immediately appeal to Wilson for peace on the basis of the Fourteen Points.

"I cannot even have till November?" Prince Max asked. The answer was a decisive "no." The Bulgarian front had collapsed and he was shown a telegram from Ludendorff received at 2 P.M. on October 1: "If by seven or eight o'clock this evening it is certain that Prince Max of Baden will form the government, I agree to the postponement till tomorrow forenoon. If on the contrary, the formation of the government should in any way be doubtful, I consider it desirable that the declaration should be issued to foreign governments tonight."

Prince Max stalled, pleading for a chance to rescue his dignity with, at least, a statement to the Reichstag before the humiliating plea to the enemy. He appealed to the Kaiser, who told him brusquely: "You have not been brought here to make difficulties for the Supreme Command." And on October 3 Field Marshal Hindenburg sent the Prince a letter: "The Supreme Command insists on its demand that a peace offer to our enemies be issued at once . . ."

It would be difficult, but obviously not impossible, for Ludendorff and Hindenburg, in decades to come, to pass over all those panicky letters and telegrams and install in the German mythology the notion that the military were prepared to fight on but were stabbed in the back by civilians of uncertain ancestry who made peace.

In his memoirs, Prince Max noted that the High Command "probably saw in Wilson's program a mere collection of phrases which a skillful diplomacy would be able to interpret at the conference table in a sense favorable to Germany."

On October 5, 1918, Prince Max sent off his first fateful note to Wilson, by way of Switzerland, asking for an armistice so that a peace might be built on the basis of the President's Fourteen Points and his various amendments and additions. Apparently forgotten were the expressions of scorn and outrage with which the German and Austrian press greeted the Fourteen Points barely ten months before. Now forced to rely upon those points as an escape hatch, the hapless Prince wrote a letter to his cousin, the Grand Duke of Baden:

"My dear Fritz,

"In a sleepless hour after midnight I write these lines . . . I believed that I had been summoned at five minutes to twelve, and find out that it is already five minutes past . . . We are already in the middle of a revolution . . . I still hope to save the Kaiser and the Hohenzollern dynasty . . . The Conservatives speak quite openly of his abdication. Thank God I have in the Social Democrats allies on whose loyalty towards me at least I can entirely rely. With their help I hope to save the Kaiser. Such is the irony of fate . . ."

That first note from the bedeviled Prince Max was received among the Allies with astonishment and some suspicion. Britain's liaison officer for the Allies, Sir Henry Wilson, commented in his diary: "What impertinence!" He told Lloyd George: "Let the Boches withdraw to the other side of the Rhine, and the Austrians get out of Italy and the Trentino, then we'll talk."

Few believed that Germany, whose armies were still fighting outside its borders and whose soil was absolutely untouched, was in fact beaten. It had been expected that the end of active fighting on the Russian front would release fresh German legions for the West. The Allied governments did not know that Ludendorff had already written off those troops because "the temptations to which the men were exposed from the corruption of Jewish traders in the east and from Bolshevik propaganda, as indeed from propaganda from home, had broken their fighting spirit."

The disaffection was born of hunger and disenchantment, fed by the manifestoes of Lenin and the speeches of Wilson, all nicely calculated to divide the people from their leaders. (The inclusion of Jews among the sinister forces was standard operating procedure in any Central European crisis and merely testified to the gravity of the situation.) Because the extent of the German collapse had been underestimated by the intelligence forces of the Allies, the note was seen in many quarters as a "peace trap" to give Ludendorff's forces time to rest and recoup.

The New York *Tribune* thundered against all talk of a peace short of total victory. On October 7 it said editorially: "We have laid down one condition of war—one only—and that is to use force, force to the utmost, force without stint or limit, until we shall have destroyed forever in this world the indecent, intolerable, criminal thing that now holds out its dripping hands." In the Senate, Henry Cabot Lodge declared: "If we agree to an armistice Germany will have the opportunity to restore and refresh her armies and to accumulate munitions, and she can sit at the council table and discuss details that are vital and refuse everything she does not like under threat of renewing the war in a more advantageous position."

As if oblivious to the warlike clamor, Wilson answered the first German note softly, requesting clarification: Did the Imperial Chancellor accept fully the Fourteen Points and its various addenda so that only their practical implementation need be worked out subsequently? Would the German Empire withdraw from all occupied zones and did the Imperial Chancellor speak for the German people?

British tempers were badly frayed when Wilson's message was read in London. Lloyd George was reported furious because he had not been consulted and because no mention had been made of Alsace-Lorraine, a point which troubled Paris even more. Neither power could comment because neither had yet been officially informed. On October 9, after a peppery meeting with his staff, Lloyd George got off a top-secret message to Washington suggesting that the Germans be warned that the Fourteen Points represented the thinking of the President alone, that German acceptance of the Wilson doctrine would put Britain in a difficult position because it had reservations about some aspects of the program, particularly the point on Freedom of the Seas. Finally he suggested that the President come to Europe promptly for consultation or else send a fully empowered emissary to talk for him.

On October 12 the Germans answered "yes" to all of Wilson's questions. The euphoric mood in the White House had faded by then under criticism from home as well as abroad, and Wilson stiffened his position. His answer, sent on the fourteenth, fell short of the war party's demand for unconditional surrender, though not by very much. However, it gave the Germans no reason to suppose that the Fourteen Points would not be the basis for peace acceptable to all powers. To do so would have negated Wilson's entire philosophical justification for the war.

He warned that the Allies would not consider peace so long as the Germans continued their "illegal and inhumane practices . . . sinking passenger ships at sea, and not the ships alone but the very boats in which their passengers and crews seek to make their way to safety." He condemned the German government for committing "wanton destruction" in the course of their retreat from Flanders and France. And he pointed out that the Wilson doctrine, which the imperial government was agreeing to accept, included the President's Fourth of July address of 1918, which called for "the destruction of every arbitrary power anywhere that can separately, secretly and of its single choice disturb the peace of the world or if it cannot be presently destroyed, at least its reduction to impotency." He ran the ramrod home by adding: "The power which has hitherto controlled the German nation is of the sort here described."

That denunciation stirred misgivings among the officials of Britain's Political Intelligence Department. In a top-secret memo, dated October 30, 1918, the P.I.D. saw "dangerous consequences." The President seemed to be suggesting a "League of democratic governments pledged to overthrow, or to prevent the establishment of, any form of government in any state, either within or without the League, that did not comply with certain principles. The League of Nations would then become a Holy Alliance of democracies."

The document warned that such a league might be used to overthrow "the present government in Russia, and whatever may be thought of the Bolsheviks, it might appear unwise to pledge the League at its inauguration to a crusade against Bolshevism."

Tracing the possible effects of such a doctrine closer to home, British Intelligence suggested that "it might also be taken so as to justify interference with the form of government in India that is certainly arbitrary: the government of India could 'separately and secretly disturb the peace of the world' in the sense that it could carry out policy which would involve a war with Persia or Afghanistan or Siam or China or Japan."

On the other hand, the War Cabinet itself breathed a sigh of relief. According to the minutes of the meetings following the dispatch of Wilson's second note, the Chancellor of the Exchequer, Bonar Law, recalled that although the President had previously expressed fears that the Allies favored overly harsh terms for Germany, now Wilson "had himself put forward demands which were humiliating and practically amounted to unconditional surrender."

In Central Europe the note produced a sense of shock and disappointment, as though a local saint had put a high price tag on salvation. The first exchange of peace notes had stirred hopes for a gentle end to the war, for shipments of food and clothing and coal. In the winter that was coming coalless stoves would add to the torment of hunger, for fuel, like food, was cut off from Europe by the blockade. And already influenza was sweeping Berlin. The strong and bitter words of Wilson's second note fell heavily on beleaguered Germany. Prince Max noted in his memoirs that "disappointment worked like the bursting of a dam."

On the German right wing, the note seemed to have had a stiffening effect. The Conservatives issued a manifesto in the daily *Kreuzzeitung:* "If once the enemy troops with their Negro hordes [a reference to French and American regiments] trample our country underfoot, the fields of the homeland will be laid waste and its people given up to abject misery. If we have to conclude peace defenseless and with our hands bound, we, our children, and our children's children will have to experience a slavery which will far surpass everything which Prussia after 1806 had to suffer from the Corsican conqueror."

The German War Cabinet met on October 17. Ludendorff by then had changed his mind and declared he could fight on to victory: "We should not exaggerate the value of the Americans," he said. "They are certainly bad enough . . . but we have beaten them up to now even where we were in a great numerical inferiority . . . Our men have no fear of the Americans as they have of the English . . . I have the impression that before we take upon us through this note conditions that are too hard to be borne, we ought to tell the enemy that they will have to fight for such conditions."

Prince Max: "And when they have been fought for, shall we not have to face even worse?"

Ludendorff: "There can be no worse."

Prince Max: "Oh, yes, there can—an invasion and devastation of Germany."

In Eastern Europe, Wilson's words sounded not like the knell of doom but like a trumpet at heaven's gate. His call for self-determination reinforced the manifestoes out of Petrograd. Count Mihály Károlyi, Hungary's impatient nationalist leader, declared: "There cannot be a single Magyar who will not cry out when he hears President Wilson's note . . . The hour has come proclaiming the independence of Hungary; let it be done today rather than tomorrow."

Echoes came from the Ruthenians, the Poles, the Southern Slavs, all equally passionate. What matter that their claims might conflict and that some people might find themselves trading one yoke for another? It was a great day dawning, and millions of starving people were shouting: "Let it be done today rather than tomorrow."

At five-fifteen on the afternoon of October 16, Colonel House opened the door of his Park Avenue apartment to Lincoln Steffens, his radical, muckraking journalist friend, who at that time had been virtually blacklisted. "Only a minute," House told Steffens. "I sail tomorrow morning. We hear that Germany has accepted everything. We get it from all quarters. So, unless the official news tonight contradicts it, we go to make peace."

House cleared the way for Steffens to go to Paris and told him: "I'd rather have you there than any man I know." The Colonel talked as he packed, and let Steffens know that "the Allies are not with Wilson on everything, and that the Germans were clever to throw themselves on Wilson's side."

On the following morning the President's friend sailed for Paris with the extraordinary assignment of persuading the Allies of the United States to commit themselves to the President's terms for peace which up to that moment had been accepted in full only by the enemy.

Two

LAURELS FOR THE
VANQUISHED

The Allies stared victory squarely in the face at the end of October 1918 and found it unbelievable. True, the Turkish and Austrian empires were collapsing, but a vast gray German army still stood astride the canals before Ghent in Belgium and along the Meuse in France. No Allied soldier had yet set foot on German soil. When the Germans fell back from the Channel ports they did so in good order, burning and looting in the ancient way. There had been no rout.

Yet now the Supreme Allied War Council was officially in receipt of the correspondence between the enemy and the President of the United States concerning an armistice. The Germans had wriggled uncomfortably on the sword point of Wilson's second note but had at last accepted it, gently disclaiming all charges of inhumane conduct and pointing out that the government was now fully representative of and responsible to the German people. The German Empire had officially embraced Wilson's points, particulars, and principles. And peace—or at least an armistice—hung on a similar acceptance by the Allied Powers.

The unreality of an apparently unbroken enemy yielding to what had been considered largely a rhetorical exercise perplexed the statesmen and generals of Britain, France, and Italy at the moment of seeming victory. Wilson's second note, difficult as it was for the Germans to accept, did not escape criticism in England. The British War Cabinet found it a "total usurpation of the power of negotiations," in the words of the chief liaison officer of the Allies, Sir Henry Wilson. And the President's scarcely veiled call for abdication of the Kaiser was thought to make Bolshevism almost inevitable in Germany. Although Lord Robert Cecil rallied to the Americans' defense, the British military on the eve of peace viewed Wilson as a "super-Gladstone and a dangerous visionary."

In Berlin, however, the new Centrist Secretary of State, Matthias Erzberger, was championing the League of Nations with the zeal of a convert (though he insisted he had always held such views as a minority member of the Reichstag). He denounced "half measures," called for all international questions—even those involving "national honor"—to be subject to a Court of Arbitration, and declared that "unrestricted selfishness in the lives of states is bankrupt." To Germany the League had become a sanctuary in the storm.

Prince Max claimed to have had word from a United States diplomat in Scandinavia who told him privately: "For God's sake do something to make Wilson strong against the Entente militarists, who are in power in France and England." Wilson would "easily be able to dispose of the American jingoes," Max was assured, "after the abdication of the Kaiser and the Crown Prince."

Prince Max told a cabinet meeting that he, like Erzberger, would "commend to our people in this dark hour the idea of the League of Nations as a source of consolation and renewed strength . . ."

A League of Nations offered neither hope nor consolation to General Erich von Ludendorff, who, on October 25, 1918, accompanied Field Marshal Hindenburg on a visit to the Kaiser at Schloss Bellevue to explain away—if this were possible—the panic which a few weeks earlier had led them to demand an immediate armistice. It had been a subtle device, said Ludendorff, to undercut Wilson by revealing to the German people the true nature of the peace the President would inflict. The excuse seemed very lame, and the Kaiser suggested coldly that they try to convince the government leaders.

The two proceeded to Berlin and, for the record, Ludendorff told the civilian politicians: "In the name of the Fatherland, I throw the shame of [the armistice] on you and your colleagues."

The next morning, October 26, they drove again to Bellevue, where Ludendorff's resignation was regretfully offered to the Kaiser, who accepted it with unceremonious alacrity. It had been demanded by Prince Max's government as evidence of the nation's break with the Prussian past, a gesture designed to please Wilson.

Ludendorff left the castle in a state of pique, largely because Hindenburg had not felt it necessary to resign with him. He refused to enter the

Field Marshal's car, and when Hindenburg asked why, Ludendorff replied : "Because you treat me so shabbily."

Ludendorff, who up to a few months earlier had virtually controlled the entire German war effort, went alone to his headquarters at Spa in Belgium. He thought nostalgically of burned and battered Liège nearby and wrote in his memoirs: "There I had staked my manhood . . ." From a refuge in Sweden, he set down his impressions of how "chaos, Bolshevism, terror, un-German in name and nature, made their entry into the German Fatherland." Then he resigned himself to await the return of "national self-discipline . . . a condition precedent to the renaissance of Germany."

Two other highly significant diplomatic events occurred in Europe on that morning of October 26, 1918, when the General paid his farewell to the Kaiser:

Emperor Karl of Austria-Hungary made a curtain speech of a different sort. He wrote to Kaiser Wilhelm:

"Dear Friend,

"It is my duty to inform you, however hard the task may be before me, that my people are neither in a position nor willing to continue the war . . . Internal order and the monarchical principle itself are in serious danger if we do not prepare at once to end this struggle. For this reason I now notify you that I have arrived at the irrevocable decision to ask for a separate peace and an immediate armistice within twenty-four hours."

The other notable event of that morning was the arrival of Colonel House in Paris. Almost at once Allied statesmen began to grind their private axes on the doorstep of the elegant mansion at 78 rue de l'Université, where the President's friend made his headquarters.

On the day of his arrival, October 26, House took his lunch while British Secretary of State Lord Milner and Field Marshal Douglas Haig sought to convince him that the military situation in no way justified Germany's surrender. Victory, if it could be called that, was far from total, and if there was to be peace now, Haig said, the Germans would have to be handled delicately.

At six o'clock that evening House tasted different and stronger stuff. The Premier of France, Georges Clemenceau, came by to assure him that Germany had been whipped and would accept any armistice terms that were offered. Here was no cool diplomat but a shaggy embodiment of history. This short, round, balding man with fierce sardonic eyes and scraggy mustache had reported the American Civil War as a correspondent and seen Wilhelm I proclaim the German Empire from captured Versailles in 1870. He had participated in the Commune. He had championed Dreyfus and published Zola's passionate defense, inventing for the series the historic headline *J'Accuse*. He bore the scars of duels forced on him when parliamentary debate touched his tender honor. He gloried in the sobriquet "the Tiger of France," given him by generations of caricaturists.

Clemenceau had been a socialist and a radical, but in his later years he summed up his political creed this way: "I have no illusions either about individuals or about the sovereign masses. What is called for convenience the People is the mobile mass of changing interests, floating on all the winds of prejudice, of atavistic dreams, of passions, of desires . . . I believe in pity, in the generous outburst of the spirit, in the thirst for justice in the hearts of isolated men."

In November 1917, when France, after four million casualties, had almost stopped fighting, when mutinies and strikes testified to the national revulsion against a war that seemed futile and inglorious, Clemenceau became Premier for the second time in his life. He beat his countrymen into line, imprisoned dissenters, stifled every manifestation of defeat or protest or even "the thirst for justice" until at last his people began to believe that victory, however painful, was possible.

Now in his floppy hat and cape, and leather gaiters, with his ever-present gray suede gloves concealing the eczema that scarred his hands, the seventy-six-year-old tiger confronted the mild-mannered Texas colonel, talking to him in a no-nonsense English that bore a marked American accent.

It was evident from the start of that conversation that Clemenceau would not be won by any principle, by any captivating vision that did not guarantee the security of France. He handed House a memorandum prepared by Marshal Foch containing the terms of an armistice which were tough, as befits those of a conqueror to a conquered enemy. Clemenceau left no doubt that he thought Germany had been beaten, even though its armies still stood in France and Belgium.

The memorandum, he told House, was for his and Wilson's eyes only. Not even President Poincaré had yet seen it. Clemenceau scorned most of France's politicians and reserved a special disdain for his President, who was known to oppose any armistice and who was held in line only by Clemenceau's threat to resign. If the Colonel wished to send a copy of the memo to Wilson, he must promise to transcribe it himself, Clemenceau warned. Not even a secretary must see it. With that he left.

The possibility of peace had begun to expose the deep divisions which had been barely concealed by the fragile mucilage of wartime comradeship. Some of these were revealed to House by General Tasker Howard Bliss, who had been representing the United States on the Allied Supreme War Council before the arrival of the President's plenipotentiary. Bliss had written a memorandum arguing that the armistice terms must require the total disarmament of Germany. He took the opportunity of showing it to Lord Milner when he met him on the terrace of the British Embassy in Paris after lunch one day. Milner studied Bliss's paper carefully, then told him he could not agree with any plan calling for the swift demobilization of the enemy's army, because, he said, these same forces might very well have to stand as the bulwark against Russian Bolshevism.

Bliss agreed that Bolshevism might present a danger of "moral penetration" but could not see any prospect of a military threat from that quarter. At that point Sir Henry Wilson put his head out the window and, seeing the earnest Anglo-American argument in progress, was about to pop inside again when Lord Milner called him over to show him Bliss's memo.

Sir Henry said he would go along with a proposal to strip the Germans of their field artillery and machine guns but would allow them to withdraw "with the honors of war . . . with drums beating, colors flying and infantry armament." He closed the conversation by observing: "To get them out of France I would build a golden bridge for them across the Rhine."

General Bliss confided his worries to House and directly to the President. He said he feared that in their anxiety over Bolshevism the British would "leave the Germans practically fully armed and mobilized, with no assurance whatever that they might not combine later against the Allies or whatever of the latter might be left" after their own demobilization. Thus Bolshevism took its place, like Banquo's ghost, at the conference table, where it was to obsess the policies of Western Europe and the United States in the months and years and decades to come.

Although the military details of the impending armistice vitally concerned all of the Allied statesmen, as well as the American generals Pershing and Bliss, they were considered almost irrelevant by Wilson and House, whose eyes were fixed on the peace they were impatient to build. The Colonel was totally preoccupied with the necessity of persuading, by threat of force if need be, the total surrender of the Allies to the Fourteen Points, above all the Fourteenth Point—the League of Nations.

The Points, however, seemed a trifle airy when one came to the specifics of diplomatic bargaining. House therefore asked Walter Lippmann, who had resigned from the Inquiry but was then in Paris on assignment with Army Intelligence, to sit down with Frank I. Cobb, editor of the New York *World*, and write an exegesis of them.

Lippmann and Cobb's "explanation" was cabled to Washington on October 29 and approved by Wilson the following day. It thus became the first definitive outline of the United States policy on the peace. It is characteristic, perhaps, that Wilson and House, concerned with eternal principles rather than the details of implementation, should have left this major refinement—not to say alteration—of policy to the hurried drafting of two journalists.

Less understandable, considering the Anglo-American emphasis on fair play, is the fact that it did not occur to anyone to acquaint the Germans with this "explanation." It was as if the enemy had opened talks for peace on the basis of the Ten Commandments and found that they had subscribed instead to a penal code distantly inspired by the original revelation.

It could be argued in hindsight that Germany was in no position to be choosy and that in any case she would have had to sue for peace accepting whatever terms were offered. Nevertheless, the switch was symptomatic of the American inclination to improvise. The key, in America's thinking, though certainly not in that of her allies, lay in the League of Nations. As long as that promise remained, unblemished and uncompromised, all other details could be arranged without fundamental loss of principle, Wilson and House told each other.

This is the way Lippmann-Cobb sought to implement the Points:

Point I. "Open covenants openly arrived at . . ." was not meant "to exclude confidential diplomatic negotiations involving delicate matters," they noted. It was designed only to rule out the "secret treaties" by declaring that once an agreement was reached it was to be made public.

Wilson had meant to say that there would be open covenants secretly arrived at—clearly a more practical concept, if far less gloriously democratic than the original phrase.

Point II. "Absolute freedom of navigation upon the seas, outside territorial waters, alike in peace and war, except as the seas may be closed in whole or in part by international action for the enforcement of international covenants," read Wilson's original text.

This sounded like the end to the tactic of the maritime blockade which had been so instrumental in starving the Central Powers into submission and which traditionally was Britain's trump card. The commentary softened the blow somewhat, by pointing out that the article should be read in the light of the new order of the League of Nations. In any future war sanctioned by the League against an outlaw power the rights of neutrals would be academic, since no League member would be neutral in such a conflict.

In limited engagements, involving no breach of an international covenant, the League would have to decide the relative rights of neutrals and belligerents, although it would be expected to favor those of the neutrals.

The rhetoric had been deflated but not sufficiently to calm British fears, and this was to become the major point of friction in the pre-armistice struggle.

POINT III. "The removal, so far as possible, of all economic barriers and the establishment of an equality of trade conditions . . ."

When this point was "explained," it proved to be no more than a declaration that no country in the League would discriminate against a fellow member. However, "a nation could legally maintain a tariff or a special railroad rate or a port restriction against the whole world, or against all the signatory powers."

POINT IV. "Adequate guarantees given and taken that national armaments will be reduced to the lowest point consistent with domestic safety."

Lippmann-Cobb: " 'Domestic safety' clearly implies not only internal policing, but the protection of territory against invasion." That definition left a loophole wide enough to accommodate all the armies and fleets of the world then existing or likely to be created so long as military power could be construed as a defense of the fatherland.

POINT V. "A free, open-minded, and absolutely impartial adjustment of all colonial claims, based upon a strict observance of the principle that in determining all such questions of sovereignty the interests of the populations concerned must have equal weight with the equitable claims of the government whose title is to be determined."

The "explanation" declared that when Wilson said "all colonial claims" he obviously meant some colonial claims, specifically those of the enemy. "Some fear is expressed in France and England," the exegesis began, "that this involves the re-opening of all colonial claims. Obviously it is not so intended. It applies clearly to those colonial claims which have been created by the war. That means the German colonies and any other colonies which may come under international consideration as a result of the war."

Having converted a sweeping anticolonial declaration into a rule of fair play in dividing the spoils, the explanation proceeded to designate Britain and Japan as "the two chief heirs of the German colonial empire." True,

Lippmann and Cobb went to some pains to explain that Germany was about to lose her colonies not because she lost the war but because "she will use them as submarine bases, because she will arm the blacks, because she uses the colonies as bases of intrigue, because she oppresses the natives."

The interests of the natives would henceforth be protected because the new management would act "not as owners . . . but as trustees for the natives and for the interests of the society of nations."

POINT VI. "The evacuation of all Russian territory and . . . an unhampered and unembarrassed opportunity for the independent determination of her own political development and national policy . . . a sincere welcome into the society of free nations under institutions of her own choosing . . ." These had been the promises of Wilson's original text.

The "explanation" said that "clearly" Russian territory should not be considered "synonymous with territory belonging to the former Russian Empire." A case could have been made for breaking up the "prison house of nations" that had been the Czar's empire, but hitherto this treatment had been reserved exclusively for enemy empires.

The Lippmann-Cobb proposal would consider Russia "a clean slate" on which new frontiers were to be drawn at the peace conference, granting recognition to "de facto regimes" representing Finns, Estonians, Lithuanians, and Ukrainians. Concerning Central Asia, it was suggested that "some power" may "have to be given a limited mandate to act as protector."

The Brest-Litovsk Treaty was, of course, declared "canceled and palpably fraudulent." Beyond that crumb of comfort, however, the Bolsheviks could salvage little of the warmth that enlivened Wilson's original text, published at a time when it was hoped that Russia would avoid a separate peace and when such talk of dismemberment would have been tactically unwise.

POINT VII. Concerning Belgium, the "explanation" stressed that it was to be not only "restored" but compensated for all damages and for its war debt.

POINT VIII. France, on the other hand, could claim damages but not reparations for its war debt inasmuch as the attack on France, by 1914 standards, had been "legitimate," whereas the invasion of neutral Belgium had been "illegitimate." Lippmann and Cobb would restore Alsace-Lorraine to France but draw the line at giving her the coal fields of the Saar Valley, because the miners were German. (This was a sore point; throughout the nineteenth century the development of France had been stunted by a lack of coal while Germany and England produced booming economies with their supplies of it.)

POINT IX. "A readjustment of the frontiers of Italy should be effected along clearly recognizable lines of nationality."

The Italians had been objecting to that unequivocal statement ever since it was uttered, inasmuch as it canceled out a bargain made in London in 1915 and would have denied Italy's ambitions to rank as a world power. Italians did not live in large numbers anywhere outside Italy, except for parts of New York City, an unlikely area for colonial aspirations.

The exegesis tried to mollify the Italians. To get around the sticky Wilsonian emphasis on ethnic factors, the explainers suggested that a security line be drawn across the "crest of the Alps." Italian forces would then "occupy the uninhabited Alpine peaks for military purposes" but the German communities would be "autonomous."

Trieste and Fiume would be "free ports." There would be "no serious objection" to establishing Italy as "the protector of Albania" so long as the "local life of Albania" was to be guaranteed by the League of Nations. Why an Italian protectorate over Albanians was to be sanctioned while a similar arrangement for Tyrolean Germans was forbidden was not made clear.

POINT X. Wilson promised the "freest opportunity of autonomous development" to the people of the Austro-Hungarian Empire.

The explanation called for a free Hungary and an independent Czecho-slovakia (with some provision to be made for the million Germans there). It left unsettled the touchy frontier problems of the newly created Yugo-slavia and, in general, expressed the policy of the United States in support of a Confederation of Southeastern Europe. This last prospect seemed most unlikely since the new states were already at swords' points over frontiers and were seeking to right all the ancient wrongs in the uncom-promising spirit of nascent nationalism. German Austria, in this American view, however, was to be permitted to join Germany, a generous act allowing the defeated enemy to expand.

POINT XI. In the article which described the rearranged Balkan states of Rumania, Serbia, and Montenegro, the "explanation" was noteworthy for allowing Bulgaria to enlarge its territory. This item did not sit well with the British either, since Bulgaria was in fact an enemy country and had fought alongside the Central Powers, even though the United States had never formally declared war against it. It seemed unreasonable to the Allies who had had to fight Bulgarian troops to see it richly rewarded.

Point XII. The section on the Turkish Empire had provided for the emancipation of all captive peoples as well as for the free passage of the Dardanelles.

As interpreted, however, the emancipation was more like a change of directorship. Armenians were declared by Lippmann and Cobb to prefer Britain over France as a "protector." Syria "has already been allotted to France by agreement with Great Britain. Britain is clearly the best mandatory for Palestine, Mesopotamia and Arabia."

Lippmann and Cobb had become clear on Britain's suitability as a Middle Eastern mandatory power largely as the result of some very emphatic enlightenment on the part of Lloyd George. The Prime Minister later recalled the arguments with some bitterness. "Except for Great Britain," he wrote in his memoirs, "no one had contributed anything more than a handful of black troops to the expedition in Palestine . . . The other governments had only put in a few nigger policemen to see that we did not steal the Holy Sepulchre! When, however, it came to signing the armistice all this fuss was made."

Point XIII. A Polish state was to be set up in territories inhabited by "indisputably Polish populations."

An "impartial census" was suggested in areas where the "indisputable" aspects were disputed. And Germans and Jews were to be given "rigid protection." This last proviso was prompted by the reports reaching London from Warsaw indicating that some Poles were celebrating the dawn of freedom with pogroms.

Point XIV. Wilson had declared in his final point: "A general association of nations must be formed under specific covenants for the purpose of affording mutual guarantees of political independence and territorial integrity to great and small states alike."

On this Lippmann and Cobb said only that "no further elucidation is required. It is the foundation of the diplomatic structure of a permanent peace."

It was indeed the only point left absolutely undiluted.

Thus, long before the Allies could force their own compromises on Wilson, his Fourteen Points had already lost some of their purity. What remained sacrosanct was not the Fourteen Points but the Fourteenth Point—the League.

This vision of the world to come had to be analyzed, digested, and accepted or rejected within a few days amid the turmoil of planning the ongoing campaigns of the war and sorting out the special interests of the Allies, whose fraternal feelings were beginning to wilt as the prospects of peace brightened. It was clearly difficult to involve in the decision making the representatives of all the Allied and Associated Powers, much less those of the new governments sprouting everywhere *de facto* or *de jure* in the shambles of defeated empires. Impossible, said the Colonel. "As soon as you get more than ten men in a room everyone wants to make a speech."

French Foreign Minister Stéphen Pichon reached for a formula that had a certain academic logic but flagrantly contradicted the reality. He proposed limiting the steering committee to those powers which had suffered invasion by the enemy. Lord Balfour demolished that proposal by pointing out that this would admit Montenegro to the inner sanctum but would exclude Britain.

In the end, the realities of power dictated the forms of the conference. Britain, the United States, France, and—as a concession—Italy would steer the victorious world. In the last analysis, however, the helmsmen were not nations but men—four men.

David Lloyd George was the youngest, only fifty-six, a cheerful and scrappy politician who had battered his way into British politics at a time when it was still a sport for gentlemen. Raised by his widowed mother and his uncle, the town shoemaker of Llanystumdwy in Wales, Lloyd George challenged the Tory establishment in his parish with fierce Welsh diatribes against the "whole kennelry of gorged aristocracy and their fawning minions." He thereby won a seat in Parliament.

When he met Colonel House in 1915 he had just been appointed Minister of Munitions. He had to ask House whether he would like to sit on the chair or on the table, the only two pieces of furniture in his newly created ministry. Lloyd George, from the vantage point of his office, proceeded to bully the country into producing the stuff of war, only to be dismayed at how the gentlemen generals were misusing it. He drove his way to the top, and the gentlemen retreated before him until in December 1916 Asquith was maneuvered out and Lloyd George in as Prime Minister. He had earned the mistrust, if not the active dislike, of the King and the generals but his capacity for manipulating people, combined with his direct approach to getting the job done, had won him a grudging respect.

Like Wilson, he reveled in the Nonconformist religious tradition, glorying in the sonorous poetry of the Old Testament and delighting in the Welsh psalm fests. But there the resemblance ceased, for Lloyd George lived fully in the world. Some who watched his way with women thought he lived too fully and nicknamed him "the Goat."

Anatole France remarked: "He speaks the same language as Wilson but he is utterly different. The other [Wilson] is a naïf. Lloyd George is a clever fellow. He reads the Bible and sings his psalms, but he serves his country and himself." Clemenceau, in one of the many inter-Allied controversies, accused Lloyd George of being an enemy of France. "Surely," Lloyd George responded, "that is our traditional policy."

Along with the giants—Lloyd George, Clemenceau, and House (standing in for the remote and pure Wilson)—was Vittorio Orlando, a man of exquisite and gentle courtesy of whom the British diplomat Harold Nicolson once remarked, "He was never able to rise to the level of his own intelligence." House found Orlando a delight to work with. He seemed to have a horror of behaving unpleasantly. This was a political disability in an Italian representative responsible for asserting territorial claims that had fallen into disrepute under the influence of Wilsonism. Orlando had to leave the tough bargaining to his Foreign Minister, Baron Sidney Sonnino, who thus was saddled with a less charming reputation.

Language was a problem for the four in informal conversation. Clemenceau was the only one at home in French and English. Neither House nor Lloyd George knew any other language fluently. Orlando could speak French, but his English, he explained, was limited to three phrases: "Eleven o'clock," "I don't agree," and "goodbye." He was to use all three formulations, but much of his charm had to be interpreted.

Frequently the Foreign Ministers would also be on deck: Stéphen Pichon of France, Balfour of England, and Baron Sannino of Italy. Sir Maurice Hankey, secretary of the British War Cabinet, also sat in on a number of meetings.

This steering committee for the world usually gathered at House's headquarters on the rue de l'Université, occasionally in Clemenceau's dingy office, or grouped about a huge desk in front of a roaring fireplace in Pichon's study at the Quai d'Orsay.

The battle of the Fourteen Points was actually joined on October 28, two days after the Colonel arrived in Paris, when Sir William Wiseman came by the rue de l'Université just as House was preparing to go to bed. What was meant to be an informal, friendly chat turned out to be a demonstration of American determination that had a touch of menace in it.

Sir William began by reporting some of the stormy cabinet sessions in London concerning the Fourteen Points and in particular the "unacceptable" second point on Freedom of the Seas, which seemed to negate the power and glory of the British fleet, on which England depended for her survival.

House was blunt: "If the British were not careful they would bring upon themselves the dislike of the world." He told Sir William that he did not believe "the United States and other countries would willingly submit to Great Britain's complete domination of the seas any more than to Germany's domination of the land and the sooner the English recognized this fact the better it would be for them." Quite forgotten were the wartime days when the United States had agreed to collaborate with the British to cut off trade with the Central Powers. Wilson and House now recalled the principles of a still earlier time when the United States as a neutral upheld the right of its ships to trade anywhere in the world.

The Colonel made his first threat of an arms race when he told Sir William that evening that "our people, if challenged, would build a navy and maintain an army greater than theirs. We had more money, we had more men and our natural resources were greater."

On the following day, October 29, House lunched with Lloyd George, Lord Balfour, and Lord Reading. He thought he had made some headway but this turned out to be an illusion bred of British table manners. When they gathered with the French and Italians at the Quai d'Orsay that afternoon, the conversation was less cordial.

Early in the discussion, Clemenceau turned to Lloyd George: "Have you ever been asked whether you accept the Fourteen Points? I have never been asked."

Lloyd George answered: "I have never been asked, either."

Then they inquired whether granting an armistice now in the light of Wilson's negotiations with the Germans would commit them to Wilson's entire collection of points.

"That is my view," said House.

"Then," said Clemenceau, "I want to hear the Fourteen Points."

Italy's Baron Sonnino added: "Yes, and the five more and all the others."

It was a gratuitous exercise, of course, since all the points had become thoroughly familiar not only to the diplomats of the world but to their peoples as well. Nevertheless, House began to read them. When he came to the second article, on Freedom of the Seas, Lloyd George broke in sharply: "This we cannot accept under any conditions; it means the power of blockade goes. Germany has been broken almost as much by the blockade as by military methods. If this power is to be handed over to the League of Nations and Great Britain were fighting for her life, no League of Nations would prevent her from defending herself . . . "

House attempted to cool the British Prime Minister. The point would not mean the end of blockade, he said. It would be merely "a codification of maritime usage that would sanctify the doctrine of the immunity of private property at sea in time of war."

The British would not accept that palliative rephrasing. The naked reality was that Britain's fleet in wartime would be inhibited by the League.

Colonel House calmly explained that if the Allies did not accept the Fourteen Points, President Wilson would have to so inform the Central Powers. The United States would then have to consider whether or not to continue negotiations with Berlin.

"That would amount to a separate peace between the United States and the Central Powers," said Clemenceau incredulously.

"It might," said Colonel House.

In his report of that conversation to Wilson, the Colonel noted: "My statement had a very exciting effect on those present."

General Jean-Henri Mordacq, the aide and friend of Clemenceau, recalled that it was a tormented Tiger that emerged from that meeting. Clemenceau came out "unnerved, exasperated . . . still pale with emotion." Not only had the genial American colonel attempted to browbeat the Allies into accepting Wilson's doctrine but, along with Lloyd George, he had seemed to reject the Foch memorandum. Though less conciliating to the Germans than were the British, House had plainly disagreed with his own generals Bliss and Pershing, who favored marching to Berlin before granting an armistice—a policy far tougher than anything Foch had proposed. The disagreement within the American team astonished and discomfited Clemenceau, who did not at once grasp the varying priorities among the Americans. House was concerned only with the Points, generals Bliss and Pershing with the Germans.

General Mordacq noted in his memoirs: "I have rarely seen [Clemenceau] so sad, so worried, so nervous."

Clemenceau slept poorly the night of the twenty-ninth, and so did House. After leaving the Quai d'Orsay, the Colonel sent off a cable to Wilson asking for full authority to insist on the Fourteen Points, an authority he knew he was likely to get from Wilson. The strategy, however, in this first battle for Wilsonism and the League would have to be worked out on the scene. And the Colonel had no guidelines from Washington.

At three o'clock in the morning of October 30, the staff at the rue de l'Université finished coding the dispatches for Washington and messengers left to rush them to the cable office. The roar of the couriers' motorcycles in the courtyard woke the Colonel and the odd circumstances of his war with the Allies kept him from falling asleep again.

"I fell to thinking about the dilemma I was in with the three Prime Ministers," he later noted in his diary. "It then occurred to me that there was a way out of the difficulty. I would tell them that if they did not accept the President's Fourteen Points and other terms enunciated since January 8, I would advise the President to go before Congress and lay the facts before it, giving the terms which England, France and Italy insisted upon, and ask the advice of Congress on whether the United States should make peace with Germany now that she has accepted the American terms, or whether we should go on fighting until Germany had accepted the terms of France, England and Italy, whatever they might be. . . . I turned over and went to sleep knowing that I had found a solution of a very troublesome problem."

Clemenceau rose on the morning of the thirtieth without so neat a tactic in mind but with an equal determination. Assuring Mordacq that he "would not let them sabotage the victory," Clemenceau set out for the rue de l'Université and an impromptu private meeting with the Colonel before the British and Italians could show up.

He sat down with House at 10:30 in the morning and before lunchtime arrived at an understanding. Agreement was rendered quite easy probably because Clemenceau did not regard the wording of the Fourteen Points and all the particulars as very significant. And House, obsessed like Wilson with words and concepts, did not regard Clemenceau's preoccupation with establishing bridgeheads across the Rhine as much more than a detail. When this became apparent the two saw eye to eye and came to a friendly tolerance that later was to blossom into something like affection. In any case, the Colonel yielded readily to the Foch point of view on military matters. And after that the Premier took a far less combative posture on the Points of Peace. The fight then narrowed to an Anglo-American duel.

House came to the afternoon session of the steering committee armed not only with Clemenceau's apparent neutrality but with some ammunition that had newly arrived from Washington. He now had Wilson's complete endorsement of the Lippmann-Cobb exegesis, which could serve as a guide in answering the Allies' demands for specific implications of the Points. Moreover, the President had sent a cable which not only provided the authority House sought but constituted a formidable bomb to be dropped into the conversation if needed.

Wilson's cable read: "I feel it my solemn duty to authorize you to say that I cannot consent to take part in the negotiation of a peace which does not include the freedom of the seas, because we are pledged to fight not only Prussian militarism but militarism everywhere.

"Neither could I participate in a settlement which does not include a League of Nations because such a peace would result within a period of

years in there being no guarantee except universal armaments, which
would be disastrous. I hope I shall not be obliged to make this decision
public."

That afternoon House did not drop Wilson's bomb but instead gave
Lloyd George the benefit of his predawn thoughts when he had been
awakened by the roars of the motorcycles. He conjured up the possibility
of President Wilson consulting Congress on whether peace might be had
now on American terms or later, at a higher cost of American lives, on
British terms. The picture was unpleasant and the Anglo-American clash
continued to no conclusion.

The situation was ironic because both House and Lloyd George had
leaned to the vision of a Pax Anglo-Americana.

On October 31, the full Allied War Council met for the first time in a
blaze of bemedaled uniforms around a huge mahogany table in a room of
the Trianon Palace, overlooking the gardens of Versailles. The talk was
formal, ceremonial, and dull. After that the Council gathered daily in the
afternoons to approve the decisions that had been taken in Paris during
the morning.

General Bliss noted that the Council's "sole function was to trim the
edges and round off the corners, in doing which there was an opportunity
to consider points raised by the smaller powers who had not been represented in the preparation of the drafts."

The General was being tactful. Although the views of the smaller
powers were occasionally heard at these afternoon sessions, few of them
were seriously considered. Occasionally the "steering committee" would
neglect to even offer their decisions for approval. Lord Milner once
pointed out this irregularity to Clemenceau.

"You draw up resolutions at your morning meetings which have not
been adopted by the War Council," he said.

"That is not necessary," growled the French Premier. "The Supreme
War Council met this morning and passed upon these questions. When-
ever the Prime Ministers and Colonel House meet, the Supreme War
Council meets, and what we do is final."

Within that select company House fought the battle for the Freedom
of the Seas, recalling for the sake of fire-breathing British admirals that
this had been an issue in the War of 1812. In less acrimonious moods he
assured the British that Point II would permit the blockading of an enemy
port in time of war so long as neutrals could sail the open seas without
interference.

Clemenceau, mindful of House's agreement not to oppose French
bridgeheads across the Rhine, lent a helping hand. "I do not see any

reason for not accepting the principle," he said. "We accept." Then he turned to Lloyd George with a disarming smile: "You do also, do you not?"

The British Prime Minister shook his head and said: "It's no good saying I accept the principle. It would only mean that in a week's time a new Prime Minister would be here who would say that he could not accept this principle."

House asked whether the British might be ready to discuss the matter at the Peace Conference.

"All I say," said the hard-pressed Prime Minister, "is that we reserve the freedom to discuss the point when we get to the Peace Conference. I don't despair of coming to an agreement." House asked whether he would put that commitment in writing for the President.

"Will he like something of this kind?" asked the Prime Minister, clutching at straws. House nodded and the battle ended. The United States had demonstrated a willingness to use its massive power even against its favorite ally for the sake of a Wilsonian concept.

By comparison the skirmish over Italian objections to the limits put to its territorial ambitions in Point IX was minor. Baron Sonnino was not concerned with the German terms at all. All of Italy's claims were against Austria, but he saw a dangerous precedent in acceptance of the total package.

"If we adopt this interpretation of the Fourteen Points as regards Germany, will it not appear that we adopt them also for Austria?" he asked.

"It has nothing to do with Austria," said Lloyd George. This flew in the face of all logic, for the Points were broad philosophical statements designed to hold true not in one case but in all cases. Actually Austria, like Germany, had called for an armistice on the basis of these same points, and the Allies had already set up machinery for the Austrian surrender.

Sonnino assured his colleagues that Italy had no objections to any of the Points as they applied to Germany. At that moment the ever-watchful Clemenceau broke into the Baron's discourse to ask: "Are we agreed regarding the reply to Germany? I accept. Lloyd George accepts." Then he turned to Orlando. "Do you accept?"

"Yes," said the agreeable Orlando, and Italy thus went on record as favoring Point IX, an action which within a few months was to figure in a new and bitter crisis.

The British generals, particularly Field Marshal Haig, fought their own battle against pushing the defeated enemy too hard, voicing sometimes the fear that, if the terms were harsh, the Germans would fight on, and at other times warning that Prussianism, however detestable, might be a necessary ally against Bolshevism. American generals Bliss and Pershing clung to their position that no armistice should be signed until Allied troops marched through a battered Germany into Berlin.

Marshal Foch expressed the French sense of urgency, unshared by the Americans: "The Government of the United States, whose army is steadily increasing and is therefore called to play a more and more important part in the war and in its consequences, may well regard a refusal of the armistice with satisfaction."

As the terms were finally drawn, the French got a provisioned bridgehead across the Rhine and their armistice. Germany would surrender most of her surface warships and all of her submarines, evacuate all occupied territory, return all prisoners "without reciprocity," and turn over to the Allies: 5,000 cannon, 30,000 machine guns, 3,000 mine sweepers, 2,000 war planes, 5,000 trucks, 5,000 locomotives, and 150,000 railroad cars.

In return they were to get an end to hostilities, the consolation that the Fourteen Points were now official Allied policy, and an assurance that ultimately a League of Nations would render justice to all.

On November 5, the Colonel chortled his triumph in a cablegram to Wilson: "I consider that we have won a . . . diplomatic victory in getting the Allies to accept the principles laid down in your January 8 speech and in your subsequent addresses. This has been done in the face of a hostile and influential junta in the United States and the thoroughly unsympathetic personnel constituting the Entente Governments." House rejoiced even in the objections that had been made because these seemed to underscore the acceptance without reservation of all other Points, including the establishment of the League. And Walter Lippmann sent his congratulations to House: "Frankly, I did not believe it was humanly feasible, under conditions as they seemed to be in Europe, to win so glorious a victory."

On November 5 the American government informed the German government that Marshal Foch was now authorized to receive their representatives and communicate the terms of the armistice.

It was not completely clear that a competent government existed in Germany at that moment. Prince Max himself was far from sure of it. The mutiny in Kiel was still out of control. The Social Democratic government sent the huge, beetle-browed, and unprepossessing Gustav Noske to attempt to keep the revolutionists in line. The Kiel sailors, who thought he had come to give the Social Democratic blessings to their movement, hoisted him in triumph to their shoulders, unaware that he had brought troops to help crush them. After acknowledging the cheers of the mutineers, Noske went off to cable Berlin: "Here an example must be made. Kiel cannot be starved out. It must be attacked in force and bombarded from the sea."

Berlin had other problems. The demand for the Kaiser's abdication was becoming irresistible. On November 7, Prince Max walked in the Chancellery garden with the Social Democratic leader Friedrich Ebert. "You know my plans," said Max. "If I succeed in convincing the Kaiser, can I count on your support in fighting the Social Revolution?"

Ebert answered: "Unless the Kaiser abdicates, the Social Revolution is inevitable. But I will have none of it. I hate it like sin."

Prince Max appealed in vain for a semblance of order in the country, while enlisted men went on firing their rifles in the air and forcing the Kaiser's officers to throw away their hated insignia of caste. Meanwhile other officers were riding in a staff car toward the front lines and Compiègne, where Marshal Foch waited in a railway car drawn up on a siding.

The delegation was made up of Count Oberndorff, General von Winterfeld, Captain Venselow, and, for spokesman, Matthias Erzberger, the Centrist Secretary of State who had fastened his hope on Wilson, the League, and the bogey of Bolshevism to ease the terms of Germany's defeat. It was odd that a civilian should even be involved in so military a matter as an armistice and still odder that German generals should so compliantly take their lead from a politician, but this was a time for generals to lie low. It was far better that a civilian politician, and a Centrist at that, be identified with the defeat; the ground was being laid for the historic stab-in-the-back theory of the disaster.

The German party arrived at Compiègne, with a white flag fluttering, at seven in the morning on November 8. The Marshal let them cool their heels until nine, when they were shown into the railway car. With icy dignity Foch asked them the purpose of their visit. Erzberger said they had come to receive the Allied proposals for an armistice.

"We have no proposals to make," said the Marshal.

Count Oberndorff pleaded for an end to the game of cat and mouse, but the Marshal relished the moment too much to let it pass so swiftly. The Count pointed out that he was not good at this sort of thing and did not know how to put the question, but they wanted to know the conditions of the armistice. Erzberger read Wilson's last note indicating that Foch was authorized to inform the German delegation of those condi-

tions. The Marshal agreed that he was so authorized if the German delegates asked for an armistice. "Do you ask for an armistice?" They
humbly asked, and then the Marshal had the terms read to them.

For three days the Germans stayed in the forest at Compiègne dispatching couriers, who found it increasingly difficult to get through their own
lines amid the wreckage of crumbling authority. Erzberger pleaded that
the Germans be allowed an army to fight Bolshevism on their home front,
which if successful in Berlin would soon infect the rest of Europe.
Clemenceau in Paris summed up the report from Compiègne in a message
to House: "[The Germans] also objected that we were taking too many
machine guns and that they would have none left to fire on their com-
patriots."

Erzberger complained that the Allies would not believe the Germans.
He told them they were making the same mistake the Germans themselves had made at Brest-Litovsk. An English officer replied: "He who has
the wind in his sails wins."

Then Erzberger asked for an immediate end to the blockade and for
the provision of food supplies to ease the Germans' hunger. The reply
was a cautious "perhaps."

When the talks began no one knew whether the Germans would accept
the terms or walk out and resume the war. But by three o'clock in the
afternoon of November 8, it became clear that the Germans, though they
might squirm and protest, were committed to peace at almost any price.
When that news came in a message from Compiègne, General Mordacq
burst into Clemenceau's office. The Tiger put his head in his hands and
began to cry.

On Sunday, November 10, French workmen at Compiègne jubilantly
exhibited the news headlines to the German delegates: "The Kaiser
Abdicates." Actually the Kaiser had only half-abdicated, retaining his
title as King of Prussia—a total absurdity inasmuch as the new Socialist
government of Ebert was proclaiming the birth of the German Republic,
including Prussia. Kaiser Wilhelm had reluctantly gone that far only after
a poll of the German generals revealed that no more than one out of
thirty-nine thought the Emperor could rally the nation to continue the
war. And when they were asked whether their troops could be counted
on to take up arms against the German Bolsheviks, twelve said "perhaps,"
nineteen said they were "dubious," and eight said "no."

At ten in the evening the Emperor climbed into a railway car at Spa
that was to take him into exile in Holland. At ten-thirty he changed his
mind and ordered a car to take him back to the villa and bomb shelter he
used as his headquarters. At five in the morning of the tenth, Hindenburg

persuaded his Emperor to bow to the inevitable and again bundled him aboard. The Dutch chastened the last of the Hohenzollerns by holding the Emperor's train at the border for six hours before admitting him to sanctuary. By the end of that month Wilhelm would be forced to forgo even the fiction of the Kingdom of Prussia under British threats to have him extradited and tried as a war criminal.

In Berlin, Prince Max had tearfully resigned. His successor, Ebert, had invited him to remain as lieutenant general, but the Prince refused, asking only that the Socialist "save the Reich." "Have you forgotten," said Ebert, "that I have already given two sons to the Fatherland?" The new regime, trying to control a runaway revolution, urged German soldiers to return to their homes peaceably and "obey their officers as in the past."

At ten in the morning on Sunday, November 10, the word from Foch was that the Germans had revealed the location of their mines in order to prevent further needless bloodshed. "Too polite to be honest," commented Clemenceau.

At eleven o'clock, Clemenceau had Mordacq telephone Foch and insist that the German delegates sign for the government in Berlin, whatever it might be at the moment, and offer assurances that the terms would be carried out.

Clemenceau kept House informed throughout that Sunday, and they agreed that food would be sent to at least some sectors of the German front as soon as the armistice was signed. House's mood was now supremely confident. He cabled Wilson urging him to go before Congress with a message to the world as soon as the armistice was finally concluded. "You have a right to assume," he wrote, "that the two great features of the armistice are the defeat of German military imperialism and the acceptance by the Allied Powers of the kind of peace the world has longed for. A steadying note seems to me necessary at this time. A word of warning and word of hope should be said. The world is in a ferment and civilization itself is wavering in the balance."

At Compiègne, Erzberger, having won the promise of food for the duration of the armistice, sought an immediate total lifting of the British blockade as well. It was the women and children who were suffering, he said, declaring this "unfair." That word, sacred in the British mythology, drew a stinging rejoinder from Admiral Hope at Foch's side. "Not fair!" he cried. "Remember that you sank our ships without making any distinctions." Then he agreed to take the matter up with his government.

At nine in the evening Clemenceau was preparing to retire when two telegrams arrived. The first reported the German acceptance; the second attached a lengthy German protest. "The Germans are always the same,"

Clemenceau said. "They know very well that given their internal situation—which cannot be more brilliant than the strategic one—they must sign the armistice. But that does not prevent them from twisting and turning . . . we must finish with it."

At 5:20 on the morning of November 11, the three German officers took up their pens to sign the document. Observers noted that they had tears in their eyes. Erzberger made one last statement: "A people of seventy million suffers but it does not die." Marshal Foch said merely: "*Très bien.*" The two sides rose from their chairs at 5:30. There was no shaking of hands.

House got the word at 5:30 by telephone from an American observer at Compiègne. At 5:45 General Mordacq came to the rue de l'Université hoping to break the news to him. To oblige him House let him think he was the first. Later the French general described how the Colonel had hugged him and said: "Our dead on the *Lusitania* are avenged."

At nine o'clock House received a message from Clemenceau:

"My very Dear Friend:

"In this solemn moment of great events in which your noble country and its worthy chief have played so fine a role, I cannot restrain the desire to open my arms to you and press you against my heart."

The State Department received the news at three in the morning, Washington time, and an official on stand-by duty telephoned the President, who commented: "That's fine. Thank you."

The President and Mrs. Wilson had been up until one that morning decoding cables. Mrs. Wilson noted later that when the President put down the phone, "we stood mute."

Later in the morning came a cable from Paris:

"Autocracy is dead. Long live democracy and its immortal leader. In this great hour my heart goes out to you in pride, admiration and love.

"Edward House"

In New York Harbor one hour before dawn the Statue of Liberty was lit for the first time since Wilson had declared war. And at the Casino Palace, five thousand delegates of the Universal Negro Improvement Association called for extension of the new doctrine of self-determination to Africans and the granting of Wilsonian liberties to blacks in America.

In London, Lloyd George declared in a speech at the Guildhall: "Empires and Kingdoms and Kings' crowns are falling like withered leaves before a gale." He caught himself in time to say that he did not refer to properly behaved constitutional monarchs like Britain's who are not "clad in shining armor."

After receiving the news Clemenceau downed a breakfast of hot vegetable soup, chicken, and wine and went off to the ministry, where he told his staff: "Yes, the Eternal Father took seven days to make the world. It is probable that we who are less clever will take seven years to put back together just one-seventh of it. In any case we've no time to lose."

In the evening the Premier went with his family through a back door into the Grand Hôtel. Hidden behind drapes in a darkened room, he watched the floodlit steps of the Opéra, where a singer, wrapped in the Tricolor, sang the "Marseillaise" to a hushed crowd. To hear better the Premier stepped out on the balcony, where the roving spotlight picked up his familiar hulking silhouette. And the throng turned to shout rhythmically, "Cle-men-ceau—Cle-men-ceau." The Tiger, grown unaccountably shy, ducked behind the drapes again.

Bells rang out in Berlin as elsewhere to announce the armistice, but there was also the rattle of machine-gun fire. The rich stayed indoors. No trains ran. No theaters were open.

The night of November 10 near Champagne in the Argonne had been cold and foggy. Although the flowers and flags of approaching peace already decorated the village, the guns continued to boom and the field hospital at Mézières had been hit in the early hours of the morning. Then at the eleventh hour of the eleventh day of the eleventh month French buglers stood up in front of the trenches and sounded the war's end. They were answered by German buglers. The French sang the "Marseillaise" and the Germans put their helmets on the ends of their rifles and shouted: "*Hoch die Republik.*"

The formal war was over and the bloodletting was now informal. Russians fought the Allies and the Germans and the Japanese and each other. Poles continued to battle Czechs over scraps of land. Ukrainians swooped on Galicia. Rumanians, Lithuanians, and Serbs struggled with each other or slaughtered the Jews among them. Lloyd George surveyed the small and brutal wars that succeeded the big one and commented: "The resurrected nations rose from their graves hungry and ravening from their long fast in the vaults of oppression."

Not all the vaults were yet flung open and British troops went on killing and being killed by Afghans, Indians, Egyptians, and Irish. Aside from pure and simple bloodshed there was hunger and cholera and the louse-born typhus and rampaging influenza.

Above the desolation came the clamor of evangels offering salvation in Leningrad and Washington and Dublin and Delhi. There were also those who sought to repair the shattered dikes of the old order. The leading steelmasters of Germany, such as Hugo Stinnes (whose fortune had

soared from thirty million marks at the beginning of the war to a billion
at the end), met with the leaders of the German trade unions to establish
a great "copartnership" against the forces of anarchy. Steel baron Dr.
Reichert noted that "in the face of the tottering state and government,
industry could find strong allies only on the side of the workers, that is,
of the trade unions . . . The sacrifice had to be made."

The meetings of Stinnes and company with the unionists were not the
only signs of the tide that ran below the surface of the revolution. When
the troops of the Western Front returned to Berlin, they did not look like
a disaffected, broken army. The officers, with Iron Crosses dangling from
their chests and their helmets garlanded with the oak leaves of victory,
took the salute on horseback to the fanfare of trumpet and drum. Ebert
greeted them by saying: "I salute you who return unconquered from the
field of battle."

Such a sight might have reassured those, like Field Marshal Haig, who
worried because there were too few dependable forces to contain the
infection of Bolshevism. The development positively alarmed Harold
Williams, Geneva correspondent of the London *Daily Chronicle*, who
shared his dismay with a British intelligence agent. He in turn passed
the memo along under a classification of "secret" to the War Cabinet.

"I am perhaps only repeating what you realize very clearly in London," Williams wrote, "when I say that the German revolution is a very
rotten thing . . . the danger is that the revolution is not in any sense a
real one. The German spirit is unchanged and the German methods are
unchanged. There is not a sign of repentance. Democracy is a new mode
now and people are simply changing their dress. They are not really
angry with the old regime. The whole thing is simply a dodge to save the
Germans' face. They don't admit they are beaten; they hate us as much as
ever, and under the new forms as long as they last, they will pursue their
old policy. I have never felt the modern German spirit so strongly as I
feel it here and now . . . As far as I can see—except perhaps among
some soldiers and sailors and workmen—there is nothing human about
this so-called revolution, nothing tragic or amusing. It is simply a dull
form of mechanical adaptation in which the heroes of yesterday are playing new parts . . ."

In the United States, some political leaders saw or thought they saw or
said they saw the symptoms of Bolshevism even at home. But there were
others who feared Wilsonism almost as much as Bolshevism.

Against the advice of Colonel House and others, the President had left
his pedestal and entered into the bitter elections of November 1918, calling for a Democratic Congress that would help him win the war. The

Republicans, who actually had scarcely interfered with the conduct of the war, enthusiastically hailed the end of the domestic political truce and assailed the President with the customary partisan vehemence. The result was a defeat for Wilson at a critical moment. Both the Senate and the House of Representatives went Republican, amounting very nearly to a vote of no confidence.

Theodore Roosevelt handed down the verdict: "Our Allies and our enemies and Mr. Wilson himself should all understand that Mr. Wilson has no authority whatever to speak for the American people at this time . . . Mr. Wilson and his fourteen points and his four supplementary points and his five complementary points and all his utterances every which way have ceased to have any shadow of right to be accepted as expressive of the will of the American people . . . Let [the Allies] impose their common will on the nations responsible for the hideous disaster which has almost wrecked the world."

Now the President was contemplating still another move in defiance of the advice of all his friends at home and abroad: Colonel House, Lord Cecil, Lord Balfour, his Cabinet. He would go himself to the Peace Conference at Paris. Regardless of Theodore Roosevelt and the Congress, the fact remained that the world had accepted the creed of Woodrow Wilson, and the League of Nations was about to be established. The peoples of Europe were clamoring for it and for him, he thought. The world, it seemed, lay ready for salvation at Wilson's coming.

On the night of November 11, 1918, after the speeches and the cheers, the President read a chapter of the Bible and went to bed.

Three
WILSON
IN PARIS

The voyage of the *George Washington* in December 1918 had an air of self-conscious solemnity becoming to an occasion so universally proclaimed as historic, but it also had the trappings of a gala Grand Tour.

Shortly after the ship pulled away from a Hoboken pier on the morning of December 4, Mrs. Edith Bolling Wilson left her husband's side on the bridge and dispatched a carrier pigeon bearing a message to Admiral Gleaves thanking him for "the beautiful arrangements on the docks."

The President's wife was entranced by her suite's "cozy dining room done in English chintz . . . a homelike sitting room in cretonne . . . a bedroom in ivory with a pink bedspread . . . the President's bedroom with sombre green curtains . . ." She noted in her memoirs her appreciation of the "wonderful meals" prepared by the renowned chef of New York's Hotel Belmont, brought along to spare the Wilsons the mediocrity of ship fare. However, the President, she observed, was "put out" by these niceties and embarrassed by the "special privileges" accorded him.

They were, in fact, out of keeping not only with the stern sense of mission characteristic of the President but with the devastated continent they were about to visit, where millions of people were looking up from the ruins of their cities to Wilson and America to put their world together again.

Wilson carried with him telegrams and letters from all parts of the world, airing ancient grievances as if this were the Last Judgment and

Wilson were the Angel of Mercy. A group of Armenians complained: "You are leaving America without having uttered a reassuring word as to the future of Armenia . . . Why should we have anything further to do with Turks . . . ?" Albanians pleaded: "We come therefore to you, Sir, as to the respected chief of the most powerful democracy, as to the man who has placed the sentiment of justice far above all interests . . . Today Albania is struggling painfully in the hands of those who wish once more to dismember her . . ."

The Keeper of Coins and Medals in Vienna wanted Wilson to preserve from the conquerors' hands the great Vienna art collection. A Korean delegation quoted Wilson's own words to him on the rights of small nations and reminded him that "under Japanese control Korea as a nation is doomed to extinction." An appeal from China said: "The cause of Christianity is largely tied up with what you advocate . . ."

Atrocity victims in Shantung laid their plight on Wilson's shoulders. The Persians brought their complaints against both the Russians and the British. The Jews looked to Wilson to guard the Holy Land and make good a two-thousand-year-old hope of Zion restored. The Ukrainians wanted him to bestow on them the blessings of American democracy and the American system of education. Poland wanted the return of archives stolen by Napoleon. Belgium thought Wilson should find Rubens' "Golden Fleece," which had disappeared in the late eighteenth century. Sweden beseeched Wilson to give her back the Aaland Islands.

In addition to the rights of nations and the wrongs of empire, there were the simple needs for food and shelter and the healing of the sick. Wilson carried with him the hopes of liberals and even radicals. Lincoln Steffens commented: "As I see it all, Wilson is up against the inability of the cynical world to credit his sincerity. Carranza [President of Mexico], Trotsky and the Germans cannot believe that he means really to make war (and peace) against Imperialism, not only German, but German, British, Italian and American imperialism."

Such hopes imposed a terrifying burden, and Wilson, on that December voyage across the Atlantic, tasted the bitterness of a messiah's foreknowledge of inevitable failure.

On the deck one evening he told his buoyant, optimistic propaganda chief, George Creel: "It is to America that the whole world turns today, not only with its wrongs, but with its hopes and grievances. The hungry expect us to feed them, the roofless look to us for shelter, the sick of heart and body depend upon us for cure. All of these expectations have in them the quality of terrible urgency. There must be no delay. . . . You know and I know that these ancient wrongs, these present unhappinesses, are not to be remedied in a day or with a wave of the hand. What I seem to see—with all my heart I hope that I am wrong—is a tragedy of disappointment."

Aboard the *George Washington* with the Wilsons were Secretary of State Robert Lansing and his wife; Secretary of War Newton Baker; American diplomat Henry White, who was to represent the Republican opposition on the peace delegation; John W. Davis, former ambassador to Britain; the French and Italian ambassadors and their wives; a bevy of admirals; the entire Inquiry team; and an array of Army Intelligence officers, who busied themselves making a documentary of the historic voyage.

For most of the trip the President remained aloof. He took his meals with Mrs. Wilson and occasionally a few invited guests in his private dining room. The Secretary of State and the ambassadors dined in the rear lounge, and the Inquiry team of scholars took over the main dining room. For the first four days the President held no conferences, not even with his Secretary of State.

He walked the decks followed by his Marine guard and accompanied by Mrs. Wilson or George Creel or the head of the American delegation's press bureau, Ray Stannard Baker. Five days out at sea, Professor James Thomson Shotwell of the Inquiry noted in his diary: "We are all perfectly in the dark as to how useful we may be when we get across. Meanwhile we are taking it easy although with some restiveness and grouching."

When the President did mix with the lower ranks it was a ceremonial gesture: shaking hands with eight hundred sailors at a "sing" belowdecks or sitting in one of the ship's two movie houses to laugh at Charlie Chaplin in *A Dog's Life.*

When at last the President called a conference with the Inquiry members who had worked for months to make available their expertise, Professor Shotwell missed the summons. He was engrossed in watching the spectacle of a presidential twenty-one-gun salute being offered by a flotilla of destroyers off the Azores. It was a pity, as Professor Shotwell remarked, because not only was this the first time Wilson called in his experts; it was to be the last until June 1919, after the signing of the Peace Treaty.

Dr. Isaiah Bowman was there, however, and took careful notes, which revealed Wilson's thoughts on the Peace Conference, the League of Nations, and the world—for the President did not call in the experts to hear their views but for them to hear his. In that shipboard conference Wilson summed up the arrogant innocence of America as he outlined the League in all the purity of his vision.

"The President remarked," noted Professor Bowman, "that we would be the only disinterested people at the Peace Conference, and that the men whom we were about to deal with did not represent their own people."

The "opinions of mankind"—to be expressed by Americans—were for the first time to dominate the decisions of a world conference and, unless the will of the people rather than their leaders won out, there would be "another breakup of the world, and when such a breakup came it would not be a war but a cataclysm."

Covenants would establish the League of Nations, which would set the new world in motion but not blueprint it. "Experience would guide subsequent action." Boundaries would be set, but these could be corrected later if any injustices were committed. "He illustrated his point," reported Bowman, "by the workings of the Monroe Doctrine, saying that what it had done for the Western Hemisphere the League of Nations would do for the rest of the world."

The days of empire were over. "England herself," said Wilson, "was against further extension of the British Empire." The German colonies were to be declared the "common property of the League of Nations and administered by small nations." The resources of each colony were to be made available to all League members.

The Council of the League, made up of "the best men that could be found," would hear all disputes. Discipline would not be maintained by military action but by boycott, the shutting off of trade and even of postal and cable facilities to a transgressor. "No nation would be permitted to be an outlaw free to work out its evil designs against a neighbor or the world."

In missionary terms he told the Inquiry members that what was needed was "a cleansing process" to "recreate or regenerate the world." The people were demanding it, he said, and "if it won't work, it must be made to work." The "poison of Bolshevism," Wilson declared, was being "accepted readily" as a "protest against the way in which the world has worked." He called on the delegation to fight for a new order "agreeably if we can, disagreeably if we must."

The United States would back the claims of a country only "as justice required." He told his experts: "Tell me what's right and I'll fight for it; give me a guaranteed position."

George Louis Beer, the Inquiry expert on colonies, did not take kindly to the notion of entrusting colonial territory to small nations, which, he thought, would be inexperienced in governorship as well as exploitation. He found it a "dangerous and academic type of thinking," and concluded that Wilson had not examined the world scene in detail. Nonetheless, Beer found Wilson "frank, witty and full of charm."

On Thursday evening after the movie, the audience, including the Wilsons, sang "Auld Lang Syne" and "God Be with You 'Til We Meet Again." At seven-thirty the following morning, Friday, the thirteenth (to Wilson, a happy omen), the *George Washington* stood off Brest while dozens of French warships queued up to pass in review, their guns firing in salute, their crews lined up at the rails, their bands playing "The Star-Spangled Banner."

The President took the salute standing on the bridge until dignitaries came out in launches to escort him ashore to the ceaseless ceremonial cannonade from the ships. It was a triumphant landing. The shore sparkled with the gold braid of the military, the white coifs of the Breton ladies, and flags draped everywhere. No other statesman or general could have commanded such cheers.

The port was placarded with grandiloquent welcomes. A deputy of the Radical party of Brest called on the people "with uplifted hearts" to greet Wilson, who had come to Europe "to found a new order on the rights of peoples, and to stop forever the return of an atrocious war which has been imposed upon us for the defense of our homes."

The socialist General Confederation of Labor posted a proclamation in bright green:

"To the France of the Workers and the Peasants! To the Workers of Paris!

"President Wilson is about to touch the soil of France.

"President Wilson is the highest and noblest representative of the great American nation, whose cooperation has been decisive in the formidable conflict. . . .

"President Wilson is the statesman who has had the courage and insight to place rights above interests, who has sought to show humanity the road to a future with less of sorrow and carnage. Thus he has given voice to the deepest thoughts which stir the democracies and the working class. . . .

"For having affirmed these principles of action, for having placed them in the center of the stage of the world, PRESIDENT WILSON HAS MERITED WELL OF HUMANITY. . . .

"For the task which remains to be accomplished, may President Wilson feel near to him the hearts of millions of men and women!

"In the streets on the fourteenth day of December the workers of France will be assembled in force.

"To President Wilson their presence will cry aloud:

"For international justice, for the League of Nations, which will make all people equal in rights and duties—for the peace that endures.

"Courage, we count on you, we are with you!"

On shore was the President's daughter, Margaret, who joined him on their triumphal train ride to Paris. (Mrs. Wilson complained, however, that "no part of the train was clean and the sheets felt damp.")

Despite the exhilarating acclaim, the President was riding into a storm. When the armistice was signed the President had declared his determination to attend the Conference as a delegate and cabled House: "I assume also that I shall be elected to preside."

While this decision was still a rumor, Clemenceau sent House a message which was promptly forwarded to Wilson. "A particularly serious question," Clemenceau wrote, "is to know whether the President intends to take part in the Conference. I ought not to hide from you that in my opinion this seems to be neither desirable nor possible. Since he is chief of state he is consequently not on the same line as ourselves. To admit one chief of state without admitting all seems to me an impossibility."

Clemenceau was particularly distressed at the notion that President Poincaré might take his cue and demand that he head the French delegation, an unendurable prospect for the Tiger, who would not be tamed by a President he heartily despised.

Lloyd George said he was "shocked" at the idea of Wilson's serving as a delegate. He feared Wilson's power and his ignorance of Europe. Of all the Allied leaders only Balfour and Tardieu had ever met the President and, despite House's denials, the word had spread that Wilson could be difficult and obstinate.

Americans, too, had opposed Wilson's coming. Lansing thought it "one of the greatest mistakes of his career" and told the President it would "imperil his reputation." Frank Cobb, who had resigned as editor of the New York *World* to act as adviser to the American delegation, sent a memo to House urging that Wilson reconsider his plans to come. "In Washington he is a dispassionate judge whose mind is unclouded by all these petty personal circumstances of a conference," Cobb wrote. "If his representatives are balked by the representatives of the other powers in matters which he regards as vital to the lasting peace of the world, he can go before Congress and appeal to the conscience and hope of mankind. He can do this over the heads of any peace conference. This is a mighty weapon, but if the President were to participate personally in the proceedings, it would be a broken stick . . . he must fight on his own ground and his own ground is Washington. Diplomatic Europe is all enemy soil for him."

Wilson reacted violently to these sentiments when House passed them along. He cabled back that the maneuvers seemed a way of "pocketing" him and that they "upset every plan we had made." His message, as officially paraphrased, read: "I infer that the French and British leaders desire to exclude me from the Conference for fear I might there lead the weaker nations against them. . . . I object very strongly that dignity must prevent our obtaining the results we have set our hearts on. . . . I hope you will be very shy of their advice and give me your own independent judgment after reconsideration."

The Colonel was in a ticklish position. To urge Wilson to stay at home would be tantamount to putting himself forward as the chief negotiator. Privately he observed in his diary that when the President "stepped from his lofty pedestal and wrangled with representatives of other states on equal terms, he became as common clay."

To Wilson he wrote only: "My judgment is that you should . . . determine upon your arrival what share it is wise for you to take in the proceedings."

Another Wilson-House conflict was brewing as well. To the Colonel, "the skeleton of the treaty was made before the President came to Paris." The armistice agreement, House reasoned, embodied in rough outline all of Wilson's Points. With some general territorial provisions, which could be refined later, it formed the basis for a preliminary peace treaty that could be signed quickly. And to the Colonel speed was vital to head off the chaos he saw looming in Europe; to reassure the people of the world; to ease the financial crises that were threatening; and to facilitate a massive relief operation for the starvation in Central Europe.

The President, however, feared that if peace were achieved without the League the incentive to establish it might well be gone, and the scheming Powers would put on the shelf the one instrument that could make the peace lasting or meaningful.

The Wilsons were put up at the palace of Prince Murat (the descendant of Napoleon's sister) at 28 rue de Monceau, a regal establishment laden with gilt and crimson damask, still bearing the Bonapartist symbols: eagles and bees. When the diminutive and unpretentious King of Italy, Victor Emmanuel, arrived to pay his respects to the leader of the world's democracies, he looked around at the splendor and said: "My God, I couldn't live in a place like this."

There were fetes, balls, receptions, parades, the presentation of gifts at the Hôtel de Ville: for the President a gold medal, and a gold pen with which to "sign the just, humane and lasting peace"; for Mrs. Wilson a pin of six doves in rose quartz. "It was a pretty conceit," she noted, "and the workmanship was unique."

The President, shortly after the welcoming rites were concluded, hurried around to the Hôtel Crillon, where House, though ill, had been overseeing the stage management of the President's arrival and easing the fears of Allied diplomats. The President sought to transmit his own euphoria to the Colonel, but he seemed not to have succeeded. He told House that he intended "making the League of Nations the center of the whole program and letting everything revolve around that. Once that is a *fait accompli* nearly all the very serious difficulties will disappear."

The first meeting between Wilson and Clemenceau seemed to bear out the President's cheerfulness. It went along splendidly, House noted, although—perhaps because—both stayed away from the heart of the matter. House's diary records: "They simply did not touch upon topics which breed discussion."

Nevertheless, within a few days of that encounter Clemenceau announced a change of mind and told House that he now hoped Wilson would stay on and head the American delegation. House thought "it might be because he believes it will pull Wilson down from his pedestal." Indeed, the Tiger's paws were scarcely velvet when a little later before the Chamber of Deputies he described the President as a man of *"noble candeur."* Literally the phrase might be translated as "noble simplicity," but to an audience of politicians, for whom innocence is a liability, the words carried the connotation of "simple-mindedness."

Beyond conferring with House—either in person or over the direct, and presumably tap-proof, telephone linking the President's study at the Palais Murat with the Colonel's bedroom at the Crillon—there was little to be done. Lloyd George was in the midst of the "khaki election campaign," in which he was rallying his country on a platform of "Hang the Kaiser and make Germany pay." The Conference would have to wait.

Belgian and French leaders had been insistently inviting Wilson to see for himself the ravaged sectors of their countries so that he might better understand their feelings. He put that painful pilgrimage off to the spring, however, much to the disappointment of the Allies. To a member of House's staff the President confided his reason: "The French want me to see red. I could not despise the Germans more than I do already."

Instead the Wilsons spent Christmas with American troops in the snow and mud of a town called Hume in northern France, to the delight of the rotogravure sections of the Sunday papers. Then, still marking time, the

President reluctantly agreed to visit Britain and Italy, by way of appeasing the clamor for celebration.

The President and Mrs. Wilson rode with the British royal family through London streets, and the aging dowager Queen Alexandra leaned out of a window of Marlborough House to wave the Stars and Stripes and blow kisses to the President. The presidential couple stayed in a magnificent but chilly suite at Buckingham Palace, which was still on wartime coal rations.

At the glittering royal banquets the band in the minstrels' gallery played "Dixie." The crowds everywhere were good-natured and enthusiastic as Wilson oratorically demolished the underpinning of half a century of British foreign policy. He assailed the theory that peace could be maintained by a balance of power, and at Manchester he declared against imperial self-interest. "Interest does not bind men together," he said. "Interest separates men. There is only one thing that can bind men together, and that is common devotion to right."

Once again, as happened so frequently in Wilson's career, he was wildly acclaimed but his words were treated as no more than pleasantries. Actually the mood of Britain was not inclined to generosity. Central Europe was down to its last scraps of food, but the *Daily Mail* headlined the story: HUN FOOD SNIVEL. Revenge and the security of the Empire were the themes that gave Lloyd George a thumping victory and a huge majority in Parliament.

However divided Britain might have been on other issues, all parties seemed to pay lip service at least to the League of Nations as an objective and to Wilson as its guiding spirit.

Even out of the ashes of defeat the Labour party echoed that sentiment, although it offered a significant warning from the left. At a meeting at Albert Hall of the Political Committee of the Trades Union Congress and the National Executive of the Labour party, Mrs. Philip Snowden told a cheering crowd: "I am as strong as anybody in this country in my support of President Wilson, the best of the bourgeois if I may call him that. . . . But what sort of a League is going to be achieved? The signs point to the almost certainty now of the formation of a new Entente, the formation of a League of Nations to oppose a League of Peoples. . . . At this coming Peace Conference will there be present Trotsky?" (Prolonged cheers and interruptions. A voice: "An absolute murderer. I can prove it, if you like.") Mrs. Snowden continued: "I am not suggesting that this man should go. This is a parable. My point is this: A League of Nations, unless we take care, will be built up on a capitalist basis, and the accumulated power of militarism, navalism and economics will be used in a more terrible fashion, not to preserve the peace, but to destroy the newborn economic system." She closed by appealing to the women of England to make a meaningful gesture by purchasing "India-rubber teats for the feeding bottles of German babies."

George Bernard Shaw then rose to speak. Challenged for his union credentials, he said he was a member of "the Authors' Society and I get my living mostly by piece work." He noted that British women, voting for the first time in history, had carried the election "by being absolutely solid for the hanging of the Kaiser." The preparations for the next war had already begun, he said, and if he were Secretary of War, he, too, would have to prepare and tell the partisans of the League: "Get your League of Nations first, and then I shall be able to dispense with preparations for war." This, he said, was the view of Clemenceau, who was being unjustly criticized for an attitude which, he said, recalled a line from Tennyson: "Half a league, half a league, half a league—onward."

He noted that even in the armistice negotiations the United States had threatened to build a fleet larger than Britain's, and concluded: "So we had to choose between the League of Nations and another war."

In the end the Labour meeting, in an uproar of cheering, approved a resolution, moved by Arthur Henderson, secretary of the Labour party, and supported by Ramsay MacDonald, welcoming Wilson, paying tribute to him, and urging the British delegation to the Peace Conference to "make the definite establishment of the League of Nations one of the foremost clauses of the Treaty of Peace."

The sentiment seemed, on the surface at least, to be unanimous in Britain, and the Wilsons left on a wave of enthusiasm, undampened by the cold January rain that pelted the umbrellas of King and Queen and President.

In Italy the air was even more intoxicating. In Turin the crowds shouted, "Viva Wilson, God of Peace." From Rome, *The New York Times* reported: ". . . the whole national life seems in suspense awaiting the arrival of President Wilson, to whom are attributed almost supernatural powers. All parties are one in this; to await the verdict of his judgment on the most widely differing subjects. No man from a far continent has ever had such a deep and powerful influence on the mind of the whole nation or has done so much to inspire them to high ideals and noble aims."

Violets and mimosa rained from balconies on the Wilsons. In the glittering sixteenth-century Quirinal, summer palace of Popes and Kings, Mrs. Wilson turned to the diminutive King of Italy and reminded him of his ascetic disdain of the sumptuousness of the Palais Murat, where the Wilsons stayed. "Ah," said the King, "but I do not live here, and all this does not belong to me any more than the White House belongs to you."

Later they visited the monarch in his own Villa Savoia and saw the spartan King's bedroom, small, uncarpeted, with little in it except two chairs, shelves loaded with war relics, and a picture of the Queen.

In Italy, as in England, the people and the deputies in Parliament listened "with intent and silent interest" when Wilson suggested that high principle might involve a sacrifice of national ambition. The deputies politely sat on their hands when he called for the independence of Italy's neighbors in the Balkans but applauded vigorously every mention of the League of Nations.

It is not easy to know how much of Wilson's own texts were based on canniness and how much on self-delusion. While all the world was aware of the crass bargain Italy had driven in 1915 to gain territorial promises for her entry into the war, Wilson told the deputies he knew "that Italy went into the war for the same exalted principles of right and justice as moved the American people."

The splendor of the Italian tour was almost demolished at the very end when it ran up against the President's unbending Presbyterian view on keeping the Sabbath. Sunday night had been chosen as the finale of the Italian tour, and for the occasion a glittering cast had been gathered from all over Europe for a gala performance of *Aida* at La Scala. The house had been sold out long in advance, though Wilson somehow had not been told of the planned event.

When informed of it he declined on the grounds that he could not attend a theater on Sunday. This prim Protestant rectitude shocked Italy. A resourceful diplomat approached the President at the last minute with the question: Could his religious convictions permit him to attend a sacred concert? Wilson agreed. A soloist sang two hymns that night before the curtain went up on *Aida* and the occasion was saved—even as the League would be—by compromise.

By the time the President was ready to return to Paris the fissures in the Allied camp were evident. Clemenceau, whose tolerance of international sweet talk was limited, had already drawn the crucial distinction between his own and the President's point of view: "America is very far off from Germany but France is very near, and I have preoccupations which do not affect President Wilson as they do a man who has seen the Germans for years in his country. There are wrongs to be righted."

On the French left, *L'Humanité* offered Wilson a warning: "We can-

not but show ourselves full of disquiet for the future. Pichon and
Clemenceau have just formulated publicly their conception of peace. It is
in brutal contradiction to that of President Wilson. . . . Do not let us
deceive ourselves; there is no longer any unity of thought among the
Allies; and in consequence, what has the Peace Conference in store for
us?"

In England, the *Herald*, a labor weekly, warned in outsize headline
type on page one: "Don't be wangled, Wilson!"

Somewhat embarrassing was the support that came from a German
aristocrat who had thrown in his lot with the Social Democrats, the new
Foreign Minister of the Reich, Count Ulrich von Brockdorff-Rantzau:
"No peace must be signed which differs by the breadth of a hair from the
principles of President Wilson's Fourteen Points, which Germany has
accepted and the Entente, willingly or unwillingly, has signed."

Lloyd George returned to Paris with a resounding electoral victory
under his belt and could with great validity claim a mandate from his
people. Similarly, Clemenceau had been handed a decisive vote of confidence from his Parliament. Wilson, on the other hand, was rapidly
running out of support at home, and his status as a minority leader was
becoming every day more obvious. The opposition made political capital
of the reports of the presidential progress through Europe.

Senator Lawrence Y. Sherman rallied the log-cabin sentiment of Americans against the Babylonian luxuries of the Old World. On the floor of
the Senate he declared: "I wish to compare the zinc garbage cans out of
which the American soldier is fed with the . . . solid-gold service and
the inlaid mahogany table from which the President and Rear Admiral
Grayson [Wilson's personal physician] are feasting in London." He described at some length Mrs. Wilson's hat, which sported the plumes of an
egret, and reminded his colleagues that that bird so callously plucked for
the First Lady was "protected in our country by the Safety and Birds
Act." Finally, after enumerating the glasses in the Murat Palace (3,000)
and noting the size of the bathroom (30 feet square), the Senator concluded: "The cables have been burdened with useless news while sleepless
mothers have been crowded off the wires in this foolish display of un-
American adulation abroad. We are further informed that the tips expected to be paid by the President at the several palaces where he is
lodged and entertained in Paris, London, Rome and Brussels will run
from $10,000 to $30,000 each for the parasites who walk backward making obeisance to guests, and other useless appendages of European pomp
and circumstance. These tips would pay for many cable messages to

anxious mothers and be of some real service when drawn from the public treasury supplied by taxes."

And three days before he died Theodore Roosevelt dictated an article for the Kansas City *Star* in which he unwittingly summed up reasons for the League's appeal to all sides in every country: "The trouble with Mr. Wilson's utterances, so far as they are reported, and the acquiescence in them by European statesmen is that they are still absolutely in the stage of rhetoric, precisely like the Fourteen Points. Nobody knows what Wilson really means by them, and so all talk of accepting the Points as the basis for peace or a League of Nations is nonsense, and if the talker is intelligent, it is insincere nonsense, to boot."

The effect on Wilson himself of the adulation, the obeisance of Kings, Parliaments, and Pope, and the thunderous ovations in the streets was to have its political consequences. Harold Nicolson, the diplomat and diarist who was a member of the British delegation, noted that the President seemed to suffer from the same delusion that had afflicted the French revolutionary leader Marat: that *"la volonté générale"*—the general will of the people—was embodied in him alone. It was probable that Wilson had cultivated that illusion long before he came to Europe, but there can be little doubt that the cheers of the millions and the florid acclamations of the press—particularly in Italy—were overpoweringly heady.

The very theatricality of the scenes in which Wilson made his stately entrances and exits served to color an image of Europe he brought with him. It was an image drawn with the broad strokes of a newspaper cartoon: Princelings of a decadent Europe forcing their people to pay for their bloody dramas of ancient prejudice and dynastic quarrels, from which the New World had been rescued by Divine Providence and the wisdom of the Founding Fathers.

In fact, however, Clemenceau's preoccupation with the security of France and his idea of a League that would safeguard that security were in an ancient but not unreasonable tradition. The French journalist Geneviève Tabouis recalled that Sully, the friend and counselor of Henri IV in the seventeenth century, formed what was called "the Great Plan." This was to be a league of small states, headed by France and dedicated to preserving the *status quo*.

In the dawn of the Napoleonic era, Abbé Sieyès adapted the Great Plan to new circumstances. "The French Republic," he said, "surrounded by vassal republics, dominating Europe by her alliances, bending it to her will, imposing peace on all states and propagating the doctrines of the Revolution among the peoples, these are the secular claims that French diplomats should defend with patient wisdom."

Clemenceau prepared to defend such claims. For France the Empire and trade were secondary matters. The prime objective of foreign policy in a peasant nation is the protection of its frontiers. French diplomacy was presented in terms of national honor and integrity.

Britain's policy had different but equally understandable antecedents and was dressed in different colors. The prime function of British diplomacy, Geneviève Tabouis points out, was to serve British commerce. To the French preoccupation with national grandeur and such aristocratic concepts as glory and honor, the British counterposed pragmatism, tempered by the honest merchant's ideal of fair play. Their pragmatism made them leery of the Frenchman's historic principles and inflexible logic. They fancied the symbols of history but preferred a policy of improvisation. In France the charitable called this devotion to flexibility "muddleheadedness"; the critical, "perfidy" or "hypocrisy."

Wickham Steed, the distinguished editor of the London *Times*, explained it in gentler terms: ". . . the great majority of my countrymen are very rarely, if ever, guilty of perfidy or hypocrisy but . . . they are almost always inconsistent. Now inconsistency is not hypocrisy unless it be conscious."

Britain needed to assure itself that the lifelines of trade and Empire would be safeguarded, that no single power would again disturb the comfortable balance of power in Europe, and that Germany would be quickly put into a position to pay its debts and resume its rightful place as a market for trade. Winston Churchill enunciated the position this way: "The time has come to remember the Roman motto: 'Spare the vanquished, bring low the proud.' "

The vanquished were German, the proud were French. And if they were proud, the French were also fearful. In 1870 and in 1914 danger and humiliation had swept easily across the Rhine, at best a feeble natural barrier, whereas Britain stood safe beyond a channel and the United States across an ocean.

General Foch declared: "We must have the left bank of the Rhine. There is no English or American help which could be strong enough and which could arrive in sufficient time to prevent disaster. . . . The Rhine remains therefore today the barrier which is indispensable to the safety of Western Europe and thereby the safety of civilization."

To the French the League of Nations was important if it guaranteed the security of civilization, defended by and embodied in France. Otherwise it was irrelevant. On January 7, President Wilson, freshly arrived from Italy, was having a preliminary encounter with the assembled Prime

Ministers of France, England, and Italy in Colonel House's suite at the Crillon.

Fearing a head-on clash over the League, the Colonel took Clemenceau into another room while the President chatted with Lloyd George.

According to his memoirs, House told Clemenceau that actually the only guarantee France might have that Britain and the United States would promptly come to the aid of France, should the Germans once again pour across the Rhine, would be the solemn undertakings implicit in a League of Nations. The League offered France an opportunity to bind France's allies to her defense. If that opportunity were missed, House said, it might never come again.

Clemenceau then placed both hands on the Colonel's shoulders and told him: "You are right. I am for the League of Nations as you have it in mind and you may count on me to work with you."

The Italians saw in the League a loophole through which their nation might creep into recognition as a power. In the half-century since Italy's unification under the Kings of Savoy, she had been driven or cozened out of every colonial foothold to which she aspired, settling finally for two uneconomic wastelands in Somaliland and Eritrea when other European nations were gobbling up Africa and Asia.

This was due in part at least to a singular lack of diplomatic expertise, epitomized by Agostino Depretis, Premier for eleven years, who said: "When I see an international situation on the horizon, I open my umbrella and wait till it has passed."

It was Depretis who led Italy into the Triple Alliance with Austria and Germany in 1882. Now, having sold out that alliance for territorial promises embodied in the Treaty of London, Italy waited for its payment and for membership in the League, where henceforth it would play a role equal to that of the Great Powers.

The Japanese came out of their crowded archipelago to enter the fraternity of empire seeking only to emulate the earlier achievements of Europeans.

Germany clung desperately to the League and Wilson as its shield and savior from vengeful reprisals.

The smaller nations, those old and impotent ones long used to being buffers, and the burgeoning new ones, many of them basing their claims to independence on freshly exhumed traditions, read Wilson's declarations as a charter for the millennial coexistence of lion and lamb, each with an equal vote.

Into this arena of contradictory hopes came Wilson, undistracted by any intimate knowledge of European history or economics, confident in the power of the Word ultimately to rout the enemies of civilization. He and Colonel House had defined that civilization as the world of Western Europe, redeemed and cleansed by America, and rendered fit to bring the lesser breeds into the age of the League of Nations.

Four

THE
COVENANT

Bedraggled and cold—amid a shortage of fuel and wine—Paris, in January 1919, awaited the most glittering diplomatic assemblage since the Congress of Vienna met to pick up the pieces after Waterloo. Heavy rains had swollen the Seine to dangerous crests, and the wine cellars along the banks were awash with mud.

Ever since the armistice, Parisians had been depositing abandoned German cannon along the Champs-Elysées and the Place de la Concorde as trophies of victory. "If snow comes," *Le Temps* warned, "our most beautiful promenade will look like a reproduction of a scene from the Retreat from Moscow." Although the victory flags were soggy, and lagging garbage collections left the streets in disarray, people danced with a manic gaiety. In homes, in cabarets, at all-night balls and impromptu street-corner celebrations, people flung themselves and each other into the tango. Newspapers called it *La Grippe Argentine*, for it spread like the flu.

The streets of the city, accustomed to the ominous quiet of wartime, suddenly came alive with traffic. In the cafés people gawked at exotic diplomats. The stately Hashemite Prince Faisal of the Hejaz, in billowing Arab kaftan, with his aide and adviser, the legendary Lawrence of Arabia; the Maharajah of Bikaner in British khaki topped by a turban; Armenian prelates in lofty black conical hats; the diminutive Baron Makino of Japan; the lean, elegant, almost boyish Wellington Koo of China—all mingled with the plainer pin-striped diplomats of Europe and their ladies.

Everywhere landlords and innkeepers reaped a harvest of francs, and prices rose scandalously. The news was full of blood and also trivia. In Germany the revolution teetered away from the brink of Bolshevism, and the Spartacist leader Karl Liebknecht, borne on the shoulders of the crowd barely two months before, was murdered along with the revolution's heroine, Rosa Luxemburg, by the police, abetted by a mob. The French Socialist paper *L'Humanité* revealed that the British Cabinet was thinking of inviting the Bolsheviks to Paris, notwithstanding the half-hearted but still sanguinary war the Allies were waging in Russia. And, as a sign of the times, some chauffeurs, waiting until four in the morning outside a fete, gave notice that they would leave en masse if their employers did not call it a night. They were appeased with *pâté de foie gras*, and the party went on.

Dance music mingled with the rattle of teacups at the Hôtel Majestic on the avenue Kléber, which housed the British delegation of two hundred diplomats and advisers, plus an equal number of secretaries and stenographers. There Sir Basil Thomson of Scotland Yard had imposed rigid security measures, restaffing the hotel completely to leave only English chambermaids on duty. He was apparently unaware that the delegation had moved all of its files, maps, and classified documents next door to the Hôtel Astoria, which continued to be maintained by French and other foreigners. British caution was evident morally as well as medically: a chaperone and an obstetrician were provided for the women on the team.

The "organizing ambassador," Sir Maurice Hankey, who presided over the arrangements from his headquarters across the street in the Villa Majestic, wrote to his wife in evident astonishment at what he had wrought: "The Hotel Majestic is a very lively place. All the most beautiful and well-dressed society ladies appear to have been brought over by the various departments. I do not know how they do their work, but in the evening they dance and sing and play bridge!"

Away from it all, in the rue Nitot, a flat had been set aside for Lloyd George, and another, one flight above it, for Balfour. Motorcycles and army cars raced furiously between the British headquarters and Le Bourget, where an airplane shuttle service had been set up, making it possible for delegates to hop to London for tea. "Oh, it was a time of miracles!" exclaimed American press officer Ray Stannard Baker.

The Americans took over the up-to-date Hôtel Crillon. The delegation and the Inquiry staff totaled more than the British two hundred, and to the corps were added some three hundred newsmen. The President stayed in splendid seclusion at the Palais Murat.

The French marshaled their teams at the various ministry offices. The other nations, in groups of fifty and sixty, set up their camps throughout the city. In all, seventy plenipotentiaries, thirty-four alternates, 1,037 delegates, their secretaries, experts, guards, servants, and retainers poured into Paris in the first weeks of January.

This tabulation did not include two impecunious delegates representing the Koreans of Siberia, who signified their intention to attend but who unfortunately had to make the voyage on foot and thus did not arrive until six months after the Conference was over.

The Clock Room on the ground floor of the French Foreign Office at the Quai d'Orsay was known as a plush but soporific waiting room. It dripped with crimson and gilt, and it derived its name from an elaborate timepiece with Indian motifs, dispatched by France to an Indian prince in gratitude for his help against British interests there, a reminder of days when the nations of the Entente Cordiale were less than cordial in colonial competition.

On the afternoon of January 19, 1919, a large horseshoe table filled the huge chamber, around which ranged chairs of ebony and crimson plush. Two gilded armchairs stood at the head of the table—one for the host, President Poincaré, the other for Woodrow Wilson. Nothing so clearly marked the position of the United States in the world as its placement at the head of that horseshoe table, occupying its position by virtue of its wealth and its glow of disinterested purity.

The American delegation, consisting of Secretary of State Lansing, Henry White, and General Bliss (Colonel House was too ill to attend), was seated on humbler plush at Wilson's side. The French, British, and Italians (reduced to three because of a ministerial crisis in Rome) flanked the Americans. Beyond them ranged the representatives of other nations in alphabetical order.

A solemn almost prayerful hush filled the room when President Poincaré rose to make the opening address. All of the delegates rose with him and continued to stand as in church—some reverent, some fidgeting throughout the twenty-five minutes of his address. He expressed the prevailing official sentiment toward the United States when he said: "America, the daughter of Europe, crossed the ocean to wrest her mother from the humiliation of thralldom and to save civilization."

At the end of what seemed a benediction, there was no applause and, after a translation into English, the French President rose solemnly and shook the hand of every delegate at the table, then left the room.

Clemenceau moved to the head of the table as temporary chairman and briskly got down to business. By prearrangement Wilson proposed him as the permanent chairman. (Protocol made such a designation inevitable in spite of Wilson's earlier assumption that he would have that honor.) The motion was seconded by Lloyd George in a jollying speech in which he referred to the seventy-eight-year-old Clemenceau as the "Grand Young Man of Europe." When the translator rendered it as the "Grand Old Man," both Clemenceau and Lloyd George in feigned indignation protested and thus lightened the churchlike solemnity of the occasion.

"We came here as friends," said Clemenceau. "We must pass through that door as brothers." A few more formalities and the infighting could begin.

When the Plenary Conference went into its second session on January 25, the diplomats continued to follow a script well prepared and rehearsed. There would be no opposition to the League in principle. It had been agreed that the structure of the organization would be hammered out in committee—certainly the most prestigious of the Conference, and that committee would be headed by Wilson himself.

In presenting the League idea for formal acceptance, Wilson outlined its aims with a prescience that was to become dramatically evident half a century later. "Is it not a startling circumstance," the President said, "that the great discoveries of science, that the quiet study of man in laboratories, that the thoughtful developments which have taken place in quiet lecture rooms, have now been turned to the destruction of civilization? The enemy whom we have just overcome had at its seats of learning some of the principal centers of scientific study and discovery, and used them in order to make destruction sudden and complete; and only the watchful, continuous cooperation of man can see to it that science, as well as armed men, is kept within the harness of civilization."

He also restated the unique disinterestedness of the United States: "In a sense, the United States is far less interested in this subject than the other nations here assembled. With her great territory and her extensive sea borders, it is less likely that the United States should suffer from the attack of enemies than that many of the other nations here should suffer; and the ardor . . . for the Society of Nations is not an ardor springing out of fear and apprehension, but an ardor springing out of the ideals which have come to consciousness in the war. . . . We are masters of no people but are here to see that every people shall choose its own master and govern its own destinies, not as we wish but as it wishes.

"We are here to see, in short, that the very foundations of this war are swept away. Those foundations were . . . the aggression of great

Powers upon small . . . the holding together of unwilling subjects by the duress of arms . . . the power of small bodies of men to work their will upon mankind and use them as pawns in a game. And nothing less than the emancipation of the world from these things will accomplish peace."

It was a stirring speech and for the President it was a personal triumph: He was here proposing a new world order to the assembled nations of the world. The vote for the establishment of the League was, as prearranged, unanimous.

The resolution, which had been painstakingly drafted at the Crillon, declared:

> 1. It is essential to the maintenance of the world settlement, which the Associated Nations are now met to establish, that a League of Nations be created to promote international cooperation, to ensure the fulfillment of accepted international obligations, and to provide safeguards against war.
>
> 2. This League should be created [the minutes mistakenly printed this word as "treated" and the error has since been perpetuated in many histories] as an integral part of the general Treaty of Peace, and should be open to every civilized nation which can be relied on to promote its objects. [The vagueness of these membership qualifications reconciled those who dreamed of universality with others who would have drawn the line at Germans or Russians.]
>
> 3. The members of the League should periodically meet in international conference, and should have a permanent organization and secretariat to carry on the business of the League in the intervals between the conferences.

A League of Nations was then, at long last, a fact. It would have to be cut and shaped to the realities of the world, and ostensibly this was to be done in committee. Hoping that the smaller powers would not get in the way, Wilson had suggested that the big powers work out the entire structure of the League, summoning the little ones only when a point under discussion might refer to their particular problems.

In the end he yielded, and the Commission on the League of Nations was composed of representatives of the United States, Britain, France, Italy, Japan, Belgium, Brazil, Portugal, China, and Serbia. The last five had been chosen by the smaller powers themselves to represent their views.

Wilson insisted that he himself would represent his country on the Commission and would, of course, chair it. His fellow delegate would be the co-plotter of the new order, the mediator between the dreams of Magnolia and the realities of Europe, Colonel House.

Before the Commission could get to work, however, an attempt had to be made to clear away some of the jungle of tangled national aspirations and conflicting philosophies. The hacking went on at two principal sites: the spacious, workmanlike suite of Colonel House at the Crillon and at the Quai d'Orsay. The ailing House kept the American legal adviser, David Hunter Miller, conferring all day with Lord Cecil and the visionary South African general Jan Christiaan Smuts, then up half the night juggling the British views with the President's drafts to arrive at an Anglo-Saxon consensus.

Prime among the ingredients to be mixed was the basic Covenant draft, which House had prepared in Magnolia and which Wilson had amended. Then there was a pamphlet by General Smuts entitled *The League of Nations: A Programme for the Peace Conference,* which had just come out in England. In addition to a ringing phraseology ("The tents have been struck and the great caravan of humanity is on the march . . ."), the Smuts pamphlet was noteworthy for refining earlier British drafts and including a proposal for converting the enemy's colonies into trust territories. Smuts had gathered some of these notions from programs of European socialists and British trade-unionists.

There was also a draft by Lord Cecil which was close to the American position, except for differences on the subject of Freedom of the Seas. Lastly there were proposals by Jewish organizations to include in the Covenant some commitment to protect the rights of minorities—a point which Wilson favored.

These were mixed into a draft which came to be known as Wilson's second, and then revised into a third draft that was still to be worked over by the Anglo-American experts.

The President, when he was not closeted at the Crillon, was wrestling with Lloyd George and Clemenceau, being soothed by the gentle Orlando or nettled by the vigorous Sonnino, and alternately enraged and encouraged by representatives of smaller powers who besieged the shapers of the world. Everywhere in Paris diplomats scurried to win a spot on eternally filled agenda or to line up support with this or that great man.

Wickham Steed, editor of the London *Times* who also ran an influential column in the *Daily Mail,* was a handy source of advice. Among those who turned to him was Eduard Beneš, Foreign Minister of the infant state of Czechoslovakia, who found himself beyond his depth in a search for recognition. His story illustrates the semantic and psychological factors on which the fate of nations depended in that season of bubbling hopes.

Cecil and Balfour had refused to accept a French formula of recognition which described Beneš's Czechoslovak National Council "as the first basis" of the future government of Czechoslovakia because it did not leave the Czech people enough leeway, they said, to choose some other form. Beneš could not understand the objection or see his way around it. Steed took the formula which Cecil and Balfour had rejected and made one correction. He crossed out the words "as the first basis" and substituted "as trustee for," then told Beneš: "Take that to the Foreign Office tomorrow and you will get your recognition."

"What does it mean?" asked Beneš.

"Don't ask, my dear fellow," said Steed. "You will never understand. 'Trustee' is a mystical word. It is legal, moral, metaphysical, anything you like, but it will do your business for you."

As Steed predicted, Cecil and Balfour accepted the edited version with no difficulty whatever, and Beneš returned to Steed, thankful, delighted, and still mystified. "They have agreed to recognize us," he reported. "They swallowed the word 'trustee' like cream, but I still don't know what it means." Steed attempted to explain:

"You must understand that we are a mystical people with a number of 'blessed words' in our vocabulary. Those words calm our moral scruples and flatter our sense of fairness. These are things which Continental peoples and governments have never been able to understand and probably never will. That is why they are always likely to be wrong about British policy . . . you will see that the Americans will accept our formula because they are still Puritan enough to know what it means."

"Trustee" was indeed a word of potent magic as long as it could be left in a rhetorical cloud. It lost its charm when hardheaded diplomats tried to define it, weigh it, calculate its meaning in profit and loss. That happened in a very nearly catastrophic encounter on January 30, 1919, four days before the League Commission was to hold its first meeting.

On that afternoon the Big Ten, with an impressive retinue of experts and aides, gathered in the spacious but dreary office of Stéphen Pichon at the Quai d'Orsay primarily to see how the word "trustee" or "mandate" would apply to the German colonies in the Pacific.

Japan was, of course, vitally interested, since it had been promised in 1915, on the occasion of its commitment to the democratic cause, that it would inherit, among other things, German isles in the North Pacific. On hand for the discussion were the representatives of the British dominions of Australia, New Zealand, and South Africa, each with an eye on a nearby piece of German property and each preferring outright, unvarnished annexation to what they regarded as euphemisms.

William Ferguson Massey, the huge and craggy Prime Minister of New

Zealand, who had demanded not one but two seats at the Peace Conference, aside from the British delegation, agreed with Lloyd George that
the Germans did not deserve to retain their colonies but argued that the
British Pacific dominions did not deserve to be fobbed off with half
measures. According to the minutes of that meeting, Massey believed
direct annexation "would be better for the European races and also better
for the native races. They would be able to proceed with the education of
the native races, not only in secular matters, but also in the principles of
Christianity, which he believed were necessary for the welfare of all
nations."

He thought that justice ought to be meted out on all sides—to those
who had broken the "law of civilization" and to those who had suffered
from that lawlessness. In plain terms this seemed to mean the direct
transfer of some of the Samoa Islands, New Guinea, and South-West
Africa from undeserving Germany to the deserving dominions.

If outright annexation were ruled out, he was prepared to accept a
mandate providing that what had been called a colony be incorporated
into the new motherland, "administered under the laws of the mandatory
state as integral portions thereof," with the promise that the mandatory
or governing state would outlaw the slave trade and all traffic in arms and
liquor and agree not to raise native armies. Those concessions, drafted as a
compromise by Lloyd George, were as far as he was prepared to go.

Wilson, in cold anger, asked whether Australia and New Zealand were
presenting an ultimatum.

Massey said, no, it was not an ultimatum but he thought he had made
himself perfectly clear, though he could not speak for Australia.

William Morris Hughes, Australia's Prime Minister, an astonishing contrast to his hulking confrere from New Zealand, was a short and desic-
cated man, who was obliged to use an electric earphone to hear the
argument, and even at that, did not do very well. He began to go over the
ground already torn up by Massey's bulldozer when Wilson broke in to
ask whether he had heard his question.

Hughes asked him to repeat it, and again Wilson demanded to know
whether the British dominions were serving an ultimatum on the Peace
Conference. Hughes paused reflectively, then said he thought President
Wilson had put the situation fairly well.

Hughes's evident antipathy to Wilsonism was based on certain embarrassing facts. He put it this way to newsmen: "The spectacle of New
Zealand administering one of the islands of Samoa under a mandate, while
the United States . . . administers two of the Samoa Islands without any
mandate, will be a particularly curious paradox."

That paradox was one of many traps history had set for Wilson. The Samoa Islands had been divided in 1899 in a friendly agreement between Kaiser Wilhelm and President McKinley at a time when many Americans had come to believe that the English-speaking and Teutonic nations were divinely ordained to be what a U.S. senator called "the master organizers of the world." Now the Kaiser, twenty years later, had lost his Samoa; and Wilson was solicitous about German Samoa's continued existence as a colony but made no offer to give American Samoa even the figleaf of a mandate.

In Hughes's mind Lloyd George was also suspect. Shortly before the armistice the Australian Prime Minister had written a letter to Lloyd George marked "Most Secret" in which he urged the British to renege on the promises to reward Japan with the German islands of the North Pacific. He reminded Lloyd George of "Australia's deeply rooted mistrust of Japan" and warned that his country's "welfare and trade are alike seriously menaced by Japan. The recognition of Japan's claims to these islands will enable her to pursue much more effectively her policy which is directed towards securing for herself the trade which Britain and Australia have built up."

Japan's contribution to the war effort was belittled. "As a matter of duty," Hughes wrote, "Japan has given us absolutely nothing. Her assistance, such as it is, has on each occasion been bought by 'considerations' and 'compensations.' "

Lloyd George answered in a crisp memo to Hughes, pointing out that in 1915, when the promises were made in order to have Japanese naval support in the South Atlantic, in the Indian Ocean, and in the Mediterranean, the governments of Australia and New Zealand had been informed and had approved, and that part of the deal had been that Japan would support the British Empire's claims to Pacific islands south of the equator. "It is clear," Lloyd George added, "that His Majesty's Government can neither now nor at the Peace Conference go back on this official assurance without committing a breach of faith."

Now, faced again with the anti-Japanese hostility of Australia and New Zealand, Lloyd George glossed over the crisis by remarking that, inasmuch as the views of everyone had been heard, the matter could wait for development of the League. Clemenceau then entered the controversy by objecting to one aspect of the matter that affected French security, the yardstick by which he measured all propositions, financial or philosophic. France, exposed to European dangers as no other member of the Allies, would be unfairly hampered in its own defense if it were not permitted to raise volunteer troops from territories it agreed to accept under a mandate.

Lloyd George assured Clemenceau that the prohibition was designed only to prevent the use of armed natives "for other than police purposes or defense of territory" and that the exceptions would clearly cover defense of the mandatory government. Clemenceau, who acknowledged France's debt to its colonial troops, said this was all right so long as everyone understood France's needs.

The minutes of that afternoon concluded:

"Mr. Lloyd George said that so long as M. Clemenceau did not train big nigger armies for the purposes of aggression, that was all the clause was intended to guard against. M. Clemenceau said that he did not want to do that. He therefore understood that Mr. Lloyd George's interpretation was adopted.

"President Wilson said that Mr. Lloyd George's interpretation was consistent with the phraseology. M. Clemenceau said that he was quite satisfied."

The unabashed conviction that Europeans were the carriers of civilization and the proper mentors of lesser breeds, voiced so bluntly on that afternoon at the Quai d'Orsay, was to have a series of violent sequels within the next two weeks and would come close to shattering the League before it was born. Certainly the prenatal experience left its marks on the infant.

At two-thirty in the afternoon of February 3, 1919, twenty-two men gathered in Colonel House's suite at the Crillon for the first meeting of the Commission on the League of Nations. The Colonel set the stage. The head of the table was reserved for Wilson with a chair at his left for House and a chair behind them for the legal adviser, David Hunter Miller. Then came the British—the tall and gangling Lord Cecil, legs sprawling before him, his suit ill-fitting and rumpled, his gleaming pate surrounded by tufts of hair, giving him the air of an ungainly bird. With him was the stern and military General Jan Christiaan Smuts, the Boer who, after he was beaten by the British at the age of thirty, retired, as he then said, "to water my orange trees and to study Kant's Critical Philosophy." At forty-nine he had offered his own concept of the League, tallying closely with Wilsonism, though hedging on general principles wherever they might confine the ambitions of South Africa.

The French were represented by that amiable and earnest "peace fanatic" Léon Bourgeois, who had put together all of the French ideas on a League and whose notion of the ideal form in which to channel a clash of nations was a lawyer's duel amid the majesty of an international court. He was visibly offended when someone at the meeting asked him whether in fact there really existed a Permanent Court of International Justice at The Hague (then just twenty years old). "Sir," he said, "I have the honor to be one of its members." He had prepared an outline of procedure for the Commission which was thorough, logical, systematic, and ignored. He was seconded by the succinct lawyer-politician Ferdinand Larnaude.

Premier Orlando lent his dreamy eyes and the weight of his office, but little more, to the Commission. There were also the Japanese Baron Makino and Viscount Chinda; the graceful Koo of China; and the gentle, courteous, and elegant Paul Hymans of Belgium, conscious that he spoke not only for the first victim of the war but for the little powers that gathered about him. Also speaking for those little powers were Jaime Batalha Reis of Portugal, somewhat distracted by an untimely revolution that had broken out in Lisbon; Epitacio Pessôa of Brazil; and Dr. Milenko R. Vesnitch of Serbia, for whom the war would not be over so long as the genial Orlando at Wilson's side nourished Italian ambitions in the Balkans. Aides and translators made up the rest of the group around the table at the Crillon.

When Miller arrived at the Colonel's suite proudly bearing printed copies of Wilson's third and latest draft of the Covenant, the Colonel informed him that they had changed their minds the night before and were going to use the draft in which Miller himself had reconciled Wilson's thinking with that of the British. No one had told Miller, and now he had to scurry to have enough copies made up for the delegates.

When the copies were distributed, Wilson announced that the draft had been painstakingly prepared by him, Colonel House, Lord Cecil, and General Smuts and that the Commission would proceed to discuss it point by point.

Léon Bourgeois suggested at least a twenty-four-hour delay to consider the document, which as yet no one outside the British-American teams had even seen. Orlando thought it ought to be translated into French. To which Cecil answered: "We must push ahead. There has already been a great deal of discussion [referring to his sessions with Wilson and House]. We must get down to the details. The whole world is awaiting the results of these deliberations."

But, the French protested, there was not even yet a secretariat, stenographers, secretaries, the essential, time-honored accoutrements of an orderly international discussion. "Unless we have a record," said Larnaude, "we shall be working in the dark."

"The important thing," said Wilson, "is to make progress. The record will take care of itself." He added half jokingly (which is to say half seriously): "I am opposed to a record being kept because I want to keep an open mind. I want to be able to say on Wednesday quite the opposite of what I may have said on Monday."

Bourgeois pointed out that he not only wanted to study the draft himself but also wanted time to consult his government. At that Wilson grew impatient. If the delegates were to consult their governments on each point, he said testily, they would never get anywhere. The governments must be presented with the plan only when it is completed. After Belgium and Portugal had endorsed the request for a chance to read the draft overnight before discussions began, the meeting adjourned amid French despair.

What, Cecil asked before the group disbanded, could be told to the press? Wilson suggested a formula: "We met to compare views as to how to proceed and decide upon a procedure which would advance the matter." That wording, slightly refined in the editing, made up the communiqué which was handed to the press, and it added to the dismay of reporters. Besides occasional authorized briefings from House and Cecil, they would have to rely on café gossip and unattributed speculation in this dawn of "open diplomacy."

Wilson yielded only on the matter of stenographers, who, beginning with the third meeting, were allowed to sit at a table considerably removed from the delegates, often out of earshot. They had to confine themselves largely to noting those present. Historians ever since have tended to rely principally on unofficial, personal notes kept by participants or aides at the conference table.

The ten meetings of the Commission, held in as many days, shaped the League largely by rolling over objections. Some of these, however, proved troublesome. The small powers very quickly and unexpectedly found themselves engaged in a bitter test of strength with Wilson, the man they had hailed as their disinterested champion. This was not due to a cynical change of heart on Wilson's part. He still viewed himself, indeed, as their champion, but he felt that only a benign autocracy could assure their democratic rights.

The small powers did not at once grasp this American point of view and in the second session bridled at the proposal that only the Great Powers would be represented on the Council of the League of Nations— its executive body and steering group. When the argument grew bitter, the small powers, with Belgium's Hymans as spokesman, proposed that the Commission itself be expanded to include representatives of four more nations: Greece, Poland, Rumania, and Czechoslovakia.

Wilson and Cecil opposed the move. They confidently put the question to a vote—and lost. The battle continued on February 5, even before the fresh reinforcements of the small powers could arrive. "I strongly urge going slow," Lord Cecil told the delegates, "on the proposal to give the smaller powers four representatives on the Council. Our purpose is, of course, to make the League a success, and that demands the support of the Great Powers. Two representatives of the lesser powers should suffice."

Hymans lost his elegant aplomb and shouted at the mild Cecil: "What you propose is nothing else than the Holy Alliance."

Vesnitch, the Serbian, remarked dryly: "It will certainly look odd to tell the world that we have decided to give five representatives in all to five nations, and two in all to the remaining forty-five."

The reinforcements joined the fray at the fourth session on February 9. They did little to turn the tide, but they brought into the arena a certain flair. There was the elder statesman with the fierce Cretan glance, Eleutherios Venizelos, who, as President of the Council in Greece, had eloquently spurned Germany's offer to join the Central Powers in exchange for a piece of Serbia. "My country is too little to commit so great an infamy," he had said then. Now his mission in Paris was to hold off rapacious Italy from the Balkans and see to it that no power less inhibited than his own dominated Constantinople. With him came Ion Brătianu, Premier of Rumania, bent on persuading France and Italy to support his country as the bastion of Latin civilization in the east, even though Rumania itself was in the throes of uprisings and pogroms; Roman V. Dmowski of Poland, often at odds with his pianist President Paderewski, uneasy at the ambitions of his little neighbor Czechoslovakia, and embarrassed at persistent reports of pogroms and anti-Jewish boycotts at home; and Premier Karel Kramář of Czechoslovakia, seeking the big powers' friendship against the prospects of Austria's union with Germany, which he foresaw as a peril to his infant nation.

This line-up of uncertain unity was not calculated to make the mighty tremble. The Goliaths endured the slingshots from the divided band of Davids and, in the end, won their way. "The Council shall consist of Representatives of the Principal Allies and Associated Powers (the United States, Britain, France, Italy and Japan) together with Representatives of four other Members of the League."

The Assembly, comprising all members, was to choose the four "non-permanent members" by a two-thirds majority for whatever term of participation it might decide. The power of the great international democracy of the League was safe in the hands of those who bore the burden and the booty of civilization.

Just how powerful the League was to be was the sticking point for the French, and the question drove Léon Bourgeois and Ferdinand Larnaude into repeated collisions with their Anglo-American colleagues. In actual fact the French position had changed markedly from the original amused disinterest manifested by Clemenceau when first the League was broached. The change perhaps dates from Clemenceau's dramatic meeting with House in which the Colonel explained that the League of Nations would actually be France's only guarantee of immediate Anglo-American aid in case of German aggression.

The combination of lofty principle and practical guarantees was irresistible. However, French statesmen reasoned, if the League were to serve the interests of France—and therefore civilization—it would have to have teeth. A toothless ideal is picturesquely quixotic but a toothless guard dog is a danger.

The London *Times* correspondent noted, "The French attitude towards the League of Nations has undergone an undeniable change. In many quarters, where, but a few weeks ago, it was looked upon as the vague dream of a retired college professor, it is now held to be an essential instrument of the present settlement, and as containing a real potentiality, at any rate the germ, of permanent peace."

Léon Bourgeois and Ferdinand Larnaude, therefore, pressed unrelentingly for a League of Nations that would have police powers, embodied either in military force of its own or in contingents of member states pledged to be available on call from the League. France wanted a general staff that would be able instantly to coordinate a military defense. In all probability, of course, the commander of such a general staff would have been the undisputed hero of the war, Marshal Foch. To the United States and Britain, at least, this would have been untenable. To put a nation's military forces under rigid international inspection and at the beck and call of a foreigner struck at the root of national sovereignty. Thus, the League, in its very infancy, had to face the question whether the Great Powers were willing to sacrifice any appreciable part of that sovereignty.

Ironically it was the pacifist Léon Bourgeois who put the case for resting the authority of the League upon military might. "A force must be created," he said, "so superior to that of all nations or to that of all alliances that no nation or combination of nations can challenge or resist it. In order that the international force should be what President Wilson desires, it must be so great that no single force can defeat it." Bourgeois quoted Wilson's gallant oration before the Chamber of Deputies in which the President had said, "The frontier of France is the frontier of the world's liberties." The French envisioned a League that would assure those frontiers.

Wilson, with a plainly wary eye on his own Congress, said that "we cannot offer more than the condition of the world enables us to give," and to the furious French insistence that the League be more than a pious covenant, he offered a pious answer: "The only method by which we can achieve this end lies in our having confidence in the good faith of the nations who belong to the League. There must be between them a cordial agreement and goodwill . . . When danger comes, we too will come, and we will help you, but you must trust us. We must all depend on our mutual good faith . . . No nation will consent to control [of arms and military preparations]. As for us Americans we cannot consent to control because of our Constitution."

Bourgeois, recalling the long wait for American support in the last war, said if help took months or years to come, it might be useless and the League would be "nothing but a dangerous façade."

There was one other slim hope for a front against aggression: disarmament. Indeed, disarmament was a consummation devoutly to be wished but not to be enforced, the British and the Americans told the French. Larnaude put the question bluntly: "Could states which refused to accept the plans for reduction of armaments proposed by the Council remain in the League?"

Cecil replied that states refusing to comply would nevertheless remain in the League. Universality was an objective upon which all were agreed. "There would be no obligations to carry out recommendations, which would be formulated merely for the consideration of the several governments."

Bourgeois then tried to solve the problem by pleading for some international inspection of arms so that at least the League could be alerted to any preparations for war. Cecil maintained that such surveillance was in fact unnecessary inasmuch as everyone had known of Germany's military preparations years in advance of the war and that no country could really prepare in secret. Larnaude recalled that at the battle of Charleroi thirty German divisions appeared out of nowhere, the Allied intelligence having greatly underestimated the extent of German preparations. When Cecil suggested that all countries were supposed to report their military strengths, Larnaude suggested that "it was quite illogical for the controller to control himself."

In the end France had to settle for a complex machinery of hearing disputes, with a possible invitation to member states to join in sanctions amounting to a sort of economic excommunication. To ease French feelings, Cecil proposed a permanent commission to "advise the League . . . on military and naval questions generally." The sop was embodied in the Covenant, but the French were scarcely reassured.

The lack of reassurance was in fact becoming general in the nightly sessions around the conference table at the Crillon, except in the Anglo-American camp, where the euphoria was irrepressible. "Practically everything originates from our end of the table," noted Colonel House in his diary. "That is, with Lord Robert Cecil and the President . . . The President excels in such work. He seems to like it and his short talks in explanation of his views are admirable. I have never known anyone to do such work as well."

Actually the Colonel, the Lord, and the President felt themselves on the verge of triumph because what they had in mind was not so much a political act as a first step toward moral regeneration. The bread-and-butter practicalities that preoccupied France and the lesser powers seemed to them to demonstrate a narrow vision and a deplorable self-interest. "It is the spirit back of the Covenant," said the Colonel, "that counts more than the text."

The spirit of the Covenant—and of Wilson the Covenanter—was to be tested yet again—this time by the Japanese, who sought what they considered a rather elementary implementation of the concept of equality of men, nations, and races.

Although the subject of the German Empire in the Pacific had come up at the Quai d'Orsay, the final disposition of these colonies was to be spelled out in the Covenant by the Commission. There the demands of New Zealand, Australia, and South Africa for outright annexation were answered with the verbal magic of the "mandate." The South Pacific islands and South-West Africa were singled out to "be administered under the laws of the Mandatory Powers as integral portions of its territory" precisely as demanded by the clamoring dominions.

France offered no objections because it expected to acquire the "mandates" of Syria and Lebanon. Similarly, Britain, it was understood, was to have the trusteeship of Palestine, Transjordan, Togoland, and the Cameroons. For Belgium there was Ruanda-Urundi. Japan, as agreed, was to receive the Marianas, Caroline, and Marshall islands in the North Pacific as well as Chinese concessions. The peoples thus mandated were referred to in the Covenant as "peoples not yet able to stand by themselves under the strenuous conditions of the modern world."

Although the Japanese had presumably proved in war that they could stand quite ably by themselves, they had not been cheerfully accepted when they emigrated or traveled abroad. Australia and New Zealand made no pretense about excluding all Orientals from their shores. The United States had been slowly shutting its door to immigration from the Far East. According to a "Gentlemen's Agreement," reached in 1907, the Japanese government agreed "voluntarily" to restrict emigration to the trickle approved by the United States. Chinese workmen, imported to help build the railroads of the West, had been lynched and their homes had been burned when jobs grew scarce and competition keen. Pressure was growing to bar formally the admission of Orientals on the West Coast. Into this swamp of racial antagonisms—which Wilson and Lloyd George were doing their best to ignore—lightly stepped the two Japanese nobles Baron Makino and Viscount Chinda.

They asked for the inclusion of one sentence in the Covenant of the League of Nations: "The equality of nations being a basic principle of the League of Nations, the High Contracting Parties agree to accord, as soon as possible, to all alien nationals of States Members of the League equal and just treatment in every respect, making no distinction, either in law or in fact, on account of their race or nationality." It seemed an inoffensive and even a logical amendment to Wilson's favorite clause proclaiming the inviolability of the human conscience and the free exercise of religion.

Intimations of the Japanese preoccupation with racial discrimination had come early in February, when the Baron and the Viscount, following the customary path of troubled diplomats, brought the problem to Colonel House. The Colonel's diary reveals that he transferred them to "the backs of the British, for every solution which the Japanese and I have proposed, [Australian P.M.] Hughes of the British delegation objects to."

The Japanese apparently found the Colonel receptive and thanked him for his "considerate sympathy," but they came away with only a hatful of words. On February 6, the Colonel noted: "Viscount Chinda brought another draft covering the race question. He found, after consultation with his legal adviser, that the one we agreed upon was practically meaningless. The one he brought today will not be accepted either by our people or the British Colonies. The Japs [sic] are making the adoption of a clause regarding immigration a sine qua non of their adhesion to the League of Nations."

Ever seeking a neat semantic reconciliation of opposites, the Colonel confided that he thought a compromise was possible "which will in no way weaken the American or British Dominions' position and yet will satisfy the amour-propre of the Japanese." This description of the race question as a Japanese foible was symptomatic of the prevailing American attitude on the matter.

As Baron Makino put it during a press conference, the Japanese had a basic problem: every time their energetic people tried to expand beyond their overcrowded island they "found the door closed against them." So far, the Baron pointed out, they had not "allowed themselves to take a morbid view of the situation, nor will they in the future. They have imagination and understanding enough to take a sympathetic view of the attitude of their friendly neighbors, although at the same time they are not unmindful of the maintenance of the dignity and pride proper to the people of a world power."

The Baron's views of his people resembled Gilbert and Sullivan's "three little maids from school" far more than the fierce Samurai of legend. "We are far less worldly-wise than we are supposed by some people," Baron Makino said. "On the contrary we are on the visionary side. Our people are idealists."

Japan did indeed have both aspects, one profile visible from Asia, the other from Europe. To the Asian, the Japanese were conquerors who had defeated the Czar, assisted the Western powers in crushing the Boxer Rebellion, seized Korea, and inflicted on China one of its "days of shame" by forcing the infant republic in 1915 to bow to the "Twenty-one Demands" which would have made it a Japanese protectorate.

In Europe, on the other hand, the Japanese, their initiation dues fully paid, waited patiently to be admitted to a respectable club. They had helped to keep the door open in China for all of the world's civilized concessionaires. They had a distinguished war record. "There was never a temptation," Baron Makino told the press, "to treat with the forces which stood for gain and spoils regardless of right. Every inclination in us drew us to the side of the Entente. There never was a moment when we regretted our decision, and never a time when we were not loyal to the core, far removed from the center of the conflict as we were."

The bill which the Japanese were handing to the victorious powers had two parts. One was to be paid in mandates and imperial concessions; the other, in the acknowledgment of racial equality, which in turn could be used to ease the discriminatory treatment of Japanese nationals.

After shuttling vainly between the Colonel's suite at the Crillon and the British offices at the Majestic, Baron Makino raised the matter formally at the meeting of the League Commission on February 13, when the article on religious freedom was up for discussion. He read from a carefully prepared text:

"This article," he said, "attempts to eliminate religious causes of strife from international relationships, and as the race question is also a standing difficulty which may become acute and dangerous at any moment in the future, it is desirable that a provision should be made in this Covenant for the treatment of the subject. It would seem that matters of religion and race could well go together." He did not pretend that the clause would in itself do much. "It must be admitted," he said, "that the question of race prejudice is a very delicate and complicated matter, involving play of deep human passion, and therefore requiring careful management." It would be merely an "invitation" to governments and peoples to "examine the question more closely." In the future, said Baron Makino, members of all races within a nation would have to foot the costs of implementing League decisions and therefore "each national would like to feel and in fact demand that he should be placed on an equal footing with people he undertakes to defend even with his life."

He recalled that in the war just concluded men of different races had fought side by side. "I think it only just," he concluded, "that after this common suffering and deliverance the principle at least of equality among men should be admitted and be made the basis of future intercourse."

The point and its phrasing were so Wilsonian that it was hard to counter it. Lord Cecil did not attempt it. Instead he paid tribute to the "nobility of thought" voiced by the Baron, but referred to "serious problems within the British Empire" and suggested postponement. Venizelos proposed that the whole question of religion and race be omitted from the Covenant and be considered by the League when it was formed. Other members, seeking a way out, applauded that strategy. Wilson was not himself present at the session, but Colonel House tentatively approved the compromise, reserving Wilson's right to raise the matter again, since the Freedom of Religion clause was so dear to the President's heart. Baron Makino also served notice that the matter might be raised again.

When House told Wilson that the only way to avoid a commitment on race was to avoid one on religion, the President agreed, all the more readily because it meant that the Commission would be ready with its draft of the Covenant on the thirteenth of February, that magical Wilsonian number, and that its articles, without the religious clause, would number exactly twenty-six, or twice thirteen.

This was indeed a victory for the President's numerological prejudices, but a sober review of the realities was less enchanting. The League was now in skeleton form, if not yet in flesh and blood. Yet even at this stage—and the draft would still have to be debated by the Peace Conference as a whole and by all the signatories in their respective Cabinets and Parliaments and Congresses—the original vision had already been compromised, on at least these crucial points:

• It was not to be a League with power to enforce its decisions beyond moral suasion. Though economic and other sanctions would be available for use against an aggressor, their application would depend on the zeal of each member.

• It was not to be a democratic League in which a little power could presume to have anything remotely resembling an equal say with the great and rich in running the world's affairs, although the powerless were assured at least a forum for their complaints.

• The colonial peoples were to be regarded as the children of the world, though some at least were listed as out of grammar school. Masters were to become mandatory powers and tutors.

• The race question had been shelved in deference to certain local customs among the civilized.

Other questions once thought to be burning in Wilson's mind were now dismissed as trivial. For example, there was the matter of Freedom of the Seas, which only two months earlier had seemed to open an unbridgeable gulf between Britain and the United States. Wilson himself had declared it to be an issue on which he would not yield, the British War Cabinet was seized with the most intense anxiety, and the fight raised the prospect of a naval arms race between the two allies, perhaps an eventual war.

On February 14, a few moments before the draft Covenant was to be revealed to the Plenary Conference at the Quai d'Orsay, Wilson wrote off that burning issue as a joke. When a reporter raised the question at a press conference, the President said: "I am glad you asked me that, for I want to tell you a good joke on myself. I did not see this joke until I came over here. Under the League of Nations there will be no neutrals. They will all be in the League, and subject to the League's decisions on the matter of the exertion of armed force. If there are no neutrals there will be no issue over sea rights, for the freedom of the seas puzzle arose over relations between belligerents and neutrals. The League will now settle all matters of naval policy. So, it might be said, 'There ain't no such thing' as an issue of freedom of the seas."

Other minor matters had been settled simply by not being raised. By the February 14 reading of the draft, the British Empire had somehow acquired six votes at the Conference and in the League: In addition to Britain itself, there would also be Canada, South Africa, Australia, New Zealand, and India. Colonel House seems to have been among the few who realized this multiplication of British voices, all expected to support the mother country, but he saw in it a possible undercover liberation of the British colonies. "When this dawns on the Conference," he wrote in his diary, "I am wondering what they will do. As far as I am concerned I shall not bring it up, and for reasons which seem to be sufficient. If Great Britain can stand giving her Dominions representation in the League, no one should object."

At three-thirty in the afternoon of Friday, February 14, in the Clock Room of the Quai d'Orsay, Wilson announced to a Plenary Meeting of the Peace Conference that the fourteen-member Commission on the League of Nations had brought in a unanimous report proposing a Covenant. He read the text and, in a speech that followed, said: "A living thing is born, and we must see to it that the clothes we put upon it do not hamper it—a vehicle of power, but a vehicle in which power may be varied at the discretion of those who exercise it, and in accordance with the changing circumstances of the time. And yet, while it is elastic, while it is general in its terms, it is definite in the one thing we were called upon to make definite. It is a definite guarantee of peace."

In closing he held up a copy of the Covenant and said solemnly: "This document is the condemnation of war . . . Force is vanquished. The peoples can now live in friendship like members of one family, and soon as brothers."

That same evening a red carpet was unrolled before the President and Mrs. Wilson for their walk to the train that would take them to Brest on the first stage of their homeward journey. It was to be a brief trip to catch Congress before its adjournment, to mend political fences, and to spike the guns of the opposition to the League.

Technically Secretary Lansing was the ranking officer left in Paris, but, according to the minutes of the Council of Ten, Wilson "asked Colonel House to take his place while he was away." The Secretary was, in fact, treated by all the Wilson camp as an irrelevance if not as an enemy within the gates. He had never concealed his distrust of Wilsonism. He inveighed against the concept of "self-determination" and exclaimed: "What a calamity the phrase was ever uttered!" He was intolerant of the lip service to equality and maintained that "even a World Court could never be constituted if the cultural as well as other superiorities of certain powers of the world were not in some way recognized."

He wanted a League that would be virtually without powers of enforcement at all, willing only to offer the "negative guarantee" of agreeing to "nonintercourse" with powers that might defy the League. In general, his memoranda were said to be virtually unread by Wilson, although, as the deliberations proceeded, the League was coming more and more to resemble his vision rather than the original so fondly explored by Wilson and House at Magnolia.

As usual, the President departed with only the haziest instructions to his subordinates, but he did inform the Council of Ten that "he did not wish his absence to stop so important, essential and urgent work as the preparation of a preliminary peace." When he left Paris, Wilson "looked happy, as well indeed he should," the Colonel noted.

It was true that in general the draft Covenant was receiving favorable publicity, but a close reading of the coverage suggested that the document was a glittering mirror in which the press of each nation found and applauded its own image. For example, the London *Times* wrote: "Those who thought that the League of Nations was only a project of international amiability will change their minds when they read the Covenant published today . . . Peace and its preservation have been brought down from the clouds; what is more, peace in this Covenant is for the first time equipped with thunders of its own. It is a cause of legitimate pride to recognize in the Covenant so much of the work of Englishmen. . . ."

In Paris, *Le Figaro* saw in the same document a triumph of French ideas: "The Commission on the initiative of its illustrious chairman, Woodrow Wilson, wisely decided not to ravish tomorrow from the eternal and confined itself to making safe the present. The mystic Society of Nations has then become a League of the Five Great Powers which beat Germany, and which, having conquered, mean to consolidate both victory and peace. A close alliance will result among the United States, England, France, Italy and Japan . . . The future is open to a better settlement, but that naturally is as yet vague and nebulous."

And though the *Giornale d'Italia* called the document "a sublime act of human solidarity," there were, of course, dissenting voices in Europe as well. The voice of the Socialists in France, *L'Humanité*, hankered after the Wilson of a year earlier before his Fourteen Points had been "explained" and "adapted": "It is clear to the dullest," said *L'Humanité*, "that we are far from Woodrow Wilson's first proposals. . . . The project cannot in any way command the support of democracies and people's parties which placed such hopes in the ideas of which Mr. Wilson constituted himself an eloquent defender."

In the United States the reaction was predictably mixed and vehement. The New York *Tribune*, lukewarm, declared: "There is no safeguarding of peace. To each nation is reserved liberty of action. There is no limitation of armaments, no international police force under the control of the League. . . . We have before us something in the nature of an Entente Cordiale such as was established between Great Britain and France when they agreed not to act together but to confer with a view to action when trouble threatened. In the recognition of this entente principle there is a great victory for French ideas. . . . On the whole there is some gain for peace."

The Philadelphia *Inquirer* declared that the United States would not "lose its national identity" under the Covenant. "On the contrary its love for liberty, independence and justice is bulwarked." But the New York *Sun* warned that to sign such a document would require an amendment to the United States Constitution.

The press was symptomatic of the country and Congress—passionately divided or else a bit bored. When the text of the Covenant was made public, Senator William Borah, Republican of Idaho, commented: "One thing is perfectly clear . . . as it stands, it is a renunciation of the Monroe Doctrine."

Senator Selden P. Spencer, Republican of Missouri, called it "brimful of glittering generalities," and added: "I favor a League of Nations, but I don't want it if it means for us the abandonment of our nationalism."

Senator William H. King, Democrat of Utah, declared that the American people would never "abdicate any of their sovereign rights. In my opinion, the Sermon on the Mount, the Ten Commandments and the Monroe Doctrine are good enough for them."

On the other side, Senator Key Pittman, Democrat of Nevada: "The President has won the greatest diplomatic victory recorded in history. He has overcome the cynical diplomat, the skeptical statesman and the hopeless materialist." And Secretary of the Navy Josephus Daniels declared that the Covenant was "a document which makes the Magna Carta and the Declaration of Independence mere forerunners of an immortal instrument that blesses all the world for all generations. . . . The draft of the League of Peace is almost as simple as one of the Parables of Jesus and almost as illuminating and as uplifting. It is a time for churchbells to peal, for preachers to fall upon their knees, for statesmen to rejoice, and for the angels to sing, 'Glory to God in the Highest!' "

The President's impulse was to meet the opposition with an address to Congress in which he would state his case eloquently and without interruption, but he acceded finally to House's warnings that the rebellious political chieftains would "take it that he had called them together as a schoolmaster." On the day of his departure from Paris the President reluctantly agreed to invite the members of the House and Senate Foreign Affairs committees to meet with him at a White House dinner to examine the Covenant point by point.

At the pier at Brest, Wilson still seemed invigorated by the glow of battle. When an American congratulated him, he told the anecdote of the optimist who leaped from the twelfth story and called out as he passed the fifth floor: "I'm all right so far." But despite the jauntiness of the President's dockside manner, Richard V. Oulahan, *New York Times* correspondent, noted: "The President is a very tired man. His fatigue was apparent to those who saw him today. . . . It is acknowledged by the intimates of the President that the League of Nations plan is not all he hoped for. He is disappointed for one thing because of its failure to include an article inviting all nations to practice religious toleration. When he proposed this he found himself involved in a snarl of racial and religious antipathies . . ."

Whatever his private misgivings about the League or his fears of the Philistines at home, the President put up a brave front when he landed in Boston on February 24. "If America were at this juncture to fail the world, what would come of it?" he asked in an address to a glittering crowd that included the Governor of Massachusetts, Calvin Coolidge. "I do not mean any disrespect to any other great people when I say that America is the hope of the world. And if she does not justify that hope the results are unthinkable. . . . Any man who thinks that America will take part in giving the world any such rebuff and disappointment as that does not know America."

The reception in Boston was less than exuberant, considering the passionate, fighting tone of the President's oratory. The congressional dinner, so ardently counseled by House, was no more successful. The archenemy, Senator Borah, declined to attend, disdaining to confront the President "off the record," an eventuality which cooled Wilson's enthusiasm for Colonel House's political advice.

Still, the performance proceeded on schedule. The White House was brilliantly illuminated for the occasion, and the President and Mrs. Wilson presided over a banquet for the thirty-six congressmen in the State Dining Room. The bitter anti-Wilsonian Senator Lodge of Massachusetts gave his arm to Mrs. Wilson to escort her into the East Room after dinner. And after the lady excused herself, the gentlemen seated themselves in an oval around the President and the business of the evening began. Senator Lodge, who was to head the Foreign Affairs Committee in the next term of the Senate, led the attack: The Covenant of the League was a blow at the Monroe Doctrine; it substituted internationalism for American nationalism and only Europe would stand to gain. If there must be a League, he said, its constitution should be prepared calmly in a time of peace, not while the war was still in fact raging in the world. "We are invited to move away from George Washington," he said, "toward the

other end of the line at which there stands the sinister figure of Trotsky."
He wanted no bridge built "to international socialism and anarchy."

Having scored very few points among the well-fed congressmen, the
President again took his case to the people in an address at New York's
Metropolitan Opera House, where he declared: "The only vision has
been the vision of the people. Those who suffer, see. . . . The men who
utter the criticisms have never felt the great pulse of the world. . . . The
great tides of the world do not give notice that they are going to rise;
they rise in their majesty and overwhelming might, and those who stand
in the way are overwhelmed."

He made no effort to disguise his strategy: "When the Treaty of Peace
comes back, gentlemen on this side will find so many threads of the
Treaty tied to the Covenant that you cannot dissect the Covenant from
the Treaty without destroying the whole vital structure."

He remained supremely confident that the opposition, no matter how
determined, would never dare reject the Treaty of Peace, and that they
would have to swallow the Covenant with it. Senator Lodge did his best
to dispel that confidence by reading on the floor of the Senate a list of
thirty-seven senators pledged to defeat the Treaty if it contained the
Covenant of the League as drafted. That number, more than a third,
would be sufficient to block the ratification of any Treaty which, under
the Constitution, requires an affirmative vote by two-thirds of the Senate.

The American opposition to Wilson and the League drew its strength
from a number of sources: There was, of course, the natural tendency of
America to withdraw from the contagion of Europe and an inevitable
desire to enjoy the fruits of peace and normal life. In addition, however,
events in Europe seemed to conspire to further America's suspicions that
it was the honest country bumpkin being taken by the wily city con man
of internationalism. The Irish rising stirred mistrust of the British—always there, however mixed it might be with admiration and emulation.
The belief that Englishmen had a major hand in the drafting of the
Covenant and the fact that the British Empire was to speak with six
voices and six votes in the Assembly of the League, led to charges that
America was to become simultaneously a "vassal" of Britain and the
unwilling inheritor of the "burdens of empire" which Britain was trying
to unload.

In addition, the 1920 election was under way and the League had been
chosen as the stick with which to beat the Democrats. The New York
Sun was already rallying Republicans against "yielding up our national
independence to gratify the vanity and to satisfy the ambition of a
dangerously impractical autocrat, the greatest autocrat of all time, in

temperament, in characteristics, and in his reach for world power, world dominion."

To top it all, America was now chasing the specter of Bolshevism. Wobblies, socialists, anarchists, linked with the world-wide wave of postwar strikes, were being jailed, mobbed, deported, or "investigated" to the running encouragement of the press. The mildest epithet applied to them was probably that of *The New York Times*, which editorially labeled them "the missionaries of eternal smash."

Vice-President Marshall told a rally of Presbyterians in Baltimore that not only should Bolshevism "and all it represents" be suppressed but "those leaders who were instrumental in trying to precipitate riot should be hanged." The news services reported that the Presbyterians wildly applauded the Vice-President's sentiments. It did not matter that the Administration was thus on record as anti-Red; Wilson's internationalism was seen as an entering wedge for "foreign ideologies," two words which traditionally rouse in many Americans the kind of horror medieval villagers felt at the whispered approach of "bubonic plague."

The President, however obstinate, realized that when he returned to Paris he would have to reopen the meetings of the Commission on the League, which he had sought so earnestly to bring to a swift conclusion under an Anglo-Saxon steamroller. He would have to compromise.

He would have to persuade France to accept an even weaker enforcement machinery in the League and to insist that the Covenant expressly acknowledge the Monroe Doctrine. Indeed, if possible the Commission members must be required to take what amounted to an oath of loyalty to it as to a sacred American household god, for all the enemies of the League and Wilson had wrapped themselves in the Monroe Doctrine as if it were the flag.

The United States must also be assured, in the body of the Covenant, that such questions as tariffs and immigration—which to some might seem to be the likeliest subjects for intergovernmental regulation—would be outside the domain of the League. Acceptance of a mandate must be clearly stated as optional, so that Americans need not feel obliged to take on any responsibility they might deem contrary to national interest. And lastly the American Congress must be given an opportunity to back out of the League whenever it saw fit.

If all these conditions could be plainly spelled out, there was a chance that the opposition in the Senate could be reconciled to the League. Without such modifications the cause had now been sadly revealed as hopeless. This was made clear to the President by the most politically astute champions of the League: Senator Gilbert M. Hitchcock of

Nebraska, Harvard president Dr. Abbott Lawrence Lowell, and former President Taft, who, despite his Republicanism, joined Wilson on the public platform and castigated the League's foes as those "who belittle America and become little Americans."

Burdened with the grim knowledge that his path would lie through a morass of ever-greater compromises and consoled only by the conviction that a League of Nations, however weak, would in the end redeem the hopes and confound the doubts, the President, with Mrs. Wilson, on March 5 again sailed for Europe aboard the *George Washington*. The second coming of Wilson was a more sober affair than the first. The Biltmore chef had been left behind. The sense of mission remained, combined now with a dogged determination. The President kept severely to himself for most of that voyage.

Five

THE SECOND
COMING

Wilson returned to Europe a prey to dark suspicions. A month before, he had left Colonel House in Paris with general instructions to promote an "interim" agreement. In fact, the working committees had evolved a consensus on military, naval, and economic terms so complete that it seemed to the Colonel and others a pity to waste it all on a temporary pact when it could well stand as the final document. This seemed to the President to smack of treason against the League, for, now more than ever, it was vital that no peace be concluded without the League of Nations inextricably woven into its fabric. Otherwise it might be fobbed off with a pious commitment to establish it at some uncertain future, and it could end by being forgotten altogether.

Ray Stannard Baker and Mrs. Wilson contended that the long knives of anti-League intrigue had been at work while the President's back was turned, but the evidence for this particular skulduggery seems less than convincing.

To begin with, Clemenceau—without whom any conspiracy would seem improbable—was not in the best condition for plotting. An attempted assassination, such as might have put less durable men out of the picture altogether, left the Tiger, not incapacitated, but certainly inconvenienced.

Émile Cottin, a man who described himself as a "solitary and scientific anarchist," had taken it into his head some months before the end of the war that Clemenceau was "the enemy of humanity" and the one most likely to start another war. Therefore at 8:55 in the morning of February 19, as the French Premier's car was pulling away from his home and rounding the corner of rue Franklin, Cottin leaped forward from the sidewalk and fired, shattering the rear-door window. Clemenceau leaned out to see what was happening, and Cottin fired again—seven shots in all before the car sped the aging Premier away, bleeding and in pain from three bullets that had found their mark. A mob set upon Cottin and was beating him with umbrellas and whatever else was handy when police rescued him.

Although two of the bullets scored only flesh wounds, one was lodged so perilously close to the Premier's lungs and heart that it could not be removed, and gave him intense pain. Stephen Bonsal, one of the few aides on Colonel House's staff who was fluent in French, was detailed to attend the wounded Tiger, whose condition was regarded as serious by everybody but himself.

Bonsal was present when top police and legal officials came to report to the Premier on their findings concerning Cottin. The would-be assassin was apparently mad, they said, and had no accomplices. They asked the Premier what sentence he would suggest for the man.

"I'm glad I'm not a judge," Clemenceau told them. "When I think of the men who are continually sniping at me from ambush, I am tempted to say that this brave fellow who faced my walking stick with nothing in the way of a weapon save an automatic pistol should have conferred upon him some prize of valor, some Grand Cross or other."

Carried away by an appreciative audience, Clemenceau elaborated on his whimsy: "But I must not be impulsive. The women and the children and all the innocent bystanders who might have been hurt while the fellow was aiming at my miserable old carcass should be considered. Then his poor marksmanship must be taken into account. We have just won the most terrible war in history, yet here is a Frenchman who at point-blank range misses his target six times out of seven. Of course the fellow must be punished for the careless use of a dangerous weapon and for poor marksmanship. I suggest that he be locked up for about eight years, with intensive training in a shooting gallery."

Cottin actually drew a ten-year sentence.

Clemenceau was kept in constant touch with Colonel House by nightly reports brought to him by Bonsal. The Tiger's mind began to prowl at midnight after a nap that consumed a good part of the early evening. In the course of one post-midnight conversation, Clemenceau discussed his relations with Wilson and Wilsonism in a way that scarcely sounded as if a conspiracy were afoot.

"I must make a peace," he told Bonsal, "based upon my belief and upon my own experience of the world in which we have to live. . . . Mr. Wilson has lived in a world that has been fairly safe for democracy; I have lived in a world where it was good form to shoot a democrat. After a few weeks of sparring I became convinced that your President wanted the same things that I did, although we were very far apart as to the ways and the means by which we could reach the desired end. When he developed his program, it seemed to me perfectly Utopian. I said to him, 'Mr. Wilson, if I accepted what you propose as ample for the security of France, after the millions who have died and the millions who have suffered, I believe, and indeed I hope, that my successor in office would take me by the nape of the neck and have me shot at daylight before the donjon of Vincennes.' After that we began to get together."

Indeed, the most bitter hostilities in Paris were between the members of the long-standing Entente Cordiale, Britain and France. At least on one occasion, when Clemenceau was defending the French need for security against the British need to revive Germany as a trading partner, Wilson had to step between an amused Clemenceau and the scrappy Lloyd George, who had squared off with fists raised. If the President had not intervened, Clemenceau said later, "I would have clipped old George on the chin."

In recalling the episode Clemenceau said Lloyd George had demanded an apology, and the French Premier had told him: "You shall wait for it as long as you wait for the pacification of Ireland."

Actually Lloyd George himself was away from Paris for at least one week of the four Wilson was gone. In defense of the theory of an anti-Wilson, anti-League plot, Ray Stannard Baker pointed to the sinister presence in Paris of Winston Churchill, to whom he attributed an avid passion for military solutions and the old diplomacy. The facts, however, reveal that Churchill, then a member of the British War Cabinet, showed up for exactly one afternoon session at the Quai d'Orsay and then flew back to London. He could scarcely be said to have left his stamp upon the negotiations, which he later dismissed as "a turbulent collision of embarrassed demagogues."

Throughout the period of Wilson's absence a certain confusion existed, so that the diplomats did not in fact know whether they were evolving a temporary or a permanent arrangement. There were pressing arguments in favor of the latter objective, however. An uneasiness had spread throughout Paris. The London *Times* reported while Wilson was still away: "The feeling that the whole business of peacemaking is exposed to sudden dislocation by unforeseen events has been growing very strong among well-informed delegates of late. All reports that reach Paris upon the condition of things in Austria, Bohemia, Poland, and Germany show that, unless the revictualing problem be promptly solved, chaos and anarchy may extend throughout the greater part of Central Europe." To the anxiety stirred by tales of hunger, riots, rebellions, and assassinations were added the disquieting news of the growing American coolness to Wilson's mission.

By March 14, when the President and his wife returned to Paris, the British diplomat Harold Nicolson noted in his diary that Wilsonism "was leaking badly." To Wilson and to some of his coterie, the Messiah legend required both betrayal and martyrdom, and, for them, the smell of conspiracy was heavy in the air as he was driven to his new quarters on the Place des États-Unis, near the Étoile. Some observers thought the President showed a certain coolness to Colonel House, who had met him at Brest and come up on the train with him. Mrs. Wilson, years later, recalled in her memoirs that after a brief chat on the train her husband had confided to her that House had betrayed all that they had fought for. It may be that Mrs. Wilson's recollection of that conversation was colored by an undeniable distaste for the Colonel, who had so captivated her husband. If, in fact, the President had sensed a betrayal on the part of Colonel House, it is hard to explain why he continued to repose trust and responsibility in him for the remainder of the Conference.

In any case, it was true that Wilson was alarmed at the progress made in his absence and he feared that he would be faced with a *fait accompli*— a peace without a League. He went into conference at once with Lloyd George, who was awaiting lunch at the President's Paris home. They were joined by Clemenceau, who, to exhibit his powers of recovery, had come to the station to greet the Wilsons. Then, to spike the rumors that had found their way into headlines, Wilson issued a statement to the press reaffirming the earlier resolution that the League was and would remain "an integral part of the Treaty."

The difficulty was that now Wilson would have to reconvene the Commission on the League so that the report might be made more palatable to Congress. He could scarcely hope to effect those changes without reopening the box he thought he had closed. Out would come the demons of debate in the form of Belgium's Hymans clamoring for more power to the little states; Japan's Makino raising again that embarrassing matter of racial equality; and those indefatigable French lawyers Bourgeois and

Larnaude with their insistence on giving this infant League the power to control nations, the very thing the United States Senate feared. Furthermore, to reopen those debates at the Crillon and the Quai d'Orsay would inevitably postpone the Treaty, so that Wilson, who wanted to bring salvation to the world, must now seem to stand in the way of relief for all of suffering Europe until the last word in the Covenant had been written and approved.

The President grimly reopened the sessions of the League Commission on March 22, one week after his return to Europe. Bourgeois promptly renewed his offensive, pressing for disarmament with at least some means of verification, if that was to be the essence of the world's security. He suggested an international control commission; Wilson replied: "A commission to discover whether nations were keeping faith or not would certainly be unwelcome in many countries."

The French fought a desperate losing battle throughout the five remaining meetings of the Commission. In the end disarmament was enshrined—not to say embalmed—in an article which commended the concept highly, deplored the private manufacture of munitions, and pledged the signatories to "interchange full and frank information as to the scale of their armaments, their military, naval and air programmes and the condition of such of their industries as are adaptable to warlike purposes."

Embarrassment over the racial issue became acute in a tumultuous meeting on the evening of April 11. This time Baron Makino sought to make his point not by means of a separate article or as an enlargement of another article. He would settle for just one more rhetorical flourish to the Preamble, where one might have thought it would have gone unnoticed. The Preamble, as drafted, pledged the nations to work for peace and cooperation by, among other things, "the prescription of open, just and honorable relations between nations." Baron Makino's amendment would have added the clause: "by the endorsement of the principle of the equality of Nations, and the just treatment of their nationals."

He explained that the wording was not intended to interfere with the internal affairs of any nation, that indeed it was far less than what the Japanese people had hoped for and represented an effort at conciliation.

Lord Cecil seemed genuinely moved as he explained that, although personally he was entirely in accord with the sentiment expressed by the Japanese, he could not vote for the amendment. "One of two things must be true," he said. "Either the points which the Japanese Delegation proposed to add to the Preamble were vague and ineffective, or else they were of practical significance. In the latter case they opened the door to serious controversy and to interference in the domestic affairs of States members of the League."

Viscount Chinda pointed out that the words of the amendment were broad but no broader than many others in the Covenant calling for curbs on the arms traffic or for improved labor conditions. Acceptance of the Japanese amendment would mean nothing except that the League of Nations was to be founded upon justice, he said. If such a clause was rejected, the Japanese people would conclude that the equality of member states was not recognized and this would make it "most unpopular." Some Japanese had already suggested that unless there was some satisfaction on this point Japan should not become a member, he pointed out.

Bourgeois said it was plainly impossible to vote against such an amendment, "which embodied an indisputable principle of justice." Orlando agreed that the principle could not be rejected. Larnaude pointed out, in an attempt to win the Anglo-Saxons over, that preambles are meant for general statements beyond strict application. And the wily Venizelos suggested to Wilson that, if this clause were inserted in the Preamble, he might bring back the article on Freedom of Religion without fear of complications. Czechoslovakia's Kramář saw no danger in the wording. Wellington Koo, who had been having some sharp differences with his Japanese colleagues in other meetings concerned with territorial rights, was a bit starchy but nonetheless gave it his blessing. He thought that "time alone can give a universally satisfactory solution" to the questions raised, but added: "Nevertheless, I should be very glad indeed to see the principle itself given recognition in the Covenant, and I hope the Commission will not find serious difficulties in the way of its acceptance."

Wilson then said he feared the controversy that would arise from such an amendment outside the Commission and therefore suggested that it would be wise not to include it. It was all implied, in any case, in the spirit of the Covenant, he said.

Baron Makino said he did not want to continue "an unprofitable discussion" on what he regarded as an irreducible compromise. He called for a vote, and won handily with eleven supporters for the amendment out of the seventeen present.

President Wilson then exploded the meeting by blandly announcing that the amendment was not adopted because the vote was not unanimous. Up to that moment there had been no such suggestion of a unanimity requirement and, at Wilson's insistence, there had been no formal adoption of any rules of procedure. This was a spur-of-the-moment stratagem. After his verdict, Wilson soothingly suggested that "no one could dream" of interpreting the rejection as a condemnation of the principle proposed by the Japanese. And Lord Cecil spoke eloquently of the advantages of "silence" on such questions. Baron Makino asked only that the number of votes for his amendment be recorded.

A pattern was emerging: The Japanese had to forgo the promise of equality to appease Australians, New Zealanders, and Americans. Within weeks Japan would send in its bill for that affront and it would be paid by the Chinese, who in turn could command compensation in no harder currency than sympathy.

To hold off the French and Japanese proposals was a necessary defensive maneuver, but the prime objective set for Wilson by the Senate opposition was to win some undeniable European commitment to the Monroe Doctrine. When President James Monroe included in his annual message to Congress in 1823 a warning that any effort by European empires to reclaim their lost colonies in the Americas would be regarded as a threat to the security of the United States, it was widely regarded by Europeans as a piece of impertinence. Now almost a century later Wilson was seeking to compel its world-wide acceptance. This exercise of might, however, seemed irrelevant, since no European Emperor any longer dreamed of replanting his flag where it had been uprooted in America. Actually, though, the Doctrine itself had been considerably extended, notably by Theodore Roosevelt, who asserted the right of the United States to exercise its tutelage over all the Americas. In an unofficial letter justifying intervention in Venezuela, Roosevelt had written to Secretary of State John Hay his version of the Doctrine updated: "It will show these Dagos that they will have to behave decently."

To complicate matters still further, the Doctrine had been coupled with Washington's cherished injunction against "foreign entanglements," so that it had become part of a formula to keep America pure and safe behind its sea walls. The President's opposition was now demanding that he get the rest of the world to endorse this American exclusivity in the context of a Covenant designed to lead the world to internationalism. Only the mightiest Anglo-Saxon powers could treat logic with such serene contempt. Miller, the legal adviser and chronicler of the American delegation, commented on the achievement: "Nothing but the results of the World War could have made such a declaration even remotely possible."

Wilson at first attempted to attach a Monroe Doctrine clause to the enforcement provisions of the League (Article X), thereby confusing it still further. To the French this clause was a very weak reed as it stood, and now the President would sap its strength still further by adding the following:

"Nothing in the Covenant shall be deemed to affect or deny the right of any American State or States to protect the integrity of American territory and the independence of any American Government whose territory is threatened, whether a member of the League, or not, or in the interests of American peace, to object to or prevent the further transfer of American territory or sovereignty to any power outside the Western Hemisphere."

Balfour and Lord Cecil drafted an alternative and simpler formulation: "Nothing in this Covenant shall be deemed to affect any international engagement or understanding for securing the peace of the world such as treaties of arbitration and the Monroe Doctrine."

The British favored such a formulation, thinking that it might someday be invoked to sanctify other arrangements, such as an alliance in the Pacific between Britain and Japan. Wellington Koo caught the drift and saw in it the seeds of an Asian Monroe Doctrine with the Chinese cast as Latin Americans.

It was the French, however, who quixotically called on logic. President Wilson had explained that the amendment was to say only that the Monroe Doctrine was not inconsistent with the terms of the Covenant. If it is not inconsistent with the Covenant, why refer to it at all? asked Larnaude. Then the French requested a definition of the Doctrine. But Cecil observed that the Doctrine had never been definitely formulated and it was better to leave it so.

The French were concerned exclusively with the possibility that some situation might arise in which the United States would cite this undefined doctrine as a pretext for not coming to the aid of a European country— France, for example—should it be attacked by another European country —Germany, for example.

It was on the evening of April 10 that Wilson had raised the matter, and the argument circled wearily until midnight, when the President launched into what has been called one of his greatest speeches. Miller reports that it "left secretaries gasping with admiration, their pencils in their hands, their duties forgotten and hardly a word taken down."

The address—thus lost to history because it was too stirring to be recorded—was later paraphrased for the minutes: "A hundred years ago the Americans had said that the absolutism of Europe should not come to the American continent. When there had come a time when the liberty of Europe was threatened by the spectre of a new absolutism, America came gladly to help in the preservation of European liberty. Was this issue going to be debated, was the Commission going to scruple on words at a time when the United States was ready to sign a Covenant which made her forever part of the movement for liberty? Was this the way in which America's early service to liberty was to be rewarded? The Commission could not afford to deprive America of the privilege of joining in this movement."

The French delegates, though appreciative of Wilson's eloquence, were seemingly immune to its spell. Patiently Larnaude renewed his lawyer's examination of the proposition. He had no doubt, he said, that the United States would again come to the rescue if absolutism threatened Europe, but not all wars are wars of liberation. Suppose, he said, that France were engaged in a struggle with an equally liberal country on a purely economic issue.

For two nights the French and Chinese experimented with a variety of formulas. Lord Cecil finally went to the heart of the matter. The one criterion for a successful format, he said, was whether it would satisfy the opposition in the United States. After that, to stifle French objections, Wilson had only to indicate that opposition to the amendment "would create a most unfortunate impression on the other side of the water."

In the final draft the Monroe Doctrine was specifically blessed in the Covenant, although, in a compromise devised by Cecil, it was not tagged on to the enforcement clause so cherished by the French, but incorporated as a separate article. Larnaude and Bourgeois were unconvinced up until the last session of the Commission, but Wilson had come to an understanding with Clemenceau—on other questions of territorial bargaining for which Germany might have to pay—and therefore he could confidently bring down the gavel and declare the article adopted.

Bourgeois and Larnaude went down fighting on still another amendment offered by the President as a sop to his senatorial critics: the right of secession. Wilson had proposed that states could withdraw on two years' notice after 1929—assuring the League at least a decade of life. But Larnaude objected: "If the people of France thought that the League was to last only ten years, they would think it had already failed."

It was difficult for Wilson to argue against a position he himself had taken a few months earlier when he opposed any withdrawal machinery. Now he was almost apologetic. National sovereignty was "a fetish of many public men," he said, and a permanent arrangement would make them feel they had surrendered their nation's sovereignty. He granted that no state would have a moral right to withdraw but only a legal right. In the end he relied on the invincible argument: the Senate would not go along with the Covenant if it had no escape hatch. The escape hatch was duly built into the framework of the League, signifying that any country could withdraw on two years' notice. No exception was made for the first decade.

There was no difficulty in inserting a paragraph to the effect that the Council would not interfere in matters regarded as "within the domestic jurisdiction" of a country under "international law." These remained discreetly undefined.

Wilson and House fought the battle of the League amendments in five night sessions at the Crillon, but during the day the President wrestled in other arenas and with other adversaries. Most of the time the battlefield was his own headquarters at the Place des États-Unis. There, in the Grand Salon, beneath a pair of Goya portraits, the President sat at one side of the great fireplace. At the other side was Lloyd George. Like two proper Anglo-Saxon andirons, they faced Clemenceau, hunched in a brocaded chair, his gloved hands folded on his lap, his skullcap and country boots making him look less like an elder statesman than a French provincial farmer "dry of soul and empty of hope with a cynical and almost impish air," as John Maynard Keynes described him. Next to Clemenceau sat the genteel Orlando, visibly pained at the occasional necessity to disagree with his companions.

What had started as the Big Ten (two each of the five dominant powers) had become the Big Five, and now, by excluding Japan from all questions save those that affected it directly, had become the Big Four.

When Wilson succumbed to exhaustion and the grippe on April 3, the meetings were held in his bedroom, with Colonel House on hand to speak for him. It was these men who had to decide the terms to offer Germany, Austria, and Turkey; whether and when the blockade should be lifted; how to renew the armistice. They had to divide the colonies; cordon off Bolshevism and forestall revolution; levy reparations; and, above all, re-draw the map of Europe. They had to do it while establishing a League. And all must be done quickly to still a mounting clamor for peace so the world could demobilize, so that food could go to the starving and the world's trade could be re-established.

The President felt compelled to issue a special statement to the press in which he tried to counter the "very surprising impression" that a preoc-cupation with the League had delayed the drafting of peace terms. As if accused of indulging a personal hobby on company time, he explained that the Covenant was being written after regular working hours. League Commission conferences, he told the press, "have been invariably held at times when they could not interfere with the consultation of those who have undertaken to formulate the general conclusions of the Conferences with regard to the many other complicated problems of peace, so that the members of the Commission congratulate themselves on the fact that no part of their Conferences has even interposed any form of delay."

The mood of the Four had declined from the ceremonial courtesies of January and February to a nervous rancor by March and April. During those months, each of the Four—and Japan's Makino—threatened at one point or another to walk out. Only one did in fact leave; ironically, it was the one diplomat most anxious to please, most upset by quarrels—Orlando.

The difficulty, in his case, stemmed from that "secret" Treaty of London of 1915 (subsequently made public by the Bolsheviks), which promised in exchange for Italy's joining the Allies to give it parts of the Tyrol and Trentino up to the Brenner Pass (a territory containing 229,261 Austrians); large parts of Yugoslavia (with a population of 477,387 non-Italians); also northern Dalmatia and a number of islands (with an additional 751,571 Yugoslavs), Rhodes, the Dodecanese Islands, and a small slice of Turkey.

Back in 1915, the British negotiators had made their distaste for the deal quite obvious, to the point where the Marchese Ingeridi, the Italian ambassador, complained to a British diplomat: "You speak as if you were purchasing our support." The British diplomat had reportedly answered: "And so we are." Now the bill was to be paid, even though such payment would make a mockery of the Fourteen Points and all the subsequent points and the Covenant that was being drafted and every principle of Wilsonism. "Our hands were tied by the Treaty of London, and we could say nothing," wrote Britain's Nicolson. "We longed for the Americans to call down fire from Heaven and to proclaim their principles . . ."

Wickham Steed, in a memorandum to his boss, Lord Northcliffe, reported a similar mood: "Balfour hates the secret treaties, knows that if they are complied with they will ruin the Conference, but simply folds his hands and says that 'England has signed and England must keep her word.' He is really trusting Wilson to get him out of the hole, but Wilson does not want to put his foot down until he is quite sure where he is putting it."

Wilson and House, bedeviled by French demands for reparations from the Saar coal fields and a bridgehead across the Rhine, were in no mood to call down celestial wrath on the charming Orlando. They evolved, instead, a compromise withholding Fiume and parts of Dalmatia but giving the Italians the Brenner Pass. Wilson was apologetic. He wrote a memo to Colonel House asking him to offer that feeble compromise to Orlando: "Perhaps you will think it best," he suggested to the Colonel, "to break this to our friend, of whom I am really fond and whom I long to help."

Orlando was crestfallen at the proposal, and his disappointment was all the greater because Lloyd George had asked the Yugoslavs to present their views to the Four. Orlando absented himself from that session and spent the afternoon with House explaining to him that Italy still regarded itself as at war with the Yugoslavs and that his attitude was rather what Clemenceau's would be if the Germans were asked to join in the discussion on the Rhine frontier.

House then devised a scheme to place Fiume under temporary League administration, leaving its ultimate disposition for a calmer season, and Wilson put the proposition to Orlando, who regretfully turned it down. The disagreement pained Wilson. Only once before, he confided to House, had he had such an unhappy interview: with a mother of one of his students whom he had to expel from Princeton.

Wilson next had the idea of appealing directly to those tumultuous Italian crowds who a few months earlier had acclaimed him as a hero, almost a god. He prepared a message, confident that his words would rally the people. House thought it worth a try, and Clemenceau and Lloyd George, though they did not approve, made no effort to stop him. Accordingly, on the night of April 23 Wilson released his manifesto to the Italian people:

"America is Italy's friend . . . she is linked in blood as well as affection with the Italian people. . . . Interest is not now in question, but the rights of peoples, of states, new and old, of liberated peoples and peoples whose rulers have never accounted them worthy of right; above all, the right of the world to make peace and to such settlements of interest as shall make peace secure . . ."

Unfortunately, the Italian people and press saw in it a betrayal by Wilson and resented his attempt to go over the heads of their leaders. The Italian delegation had no choice, of course, but to return to Rome, where, said Orlando, the Italian people must "choose between Wilson and me." On that operatic note he made his exit. There was nonetheless a *sotto voce* aside to House: the Prince di Scordia, Orlando's secretary, came by the Crillon to express Orlando's regret that he did not have the chance to say farewell and to convey assurances of "a warm feeling of friendship."

Around the fireplace at the Place des États-Unis the Three resumed their crises, with brief excursions into the public arena to taste the bitterness in the air.

On April 28 the Conference met in plenary session to hear the revised Covenant of the League of Nations. It was a dispirited meeting with little of the glittering, hopeful rhetoric of the first reading. Wilson's speech was pale compared to the rousing oratory with which he presented the

February draft before it had been picked at by senators and before he himself had had to dilute it still further. As if by sleight of hand, in the reading he included an amendment to Article V that had not been seen even by some members of the Commission. It said: "Except where otherwise expressly provided in this Covenant or by terms of the present treaty, decisions at any meeting of the Assembly or of the Council shall require the agreement of all the Members of the League represented at the meeting . . ." Thus, to forever bury Makino's troublesome resolution on race, was the rule of unanimity embodied in the League, foreshadowing the veto power that would characterize the organization and its successor in later decades.

No one seemed to notice the enshrinement of the veto. The delegates were too busy restating all the objections that had been made in the sessions of the Commission: Bourgeois on the deplorable lack of teeth in the League, and Hymans on the right of small powers. Latin Americans wanted a definition of the undefinable Monroe Doctrine. Rustem Haidar of the Hejaz spoke for the Arabs who had dreamed of a United Arabia, only to see the Middle East again divided by new conquerors. And Baron Makino expressed the "poignant regret" of his government and his people that their proposal to embody the principle of racial equality had failed of adoption, "although it obtained, may I be permitted to say, a clear majority in its favor."

The general unhappiness marred the glory of the hour, but nonetheless Wilson had his Covenant tailored to appeal to the United States Senate, whatever the Hejaz and Japan might think of it. Wilson's uneasy conscience would find a way to compensate those whose rights or territories had been compromised.

The Japanese were to be placated by affecting yet another "secret" treaty provision, one which had purchased its naval support in 1917. In addition to the German islands of the North Pacific, Britain had promised to turn over to Japan the German concessions in Shantung Province and at Kiaochow. China, which had also entered the war on the Allied side at the same time that Japan did, had expected that victory would put an end at least to the German concessions, if not to those held by its allies, the English and French.

Wilson and House pondered the problem. They had been unfair to Japan on the race clause; they must make up for it—even at the expense of China, who was powerless and therefore patient. Moreover, Japan was threatening to withdraw and the Conference could not afford another walkout, what with Orlando still in Rome. Also, might not the Japanese make their own deal with a renascent Germany? "I know that I shall be accused of violating my own principles," Wilson told Ray Stannard Baker, "yet nevertheless I must work for world order and organization against anarchy and a return to the old militarism. . . . The only hope was to keep the world together, get the League of Nations with Japan in it, and then try to secure justice for the Chinese, not only as regarding Japan but England, France, Russia, all of whom had concessions in China."

The Japanese, moreover, were in a mood to make things easy for the perplexed spirits of the Americans. They insisted on the formal cession of Shantung but solemnly promised that Japan would then turn the sovereignty of the province back to China, retaining only the economic rights formerly enjoyed by the Germans. These included, among other things, the railway. And Baron Makino threw in the promise that the railway police, to be composed of Chinese—with Japanese instructors and advisers—would be used for no other purpose than ordinary railroad security.

Baron Makino had a disarming manner when he spoke to the Council of Four-minus-one before the fireplace at the Place des États-Unis. "In the past," he said, "international relations with China were not always conducted according to the principles of justice. It is better not to seek those who bear the guilt for that; one began it and the others followed it. As for us the principal direction of our policy will henceforth be based on equity and a desire for friendly relations. The Marquis Yamagata, who is one of our leading capitalists, told me recently that, in all our enterprises in China, we must see to it that we share the profits equally with the Chinese. If we have the open door in China, that is all we ask."

The promises and fair words were all that Wilson and House needed. House noted in his diary: "The concessions the Germans obtained from China in the first place, and which the Japanese have taken over as part of the spoils of war, is bad enough; but it is no worse than the doubtful transactions that have gone on among the Allies themselves and, indeed, that are going on now. They are dividing up the Turkish Empire just as the Japanese are trying to secure a sphere of influence in China, but with this difference: the Allies intend to hold what they take in Asia Minor, while the Japanese have promised to return the concessions to China provided the Allies permit Japan to save her face by first taking them over."

On April 22, Dr. Wellington Koo and Mr. Lou Tseng-tsiang were summoned to the meeting of the Council of Three, and there President Wilson offered them the justice that would ultimately come with the League: "As soon as the proposed League of Nations is established, we will give China all our assistance and aid to remove all present inequalities and restrictions upon her legal rights, so that the Republic of China shall truly become a perfect, independent, sovereign great state. . . . Such sentiments, I am happy to state, are shared by Baron Makino, who will likewise be glad to assist in this worthy direction."

During the Japanese crisis the President was showing the strain of seeing his "victories" tarnish before his eyes. "These are terrible days for the President physically and otherwise," Admiral Grayson cabled Washington. "President putting up a great fight against odds."

A mood of frenzy, almost despair, gripped the high-minded experts at Paris. Nicolson recalled in his memoirs the demoralization among the staff at the "almost panic realization" that the prophet of the White House not only was unwilling to call down fire from heaven, but displayed an equal disinclination to call for memoranda from his own experts.

There could be no systematic prearranged agenda at the fireside of the Place des États-Unis because the Three were not the only shapers of the world. Often it was all they could do to keep abreast of events. When Bolshevism leaped the firewall around Russia and blazed in Budapest, lesser statesmen panicked. Calls for intervention against Béla Kun's "Red Terror" rose on all sides. At the Place des États-Unis the generals were called in to guide the Three. Foch clamored for Allied occupation of Vienna to bring law, order, and food. Sir Henry Wilson agreed, joining with Foch in an acidulous scorn for civilian statesmen. (He was fond of repeating Foch's comment that a day with Lloyd George "was only valuable in that it showed you that his bag was empty," adding his own barb to the effect that on the basis of his chief's activities at the Peace Conference, it was hard to say whether he was the Prime Minister of England or Silesia.)

The American general Tasker Bliss, though he bore himself like an animated ramrod, had a more flexible mind and shared none of his colleagues' military snobbism. He told the Big Four that their thinking was distorted by the word "Bolshevist." "If we replace it with the word 'revolutionary,'" he said, "things perhaps would be clearer. . . . A *cordon sanitaire* could stop the Bolsheviki but not Bolshevism, and to set up a real barrier we would have to deploy very sizeable forces from the Baltic to the Black Sea. I don't believe we need take that way out unless we are certain there is no other way. I see two other ways: peace, with a delineation of frontiers, concerning which the very uncertainty creates a great deal of trouble and unrest among the people; and secondly, the lifting of the blockade and the creation of the possibility for everybody to go back to work."

When the generals left the room Wilson took up where Bliss had left off: "In my opinion," the President said, "to try and stop a revolutionary movement by regular armies is like using a broom to stop a flood. Besides, armies can be infected with the Bolshevism they are sent to combat. . . . The only means of acting against Bolshevism is to make its causes disappear. This is difficult, however, because we cannot even be sure of what the causes are." He cited, nevertheless, the growing joblessness and hunger and said the only answer was to "fix the frontiers and reopen commerce." Wilson said it was impossible for Americans to occupy Vienna because that would be contrary to the armistice terms, and he was opposed to marching into Hungary because "if Bolshevism stays within its frontiers, it's none of our business." He would go along with support for Rumania against any hostile Hungarian action.

Orlando, before he walked out, had posed the predicament of the Western Powers: "In Russia we must choose between two policies equally logical and tenable. The first is intervention: go all the way to Moscow if necessary and crush Bolshevism by force. The second is to regard Bolshevism as a *de facto* government and establish relations, if not cordial, at least more or less normal. Up to now we have followed neither policy and we have therefore suffered the worst consequences of each. Without making war, we are in a state of war with Russia. Up to now the Russian or Ukrainian Bolsheviks are only defending their territory."

Clemenceau agreed with Wilson that it was only necessary to bolster Rumania's armed forces.

Lloyd George went further than all the others: "There is talk of suppressing the revolution in Hungary. I don't see why we should do it: there are few countries that need it more. Today I talked with someone who has visited Hungary and knows it well. He tells me that it is a country with the worst landlord regime in Europe. The peasants there are oppressed as if they were in the Middle Ages and the right of the first night still exists there."

The conversation was high-minded and inconclusive on matters which were beyond the immediate concern of the big powers. What drove them to the point of walking out were controversies that touched their own national security, economics, or pride.

When the discussion involved reparations or the punishment of Germany, the mood would grow anguished. Wilson, clinging to at least a shred of his Fourteen Points, would demand a policy of no indemnities. (The correlative principle of no annexations had already been whittled away with the Italians taking the Tyrol and sulking because they could not have all they hoped for in Yugoslavia, with the Japanese clutching Shantung, the Australians and New Zealanders picking up island "mandates," and Britain and France dividing the Turkish Empire.) Now here was Clemenceau threatening momentarily to leave the cozy hearth and roaring: "We were attacked. We are victorious. We represent right and might is ours. This must be used in the service of right."

And Lloyd George at one moment would remember his own campaign pledge to hang the Kaiser and make Germany pay, while at the next he would worry lest Germany refuse to sign so tough a treaty. "We must have a Government that will sign," he said at one meeting. "The one now in power is but a shadow. If our terms are too severe it will fall and then look out for Bolshevism."

André Tardieu, Clemenceau's right-hand diplomat, wrote in his memoirs: "By the end of March this obsession [of Lloyd George's] became so threatening to the most vital clauses of the Treaty that M. Clemenceau felt called upon to meet it with uncompromising directness, which Anglo-Saxons accept because they consider it fair and which impresses them far more than shifting resistance."

The mercurial Prime Minister, forever worried about his parliamentary hecklers, blew hot and cold that spring, and when Clemenceau demanded that the frontier be fixed on the Rhine, Lloyd George threatened to head for London.

On April 6 it was Wilson's turn to hold the walkout gun at the heads of his fireside companions. He did not do so directly but sent a wire for the U.S.S. *George Washington* to proceed to Brest. The order found its way into the papers and produced a momentary calm at the Place des États-Unis.

Even Belgium, the prime victim, who for years had seen itself cartooned as the beautiful maiden ravished by the Hun, found its rescuers less than gallant and at the end of April threatened a walkout. The Belgians were disappointed because they had lost their fight for priority in reparations and because Brussels had been turned down as the site of the League of Nations. Although Wilson had originally vetoed Geneva as the locale of the Peace Conference because it was a morass of rumors and plots, he had turned about and favored it as the capital of his League. Brussels, he said, would forever remind diplomats of the fierce partisanship of war, whereas neutral Geneva would create a mood of neutral peace. The Belgians argued, in vain, that Geneva did not deserve such honor because it had not shed a drop of blood to gain the victory.

In the first week of May the draft of the Treaty was ready. It pleased no one very much. Germany was effectively disarmed and its fleet was due to be surrendered, but France had lost its fight for the Rhine frontier. The League was incorporated as Article I of the Treaty, but it was a patchwork of compromises and was riddled by evasions; not quite a Holy Alliance of the Victorious Powers, not quite a Charter of the Rights of Man, but something in between, rigged to make it acceptable to the United States Senate. Reparations were accepted in principle, but the figures were left for a later accounting. Central Europe was redrawn, but no one was persuaded that all the boundary lines were just or in the long run even viable.

Nevertheless, it was ready. The Italian delegates were still sulking in Rome. The Three considered a forty-eight-hour ultimatum ordering the Italians to appear or face the prospect of a Treaty without Italy's signature. Clemenceau and Lloyd George were against that proposal, not because they thought that it might fail but because they feared its success. If Orlando and Sonnino rushed back in time they might reopen the whole Treaty of London, and the British and French might have to acknowledge their bargain.

Orlando and Sonnino, however, sent word that they would return without conditions in time for the Plenary Session of the Conference set for May 6, and Clemenceau took the liberty of attaching Italy's name to the Treaty the night before.

For eight days a German delegation of one hundred and eighty, plus a corps of newspapermen, had been waiting in three hotels in Versailles. They had been preparing for negotiations ever since the armistice and had filled thick dossiers with German proposals for the peace to come. Through January, February, and March they had waited in Berlin for some nod from Paris. When at last the invitation came, on April 18, the Foreign Minister, Count Brockdorff-Rantzau, who had a flair for irony, suggested that he send three officials to bring the text of the Treaty to Germany so the government could consider it. The Allies sent a second note demanding that the German delegation come to Paris and that it include plenipotentiaries who could sign on the spot.

Accordingly, the one hundred and eighty diplomats and advisers and translators left Berlin in a special train on April 28 and reached Versailles on the evening of the twenty-ninth. The Count and his top aides and chief delegates were quartered at Mme de Pompadour's old palace, which had become the Hôtel des Réservoirs. They were allowed to roam freely in the Parc de Trianon, but when they went into Versailles the French provided a military escort for their protection, and after May 1 fences were built so that they could go back and forth between their hotels safe from the curious as in a protected warren.

On May 5 the Count was informed that the peace terms would be handed to him at three o'clock in the afternoon of May 7 at the Trianon

Palace Hotel. There would be no discussion, but the German delegates could present their observations in writing—in both French and English —within fifteen days.

At the Trianon Palace Hotel on the date set, the Germans were seated at one end of a rectangle of tables, facing Clemenceau in the middle of what seemed to them the judges' bench. At his right sat Wilson and Lansing; at his left, Lloyd George and Bonar Law. Around the rectangle ranged representatives of the other nations who had emerged on the winning side. In the middle of the tables between the Germans and their judges sat the interpreters. Clemenceau rose and spoke briefly, in what seemed to a German observer "anger and disdain." There would be no discussion, he said. The Germans would have the right to convey their objections in writing. Then he handed over the peace terms, which in fact had been seen in their entirety by very few persons beyond the Big Three, though the document claimed the adherence of all of the Allied and Associated Powers.

Then Count Brockdorff-Rantzau shocked the assembly by speaking from his chair, not deigning to rise as Clemenceau had done, because, as it was later explained, he did not wish to seem like a prisoner in the dock who is expected to stand during the sentencing. He spoke calmly and precisely, in German, pausing so that each sentence might be translated into French and English as he went along. "We know that the power of the German army is broken," the Count said. "We know the power of the hatred which we encounter here, and we have heard the passionate demand that the vanquishers make us pay as the vanquished and shall punish those who are worthy of being punished.

"It is demanded from us that we shall confess ourselves to be the only ones guilty of the war. Such a confession in my mouth will be a lie . . . we energetically deny that Germany and its people, who were convinced that they were making a war of defense, were alone guilty . . . In the last fifty years imperialism of all European states has chronically poisoned the international situation. . . . I do not want to answer by reproaches to reproaches, but I ask [the Powers] to remember when reparation is demanded, not to forget the armistice. It took you six weeks till we got it at last, and six months till we came to know your conditions of peace. Crimes in war may not be excusable, but they are committed in the struggle for victory, and in the defense of national existence, and passions are aroused which make the conscience of peoples blunt.

"The hundreds of thousands of noncombatants who have perished since the eleventh of November by reason of the blockade were killed with cold deliberation, after our adversaries had conquered and victory had been assured them. Think of that when you speak of guilt and punishment."

Count Brockdorff-Rantzau spoke not only with a righteous—some called it self-righteous—anger but with a sense of irony. "In this conference," he said, "where we stand toward our adversaries alone and without any allies, we are not quite without protection. You yourselves have brought us an ally, namely the right which is guaranteed by the treaty, by the principles of peace . . . The principles of President Wilson have thus become binding for both parties to the war, for you as well as for us, and also for our former allies." He acclaimed the League as "the sublime thought to be derived from the most terrible disaster in the history of mankind" and called for opening it "to all who are of good will."

He closed with a warning: "The peace which may not be defended in the name of right before the world always calls forth new resistance against it."

It was not the contrite speech of a prisoner brought to book. And it disturbed many of those who heard it. The Wilsonian tone of some passages did not excuse it even in the eyes of Wilson himself, who turned to Bonar Law and said: "I see it had the same effect on you as on me. You're red in the face." Lloyd George remarked: "It is hard to have won the war and have to listen to this." Tardieu wrote that the Count had come "draped in brutish insolence." He called him a "delirious swine," and added: "At least may this true Boche receive our thanks for his shameless frankness which dispels any illusions about the German cause." But Colonel House thought that perhaps the Count had been too nervous to stand and that the speech was "an able one but . . . out of place." He added that if he had been in the Count's position he would have said: "Mr. President, and gentlemen of the Congress: War is a great gamble, we have lost and are willing to submit to any reasonable terms."

Sir Henry Wilson also thought the Count's speech "quite capable" and one calculated to shock "our frock-coats."

Clemenceau, in no mood to applaud a German performance, or participate in gamesmanship, brought the session hurriedly to a close. It had lasted barely half an hour. The Count paused to light a cigarette before he made his exit.

It was purely fortuitous that the assembly took place just four years to the day after German U-boats sank the *Lusitania*.

That evening Johann Giesberts, a fat and jowly little man representing the Catholic Centrist party, came into the Hôtel des Réservoirs and announced: "Gentlemen, I am drunk. That may be proletarian, but with me there is nothing else for it. This shameful treaty has broken me, for I had believed in Wilson until today . . . Right now if I had those fellows here, who this afternoon were sitting opposite—Wilson, Lloyd George and Clemenceau—they would hit the ceiling so hard they'd stick to it. I am telling you this, gentlemen, if those fellows think that the German laborers are going to work hard for that capitalist gang, they're wrong, and when they march into the mining district, the few hand grenades that'll be needed to flood every mine, will be on hand."

In Weimar, the President of the German National Assembly declared: "The unbelievable has happened. The enemy presents us with a treaty surpassing the most pessimistic forecasts. It means the annihilation of the German people. It is incomprehensible that a man who has promised the world a peace of justice, upon which a society of nations would be founded, has been able to assist in framing this project dictated by hate."

Count Brockdorff's intimate adviser at Versailles and the German delegation's chief administrative officer was Dr. Walter Simons, a chief justice under the Kaiser. In writing to his wife early in May, he interrupted a delicate description of the mockingbirds and nightingales, wisteria and azaleas of the Trianon Park in order to outline the horrors of the Treaty. He wrote: "The Treaty, which our enemies have laid before us, is, insofar as the French dictated it, a monument of pathological fear and pathological hatred: and, insofar as the Anglo-Saxons dictated it, it is the work of a capitalistic policy of the cleverest and most brutal kind."

In commenting on a Treaty which—whatever its merits and demerits—did impose severe restrictions on the German state, Dr. Simons chose one "trifling example" to illustrate the humiliations imposed: Germany was required to surrender to the British the skull of the Sultan Kwakwa, a rebel chieftain of what had been German East Africa.

The German delegation resolved to play for time. Dr. Simons confided the strategy to his wife: "Every week that we gain will weaken the position of our opponents. The better this treaty becomes known, the more impossible will it be to put into effect. We must avoid the breaking off of negotiations, which would give our opponents the desired opportunity to gain honors and the spoils of victory by a last military drive, which would once more whip up the dying military instincts of their people, the kind of result that was brought about by our astounding attack in the East after Trotsky had broken off the negotiations at Brest-Litovsk."

By May 30 the indefatigable team under the Count had submitted piecemeal more than three hundred pages of objections and counterproposals to the terms of the Treaty.

The hopes of the German delegation were beginning to grow out of the divisions of the Allies. The United States Senate was expected to publish the text of the Treaty, which might, the Germans hoped, swing American opinion round to sympathy with Germany. In addition, Dr. Simons foresaw the fruits of Italian and Japanese disappointment, though these would take longer to ripen than he imagined. "Italy," he wrote on June 12, 1919, "is waiting for the first opportunity to join with us, and trembles lest we sign. Japan has, indirectly, given us warning not to sign, because she needs us later." And with that dim prevision of an axis, Dr. Simons urged the Count not to put his name to the Treaty, even though such refusal would mean the destruction and occupation of much of Germany, in some cases at least by the dread "black troops" of the enemy. If that happened, the occupation would not last, he said, because the Allied troops would mutiny and their statesmen would realize that they "need a Germany that will be an economic unit from which to get their reparations."

Under the Treaty, Germany was to lose one-tenth of its iron foundries, a third of its blast furnaces, three-quarters of its iron ore and zinc. As it was, Germany's raw materials had been drastically depleted by the war, except for its coal and iron stocks. The land had been ravished to assuage the famines and there was a shortage of fertilizers to replenish it.

Labor would be in short supply, not only as a result of the war losses but because Germany henceforth could not draw on cheap Russian and Polish manpower, a work force on which it had relied before the war and appropriated during the war. In addition, the loss of Alsace-Lorraine deprived it of some excellent farm land and a sizable population. Germany was to lose the coal of Upper Silesia to the new Poland, according to the original terms, but, in one of the few concessions made to Germany as a result of its objections, the ultimate disposition of that region would be decided by a plebiscite, as would that of the Saar. The Rhineland, though it was to be occupied for fifteen years, would ultimately be Germany's, despite the frantic pleas of the French that this was a vital gap in their defenses.

The German colonies—covering about a million square miles and including some twelve and a half million people—were to be parceled out as "mandates" among the victors; the fleet was to be surrendered to the British, and Germany was to be left demobilized and disarmed. (In another concession the final draft suggested that in this respect Germany was but paving the way to a general world-wide disarmament.)

The actual bill for reparations had not yet been computed in the spring of 1919 and it hung over Germany like a cloud.

The German delegates at Versailles, feverishly filling pages with their objections, saw themselves cheated of the Wilsonian promise of a "peace without victory." They were appalled to find that they were being given almost the same kind of peace terms they themselves had handed out at Brest-Litovsk fifteen months before and in Paris forty-nine years earlier. They protested that this was not the evil old imperialist Germany, which, they implied, might have deserved such treatment, but the new popular, democratic, socialist Germany, the innocent heirs of the Allies' vengeance.

"In the peace document laid before us," they declared, "a moribund conception of the world, imperialistic and capitalistic in tendency, celebrates . . . its last horrible triumph."

The objections filed by the delegation asserted the right to maintain intact the German Empire—even under popular, democratic, and socialist auspices. "As a great civilized nation," the German negotiators wrote, "the German people have the right and duty to cooperate in the joint task which devolves upon civilized mankind of exploring the world scientifically and of educating the backward races. In this direction she has achieved great things in her colonies."

It was not clear why the new Germany chose to defend the imperial policies of the old, but in any case it was unfortunate, for the Allies delighted in quoting the exposés of reformers, including some of those in the new German government. Matthias Erzberger himself, it was pointed out, had charged that the German plantations had been made profitable by being "manured" with the blood of Africans. The Herreros of South-West Africa had been almost extinguished as a people by a genocidal suppression of their revolt. The Cameroons had become known as the "land of the 25" because that was the number of lashes with a rawhide whip administered by German authorities for the most minor offenses. German reformers in earlier years had documented the policies which had depopulated vast regions, broken ancient tribal and family relationships, and accomplished a "recruitment" that much resembled the raids of slavers in earlier days.

Concerning the new Poland, which might inherit part of the Silesian oil fields, the German negotiators said, with a tinge of the old imperial scorn, that it "possesses no or insufficient qualifications for the welfare of workers."

When they came to the provision denying the right to *"anschluss"* with Austria, the German experts wrote: "Germany has never had, and never will have, any intention of shifting the Austrian-German frontier by force. However, should the population of Austria . . . desire to restore the national connection with Germany . . . Germany cannot pledge herself to oppose that desire of her German brothers in Austria, as the right of self-determination should apply universally and not only to the disadvantage of Germany."

To that the Allies answered that they would "take note of the declaration in which Germany declares that she 'has never had and will never have the intention of changing by violence the frontier between Germany and Austria.' "

Even the League, which had been held out to the Germans as their guarantee of a new and different world, would not at once be available to them. They learned that they would first have to demonstrate proper behavior in a term of probation. To this also they objected vociferously and at length.

On disarmament they argued that if Germany is to lay down its arms it must expect similar disarmament on the part of the Allies and the end of compulsory military service.

How these points were received by the Allies is revealed in a remarkable series of conversations in the Council of Four, recorded by the interpreter and diplomatic observer Paul Mantoux. These indicate the fears that beset the victors that the vanquished might not remain vanquished; that the Germans, if pushed too far, might not sign and the war might have to begin again. The exchange on June 7, 1919, carries the flavor of these fears. President Wilson began that session by reading the draft of a proposed reply to the German demand for admission to the League of Nations immediately on the signing of the Treaty of Peace. He proposed not a surrender to German terms but a conciliatory statement that read in part:

"The intention of the Allied and Associated Powers is not at all to exclude Germany from the League of Nations. As soon as they are convinced that a democratic government is solidly established in Germany and that the German people is animated by a peace-loving spirit, they will admit Germany into the League. They hope that this will happen a few months from now."

Clemenceau: "Ah, that's saying a lot."

Wilson: "We could put in place of the last words 'in a short time.' "

Clemenceau: "We will see about that."

Wilson thereupon resumed reading from his draft reply to the Germans: "In answer to the German comments on general disarmament, it is declared that the Covenant of the League of Nations foresees the general reduction of armaments and also foresees the mutual guarantee of obligations undertaken in this respect by members of the League. This question includes that of compulsory military service, which will be one of the subjects in forthcoming discussions."

Lloyd George: "I don't know whether this dish is done to M. Clemenceau's taste."

Clemenceau: "I'll have no trouble digesting it because I won't swallow it. Lord Robert Cecil can make the peace by himself if he likes."

Lloyd George: "This comes from the League of Nations Commission—M. Léon Bourgeois, in other words . . ."

Orlando: "It's going a bit too far to promise our disarmament even before that of the Germans is effective."

Wilson: "Let's take this thing seriously. We must choose between issuing an ultimatum or making concessions."

Clemenceau: "I think that one can come to a point between an ultimatum and capitulation, but this text does not represent my way of going between the two."

Lloyd George: "Surely, the words 'within a few months' when applied to the admission of Germany into the League of Nations is going a bit too far."

Wilson: "My opinion has always been that we will do better with the Germans inside the League of Nations than if they stay out."

Clemenceau: "You'll never hold them. I know them well. . . . Lord Robert Cecil is ready to open his arms to them."

Wilson: "I think I must defend him. He does not deserve that reproach."

Clemenceau: "I have the greatest respect for him, but I am not obliged to feel as he does."

Although Wilson, Lloyd George, and Orlando feared that the Germans might yet refuse to sign, and though Count Brockdorff-Rantzau and Dr. Simons were determined to preserve their honor and withhold their consent, other factors were forcing Germany's signature.

The blockade was continuing to starve the German people and blight the dreams of German industrialists for a restoration of their once-powerful position in world trade. With the end of arms orders the factories of Germany were closing down. The soldiers and sailors were being discharged into breadlines of unemployed. Though capital had begun to flow out of Germany, the most powerful industrialists had retained their empires. Now, in the most formidable concentration of wealth Germany had ever known, they held the future of the country in their hands.

These men ranged from Karl Helfferich of the Deutsche Bank and

Alfred Hugenberg of the Krupp Enterprise, politically on the far right, to the "liberal" millionaires: Hugo Stinnes, the steel magnate, Wilhelm Cuno, the head of the Hamburg-American Steamship Line, and, among the most powerful, Gustav Stresemann, former general secretary of the Union of Saxon Industrialists. Right or left, all of them needed peace and a resumption of friendly relations with the commercial powers and markets of the world if they were to preserve their fortunes.

Of lesser importance as a prod to peace, though indicating the universal jitters, was the attitude described by the delegate from the South German States: "If the Treaty is not signed the Allied armies now waiting on the Rhine will march into Germany. We shall be the first to suffer invasion. Rather than submit to this, we shall make our own terms with the Allies and secede from the Reich."

Accordingly, on June 21, the government of Philipp Scheidemann fell and a new Cabinet was formed under Gustav Bauer with a mandate to sign the Treaty and get it over with. On the same day German honor was appeased with a watery sacrifice. The once-dreaded High Seas Fleet, the jewel in the Kaiser's crown, which had been surrendered intact the previous November and interned at the Scottish port of Scapa Flow, was scuttled by its crews. The German warships sank to the bottom of the bay, forever saved from flying the British flag.

On June 22, as Count Brockdorff-Rantzau, who had refused to sign, was leaving Versailles, the Allied and Associated Powers were officially informed that Germany would accept the Treaty. The new government attached only one proviso: that Germany be spared the stigma of exclusive guilt in starting the war and that the Kaiser not be brought to trial.

Wilson, Lloyd George, Clemenceau, and Orlando met at the British Prime Minister's flat on the rue Nitot to consider this last German plea. There was now no point in conceding anything. Though the Kaiser was safe in Holland (which was unlikely to extradite him), there was no need to seem "soft" or to cater to Germany's wounded pride. They sent word insisting on total compliance with the terms already laid down and set a deadline of seven in the evening of June 23.

Hours before that time, the Germans indicated their willingness to sign, but asked for an extension, which was promptly refused. At five-twenty in the afternoon flags were raised over the Crillon and the Majestic hotels in Paris, signifying the formal German surrender.

On June 27 Clemenceau permitted himself a small act of reassurance to the enemy. He sent word that the blockade which had starved and humbled Germany not only throughout the latter years of the war but throughout the tortured winter and spring that followed the armistice, would be lifted just as soon as the German legislature ratified the Treaty.

On the following day the stage was set at the Palace of Versailles. The captured German cannon which had hitherto littered the great Cour de Marbre had been removed. In their place stood French infantrymen in sky-blue parade uniforms, cavalrymen on splendid mounts, and cuirassiers in plumed helmets and gleaming breastplates, saluting with naked swords.

The diplomats of the victorious powers filed between their ranks—all but the Chinese, who had sent word they would not sign or even attend the ceremony because their rights had been ignored and their province of Shantung had been taken from the Germans only to be given to the Japanese.

Any notion that the document to be signed that day would signify a peace without victors or vanquished and without the un-Wilsonian passion of revenge was dissipated by the French choice of setting. The ceremony was to take place in the great Hall of Mirrors where Bismarck had proclaimed the German Empire in 1871.

At three o'clock in the afternoon, four officers of the various Allied armies entered the hall followed by two German representatives in black frock coats. The Germans were seated before a rosewood and sandalwood table on which reposed the Treaty, bound like a book, its text almost unchanged since it had been handed to Count Brockdorff-Rantzau on May 7. Clemenceau rose to his feet, and putting no polish to the business, invited the Germans to sign. They rose to do so, bowed, but were then waved back to allow Clemenceau's brief speech to be translated. The translator came to the words "German Republic" and Clemenceau held up his hand to curtly correct him. The expression, he said, was "German Realm."

Then at last the Germans signed, and the parade of delegates from thirty other nations followed with Wilson leading all the rest. As the pianist-statesman Paderewski signed for Poland, the guns began to boom. At three-forty the ceremony was over and the fountains of Versailles, which had been still since 1915, leaped and sparkled.

In years to come the peace that was signed that day would be called "Carthaginian," though Germany would learn to live with it and even thrive. Some would fasten on it the blame for German hostility in later decades, though it was not the Treaty but a world depression that was to stir the discontent of Germans.

Harold Nicolson wrote this obituary for the Versailles Treaty: "The Continental powers desired a solution which should satisfy not their greed . . . but their anxiety."

An American observer on the scene, Charles Seymour, commented: "It was not so much a duel as a general melee in which the representatives of every nation struggled to secure endorsement for their particular methods of ensuring peace. . . . Our geographical position was such that we could advocate disarmament and arbitration with complete safety. Wilson's idealism was in line with a healthy Realpolitik . . . According to the American program we ourselves gave up nothing of value, but we asked the European nations to give up much that seemed to them the very essence of security."

The compromises and vacillations, the easy sacrifice of little peoples and non-Europeans, dimmed the uncertain glory of that day in Versailles, and the kindliest critics then or since have blamed its defects on haste and muddleheadedness.

What would come out of that document on the rosewood table in the Hall of Mirrors, no one knew. Only two things were certain: The world was no longer at war—in a formal sense at least; and Wilson's League of Nations—makeshift and ramshackle—was launched.

Six

ORPHANED
AT BIRTH

Throughout the negotiations at Paris a discreet and unassuming figure hovered at the elbow of Lord Balfour. Timely reminders would be whispered in the Foreign Minister's ear, and memoranda would materialize before him, complete with the very data for which his Lordship might be fumbling. The shadowy presence operating with such unobtrusive efficiency was Sir Eric James Drummond, a lean, sad-looking, and altogether unimpressive forty-two-year-old man with a long nose, prominent Adam's apple, and pale gray eyes.

Sir Eric had been a fixture in the British Foreign Office for nineteen years, during which time he had acquired a passion for anonymity along with a scrupulous regard for the minutiae of diplomacy. He habitually wore the prescribed gray-striped trousers of the junior diplomat and carried his umbrella tightly rolled. An impecunious younger brother of the Earl of Perth and heir to the title (distinguished in Scottish history for a fierce and improvident loyalty to the Stuarts), Sir Eric Drummond reminded the caricaturists at the Peace Conference of a "loyal wire-haired Scottish terrier." Actually, however, he was far more than a mere appendage to Lord Balfour (who once thought he was honoring him by calling him "the perfect private secretary"). Balfour had found Wilson's League fixation something of a bore, and turned over most of the work on that subject to Drummond, who responded enthusiastically—within the limits of his reserve—to the League, to Wilson, and to Colonel House.

The Americans came to value his judgment as well as his efficiency and treated him as a trusted confidant.

At the Conference table in Paris it was at first thought that the Secretary-General of the League would be, in a sense, the Chancellor of the world, with wide political powers. Drummond later commented: "When they found they couldn't get the highest calibre man for the job they had second thoughts about it. . . . They decided they didn't want an International Dictator."

They settled then for a Secretary-General, more an administrative position than the political post of Chancellor. So it was that Sir Eric became the only individual to be mentioned by name in the historic Covenant of the League of Nations, designated as its first Secretary-General. It was evident, however, from the start that the post could not be a purely administrative one and that the "perfect private secretary" was quite capable of political initiative. His political aspect, however, would have to be as unobtrusive as possible, and that appealed admirably to Sir Eric. "Behind the scenes activities," he recalled in later years, "suited my temperament and previous experience. I was neither a parliamentarian nor a politician."

He went to London as soon as the Treaty was signed and set up shop at 117 Piccadilly, where he proceeded to recruit for the world's first international civil service. The service began with two young men, an American and a Frenchman who were to be Sir Eric's deputies, confidants, and fellow architects of the world secretariat: Raymond Fosdick, who at thirty-five had already served as the civilian adviser to General Pershing, commander in chief of the American forces in France; and Jean Monnet, the thirty-year-old head of the French supply organization based in London.

In a routine gesture toward a diplomatic balance, Drummond named two more deputies—an Italian, international lawyer Dionisio Anzilotti, and a Japanese liberal statesman and educator, Inazo Nitobe. The last two, chosen to keep the big powers unruffled, never worked as closely with Drummond as did Fosdick and Monnet in those early months.

Within days Sir Eric and his deputies worked out a structure for the Secretariat which was to last intact throughout the life of the League. The list of departments showed the scope of the League's work as envisioned by that little group of young men in London. A Mandates Section was originally offered to George Louis Beer of the American Inquiry team, but when he fell ill the job was given to a Swiss, William Rappard. The Economics and Finance Section was assigned to British economist Arthur Salter. The Section on Social Problems—dealing principally with the illegal traffic in drugs and women—was entrusted to Dame Rachel Crowdy, who had been working throughout the war behind the front lines in Belgium and France. (She was to be the only woman ever given so high a rank in the Secretariat throughout the League's history.) The Political Committee, charged with assisting the Council in its frontier drafting, was placed under Paul Mantoux, that extraordinary translator-diplomat-confidant who not only bridged the language gap among the Big Five, Four, and Three but also provided a discreet and valued expertise.

A Dutch lawyer, Joost van Hamel, was recruited to run the League Section responsible for setting up the newly formed International Court of Justice, as well as for registering and publishing treaties. Erik Colban of Norway was given the Section on Minorities—under the Peace Treaty the League was charged with protecting such people from overweening majorities in all the countries of the world. Italy's wartime expert on shipping, Bernardo Attolico, headed the Section on Communications; Sir Herbert Ames, a Canadian M.P., was made Treasurer; and the French journalist Pierre Comert was put in charge of the Press and Information Section. Left unfilled in the early days was the significant chairmanship of the Administrative Commission, which would have the task of dealing with League agencies set up to administer the free port of Danzig, destined to be a small depot of political dynamite, and the Saar Basin pending the plebiscite that was to settle its future.

In addition to these department heads there was to be a librarian and a small corps of translators and interpreters. (The League was to have two official languages, English and French.)

For thus inaugurating a World Cabinet, a civil service, and head-quarters, Sir Eric was given a small shoestring for a budget and virtually no directives save to avoid treading on sensitive political toes.

How slender that shoestring was could best be seen in the austere headquarters of the infant League that some people, at least, looked upon as the hope of the world. The first secretariat building, at 117 Piccadilly, was described in a letter to Paul Mantoux while he was still in Paris, from a friend who wrote to prepare him for the shock of austerity after the glitter of Versailles: "The offices are big enough . . . for a provisional organization, not much luxury, a Spartan simplicity, few keys, doubtless because of the principle that the League has twisted the neck of secret diplomacy. On your arrival you will have . . . a telephone and very few pieces of the absolutely necessary furniture but not much else."

Even when Drummond found new quarters in Sunderland House on Curzon Street, the atmosphere of maximum inconvenience and unremitting pressure was preserved. Sunderland House was described by

visitors as ugly, pretentious, and unsuitable. Throughout the summer of
1919, Sir Eric and his staff worked at top speed because, when the curtain
fell on the play of fountains and the celebrations at Versailles, it had been
universally expected that the first Assembly and Council meeting would
take place in September of that year in Washington. There was even talk
of chartering a special ship to take the European delegates across the
Atlantic. After that would come the hunt for a commodious palace in
Geneva, and the League would be under way. All that was needed was
American ratification.

Unfortunately, the news from Washington was disconcerting. The
general feeling was that the Secretariat had better tread as if on glass. The
staff meeting in Sir Eric's office on the afternoon of August 27, 1919, was
typical.

The Secretary-General announced that "it was more important than
ever for the Secretariat of the League to avoid doing anything which
could provide ammunition for its opponents in America. For this reason it
would be best for the present not to make any further appointments to
the staff."

Fosdick, the only American present, tried to bolster the jittery spirits
of his colleagues. Even if the United States did not come in this year, he
said, "she could not possibly remain out long." The only appeal that
could be effective from outside the United States, he thought, would be
one from Belgium, the original and most appealing victim of the war.

Reports from Switzerland, the future host country of the Secretariat,
also lacked the warmth of welcome. The Swiss Socialists, Sir Eric reported on that cheerless August afternoon, had just come out against the
entry of their country into the League, and it would be impossible to plan
to set up shop in a nation that was rejecting the organization. Although
the Peasant party had gone on record in favor of entry, their rank and file
in the rural cantons were known to be wary of the seductive ways of
foreign diplomats and to cherish their neutrality as they would their
honor. (The two are often taken as synonymous in Swiss politics.) In
view of the uncertain shifts in Swiss opinion, it had been decided to
postpone the referendum which, in Switzerland's system of direct democracy, would have to decide such things. At best, therefore, it looked as if
the Secretariat would have to settle in gloomy Sunderland House until
the spring, by which time, it was hoped, a thaw might have set in among
the chilly Alpine farmers who would decide whether or not to open their
tidy little society to the designs and purposes of the great world outside.

During that spring and summer the little band of world civil servants
not only were concerned with the details of where and how they were

going to work; they were trying to see the way ahead for an organization that was born, some thought prematurely, after a most difficult labor, in a world where international ideals suffered a very high infant mortality. The team in London was neither cynical nor visionary. For example, a confidential memorandum from Arthur Salter, the Secretariat's economic expert, to Drummond in May 1919 outlined the possibilities and perils of the League more realistically than ever Wilson and House had discussed them at Magnolia, or Clemenceau and Lloyd George appraised them in Paris.

There were two possibilities, Salter wrote: a League that would not touch political questions unless and until they became serious international disputes, but would handle "a mass of non-contentious business—postal conventions, supervision of waterways, etc."; or a League which eventually would become "an integral factor in the determination of the policy of every National Government in the world so far as it affects other countries, both the government and the administration of the world in international affairs becoming gradually, but really and effectively international."

He thought that even by the least ambitious forecast the League would "doubtless go beyond the first conception and on the most ambitious it will certainly for many years fall far short of the second." Still, he told Drummond, the League from the start had to choose between the two objectives. He opted for the second, but added this warning: "The League starts towards internationalism from a nationalism that is in some respects more developed and more intense than before the War commenced."

Salter was afraid that Switzerland would finally say "yes" to the League and condemn it to rot in a backwater of the world. He foresaw the danger "that we may see the League represented by a denationalized staff, living in a provincial capital, cut off from any live contact with any of the real instruments of government throughout the world, inadequately supplied even with information as to the proposals and contemplated policies of the several National Governments in all the questions that really matter, handling and coordinating a great mass of dull and useful work which is given to them because it is non-contentious in character and for that reason quite irrelevant to the future peace of the world, and then when a dispute has actually broken out, intervening at the last hour as a somewhat improved Hague Tribunal. . . . The great danger of the League, in a word, is that it will die of dullness. Geneva will be a suburb, not a centre, in the world's government."

He thought, however, that if public opinion could be brought around to back it, the League might, even with the handicap of Geneva, become meaningful, not as a super-government or as a mere forum, but as a vital point of contact. He suggested that each country keep representatives in Geneva and at the same time keep "home secretaries" for League activities at their own capitals who could bring League policy to bear on national problems and rally public support for the League.

In actual fact, Drummond's own technique of off-the-record diplomacy, quite different from the legalism of the French approach or the rhetoric of Wilson, was compatible with Salter's ideas and was to guide the Secretariat throughout the early years. The difficulty was that the world had been led to expect another sort of League, and it was that mythical super-state that stirred great expectations in some circles and great fears in others; its failure to materialize stirred commensurate relief and disappointment.

Even Clemenceau, presumably immune to the enchantments of Anglo-Saxon rhetoric, in that summer of 1919 seemed a prey to easy optimism. He spoke with the buoyancy of House and the passion of Wilson. The Colonel was staying in England through the summer, charged by the President with putting the finishing touches to the business of converting the late German Empire into a system of mandates and with continuing to serve as the presidential eyes and ears abroad. Clemenceau wrote to him in London on September 4 to impress him with the "urgent need for convening the first Assembly of the League as soon as possible in Washington, to be presided over by your President."

Clemenceau, who had been accused of tigerish ferocity and an unparalleled cynicism, was now purring with enthusiasm and talking like an Anglo-Saxon preacher: ". . . neither the action of the Governments nor even that of the League of Nations can be effective unless preceded by a moral preparation of the people, which will furnish both the condition and the sanction of the necessary results. Moreover, in the midst of the thousand difficulties which are appearing or have already appeared to all the Governments, it is necessary, in my opinion, that the League of Nations, endowed with a recognized personality, should be able to recommend and enforce all solutions of 'fair play' in the current order of life. . . . No man is better qualified than President Wilson to recall to the nations, upon the opening of the First Assembly, that the League of Nations will have prestige and influence only if it succeeds in maintaining and developing the feeling of international solidarity of which it was born during the war upon the call of the President."

The Colonel forwarded Clemenceau's letter to the President with the optimistic comment: "It indicates a growing enthusiasm for the League."

That was in September, when the busy exchange of correspondence between the President and the Colonel was as affectionate as ever, belying any notion of distrust. On August 26 the Colonel reported the usual spate of rumors of a rift between them. "Our annual falling-out seems to have occurred," he wrote, and the President cabled back: "Am deeply distressed by malicious story about break between us. . . . The best way to treat it is with silent contempt."

When the British diplomat Sir William Wiseman lunched with the President in early September, the talk turned to Colonel House and Sir William remarked that the Colonel "is trusted by all the statesmen of Europe." To which the President responded: "And rightly, for he is most trustworthy."

Sir William noted also that the President looked gray and drawn and that the nervous twitch of his face had become almost uncontrollable. Wilson was then engaged in a battle against adversaries far more bitter than any he had encountered in Europe.

Europeans had come to identify their own self-interest with a League of Nations of some sort, but the pro-League Americans argued for it as an outlet for their generous instincts, as America's gift to the world. And those who were against it saw in the League a cunning temptation set to beguile Americans away from their private Eden. Few proponents argued that America needed the League for its own security or well-being.

On May 26, while Wilson was still in Paris, Senator James A. Reed, Democrat of Missouri, waved a list of the member states of the proposed League of Nations and declared: "Ninety per cent of them are a mixture of Negroes and Spanish mulattoes. Yet, you men of the South, you lily-whites, you gentlemen who say that white men alone should control in your own states are willing to allow this meagre population, ninety per cent of whom are Negroes and mulattoes . . . to have a vote equal to the total vote of the United States in the League of Nations . . . This is a colored League of Nations."

On June 20, Senator Lawrence Y. Sherman of Illinois, a Republican, reclassified the nations of the world and came up with still another scandal. He found that out of forty League members twenty would be Catholic states. "The Covenant of the League of Nations bears within its folds a reactionary power more fatal and insidious than a Prussian helmet, more dangerous than future war," he warned his colleagues. ". . . While the evidence is circumstantial it all tends to connect President Wilson with influences . . . inimical to the future welfare of the United States."

The American people were being assaulted by still other bogeys. For example, a pamphlet was circulated in the hinterlands of America under the folksy title *League of Nation* [*sic*] *Joe—The Backwoods Farmer from the Ohio Hills*. In it the author, Lewis P. Showalter, warned: "If there were twenty nations in the League we could control one-twentieth of our own affairs. If the Japanese would choose to send Japanese workmen over here to crowd out our workmen from our factories, shops, mills, etc., we could not say no . . . as we could by the League control only the one-twentieth of our destinies. . . . If the Japanese choose to come over here, seize upon our farms and homes, or take them by taxation, you could not say no, as you had signed your death warrant when you went into the League; placed your country in the hands of other nations, to do with you as they saw fit to do. If they choose to rob you, turn your wives and children as beggars upon the public highway, you could not say no; you would be in their hands and at their mercy, all for the sake of the League."

At the other end of the political firing line were those of the liberal and the radical left, some of whom in the early days were more Wilsonian than Wilson, but who now assailed the League and the Treaty because they saw in them a shoddy compromise with a great promise and a betrayal of their hopes. *The New Republic*, for example, declared that "the only concrete political expression which can be given to the American sense of the treaty's immorality and intrinsic unworkableness is to withdraw from all guarantees under the Covenant which pledge America to maintain the situation created by the treaty. This withdrawal is dictated not only by good faith but by common prudence and a decent regard for American safety in a hopelessly embroiled settlement."

The gentle muckraking radical Lincoln Steffens, referring to "House's policy of infinite compromise," said: "It amounts to surrender. He gives up the objects of his League to get the League." And Socialist Victor Berger, who went to prison for his antiwar convictions, was calling the League "a capitalist scheme" that would bring only "more wars and more armaments."

Wilson's runaway rhetoric had stirred expectations far beyond the ability of any League to gratify. American Negroes, for example, took seriously the promise of liberty without distinction based on race or creed, and thought that if this was to be granted to minorities in Europe a portion of it might also be dispensed in America. William Monroe Trotter, secretary of the Equal Rights League, delivered an eloquent appeal to the Big Five meeting in Paris:

"Hear ye our petition that the same protection of equal rights and life for the ethnical minorities which you require for the Jews in vanquished Austria and restored Poland, you agree in your compact and League of

Nations shall be vouchsafed to the citizens respectively of the allied and associated powers.

"For so long as a woman advanced in holy pregnancy can be hung with impunity, by her heels, to the limb of a tree by the mob, her abdomen ripped open and the head of the babe crushed under heels of the lynchers, as suffered by the late Mary Turner, in Georgia, in the last year of this world war, the world has not been made a 'fit place to live in,' nor has frightfulness vanished from the earth with the Prussian empire."

Trotter got a polite hearing but no more. He brought the petition before the Senate Foreign Relations Committee and he and his colleagues were given half an hour to state their case. Their petition was entered into the record and there it died.

The ringing phrases of the League did not in fact put an end to the pogroms in Poland any more than they forestalled lynchings in the United States.

Lenin's alternative trumpet call to liberation sounded more convincing to many on the left than the voice of Wilson. They saw a revolutionary surge being walled in by the *cordon sanitaire* of buffer states in the Baltic and the Balkans and along the Rhine and, as Walter Lippmann put it, "the whole thing guaranteed by an alliance with Great Britain and America disguised as a League of Nations."

Apart from the know-nothings on one side and the liberals who knew too much on the other side, were the politicians of the opposition, ready to take the high road or the low road to Wilson's defeat. There was the aristocratic and elegant senator from Massachusetts, with trim goatee and wavy hair, Henry Cabot Lodge, the heir of Theodore Roosevelt, maintaining his devotion to a League that would preserve America's sovereignty, national prerogatives, and national ambitions and that would not bear upon it the stamp of Woodrow Wilson. As chairman of the Senate Foreign Relations Committee, he was determined to amend the League Covenant to the point of innocuousness or to leave it as an albatross to hang forever around Woodrow Wilson's neck.

There were William Borah of Idaho and Hiram Johnson of California, men who came to the Senate as free-swinging antitrust insurgents at a time when Theodore Roosevelt defined an insurgent as "a progressive who is exceeding the speed limit." Now they were the giants of the Republican party, tuned to the isolationism of middle America, leaders of the "irreconcilables," the bitter-end foes of any League, Lodge's or Wilson's.

There was Colonel George Harvey, who had been among the first to acclaim Wilson's political potential, who worked for his election to the governorship of New Jersey and to the presidency only to be thrown over as tainted with Wall Street money at a time when Wilson was wooing the populist William Jennings Bryan. (And Colonel Harvey was as unlikely as Wilson to forget a slight.) He gathered money from the Mellons and the Fricks for the anti-League war chest. In the ranks of opposition senators there were highly principled men, though their principles varied from whooping imperialism to sober prudence. There were also the spleenful anti-Wilsonians like Philander C. Knox of Pennsylvania and Medill McCormick of Illinois, who would not even rise when the President entered the Senate Chamber to address them on his return from Versailles.

The tactics were full of the rough-and-tumble of the United States political warfare, in which few of the combatants ever questioned the source of the ammunition they used. When Borah produced a text of the Versailles Treaty even while it was under supposedly secret discussion in Paris, it was generally thought to have come direct from the German delegation at the Hôtel des Réservoirs in Versailles, and there is some evidence that tends to confirm that accusation. (See Walter Simons' letter to his wife, page 125.)

The Senate Foreign Relations Committee, in the ordinary course of affairs, would be expected to hold public hearings on the Treaty, including, of course, the Covenant. And they were unsparingly conscientious about it. At ten in the morning of August 19, they came to the East Room of the White House to question Woodrow Wilson on every aspect of what many of them were treating as an un-American conspiracy. Around the President on that morning was a ring of his enemies. Their mood was rendered even less congenial than it might have been by the President's own acerbic disdain. He had habitually voiced his contempt for them as "poor little minds that never got anywhere but run around in a circle and think they are going somewhere."

Lodge and Borah and Johnson were there. A few friendly faces, such as that of Gilbert M. Hitchcock of Nebraska, were in the group as well, but these men could offer small comfort in the midst of the inquisition. The attackers probed the sensitive spots: the Secret Treaties, the concession of Shantung to Japan, the race question.

Borah asked: "When did the Secret Treaties between Great Britain, France and the other nations of Europe with reference to certain adjustments in Europe first come to your knowledge? Was that after you had reached Paris . . . ?"

Wilson: "Yes; the whole series of misunderstandings were disclosed to me for the first time then."

It has been variously suggested by Wilson's friends and supporters that he was ill, rattled, or phenomenally forgetful that August morning. In view of the wartime White House meeting with Balfour and the subsequent correspondence concerning the Secret Treaties, and considering that millions had read the texts of those agreements in *Pravda*, the Manchester *Guardian*, and *The Nation* as well as in other periodicals long before Wilson went to Paris, the kindliest interpretation that can be put upon the President's reply to Borah is that a stag at bay thinks with his antlers.

The President seemed to be disarmingly naïve when the senators asked about Japan's promise to return full sovereignty to China after being given the concessions formerly held by Germany, retaining only the economic rights enjoyed by the other powers in that prostrate nation.

"When is the return to be made?" Senator Johnson asked.

Wilson: "That was left undecided, Senator, but we were assured at the time that it would be as soon as possible."

Johnson: "Did not the Japanese decline to fix any date?"

Wilson: "They did at that time, yes; but I think it is fair to them to say not in the spirit of those who wished it to be within their choice, but simply that they could not at that time say when it would be."

Johnson: "The economic privileges that they would retain would give them a fair mastery over the Province, would they not, or at least the Chinese think so?"

Wilson: "I believe they do, Senator. I do not feel qualified to judge. I should say that was an exaggerated view."

Johnson: "But the Chinese feel that way about it, and have so expressed themselves?"

Wilson: "They have so expressed themselves."

Here Senator Knox of Pennsylvania joined the argument: "Mr. President, the economic privileges that [the Japanese] originally acquired in Korea, and subsequently in inner and outer Mongolia, and in northern and southern Manchuria, have almost developed into a complete sovereignty over those countries, have they not?"

Wilson: "Yes, Senator; in the absence of a League of Nations they have."

Senator New of Indiana: "Mr. President, does not this indefinite promise of Japan's suggest the somewhat analogous case of England's occupation of Malta? She has occupied Malta for something like a century, I believe, under a very similar promise."

Wilson: "Well, Senator, I hope you will pardon me if I do not answer that question. . . ."

Senator Porter J. McCumber of North Dakota: "In those conversations it was fully understood that Japan was to return Shantung as soon as possible?"

Wilson: "Yes, sir."

McCumber: "Was there anything stated as to what was meant by 'as soon as possible'?"

Wilson: "No, sir; no. We relied on Japan's good faith in fulfilling that promise."

The senators appeared in the course of that morning as the champions of China.

Senator Johnson: "Did China enter the war upon our advice—the advice of the United States?"

Wilson: "I can not tell, sir. We advised her to enter, and she soon after did. She had sought our advice. Whether that was the persuasive advice or not, I do not know. . . ."

Johnson: "Do you know, Mr. President, whether or not our Government stated to China that if China would enter the war we would protect her interests at the Peace Conference?"

Wilson: "We made no promises . . . She knew that we would do as well as we could. She had every reason to know that."

Johnson: "Pardon me a further question: You did make the attempt to do it, too; did you not?"

Wilson: "Oh, indeed I did; very seriously."

Johnson: "And the decision ultimately reached at the Peace Conference was a disappointment to you?"

Wilson: "Yes, sir; I may frankly say that it was."

Johnson: "You would have preferred, as I think most of us would, that there had been a different conclusion of the Shantung provision, or the Shantung difficulty or controversy, at the Paris Peace Conference?"

Wilson: "Yes; I frankly intimated that."

Under continued questioning Wilson declared that the Conference was forced to yield on the Shantung provision because otherwise Japan would not have signed the Treaty or joined the League. Then the Committee read aloud to Wilson from the testimony given earlier by Secretary of State Lansing, and the conflict between the President and Lansing moved closer to open hostilities. For ardent Wilsonians, the brand of treachery was on the excerpted testimony read that day:

Lansing had been asked: "Would the Japanese signatures to the League of Nations have been obtained if you had not made the Shantung agreement?"

Lansing: "I think so."

Senator Johnson had persisted: "So that even though Shantung had not been delivered to Japan, the League of Nations would not have been injured?"

Lansing: "I do not think so."

Johnson: "And you would have had the same signatories that you have now?"

Lansing: "Yes; and one more, China."

Johnson: "One more, China. So that the result of the Shantung decision was simply to lose China's signature rather than to gain Japan's?"

Lansing: "That is my personal view, but I may be wrong about it."

Johnson: "Why did you yield on a question on which you thought you ought not to yield and that you thought was a principle?"

Lansing: "Because naturally we were subject to the direction of the President of the United States."

Johnson: "And it was solely because you were subject to the direction of the President of the United States that you yielded?"

Lansing: "Yes."

Wilson listened to the reading of that testimony and then said: "Well, my conclusion is different from his, sir."

At that moment in the East Room of the White House it would have been difficult for any man to reconstruct the tangled affairs and the perplexed state of mind of Paris a few months earlier. Wilson could not explain that, having gone against his principles to deny Japan her plea for a statement on racial equality, he had felt impelled to yield to her on Shantung even at the sacrifice of other principles. One cannot, after all, re-create the frenzy of a market place or a battlefield in the quiet of the East Room in the White House.

Johnson raised the matter of the racial question and pressed Wilson to reveal the voting at the League Commission, where he had vetoed the majority in order to placate Australian and New Zealand racism and to make the League more acceptable to Americans. Johnson put the question this way: "May I ask, if permissible, how the representative of the United States voted upon that particular proposition?"

Wilson ran to cover, saying: "Senator, I think it is very natural you should ask that. I am not sure I am at liberty to answer, because that touches the intimacy of a great many controversies that occurred in the Conference, and I think it is best, in the interest of international good understanding, that I should not answer."

Thus while Colonel House could write encouraging letters from London, and Clemenceau could sound like a convert to a pristine Wilsonism, the President was being persistently reminded of the myriad blemishes that marred what he had so long believed to be his life's work.

He would not stay in Washington and argue over details, for which he had never had much patience, with men for whom he had never had much respect. Instead he would go to the final arbiter, the people, in whom he had always professed a profound faith and in whose name he had sought to erect a structure of peace. He would go to them and seek to rekindle an enthusiasm for a vision that was being sullied by what he conceived to be a pettifogging cross-examination.

On the evening of September 3, Wilson, his face looking gray and old, distorted into spasms by the recurring nervous tick, plagued by almost incessant headaches, boarded the blue-painted *Mayflower*, the presidential car at the end of a seven-car train. With him went Mrs. Wilson and Dr. Grayson, a maidservant, and a valet. Up ahead the cars were filled with the Secret Service and the press corps. The trip was to wind through the Midwest, the Northwest, down the Pacific coast, and through the Southwest in twenty-seven days, on a schedule calling for twenty-six major speeches and scores of whistle stops where the President would have to speak smilingly and shake hands and win friends for the League. It would have been a grueling ordeal for a man half Wilson's age in prime condition.

For Wilson it seemed a suicide mission undertaken as a self-sacrifice to preserve what he believed in, to secure his place in history, and to defeat the political opposition whom he had come to loathe and whom he publicly stigmatized in Kansas City as "contemptible quitters."

Through Missouri, Ohio, Kansas, Indiana, Nebraska, Montana, Wyoming, Washington, California, Nevada, Utah, Colorado, the presidential special ran. The President took heart from the crowds, gawking, yelling, cheering, pleased that he had come so far to see them and merciless in their hospitality, reaching to shake hands with a man who scarcely had the strength to respond.

Borah and the oppositionists had also taken to the road and were stumping the country to rally Americans against the allegedly sinister plots of the world outside.

It was while he was in Washington State that Wilson got the news of what seemed like fresh betrayal.

William C. Bullitt, who had served on the staff of the American delegation at Paris and had journeyed through Russia with Lincoln Steffens, was testifying before the Senate Foreign Relations Committee. Bullitt had made his views crystal clear to Wilson before, when he resigned in May, denouncing in writing the policy of the Powers with regard to Russia, Shantung, the Tyrol, Thrace, Hungary, Danzig, and the Saar, all of which, he said, would "make new international conflicts certain." He closed his letter by granting the President the faint praise of good intentions while double-damning his strategies: ". . . if you had made your fight in the open, instead of behind closed doors, you would have carried with you the public opinion of the world, which was yours; you would have been able to resist the pressure and might have established the 'new international order based upon broad and universal principles of right and justice' of which you used to speak. I am sorry that you did not fight our fight to the finish and that you had so little faith in the millions of men, like myself, in every nation who had faith in you." With that farewell message in mind Wilson had no illusions about Bullitt's thinking. The shock came when he heard Bullitt quote a conversation with Lansing. Bullitt read notes of the conversation to the Committee:

"Mr. Lansing then said that he, too, considered many parts of the treaty thoroughly bad, particularly those dealing with Shantung and the League of Nations. He said, 'I consider that the League of Nations at present is entirely useless. The great powers have simply gone ahead and arranged the world to suit themselves.' We then talked about the possibility of ratification by the Senate. Mr. Lansing said: 'I believe that if the Senate could only understand what this treaty means, and if the American people could really understand, it would unquestionably be defeated but I wonder if they will ever understand what it lets them in for.' "

Questioned by reporters, the Secretary of State declined to comment, leaving the plain implication that Bullitt had quoted him correctly. When Wilson was told the news he exploded and characteristically saw only a personal betrayal, not political disagreement. "This from a man whom I raised from the level of a subordinate to the great office of Secretary of State of the United States!" he exclaimed. "My God! I did not think it was possible for Lansing to act in this way."

All through the swing around the Northwest and down to California, fatigue and the remorseless headaches plagued the President, who would not stop for a day's rest until the night of September 26. They had left Pueblo, Colorado, and were rolling on to the next stop, Wichita, Kansas, when Wilson yielded to his doctor, his wife, and his aides. He had no choice. The left side of his face hung loose, paralyzed by a stroke. The President cried at the surrender cruelly dictated by the infirmity of his body.

Grayson told reporters that the President had suffered a "nervous breakdown." The blinds on the *Mayflower* were drawn. A pilot engine was sent ahead to clear the way and the presidential special raced toward Washington.

Throughout the weeks and months that followed, while the President wandered about the White House in a daze of headaches, his left side partially paralyzed, the nation was given only the vaguest medical bulletins. On October 4, Mrs. Wilson found him lying on the bathroom floor, suffering from a second and more serious stroke.

In France, on October 5, the Chamber of Deputies voted 372 to 53 to ratify the Treaty, League and all. That day might have been a triumph for the team of Wilson and House, for whom only a few years earlier the League had been an airy dream spun in the summer months on the lawn at Magnolia. But Wilson was cut off from the world in a private agony. And Colonel House lay ill aboard a ship bound for New York. He was suffering from gallstones but his doctors found him too weak to undergo surgery. On October 12 he was carried off the boat on a stretcher and then noted in his diary: "At a moment when energetic action is imperative I am bedridden and all we fought for is in grave danger."

The Colonel had taken precautions months earlier to send Stephen Bonsal to Washington to keep his ear to the ground and to probe the subtle mind of Senator Lodge. Bonsal had a happy facility of retaining the friendship of Lodge while acting as House's aide, betraying neither.

On October 30, expecting to be summoned before the Committee, the Colonel wrote to Bonsal: "The President is absolutely incommunicado. No one is admitted except Mrs. Wilson and now and again a tight-lipped doctor. You know Lodge, and while you like him personally, politically you abhor him and all his deviltry, as I do. But dissemble, touch him with asbestos gloves, and secure for me a respite, a cooling-off period."

When Bonsal tactfully approached Lodge, the Senator radiated a genial self-assurance, sending his respects, thanks, and best wishes for a prompt recovery to the Colonel while he indicated that the Senate in fact had no need of him. "The record is made up," he told Bonsal. "We think we know all the facts, and it looks as if everyone has made up his mind how he will vote."

The Senate Foreign Relations Committee under Lodge's guidance had included a series of "reservations" in its report which totaled a neat fourteen to balance Wilson's original points. If these were adopted, he and his followers would vote for the Treaty and the League, Lodge maintained.

Lodge laid his greatest stress on Article X, which for Wilson was the "heart of the League." Lodge was not advising that the heart be cut out but that it be ordained to beat only at the will of Congress. Article X, as drafted in Paris, committed all signatories to "respect and preserve" the territorial integrity and political independence of all other League members against any external aggression. If such aggression took place, the Council of the League was to "advise upon the means by which this obligation shall be fulfilled."

To this Lodge would have added the stipulation that the United States undertakes no obligation to interfere in any controversies between countries or to safeguard anything unless in each case Congress approves the contemplated action.

Nothing so plainly reveals the difference in approach between the Americans and the Europeans as does the battle over this article. The Americans saw in it a door to heaven or to hell, depending on whether one was a Wilsonian internationalist or a Lodge "reservationist." Wilson declared the article absolutely crucial to the undertakings implicit in League membership, and warned that any change would serve to destroy the whole structure. The opposition said that Article X was the beginning of the end—if not the end itself—of the American Constitution.

The Swiss were debating the same matter and ultimately were to come to a vastly different conclusion. The Swiss Federal Council examined the Covenant, word by word, as if they were dissecting a watch. In a report of 409 pages, they concluded that Article X was "not a very heavy obligation to the members of the League," that, even in the most extreme circumstances, the Council was empowered only to "advise" and not to command governments. That was in fact all the article said; it left the sovereignty of League members unthreatened.

Lodge's other reservations, included in the Senate Committee report, ran along similar lines: The right to withdraw from the League would be left to Congress. The United States was not to accept any mandates without the approval of Congress. Congress would decide what questions were domestic American matters and hence out of the League's jurisdiction. Examples of domestic questions included immigration, labor, tariffs, the illegal traffic in women and narcotics. It would have barred the League from considering all questions "relating wholly or in part" to the internal affairs of the United States. (David Hunter Miller pointed out that a question which was "in part" domestic must be "in part" international, but this subtlety did not enter the political debate, which was generally fought with brickbats rather than rapiers.)

The Committee wanted also to exclude the League from any question involving the Monroe Doctrine. It would repudiate the Shantung settlement, and declare that if the United States reduced its arms under any international agreement, it would feel free to rearm if it were threatened or invaded. The report declined to make any commitment to wage economic warfare at the behest of the League or to undertake any commercial policy at variance with American laws. It warned that Congress would have to approve the International Labor Organization before Americans could participate in it and, finally, it declared that it would never be bound by any decision in which the British Empire had more than one vote.

There is considerable evidence to indicate that these fourteen counterpoints were regarded by Lodge as a maximum demand put on the record largely as a bargaining position and that he was prepared to accept far less.

Early in November, Bonsal had several encouraging talks with the Senator, all of which were fully reported to Colonel House, who in turn joyously summed them up in communications to the President, but not a single comment emerged from the silent sickroom in the White House. In one conversation with Bonsal, Lodge had penciled in on a copy of the Covenant the amendments he thought necessary for ratification. Bonsal reported that they amounted to about forty word changes and inserts totaling no more than fifty words. To Bonsal these changes "were more concerned with verbiage than with the object and intent of the instrument." They would have modified principally Article X, leaving Congress free to decide whether it would appropriate funds for any American policy undertaken in connection with League decisions.

Bonsal argued that this power "goes without saying." To which the Senator answered: "If it goes without saying there's no harm in saying it—and much advantage." Then the elegant—if somewhat pedantic—Bostonian gently criticized Bonsal's phrase "it goes without saying" as a "barbarism" and went on to condemn the literary style of the Covenant. "As an English production it does not rank high," Lodge told Bonsal. "It might get by at Princeton but certainly not at Harvard."

Bonsal sent off to House a copy of the Covenant annotated in Lodge's own hand. He telephoned the Colonel to tell him that Lodge foresaw no difficulties in securing ratification if these minimal changes were made. Bonsal noted in his diary that he had been "rewarded by a whoop of joy" from the Colonel at the other end of the line.

That copy with Lodge's notes, which might have been the key to American participation in the League, was sent to the White House, according to the Colonel, but it vanished into the guarded sickroom and has been lost to history. House waited anxiously for the customary invitation to confer with the President, and this time he waited in vain.

Actually, the changes required by Lodge in his conversation with Bonsal were not much different from those Wilson himself had suggested in a memorandum to his spokesman, Senator Hitchcock, before the catastrophic swing around the West. In that memorandum he agreed to four stipulations: Article X was to be regarded as empowering the League Council to "advise" only, leaving each country free to accept or reject that advice; there would be no limitation on America's right to withdraw from the League; immigration, naturalization, and tariffs were to be considered domestic matters and out of the League's jurisdiction; nothing was to interfere with the application of the Monroe Doctrine.

When Hitchcock offered these as his own suggestions, as per Wilson's orders, Lodge saw in them the hand of Wilson and for partisan reasons wanted them to come from Republican sources, and to be seen by the nation as Wilson's surrender. Those terms Wilson would not accept. On the eve of the Senate vote on ratification, Hitchcock sent out an anguished plea for help. He told Bonsal: "I and most of the members of our Party in the Senate are personally in favor of getting the Treaty ratified in almost any form. In any form if even in one of the least desirable forms, it would, we think, end the present disastrous anarchy that prevails in world relations. I have to act under instructions, but those in control at the White House prevent me from receiving instructions direct. I am merely told 'the President will not budge an inch.' His honor is at stake. He feels he would be dishonored if he failed to live up to the pledges made to his fellow delegates in Paris . . ."

Lodge, he told Bonsal, maintained a deep hatred of Wilson and a resentment of the fact that the Republicans had not been involved in the drafting of the Covenant in Paris. Still, Hitchcock said of Lodge: "I think he would like me to offer changes and concessions. Of course, by my instructions, although, owing to the President's illness, they are somewhat out of date, I am precluded from doing so. So my conviction deepens that whatever may have been his purpose two months ago, today Lodge has decided to defeat the Treaty and the Covenant—if he can. Please tell Colonel House that this is my firm impression and further assure him that unless we agree to compromise on what so many of us think are minor points, the Treaty will fail of ratification."

All efforts to break through the wall of silence about the President failed. The President's last instructions had been to resist all amendments as the work of those who would not ratify but "nullify" the Covenant. In the vote on November 19, Wilson's supporters joined with those "irreconcilables" who would not accept even Lodge's League. The loyal

Wilsonian, pro-League Hitchcock voted along with the bitter-enders Borah, Sherman, Johnson, and Knox. Ratification of the Treaty and the Covenant with the Lodge reservations was lost 55 to 39.

If the pro-League Wilsonians had voted along with Lodge instead of Borah, the Treaty and the League would have been ratified by a vote of 81 to 13—more than would be needed for the two-thirds majority required to ratify.

Ratification without reservations was, of course, a lost cause and went down to defeat 53 to 38.

A week after the vote, House told Bonsal: "We do not know that the President ever saw the Lodge reservations . . . We do not know if the President received the numerous letters and petitions, from scores of men who had been his lieutenants and supporters in all the League battles, urging him to accept the Treaty even with important modifications—and so avoid world anarchy." House concluded his conversation with Bonsal by asking "the question that cannot and should not be avoided: who was the President of the United States during these crucial weeks when decisions vital to the security of our country and to the peace of the world, had to be and certainly were, made? Who acted in his name in the days and weeks when the President was not in touch with his constitutional advisers?"

Colonel House wrote two letters to the President in the first few days after the vote. On November 24 he urged the President to return the Treaty to the Senate at the opening of the next session and simultaneously advise Hitchcock and his supporters to go along with the reservations. Then, the Colonel suggested, the President could submit those reservations to the Allies. If they rejected them, Wilson's stand would be vindicated. If they accepted, Wilson's "conscience will be clear." "Afterward," the Colonel assured the President, "it can easily be shown that the Covenant in its practical workings in the future will not be seriously hampered and that time will give us a workable machine . . . To the ordinary man, the distance between the Treaty and the reservations is slight . . . The supreme place which history will give you will be largely because you personify in yourself the great idealistic conception of a League of Nations . . . Today there are millions of helpless people throughout the world who look to you and you only to make this conception a realization."

Three days later he wrote again to clarify the proposal, and to assure the President that he had talked with other League supporters. These, said the Colonel, agreed that if he followed this advice "it will probably ensure the passage of the Treaty and probably in a form acceptable to both you and the Allies." Again he sought to reassure Wilson of the view history would take of him: "On the one hand your loyalty to our Allies will be commended, and on the other your willingness to accept reservations rather than have the Treaty killed will be regarded as the act of a great man."

Neither letter was answered, and House, shut out from the sickroom, was never again to see or hear from Wilson. Nor was he to know again the quiet glory of the wirepuller, the "friend" of the President, and the confidant of the great men on the stage of the world.

During that winter and spring other appeals came to the White House from Wilson's staunchest supporters. For example, Ray Stannard Baker, the President's hero-worshipping press attaché, Isaiah Bowman of the Inquiry, and David Hunter Miller, his legal expert, were among the signers of a plea that said in part: "You have performed your duty of honor in endeavoring to obtain the ratification of the Treaty as you signed it at Paris. The responsibility for the reservations and their defects rests with their authors and not with the author of the Covenant. But even with the reservations the Covenant with the moral force of the United States under your leadership behind it, is of such value to humanity at this moment that we look to you to carry it into effect and to lead the world's opinion in its operation."

David Lawrence, Wilson's admiring biographer, later commented: "The United States would today [1924] be in the League officially if the President had been able to get the advice he so much needed in his enfeebled condition. On his sick bed he almost agreed to accept the Lodge reservations, but someone urged him to make an issue of it in the 1920 campaign and in January, 1920, he asked that a solemn referendum be taken."

Whoever urged the President to put the question to the people and stake ratification on an election could not have stirred far from the White House in those months. For the current of American public opinion was running fast against the League, internationalism, and Wilson. America was distracted by drinking toasts with bootleg whiskey to the newly passed Prohibition law, and beset by a fear of Bolshevism and anarchism which it identified as foreign imports. In some quarters at least, it seemed vital that America be guarded against the contagion of European ideas. Clearly, it was a poor season in which to hope for a massive popular vote based on an understanding of the interdependence of nations.

Throughout the winter and spring of 1920 the Lodge forces and the more obdurate Borah forces, not to mention the rabid fringe groups of the isolationists, had grown in strength and their position had hardened.

They had added another reservation, shattering the neat symmetry of Lodge's fourteen counterpoints. This one declared for Irish independence. It was designed to win the Irish vote and humor the anti-British mood, always present in American politics and now in high fashion. A few of the earlier reservations had been modified to suit one or another of the rival factions within the anti-League coalition.

The Wilson forces in the Senate were still denied the leadership of the President and deprived of the freedom of action that might have led them to compromise. The President himself was cut off from contact with his friends and enemies alike, while rumors outran denials that he was mad or stricken with venereal disease. The denials were not always convincing. The President's staff throughout the months of the President's illness had kept up a semblance of orderly government. Lansing, as Secretary of State, called the Cabinet together each week. He passed over in silence the fact that the Cabinet had been reshuffled from time to time by the President's wife, who made the appointments over tea.

On February 7, 1920, Lansing did at last hear directly from the President in the form of a letter in which Wilson asked an astonishing question: "Is it true, as I have been told, that during my illness, you have frequently called the heads of the executive departments of the government into conference?"

Lansing not only admitted the accusation but contended that his actions had been vitally necessary. The President replied: "I must say that it would relieve me of embarrassment, Mr. Secretary, if you would give your present office up."

When Lansing, on resigning, released the correspondence, the Los Angeles *Times* headlined the story "Wilson's Last Mad Act." The New York *Evening Post* said: "We have been repeatedly assured by those surrounding the President during his illness that Mr. Wilson at all times has been in perfect mental condition and in touch with what was going on in the land. If this is so, is it at all conceivable that Mr. Wilson never stopped to inquire how the business of the country was being carried on during his illness? Was he ignorant of Cabinet meetings at which coal strikes and Mexican complications were discussed? The indignation at a sudden discovery implied in Mr. Wilson's letters is incomprehensible."

Wilson's choice of a successor to Lansing was no less incomprehensible. He plucked a lawyer, Bainbridge Colby, from an obscure position on the Shipping Board to offer him the post. Colby's qualifications for the top cabinet position consisted of a brief period of service with the Inquiry team at Paris. All that was known of his attitude toward foreign affairs was an abiding hostility to the Soviet Union and a personal devotion to Wilson.

The impression of presidential instability was enhanced by Wilson's apparently absurd crotchets. For example, when his Pierce-Arrow was being repaired, the President angrily refused all proffered substitutes—including Cadillacs—for his occasional drives, and insisted on going out in a horse-drawn victoria.

Mystifyingly, he still commanded the unswerving loyalty of his followers in the Senate. The Wilson line of November still stood: that any reservation was tantamount to nullification and that ultimately—in the 1920 elections—the people would overrule the Senate and vindicate the pure Wilsonian position. "I hold the doctrine of Article ten as the essence of Americanism," he wrote Senator Hitchcock on March 8. "We cannot repudiate it or weaken it without at the same time repudiating our own principles."

The Hitchcock pro-League forces in the Senate were demoralized and torn between the need for compromise and the habit of loyalty to the President. Even those who favored compromise wondered how much to trust the elegant but capricious senator from Massachusetts.

On the morning of March 19, 1920, the day when for the second time the Senate was due to vote on the ratification of the Treaty and with it the League of Nations, Corinne Roosevelt Robinson, the sister of Theodore Roosevelt, took breakfast with Senator Lodge. Later she recalled the conversation: "He told me that he was going to come back that afternoon with the promise of the signing of the League and I asked him if he was sure of it. He said that he was sure of a certain number of Democrats who would vote with a certain number of Republicans for the United States to go into the League with strict reservations, but to go into the League."

The vote that afternoon did not quite repeat the November story. The Senate voted 49 in favor of ratification, 35 against, with 12 abstentions. Ratification would have required a two-thirds vote, or 64 in favor. Although there were some break-aways from the all-or-nothing Wilson forces, most of the organization held firm. Hitchcock led the way, again voting with Borah, Brandegee, Knox, Johnson, and the rest of "the irreconcilables."

Mrs. Robinson was there when the senator from Massachusetts returned home from the Capitol. "I was at the door to meet him when he came back," she said, "and he went into his library with a heavy brow. He said, 'Just as I expected to get my Democrats to vote with my Republicans on going into the League, a hand came out of the White House and drew back those Democrats, and prevented our going into the League with reservations.' "

Whether Lodge was in fact that disappointed remains something of a mystery. Mrs. Robinson's version has been supported by the Senator's grandson and successor to his name and office. The younger Senator Lodge added parenthetically to his confirmation that he wished his grandfather had been an "irreconcilable" but unfortunately he was not.

Lodge's daughter, Mrs. Clarence C. Williams, insisted, however, that the reservations had been designed by her father to "emasculate the Wilson pact" so that even if it did pass it would be worthless. "My father never wanted the Wilson League, and when it was finally defeated he was like a man from whom a great burden had been lifted."

Whatever Lodge's motives and disappointments, he had successfully defeated his archenemy Wilson, and the League now would await the final decision by the electorate. That summer the Republicans nominated a man who had followed the Lodge line. He was a genial ex-journalist, Senator Warren Gamaliel Harding of Ohio. His running mate was the equally unimpassioned Governor of Massachusetts, Calvin Coolidge, fresh from his triumph in breaking the strike of the Boston policemen. The Democrats chose two Wilsonians, James M. Cox of Ohio and Franklin Delano Roosevelt, a promising young Assistant Secretary of the Navy.

When the Democratic team called on the President, he urged them to peg the campaign on the League issue, for Wilson the only issue.

Harding viewed the League of Nations as an alderman might approach a sewer contract, confident that he had the political strength to get it on his own terms. In July 1920, he confided to Professor Irving Fisher of Yale: "I want the United States to get into the League just as much as you do. Of course, I am opposed to the Wilson League, as I have always said, but the League can be changed. My idea is to call the nations together and ask them to make such amendments as are necessary to secure the approval of the United States." The nations of the world, he added, would be "only too glad to get us in on any terms."

Two weeks before election day, Wilson seemed confident that the people would once again acclaim him as their tribune and vindicate his cause. Whether in Rome, Paris, London, New York, or Washington, the President had always tended to read too much into the cheers of crowds. He told Secretary of Agriculture David F. Houston: "You need not worry. The people will not elect Harding."

The electorate handed an overwhelming victory to Harding and Coolidge—a record-breaking plurality of over seven million. The Socialist candidate, Eugene V. Debs, running for the presidency from a jail cell in Atlanta, polled close to a million votes. (Wilson had resisted appeals by liberals and radicals to pardon Debs for his antiwar stand.)

For Wilson and for much of Europe the balloting, which recorded an unprecedented turnout of twenty-six million voters, was seen as a repudiation of Wilson, the League, and internationalism. There is reason to believe, however, that both Wilson and the diplomats of Europe here fell into the trap of assuming a clear ideological meaning in an American election. League partisans in many places were returned to Congress with thumping majorities by the same voters who gave Harding a landslide. Walter Lippmann later summed up the vote this way: "The Republican majority was composed of men and women who thought a Republican victory would kill the League, plus those who thought it was the most practical way to procure the League, plus those who thought it the surest way offered to obtain an amended League. All these votes were inextricably entangled with their own desire or the desire of the other voters to improve business, or put labor in its place, or to punish the Democrats for going to war, or to punish them for not having gone sooner, or to get rid of Mr. Burleson [the unpopular Postmaster General], or to improve the price of wheat, or to lower taxes, or to stop [Secretary of the Navy] Daniels from outbuilding the world, or to help Mr. Harding to do the same thing."

Regardless of how others might interpret the oracular pronouncement of the American electorate, the lame-duck Wilson State Department assumed that America had abruptly retired behind the Atlantic wall. There seemed little alternative. The machinery being put together in London and Paris was devised to carry out the provisions of the Versailles Treaty and, as part of that pact, to establish the League of Nations. Now the United States had refused to ratify the Treaty. It was still technically at war with the Central Powers and would remain so until it chose to make a separate peace. Without ratification of the Treaty, League membership seemed impossible.

On December 15, Roland W. Boyden, who had been serving as the unofficial American representative on the Reparations Commission in Paris, received "for personal information" a confidential cable from the State Department: "Department has practically decided upon full withdrawal of participation by United States on Reparations Commission as well as other Commissions in Europe. If you have opinions and suggestions for best carrying out such decisions, Department invites you to send them."

On December 20, Boyden replied with this plea: "Any method of withdrawal from the Reparations Commission by this Administration would, it seems to me, appear undignified. Only the election has occurred to change the situation, and this may be interpreted to mean modification or even abandonment of the League, or it may be thought inconclusive, depending chiefly on the opinion of the interpreter." Boyden argued that continued association, however unofficial, with the League and Treaty mechanisms would be vital for America and Europe. "The particular demands upon Germany and especially the fixing of the indemnity are a case in point. For unless indemnity and deliveries and particular payments are subject to some limitation financially and economically, Germany cannot remain solvent, and German solvency, which is still possible, is of importance to us. And finally, whatever action the new Administration may take in regard to the League, it must arrange new settlements with the Allies and Germany or ratify Treaty with or without change. To leave behind it favorable conditions for a settlement is probably sound policy for this Administration. . . . To embarrass the new Administration for political purposes will inevitably appear to be object of withdrawal."

On February 10, Boyden was informed of the final decision, taken after consultation with President Wilson. He was not to attend any conferences because "it is impossible that your words and even your silence would not be considered as in some degree reflecting the attitude of this Government which it would be difficult to do authoritatively as its official mind not being made up is therefore incapable of expression or interpretation."

On Boyden's views concerning the election results, the State Department, citing presidential concurrence, wrote: ". . . you doubtless recall that an attempt was made in 1919 to obtain the consent of the Senate Foreign Relations Committee to our being represented on the Reparations Commission. Congress evinced no interest then, nor has it subsequently, in our being represented on the Commission despite the important and tangible advantages which your presence there has afforded to American interests . . . Some of the Senate leaders have informed me that the first step under the new Administration will be to conclude a separate peace with Germany. This would automatically eliminate this country as a party of the program of reparations provided for under the Treaty of Versailles and would also automatically eliminate you from the Commission."

Boyden finally secured permission to stay on in Paris in no official capacity and file reports on whatever information he could informally pick up without committing the old or new administrations to any position whatever.

Actually it was not until the spring of 1921 that the Americans seemed irrevocably lost to the League. A new American ambassador arrived in London and by his very presence exorcised the preacher-like ghost of Wilson and the urbanity of House. The representative of the new Harding administration was Colonel George Harvey, that unforgiving politician whom Wilson had used and later scorned. On being welcomed to London by the Society of Pilgrims, Colonel Harvey sounded what he thought was the knell for Wilsonism.

"Anybody could see," he said, "that it follows then inevitably and irresistibly that our present government could not, without betrayal of its creators and masters, and will not, I can assure you, have anything to do with the League or with any commissions or committees appointed by it or responsible to it; directly or indirectly, openly or furtively."

Colonel Harvey seemed to have slammed America's front door, but in fact the back door was open. For decades afterward, the United States, like Wilson in his more saintly moments, remained in the world although ostensibly not of it. The American diplomacy of the open back door called for a style admirably suited to the Secretary-General of the League of Nations, Sir Eric Drummond.

Seven

THE SMALL TRIUMPHS OF YOUTH

"January 16, 1920, will go down in history as the date of the birth of the new world," declared the grandiloquent Léon Bourgeois as he opened the first Council of the League of Nations on the morning of that momentous date in the Clock Room of the Quai d'Orsay.

One hour and twenty-five minutes later, when the entire agenda of one item—the appointment of a commission to trace the boundaries of the Saar—had been completed, Léon Bourgeois adjourned the meeting, noting, a bit ruefully, that "public opinion will perhaps be surprised that we have today made no greater stride and left no deeper mark upon the world."

Actually, if there was any general surprise it was that the infant League was still alive. Woodrow Wilson had formally convoked the Council in conformity with an article in the Covenant which provided that the President of the United States should summon the first Council and the first Assembly to meet.

When that article was drafted, the League was considered above all to be Wilsonian and American. Now the United States Senate had driven Wilson from the stage of the League and, unwittingly, had contrived a similarly shabby exit for Clemenceau. The Tiger of France had become an ardent convert to the League because coupled with it was the promise of an Anglo-American pledge of assistance to France in time of need. For the sake of that promise Clemenceau had yielded his demands for a permanent French bridgehead across the Rhine to stem some future German tide. By rejecting the Treaty, the Senate had canceled out Wilson's promise of help, and Britain's was no longer valid since it was made contingent on simultaneous American action. The Rhine would be in German hands; France seemed once again exposed, and Clemenceau betrayed. The fierce champion of France was made to look like a pawn who "had won the war and lost the peace."

On January 17, 1920, the French National Assembly defeated Clemenceau in the vote for the presidency of the Republic and chose Paul Deschanel, a man whose talents and political record were so lightweight as to make his victory doubly galling to Clemenceau. (Actually, within nine months Deschanel had to be removed from office for manifest incapacity, after being caught climbing trees in the Elysée and bathing in the fountains.) The military chiefs whom he had kept in line now turned on Clemenceau, and both Marshal Foch and Marshal Henry Wilson could afford to vent their spleen against the worn, old "frock-coat." Unreconciled to defeat, Clemenceau told a sympathetic Lloyd George, "I still have my teeth." And Lloyd George commented: "Now it is the French who are burning Joan of Arc."

Orlando, too, was out of office because that genial diplomat had returned from Versailles with not quite enough to justify Italy's war casualties or satisfy its imperial hopes. The Japanese delegates to Versailles had to be protected by police from Tokyo crowds, who felt humiliated by the defeat of the racial-equality clause and the general treatment of Japan as a second-rate power.

Lloyd George still clung to office in England, but his coalition was threatening to come apart at the seams. The discreet Balfour survived, but Lord Cecil, having taken the side of Asquith against Lloyd George, was out of favor.

It was, in short, a hard time for heroes. Most of the leaders, who a year earlier were being feted as saviors, now found themselves outmoded while the world prepared to live out the consequences of their dreams.

The immediate consequences were scarcely reassuring. Poles and Russians were fighting on a wide front; Estonia and Latvia were battling the Soviet Union; Lithuania was alternately under Polish and Russian flags; Mustafa Kemal Pasha was dreaming of a new Turkey and fending off the Greeks. The Allies were occupying Constantinople. Persia was engaged in a desultory border war with Russia and there was fighting in Hungary. The Japanese had occupied the Russian maritime provinces; the Chinese in Shantung were engaged in an anti-Japanese boycott; the Poles and Germans were battling in Upper Silesia; the Poles and Czechs in Teschen; the Italians and Yugoslavs at Fiume. And starvation hovered over all.

In June 1920, Paul Mantoux had a chat with Lord Cecil on the peace that looked like war, and afterward summed up the conversation with these notes: "Threats of war from all sides . . . if these are fulfilled, catastrophe is inevitable. . . . Don't lock the League of Nations into a judiciary role. It is better to prevent conflicts than to settle them. The League of Nations still has credit which it must use. This is the interest of each government considered separately. And don't be afraid of discussions and crises; these are better than a polite silence broken by the sound of cannon."

Presiding over Europe at this juncture was the Conference of Ambassadors, which had inherited the mantle of the Supreme Council and the habits of thought which had converted that body to the Big Five, then Four, then Three. The Conference members quickly learned to utilize the League as a convenient receptacle for problems too unimportant for their august attentions or too complicated to be resolved by them. Memoranda from the diplomats would instruct Sir Eric's busy little office at Sunderland House to explore the question of disarmament; to supervise some aspects of the Free City of Danzig; to administer the Saar until a plebiscite could be held; to organize the orderly transformation of the German colonies into mandated territories; to do something about the Armenians and the Albanians and Lithuanians; to investigate conditions in the Soviet Union (with which neither the League nor any of the Great Powers had diplomatic relations). Although the Great Powers yielded scarcely any authority to the League, they loaded it with responsibilities—a recipe for frustration. In the first three months of the League's existence it was so beset by problems that, at the Council meeting of March 13 in Paris, Balfour, according to the minutes, said "he did not fear that the League would be neglected, but rather that the Governments and peoples of the world would throw upon the League a burden at least as heavy as that which it is able to bear."

Despite the major preoccupations of the League there was an air of marking time at Sunderland House. No one was yet prepared to accept the departure of the United States as final, even after the second vote of Congress in March. And it was not until spring that Sir Eric and his team could be sure of where they would set up house. The Swiss finally voted to join the League, although not without a special reservation safeguarding their political, military, and economic neutrality "in perpetuity."

Sir Eric thereupon descended upon Geneva to establish a Secretariat and to arrange for the first Assembly of the League in November. He came across the sprawling Hôtel National on the shores of Lake Geneva at a moment when the management was freshening up for the expected post-war tourist boom, which seemed to require, among other innovations, the installation of eighty-two new bathrooms. Sir Eric offered a check for five and a half million Swiss francs to the owners, the Société de l'Industrie des Hôtels, and ordered the new bathrooms demolished and the plumbing ripped out.

He kept the cast-iron African maiden who held aloft an unlit lamp over the gardens that sloped down to the lake. He hired the hotel's director, M. Hottop, as the first concierge of the League and retained the hotel's huge St. Bernard as a mascot. He chose the glass-roofed dining room as the new Council chamber, and settled in.

The Republic and Canton of Geneva seemed eminently cooperative. Their leaders promised to improve the service of the No. 4 trolley to the Secretariat building (although the street was too narrow for double tracks). They enlarged the railroad station, scheduled first-class service between Geneva and Paris, set up a marquee to shelter distinguished diplomats, and made efforts to arrange daily air service to London. (Geneva's autumn fogs canceled that plan.)

They repainted the ancient Salle de la Réformation, substituting chairs for the old pews; doubled the number of heaters; removed a ponderous bas-relief of the city of Jerusalem in the basement to make room for toilet facilities; and broke three passageways into the Hôtel Victoria next door, the Assembly headquarters. "The acoustics are good," Sir Eric was assured by the city's representative, "if the speakers will raise their voices a little." The Genevois set aside the Pic-Pic Building, with an underground passageway to the elegant Hôtel des Bergues, to house forty-two delegations, a telegraph-and-telephone center, a stationery store, and a photo shop.

By November the stage was set in Geneva. But the timing was unfortunate, for Warren Gamaliel Harding had just been elected President of the United States. Cox and Roosevelt had gone down to humiliating defeat and with them Wilson and the League. The Assembly opened to a press damning enough to close any show after the first night.

"Eighteen months ago, when the League was born," commented Britain's *Daily Herald*, "there were very many who looked forward to the meeting of its Assembly as a historic event of profound significance. Today there are very few who do not see it as a sorry farce."

Die Züricher Post laid down impossible conditions by which the League could save itself from doom: "If the Assembly does not recognize that its first duty is to free itself from the fetters of the Treaty of Versailles, it will never succeed in founding a League of Nations . . . It is not possible to speak of the League of Nations unless great and powerful America becomes a member."

And from the left came jeers:

L'Avanti of Rome: "Nothing serious or practical can come of the solemn discussions of the Assembly because the peoples are absent from it. The proceedings will therefore be confined to useless talks between personages without authority."

And the French Socialist leader Marcel Cachin wrote in *L'Humanité*: "The defeat suffered by Wilsonism in the United States strikes at the very existence of the League of Nations, the keystone of the ex-President's conception of Peace. America's place will remain empty at Geneva, and the two countries that dominate this paradoxical organism, France and Great Britain, are divided on almost every one of the objects to be discussed."

With lofty disdain, René Viviani, heading the French delegation, dismissed the critics' carping. In an interview with *L'Indépendance Belge* of Brussels, he said: "All great enterprises have been cradled in mockery. If, nevertheless, they had not been continued, where would mankind be now?"

It cannot be said, therefore, that the League entered upon its official life in an atmosphere of high illusions. Actually, it seemed to be founded upon a swamp of disenchantment. The League idea found little support in the political mood of any major power. Lord Cecil, one of the few who kept his faith in the League unsullied, gave this dour view of the British political scene: "The Liberal Party was shattered by the quarrel between Mr. Asquith and Mr. Lloyd George, so that such opposition as existed was predominantly Labour. An experienced observer said that when he looked at the right of the Speaker's chair he thought he was attending a Chamber of Commerce. When he looked at the left he thought it was a Trades Union Congress. All or almost all of the House professed support of the League; very few knew anything about it. Some of the Conservatives in their hearts disliked it, many disbelieved in it. Even the Labour members were at that time doubtful. The Liberals in the opposition were its best friends and they were powerless."

The possibility that Britain might follow the United States out of the League worried Sir Eric throughout the early years. On June 29, 1921, on the eve of an Imperial Conference, he wrote to Balfour outlining his fears and subtly pointing out to his former superior how the League might serve Britain's classic policy of drawing closer to the Americans and keeping aloof from Europe, while balancing the continental powers to prevent the emergence of any single and formidable force.

He noted the ominous signs of disaffection from England: "We have had a speech by the Prime Minister, not altogether favorable to the Covenant, followed by a similar but stronger one by the Foreign Secretary; a leader in the *Daily Chronicle* stating that there was no intention of scrapping the League, but that it must walk very cautiously and confine its activities within somewhat narrow limits; and lastly a statement by Smuts in which he spoke of the League and an Association of Nations [Harding's plan] as equally admirable alternatives."

Sir Eric suggested that those who pursued this trend were neglecting the League as a tool of British diplomacy, admirably suited to serve British objectives: "To keep peace and to prevent predominance by any one Power," Britain must "speak with a voice of great authority in Europe," Drummond wrote. A platform was being given it to do exactly that in the Council of the League of Nations at very little price. Drummond emphasized, as the Swiss had noted earlier while the Americans were frightening one another with paper goblins, that "the obligations under the Covenant, when they come to be examined, are extremely light." There was "much loose talk about these obligations," the Secretary-General continued, "but after careful examination they are, I believe, reduced to one thing, viz., that if a Power breaks the solemn engagements she has entered into under the Covenant, Great Britain will have to break off financial and economic relations with that Power. But even here there is a safeguard, since it is the British Government who will judge whether the Power has or has not broken those engagements."

Concerning Britain's desire to work closely with the United States, Drummond reminded Balfour that "some two years ago, eighty percent of American citizens were strongly in favor. It may be that the present Administration would like to see Great Britain leave the League, or allow it to fail for want of support, but in America when the reaction in the League's favor comes, as it undoubtedly will, a bitter feeling will certainly arise against Great Britain, who is looked upon as one of the League's champions, for her defection at the critical moment."

Drummond then added this comment: "I agree that this would be most unreasonable, but as you have often told me, our friends over the water are not always ruled by their intellect."

The letter is interesting because it reveals the practical-minded British orientation of the very acute Secretary-General; because it cuts through the grandiose rhetoric of Wilson, which still found echoes in Assembly oratory; and, above all, because it reveals that, in Sir Eric's mind at least, the League had taken on the characteristics previsioned by Salter, who thought that its maximum effectiveness would lie in its ability to serve as a corridor in which national policies and ambitions would be channeled and not superseded.

Balfour may have taken Drummond's letter to heart, for at the 1921 Imperial Conference, which agreed to accept an invitation to the Washington Disarmament meeting, he deftly squelched any move to shelve the League. If the League were abandoned, Balfour said, "it is not in the lifetime of this generation that a serious effort will again be made to substitute the rule of justice in international affairs for that of force, and the horror of five years of war will have been endured in vain."

Balfour's conduct thereafter in the Council and the Assembly left little doubt that he saw in the League a vehicle for the advancement of British policy. In this he differed with those like Lord Cecil who seemed to have taken Wilsonism seriously to the point of imagining that national policies ought at times to be subservient to the needs of the League—as if that entity existed beyond the aspirations of its members.

The aristocratic Cecil, who had become discouraged with postwar British politics because it was dominated by "the commercial class," narrowly missed being left out of the first Assembly altogether. As it was, he appeared as the representative not of England but of South Africa, chosen by General Smuts, who had gone on to the premiership of that country. Cecil, who, it was said, "was the kind of liberal who could see the better side of dynamite," tried to derive a high moral lesson from the political foul play that kept him off the British delegation.

He told the Assembly:

"General Smuts not so many years ago was one of the most redoubtable and successful commanders of the Forces of the Boer nation when they were in arms against the British Empire, and I was the son of the Prime Minister who conducted the war on behalf of the British Empire. And yet it now comes about that the General of the Boers goes to the son of the British Prime Minister and asks him to appear before the Assembly of the League of Nations as the best exponent of the General's views on international subjects." The turnabout, he said, had its origins in the British capacity to be gentlemanly following the Boer War. He drew a moral: "Do not let us shrink from even strong measures of pacification and reconciliation . . . Be just and fair."

In fact, Lloyd George was seeking to make Cecil pay for his "treason" in shifting his parliamentary support to Asquith. London's *Daily News* said that Cecil's exclusion "bears the impress of a calculated policy." And

Cecil himself spoke of the high-powered pressures applied to force him to turn down Smuts's offer.

Cecil's place on the British delegation was taken by a scrappy, acutely nondiplomatic trade-unionist and Laborite cabinet member, George Nicoll Barnes, who lay about him with a cudgel and greatly enlivened the debates in the first Assembly, which was, inevitably, his last. Although in principle Lloyd George liked to conciliate the Laborites with diplomatic posts, Barnes never mastered the proper stance. After he was replaced, Cecil commented: "The reason for the change was that Mr. Barnes claimed a certain amount of liberty of speech in the Assembly which shocked the bureaucracy in London. . . . As an exponent of the point of view of the average Briton, Mr. Barnes was hard to beat."

On disarmament, for example, Barnes insisted on pointing to where the arms were piling up. "I respectfully submit," he told the Assembly, "that the ex-enemy powers have ceased to be a menace to the world for the next generation, and that we ought to concern ourselves more with putting our own house in order . . ." He called for disarmament "not on the part of the ex-enemy powers who are now very largely disarmed, but upon the part of all the members of the League."

Barnes objected to the ceremonial laying of a wreath on the monument to Jean Jacques Rousseau, Geneva's favorite son (on the grounds that his ideas motivated Napoleon), demanded the admission of Germany, told the Council to stop spending time on abstruse economic problems and get on with settling the world's trouble spots and, furthermore, to do it without spending so much money.

The League's modest budget (fifteen million Swiss francs) was vigorously assailed, and Sir Eric's own salary of £10,000 a year came under the heaviest attack. New Zealanders protested that this was five times the pay of their own Prime Minister. The Secretary-General was saved from a pay cut only by Lord Balfour's gentle reminder that many American businessmen got far more.

To Barnes and others—principally in the British Empire bloc—who scoffed at the notion of the League's concern with broader economic questions such as the distribution of raw materials, Tommaso Tittoni of Italy pointed out that "on the solution of this question depends the future of peace or war." He drew vigorous applause and then went on to make a plea, the first of many such vain efforts: "I do not intend to propose any method of solving these tremendous problems. I only appeal to those powers who are the fortunate possessors of raw materials, to those powers who are rich, not to wait for the poorer powers and the powers who are dependent on them, but to come before this Assembly and say that they will waive their national interests and national egoisms in the general interests of humanity, justice and equality."

The applause was thunderous, and Brazil's Gaston Da Cunha shouted, "*Très bien.*" But no one that year or in the years to come appeared to waive any national interest or national ego at the Assembly of the League of Nations.

The first Assembly was made noteworthy by the revolt of the non-Europeans. Newton W. Rowell of Canada declared that his people were not prepared to send their top leaders across the ocean to Europe for frequent meetings, nor were they prepared to entrust their future to European leaders. "You may say that we should have confidence in European statesmen and leaders. Perhaps we should, but it was European statesmanship, European ambition that drowned the world with blood and for which we are still suffering and will suffer for generations . . ."

At that point Gabriel Hanotaux, speaking for France, cried out: "I say Europe fought for the world, Europe fought for humanity." The applause came mainly from Europeans.

Argentina led the fight to democratize the League from the start. The fiery Honoria Pueyrredon read a virtual ultimatum to the Assembly demanding that the Council be elected by the Assembly and responsible to it, that all sovereign states be admitted at once, and that even the smallest be represented—if necessary without a vote. He further called for a Court of Justice with full power to enforce its arbitration decisions. When the Assembly declined to approve the changes which would have swept aside all the careful hedging that had consumed the wiliest brains of the world in 1919, the Argentine delegation walked out.

Some thought they heard in Pueyrredon's speech not the revolt of the New World but the echo of the Harding administration in Washington. The League Assembly named commissions and heard reports and lambasted the Council, but, despite the businesslike air, it was bedeviled by the empty chair that waited for the United States. Then, and throughout the first three years of the League's existence, that prodigal son seemed bent on a policy of calculated obstruction. "We are out to kill the League," was the terse policy summation attributed to United States ambassador to Britain, Colonel Harvey, still attempting to exorcise the ghost of Woodrow Wilson.

Actually the Harding foreign policy kept the League on a grid of nervous anxiety. In the summer of 1921 the United States quietly signed separate peace treaties with the former enemies, all of them virtual replicas of the Versailles Pact, the iniquities of which had been so painstakingly stigmatized and hurled at the head of Wilson. The League Covenant was thus the only part of the Versailles Treaty disclaimed by the United States.

Harding flirted with the project of a competitor to the League, an Association of Nations with a less powerful Council and Assembly but with a more potent Court. He was certain that the mere presence of the United States would at once win the nations of the world to his Association, just as the absence of the United States would assuredly doom the League.

In February 1921, during the twilight between Harding's election and his inauguration, a confidential memorandum was sent to Drummond by Arthur Sweetser, that ardent American champion of the League and acute observer of American politics.

Sweetser sketched the scene in Congress: "The Republican Party, which was able to hang together throughout the campaign on the anti-Wilson issue, is torn by a civil war between the pro-League group, headed by Root, Taft, Hoover, etc., and by the Irreconcilable group, headed by Johnson, Borah, McCormick, etc. . . . In addition there are the Democrats. They control a little over a third of the Senate, or quite sufficient to block any action by the Republicans if they set out to be merely obstructionist. They feel extremely bitter over the recent campaign, especially over the Republican attitude toward the League, and have shown by recent private correspondence of their leaders that they intend to make an intensive fight for the League, which may possibly be as embarrassing as it will be helpful."

Sweetser discussed the possibility of amendments to the League Covenant to win American support, and said the Americans were unanimous in demanding such changes, though "not one man in ten knows what these changes are, with the single exception of Article ten." (That article constituted a collective guarantee of each member's territory against aggression and so stirred fears of too great a commitment to action.) Sweetser noted two other aspects of the League which interested Americans: "First, is the International Credit scheme which American business interests have taken hold of with the keenest possible interest. If this plan is pushed through successfully by the League, there is a very strong possibility that it would bring about the support of the great preponderance of American business interests, which in themselves are sufficient to turn the Government. The second is the question of mandates, especially over Mesopotamia, where the feeling has been created that the United States is being deliberately excluded from oil resources. It should be easy to dispel this feeling."

He thought that a "solution in the United States will take a long time, very possibly two years," and warned: "What has done more harm to the League than anything else has been the apparent waiting around and inactivity on the theory that nothing can be done without the United States."

Most significant, however, in the light of what was to come, were Sweetser's comments on the disarmament outlook:

"Recently," he told Drummond, "the Irreconcilables have interjected a new element through the Borah resolution, calling for an agreement between the United States, Japan and Great Britain for a fifty percent reduction in naval appropriations. This is a most clever move because it at once converts the Irreconcilable group from the role of sheer obstruction, which their opposition to the Treaty and the League has forced them to, through the past year, into the position of an extremely liberal and constructive group.

"The new Administration will undoubtedly follow up this suggestion with a call for an international conference on Disarmament. If Disarmament can be secured by the United States acting on its own initiative and outside the League of Nations, the one really powerful argument for joining the League will have been shattered."

Out of this strategy, hatched by the Irreconcilables to undercut the League, came the call on August 11, 1921, for a Washington Conference of the Big Five—Great Britain, France, Italy, Japan, and the United States—to discuss "limitations of armaments and other problems which have arisen in the Pacific Area."

The Conference, scheduled for November 12, lay like a cloud over the second Assembly of the League, which convened on September 5, 1921, only three weeks after the summons from Washington, which seemed to the delegates to be Harding's most formidable challenge.

The disarmament question was not the only arena in which the United States had seemingly pitted itself against the League. Even in the final days of the Wilson administration, Washington had served notice that it would have to be consulted on the mandates question and the League had asked that a United States representative sit in on the Council so that the American views could be heard. Harding refused, however, and instead sent still further protests to Geneva.

American delays and reluctance to answer League communications were hampering the League's credit scheme to bail Austria out of economic disaster. (The United States had lent Austria twenty-five million dollars and, for the scheme to have any effect, the United States would have to agree to extend the loan for twenty years.) Harding's aloofness was also blocking the necessary international agreements that would allow the League to do something about the traffic in opium and in what was then euphemistically known as "white slaves"—meaning women. On immigration, a matter of top concern to the United States, which was considering the establishment of the quota system, the Department of Labor did actually assign a representative, who got as far as London. He was then sent home by Colonel Harvey, who saw in such a mission an unwholesome recognition that the League of Nations did actually exist.

That the League was indeed a reality seemed unarguable in the early days of September 1921, as the delegates gathered once again at the Salle de la Réformation for the Assembly, and for their Council meetings in the Palais that had been the Hôtel National. Léon Bourgeois had grown stouter and wearier and leaned upon his secretary, a woman almost equally aged. Balfour was as jaunty as ever with hat at an angle and walking stick under his arm. Paul Hymans of Belgium was described by a correspondent as "pirouetting" gracefully to beam at myriad friends. Wellington Koo, President of the Council at thirty-seven years old, carried an elegant light-gray hat and nodded in dignity at the elders about him, who so admired this cool and quiet spokesman for distracted China. In and out of the Palais corridors sped Sir Eric Drummond shepherding his flock of statesmen, summoning this one or that to private conferences to oil the machinery of his League.

The Assembly ran on words. Many of them were without consequence, but uttered grandly and solemnly for the record or for a constituency. Some expressed a personal agony. For example, there was this portentous cry from Henri Lafontaine of Belgium: "Everywhere in the world we see misery. There are six million unemployed in the United States. There are thirty million people suffering from famine in Russia. Armenia is at her last gasp. Georgia calls out for help. The Greeks and Turks are continuing a war of massacre. Everywhere commercial and economic relations are troubled . . . We read in the papers of aeroplanes that carry eggs with them, like birds, but eggs with terrible contents—a ton of explosives—which would have a disastrous effect, and which could sweep away whole suburbs of cities . . . a war against women, children and old men . . . There ought to be no more frontiers guarded by the bayonets of the soldiers. If we do not take up the task of speaking in the name of the world's conscience, then I am afraid, we shall have the role of being the gravediggers of the world's hopes."

Or there was the extraordinary performance of Srinivasa Sastri of India, of whom the correspondent of the French paper *L'Oeuvre* wrote: "He transforms the guttural tongue of his conquerors [English] into a harmonious language. One seems to listen to a rhythmic chant, strange and smooth, accompanied by slow caressing gestures." He warned the Assembly that some of the powers to whom mandates had been allotted "do not hesitate to subject colored populations within their areas to certain hardships and, I am sorry to add, even indignities. . . . Let us remember that . . . the Germans did not make a color bar or introduce these invidious distinctions." He expressed the hope that neither the Indian nor the Japanese representative "will find it necessary to come on this platform and tell the Assembly that we are worse off than we were under the Germans."

Unfortunately few delegates heard that warning, inasmuch as Sastri's peroration had run into the lunch hour. In any case, such declarations were treated in those early years as pious irrelevancies. The League, struggling to survive, was weighted down with more immediate problems.

Many of those who had scoffed a year earlier at the first Assembly marveled at the second one, that this organization, even without the United States and Germany, had lasted through the year and somehow grown in stature and confidence.

Paul S. Mowrer, covering the session for the Chicago *Daily News*, wrote: "In my opinion few less justifiable errors have ever been committed by responsible politicians than that of certain American leaders in assuming that the League of Nations was doomed either to early disintegration or to lingering paralysis, and that we could, therefore, well afford to ignore its existence. The fact is that the League is neither dead nor dying."

The lavish praise showered upon the infant League was more for its sheer survival than for actual accomplishment. Still, there were victories as well as defeats and draws. These, continuing throughout the first half of the 1920's, gave an impression of vitality.

True, in the matter of disarmament, Washington decidedly stole a march on the League. However crassly political may have been the original motivations of the Washington Conference of 1921, it succeeded brilliantly, to the astonishment, almost the alarm, of the world's statesmen. Secretary of State Charles Evans Hughes opened it on November 12 by proposing, with unheard-of directness, that the first business of a disarmament conference was to disarm. "One program [of naval armaments] inevitably leads to another," he said, "and if competition continues, its regulation is impracticable. There is only one adequate way out, and that is to end it now."

The delegates then worked out a proportion of naval strengths in the Pacific, putting Britain and the United States on a par and setting Japan's strength at an inferior level—a formula that lasted until 1938. In return for this concession and for observing its promise to return Shantung to China, Japan was allowed to inherit Russia's former concessions in Manchuria and, what made it all worth while to Japan, the United States and Britain promised not to increase their naval bases in the Pacific, although the agreement did not affect the British bastion at Singapore.

That a certain measure of disarmament should actually flow from a disarmament conference was an event not only unprecedented at the time, but never to be equaled in the long, tortuous, and quixotic disarmament efforts of the League, which must be chronicled in a later chapter.

What inspired a measure of hope for the League in the early 1920's was its handling of an array of crises that bubbled in the aftermath of the war. The fortunate aspects of one of the first crises, the Aaland Islands problem, was that basically it concerned two small countries with a marked taste for international law and order, and involved no vital interest of any major League power. This made a solution eminently possible.

The three-hundred-island archipelago of the Aalands lies off the southern and southwestern coasts of Finland. The 26,000 islanders, all of whom were Swedes by descent and spoke Swedish, had been ruled by the semi-autonomous Grand Duchy of Finland under the overlordship of the Czars. (The Aalanders contended that they had never voluntarily submitted to the Czar as the Finns had.)

The islands' only claim to world attention lay in the fact that, if fortified, they would command the entrance to Russia's major northern port, Petrograd. Inasmuch as Russia was not a member of the League or recognized by any member at the time, it could not be consulted, and so the chess match would be played without the king.

When Finland, Latvia, Estonia, and Lithuania declared their independence, the Aaland Islanders, seizing upon the slogan of self-determination, clamored to return to the Swedish crown.

The Finns would have no part of the Swedish proposal for a plebiscite. The Aalanders would have no part of the Finnish offer for autonomy. In a letter to Drummond dated July 22, 1920, farmer Johannes Eriksson and farmer August Karlsson, in behalf of the Aaland Provincial Assembly, declared: "Our fears that a foreign race should invade our Island is based on the experience of how the Finnish race suffocates the Swedish mind, and no law can give us the protection against this, as our national existence is demanding."

Two companies of Finnish troops armed with machine guns went ashore on the islands and arrested two advocates of union with Sweden, charging them with high treason. Sweden severed diplomatic relations. Inasmuch as Finland was not yet a League member, Britain's Lord Curzon brought the matter to the attention of the Council and Finland was invited to send a representative to sit in on the sessions.

Sir Eric, in reporting the affair to the first Assembly, said that the Council "would naturally desire to hear the views of Russia on the subject when she had emerged from the exceptional position in which she found herself."

Before taking any action, the Council heard the opinions of three international jurists, all of whom agreed that it had full jurisdiction over the question. It then dispatched a commission to the islands, to Sweden, and to Finland. In the end, the Council, seconded by the Assembly, gave the islands to Finland but exacted strict guarantees of autonomy and a pledge of noninterference with the use of the Swedish language or customs.

The Council further proposed an international pact for the perpetual neutrality of the islands. In October 1921, representatives of Great Britain, Italy, Latvia, Poland, Sweden, Denmark, Estonia, France, Finland, and the League signed an agreement guaranteeing the islands' freedom from fortifications. No invitation was sent to Moscow on the grounds that no diplomatic machinery existed to reach powers beyond the pale.

Sweden accepted the decision but held that it was contrary to the principles of the Covenant. In the Assembly of 1921 Sweden's Hjalmar Branting voiced "the hope that the day will come when the idea of justice shall have so permeated the conscience of the peoples, that the claims inspired by such noble motives and a national feeling as deep as that of the population of the Aaland Isles, will be triumphantly vindicated."

Whatever may have been the feelings of the islanders, or the Swedes or the Finns, for the League it was undeniably sweet to be denounced as unjust but still to be accepted as the ultimate authority.

The case of the city of Danzig did not involve the League as judge but as a watchdog and go-between in the city's relations with Poland. Though in later years the situation was to have the grimmest consequences, in the early 1920's the League's handling of it seemed to be a triumph for Drummond's thoroughness and beneficent paternalism.

The city of some 350,000 people, about 42.5 percent of whom were ethnically German, had been one of the forfeits Germany paid for losing the war. Frederick the Great had originally taken it from Poland in 1772, declaring that "whoever holds the course of the Vistula and Danzig is more fully master of that country [Poland] than the King who reigns over it."

Poland, now freshly re-created, had demanded it back as a matter of simple historical rectification. But such a proposal would have run counter to the Wilsonian doctrine of ethnic considerations in self-determination and it would have wrecked Germany's flow of commerce to the Baltic. In an effort to be fair, therefore, the map makers at Versailles gave Poland a corridor running one hundred miles through West Prussia to the sea, and declared that Danzig and an area of seven hundred and fifty square miles around it would be a "free city" protected by the League. Both solutions were to create formidable problems.

In very short order the League established its High Commissioner in Danzig and supervised elections for the Senate and Parliament that were to rule the town until a Constitution could be drafted. Danzigers bridled at the necessity for League approval of the election machinery and at the Council's orders to close down a German rifle factory. (The manufacture even of hunting rifles was banned, as was any step that might even indirectly involve the League's protégé in complicity with military adventures.)

By October 1921, the League's High Commissioner in Danzig, Sir Richard Haking, conferred a kindly pat on the heads of the city's senators and held up a warning finger against playing under the table with the Germans. "Danzig has now got an opportunity of getting her economic and financial affairs stabilized," he told them, ". . . but she must drop any outside dealings she may contemplate with Germany, she must act independently as a Free City, she must pass laws to reduce the deficit of her Budget, and she must arrange her dealings with the Government of Poland so as to assure the full commercial use of the great hinterland which is served by her harbor. If the Danzig government tries to be clever, tries to get something for nothing, she can expect no help from the Allies, her economic and financial condition will get worse instead of better, and the world will think that she is incapable of self-government."

In those early years the Danzigers listened to the advice and the implied threats of the League and gave no trouble to the High Commissioner, who was empowered to guide their relations with Poland. The experiment seemed to be working.

It was more difficult to implement the Versailles Treaty in the coal fields of the Saar, which lay like a time bomb with a fifteen-year fuse between Germany and France. The Treaty had provided that during that time France would operate the Saar mines in part payment for German destruction of French resources and that the League would administer the territory of over 700,000 people.

This was to be no paternal vice-regency over an elected Senate as in

Danzig. It was to be naked rule by the League directly over one of the prizes of the war, where French and Germans continued to confront one another. The Council established a Commission of Five to govern the Saar, backed by a garrison of French soldiers and a French police force. From the start Germany swamped the League Commission office with frantic protests against the "occupation" by French troops, against expulsions of Germans, against the use of French courts-martial.

The Commission's reply to all these charges, as reported by Sir Eric to the League Assembly, seemed on the surface to be self-contradictory. The French troops, it was explained, were "not in occupation but in garrison." They were there only temporarily until a gendarmerie could be recruited locally, an eventuality which, it admitted, was not likely to prove practical in the foreseeable future. French courts-martial had no control whatever over the Saar inhabitants, the Commission asserted, adding, astonishingly, that this nonexistent control would cease once a Supreme Court of the Saar was established.

Germany protested what it called "mass expulsions," but Sir Eric told the Assembly that only "about one hundred notorious Pan-Germans, mostly foreign to the territory," had been expelled. This took place during a strike of Saar officials when the Commission had been forced into the time-honored expedient of declaring "a state of siege" and empowering the French military commander to "ensure order."

Germany protested the use of the franc instead of the mark in the Saar and in general insisted on assuming that the Saar was and would remain German territory. Still, the mines continued to operate and an uneasy peace prevailed despite the drumfire of German protest and the presence of French troops.

For the Council's cool efforts at political rule in the trouble spots of Danzig and the Saar, the League won the Assembly's approval. Lord Cecil, in a mood of modified rapture during the Assembly of 1921, conferred the honors: "I do think that this is a work which—I do not say faultless, we are talking of human things—but in the highest degree creditable. When we compare it with the other experiments in international administration which have been made in past times, experiments which have been a byword of inefficiency, I think we may congratulate the Council of the League in having carried through so far an exceptionally difficult task with credit and with success."

Of all the early crises which beset the League, Poland presented the most troublesome and the most risky ones. The difficulty was compounded by the fact that the new state was simultaneously embroiled with Russia, Lithuania, Czechoslovakia, and Germany; that these conflicts were not verbal but violent; that France and England were bitterly at odds in the area; and that Poland itself was in the hands of a flamboyant warlord.

Józef Pilsudski, as a boy, ran fiery pamphlets off his printing press for a group with vaguely anarchist revolutionary sentiments. For the same cause, he held up a train carrying gold bullion and received repeated sentences in Czarist prisons, from which he would periodically escape. The resultant antipathy to Russians lasted his lifetime, and he made no distinctions between Czarist Russians and Bolshevik Russians.

When the war broke out, the Czar offered Poland a form of autonomy, but Pilsudski scorned it and went over to the Kaiser, organizing a "Polish Legion" to fight on the Eastern Front. He bridled at the snobbish views of the Prussian High Command, rebelled, and was tossed into a German jail. Released at the armistice, he fitted in quite nicely with the needs of the hour from the viewpoint of the Allies: a Polish hero with an antipathy to both Germans and Russians.

At the age of fifty-three Pilsudski was the Marshal of Poland, the unquestioned power in his country. He was enthusiastically backed by the Western democracies although he knew little and cared less about Western Europe (he had never been there) and entertained an absolute scorn for the democratic process. An admiring biographer, Rom Landau, wrote of him: "He was entirely devoid of respect for bourgeois morality, and could infringe any customary and acknowledged code. He believed laws made for mediocrity to have no application to himself."

This disdain for ordinary scruples made his whims dangerous. For example, the Marshal's sentimental fondness for the city of Vilna, Lithuania, where he passed his childhood, was transformed by his forceful but devious temperament into a major crisis for the League of Nations.

Vilna was an ancient city with a long and tortuous history. At the end of the World War, if one seriously tried to apply the Wilsonian criterion of ethnic self-determination, the city would probably have been turned over to the Jews as the largest single component of the population. Poles and Lithuanians were about equal in number.

In 1919 Polish forces, with English and French help, drove Soviet troops out of Vilna. In July 1920 the Russians returned, drove the Poles out, and turned the city over to the new Lithuanian government. The Russians and Lithuanians thereupon drew their own maps, which differed markedly from the ones being charted in Paris. There the peacemakers drew an eastern boundary for Poland—the Curzon Line—but omitted to fix any western limits for the new Polish state. The question was tricky because in a treaty with the Czar in 1917 shortly before the Russian Revolution,

France had agreed that Russia would have undisputed claim to all of Poland. The very existence of Poland was thus a consequence of the Bolshevik Revolution. Now with the Bolsheviks an uncertain ally against the primordial enemy, Germany, France saw merit in a Poland with an elastic frontier. The Russo-Lithuanian map, however, allowed Lithuanian troops to take up their positions west of the Curzon Line, and Poland thereupon appealed to the League.

The League Council succeeded in persuading the Lithuanians to withdraw behind the Curzon Line in return for a Polish promise to respect Lithuanian neutrality. At that moment in September 1920, there erupted the Zeligowski affair, which threw the League into confusion.

Pilsudski plainly decided that Poland's renunciation of Vilna was an agreement made for mediocrities. He gathered his generals around him in the city of Lida and told them that, in view of this awkward agreement with the League, he could give no express orders to take Vilna but that he thought it should be taken and that the military should assume responsibility. His eye lighted on a general named Lucian Zeligowski, who, like the Marshal, came from Vilna.

Zeligowski, described by Polish writers as "a swashbuckler of another century," had fought the Russians with saber and pistol. His philosophy, not uncongenial to the Marshal, was summed up this way by Landau, Pilsudski's worshipful biographer: "The world was a place either of good men to drink with, or of the others into whose bodies one emptied lead."

Zeligowski hesitated to accept full responsibility for the taking of Vilna, demanding a direct order from his chief, which he would then carry out with a whole heart as well as saber and pistol. The discussion, which continued for twenty-four hours, broke up when the Marshal shouted at Zeligowski: "I wanted to make you a D'Annunzio, and now I see you're nothing but an ox!" With that the chastened Zeligowski took his unofficial orders and marched on Vilna, declaring: "We haven't come to fight. We're coming home." He termed the regime he established "the Government of Central Lithuania."

Polish delegates to the League declined to take any responsibility for General Zeligowski, who was described as a "rebel," but on the other hand they could not promise to suppress this rebellion, on the grounds that the General's action in Vilna had received "the unanimous support of Polish public opinion." The League Council suggested a variety of solutions, all of which foundered on Polish obstinacy or Lithuanian fears, mixed with legalistic pettifogging. A plebiscite was planned under the supervision of an international police force, with contingents from England, France, Belgium, Spain, Sweden, Denmark, Norway, and Greece. It would have been the first venture of a League military expedition coupled with a democratic solution. But Switzerland decided that no contingents could pass through its territory, lest they violate its neutrality. In any case, the Poles and Lithuanians could not agree on who was to be polled.

In despair Drummond passed the buck to Paul Hymans of Belgium, who listened to all arguments with great care and proposed a variety of solutions, none of which could please both sides at the same time. And Zeligowski stayed in Vilna.

"The lamentable controversy," as Balfour called it, dragged through 1920 and 1921. In the Assembly of 1921, Balfour told the story of Paul Hymans' agony, how the Polish and Lithuanian representatives "occupy no small part of their time and of the time of M. Hymans in mutual recriminations and in going over and over again the sad and ancient story of their differences. . . . To this day it is very difficult, even for the most impartial spectator of events, to know precisely what the attitude of the Polish Government is to the ex-Polish general [Zeligowski]. Is he a rebel deserving military sentence? Is he a patriot deserving the patriot's crown? We know not. Whenever the exigencies of debate require one answer to that question, that answer is given; when they require the other answer, the other answer is given."

In 1923 the Conference of Ambassadors, proceeding on the notion that *de facto* possession might as well be tidied up into a *de jure* occupation, awarded the city to Poland. (With the same realistic approach to power as opposed to law, the Conference decided in the following year that Memel, an area which the peacemakers delivered from Germany but failed to indicate where it was to go, would henceforth be Lithuanian because a Lithuanian army was already in possession of it.)

By the time Vilna was declared to be Polish, Pilsudski had already admitted to a group of diplomats that he had ordered Zeligowski to take the city. "I had a great deal of trouble," the Marshal said, "before I could persuade him to dispense with my giving him instructions in writing to rebel."

The matter came to a head again in 1927 and brought the aging Marshal of Poland to Switzerland for the first time. He was then nominally in retirement but continued to select the Polish President, Premier, and President of the Council. He came because General Augustinas Voldemaras, the President and dictator of Lithuania, a scrappy, passionate, fierce little professor of history who, as one observer remarked, "looked like a peasant at a funeral," had threatened to march on Vilna if the Council did not turn the city back to the Lithuanians.

Pilsudski, ill at ease in civilian clothes, nevertheless terrified a diplomatic luncheon at the Hôtel des Bergues by asking the German delegates what ever happened to the officer who had taken him off to a German jail.

He was no more tactful in the formal Council sessions of December 10, 1927. He interrupted the reading of a long and involved resolution to roar: "I want to know whether we are going to have peace or war. If it is peace I shall telegraph Warsaw for a Te Deum to be sung in all the churches and for the ringing of all the bells."

Around the table the eyes of the diplomats turned to Voldemaras, who could only respond: "Lithuania wants peace." Poland and Lithuania thereupon signed yet another document guaranteeing the inviolability of each other's borders. That left the Vilna question up in the air, and Vilna stayed in Polish hands, where it remained until 1939, when the Soviet army restored it to the Lithuanians, as a by-product of its march into Poland.

It was difficult to call the Vilna question a victory for the League and for sweet reasonableness. Still, it was said that the League had prevented or limited the bloodshed.

Behind the shenanigans of Pilsudski and Zeligowski lay a conflict, made manifest on the flexible Polish borders, but far exceeding that issue in gravity. This was the clash of English and French views, policies, philosophies, and temperaments. It raised the question whether France had won or lost the war.

France had received none of the guarantees of security it sought and without which the war itself seemed to have been in vain. The Rhine would shortly lie open to the Germans; the pledges of assistance from Britain and the United States had been buried along with Clemenceau by the United States Senate; France saw in the League the last remaining mechanism for enforcing the Treaty of Versailles, and it trembled at the slightest tampering with its provisions. It depended on the strictest possible interpretation of the Treaty to collect its reparations. To England this attitude appeared to be crass and grasping, but *Figaro* put the Anglo-French differences bluntly: "After the Armistice and by virtue of the Versailles Treaty, England was paid on the nail, France had to accept payment by installments . . . Everything which a victorious England could obtain from a defeated Germany she has already had: Colonies, Navy and mercantile tonnage. . . . We, on the other hand, have been paid in promises. We hold pledges that it will take twenty years to redeem. Should this redemption be avoided we should face bankruptcy. England, the world's most able business nation, must be aware of this."

France was doubly alarmed at the first appearance of the specter of Russo-German collaboration. Berlin and Moscow were in fact on diplomatic speaking terms and in East Prussia German volunteers were signing up to fight with the Bolsheviks against the Poles. To a jittery and largely betrayed France this spelled the most appalling doom.

It was then that France decided to send military support under General Weygand to Poland. (The British High Commissioner at Danzig refused to allow French munitions to be unloaded at that port.) On top of this France recognized the insurgent White Guard General Wrangel.

England, on the other hand, thought that the entire Polish-Lithuanian uproar an unreasonable obstruction to the major business of the world, which was to get down to business again.

Geneviève Tabouis, the diplomatic journalist (some accused her of being a journalist diplomat), wrote that Lloyd George "showed himself willing to endorse any violation of Polish independence and integrity if only Poland would be good enough to subscribe to it."

Aside from those who took a commercial view of the world, there were others in England who detested the intervention in Russia, either because it seemed an unwarranted interference in the internal affairs of another country or because they saw in it a conspiracy to strangle an experiment that held the promise of working-class emancipation.

Poland's attitude toward the varying approaches of Western Europe was best summed up not in the ferocious histrionics of Marshal Pilsudski but in an urbane letter written to Sir Eric Drummond in June 1920 by a professor of law at the University of Cracow, who served as president of the Polish Society for the League of Nations and as Sir Eric's eyes and ears in that city.

"Peace with Russia," Professor M. Rostworowski wrote, "is another serious problem which troubles us, but to imagine the reaction such talk might arouse in Poland, you have only to recall how a proposition of peace would have been received in France in the spring of 1918 [a time of German military success]. The spectacle of the Bolsheviks finding allies not only among the Germans and their client states, but among statesmen in the camp of *our* allies—is not exactly one to fill us with enthusiasm, but we must not forget, on the one hand, that 'business is business,' and on the other, that doctrinaire pacifists are the enemies of the human race."

All of these fears boiled to the surface in the coal and iron fields of Upper Silesia, an area almost as important in economic terms as the Ruhr.

Within the preceding five hundred years the territory had been, at various times, Polish, Bohemian, Austrian, and Prussian. About two-thirds of its two million inhabitants at the end of the war were Polish, and the rest were German, but the great industry that made the area of key importance had been built by German capital and constituted a major factor in the German economy.

The peacemakers in Paris in the spring of 1919, finding the Silesian problem too touchy for a quick Wilsonian solution, had fallen back on the device of a plebiscite. Allied troops occupied the region under an inter-Allied commission delegated to run the balloting as fairly as possible, while seeing to it that in the meantime Germany would receive 500,000 tons of coal a month from the mines.

The vote on March 20, 1921, yielded a clear majority for union with Germany: 707,605 against 479,359 for Polish nationality. The vote settled nothing, however, since the Poles at once charged fraud and coercion, accusing German employers of pressuring their Polish workers into voting for Germany. And the inevitable Polish "irregulars" appeared on the scene, this time under a man named Korfanty, who seemed to be patterning his role after that of Zeligowski.

Lloyd George, under the impression that the French and Poles had gotten away with larceny at Vilna, proposed giving all of Upper Silesia back to Germany, despite the fact that this would plainly have violated the Versailles Treaty and driven the French to utter distraction. The Prime Minister, fortified with a glass of port, would regularly use the House of Commons to blast the French and Poles. His admiring secretary (and subsequently his wife), Frances Stevenson, voiced the general British sporting approach in her diary after a speech by her boss on May 13, 1921. "I think D [for David] was right," she said, "though we nearly had a row over the things he said about the French. But they are certainly not playing the game in this instance. And the Germans will—and are—making the most of D's speech."

Sir Eric described the situation in different terms. In a letter to British diplomat P. H. Kerr, he wrote: "In Paris they had just got to a point where Upper Silesia seemed likely to cause a definite breach between England and France with, to my mind, incalculable results for the peace of Europe for a considerable time to come. What was to be done?"

What was done, in fact, was that the diplomats turned, in a mood of rage and exasperation, to Sir Eric and the League. On August 12, 1921, the Conference of Ambassadors asked for recommendations for a solution to be formulated with the "utmost urgency."

Sir Eric's first thought, as he wrote to Kerr, was to establish a commission, as in the affair of the Aaland Islands. To carry weight in so touchy a situation, however, its members would have to be both eminent and neutral. This proved impossible, Drummond noted, because "all the countries of Europe were more or less concerned in this dispute, either directly or because they wished to stand well with England or with France or alternatively with Poland or with Germany. The Governments of what may be called neutral countries were not willing to allow any of their nationals to serve."

Using a commission of experts, representing not their nations but themselves, the League Council tried to draw a boundary in Upper Silesia that would do the least amount of violence to ethnic sentiments and economic effectiveness. However, when the communities of pro-German and pro-Polish leanings were pinpointed on the map, it looked like a mosaic, defying any simple boundary. The League experts, bitterly assailed by partisans of all sides, took volumes of evidence from both German employers and Polish workers. Sir Eric explained the precedent-shattering nature of the procedure: "These people who came to give evidence were very grateful, and said that it was the first time that the views of delegates from the territory itself had been represented." The League experts did not, however, go into the area itself, where terror and counter-terror raged, because, as Sir Eric pointed out, "both the Germans and Poles earnestly begged the two experts not to go to Upper Silesia to take evidence locally, as they considered that this might lead to grave disturbances, and that they would not obtain impartial evidence on the spot."

In the end the League devised a line which, with some minor and voluntary adjustments of population and industry, would satisfy 64.5 percent of Upper Silesians. The astonishing nature of this feat was attested to by an authority on plebiscites who estimated that, theoretically, the most satisfactory line imaginable—without reference to industrial considerations—could please no more than 70 to 75 percent. The League specified the manifold problems of transition and proposed that Poland and Germany sign an agreement embodying all the procedures. Until that was done an inter-Allied commission with German and Polish representation ruled the territory.

German and Polish negotiators thrashed the matter out at Geneva under the patient guidance of the Swiss chairman of the League-invented Upper Silesia Conference. In May 1922 they formulated the agreement in a document of over six hundred articles, more massive than the entire Treaty of Versailles. The British put up a small rear-guard action but in the end accepted the solution offered by the League in a touchy situation which the big powers themselves had failed to solve.

The League Council tried to disentangle the powers from their own confusion in Albania as well, but with far less success than in Upper Silesia. Albania had been virtually conceded to the hegemony of Italy by the peacemakers at Versailles, but Italy in the early 1920's was in no position to digest the morsel. Even while the Peace Conference was proceeding in Paris, Gabriele D'Annunzio, that flamboyant poet, lover, opera tenor, and amateur statesman, had seized the Adriatic port of Fiume. He held it for a year, treating his followers to speeches of a torrid nationalism. A fervent and equally synthetic nationalism was being drummed up by the Fascisti in Rome.

To Paul Mantoux in Geneva came messages that revealed the difficulties Italy would have in swallowing whatever crumbs had been left to it at the feast of Versailles. On November 12, 1921, Dominick Veré, the League's man in Rome, wrote to Mantoux: "The situation is peculiar; the Ferrovieri [railroad workers] are on strike because of the doings of the Fascisti in Rome. But the Fascisti cannot leave Rome as long as the Ferrovieri are on strike. C'est l'impasse complète! . . ."

On the matter of Albania, Veré reported that the Italians "hope to keep Albania alive until better times—better times for Italy, I mean. In other words they hope to keep things going till the Italian government and the nation be ready to take a lead in the inevitable liquidation of that country. Why is the Italian government so pessimistic? . . . It is Albania herself whom they distrust or rather the Albanians . . . So many 'prominent Albanians' have offered to sell their country—or bits of it—to Italy, to Yugo-Slavia and to Greece (or to anyone else) that Rome hardly dares place any more hope in the country's more honest representation . . . An 'accorda di Londra' [referring to the Secret Treaty of London] has recently been reached between England, France and Italy, in view of that most undesired and undesirable—but perhaps inevitable—event: the liquidation of Albania. Italy's allies have recognized her preponderant interests and her right to act in their defense. But does Italy want to act? Heaven forbid!"

Albania's borders were being chewed by Serbian and Greek military incursions, taking advantage of Italy's internal preoccupations. Veré told Mantoux that the Yugoslavs were for liquidating Albania at once while "they hold—as we say here—the knife by the handle. Can the Allied government or the League wrest it from them? Qui vivra verra [Time will tell]."

Italy's delegate to the Conference of Ambassadors, according to Veré, was instructed "to reach a favorable solution with the least expenditure of force . . . In other words the poor man will be told to make bricks without straw."

The fate of Albania was not at first the concern of the League, inasmuch as the Council of Ambassadors was then taking a direct hand in the Balkans. It had established an Inter-Allied Delimitation Commission to fix Albania's borders, and in deference to Italy's "preponderant interests" this consisted of three Italian officers. On August 27, 1923, the three Italian Commissioners and their Italian chauffeur and Albanian interpreter, while riding in Greek territory, were ambushed and killed by unknown gunmen.

Italy at once dispatched an ultimatum to Greece demanding, among other things, the payment of fifty million lire as an indemnity within five days. The Greeks countered by offering to pay "equitable compensation" to the victims' families. Four days later the Italians answered by bombarding the Greek island of Corfu, then crowded with Greek refugees from Turkish persecutions. The Italians followed up their bombardment by occupying the island and declaring their intention to hold it until the indemnity was fully paid.

The Conference of Ambassadors characteristically fumbled, devoting itself to the assertion of its own rights in the matter. It demanded an inquiry into the assassinations—to which Greece immediately acceded—and reserved the right to fix the indemnity because the murdered officers were acting as agents of the Conference of Ambassadors.

Greece thereupon appealed to the League. The League Council met at once, but Italy challenged its competence on the grounds that the matter was being considered by the Conference of Ambassadors. Here, then, was a jurisdictional question of immense and precedent-setting proportions.

The Council again turned for advice to a committee of jurists, who, although they thought the Council was competent, struck a curious and far-reaching note. They declared that "coercive measures which are not intended to constitute acts of war may or may not be consistent" with the Covenant. This loophole, as wide as a barn door to diplomats seeking to justify warfare in the name of peace, was spotted by the Swedish and Uruguayan representatives. These diplomats filed formal reservations on the point, and the Czechoslovak delegate expressed informal doubts, but the British, French, Belgian, Italian, and Japanese delegates delightedly swallowed the report in its entirety, apparently relishing the questionable proviso as potentially useful.

Then, having asserted its competence in the matter, the Council surrendered on the issue itself, leaving it up to the Conference of Ambassadors.

There the big powers, playing the Italian game, ordered Greece to pay the fifty million lire because the actual murderers had not been found. The Italians withdrew from Corfu, their honor seemingly satisfied.

The issue itself was not major, although—with Sarajevo still fresh in people's minds—the Balkans were considered a touchy spot for assassinations. Nevertheless, the League's surrender of authority to the big powers, coupled with the jurists' loophole, and the yielding to military force in Vilna were all ominous signs.

The omens, however, did not seem so gloomy in that period of rising hopes. For the League had demonstrated its usefulness, not only as an oratorical outlet and a diplomatic proving ground, but also as an extraordinary mechanism for negotiation and arbitration. It was not a super-state or the basis of a great world order of law, but it had been eminently helpful—even without the presence of Americans or Germans or Russians. This was a success far beyond the expectations of most observers, who thought that the League had been a victim of infanticide at the hands of the American electorate.

Eight

THE SAINTLY
SIDE

The League of Nations in its youth bore not only the face of a statesman but that of a saint as well. It was a weather-beaten saint, with tanned, creased face, shaggy gray mustache, and melancholy eyes. It was a saint who, at the age of sixty, sailed his craft on the Lake of Geneva, danced with pretty women in the livelier restaurants, played tennis, took ice-cold baths in chilly winter and then walked coatless up the Quai Wilson. It was a saint who sprang nimbly up the steps of the dais time after time to rouse the Assembly to some action in behalf of millions dying of starvation or in flight from terror. The League's private saint and conscience was Fridtjof Nansen of Norway.

Before he was thirty, Nansen had explored the Arctic (in 1889–91). By the beginning of the century, after a second epic conquest of the Far North, he had become a national hero and a world-wide legend. He served as his country's ambassador to England and he could have been Prime Minister if he had not decided that politics was not his métier.

In April 1919, Nansen, in Paris as Norway's "observer" at the Peace Conference, lunched with Lincoln Steffens, who had just returned with William Bullitt from a trip to Russia. Steffens was horrified by the dreadful sights of the famine but also afire with the promise he saw there for a fresh approach to the world. The view from Moscow contrasted with the disenchanting spectacle of Paris as Steffens saw it: "Righteousness and impossible desires, which are not pro-German, but just plain German:

Imperialism." His approach, which he discussed with Herbert Hoover as well as with Nansen, called for humanitarian and commercial contacts rather than political solutions. Nansen, apparently impressed, dashed off a letter to President Wilson in which he wrote: "The present commissariat conditions in Russia, where thousands are dying every month of starvation, constitute a problem that must affect the heart of mankind." He proposed a relief operation, but the Peace Conference agenda was crowded with the hopes and fears of nations, rather than of people. The French diplomat René Viviani sadly reflected that the Allied victory "has given glory to all the world but it has not put bread in men's mouths."

Nansen's relief proposal was shelved until Philip Noel-Baker, then a member of the League Secretariat, arrived in Christiania in the spring of 1920. He telephoned Nansen at his country home in Polhøgda to make an appointment with the hero of Norway. A half-hour later the hero himself drove up to Noel-Baker's hotel in a rattletrap Ford. The League emissary had come to ask Nansen whether he would undertake the League's work of rescuing the refugees of Russia, and Nansen agreed. "I remember," Noel-Baker wrote later, "that we had to push his Ford down the hill to get it to start."

Later Nansen told the biographical essayist Emil Ludwig just how it was that in 1921 he entered Russia in behalf of an organization whose member states had chosen either to ignore or to combat the government there: "The League of Nations asked me if I would go and bring back half a million prisoners who were detained in Russia. But why ask me? I had no idea. Hoover seems to have told them something. I had done some business with him over there during the war. They wanted a neutral, and possibly they thought that a diplomat would not have the courage to go, even though in reality no courage was necessary.

"When I reached Moscow, Chicherin [G. V. Chicherin, second to Trotsky in the Soviet Foreign Office] at once refused to recognize the right of the League of Nations to meddle in the affair. Within two hours I had sent a special train [which had brought Nansen to Moscow] back to the frontier. Then he calmed down and agreed on the condition that I obtain special authorization from each of the countries concerned. Perhaps these credentials arrived within six months or so, and perhaps they never came. However, I had completely fulfilled my mission in the meantime."

By March 1922, Nansen and his team of three assistants had dispatched 430,000 men to their original homes in twenty-six countries. In the process two of his assistants died of typhus in that year. Beyond that, the cost was unbelievably slight—roughly £1 per P.O.W. The Soviet government had already freed the men but, without help, could do little to speed them across a countryside wracked by famine, where trains and the fuel to run them were almost as scarce as food. Nansen scrounged rolling stock to take the men to Baltic ports and a fleet of fourteen ships to carry them home.

More discouraging to Nansen than typhus, however, was the reaction of the big powers to the tragedy of the Russian famine. Many statesmen at Geneva applauded when he spoke, and grieved with him at the senseless loss of life, but offered little help. Some were openly hostile or cynical.

On September 9, 1921, Nansen went before the Assembly to point out an unfortunate omission from the Secretary-General's report on the work of the Council: there was not a word about Russia. Diplomatically that vast nation was in limbo.

"After all," he told the delegates, "the Russian problem is the greatest question in the world, or at least in Europe at this moment. It is a certainty that Europe cannot go on without Russia. Russia is, if you will look at it from a purely political point of view, an economic necessity for Europe. We cannot expect to be able to put Europe on her feet again unless we do our best to help Russia onto her feet again."

He emphasized the cooperation he had received from the Soviet government, noting that it had permitted him to transport food parcels to prisoners of war across the country while Russians themselves were starving. "Not a package was missing," he reported.

He estimated that twenty to thirty million lives were at stake in the famine, and quoted Lloyd George's appeal to the House of Commons: "We must help. This is so appalling a disaster that it ought to sweep away every prejudice out of our minds, and appeal to only one emotion, that of pity and human sympathy."

Delegates, one after another, rose to utter the tenderest sentiments. The Danish paper *Politiken*, however, caught the drift: "[Nansen] produced a particularly deep impression when he insisted on the loyalty of the Soviet government, but he simultaneously provoked ironic smiles. In the Russian question every kind of conflicting interest comes into play, and many think only of politics and intrigue while their words are full of charity."

After Nansen resumed the fight from the rostrum on October 8, pleading for massive aid, the Serbian delegate, Dr. Spalaikovitch, laid down one prerequisite: the suicide of the Soviet regime. "I think that of the two scourges, famine and Bolshevism," he said, "Bolshevism is the worse."

With nominal support of the League but with only a little office on the rue de Rhône in Geneva and very little money, Nansen returned to Russia and engineered the rescue of several million people from famine.

When he appeared at the League Council table on May 17, 1922, he appealed for action in Russia as a matter of national self-interest: ". . . in doing this my Government have been moved by considerations not of politics nor of humanitarian feeling, but by considerations of the economic welfare of the world. And in what I have to say to you, I wish to confine myself to economic considerations and economic considerations alone. I do not wish to harrow your feelings with an account of the things which I myself have seen since I met you last at the Assembly. I do not wish to tell you of the millions who have died in torture on the Volga and the Ukrainian plains. I do not wish to give you any account, however brief, of the brutish horrors by which the progress of the famine is everywhere accompanied. I do not wish to tell you of the stories which come from our agents in Saratoff, in Samara, in Buzuluk, in Kharkoff, in Odessa; stories the truth of which we cannot doubt; stories of salted human flesh sold in the market places of the towns; stories of a fourteen-year-old girl who killed her brother and ate his flesh to save herself from death; stories of every degree of savage horror. . . . I do not wish to be hysterical . . ."

The failure of the League to respond to its conscience can be read in Nansen's deepening melancholy. The spokesmen for the major powers in the League squirmed and temporized. They perfected their facility at referring the question. The economic aspects, the Council decided, should be discussed at the Economic Conference, which was then breaking up in fruitless talk at Genoa; epidemics might be a proper question for the League's new Health Organization; famine was a matter for the Red Cross.

When in 1923 Nansen was awarded the Nobel Peace Prize he detailed his disappointments and some of the ways in which he had carried the League's banner despite the League. "Let me say a few words about helping Russia," he said. "The League of Nations was not in favor of this, to my regret . . . There was more than enough wheat in the world then, as there is today, and there was no lack of transport. Our problem was to get enough money . . . As the European governments refused us a loan of £ 10 million sterling, which I considered absolutely essential if we were to save Russia's starving millions, and stave off the terrible calamity of famine, not only in that country but in Europe as a whole, there was nothing for it but to see what could be done privately, by making an appeal to private beneficence all the world over."

He noted that the response had been "magnificent," particularly from American sources, then resumed his sad catalogue of the failure of statecraft. "How was it that some people refused to help? Well, you must ask them. Chiefly for political reasons. They represented that barren self-sufficiency, with its absence of any wish to understand other points of view. They call us fanatics, soft-heads, sentimental idealists because we have, it may be, a grain of faith that there is some good in our enemies and believe that more can be done by kindness than severity. Admitting that we believe in kindness, I don't think we are really dangerous. But the people who are ossifying behind their political platforms, and who hold aloof from suffering humanity, from starving, dying millions—it is they who are helping to lay Europe waste."

There was more misery to harry the conscience of the world and occupy the attention of the League's saint. Much of the problem stemmed from the prostrate body of the Turkish Empire, the most thoroughly beaten and humiliated of all the vanquished powers. While critics of the Versailles Treaty bridled at the slightest infringement upon Germany's sovereignty and bewailed the burdens put upon that defeated country, the Middle East was put up for grabs, with rival armies making peace a greater hell than war. Yet no John Maynard Keynes arose to talk of a "Carthaginian" peace on the Bosporus.

The division of the Ottoman Empire had all been neatly arranged in the Secret Treaties at the start of the war, but the fall of the Czar, the publication of the agreements by the Bolsheviks, and the general disrepute into which these arrangements had fallen, left the area in confusion. Matters reached a high point of absurdity when the British Foreign Office found that it was backing King Husein, the Sherif of Mecca, as the satrap of Arabia while the British India Office was supporting an opposing faction. A potential war between the departments was averted only by the intervention of the British Treasury, which cut off funds for both sides.

While British, French, and Italians maneuvered over the fallen Ottoman Empire, the wily Venizelos of Greece proposed that his country hold a part of the Turkish territory in question until such time as the Powers could decide the proper disposition. Not only was the idea practical but it could be given a Wilsonian coloration inasmuch as the Greeks were in fact local residents. Accordingly, the Greeks, backed by a fleet of Allied warships, took Smyrna from the Turks on May 15, 1919, thus shelving the question.

The Turkish sultan Abdul-Hamid was apparently willing to be put upon the shelf or at least he seemed powerless to do much about it. But a nationalist movement arose, motivated in part by Turkish loathing for the Greeks. Led by the Turkish war hero Mustafa Kemal, the movement soon commanded a majority in Parliament and was demanding all of Asia Minor for a renascent Turkey. The Allies thereupon seized Constantinople and banished some of the Nationalist leaders. Kemal, however, fled into the interior and established a government which opened friendly relations with the Bolsheviks, a move which, for the Allies, made him doubly devilish. The Greeks pursued Kemal into the interior, but by this time Venizelos' government had fallen. The former King Constantine, who was never very friendly to the Allies, returned to power. After that France and England looked upon the affair as a Greco-Turkish war. They declined to participate beyond holding Constantinople, an occupation unblessed by treaty. The League was not in fact "seized" with the problem and paid it no mind. The Treaty of Sèvres dividing the Turkish Empire had not been signed in the early 1920's and the occupation could be legally regarded as a war measure beyond the purview of the Council or the Assembly.

The Middle East question might never have reached the League were it not for the fact that in the crucible in which Kemal was preparing the new Turkey, the Armenians were perishing by the tens of thousands. For years before that, the Turks had been slaughtering the Armenians when there were no Greeks at hand. Kemal, dreaming of an ethnically unified Turkey, mitigated but did not altogether stop the slaughter, which seemed likely to achieve a Turkish unity by means of an Armenian genocide.

It had been hoped that the United States would take the entire problem on its shoulders by accepting a mandate for Armenia, but that became impossible after the League was rejected by the Senate. The Powers thought the League itself might accept such a mandate, but Drummond painstakingly pointed out that the Covenant provided only for League supervision of a mandate. The notion that the League Council, without forces, weapons, or money, could step into blazing Anatolia to govern an unborn state horrified Sir Eric.

He left the matter to the Assembly. For weeks in November and December 1920, the Assembly debated the fate of the Armenians. Andreas Winding, the correspondent of the Danish paper *Politiken*, reported the way in which life and death were weighed in Geneva:

"The world's most eminent politicians were in the tribune: Balfour, Cecil and Viviani, but the only one who seemed to be really thinking about Armenia was Fridtjof Nansen. . . . Nansen, who goes under the affectionate name of 'the Polar Bear,' pleads with the Assembly in powerful English to raise sixty thousand men and a loan of £20,000 to help the Armenians. . . . After some subtle considerations which were intelligible only to the most cunning parliamentarians, the Assembly passed both resolutions [recommending but not insisting upon aid] . . . 'It is a victory for Viviani,' declared the French, the Little Entente and the South Americans. 'A victory for Cecil,' say the Anglo-Saxons and the Scandinavians.

" 'What do you think?' I asked Nansen whom I met at the door. 'If they would only act,' said Nansen, and shook his arctic fist at the grey November sky. During the proceedings a representative of a Great Power came to a Scandinavian delegate and asked him to go to the rostrum and say, 'The worst of it is that we have divided up Turkey between us, so that there is no one to negotiate with.' "

It was Viviani of France who suggested that, if the Council could not find a nation to accept the Armenian mandate, it might at least find some power willing to negotiate a settlement. "If we cannot even do this, then let us continue our academic and theoretical debates, but let us recognize that we are unable to do anything to help suffering humanity."

Balfour, who described Kemal as a "barbarian" and "the head of an irregular band of brigands," told the Assembly: "Negotiation is a discourse between two civilized Powers in which one offers something to the other with a mutual accommodation of interests . . . Can we treat Kemal as a civilized Power; have we anything to offer him which he will take? . . . You can offer him money or you can offer him territory." Some delegates argued for the dispatch of an expeditionary force, but these were from countries—Greece and Rumania, for example—which, coincidentally, had ambitions in the area that tainted their daring proposals with a suggestion of self-interest.

Actually the Council's committee of six did succeed in turning up volunteers to negotiate the settlement. Conspicuous among them was Woodrow Wilson, now a lame-duck President. He set about the task as his final gesture of humanitarian statecraft, but before he could arrange even a preliminary talk, the Armenian leaders turned from the League's chorus of futility to the only practical solution that presented itself: integration within the Soviet Union. Wilson went on to complete his task—which included the drawing of boundary lines for an Armenia that never was or would be. In February 1921, the League Council took note of these mythical lines and decided that "until the situation in Asia Minor had become clearer, and, in particular, until the various questions in regard to the Treaty of Sèvres [ending the war with Turkey] had been settled by the Allied Powers, no further action was possible."

There remained the refugees. While many flocked to Erivan in Soviet Armenia, others, unable or unwilling to pass over the line into Bolshevism, put all they owned on their backs and took to the road.

When the League Assembly again considered the problem in September 1921, the Greek delegate, Seferiades, warned the delegates: "If you once more utter a platonic resolution it will only be a signal for a fresh massacre. If you mean to act, act! But on behalf of humanity which we represent here, let us have no more platonic resolutions, for—and I declare it from this high and impartial tribune—on our head will be the guilt for the blood of the massacred."

The League thereupon modestly averted its gaze from the tragedy and followed Cecil's mournful formula: ". . . the best thing to be done is to continue the policy laid down by the Council in February last, and to ask them to continue to watch over the situation and to take every opportunity of intervening, if they should think it possible, in order to secure such a settlement as we all desire."

In time the Armenians who had not died or fled to the Soviet Union resumed their lives, and the massacres petered out. Kemal, busy with modernizing Turkey, was more concerned with fighting the Moslem priesthood than the Armenians. He encouraged women to walk the streets without the veil and ordered all men to wear Western-style hats with brims at all times, indoors and outdoors. (This was no mere whimsy of the great secularizer—it effectively prevented one from observing the Islamic ritual of touching the ground with the forehead while keeping the head covered, a ceremony possible only with the brimless fez.)

As the revolution stabilized in Turkey the "brigand" became a statesman. When finally Kemal led his country into the League—in 1932—his assailants of the early years ate crow and swallowed Turkey.

Other refugees were also on the road, seeking escape from terror. More than a million White Russians were fleeing the Red Russians. Some of these found sanctuary in Poland, but the Poles, in turn, were forcing Jews to flee. Other Jews had to escape Rumanian terror. Greeks and Turks fled each other. Some reached Paris or Berlin. Others trekked all the way to the ports of China. Some ninety thousand of them—mostly White Guard troops in the south of Russia—poured into Allied-held Constantinople. These and the other millions scattered from Harbin to Paris were destitute, prone to rampaging epidemics, and in most cases lacking that minimal requirement of human dignity, a passport.

The League thereupon consulted its conscience, Nansen, and conferred upon him the title of High Commissioner of Refugees. He solved the problem of statehood for the stateless with what came to be known as the

Nansen passport. Because Nansen's prestige in some parts of the world was far higher than the League's, the certificate bore his name and photograph, while the words "Société des Nations" appeared in an inconspicuous size.

Feeding the refugees, clothing them, moving them out of the jammed and typhus-ridden centers, settling them into jobs—this was a mammoth undertaking, complicated at times by some delicate diplomatic considerations. For example, in October 1922 Drummond wrote to Nansen, then in Constantinople, to be careful to absolve the League of any responsibility for the massacres, to make it clear that although the powers that made up the League may be held to blame, the League's skirts must be kept clean. In a postscript, Drummond explained: "Responsibility for protection of minorities now and till the new order of things ought to be placed where it belongs, namely on the Allies and not on the League."

An example of how Drummond sought to ease Nansen's tortuous diplomatic path was the affair of the Boy Scouts unaccountably murdered in Anatolia in the autumn of 1922. Sir Robert Baden-Powell, the founder of the Scouts, had sent a sharp telegram to Drummond demanding that the murders be discussed immediately before the Council of the League. But at that moment Nansen was faced with the problem of some 750,000 refugees from Turkey who, it seems, could not be absorbed in Greece. It was felt that Nansen might have to negotiate for their return to Turkey under some guarantee of safety. Drummond therefore had to put off Sir Robert. He wrote to him on October 12, 1922, explaining the delicate state of Nansen's negotiations and adding: "Would it not therefore be somewhat dangerous for the League to take any action, however justified, which might imperil or render more difficult negotiations which will have to be taken to assist great bodies of people who will have to go on living in Turkey or recover or be compensated for property left behind? . . . An appeal to the League might well endanger the interests of the living and I hope you will agree that these interests must prevail."

It seemed a reasonable position at the time, but the decision to let murder go without a murmur of protest in order to stave off still other deaths was an ominous tactic. Nansen and Sir Eric were being bombarded with appeals: the League's archives, examined almost at random today, reveal the human wretchedness that haunted the Secretariat throughout the 1920's.

An example was a report to Nansen from James A. Grieg, stationed in Kirin, Manchuria, one of many that made all Nansen's efforts seem like the tossing of a single life preserver into a sea of drowning victims. Writing on June 27, 1924, he said: "The high hopes which were expressed when the High Commission extended its activities to the Far East have not been realized . . . One day a wire comes from Eastern Turkestan that three hundred Russian refugees are absolutely destitute of food and clothing. Next day an urgent letter from Chang-chun is received of an outbreak of typhus fever and no medical supplies available . . . To all such piteous appeals for help I have to say that the High Commission has made no appropriation for rendering substantial help . . . the splendid work done by the High Commission for the Greek refugees justifies the expectation that this smaller group of refugees . . . may not be left in their misery when the helping hand of the Assembly could save them."

France was the only European country able to absorb foreign labor at the time, and some sixty thousand refugees, ranging from Czarist dukes to Polish Jews, found a haven there. France was also one of the few nations to accord full recognition to the Nansen passport. Outside Europe it was no better. The United States had shut its doors with a quota system that would admit only the merest trickle of non-Anglo-Saxons and barred Orientals outright.

Nansen strove heroically, with little funds and under maximum harassment, to settle the wanderers where he could. There were little islands of hope like "Nansenheim" in Berlin, where refugees who could not earn a living might be fed and housed. He himself donated his Nobel prize money to projects in Russia that seemed to promise resettlement hopes for Armenians.

American relief teams and private organizations such as the Joint Distribution Committee and the Quakers pitched in, but in Geneva the delegates of the Great Powers did little more than pass mournful resolutions and pay tribute to their private saint, Nansen.

Some of the refugees were more troublesome than others. The troops of the White Guard General Wrangel, for example, who had the support and encouragement of the Allies in more promising days, expected handouts to continue after their defeat. The Bulgarians angrily accused them of setting up "a state within a state." And the Rumanians charged that they were absolutely unemployable. Most of them flocked into teeming, disease-ravaged Constantinople.

There, Lieutenant-General C. H. Harrington of the British garrison noted that, within a few days in November 1920, 140,000 members of the defeated White Army arrived, and that Greek vessels also were coming in by sea, carrying smallpox with them. "I saw one myself," he later recalled, "with seventy cases aboard, of which twenty-four died before help could be given. . . . Greek doctors were dying fast." At the height of the crisis in Constantinople the death toll among the refugees reached fifteen hundred a week.

Nansen grew weary and disenchanted in the years before he died, in 1930, at the age of seventy. The Armenians remembered him as a veritable angel, but the diplomats—except for Lord Cecil—tended to regard him as irrelevant. Nansen summed up his disappointment in his book *Russia and the Peace*: "We had hoped for a disarmament of souls: but the spirit of hostility and national hatred is growing worse than ever between former enemies and even between former allies. Everything that happens seems to hasten the catastrophe. We have decided for a policy of words."

There was another face to the League that bore neither the humanitarian look of Nansen nor the diplomatic smile of Drummond. The League's answer to Lenin was embodied in Albert Thomas, a stout, bearded, twinkling-eyed French socialist.

Greatly influenced in his youth by the socialist Jean Jaurès, Thomas launched his own trade-unionist weekly, *La Revue Syndicale*. When the war broke out he was on the staff of *L'Humanité*, and the government saw in him a force with which to mobilize the working class behind the war. It employed him with singular effectiveness as Undersecretary of State for Munitions. He was permitted to set up workers' delegations with a say in the operations of defense plants, which gave the war a gloss of working-class interest. When the Czar's military forces were crumbling, the French dispatched him to rally the Russian workers as he had done at French factory gates.

After the Bolsheviks had proclaimed the alluring slogan "peace without annexations and indemnities," Albert Thomas was assigned to meet the challenge. "I know my socialists," Thomas said. "They will shed their blood for a formula. You must accept it and alter its interpretation."

"Annexations" thereupon was translated as "restitutions," and "indemnities" as "reparations," in the lexicon of Versailles. Thomas went up and down the front during the Kerensky days: in repose, a curé peering from behind gold-rimmed glasses; in action, a ferocious revolutionary. He would tear off his collar and rip open his coat and sweat would pour down his face even in the cold of a Russian winter, as he harangued the troops to stay in the war until the Allied victory. The difficulty was that his choicest oratory was somewhat wasted, inasmuch as it was all in French and the Russians could understand only his passion. He was nonetheless effective. "The only phrase," he explained later, "which excites enthusiasm during the translation of the interpreter is my reference to the League of Nations."

Thomas combined the ingenuity and the charm of the drawing-room diplomat with the fire of the street revolutionary, and he spoke the language of Marx. He was therefore the ideal man to take in hand the International Labor Organization, which the Paris Peace Conference had designed to meet the clamor of the world's working classes.

The I.L.O. traced its lineage back to the proposals of Swiss Socialists in the 1880's which culminated in an International Association for Labor Legislation. By 1905 this organization, backed by the Swiss government, had won a general acceptance of legal limits to the workday at a time when twelve hours and more was not uncommon. The I.L.O., mandated by the Treaty of Versailles, took the preamble of that document as its charter and, under the energetic leadership of Raymond B. Fosdick and Harold Beresford Butler (chosen by Drummond), moved to carry out the Peace Conference's explicit instructions to convene its first assembly in Washington.

The timing was so awkward that less forceful leaders would have found good reason to temporize or shift the locale of the opening session. Washington seethed like the crater of an active volcano. The United States was wracked by strikes; Congress was busily using the I.L.O. meeting as a stick with which to beat the League and Wilson, charging that it was dominated by Bolsheviks and that it symbolized the menace of internationalism. Congress had refused to authorize Wilson to invite delegates or appoint any American representatives. Neither money nor facilities were appropriated.

Before the I.L.O. delegates could gather, Wilson himself had been stricken and lay helpless. Fosdick and Butler found that there were no offices, no typists, no messengers to serve the delegates of thirty-nine countries who were even then on their way to Washington. They finally obtained the use of a hall in the Pan-American Union Building; the British trade unions raised $50,000 for the meeting; and an embarrassed Congress was moved to put up another $65,000. Franklin Delano Roosevelt, Assistant Secretary of the Navy, gallantly turned over his offices to the organization, and the first meeting of the International Labor Organization was scheduled for October 29.

Then came the matter of the honorary presiding officer. Who, in such hostile territory, would represent the host country? Secretary of Labor William B. Wilson was the logical man, but he dared not move without authorization from some quarter, lest the wrath of Congress fall on his head. At last that authorization came, not from the stricken invalid of the White House, but from Mrs. Woodrow Wilson, who "ordered" the Secretary to do the honors.

From the start, the I.L.O. demonstrated a disregard of the diplomatic niceties. The Swiss and Scandinavian delegates, for example, promptly threatened to walk out unless invitations were sent to German and Austrian workers' representatives. And Léon Jouhaux of the French delegation joined them, arguing that "we cannot pretend to exclude any nations from our deliberations today and then expect them to apply our decisions tomorrow." Invitations went out, and the Powers, then still functioning through the Supreme War Council, decided to "put no obstacle" in the way of the ex-enemy workers; but by then it was too late for the Germans and Austrians to make the trip.

The I.L.O. was not envisioned as a workers' international. On the contrary, it was designed to replace the war cries of class conflict with the harmonies of class cooperation. A tripartite organization representing government, capital, and labor, its aim was to achieve what the Treaty Preamble termed "social justice."

The three sides specified in this formula for class peace did not, however, form an equilateral triangle. To guarantee that governments would not be forced to change their policies, a 2–1–1 voting ratio was established; the governmental delegation could always equal the combined strength of the labor and employer delegations. A Governing Body was established with twelve governmental representatives (nine of whom were Europeans and mainly from the most advanced industrial countries), six employers (all European), and six workers (five of whom were European). The Indians, insisting their country was industrialized, clamored for more Asian representation but lost.

To stand at the apex of this triangle the Washington conference chose as director Albert Thomas, diplomat and exponent of socialism through orderly and harmonious collaboration.

Actually the promise of that first Washington meeting seemed to be fulfilled in the 1920's. Out of the I.L.O. came not only the theoretical acceptance of the eight-hour day but a vast array of schemes for free employment agencies, unemployment benefits (including foreign workers), restrictions on night work for women, rights to maternity benefits, minimum-age legislation. Not all were applied with universal effectiveness, but still Thomas could exhibit a record of achievement that made the political victories of the League look derisory and its defeats tremendous.

Even his headquarters far outshone that of the League itself. Within three years he had installed the I.L.O. in an elegant building on the shores of the Lake of Geneva. It had the Renaissance flair and grace of a well-endowed abbey. It was furnished in rare and expensive taste, thanks mainly to the persuasive powers of the genial Thomas, who traveled much in those years and could talk governments into generous donations: tapestries from Belgium and France, wood paneling from the Pacific islands, stained glass from Germany. His own study was adorned with Goya etchings. Not only governments but foundations succumbed to his blandishments and swelled the budget of the I.L.O. It was said at one point that Thomas had a salary larger than that of the President of France.

Although the I.L.O. was actually a department of the League of Nations, in Thomas' eyes it was an independent principality, and he was its Grand Duke, smiling away with impeccable manners all attempts to control him, the I.L.O., the I.L.O.'s finances or its policies. His approach to Sir Eric always had a touch of irony in it.

For example, when some of the refugee employment problems were to be transferred to the I.L.O., Thomas firmly limited the commitment. He did not aspire to Nansen's halo. He told Drummond that his organization would do no more than investigate the employment possibilities of the refugees. "It is understood," he added, "that there can be no question of providing relief or paying the fares [to where the jobs were] of the hundreds of thousands of refugees out of the small funds allotted. It is also understood that it is entirely a temporary service which will be terminated as soon as possible."

The League's other, noncontroversial departments were organized with less fanfare. There were no debates in the Assembly on the antimalarial campaigns, the research into leprosy, or the technical assistance offered to farmers in rural hygiene, all sponsored quietly and unassumingly by the Health Organization. A series of conventions on opium, transport, and navigation rights were duly signed and sometimes observed.

More spectacular—though scarcely more productive—was the judicial wing of this non-state. The Court system was not born full-blown in the minds of the statesmen at Versailles. Actually its progenitor was Czar Nicholas II, who, in 1898, summoned a disarmament conference at the most neutral capital he could find, The Hague, in Holland. The diplomats of the day met in the spring of 1899 and in diplomatic fashion referred disarmament to a committee, which in due course came up with a pious wish and some conventions on a more "humane" conduct of war. The Czar's conference also provided for the establishment of a Court of Arbitration at The Hague to genteelly remove the causes of war.

Eight years—and several wars—later, in 1907, still another conference at The Hague launched the Court on its career. Arbitration was not compulsory, but the forty-four powers who signed the founding agreement declared it to be eminently desirable. The Court proceeded to settle occasional arguments over fishing rights and suchlike matters.

The peacemakers in 1919 added a refinement in an effort to fulfill one of the promises of Czar Nicholas' conference. The Court of Arbitration would continue to function, but The Hague would also be the seat of a "Permanent Court of International Justice." Unlike the Court of Arbitration—where the conflicting parties select the judges—the Permanent Court, with its august, appointed justices, would hand down its decisions with all the majesty and finality of law.

Unfortunately, the Covenant of the League was somewhat vague on the powers of the Court to assert its jurisdiction. International disputes might be brought to the Council or the Assembly or the Court of Arbitration at The Hague or the Permanent Court of International Justice. The nine justices of the Court were appointed from the most renowned jurists of the world. (The Council and Assembly, meeting separately, would vote simultaneously, and those candidates appearing on both lists would form the Court.) Their opinions were often weighty and set great legal precedents, but they never shook off the stigma of a small-claims court.

The Court's calendar was scarcely crowded. In the eighteen years between 1922, when it opened at the Palace of Justice in The Hague, and 1940, when German invaders made its work for justice academic—the Court sat on a total of eighty-three cases, many of which were mere requests for "advisory opinions." It probed questions such as the competence of the I.L.O. in agricultural employment, the status of a monastery on the Albanian frontier, the application of laws against night work for women administrators, the responsibility for deaths by negligence in international waters. The most far-reaching decision of the Court was its condemnation in 1931 of the customs union between Germany and Austria as contrary to provisions of the Treaty of Saint-Germain (Austria's version of Versailles). But the effect was soon nullified by subsequent military events.

It was plain that the Court, the global efforts at better health, the compacts on transit and the mails—important as they were—did not require for their effective functioning a full-blown League of Nations. The League had another purpose: the orchestration of world politics.

Nine

DUCKLING AT
THOIRY

On the weekend of June 21, 1924, two socialists, each newly come to power, met at Chequers, the official country home of British Prime Ministers.

The new tenant of Chequers was Ramsay MacDonald, the son of a sailor and a farm girl; a former chemist, bus driver, journalist, and warehouse clerk who in tweedy plus fours took on the air of a country squire. His weekend guest was Edouard Herriot, the charming, ardent poet-professor who, when asked by a reporter for a statement on his electoral victory as head of the left coalition in France, characteristically held aloft a half-opened rose and said: "This symbolizes the situation."

The two were even farther apart in personality and outlook than British socialism was from French socialism or British Tories from French conservatives. The Premier of France, like the Prime Minister of England, had come up from working-class origins but had struggled through the university, tempering his brand of socialism with an academician's precision and a Frenchman's idealism. MacDonald had imbibed his early knowledge of the world from stern Scottish preachers. He prayed every Sunday, and his speeches, even in the heat of an election campaign, had the flair of a sermon. "For Herriot," the French historian Georges Suarez wrote, "peace is a sentiment; for MacDonald it is a dogma. Herriot makes it a human function; MacDonald makes it a divine one." MacDonald himself told Herriot during that June weekend: "Your regicides were atheists. Our Cromwell believed in God."

Still, the weekend seemed an idyll of Anglo-French harmony. Herriot left Chequers convinced that the Entente Cordiale, which had been steadily deteriorating, beset as it was by the conflicting needs of French security and British commerce, had been renewed in the glow of a common socialist objective which would include a new charter of peace. On his way back to Paris, Herriot stopped in Brussels and in an interview with a reporter from *L'Indépendance Belge* revealed that he now had the assurances of an Anglo-French-Belgian defense pact. Herriot, however, had clearly read into MacDonald's pious wishes a political commitment that was not there. Under questioning in the House of Commons on June 26, MacDonald expressed astonishment at the distortions of the Belgian press and sternly denied that any such commitment had been made in his talks at Chequers.

This misunderstanding was not the most hopeful background for the opening of the League Assembly on September 1 of that year, an Assembly that was to unfold a glittering prospect—a new and more vigorous guarantee of world peace. Still, Herriot's euphoria seemed undampened.

For the opening session, with derby hat perched on his head, stubby pipe in his mouth, and his hands plunged in the bulging pockets of his baggy black suit, Herriot walked from the Hôtel des Bergues across the Rhône to the Salle de la Réformation. MacDonald came up in a hired car from the Beau Rivage surrounded by a bevy of secretaries. His flowing hair and austere good looks made him a target for photographers. When MacDonald entered the hall Herriot rose from his seat and walked over to greet him. The aloof, reserved Prime Minister faced the ardent French Premier, and then Herriot seized both of MacDonald's hands in his as the delegates cheered.

Herriot was determined to make Anglo-French solidarity the foundation of an organization for peace which would not only reinforce the League but consolidate the uneasy political coalition that had brought him to power in France. To an English colleague he said wistfully: "Why did Joan of Arc spend so much energy driving you out of France? In a few generations we would have assimilated you; what a marvelous people we would have made!"

On September 4, MacDonald preached to the delegates: "Ah, my friends, the emotions that come to one as one stands here . . . The late war was commended in my country as being a war to end all wars. Alas! the human eye sees but little prospect of that hope and that pledge being fulfilled. I do not know what the Divine eye sees . . ." His speech, florid but less than stirring, called for Germany's admission to the League and hailed arbitration as the panacea that would forever outmode the ancient trial by combat.

Herriot was wittier in style and more far-reaching. He combined with arbitration the concepts of security and disarmament, proclaiming the three to be inseparable, although even this trinity "would be but empty abstractions if they did not stand for living realities created by our common will." He roused a storm of applause when he said, "Arbitration must not be made a snare for trustful nations," and when he quoted Pascal to reinforce the unwavering French stand for a League with teeth: "Justice without might is impotent. Might without justice is tyranny."

The high point of the day's oratory was reserved for the William Jennings Bryan of the French delegation, Joseph Paul-Boncour, that superb showman with silver mane and a face he himself fancied resembled Robespierre's. He spoke with a voice that was operatic in range and power, and he gestured gracefully with his delicate hands.

He called for uprooting the economic causes of war and reached his peak in a thundering peroration: "I call the living to life, freed at last from the terrors of war. I mourn the dead, all the dead of every clime and country, united at last in the brotherhood of the tomb; I shatter the thunderbolts, the powers which seek to let loose upon the world the horrors of war."

Then it was time for the lawyers to take over from the English psalmists and the French singers of arias. The task of formulating the common will and providing the necessary teeth for the League was assigned to two committees: one headed by the Greek diplomat Nikolaos Politis, which was to see what amendments might be required to toughen the Covenant's peacekeeping machinery; and the other under the leadership of Czechoslovakia's Eduard Beneš, which would probe the fundamental questions of arbitration, security, and disarmament as proposed by Herriot.

Much of the edifice which was built in that Assembly session was designed by Beneš, that tough, pedantic, dogged nationalist who forsook Marxism to base his life on the future of a Czechoslovak state. His chief instrumentality was the League of Nations, which he saw as a bulwark against the restoration of the Hapsburgs.

Early in the war, when Tomáš Masaryk, the ideologue of Czech independence, had to leave Prague for Vienna, Beneš took over command of the underground. When he, too, had to flee, he stationed himself in Paris, where he ceaselessly nagged the Allied diplomats for a mention of an independent Czechoslovakia in the war aims. When the Allied cause wavered before the German advance, and some of the Czech exiles prepared to decamp to America, Beneš calmly announced his own plan in case of disaster: "I shall go to Switzerland for a six-month cure for my nerves, and then I shall begin all over again."

He formed the Czechoslovak National Council as a sort of government-in-exile. Calculating that even the best of manifestoes gets a readier hearing if suspended on the point of a bayonet, he formed the Czech Legion to fight in Russia, and thereby endeared himself and his nation to the Allies.

Beneš had been his country's underground Foreign Minister and when peace came he emerged carrying the same portfolio, which he never let go for the rest of his life. His politics within the new regime were less eloquently expressed than Masaryk's but had a bulldog consistency. He talked quite frankly, for example, to the Czech communists. "Gentlemen," he told them, "be logical and courageous. My business is to defend order, but I do it effectively. If you are revolutionaries, start your revolution. It is your duty. And I shall do mine, which will be to crush you."

His political life—and to Beneš there was little of any other life—had taught him to detest Germany, to dislike the Bolshevist doctrine, to suspect Italy and distrust Britain. That left France and French policy as the keystone of the structure he set out to build in his committee sessions in that autumn of 1924.

While the committees worked, the star performers of the opening scenes retired to their respective capitals leaving the stage to their second string, a group of quite remarkable men in their own right. On the British side there was Arthur Henderson, a conscientious Labour party man and ex-iron molder with whom MacDonald had a running feud. The antagonism was scarcely cooled by the fact that Henderson had gallantly refused to scuttle his chief in an inner-party fight that could have kept MacDonald from party leadership and, hence, from the prime ministry. By way of small thanks MacDonald gave Henderson the distinctly lower-echelon post of Home Secretary, taking for himself the Foreign Office along with 10 Downing Street. Henderson was allowed to come to Geneva, but once there, MacDonald ostentatiously ignored him, preferring the advice, confidence, and companionship of *Times* editor Wickham Steed.

More important for the future of the League was the man who was second in command to Léon Bourgeois in the French delegation. He was Aristide Briand, a short and shaggy man, all grizzly mustache and straggly hair, usually seen with cigarette dangling from his lower lip and with his eyes half closed. Although he was meticulous in his language and his concepts, his manner of dress, of handling statistics, of keeping appointments suggested a capricious camel in the moulting season.

As a boy Briand had wanted to be a river pilot like his uncle, but when that early model drowned in the Loire, his father, an unprosperous innkeeper, forbade him to nourish such ambition. As a result, Briand had to settle for a life as lawyer, politician, journalist, deputy, and, at intervals, Premier and Foreign Minister of France. In his childhood he had known Jules Verne. In his youth on the Left Bank he had been the friend and cabaret associate of Sarah Bernhardt, Victor Hugo, and Maupassant.

He had fought for Dreyfus and collaborated with Jean Jaurès, the legendary French socialist. He had helped to defeat Clemenceau, and at the age of sixty-two he was having his first view of the League in action. He came to it with the familiar French preoccupation for security. "The right to security," he wrote in the September 18 issue of *L'Europe Nouvelle*, "is as vital as the right to bread, the right to work, the right to education."

For him the document being drafted was to be quite simply "a mutual-aid pact among large and small nations following a peaceful line of international collaboration."

On October 1, the professorial Beneš—who spoke five languages fluently if inelegantly—chose French to present the document known as the "Protocol for the Pacific Settlement of International Disputes." He presented it dryly, peering at the delegates through tortoise-shell glasses, conscious of the gravity of the moment in which the League of Nations was about to enforce Wilsonism and protect the little nations.

The Protocol, which was to be open to all powers in or out of the League, drew none of the Covenant's distinctions between permissible and impermissible wars. It labeled an aggressor any nation which failed to abide by arbitration. The only exceptions would be those so declared by the unanimous vote of the League Council. If there were any doubt as to the aggressor, the Council would nevertheless impose an armistice and fix the terms, which would require only a two-thirds vote. The sanctions to be invoked against an aggressor would go far beyond economic penalties to include military measures devised by the Council and enforced by the signatories of the Protocol. The Protocol was not to come into effect until after a world disarmament conference, open to all countries of the world, and set for Geneva, June 15, 1925.

The atmosphere in Geneva was jubilant. There was not the whisper of a reservation, not an "if" or a "but." The vote was unanimous: forty-eight nations approved it. There were only six absentees: Abyssinia and five Latin American states (whose restrained participation in League affairs was generally held to reflect the aloofness of the United States).

Although officially voted by the Assembly, the Protocol had yet to be signed and ratified. As soon as the vote was announced, Briand, taking the place of Bourgeois, who was ill, rose and declared: "France adheres to the Protocol. France is prepared to sign it." Then he put his name to the document and also signed the companion piece, accepting for France the compulsory jurisdiction of the Permanent Court at The Hague. Only seven other delegates followed the French lead to sign on the spot. These represented Albania, Greece, Latvia, Poland, Portugal, Yugoslavia, and Estonia. France was alone among the Great Powers. It was a French victory and the heady emotionalism of the moment was French.

The Assembly closed in a mood of buoyant optimism which lasted not much longer than the time it took the diplomats to return to their capitals. The world, which had looked so rosy at the height of the party, took on the customary gray and muddled aspect of the morning after.

MacDonald found himself in deep political trouble at home, beset primarily by an economic crisis of vast proportions to which was added the political fillip of the Zinoviev letter. Grigori Zinoviev, People's Commissar in command at Leningrad, had allegedly written a letter to British socialists urging them to overthrow their country's institutions, stir up the rank and file of the army and navy, commit sabotage, and in short behave precisely as the most fervent anti-communists had long predicted they would. While the letter—the authenticity of which was long debated—had no visible effect on the Labour party, the very existence of it was enough to send tremors throughout England. To make matters worse, MacDonald tried to conceal the existence of the document and then, when questioned in the Commons, responded by calling for new elections.

Precisely how much weight the letter had in the minds of voters was a matter for speculation, but in any case Labour lost the support of the Liberals and went down to a humiliating defeat. Swept into office was Stanley Baldwin, the new Tory Prime Minister, whose Cabinet included names that were to carry a considerable weight of history: Sir Austen Chamberlain as Foreign Minister, his younger brother Neville as Minister of Health, Sir Samuel Hoare as Air Minister, and Winston Churchill as Chancellor of the Exchequer.

The British team had undergone a lightning reversal to aristocracy. MacDonald and Henderson could only console themselves with the prophecy of their mentor, the British socialist Keir Hardie, who in 1905 reportedly surveyed the genteel members of the House and remarked: "Yes, it will take the British working man twenty years to learn to elect his equals to represent him. And then it will take him another twenty years not to elect his equals."

Sir Austen Chamberlain was a meticulous early-nineteenth-century aristocrat. He prized Talleyrand as a diplomatic model, not for his corruption but for the urbane and gracious values that corruption sought to preserve. When asked how he could possibly accommodate himself to the continental habit of promiscuous handshaking, he resignedly replied: "It is my task to shake hands which my sovereign would not touch."

His father, Joseph Chamberlain, had dedicated his service as Foreign Minister to the glory of the Empire and, in the long prelude to the war, had sought without success to bring about an alliance with Germany. Sir Austen as a young man had dined at Bismarck's table and sampled German student life, which depressed him exceedingly. He came away with the feeling that, however dangerous the German old guard might be, the German universities were preparing far worse. Of the up-and-coming generation in Germany before the war, he remarked: "When they come to power, let others beware."

He found the French far more congenial. He said that he loved France "as a man loves a woman" and went so far as to learn to speak the language of his love with a facility that the French found astonishing in British diplomats, known for their insular aversion to foreign sounds. At the age of sixty-one, when he came to the Foreign Ministry, Sir Austen was tall, stiff, and seemingly austere, surveying the world through an elegant if antiquated monocle. Although he had found much to admire in the French, he remained unshakably addicted to the British distrust of political theory. "His wisdom," a French writer noted, "resembled divination, and was no more than an intelligent alertness to events."

The Protocol of Geneva, which he inherited at the beginning of his ministry, was thus completely antithetical to the Chamberlain policy of improvisation, which continental critics called muddleheadedness. It is doubtful, however, that the Protocol would have fared better on second thought in Britain, no matter who was in office. In December, Sir Austen attended the Council meeting in Rome and assured his colleagues that Britain's delay in signing the Protocol did not necessarily indicate a change in attitude but only that the new government had not yet had the time to assume a position on the matter.

Although this was taken at the time to be an evasion, it was actually quite true. In that same month Britain was engaged in sounding out the dominions on the Protocol, and the responses were violently hostile.

The Big Three of the peace conference stroll down the Champs Elysées: Lloyd George, Clemenceau, and Wilson.

The peacemakers—Class of 1919. Seated in the middle is England's Lord Cecil between Léon Bourgeois of France, on the left, and Vittorrio Orlando of Italy, on the right. Directly behind Cecil is Wilson, with South Africa's General Jan Christian Smuts to his left and Paul Hymans of Belgium to his right. The Japanese delegates Baron Makino and Viscount Chinda are seated at far left, with Colonel House standing behind them. Their opponent in League clashes, Wellington Koo of China, is seen at the right of Hymans. Many of the dignitaries obligingly autographed this photo, which hangs in the League Museum in the Geneva headquarters of the United Nations.

Colonel Edward Mandell House, whose most persuasive credentials referred to him only as "the President's friend."

Wilson on the bridge of the S.S. *George Washington* as he sailed for Europe. "Never had a philosopher held such weapons with which to bind the princes of the world," wrote John Maynard Keynes.

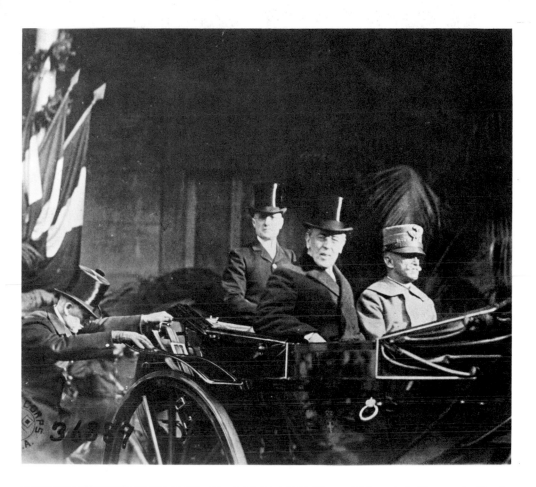

Triumph in Rome: the President and Italy's King Victor Emmanuel III ride in state from the railway station to the Quirinal Palace.

The President and the King of Italy. To the left of the King stands the Queen and, at far left, Mrs. Wilson.

Top« Triumph in London: the President and King George V. Mrs. Wilson is at the right.

Bottom« Triumph in Paris: Wilson in the ritual coach with France's President Poincaré.

Returned to battle in New York, Wilson leaves the pier to head for Washington and the fight to win congressional approval of the League's Covenant.

Aboard the *Mayflower*, the special train that took Wilson on his fateful swing around the country to rally enthusiasm for the League among a people who were already disenchanted with all things foreign. It was a grim ride that ended with a stroke that paralyzed the President and the presidency.

Top« Sir Eric Drummond, League First-Secretary, a diplomat who did his work off-stage.

Bottom« Geneva's Hôtel National before Sir Eric bought it, had the freshly installed bathroom plumbing torn out, and converted it into the League Secretariat—later known as the Palais Wilson.

Top« In the gauzy, gazebo-like Council Room at the Secretariat a League commission considers the problem of the "white slave traffic."

Left« Fridtjof Nansen, the League's saint.

Right« China's dapper Dr. Wellington Koo.

Right« Sir Eric Drummond on tour in Warsaw. At far left, the man with a wrestler's build is Sir Eric's astute deputy, Japan's Yoturo Sugimura.

Bottom Left« Lord Cecil grew more gangling and more stooped but never retired from his battle for the League.

Bottom Right« Lloyd George, in happy retirement, kicks a nonpolitical football.

Belgium's Paul Hymans, champion of the little powers, leads a parade of diplomats from the Secretariat grounds in Geneva in the days when top hats and cocked hats lent a ceremonial dash to League activities.

Below «
Baron Makino, at right, practices a Western brand of public relations.

Right « France's Aristide Briand addresses the Assembly while Sir Eric Drummond presides.

Middle « Briand presides in the Clock Room of the Quai d'Orsay. Drummond is to his right, France's Joseph Avenol behind him.

Bottom « Germany's Gustav Stresemann in his convertible outside the Métropole in Geneva.

Top« Stresemann makes his maiden speech before the League Assembly as Germany is admitted.

Bottom« Mrs. Woodrow Wilson (directly above the X) watches from the gallery as Germany enters the League of Nations.

THE CONFERENCE EXCUSES ITSELF.

Top« Disarmament: a British comment by Low.

Left« Disarmament: an Italian comment— ". . . dancing on the edge of a volcano."

Right« Sir Austen Chamberlain: "It is my task to shake hands which my sovereign would not touch."

Top Left«   Louis Barthou, an elfin wit
slain in another's murder.

Top right«   Whispering in a corridor of
eavesdroppers: France's Henri Bonnet has
the ear of Edouard Herriot.

Bottom«   The Soviet's Maxim Litvinov
responds volubly to France's Pierre Laval.

Top« While a German delegation explains Hitler's move into the Rhineland to a special meeting of the League Council in London, Secretary-General Avenol (wearing glasses) ponders the coup with chin in hand and Litvinov ostentatiously loses himself in a Russian newspaper.

Bottom« Haile Selassie arrives in Geneva by train to ask the League not to abandon his country.

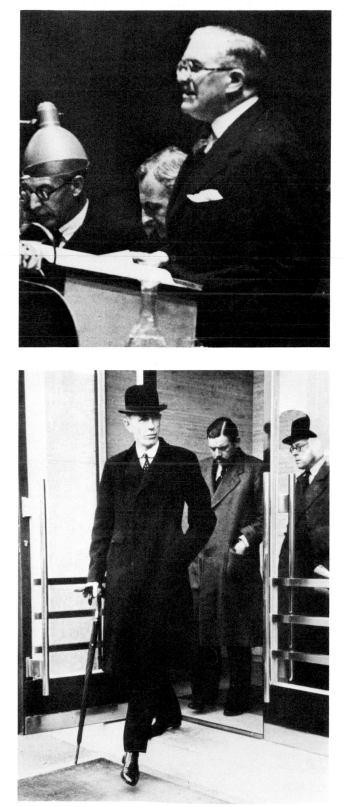

Alvarez del Vayo pleads Spain's lost cause from the rostrum of the League Assembly.

The elegant Lord Halifax steps from the new League Assembly building, reconciled to the loss of lesser causes for the sake of a promised peace.

The League's last Secretary-General, Sean Lester, scribbled a comment on a photo of himself torn from *L'Illustré:* "J. A. [Joseph Avenol, Lester's appeasement-minded predecessor] made the wrinkles."

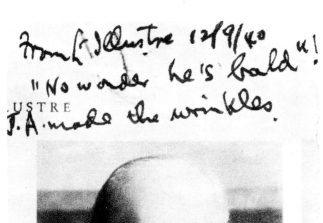

Canada and South Africa saw in it an intolerable limit to their new-found sovereignty and a trap to involve them in still another European shambles. Canadians were also worried about the possibility of applying sanctions which might not have the blessings of the United States, so mighty and so close. New Zealanders were experiencing the nightmare of being ordered by the Court at The Hague to admit colored immigrants. And all of them shared the horror of British military circles at the thought that the British Fleet, on which they all relied, might be set in motion—or restrained—at the bidding of a Council of foreigners.

The Protocol was therefore doomed, but before burying what after all had been an Anglo-French offspring, Sir Austen looked about for a way to console the mourners.

At first Sir Austen failed to appreciate the diplomatic opportunity that was offered early in 1925 in dispatches from Berlin. It was a cautious approach from Germany looking toward a pact with England and France that would exorcise the ghost of German aggression and render unnecessary further Allied occupation of the Rhineland.

"Unwise and premature," was Chamberlain's quick, curt reply. That response occasioned a strained and anxious dialogue at the Foreign Ministry of the Reich. The conversation was between the exasperated Foreign Minister Gustav Stresemann and the man whom reporters called "the *de facto* Foreign Minister of the Reich," the British ambassador, Lord D'Abernon.

Lord D'Abernon, who had planned the German approach and persuaded Stresemann to go along with it, was imperturbable. The Ambassador was a huge man, whose size seemed magnified by a habit of wearing clothes that were grotesquely large, even for him. With his tie awry and his white hair straggling about his head, he seemed absurdly out of place in punctilious Berlin. He sat listening to the Reich Foreign Minister explode and casually took notes on his stiff shirt cuffs, as was his habit.

The D'Abernon policy, however, was neat: to keep Germany from any alliance with the Soviet Union; to win acceptance for it in Western Europe; and to restore it as a trading partner for England. To effect this policy he had to manipulate both the German Foreign Ministry and his own. Since Whitehall was wrapped in its traditional fog, he frequently operated at cross purposes with his superiors.

Gustav Stresemann was similarly monumental, but he exuded a sense of order. His neck bulged from the confines of his stiff collar and tended to grow purple under stress. His bulletlike head, with hair so cropped it seemed shaven, emerged from a massive square frame. His eyes were restless and his voice was shrill. Not even his admirers could call him attractive. However, he was convivial enough over brandy and cigars and he had a hearty, rolling laugh.

Like Briand, Stresemann was the son of an innkeeper, which no doubt accounted for the fact that his doctoral thesis concerned "the economic uses of old beer bottles." He had lived the student life to the hilt, complete with duels, beer fests, drinking songs, and nature walks, for all of which he entertained a life long nostalgia. He got his start as secretary to the Association of Chocolate Manufacturers in Saxony, and when he entered the Reichstag as its youngest deputy (he was twenty-nine) he quickly became known as "Stinnes' young man," for he dutifully followed the thinking of Hugo Stinnes and the cartel of mighty industrialists he represented.

Throughout the war Stresemann remained an ardent monarchist and preserved a loyal belief in the invincibility of the General Staff. Though he was impressed by the revelations of military and bureaucratic inefficiency in the shambles of defeat, Stresemann retained a sentimental fondness for the Kaiser, and he was instrumental in securing the return from exile of the Crown Prince.

Like Chamberlain, Stresemann was attracted to the French but not for any aesthetic reasons. He was passionately devoted to Napoleon, for whom he reluctantly forgave the French nation its manifold improprieties. He was thus temperamentally attuned to the pro-Western arguments of his friend Lord D'Abernon and could resist the pressures from the increasingly militant right in Germany for a rapprochement with the East. To the ultranationalists, an opening to the East seemed a way in which to avoid the humiliations of seeking acceptance by the authors of the Versailles *Diktat*. Though Stresemann toyed with a Russian alliance, it was largely as a bargaining counter in his play with England and France or as a sop to the German right.

Stresemann had been having a difficult time with the German right wing ever since he had taken office, although he tried to convince them that the differences between them and himself were no more than tactical. Speaking at a rally of his Deutsche Volkspartei at the Schauspielhaus in Berlin on November 29, 1924, Stresemann had said: "It is the policy of force which in the end will always carry the day, but when one does not have the force, one must also fight by means of ideas."

He came to office at a time when the reichsmark was in catastrophic collapse and when the great mines of the Saar were idle because of the "passive resistance" organized by the Germans against the French occupation. It was Stresemann's painful duty to call an end to that resistance, bringing upon his head the full fury of the German right, which threatened to arraign him for treason. He stood his ground, knowing that he must get the mines to work again or face economic disaster.

At about the same time Lord D'Abernon suggested the institution of the gold mark, which miraculously overcame the currency crisis and quickly halted the flow of worthless money from the printing presses.

And now the disheveled British lord had masterminded another plan, which promised not only to give Germany a respectable position among the great Western powers but also to end the occupation of the Rhineland, which under the Treaty of Versailles was to run to 1934. Under Lord D'Abernon's patient tutelage Stresemann renewed his pressure for a Rhineland pact in both Paris and London.

The proposal, however fuzzy, was still alive when Sir Austen Chamberlain needed a word of comfort to give Herriot after the British Cabinet formally voted on March 3, 1925, to reject the Protocol of Geneva. He met the French Premier at dinner shortly after the meeting and could temper the bad news with the promise of a nonaggression pact that might even include Germany as well as Britain and France.

It also made it easier for Sir Austen to go before the League Council three days later and announce that Britain must kill the Protocol which less than a year earlier its representatives had so ardently cosponsored. The execution was performed with surgical neatness. He told the delegates that the Protocol, designed to perfect the Covenant, would in fact "destroy its balance and alter its spirit."

Sir Austen was alarmed at the possibility of enforcing the peace: "The fresh emphasis laid upon sanctions, the new occasions discovered for their employment, the elaboration of military procedure, insensibly suggest the idea that the vital business of the League is not so much to promote friendly cooperation and reasoned harmony in the management of international affairs as to preserve peace by organizing war, and—it may be— war on the largest scale."

He granted the possibility that war might be necessary to punish or control an aggressor, a violator of League principles, then added: "But such catastrophes belong to the pathology of international life, not to its normal condition. It is not wholesome for the ordinary man to be always brooding over the possibility of some severe surgical operation; nor is it wise for societies to pursue a similar course. It is more likely to hasten the dreaded consummation than to hinder it."

Aristide Briand, as French Foreign Minister, responded to Chamberlain with that elaborate and elegant irony with which French diplomats customarily accepted defeat. "The document which has been read to us," Briand said, "is instinct with a serene aloofness and a gentle philosophy which I hesitate to affront in the discussion which I am about to initiate. I, too, like yourselves, feel and appreciate the nobility and gentleness of the spirit of this philosophy, and I ask myself whether my own philosophy, which is necessarily somewhat more of this earth, is worthy to place beside it."

On the warlike tone which Chamberlain detected in the Protocol, Briand said: ". . . in my view, peace is for all practical purposes no more than the absence of war, and . . . an institution which aims at peace must if it is determined to maintain peace, explore every avenue and every means best calculated to prevent war. It was in view of this unfortunate and somewhat humdrum necessity that the authors of the Protocol felt obliged to speak of war much more often than they would have wished." However, he suggested, "putting a lightning conductor on a house does not produce lightning."

Despite Briand's wit, the Protocol was pronounced dead at the Council, but burial was put off to the regular Assembly meeting set for September. In the meantime each capital was seized with its private bugaboos. Stresemann and Lord D'Abernon in Berlin feared lest Chamberlain console France with too close a pact. Briand worried about Germany's flirtations with the Soviet Union and bolstered the wall of paper pacts with nations on Germany's eastern frontiers. He also answered the domestic critics of his peace policy by noting that "the pens which write these attacks are made from the same metal as the armaments of war." In England, Chamberlain groped for some formula which might atone for the murder of the Protocol, preserving the hope and the high-mindedness of that document without affronting the dominions or putting the glorious ambiguities of English improvisation into the straitjacket of French logic.

In the spring of 1925 Stresemann was busily corresponding with both Chamberlain and Briand. What was shaping up was a pact by which Germany would agree to demilitarize the Rhineland and reaffirm the decisions of Versailles as regards Germany's western frontiers, including the French sovereignty over Alsace-Lorraine.

Briand, seeing still another chance at security by means of yet another piece of paper, drafted a note to Germany, welcoming the proposals in general. He suggested that his answer be signed by all of the former Allied Powers. Chamberlain was cool to the notion, and when he received Briand's draft he went at it with a murderous blue pencil. He left not a line, scarcely even a word, untouched. The French Foreign Office and press were indignant at this affront not only to French policy but to French style. Briand, however, outfoxed his editor by cheerfully accepting all of the British corrections and amendments, thereby making it impossible for Chamberlain to raise further objections. The note, ultimately dispatched as an Anglo-French message, was, despite its ambiguity and reservations, an acceptance in principle of a Rhineland pact.

So it was that on September 1, 1925, when the Assembly of the League gathered in Geneva, the euphoria that anticipated the reconciliation of ancient enemies made for a merry wake following the interment of the Protocol. The pact to come figured in Chamberlain's funeral oration over the Protocol, as the hope of future salvation adorns most such ceremonies. Briand, already bemused by the new treaty which he was seeking to bring into the mechanism of the League, was not on hand. Instead, the French Premier, Paul Painlevé, a mathematician when he was not in politics, delivered for the record a cold and listless appeal for the Protocol as it was laid to rest. As the Zurich paper *Der Bund* put it on September 8, "Mr. Painlevé as a speaker melts no ice and brings no dead branches to blossom."

Within the British camp, Lord Cecil, that venerable champion of a pure untarnished League, kept up a gallant rear-guard action. When the dominions had risen against the Protocol, Lord Cecil dropped his committee work on the opium traffic and hurried to London to try to save the pact. He had been allowed to sit on the British delegation at the March Council meeting when Chamberlain doomed the Protocol. He complained bitterly at the time that he had been completely ignored. Now he sat at Chamberlain's elbow in the Assembly and listened to Paul-Boncour vent his outrage in a lyrical stream. Later Lord Cecil recalled that dismal day: "I remember whispering to Sir Austen that the speech made me feel very mean, since I really agreed with every word of it."

Le Quotidien of Paris fired a parting shot: "A nation, however great, must to some extent be considered arrogant if it tells all the other nations who have come to hear it that their conscientious and enthusiastic efforts must purely and simply be dismissed if they do not correspond with the political psychology of Great Britain. If the activities of the League are really to vanish and reappear like Mont Blanc behind the clouds in response to the atmospheric changes in British policy, the League will end by being discredited in the eyes of public opinion."

The lesser powers, led by Beneš to believe in the imminent coming of the peace of the Protocol, relapsed into a gentle disenchantment. Ironically *El Liberal* of Madrid commented: "One must come to Geneva as to Lourdes, filled with faith."

Almost immediately after the curtain fell on the death scene at Geneva, it rose again in a resurrection tableau in the spa resort of Locarno, on the

shores of Lake Maggiore in the Italian canton of Switzerland. The first
encounter of the ex-enemies in the Locarno Palais de Justice was awkward but it ended well. With Stresemann came Chancellor Hans Luther,
a cold and strait-laced man lacking the hearty conviviality of his Foreign
Minister. In precise but graceless French the Chancellor began their first
session with a recital of Germany's sufferings. Briand watched, as he later
recalled, "the shadow of discontent steal over the countenance of Chamberlain," and he felt that soon he himself would have to answer with a
catalogue of French sufferings. There would be no end to the matter and
no beginning of peace.

Briand interrupted Luther, put a hand on his shoulder, and said, "Do
not go on. You will make us all weep." The Chancellor gaped in astonishment, but Stresemann broke into a gale of laughter at his superior's
discomfiture.

"It was then," Briand later observed of Stresemann, "that I knew he
was a man."

From the start Briand was predisposed to get along with Stresemann
because he passionately desired some agreement that would allay the fears
of another German sweep across the Rhine. At least Stresemann was not
an aloof Prussian warlord or a mirthless machine like Luther. He was the
son of an innkeeper with a partiality for brandy, which betokened a
certain humanity.

Still, the first conversation after Stresemann stopped laughing was a bit
of a shock. The German minister demanded as the price of a lasting
peace: a lifting of the stigma of war guilt from Germany, a reduction of
all troops in the Rhineland to the level of the garrison Germany had
formerly maintained there, and the immediate removal of all "black
troops," whose presence offended German dignity; acknowledgment of
Germany's right to have colonies; admission to the League on Germany's
terms as a first-rate power with a permanent seat on the Council; and
quick general international disarmament to Germany's level.

Stresemann noted in his diary: "Briand almost fell off the sofa when he
learned all that I had asked. He said that he admired my audacity, which
verged on boldness, and that, according to me, the Treaty of Versailles
might as well cease to exist."

Briand rallied from the shock and prepared to woo the Germans. He
went off to the fishing village of Ascona for a lunch with the stiff and
suspicious Luther. It was meant to be a secret meeting and for a while on
the terrace of a small café they had only a cat for company, but presently
the unmistakable silhouette of Briand drew some camera-clicking tourists.
The two withdrew, but not until Briand had forcibly impressed the

Chancellor. "You are a German," Briand told him. "And I am a Frenchman. You can be a German and a good European. Two good Europeans must understand each other."

Briand played that theme relentlessly for a week in conferences in hotel suites and aboard the yacht *Orange Blossom*, which took the diplomats on a lake cruise, ostensibly in honor of Mrs. Chamberlain's birthday. (Stresemann let it be known among his German critics that he spent the entire five hours locked in a cabin with Briand and Chamberlain, all hard at work.)

Among other things, Briand told Stresemann a bit of the story of David Copperfield. The German Foreign Minister was therefore not wholly at a loss at the French Foreign Minister's note indicating his acceptance of an arrangement he obviously considered to be matrimonial if not amorous. "Barkis is willin'," the note read.

A week of haggling was over, the terms were agreed upon: Germany was to be admitted to the League with full honors and a permanent Council seat; Germany was to recognize French sovereignty in Alsace-Lorraine; the Rhineland was to be demilitarized. The pact would be guaranteed by Germany, France, England, Belgium, and Italy.

On October 14, Mussolini dashed to the scene in a display of athletic showmanship. A special train carried him from Rome to Milan, where he picked up a racing car and drove at top speed along cleared highways to Stresa. There—as if in a cinematic chase scene—the dictator of Italy leaped into a speedboat and tore across the lake to Locarno. His agility on the road was matched by his mental tergiversations. Only weeks earlier he had referred to the Germans as "the barbarians of the North" who threatened to convert Italy into a mere "geographic notion," but now he hailed the pact with them as "a work which consecrates a new Europe."

Luther and Stresemann were the first to sign the Pact of Locarno on October 16. Briand walked over and held out his hands to Stresemann, who murmured his gratitude for the kind and flattering words Briand had used to his late enemy and new-found partner. "No," said Briand, "don't speak to me of words. I will prove to you that this is not a matter of words but of deeds."

What Briand did not know then, and was never to know in his lifetime, was that five weeks earlier, on September 7, 1925, Stresemann had written a highly confidential note to the Crown Prince outlining his true aims lest the Prince be misled by the spirit of Locarno:

"In my view," Stresemann wrote to the Prince, "the foreign policy of Germany has for the short-term future three main objectives: First, a solution to the Rhine question favorable to Germany, and the assurance of peace, without which Germany will not be able to regain its strength. Second, the protection of ten to twelve million Germans living under the foreign yoke. Third, the rectification of our eastern frontiers [scrupulously omitted from the Locarno negotiations], the recovery of Danzig and the Polish Corridor, and redrawing of the boundaries of Upper Silesia. In the more distant future the reuniting of Austria with Germany, although I am aware that this will not bring only advantages to us but will greatly complicate the problem of our organization."

Germany's entrance into the League seemed to Stresemann to be all-important because only the League could act on the "burning" questions of Danzig, the Saar, and the war guilt "and a capable orator could present these questions to the Assembly of the League in a way to create serious disagreements within the Entente." He emphasized for the benefit of the Crown Prince, who favored an alliance with Russia, that "entry into the League of Nations does not mean that we are choosing the West and turning our backs on the East. We can only choose when we have behind us a military force . . . We must first get the stranglers to relax their grip. That is why German policy must at the start follow the policy which Metternich, I believe, adopted in Austria in 1809: be devious and balk at big decisions."

While the follower of Metternich smiled and kept his diplomatic secrets under wraps, the admirer of Talleyrand, Sir Austen Chamberlain, rode to the celebration in a flaming-red Rolls-Royce, with silvery horns that looked like trumpets. (It had been made for a maharajah but was available for hire from a Swiss rental agency.) Crowds came down from the mountains to fill the churches in prayers of thanksgiving for the coming of peace. The treaty document was framed and floodlit in a window of the Town Hall for the benefit of the crowds who gathered as before a miraculous relic. When the last signature, that of Mussolini's, was appended to the document, the church bells started to ring. They rang all night while the townspeople, the mountaineers, and the members of the delegations sang, drank, and hailed the advent of peace. Briand, however, who had no taste for celebrations, was in bed and asleep at nine that night.

The entire Cabinet came down to welcome Briand when his train came into Paris. And in England the King promptly made Sir Austen a Knight of the Garter for his part in the "miracle of Locarno."

But Stresemann returned to a different sort of welcome. The time of his arrival was kept secret and police occupied the railway station as if prepared for a full-scale assault. No German politician was on hand to greet him. There was only the faithful Lord D'Abernon, for whom

Locarno was a triumph, and a handful of other foreign diplomats. The Foreign Minister was whisked into a car and driven to his house by circuitous routes to avoid possible ambushes by right-wing opponents who misunderstood Stresemann's objectives.

Speaking for the obsessive nationalists, Colonel von Rodenberg wrote in the *Preussische Landeszeitung:* "If the Imperial Cabinet has agreed that Stresemann shall state his views of Locarno before the Committee for Foreign Affairs, it is merely allowing him the right of defense that is conceded to any murderer or similarly unprofitable member of the community; though it is possible that there are many members of our party who regard Stresemann as something worse than a murderer, we consider nonetheless that the Cabinet were right in their decision to permit Stresemann to defend himself."

The *Lokalanzeiger* called Stresemann "Germany's evil genius." And the press lord and industrialist Alfred Hugenberg remarked: "Stresemann has a unique opportunity of becoming the bane of Germany."

Other right-wing papers explained Stresemann's un-German behavior at Locarno by claiming (falsely) that his wife was the sister of the most anti-German of French politicians, Raymond Poincaré, and that he had himself been bought out by the Jews.

Stresemann's critics concentrated their fire on his renunciation of Alsace-Lorraine, a concession which Stresemann heatedly denied although the pact he signed at Locarno specifically pledged him to a complete acceptance of the territorial boundaries in the West. When he was not denying the plain fact of his renunciation he was justifying it on the grounds that, when one is weak, one signs documents which one may tear up when one is strong.

In the end Stresemann carried the day when one of his most energetic opponents, Minister of the Reichswehr Otto Gessler, admitted: "You can't call it renunciation when a one-legged man is asked to promise that he won't take part in any more dancing competitions."

Stresemann and Lord D'Abernon congratulated each other and prepared for the triumphal entry of Germany into the League of Nations at a special Assembly scheduled for March 1926. Never had the League's prestige been so high. Not only was it about to take a significant step toward that universality which had been its cherished hope, but it was proudly wearing the plumes of victory. The previous autumn, by its own prestige and by an unprecedented swiftness of decision, the League had stopped war dead in its tracks and, to make the affair more dramatic, had done this in the much-touted "cockpit" and "powder keg" of Europe, the Balkans. It allowed League proponents to point to the victory and suggest that if the League had been in existence in 1914 the assassination of the Archduke at Sarajevo would have been no more than a Sunday-supplement sensation.

The victory of the League had happened this way. At one o'clock in the afternoon of October 23, 1925, Sir Eric Drummond received an appeal from Bulgaria. Greek troops had crossed the frontier and were battling their way into the country. Four days earlier there had been a quarrel over a card game at the border post of Demir-Kapou; a Greek soldier had been killed and a Greek officer coming up to settle the matter under a white flag of truce had also been gunned down. And now the Greeks were attacking in strength; Bulgarian reinforcements were being rushed up, and a declaration of war was expected imminently.

Drummond telephoned Briand, who was then President of the Council. Briand promptly telegraphed both sides, urging them as League members to cease hostilities and withdraw their forces. Simultaneously he convoked a Council meeting for the following Monday, October 26. Miraculously both sides complied. Invasion orders were countermanded. Troops remained in the positions they had taken when Briand's telegram had arrived.

Delegates felt the urgency of the crisis so keenly that they flew to Geneva for the Council meeting. Swiftly they issued the League's first ultimatum: Both sides must order the withdrawal of their troops in twenty-four hours and complete the pull-back to behind their borders within sixty hours, or face "severe sanctions." British, French, and Italian military attachés in the Balkans were assigned to check the withdrawal. There was to be no discussion of causes, of rights or wrongs. War itself was the only issue and the only international crime. By ten in the morning of Wednesday, October 28, barely five days after the appeal had reached the League, the war was over. Greece was ordered to pay indemnities for the damage committed during the brief incursion into Bulgaria in conformity with the "great principle" which Briand formulated this way: ". . . in the case of a territory violated without sufficient reason reparations are due, even if at the time of the event the party committing the violation believes that the circumstances justified his act."

Never before had the principle been stated so explicitly or implemented so effectively. The victory and glory were a heady tonic for the League and its champions. That none of the Powers had the slightest interest in the Bulgaro-Greek affair was surely pertinent; but comments to that effect were ignored.

The League had flexed its muscles, thus refuting the widespread impression that it had none. This created the proper mood for what was scheduled to be a purely ceremonial occasion marking the restoration of the enemy to the status of a partner.

Briand had set the tone at the formal signing of the Locarno Pact in the British Foreign Office on November 30, when he declared: "We will die together or we will rise again together."

The German delegation, with Stresemann at its head, arrived in Geneva on March 7 and settled in at the Beau Rivage to await the call. Count von Bernstorff, the old prewar ambassador to the United States, had been functioning as Germany's observer in Geneva, attempting to smooth the way as he had with Wilson and House.

There was another item of business planned for that special session. Spain, Brazil, and Poland had asked for permanent seats on the Council and offered persuasive arguments on their own behalf. The Spanish delegations had been stalwart work horses of the League's committees ever since the inception of the League, and their nation yearned for entry into the club of the big powers as the representative of the neutrals. Brazil felt itself entitled to membership on the Council as a spokesman for the Americas; and Poland staked its claim as the child of the League and as a representative of the new-old countries of Europe. Germany's entry into the Council, it was felt, offered a fitting opportunity to enlarge and reorganize that body to make it more broadly representative. There were no strong objections from the dominant powers, France and England.

However, Stresemann, on being informed of the proposal, at once threatened that if any changes were made in the Council structure before Germany's admission it would withdraw its application for membership. That eventuality not only would frustrate the League's aspirations for universality but would in effect wipe out the hope of Locarno, the first article of which called for Germany's joining the League.

Briand had been in Geneva barely twenty-four hours when the crisis broke, but almost at once had had to return to Paris to handle a domestic ministerial upheaval. By the time he returned to Geneva four days later, on March 12, the atmosphere had deteriorated. Brazil had openly threatened to oppose the admission of Germany if its application was denied and from its temporary seat on the Council could enforce its will with a veto.

Briand offered a compromise: Poland would take its seat temporarily and Spain and Brazil would wait until the regular Assembly session in September, provided Germany made it clear in advance that it would offer no objections when the matter came up for debate. Stresemann bluntly refused and offered no compromise.

The effect was shattering: Germany, not yet in the League, was wielding policy with a sledge hammer and issuing an ultimatum. Here was no rehabilitated truant promising to behave. Those who counted noses at Geneva observed that before Stresemann had delivered his ultimatum, three-fourths of the League enthusiastically supported Germany's admission, but that afterward nine-tenths were opposed.

At last, on March 14, Stresemann agreed to leave the matter of enlarging the Council up to a committee composed of the Council members plus twelve additional delegates chosen by the Assembly, who would deliberate after Germany was admitted. The Swedish delegation's first angry reaction to Germany's ultimatum was to oppose *any* enlargement of the permanent Council—including a seat for Germany. Now Sweden joined with Czechoslovakia in declaring their willingness to give up their own Council seats at the year's end and appeal to the Assembly to turn one of them over to Poland.

There was no moving Brazil, however. Brazil's delegate, Afranio de Mello Franco, explained: "It would be a most unfortunate mistake to assume that our policy . . . was actuated by misguided national pride. That . . . is wholly untrue. I desire to reaffirm in this Assembly what I have always maintained in the Council, that, in view of our right as an American nation, we claim that America should be represented more equitably and more fully on the Council."

In vain Briand pleaded that "the loyal and sincere pact of peace" signed at Locarno could not become effective "except under the aegis of the League of Nations." Brazil was firm, and a little power had its day, however brief. Sadly Sir Austen Chamberlain admitted defeat: "It is a bitter disappointment to me that that which seemed well within our grasp and capable of realization here and now must be postponed . . ." In rage and humiliation the German delegation packed their bags and left for Berlin.

The Locarno spirit and the prestige that had flowed from the firm handling of the Greco-Bulgarian crisis were visibly fading. The American ambassador in Berlin, Alanson B. Houghton, reported to the State Department that "Europe has learned nothing from the war and the League of Nations was incapable of guaranteeing forty years of peace."

Germany reminded the world of the trump it continued to hold: the possibility of a turn to the East. On April 24, Stresemann, who only a little while ago had warned that the Soviet Union lived in hopes to Bolshevize Europe up to the Elbe and leave the rest of Germany as a granary for France, now signed an agreement confirming the Treaty of Rapallo. That nonaggression pact had been signed during a moment of frustration at the Genoa Economic Conference of 1922, when German diplomats slipped away from the tiresome negotiations to talk in a frank and friendly way with a Russian representative, as one outcast to another. The two nations agreed to establish formal diplomatic relations in return for a Russian waiver of all reparations claims. What is more, Germany promised verbally that it would not enter the League without the Soviet Union. The Western Powers at that time viewed with horror the possibility of a union of "outlaws."

Now Stresemann revived that fear and played upon it, declaring to the Russians: "For us Locarno has always been synonymous with the pacification of Europe and has not constituted a political alliance against any state whatever. . . . It was established in the course of negotiations at Locarno that the League of Nations is not an institution designed to prepare a crusade against Russia."

On May 10, the commission empowered by the Assembly to come up with a solution to the problem convened with a German representative included among its members. It produced a remarkable compromise. Up to that point the Council had had two categories of members: permanent and temporary. The Covenant specified that permanent seats would go to the United States, England, France, Italy, and Japan. Four nonpermanent members were to be elected by the Assembly "from time to time in its discretion." Although the United States had refused to come in, its seat remained vacant and ready for it at any time. In actual practice though, there were four permanent and four nonpermanent members.

Now the commission proposed increasing the Council to fifteen members. There were to be six permanent seats, thus accommodating Germany and still leaving the United States chair temptingly unoccupied. Each year three of the remaining nine Council seats would be up for election for three-year terms. Furthermore, any nonpermanent member could be re-elected by a two-thirds vote of the Assembly. These amendments allowed the commission to coin a new designation—the "semi-permanent" members of the Council.

The semantic solution did not quite satisfy the national aspirations of the Brazilians, who informed Sir Eric Drummond, on the very day the compromise was announced, that they were withdrawing from the League. Spain later adopted a less drastic and more Spanish attitude, declaring that it would retire to a "dignified abstention" from League activities. Poland accepted its seat while ridiculing the proposition.

On the eve of the regular Assembly meeting in September 1926, the Polish paper *Kurjer Porauny* called the innovation of the semi-permanent council seat "an important discovery" comparable to that of "the existence of the semi-virgin. What a pity that our ancestor Adam and his wife did not content themselves with a semi-apple, thus committing an original semi-sin. The evolution of humanity would have been different: half-expelled from Paradise, it would doubtless have experienced the felicity now reserved for Poland in the League of Nations."

Despite such heckling the way was cleared for Germany's triumphal entry into Geneva. It came in with no more than a wave of the hand and a coquettish smile to the East. The *Deutsche Allgemeine Zeitung* expressed the hope "that Russia, this great and mighty state, should also make her entry into the League and its Council." So much for Rapallo.

Still, the German flags were flying in Geneva, and the Salle de la Réformation was jammed to greet the prodigal son's return to the fold. From the front row of the gallery, Edith Bolling Wilson, two years a widow, watched the ceremonial passing of a milestone on the way to her husband's vision of a reconciliation that would mark the definitive end of the war.

The German delegation filed into the hall headed by the beak-nosed, bald von Schubert, permanent undersecretary at the Wilhelmstrasse. Stresemann dramatically brought up the rear. He seemed uncomfortable in his moment of triumph, appearing to burst out of his tight black morning coat, his neck bulging beyond his stiff white collar, but he smiled ingratiatingly.

The cheers from the gallery considerably exceeded those from the delegates. The President of the Assembly, Dr. Momchilo Nintchitch of Yugoslavia, declared: "I am glad to see Germany take her rightful place amongst us as a great nation desirous of supporting our work for international security and understanding." Then Stresemann gave his maiden speech. Though his voice was shrill (a quality it always took on when he was nervous), his words were disarmingly mild.

"Today," he said, "Germany enters a circle of states to some of which she has for decades been attached by unbroken ties of friendship, whereas others were allied against her during the Great War. It is surely an event of historical importance that Germany and these latter states are now brought together within the League of Nations in permanent and peaceful cooperation. It is a fact which indicates more clearly than any mere words or programs that the League of Nations may in very truth be destined to give a new direction to the political development of mankind."

The oratory concealed Stresemann's private view of the event, as expressed to less ardent Germans on the political right and left. "A League of Nations is intended to disguise the existing leagues among its members," he had said. "We have no other platform from which we can address the world."

Briand, as was expected, brought passion to the occasion: "Peace for Germany and for France," he proclaimed. "That means that we have done with the long series of terrible and sanguinary conflicts which have stained the pages of history. We have done with the black veils of mourning for sufferings that can never be appeased, done with war, done with brutal and sanguinary methods of settling our disputes. True, differences between us still exist, but henceforth it will be for a judge to declare the law . . . Away with rifles, machine guns and cannon. Make way for conciliation, arbitration and peace . . . With the League goes Peace! Without it, the menace of war and blood which the peoples have suffered too long!" A common political appraisal was voiced by *Unità Cattolica:* "Thus vanishes the most serious threat on the European horizon, the Russo-German alliance."

Izvestia, in an editorial in the September 11, 1926, issue, said that the Soviet Union had tried in vain to warn Germany against the League: "So long as the members of the League are bourgeois states whose deepest moral principle is the famous phrase 'homo homini lupus' [man, a wolf to other men], the League is bound to remain the arena in which a motley crowd of capitalist wolves are trying to tear each other's throats. Now Germany has entered the guilty company of the Geneva League. That is her business. We, on our side, can only express the hope that Germany's membership in the League of Nations will not prevent her from scrupulously fulfilling all the obligations she has undertaken with regard to the Soviet Union. We also hope that Germany, in spite of her membership in the League of Nations, will live in peace and friendship with our country."

The blast at the League from *Izvestia* was expected as a routine gesture, but by that time the Secretariat was already aware of a change in the wind in Moscow. Almost a year earlier, while Germany was being wooed at Locarno, feelers had been put forth from the Soviet Union via the French Embassy there, to sound out Drummond on the possibility of admitting an official Soviet observer to the League.

A letter dated October 22, 1925, from a French diplomat in Moscow named Herbette, conveyed the suggestion and intimated that this might be a first step toward applying for membership. He described the Soviet internal difficulties involved in such a turnabout: ". . . a sizeable section of the leaders of opinion would be outraged or at least disoriented in this country if the government of the Soviet Union suddenly announced that it was going to enter the League of Nations, until now depicted as an association of states socially and politically opposed to the U.S.S.R." However, Herbette pointed out, if Germany joined, the League could no longer be characterized as a combination of "victorious and conquering states, founded to oppress the vanquished."

Drummond, in a memo to Paul Mantoux on the Herbette letter, offered the facilities of the League to a Soviet observer, who wished merely to "follow the work of the League . . . as we did for the German consul here." Drummond added, however: "Frankly, if Germany joins, I should prefer to wait a year or two so as to allow the absorption of Germany by the 'Geneva atmosphere' before attempting to assimilate Russia. The two together would be excessive. I think perhaps a reply on these lines by safe channels [underscored] to Herbette might be useful."

Another subterranean flow of correspondence was going on before and during the ceremonial Assembly. Stresemann was bent on pinning down Locarno, on winning an immediate reduction of occupying forces in the Rhineland, on negotiating a return of Eupen-et-Malmédy as the price of a security pact with Belgium and France, on promoting commercial liaisons between German and French industry.

Briand at the same time was having domestic difficulties that obliged him to respond somewhat hesitantly to this too ardent wooing from Stresemann. Seven years after the war, France, burdened with war debts (mainly to the United States) and the costs of policing the Ruhr and the Rhineland, found itself in worse financial shape than the ex-enemy whom it was accused of saddling with a brutal Carthaginian peace. Germany had been bailed out of the more stringent Versailles terms by a variety of payment plans and loans from abroad. The mark, resting on gold now, was stronger than the franc.

The French public, already irritated by this contrast, also watched with mounting uneasiness the proliferation of highly jingoistic paramilitary organizations in Germany, a matter which Briand felt obliged to raise, although he put it as tactfully as possible.

Stresemann belittled the patriotic societies: there were only 20,000 Vikings and Werewolves; the Stahlhelm and the Junge Deutsche Orden were bigger but purely anti-Bolshevist, he assured Briand. Surely there was no need to fret about patriotic marching societies with a harmless taste for uniforms.

Stresemann suggested to Briand a quiet conference away from Geneva, at which the two of them could talk frankly and privately. On the night of September 16 the rendezvous was arranged. The following morning Stresemann left the Beau Rivage in a limousine at about the same time Briand climbed into his car in front of the Hôtel des Bergues.

Newsmen pursued both cars but lost the trail at the water's edge. Stresemann and Briand boarded separate speed launches and struck out in divergent courses across the lake. They met by prearrangement at an unpretentious inn run by a man named Léger in a French town called Thoiry about ten miles from Geneva. Innkeeper Léger, apparently equal to the task history had thrust upon him so suddenly, shook hands with the statesmen and led them upstairs to a room unremarkable except for its startling pink walls. On coarse crockery and out of chipped pitchers he served a state banquet for the two and their interpreters, who were necessary because Briand's German was skimpy and Stresemann's French almost nonexistent. M. and Mme Léger produced a flow of dishes: Lyons sausage, baked trout, partridges, a tasty duckling, an assortment of wines. The making of history was not permitted to disturb the lunch, for not until the coffee came did the talk begin, with each participant glowing, well fed, and in a proper mood for the reconciliation of differences.

Briand produced the military manual of the Stahlhelm which his aides had given him and asked why the German government did not suppress the organization.

Stresemann explained: ". . . a great army does not abolish its spirit overnight. The memory of comradeship-in-arms remains alive in these organizations of old soldiers . . . With us the Republic does not fully satisfy the psychological needs of the masses. It dresses in a boring black frock coat. The crowd wants bright colors, joy, motion." The Stahlhelm fulfilled those needs, nothing more. There was no danger, he assured Briand.

The talk turned to other topics: a speedier end to the occupation of the Ruhr and the Rhineland, perhaps the return of the Saar, a thoroughgoing collaboration between French and German industrialists and businessmen. As a concession by Stresemann, Germany would float a bond issue of one and one-half billion marks, earmarked for the French to bail out the franc.

At the end Briand voiced the fear of the politician in the face of the suprapolitical industrialist. He told Stresemann: "If we do not combine together we shall be swallowed up by international capitalism. Look at the growing importance of the great vested interests, the industrial cartels. They will soon dictate to us the policy we shall follow. We politicians must not allow the direction of affairs to be taken out of our hands . . . It is lucky we are in agreement. Otherwise, the American bankers would have taken the last shirt from our backs."

The understanding of Thoiry was between Stresemann and Briand. It could have no effect until approved by their respective governments. They agreed on a noncommunicative communiqué for the reporters awaiting them at Geneva. It said that the two had "examined all outstanding questions" and "reconciled their points of view." If their governments approved, they would "resume their collaboration toward desirable ends."

That afternoon Stresemann suffered a mild heart attack. His doctor ordered him to bed, but after a brief nap he rose, dressed, and sauntered over to the Bavaria, a favorite café of his where he could drink beer with reporters, who were allowed to call him Gustav. He was in too exuberant a mood to be ill. He discussed the negotiations at Thoiry in such detail that later Briand had to caution him: "Do not get so excited, my dear Stresemann. Politics is not a cinema."

Two days later the ebullient Stresemann committed a more serious gaffe. Speaking at a meeting of the German colony in Geneva, he told them that the admission of Germany into the League demonstrated that the world did not really believe the accusation of German war guilt; that Germany insisted on the right to have colonies; that occupation of any territory of the Reich was incompatible with its League status, and this included the Saar Basin.

These views were widely interpreted as a revelation of the terms reached over the Thoiry duckling and, since the actual understanding could not be revealed prior to government consultation, Briand's denials inevitably sounded lame. When Poincaré thereupon felt it necessary to repeat his conviction that Germany must bear the major responsibility for the late war, it sounded very much as if Briand had been disowned by his Premier.

Still, for most of the world the rendezvous at Thoiry was a continuation of Locarno, a love feast that marked the end of the war. "Conversation at Thoiry" was a hit act at Paris cabarets, and in December 1926 the Nobel Peace Prize was divided among Stresemann, Briand, and Chamberlain—for the Locarno Pact—and the American Charles Gates Dawes—for his celebrated plan that made German reparations feasible.

The Thoiry accord remained on ice but did not keep very well. For the French it lost a good deal of its savor after the United States let it be known that it disapproved of earmarking a German bond issue for France until the latter had paid its debts. Briand urged patience on Stresemann and continued to dream of a French security within a large and lofty-minded confraternity of the Western world.

The United States, some thought, had been edging closer to Geneva. The Senate was beginning to formulate the conditions under which there might be some recognition of the Permanent Court at The Hague. American financial experts had been chiefly responsible for straightening out the tangled reparations, and American investors were heavily involved in the economic recovery of Germany.

On April 6, 1927, the tenth anniversary of the American entry into the war, Briand seized the occasion of an interview with the Associated Press to launch a new effort at enticing the Americans. "France would be ready to publicly sign with the United States a mutual pact tending to 'outlaw war,' as the American expression goes," he said. The proposal caught the fancy of America, as it had begun to turn from the strict precepts of isolationism. Briand expanded on the notion in conferences with U.S. Ambassador Myron T. Herrick. By the end of the year Coolidge's Secretary of State, Frank B. Kellogg, added a generous American touch by suggesting that France and the United States jointly invite all the powers of the world to join in the pact.

Briand raised briefly and in vain the old questions of distinguishing between aggressive and defensive wars, but yielded at last to American pragmatism, which scorned the technicalities in favor of a declaration as unobjectionable as the Boy Scout oath and probably as effective.

Whatever the diplomats may have felt concerning the effectiveness of the Kellogg-Briand Pact, it brought an American Secretary of State back once again to the Clock Room of the Quai d'Orsay for the first time since the days of Lansing and House. And President Coolidge cheerfully gave the American blessing in a message to French President Gaston Doumergue, in which he said: "The idea of M. Briand is as big as the world."

On August 27, 1928, the crowds in Paris, waving an assortment of flags, shouted cheers for Kellogg and for Stresemann. The representatives of fourteen nations, including Germany, France, England, the United States, and Japan, put their signatures to a document which said: "The high contracting parties in the name of their respective peoples, solemnly condemn the recourse to war for the settlement of international disputes and remove it as an instrument of national policy in their mutual relations."

For the public the ceremony carried a reassuring Wilsonian echo. For most diplomats and for the Secretariat of the League there was sentiment but little reassurance in the document at a time when assurance seemed plainly needed.

The signs in Germany were disquieting. The Secretariat of the League had been uneasy ever since the election of Hindenburg in 1925. In a memo to Drummond, Paul Mantoux wrote that he was not impressed by the arguments that Hindenburg was the incarnation of Prussian military honor, because he recalled that the Prussian code required that civilians get off the sidewalk when an officer walks down the street. But granting that the Marshal may be the soul of honor, Mantoux wrote, the significance of the election lay elsewhere. "Germany had to choose between two candidates, one of whom represented a certain democratic orientation and a certain desire to carry out a foreign policy of conciliation while the other was ardently supported by the most extreme elements of German chauvinism . . . The Germans preferred the second candidate. . . . I do not think that even Ludendorff himself, if he were the head of the Reich, could unleash war immediately . . . The question is: are we approaching it or not? From this point of view the election of Marshal von Hindenburg is a bad omen."

There were other discouraging signs. The paramilitary groups were marching and demonstrating, this time for *Anschluss*—union with Austria. Stresemann, obviously ill, had come to Paris in August 1928 with no illusions or reservations about the Kellogg-Briand Pact he was to sign. He commented: "It is one of those questions to which a decent man cannot give the answer 'no,' but like all questions of conscience to which there is only one answer, its moral value is greater than its practical significance. If I asked a murderer of tomorrow whether he approved of murder in principle, he would answer 'no.' But will such a question prevent the murder?"

Stresemann took advantage of his trip to Paris to discuss more practical questions. He pressed Briand on ending the occupation of the Rhineland and drew an ambiguous, somewhat tormented reply: "We will find something . . ." It was after that that Stresemann noted in his diary: "Thoiry is dead."

In a long conference with Poincaré, the ailing Stresemann explained the street demonstrations for *Anschluss*—a union strictly forbidden by the Treaty of Versailles. Vienna and all Austria, he said, "makes us think of Mozart and Schubert. In Austria life has always been more refined and more endowed with grace; theater and literature are more appreciated there than are boxing matches . . . we seek the soul we have lost in this people who are of our blood . . ."

Germany was losing its soul, he complained, because it was being too Americanized. "We in Germany are today more Americanized than any other people in Europe, but at the bottom of our hearts we feel that in the stress of modern life we have lost a fragment of our soul."

Poincaré offered no encouragement to the German thirst for Austrian *Gemütlichkeit*, but on the subject of the alleged American threat to the soul of Europe, he said, as Briand had: "I agree with you that in the face of the powerful influence of the United States it is necessary to preserve the individuality of every European state . . . More or less we in Europe are all finding ourselves under the same flag vis-à-vis the United States."

That was the current that ran in Paris behind the formalities of the Kellogg-Briand Pact, behind the cheers for the renewed collaboration of American diplomats with Europe.

By the end of the year Stresemann was too ill to take the damp winds of Geneva. To accommodate him, the League Council met in December at warm and sunny Lugano. There the ailing Foreign Minister of the Reich, whose clothes had begun to sag about his shrunken frame, permitted himself the most violent demonstration of his diplomatic career. Stresemann for some time had wanted to appear the champion of German minorities in various countries in order to appease the right wing at home. When the Polish delegate Zaleski referred to certain activities of the Deutscher Volksbund in Upper Silesia which he found subversive of peaceful relations, Stresemann leaped to his feet, seemingly out of all control. He pounded the table and shrieked at the Polish representative. It was an impressive display. Stresemann could turn his anger on and off with remarkable ease.

Stresemann appeared once more at The Hague Conference of 1929 to put the finishing touches to the Young Plan, a refinement of the Dawes Plan on reparations. The scheme was to be tied to the evacuation of the Rhineland, which the ailing Foreign Minister of the Reich had sought as his monument. He squirmed in an agony of frustration while the British expert Philip Snowden delightedly demolished the French Finance Minister, Henri Chéron. Chéron had the reputation of being as honest as he was incompetent.

At one point Snowden had brutally termed the French proposals "grotesque" and "ridiculous." Chéron, whose English was inadequate, had the impression that Snowden had complimented him gracefully. When he heard the translation he demanded an apology. The conference almost broke up when Snowden gave his answer at a press conference. "Cockahoop," said Snowden. "Tell them in England that the British delegation feels cockahoop." The expression could not be translated for Chéron or Stresemann, but the wrangle subsided.

Stresemann tried in vain to interpose the Rhineland in the midst of the prolonged semantic confusion. In the end the evacuation was promised as part of the Young Plan's terms. Actually it was one of the few aspects of the plan that took effect, the rest were shortly to be swept away in the Hoover debt moratorium. But implementation of the evacuation came too late for Stresemann. He suffered a paralytic stroke and died in October 1929. He knew well the direction of his country and his time. Shortly before he died he told the Italian diplomat Dino Grandi, with whom he was having a champagne nightcap: "I am an old man and I am dying, but you are young and you will live to see the second Punic War."

Stresemann's death brought to an end Briand's hopes to achieve security in a Franco-German entente. It was the dead end of the road that began at Locarno and went through Thoiry. France had sought a broad general security in the framework of a strong Covenant and when that was denied it had tried to rally the world to the Protocol of Geneva. Now Briand turned to yet another scheme to bolster the League's flawed structure of peace.

He broached it during a debate in the Assembly on September 5, 1929, when Belgium's Paul Hymans gave him an opening in a plea for "economic disarmament." Ever since 1922 Briand had advocated a form of European union. Now he proposed a "sort of Federation," an idea which, he said, had been "called 'generous' perhaps to avoid characterizing it as 'rash.' "

He spelled out the idea at a private dinner in Geneva for the delegates of twenty-seven nations, and on May 17, 1930, circulated a note to the governments of Europe (which, by Briand's definition, did not include Russia and Turkey) calling for a European Union to face up to a "collective responsibility in the face of the danger which threatens the peace of Europe." The response was unenthusiastic to the point of yawning apathy. Britain saw in it a conflict with its Empire ties and plainly leaned to the Empire. Italy and Germany temporized, asking that Russia and Turkey be included. Yugoslavia was the only country to promise unconditional adherence.

On September 8, 1930, at another meeting of the twenty-seven European nations, Briand read the future of his idea in the polite evasions of his audience and noted that it was being prepared for entombment "in the museum before it had been allowed to come to life." He slammed closed his dossier on the European Union and announced that, inasmuch as his project did not appear to satisfy his colleagues, he did not consider it "useful to continue the discussion."

The era of grand schemes for collective security and the enforcement of peace was at an end. The League would henceforth play its crises by ear. The day of French grandeur—not to say grandiloquence—was over, and the time of English expedience was dawning.

Ten

EXEUNT
SAMURAI

Sir Eric Drummond was seized with gloomy reflections on the future of the League as it entered its second decade. True, it had survived. It had successfully performed a number of the chores set for it by the big powers. There had been pacts and conferences. Nevertheless, an air of inadequacy clung to the organization. The Secretary-General knew only one remedy for it: the Americans must be persuaded to take that seat at the Council table which had remained mockingly empty for ten years.

"If the United States could be induced in any way to become a member of the League," he had written earlier in a confidential memorandum to Paul Mantoux, "the future would be assured, since all countries, with the sole exception of Russia, would immediately either resume or obtain membership and remain members."

The walkouts by Argentina and Brazil rankled, and Drummond ascribed those actions and the lack of Latin American enthusiasm to Washington's influence. "In spite of the assurances given by officials and others in the United States that they have no hostility to the League," he continued, "it is certain that private or even semi-official action of the United States is directed against new application for entry into the League, against the countries of South and Central America taking much active interest in the League, and if a country in that Continent leaves the League (an event which causes them no sorrow) against its return."

"How much would the League have to pay to attract American

membership?" Sir Eric asked in his memo. He tried reckoning the cost in Covenant amendments and suggested that Mantoux make soundings to see what would be required. "Without some such arrangement," he concluded, the League would be in "real danger of dwindling and becoming only a minor factor in world affairs."

The soundings produced no cheery echo from the Hoover administration in Washington, beset as it was by deepening economic catastrophe. Yet events were being prepared at the other side of the world that would bring the Americans to Geneva, if not in any solemnized union with the League, at least in a liaison of promising intimacy.

Lord Cecil, perhaps the only member of the original Wilsonians still active in the League, was on hand to open the Assembly on September 10, 1931. Cecil was now a fixture in Geneva, embodying the purest belief in internationalism. A caricaturist depicted him as Moses to celebrate his ancient and honorable standing. When Lady Cecil saw the drawing she told the somewhat abashed artist, "Oh, he's just like that. . . . Always playing about with the Tablets of the Law."

In his opening remarks Cecil indeed played the risky role of prophet. "I do not think there is the slightest prospect of any war," he said. "I know—and history tells us—how rash it is to prophesy as to the future of international affairs. But nevertheless I do not believe that there is anyone in this room who will contradict me when I say there has scarcely ever been a period in the world's history when war seemed less likely than it does at present."

It took only eight days for Lord Cecil's prophecy to explode. On September 18 Japanese troops seized the Manchurian city of Mukden.

Both Japan's dour delegate, Kenkichi Yoshizawa, and the professorial Dr. Sao-ke Alfred Sze of China apparently were caught unawares by the development. They told the Council they would have to request further information. Sze added that he was "greatly disturbed." Yoshizawa puffed on his customary outsized cigar and commented that, even though he knew nothing about the affair, he was certain that all measures were being taken to "prevent the local incident from leading to undesirable complications."

In the days that followed, Dr. Sze read a stream of messages from Nanking and Mukden that drew a picture of a massive assault on Manchuria. He pleaded for some decisive response by the League. By way of answer, Yoshizawa transmitted reassuring cables from Tokyo and generally contented himself with answering the Chinese declamations with the statement *"Malheureusement, je ne suis pas de cet avis"* (Unfortunately, I am not of that opinion).

The Chinese messages, read in fluent English and with restrained indignation by Dr. Sze, reported the Japanese pushing into Kirin: "Besides killing several Chinese officials, Japanese soldiers . . . also slew their families and buried alive over one hundred wounded Chinese soldiers. . . . Conditions at Huangkutang even worse; communication organs, banks and money exchanges confiscated. . . . Japanese soldiers after setting fire to Changti camp, put to death over one hundred soldiers. . . . Two Japanese cruisers dispatched to Chefoo and Longkow."

Yoshizawa maintained that the incident had been touched off by a group of Chinese who blew up a section of the South Manchurian Railroad, which the Japanese were then running under provisions of a treaty wrested from the old Chinese Empire before it collapsed. The incitement had apparently been compounded by the murder of a Japanese Captain Nakimura, he went on. In any case, he promised the Japanese would withdraw all troops as soon as possible and declared that his government held no territorial designs whatever on China. This assurance, plus the fact that reports from Tokyo described Prime Minister Wakatsuki and Foreign Minister Shidehara as "indignant" at the behavior of their runaway military men, lulled the Council into a belief that the incident was part of the general chaos in China and would be forgotten in a fortnight by all but the victims.

Actually China had been living in chaotic violence ever since the last Manchu Emperor had retired in 1911 behind the walls of the Japanese concession at Tientsin. Every spring, along with the floods and famine, came a renewal of civil wars and the rampages of warlords. The Kuomintang, heirs of Sun Yat-sen, ran a dim central government that clearly did not have the "Mandate of Heaven," by which phrase the Chinese signify the acceptance of a regime which can demonstrate its wisdom and its ability to fulfill its obligations to the people.

The Chinese delegates at Geneva presented a brave aspect as the representatives of enlightened, democratic government that was leading a united nation against unconscionable aggression, but the embarrassing fact was that the writ of Chiang Kai-shek and the Kuomintang did not run very far in China. The old warlord of Manchuria, Marshal Chang Tso-lin, for example, had once calmly disavowed the right of the central government to set foreign policy for him and insisted on making his own treaty with the Russians. His son and heir, "the Young Marshal," Chang Hsueh-liang, carried on in his father's tradition, running the affairs of Manchuria by a series of reciprocal obligations. Although these might seem to a Westerner to resemble the machinery of a Mafia, the deals were actually closer to a feudal pattern. The Young Marshal came to terms with provincial governors, who came to terms with itinerant tax collectors and wandering banditti. It worked after a fashion: schools were built, settlers accommodated, and a rough and bloody justice meted out.

The Young Marshal lacked his father's ferocity (some writers labeled him "effeminate") and, although he thought nothing of challenging Chiang Kai-shek, he offered scarcely any resistance to the Japanese.

Aside from this, the Communists, who had escaped a massacre by Chiang in 1927, were in a state of war with him for the soul and soil of China. The Japanese had not yet encountered the Communists, who, even then, were on less than happy terms with the Russians. The West had scarcely heard of the men who led them, among others a poet named Mao Tse-tung.

Even while talk continued at Geneva the central government was temporarily dissolved in Canton. This intermittent, ineffective regime met the Japanese onslaught with a series of elegant, ironic, gallant, but useless gestures. For example, at a time when millions of Chinese were homeless and starving as a result of the Yangtze floods, the government rejected Japanese relief contributions that came while the military were pushing deeper into Manchuria. "It would be bitter bread for the flood sufferers to swallow," wrote T. V. Soong, chairman of the National Flood Relief Committee, "were we to accept your assistance now and should thus ill requite the genuinely sympathetic feelings of civilian Japanese."

Chinese diplomats at Geneva and elsewhere thus performed with the exquisite grace of figures on a porcelain vase, detached from crude contemporary reality. Similarly, the Japanese, fervently reiterating their loyalty to the League while assaulting the fundamental principles of the Covenant, would appear to be indulging in another kind of incomprehensible ritual, if one were not aware of the critical problems posed by the silkworm and the Samurai.

The depression had produced a devastating fall in the prices for raw silk, the mainstay for the Japanese farmers, who constituted 52 percent of the nation's population. The army was not an elite corps of technicians up for sale to a demagogue, and its officers were not the brass hats familiar in Europe. It was a conscript army which drew heavily from the peasantry, offering the farmer a chance to rise at least to junior-officer rank. It was these junior officers who spearheaded the defense of the poverty-stricken silk farmer and, like him, detested everything connected with industrialism, financiers, and city folk. They saw themselves riding out of the mists of Japanese chivalry to preserve the ancient rural traditions and the welfare of the humble peasants against the banker, the bookkeeper, and the materialist-minded Westerner. When the yen was devalued in the fall of 1931, the cities made money and the military denounced such profit taking as sinful.

They apparently saw no contradiction between the pure romance of their mission and the necessity to have Western arms, Western factories, and the most modern military techniques, offered by German instructors. Actually such dependence on Europe and the United States was wedding them closer to all the coarse twentieth-century forces they so despised. They did see, however, that the only thing that could make the misery in Japan endurable was the heady restorative of war and the call to glory. The war news helped to blot out domestic tribulations. The starving silk farmers could read in their papers about an officer's gallant wife who committed suicide when her husband was sent to the front. She carefully explained beforehand that she was acting not out of a self-pitying despair, but in order to leave her husband free to devote himself completely and without distractions to his country's service.

Samurai tradition sanctified not only suicide but murder in the cause of honor. Shortly before the assault on Mukden, former Premier Hamaguchi died of wounds received in an assassination attempt some months earlier. The events were not unrelated, and in the months to come, while the Japanese forces carried the flag in China, the habit of murdering politicians grew so prevalent that the Geneva post was to seem a sanctuary to Japanese statesmen.

To Americans, a crisis in the Pacific seemed more immediate and less complicated than European troubles. The spectacle of a rampaging Japan brought tremors to the Philippines, then under United States control, and even to the Pacific coast of the United States itself. Washington had signed away its right to strengthen its fortifications at Guam and Manila in return for a Japanese assurance of an "open door" in China and a lower naval ratio. The Nine-Power Naval Treaty left the United States and Britain without a base from which to strike Japan, whereas Japan's powerful fleet could easily reach Guam or Manila at a moment's notice.

Furthermore, China, chaotic as it was, provided commercial opportunities in hard times when trade was foundering everywhere.

Lastly, the United States had a stake in the only type of "foreign entanglement" then acceptable to the American people: the Kellogg-Briand Pact, which outlawed war as a means of settling disputes and enshrined the principle, however vague, of collective security.

By contrast, Britain and France in the fall of 1931 seemed very uninterested in exotic outposts. The glory of the Empire was fading in Britain and this occasioned considerable resentment among the Old China Hands and the Old India Hands. The resentment was turned against the Chinese and Indians, who were challenging the idea of Empire, not against the Japanese, who were showing the good sense to carry the flag that had dropped from the falling hands of the British Raj. While Hong Kong remained a treasured foothold, and the International Settlements at Shanghai were valued as a channel of trade, Manchuria was far away from either.

France had Indochina but, unlike the United States, saw in an invigorated Japan a possible ally, should trouble there get out of hand. Moreover, just as the United States understood collective security to be valuable mainly in the Pacific, France saw merit in the principle only where it felt threatened—in Europe.

Germany, for perhaps the only time in recent history, shared France's view. It had lost all its islands in the Pacific and its leased territories and concessions in China as a result of the war, and so had no economic stake in the area at all. The Weimar Republic saw no reason whatever to pick a fight with a potential ally. Also, as British historian Arnold Toynbee has pointed out, Germany, still struggling out of pariahhood, "had a fellow feeling for a fellow outlaw."

The Soviet Union felt a noticeable anxiety because it shared a two-thousand-mile border with the Manchurian provinces in which Japanese forces were operating. The Russians also recalled that, in the days of the Allied intervention, Japan had penetrated all the way to Lake Baikal. And it had taken all the diplomatic talents of the United States and Britain to persuade Japan to leave the Maritime Province of Siberia. They clung to it, in fact, as late as 1922.

The United States in its search for allies clearly had geopolitical reasons for turning to the Soviet Union, but this was plainly impossible at a time when the United States was still refusing to recognize the Bolshevik Revolution.

The smaller powers, which had looked to the United States as a champion in the Wilsonian days, would again have rallied behind an American-led movement for genuine collective security, of which they felt chronically in need. However, they had only one forum and that was the League of Nations, from which the United States had exiled itself.

To United States Secretary of State Henry L. Stimson, it was clear from the start that Chinese resistance to the Japanese advance in Manchuria was likely to be high-minded, strictly verbal, and ineffective. Within hours of the time the first Japanese soldiers moved into Mukden, Stimson had on his desk a confidential telegram from the United States minister to China, relaying a report from W. H. Donald, the Australian adviser to the warlord of Manchuria, Marshal Chang Hsueh-liang:

"Donald stated that the Marshal has ordered all Chinese soldiers within barracks, depoted all arms and forbade retaliation, adding that Japanese soldiers had apparently run amok, Japanese authorities being powerless."

In Geneva, Dr. Sze declared that China "was very unwilling to become a militarized nation." And in Nanking, Generalissimo Chiang Kai-shek greeted the Japanese invasion of Manchuria with a ringing call to quiescence: "As we have entrusted our case to the League, the National Army has received the strictest orders to avoid all possibility of a clash with the invaders. We exhort the entire nation to maintain dignified calm."

On September 21, the United States minister to China, Nelson T. Johnson, wired Stimson another report, suggesting that the Japanese soldiers were not in fact "running amok" but committing a premeditated assault. He cited a conversation he had had with his British opposite number, detailing the "maneuvers" by Japanese troops within their railway zone weeks before the Mukden outbreak:

"Guests in hotels state that during such sham fighting Japanese soldiers would enter hotels, seek out vacant rooms, plant machine guns on windows and roofs and immediately commence firing to the disturbance of everyone. It is my present belief that much of this was deliberately staged for the purpose of accustoming the populace to the maneuvering of Japanese soldiery day and night and to the sound of machine guns. . . . It seems to me absurd to believe that mere destruction of railway tracks would warrant occupation of Manchuria."

In another message on September 22, Johnson told Stimson: "It is my conviction that the steps taken by Japan in Manchuria must fall within any definition of war."

The word "war" was confined to confidential communications. Stimson, the Chinese and Japanese statesmen, and all the diplomats at Geneva joined in inventing euphemisms. Once when the Japanese delegate slipped and used the forbidden word, the League's translators deftly rendered "war" as "incident."

Stimson quickly staked out two strategies: to bolster the civilian government of Japan against the military, and to work as closely as possible with the League without arousing the suspicions of the fiercely isolationist press and public in the United States.

Four days after the outbreak at Mukden, Stimson summoned to his office the Japanese ambassador in Washington, the mild-mannered Katsuji Debuchi, who never ceased to be excruciatingly embarrassed by the ferocity of his country's military. In a memorandum dictated after the conversation, Stimson said he had told Debuchi that he had learned of "a sharp cleavage between Shidehara and some of the militaristic elements of his government. [Debuchi] said that was so." Stimson continued: "I said that what I was now doing was seeking to strengthen Baron Shidehara's hand and not to weaken it. The Ambassador said he understood perfectly."

The Secretary of State then recorded how he had read a note he was preparing to send to Shidehara. He read it to Debuchi "very slowly, paraphrasing it in more simple words." The note described the situation as "very unfortunate" and "no doubt embarrassing to the Japanese government." It also contained a warning: "It is not exclusively a matter of concern to Japan and China. It brings into question at once the meaning of certain provisions of the Nine-Power Treaty of February 6, 1922, and the Kellogg-Briand Pact."

Stimson dispatched identical notes to Japan and China expressing the pious hope that "they will cause their military forces to refrain from any further hostilities." He followed this evenhanded diplomatic approach out of solidarity with the League Council, which had decided to approach the question delicately without drawing any distinction between aggressor and victim.

For the second phase of his strategy—cautious cooperation with the League—Stimson relied on two men: Drummond, who was delighted at the prospect of bringing Washington closer to the League, and Prentiss Gilbert, whose official title as American Consul in Geneva scarcely did justice to his actual mission or to the delicacy with which he carried it out.

Prentiss Gilbert was, in fact, the State Department's ear at the Geneva listening post and the American watchdog set over the League. For Sir Eric Drummond, Gilbert was an invaluable channel for a private exchange of views with Washington.

This tall, sad-eyed American became a familiar figure as he strolled on the quays of Geneva, informal, hatless, with hands in pockets. He would pointedly cross the street when he passed the Palais Wilson lest some watchful observer report to the eternally suspicious American press that he was having illicit relations with that embodiment of internationalism. He was available, however, for unofficial chats at the Brasserie Bavaria.

His consulate was staffed far in excess of any requirements imposed by the demands of the American business community in the city, for Prentiss Gilbert served in other capacities as well. He ran in effect a training course for ambassadors. Among his illustrious alumni were

Llewellyn E. Thompson, who went on to serve as American ambassador to Moscow, Jacob Beam, who went to Warsaw, and James W. Riddleberger, who made a distinguished diplomatic record in Athens.

An intellectual with a flair for adventure, Gilbert came to the State Department after years of service as an intelligence officer in World War I. That, however, was not his first war. At the age of sixteen he enlisted to fight in the Spanish-American War. He had spent the time between wars in roaming the world, settling down for brief stints as a teacher of dramatics, first at the University of Rochester and later at Columbia University.

Gilbert was now in a position to serve as the link between Stimson and Drummond. It was through him that Stimson transmitted the first direct promise of United States support for League action in the Manchurian crisis. On October 9, 1931, Stimson cabled Gilbert a message to be transmitted to Drummond with the assurance that he might "feel free to communicate it confidentially to Council members."

The note declared that from the United States point of view it was "desirable that the League in no way relax its vigilance and in no way fail to assert all the pressure and authority within its competence toward regulating the action of China and Japan . . . On its part the American government, acting independently through its diplomatic representatives, will endeavor to reinforce what the League does and will make clear that it has a keen interest in the matter and is not oblivious to the obligations which the disputants have assumed to their fellow signatories in the Pact of Paris [otherwise known as the Kellogg-Briand Pact] as well as in the Nine-Power Pact should a time arise when it would seem advisable to bring forward these obligations."

As the tide of communications grew between Washington and Geneva, with Stimson relaying reports from China and Japan, Gilbert had to caution his chief on Drummond's inability to use information classified as "confidential." Gilbert wrote in October 1931 reporting a conversation with Sir Eric: "In regard to this valuable information you have supplied, he remains handicapped in his use of it in any practical fashion so long as he is restrained by the injunction not to reveal its source. Should he communicate it to anyone, the first question he would be asked would be as to the source of the information. From the kind of reply he would give the information either would not be accorded its full weight or its source would be surmised."

There is nothing to suggest that Stimson took the admonition seriously. His communications to Drummond via Gilbert continued briskly as the crisis deepened and many were prefaced by careful advice on maintaining top secrecy. Meanwhile Gilbert was transmitting Drummond's own suggestions. When Stimson urged that the League Council invoke the Kellogg-Briand Pact against Japan, Drummond countered with a gentler approach, suggesting that Stimson raise that matter with both China and Japan in separate notes. Apparently convinced, Stimson fired off virtually identical notes to both sides, which in due course were answered by disclaimers of any intent to violate the provisions of any treaty.

Despite the disclaimers, on October 8 twelve Japanese planes (on a reconnaissance mission, according to Yoshizawa) dropped bombs over Chinchow and scattered leaflets upon the terrified inhabitants.

Dr. Sze read a translation of the leaflets to his colleagues at the Council table: "The Imperial [Japanese] Army, which, in accordance with the principles of justice, is endeavoring to safeguard its interests and to protect the masses, will never recognize the Provisional Government of Chang Hsueh-liang at Chinchow, and therefore is obliged to take drastic measures to suppress such a government. The people of Chinchow should submit to the kindness and power of the Great Japanese Empire and should oppose and prevent the establishment of Chang Hsueh-liang's government, otherwise they will be considered as decidedly opposing the army of the Great Japanese Empire, in which case the army will ruthlessly destroy Chinchow."

At Geneva, Japanese delegate Yoshizawa not only evinced the "kindness and power" of the Japanese Empire but added a dash of courtesy and a willingness to cooperate. He cited, in defense of Japanese actions, the chaos of China, and the highly effective anti-Japanese boycott, which he described as "ill treatment and an outrage." But still he promised that Japan would withdraw all of its forces as quickly as it could with due regard for the safety of its troops and civilian nationals.

He opposed an on-the-spot investigation by the Council, which then tried to establish a system of gathering reports from the consuls of member states. These yielded considerably less information than the daily papers were carrying.

Yoshizawa—and indeed the government at Tokyo—publicly and profusely joined in the Council's only firm action of that period: deploring such outrages as the bombing of Chinchow. In this first test of the League's ability to restrain a major power, the "guilty" party maintained its adherence to League principles and the cause of peace. The Japanese government and its spokesman at Geneva seemed to be unshakable adherents to the League despite the capricious army then rampaging through Manchuria.

The Chinese, too, declined to play the role of belligerent. Dr. Sze told the Council: "China has . . . offered no resistance, withdrawn her troops, and maintained an attitude of dignified calm. She has done so because she is a loyal Member of the League of Nations and has put her trust in the League. The Covenant and the Pact of Paris are our two sheet anchors to which we have moored our ship of State and with the help of which we believe we shall ride out the storm."

Drummond meanwhile began to sound out the possibility of bringing a United States representative formally and openly into the Council, not as a substitute for the back-door negotiations but as a demonstration of American involvement.

Stimson agreed, and explained his reason to Ambassador Debuchi, who turned up frequently at the State Department in those weeks, either by invitation or on his own initiative. Prentiss Gilbert would be instructed to sit with the Council, Stimson told Debuchi, because "I wanted it to be clear that we stood not alone vis-à-vis Japan but with the other nations of the world."

With the script thus cleared, Aristide Briand took the stage at the Council session and proposed that the United States be invited to send a representative to attend Council meetings, on the grounds that the Kellogg-Briand Pact and other treaties outside the scope of the League were involved in the Manchurian affair. Yoshizawa then indulged in a series of rapid tergiversations to avoid bringing in the United States, which, he feared, would so invigorate the Council that it would shatter beyond repair the pleasant tearoom atmosphere.

He was worried, he said, about the precedent that might be set by permitting nonmembers to use the clubhouse. When this point had been argued relentlessly for days, he suggested that the Council should appoint a committee of legal experts to explore all the constitutional aspects.

Lord Reading, a pronounced conservative, who had been sent by London to supersede Cecil, gently remonstrated: "If my Japanese colleague will forgive me for saying so, that is hardly a constitutional matter." His Japanese colleague forgave him at considerable length but would not budge on the question. Finally Briand asked whether the Japanese colleague would agree to accept any ruling brought in by the committee of experts. No, the Japanese delegate could not offer any such commitment but insisted nonetheless that the legal experts should be chosen and put to work.

The matter of an American presence at Geneva was, however, sufficiently important to move the Council to a decision. Over the dissenting votes of Germany and Japan, it voted to cut the debate and invite the United States representative.

Accordingly, on the sixteenth of October, Prentiss Gilbert departed from his customary practice of crossing the street in front of the Palais, strolled casually into the Council Chamber and seated himself as the first United States representative ever to officially attend a Council meeting.

The stage managers of that historic event miscalculated in one crucial particular, however. The eager, enthusiastic welcoming speeches for Prentiss Gilbert made it apparent that the presence of a United States spokesman was of even greater historic importance than the crisis that brought him there. The point was not lost on the press, and Stimson was barraged by anguished cries from congressmen and editors. To isolationist America, the enthusiasm at Geneva was the glad eye from a lady of doubtful virtue.

Gilbert was under instructions to make it absolutely plain that his government would take no action whatever under the League Covenant, but that it would give its moral support and the benefit of its counsel on questions relating to the Kellogg-Briand Pact.

He was permitted to make only two kinds of speech: a repetition of his instructions and a polite thanks for kind words. Even then the pressure from those who feared that American diplomats were being lured by the fleshpots of Europe was such that within a week Stimson was on the verge of ordering Gilbert to desist even from that exercise. The Secretary was narrowly dissuaded from doing so only by the fear that it might further incapacitate the League in a crisis in which the United States plainly had a stake of major proportions.

Gilbert actually attended no more than half a dozen sessions and then retreated quietly to his customary role in the wings, having been the first and last American to participate openly in the Council's deliberations.

Off-stage activity now grew so feverish that little time was left for open diplomacy at the Council table. Drummond was locked in almost constant conference with Yoshizawa or Sze or Briand or Lord Reading or Italy's Dino Grandi, or any combination of these that seemed to fit the needs of the moment. At one point newsmen and the representatives of the little powers were growing so suspicious of the closed doors that Briand was obliged to call a public session of the Council, which, since rehearsals had not been completed, accomplished little but tiresome restatements of position.

A significant break did come, however, in one of Drummond's private talks with Yoshizawa. Japan had been demanding, as a prerequisite to troop withdrawal, not only guarantees of safety for Japanese personnel but full Chinese confirmation of railway rights granted Japan under treaties with the old Chinese Empire. When Drummond suggested that troop evacuation might proceed while the treaties were being negotiated, Yoshizawa unexpectedly agreed.

That this mood of sweet reasonableness was more than a passing fancy of Yoshizawa's was indicated by a seemingly casual encounter in Washington between Ambassador Debuchi and Undersecretary of State Castle. Debuchi, who had dropped into Castle's office for a chat, itemized the package which Shidehara was prepared to offer in negotiations with the Chinese: a mutual declaration of nonaggression in Manchuria; an agreement by both sides to suppress "hostile agitation"; protection for Japanese subjects in China; arrangements to prevent "ruinous railway competition and to carry into effect existing railway agreements"; a Japanese reaffirmation of the "territorial integrity of China, including Manchuria." Castle passed along the word to Stimson, who sent it through Gilbert to Drummond.

Eager to take advantage of the new wind from Japan, on the evening of October 22 Drummond sent Yoshizawa to find Lord Reading and win Britain's blessing for the new move. However, Lord Reading threw cold water on the entire plan and refused even to discuss the matter. Lord Cecil later acknowledged that Britain was in deep financial trouble and that, to Lord Reading and the policymakers in Westminster, "it seemed a matter of relatively small moment what happened in Manchuria, where Britain had no territorial interests and very little trade."

Drummond then cornered Yoshizawa again and suggested that he ask Sze in a public session of the Council whether China was prepared to carry out its obligations under the treaties. If Sze agreed, as might be expected, Yoshizawa could then cable Tokyo that he had scored his point and evacuation could proceed. If the treaties were later contested, the matter could be taken to The Hague, Drummond suggested.

The wind from Tokyo had changed again, however, and Yoshizawa told Drummond that his government had no confidence whatever in The Hague. Drummond maintained that he thought The Hague probably would have ruled in Japan's favor. The Japanese government, however, embattled by its rebellious military, felt that this was not the time to step out on that particular limb, and so ended its brief flirtation with peace.

By November, Drummond began to have grave doubts that anything short of total conquest could satisfy the Samurai spirit of Japan's warrior class. On November 6, he wrote to his Deputy Joseph Avenol: "The Japanese aims are now quite clear. They are: 1) to obtain the recognition by China of certain Manchurian agreements which China has up to now contested; and 2) to subtract Manchuria from any dependence on Nanking. Obviously China can never agree to such demands, nor are the methods used to obtain them in accord with the principles of the League. Further, if the League fails in this matter, not only is the value of the peace-keeping clauses of the Covenant destroyed . . . but also the disarmament conference [scheduled for the following February] is seriously endangered . . . This is why I regard this matter as absolutely vital from the League point of view and for the general principles for which the League stands."

Contributing to Drummond's depression in that bleak November was the sniping from within the camps nominally on the side of the League. In another letter to Avenol, dated November 10, Drummond expressed his conviction that in virtually every country the overheated nationalist press and the munitions makers' lobby were "clamoring against further pressure being put on Japan in the present circumstances; and it is these elements which are equally opposed to any successful issue being found at the disarmament conference."

Actually, Avenol himself was in disagreement with Drummond both on his method and on his view of the merits of the Japanese position. The conflict of style and policy between the two men exploded in the following weeks.

On November 13, 1931, Drummond wrote in pained discomfiture, though not in anger, to Avenol: ". . . there is one thing that rather alarms me in your suggestions, viz., that the conversations should be directed in order to obtain negotiations on the substance of the matter between China and Japan. Now, the Chinese—and I think rightly—have said that they will not have direct negotiations . . . as long as they are under pressure of military occupation . . . On such a point I do not think that we can possibly press the Chinese to give way, as if we do, we cannot but create a precedent for the future, of a most dangerous character. In fact, I can see the military elements in certain countries applying the same reasoning and thinking with joy of the results . . ."

Drummond also took issue with Avenol's position upholding the Japanese view that the Chinese government was unable to maintain order in its Manchurian territories. "I am not so certain that this is so," Drummond told Avenol. "They were ready to send up a large number of picked and reliable troops, and it seems that these would be as capable as the small Japanese forces of maintaining order, if the Japanese would allow them to do so."

This note of Drummond's was followed less than two weeks later by a bitter blast from Avenol. "For the first time in nine years," Avenol wrote to his chief on November 26, "I have not been admitted to a secret meeting of the Council which on this very occasion took place in the offices of the Minister of Foreign Affairs of France.

"After the first surprise, reflection showed me that this incident was the logical culmination of the situation. . . . In undertaking yourself the work concerning the Sino-Japanese conflict you have undertaken to assume by yourself alone the relations of the Secretariat with the two parties concerned and with the American observers . . . This is a considerable personal effort to which I render homage and which I sincerely hope will end in the interests of the League of Nations.

"I permit myself, however, to point out that this is not without risk of weakening the confidence, based on collective action, of the Secretariat and on the organic division of labor. I came here in the hope of assisting you at a difficult period. Since my arrival I have remained in complete ignorance of your actions and your plans."

Outside Drummond's official family criticism was even harsher. The commentator Pertinax wrote in *L'Echo de Paris:* "Japan has been goaded into taking extreme measures by the provocations of the League of Nations." In fact, the closest the League came to firmness, much less to provocation, was a resolution hatched by Drummond and formally proposed in the Council by Briand. The resolution called on Japan, whose delegate had repeatedly assured the Council that it would pull out its troops, actually to do so within three weeks' time. It would then sit down to negotiate all outstanding problems with the Chinese. Under the particular article of the Covenant chosen by China as the legal basis for its case, Article XI, the unanimity rule could be invoked. Japan, unlikely to overlook so formidable a weapon in its arsenal, wielded its veto effectively and the motion was lost.

(That veto was promptly immortalized in a play entitled *Yoshizawa's "No" at Geneva*, which ran throughout the winter and spring in Tokyo and added to the war fever.)

It was at least possible that, by using existing precedents or by shifting the legal basis of the discussion, Britain and France, with United States support, might have circumvented that veto. The willingness was all and the willingness was plainly lacking.

Presiding over these paralytic deliberations was the newly designated chief of the British delegation, Sir John Simon, a brilliant lawyer with a mind keenly tuned to the diplomacy of the nineteenth century, determined to offend no power and to play the subtle balancing games that had been the very stuff of international maneuvers in centuries past. Lord Cecil still tried to uphold the League, collective security, and British fair play, but he wielded little power.

Sir John Simon made it abundantly plain that Cecil, who headed the British League of Nations Union and was of too aristocratic a lineage to be shelved, was being retained at the League to keep him away from the Disarmament Conference. When Thanassis Aghnides, then secretary of the Disarmament Commission, suggested in a private conversation that Cecil be put on the British disarmament team, Sir John told him why it was impossible: Cecil was so convinced a disarmament advocate and so little concerned with partisan politics that he would bring down the government at Westminster, if necessary, to gain his objectives.

Cecil himself complained that Sir John was "not prepared to take any step to compel Japan to leave China—not even to urge that a diplomatic protest should be made by withdrawing the envoys of League powers from Tokyo."

In the stalemate which followed Yoshizawa's "No," the Council met in Paris. Drummond went along with a coterie of experts from the Secretariat staff and set up headquarters in a hotel along the Quai d'Orsay. To maintain the behind-the-scenes contact, Stimson wired Charles G. Dawes, United States ambassador in London, to take a suite at the Hôtel Ritz. The veteran diplomat, who in 1924 had helped engineer the plan to ease German reparations, was known to be unsympathetic to the League. Stimson's instructions, however, were plain: "You should be in Paris available for conferring on matters which affect treaty rights and general interests of the United States. . . . I do not want to push or lead in this matter. Neither do I want the American Government to be placed in a position of initiating or instigating League action."

Stimson sent word to Dawes at the Ritz that, if the Council decided on sanctions against Japan, United States public opinion would support it and Washington would not interfere. This green light might or might not have emboldened Britain and France, but in any case Dawes apparently failed to transmit the signal and the session accomplished little, either on or off stage. Dawes's failure to communicate was apparently characteristic. When his advisers suggested that he might consent to see one or two members of the Council in private, he said curtly: "I have no use for a town meeting."

The mood of the French public that had worried Drummond became unpleasantly clear when Lord Cecil went to the Trocadero, Paris' favorite hall for political confrontations, to address a pro-League rally. As expected, hecklers from the far right turned up in force and howled down every speaker except Cecil—possibly out of deference to Britain's popularity in anti-League circles—and the Italian representative, who carried impeccable Fascist credentials from Mussolini. As the meeting continued, brawls broke out all over the hall in what Cecil described as "the kind of light-hearted ferocity which a French crowd seems to enjoy." The unperturbed attitude of the gendarmes at the Trocadero seemed to Cecil to reflect the approval of such antics by the government of Premier Pierre Laval.

To break the impasse Drummond dispatched his undersecretary, Frank Walters, to Tokyo to persuade Japan of the value of a conciliatory gesture. The evidence of Walters' success is only circumstantial, but in any case it was shortly after his mission that Yoshizawa accepted another Drummond invention: a fact-finding commission to Manchuria. It was to be headed by Japan's friends, the Great Powers, and would include United States representation to assure the little powers that there would be no whitewash.

The idea was made attractive to Japan by a threat and an inducement. Stimson, in Washington, alarmed Debuchi by suggesting that he might release all of the confidential memoranda between them, which, with its evidence of broken promises to withdraw and repeated apologies for the runaway military, would have produced a sensation in Tokyo. The inducement lay in the fact that formation of the Commission would give Japanese diplomats some breathing time while the military machine might continue on its way. (It was that very factor of delay, however, that made the usually amenable Dr. Sze rebel at last. It took innumerable hours of argument and the combined pressures of Drummond, Britain, and France to win him over.)

When the commission proposal emerged on stage, Japan took the role of proponent, introducing the resolution on November 21 as if it had come from Tokyo or had been born in Yoshizawa's brain.

Then ensued weeks of weary comma chasing and word-by-word bickering over the "terms of reference," with Japan quite aware that the Council could not break off negotiations no matter how long they dragged on. The resolution, as finally approved, set up a commission whose only duty would be to "study and report." It was to have no authority to arbitrate, mediate, or control any of the developments which then seemed to be swiftly moving Japan's way.

To the small powers the Commission seemed painfully inadequate. Panama and Colombia, which had unwillingly entertained landing parties of United States Marines, considered it ominous that the massive invasion of one state by another should be fobbed off with the appointment of a toothless investigating commission.

Adding to the frustrations of the year's end was the retirement of

Aristide Briand. The announcement of his withdrawal from active diplomatic life was anticlimactic, acknowledging formally a decline that had already become painfully obvious.

He had been defeated not only in Geneva but in Paris as well. In the spring of 1931, at the age of sixty-nine, Briand had aspired to the presidency of the Republic. He had carefully planned his bid, assuring himself of the support of the most powerful kingmakers in France, the veteran politicians André Tardieu and Pierre Laval, but at the last moment it became clear that he had been lured into a fatal trap. After Briand was committed to the race, Tardieu shifted his support to Paul Doumer and Briand suffered a humiliating defeat. Politically he was destroyed.

In Geneva, his decline was obvious and pathetic. France's Undersecretary for Foreign Affairs, André François-Poncet, would sit next to Briand at Council meetings and present him with typewritten instructions for every point on the agenda. In private conference Briand could still assist Drummond, but he was plainly a lion whose teeth had been pulled, left to be a target for ferocious French editors. By the end of 1931 he was physically and spiritually drained. With formal regrets, Briand's resignation was accepted in January 1932 and by mid-March he was dead.

As 1932 opened, Drummond himself came under the same type of fire that had formerly been leveled against Briand. The British anti-League press assailed him as an intriguer for internationalism. The pro-League press denounced him for working with his Japanese undersecretary, Yoturo Sugimura, to protect Japan from any outright condemnation. Even Lord Cecil wrote privately to him to warn of the perils of the diplomatic game.

"I cannot tell you of the harm the secret negotiations have done in this country," Cecil wrote from London. "For the first time there is a real movement against the League which has extended to the Disarmament Conference . . . If I could believe with you that secrecy materially assists success . . . that of course would have to be considered. But I confess the evidence . . . seems to be slight. Unless you struggle against it, the tendency of all Foreign Offices will always be in favor of secrecy and most foreign ministers will share these views because it seems safer and besides, increases their personal importance."

Drummond's answer was an outspoken defense of his belief in open covenants privately arrived at: "Unhappily I agree with you that the Manchurian affair has dealt a severe blow to the League but I cannot but disagree entirely when you suggest that this is due to the secrecy of the recent negotiations . . . It is my absolute belief, and I think I have had more to do with the negotiations than anybody, that if we had tried to negotiate in public we would never have gotten anywhere . . . Of this I am quite content to take the responsibility, but I am not prepared to take it as regards the limits with which the great powers, and chiefly Great Britain, forced us to work . . . We must do our best to pull through in circumstances which are going to be exceptionally difficult."

When on January 23, 1932, Drummond served notice of his intention to resign, it was logical to assume that he was doing so under fire and as a confession of failure in the Manchurian crisis. He insisted, however, that he was preparing to retire for purely personal reasons and, though these were never spelled out, considerable credence was given to them.

Gilbert wrote to Stimson on January 30: "Speculation is of course, rife as to the 'political' reasons, particularly those connected with the Manchurian affair or disarmament, governing Drummond's resignation coming at this juncture. While it is probably inevitable that his action will have political consequences, I am personally convinced through having had knowledge of his intentions for some time and from conversations with him that his decision to resign is based almost entirely on personal considerations."

His resignation was not to be effective for another eighteen months—until June 30, 1933—and in the meantime Drummond redoubled his efforts at quiet diplomacy, working in close collaboration with Stimson.

Stimson himself was under attack now, not only from the isolationists in Congress, such as senators William E. Borah and Hiram Johnson, but from the Japanese as well. His obviously friendly feelings toward Shidehara and his civilian regime was becoming an acute embarrassment and stirring violent reactions from the Japanese military.

Ambassador William Cameron Forbes in Tokyo alerted Stimson to the frenzy of the continuing attacks on Shidehara. The Seiyukai, a party in Japan somewhat closer to the officer class, "had even threatened to bring [Shidehara] into court for revealing military secrets," Forbes reported.

Within a few weeks the Seiyukai had toppled the Shidehara government—oddly enough while the Diet was not in session—and Ki Inukai, certainly more friendly to the military, though not completely in their pocket, assumed the premiership.

On a Saturday afternoon toward the end of December, the new Premier came by the American Embassy in Tokyo and patiently listened to a sermon from Ambassador Forbes, who later reported to Stimson: "I quoted the words of an observer who had told me that in Manchuria, Japan was creating a situation which was fraught with the certainty of future war, for with the alienation of Manchurian sovereignty, China would not rest a gun. I was assured by Inukai that never would Japan allow such a situation to arise and never would Chinese sovereignty be impaired."

At the same time on Stimson's desk was a cable from Minister Johnson in Peiping: "Marshal Chang Hsueh-liang at 9:30 this evening ordered withdrawal of all Chinese forces from Manchuria stating that he was motivated by a desire to deprive Japan of any excuses for further aggression in North China . . . This ends Chinese administration in Manchuria." In a conversation with Forbes, Premier Inukai blandly expressed sympathy for Chang, that "hot-headed young man" who was naturally upset at being deprived of his powers as "king of Manchuria."

Yoshizawa, whom the new Inukai government had summoned home from Geneva to assume the Foreign Ministry, seemed very cordial to the American ambassador and spoke glowingly of the sacred "open door."

"He laid great stress upon the open door so often," Forbes cabled Stimson, "that when I commented on its not being open now he said this was merely during the period of suppressing banditry. I told him it took us six years to suppress banditry in the Philippines where we exercised sovereignty and intimated that the door might be closed for quite a while. But he emphasized the desirability of attracting American capital and business cooperation to Manchuria."

In Geneva members of the Commission of Inquiry were being recruited and passing muster before the horseshoe table: Lord Lytton of England; General Frank McCoy, who had fought with Pershing in France, representing the United States; General Claudel of France; Count Aldrovani-Mariscotti of Italy; and Dr. Heinrich Schnee of Germany. With Lord Lytton as chairman, the Commission got off to a painfully slow start. While Chinese delegates chafed, the Commission spent an inordinate amount of time apparently in packing its bags, and did not start for China until February 3. Instead of taking the shortest possible route—via the Trans-Siberian Railroad—the Commission chose to head westward, by train and ship, with liberal stopover time in Tokyo, Shanghai, and Nanking; it did not reach Manchuria until April, four months after the Council had authorized the mission.

While the Commission was proceeding with glacial speed, diplomatic moves were writing at least footnotes to history.

In the first week of January, Stimson, prodded by Drummond, issued a dramatic unilateral declaration to the effect that the United States would not recognize any Sino-Japanese agreement that might impair any rights of the American government or its nationals in China, or any situation produced by violent means contrary to the Kellogg-Briand Pact.

Stimson forwarded copies of his statement (thereafter known as the Stimson Doctrine) to London and Paris, inviting the governments there to make similar declarations. The answer from London was so cool that it chilled Anglo-American relations for years.

"His Majesty's Government stands by the policy of the open door for international trade in Manchuria," the reply said. Japan had "given assurances" that it would maintain that open door. Hence, the brief note concluded, there was no need to send any such expression of opinion to the Japanese government. France added its eloquent silence, and Japan, seeing the green light flashing from Europe, allowed a week to elapse before dispatching a model of ironic prose to Washington:

"The Government of Japan were well aware that the Government of the United States could always be relied on to do anything in their power to support Japan's efforts to secure the full and complete fulfillment in every detail of the Treaty of Washington and the Kellogg Treaty for the Outlawry of War. They are glad to receive this additional assurance of the fact . . . It might be the subject of an academic doubt whether in a given case the impropriety of means necessarily and always voids the ends secured, but as Japan has no intention of adopting improper means, that question does not practically arise . . .

"At the present juncture, when the very existence of our national policy is involved, it is agreeable to be assured that the American Government are devoting in a friendly spirit such sedulous care to the correct appreciation of the situation."

To historian Arnold Toynbee, the Japanese note "came within an ace of insolence," but the London *Times*, which had given Stimson's message a very bad review, found Tokyo's response "courteous in tone" and "reassuring." It went on to advise the British government that it does not seem to be "the immediate business of the Foreign Office to defend 'the administrative integrity' of China until that integrity is something more than an ideal."

The official Chinese reaction was one of gratitude to the United States, but unofficially a Chinese spokesman saw in the message from Washington a suggestion of further foreign intrigue over the prostrate body of China, and, in any case, no sign of immediate rescue. "It has the head of a dragon," he said, "but the tail of a rat."

"I seemed doomed to inaction," Stimson wrote later in recalling his frustrations.

The League might have resigned itself to total impotence had not some workers in a Shanghai towel factory taken a hand in the matter. On

January 9, the *Min Kuo Jih Pao* (*Daily News*) of Shanghai reported the failure of an assassination attempt on the Emperor of Japan by a Korean and commented on what a pity it was that the would-be assailant had picked the wrong car in the imperial parade. The Japanese colony in Shanghai considered this editorial note to be in bad taste, and their consul-general, Kurumatsu Murai, demanded an apology.

Nine days later five Japanese Buddhists, including two priests, were walking past the Sunya towel factory when they were jumped by a group of Chinese, who left three of them injured and one dead. A band of fifty members of the Japanese Youth Protection Society retaliated by burning the Sunya towel factory to the ground. The Japanese in Shanghai began to hold mass meetings calling upon Tokyo to send in reinforcements. Promptly a Japanese cruiser and several destroyers steamed into the harbor.

There were swift repercussions in Geneva, London, Paris, and Washington. Shanghai, a world trading center, was a very different matter from the remote hinterland of Manchuria. Each of the leading commercial powers of the world held a sector of Shanghai, with its own military and police forces, through which they channeled a profitable China commerce. On hand in this Chinese port when the towel factory burned down were 1,200 United States Marines, 2,300 British troops, and 2,000 Japanese sailors and marines.

Admiral Shiozawa, reflecting a certain tendency among Japanese naval officers to envy the army its share of glory in Manchuria, took a very firm position. He handed General Wu Te-chen, Mayor of Shanghai, an ultimatum calling for withdrawal of Chinese forces in the tenement district of Chapei, where they allegedly posed a threat to Japanese nationals.

At first Mayor Wu demurred, objected to a clause here and there, and played for time. The United States consul-general in Shanghai, Edwin S. Cunningham, sent a reassuring message to Washington that Admiral Shiozawa had promised not to order his men into action without consulting authorities of the International Settlements, whatever else he might do with the Mayor. On January 27, Mayor Wu capitulated and Japanese Consul-General Murai was fully prepared to call the incident closed. However, he was not reckoning on the pride of the navy. At eleven o'clock that night Admiral Shiozawa announced that his marines were going into Chapei to protect Japanese nationals and that he hoped the Chinese would withdraw what he termed, with delicious absurdity, their "hostile defenses."

In Geneva, the atmosphere of the Council Chamber was tense as the clock on the wall signaled the end of the Admiral's ultimatum. Shortly thereafter secretaries poured in with telegrams reporting panic in Shanghai and hospitals under bombardment.

Allowing no time for a possible withdrawal of any defenses, the Japanese forces had opened fire on Chapei. The bombardment lit up the sky and killed thousands of Chinese civilians. This time the atrocity was undebatable. It shocked the world into awareness that this was not an "incident" but "war in all but name," as one British delegate at Geneva, R. H. Thomas, termed it. Public opinion in Japan also began to register doubts.

The Chinese, fighting in the beginning with no more than small arms, resisted the Japanese assault for a month. It was the first major armed resistance of the war, and the heroism of the civilian fighters, later supplemented by units of the Ninth Route Army, did more to unify China than all the lofty sentiments of its diplomats.

The major powers were galvanized by the spectacle of war amid their own international enclaves. Within two weeks of the outbreak of fighting in Shanghai, the United States had sent the cruiser *Houston* and a flotilla of destroyers from Manila along with the 31st Infantry and about six hundred Marines. The British and French also began to bolster their Shanghai garrisons.

Stimson sent a stream of messages to Forbes in Tokyo ordering him to deliver strong oral protests to Yoshizawa. He told him to voice the "deep concern" of the State Department; to express fond hopes that the Japanese contemplated no action "in contravention of the interests and rights of other nations, China included"; to announce ship movements from Manila; and to warn that the United States would "view with deep regret" any interference with the R.C.A. transmitters controlling Chinese communications from Chenju, seven miles from Shanghai.

Yoshizawa told Forbes that Japan had no intention of interfering with anyone's interests in China but maintained that anti-Japanese agitation in Shanghai had reached an "extremity." Forbes reported that Yoshizawa had told him that "the Japanese people were so stirred up by the organized anti-Japanese movement in China that failure to take a firm stand would result in the immediate fall of any cabinet."

For all of these protests Forbes had to wait his turn in the queue which formed at Yoshizawa's office as diplomats of other nations lined up to register verbal blasts.

Meanwhile, incendiary bombs continued to fall on Chapei and bitter hand-to-hand fighting raged between the well-armed Japanese and the

Chinese irregulars. At the same time the entire United States Navy found itself in the Pacific for a series of maneuvers that were to last all spring.

At the Palais Wilson, Drummond had formulated a plan for an emergency committee of big-power consular representatives in Shanghai to handle the emergency. At first Stimson had grave reservations and wired United States Consul Cunningham in Shanghai instructing him not to participate in the round table. "I do not desire . . . to be drawn into proposals," he said, "which will appear unfair to China or as an endorsement of Japan's position."

Within days, however, Stimson rescinded those orders and permitted Cunningham to join the British, French, Japanese, and Chinese representatives in the talks aboard the British flagship *Kent* in Shanghai harbor. He insisted, however, that the agenda be limited to the immediate military problem in Shanghai.

Meanwhile, the Assembly, then in session in Geneva, had finally asserted itself and made a tentative stab at taking the management of the crisis away from the Council and the Great Powers that controlled it. What gave the Assembly its opening was a move by China (at Drummond's prodding) to shift the legal basis of its claim from Article XI of the Covenant to Article XV.

This article in effect transferred the scene of action to the Assembly, thus eliminating the threat of a veto, and carried the theoretical possibility of sanctions against Japan. That possibility of direct League intervention was academic, however, inasmuch as the big powers, the only ones capable of implementing such a step, remained set against it.

Article XV required the Assembly President, Paul Hymans of Belgium, to try once again to arrange a "settlement" before any action could be taken. This meant another go-round of the verbal battle, and this time it ended only in a decision to await the report of the Lytton Commission.

However, the Assembly did set up a committee to deal with the problem in competition with the Council. This step was plainly meant as a criticism of the big powers, who had up to then controlled negotiations, but in order to reduce the sting, all Council members were included on this committee along with six others from the Assembly. It was chaired by Assembly President Hymans. The "Committee of Nineteen," as it came to be called, set a precedent by taking over the Council's horseshoe table for its meetings.

For the moment the Assembly committee could do little more than maintain constant contact with the wardroom of H.M.S. *Kent* in the harbor of Shanghai. The League, however, was no less affected than it would have been had the parleys taken place in the glass-walled Council Chamber. Subsequent debates, maneuvers, plots, and counterplots in Geneva would be intelligible only in the light of what was happening in Shanghai.

On February 28, the urbane and diplomatic commander of the *Kent*, Sir Howard Kelly, sent word to the Committee that "the discussions were most friendly throughout" and that "the principle of mutual and simultaneous withdrawal was agreed to."

Three of the signatories to that agreement had to do their signing in Shanghai hospital beds. Two of the Japanese commanders had been injured by a bomb, tossed by a Korean during a military review in Hongkew Park to mark the Emperor's birthday. The Chinese signatory was being treated for injuries suffered in an assault by Chinese students who were critical of the armistice terms.

The Chinese in Chapei—those who had survived the fighting—withdrew in good order to previously prepared and fortified positions. The Japanese, after a face-saving occupation of the tenement rubble, evacuated all but a small garrison from Shanghai without punishing the Chinese. The denouement had a most invigorating effect on the anti-Japanese boycott.

Throughout China there were "victory" celebrations which, according to custom, involved noisy fireworks. At Nanking one such display panicked the Japanese forces, who, thinking they were under fire, proceeded to shell the Chinese capital from their gunboats in the Yangtze. The bombardment did not last long but sufficed to persuade Generalissimo Chiang Kai-shek to decamp with his entire government.

The results of the Battle of Shanghai electrified Geneva. All the powers on the Council who, barely six weeks earlier, had disdained Stimson's pleas now did an about-face, dispatching an urgent appeal to Japan, this time without the absurd fiction of an identical note to China. The message was polite but pressing. It recalled Japan's record of punctilious behavior in the League and appealed to its "sense of honor." It also reminded Tokyo, as Stimson had done, that no infringement on the territorial integrity or independent status of a League member was to be recognized if brought about by external aggression.

Toward the end of February, Stimson fired another verbal salvo. He sent a letter to Senator William E. Borah of Idaho, chairman of the Senate Foreign Relations Committee. Plainly meant to be read in Tokyo, Geneva, London, and Paris, it lumped all of the complex system of treaties in the Far East into one indivisible structure and announced that a violation of any one of them would mean a nullification of them all. He underlined the point by declaring:

"The willingness of the American government to surrender its then commanding lead in battleship construction and to leave its positions at Guam and in the Philippines without further fortification was predicated upon, among other things, the self-denying covenants contained in the Nine-Power Treaty which assured the nations of the world not only equal opportunity for their Eastern Trade but also protected them against the military aggrandizement of any other power at the expense of China."

The implied threat to Japanese domination of the Pacific shocked naval circles in Japan. An unnamed spokesman for the Japanese fleet was quoted in the press as saying that it would be "extremely serious for Japan if Mr. Stimson's note could be interpreted as implying that the United States had resumed its right to fortify Guam . . . The Japanese Navy could not believe that Mr. Stimson meant to convey such a threat."

Viscount Ishii, one of Japan's aristocratic elder statesmen, warned that if the United States attempted to block Japan's "pacific and natural expansion in this part of the world, then, indeed, a grave situation would be created."

The Japanese, however, had reason to doubt that any thunder from the West would be accompanied by lightning bolts. They had heard the thunder before and also the cries of the isolationists. The Philadelphia *Record*, for example, had declared: "The American People don't give a hoot in a rain barrel who controls North China."

For the Japanese there was disquieting news from Moscow as well, which up to now had beheld the Japanese advance toward its Siberian borders in nervous silence. Early in 1932 the Russians resumed diplomatic relations with China, which had been broken off five years before, after Chiang Kai-shek turned on the Communist wing in the Kuomintang and sent out of the country every Russian diplomat he could find.

Now, having failed to secure a nonaggression pact with the Japanese, Moscow moved closer to the Generalissimo, who was looking for a friend himself. The Chinese Communists were less than enthusiastic about the development. The Japanese voiced a certain alarm but sought to turn the situation into a propaganda advantage. "The news is most unwelcome," a spokesman for the Ministry of Foreign Affairs told newsmen. "The elements most disturbing to the peace of the world have now joined hands and Japan stands squarely against these forces."

At this point Japan's domestic front became more troublesome and chaotic than any sector of its military or diplomatic campaigns abroad. The nation seemed to be undergoing a slow coup by assassination at the hands of the Samurai-agrarians. In February a "Death Band" had been founded by a Buddhist priest and a naval airman who fed each other's appetite for medieval heroics when they first met at the London Naval Conference in 1930. (The airman died in the Battle of Shanghai but the Band carried on.) In February, Junnosuke Inouye, a former Minister of Finance, was shot to show the Death Band's disdain of politico-financiers. Then came the turn of Baron Takuma Dan, marked as a symbol of big business since he was the general director of the giant Mitsui firm.

In March a group of uniformed officers entered a Tokyo hospital and seized ex-Senator Dr. Inazo Nitobe, who had served as the Assistant Secretary-General of the League of Nations from 1919 to 1926. They whisked him off to the headquarters of the Army Reservists' Association, where he was asked to explain statements attributed to him to the effect that militarism was as dangerous as Communism. Dr. Nitobe convinced them that he had referred only to Chinese warlords, not Japanese officers. The Band let him go and he promptly took off for a pro-Japanese lecture tour in the United States, thereby probably avoiding any subsequent attentions of the Death Band.

On May 15 Premier Inukai was chatting with his daughter-in-law in the drawing room of his home when he heard the sounds of scuffling at the front door. His daughter-in-law pleaded with him to take shelter in the cellar or to escape out the window. Instead, Premier Inukai, a bit of a Samurai himself, flung open the door for his assassins, lectured them severely, and dared them to kill him. They did.

At the same time six other members of the Band, all officers, toured the city, blowing up headquarters of the ruling Seiyukai party (apparently not quite warlike enough for them), the main police station, the Bank of Japan, the Mitsubishi Bank, and the home of the Lord Keeper of the Privy Seal. Attempts were also made on the power stations but these were less successful.

When they were not tossing bombs, the group scattered leaflets identifying themselves as "Young Officers of the Army and Navy and the Farmers' Death Band."

Actually, with all the bombing and shooting, the Premier was the only fatality, although scores were injured. When it was all over, seventeen members of the Band turned themselves in to the military police in accord with the traditions of Samurai honor and to distinguish themselves from criminals. Their punishment was light, the sentences nominal, and it is doubtful that any of them actually served time.

High military officers disclaimed responsibility but were clearly sympathetic to the gallant murderers. On the day after the assaults, *Asahi*,

Tokyo's largest daily, commented that "it is doubtful that discipline could be maintained if the high officers were associated with the politicians who lack the country's confidence. The nation should therefore get rid of corrupt party governments and demand a strong national government able to cope with the present situation."

Prince Saionji, one of the few remaining elder statesmen, bowed to the winds of change and advised the cloistered and largely impotent Emperor Hirohito to invite Admiral Saito to form a government. Saito had been known as a liberal, but he was now prepared to knuckle under to the military. The difficulty was that the Samurai code was eloquent on sacrifice and honor but silent on the mysteries of governing a twentieth-century state reeling amidst the world-wide economic depression.

The agrarian knights-in-armor insisted that something must be done about the wretchedly impoverished silk farmers, whose condition continued to worsen, but they offered no clear program. In midsummer Count Koken Tanaka, an ex-minister of the Imperial Household, then nearing ninety, jolted the country with another dramatic gesture. He threatened to commit hara-kiri unless the farmers were helped. The Diet was called into extraordinary session to prevent the suicide and promptly voted measures costing some two hundred and fifty million yen. These sums saved the Count's life and honor but left the silk farmers not much better off than they were before.

In Manchuria the military spirit was clearly in better shape to handle the situation. Meeting only the most ineffectual resistance from remnants of Chang Hsueh-liang's forces, the Japanese were quickly bringing all of the three northern provinces under their control.

They had installed Henry Pu-yi, their unemployed Manchu Emperor, first as President-for-life, then as Regent, and finally as the Emperor Kang Teh of Manchukuo. He was a slim, young-looking man with thin gold-rimmed eyeglasses, who could look passably imperial in a uniform hung with ribbons and medals. His Empress, dressed in traditional Chinese-doll costume, was equally serviceable.

The Japanese always insisted that there had been a spontaneous cry from the Manchu masses for their beloved royal family, but, in the mountain of documents on the question, there is almost no hard evidence of such a clamor. And the heavy Japanese garrison needed to maintain Pu-yi did not reflect wide popular enthusiasm. When Pu-yi announced to the world the founding of his new state based on "morality, benevolence, and love," not a single nation responded except Japan, which promptly sent a delegation to sign treaties of nonaggression and eternal friendship. Actual recognition was postponed until the fall.

The puppet play was eminently useful. If Manchukuo could be regarded as independent, its goods could be kept out of the Japanese domestic market, to which it would have had unrestricted access if it were considered a Japanese overseas territory. At the same time its exports could be used to break into new foreign markets. The fiction of independence was also useful in appeasing Japanese public opinion, too much in love with "honor" to accept a naked land grab. It enabled Japanese delegates in Geneva throughout that year to maintain with the straightest of faces that their government coveted no part of Chinese territory.

Throughout the spring, meanwhile, the League's fact finders, under Lord Lytton, had been making their way to Manchuria. They had arrived in Shanghai too late for the battle but in time to pick up eyewitness accounts after the event. Their deadline had originally been set for July, but it had to be postponed, causing mounting uneasiness among the small powers, who feared that history would be made by military aggression while the League, their only defender, was searching for the truth amid the rubble.

Fact finding in Manchuria had certain difficulties—at least for the Chinese observers. L. T. Chen, a Shanghai banker, Y.M.C.A. official, and lecturer, who held degrees from both Yale and Harvard, joined the Commission when it passed through his city. He was chosen to assist Wellington Koo, the Chinese observer—or "assessor," in Geneva terminology—by Lord Lytton, who was struck by Chen's unfailing cheerfulness and wit, as well as his knowledge of Manchuria.

Chen later reported to the Shanghai Rotary Club that he had spent "two of the most leisurely weeks I remember in my life," confined to the Yamato Hotel in Mukden, where he admired the Japanese waitresses and the plum blossoms. He had perfected his billiard style "when life became so dull and I was driven to look for activity."

The Japanese informed Mr. Chen that he would have to report to the police every time he left the hotel so that bodyguards could be assigned, and that under no circumstances was he to go beyond the Japanese settlement. He was allowed no visits from Chinese Manchurians. "Any Chinese who came within the precincts of the hotel," Chen said, "was liable to arrest and at least three cases were known who were carried off to Police Headquarters, under suspicion of attempting to see the Commission or the Chinese assessors."

He pointed out that "this courtesy was extended to all members of the Chinese delegation. . . . So for the time we lived in Mukden we lived like an Emperor who dwelt in his forbidden quarters." He thought the hotel service splendid, the food excellent, and came back fifteen pounds heavier even if no better informed. The non-Chinese members of the Commission put up with these restrictions on their colleagues in order to have some of the investigative freedom they sought for themselves.

In mid-July, the work finished in Manchuria, the Commissioners stopped off in Tokyo. Ambassador Joseph C. Grew, who in the meantime had replaced Forbes, talked with General McCoy, the American member of the Commission. The general called Manchukuo "a festering sore which will inevitably lead to future wars with China and Russia and a case of irredentism much worse than that of Alsace-Lorraine." The Japanese were running Manchuria more efficiently than had the Chinese, McCoy admitted, but he saw in that no justification for the conquest. The tone of the Lytton Report was forecast as tactful but tough.

Grew warned Stimson that any United States effort to oppose Japanese recognition of its puppet state might play into the hands of the military. "Apropos of this," he wrote, "a prominent peer recently said to a member of my staff, referring to the military, 'I hope they will change their minds before they wreck the country.'" Grew said Japan's economic plight was "serious and it may become desperate." The farmers were in a bad way, unemployment was rising in the cities, and the yen was falling. He had heard, he said, though he could not confirm it, that Japan had unsuccessfully sought loans from England, France, and Holland.

The answer of the military, Grew noted, was to pour oil on the flames of anti-American sentiment and rely on "patriotic nationalist frenzy" to obscure the grim economic facts, "as in Germany in 1914."

The Japanese war machine, he added, "is built for war, feels prepared for war and would welcome war. It has never yet been beaten and possesses unlimited self-confidence. I am not an alarmist but I believe that we should have our eyes open to all possible future contingencies. The facts of history would render it criminal to close them."

Despite the pressure from Japan's vainglorious army, the Japanese statesmen were concentrating not on a military showdown but on the decisive diplomatic confrontation looming in Geneva in the fall, when the Lytton Commission was expected to submit its report. At this point attention turned to Yosuke Matsuoka, a man whose personal qualifications and career seemed to destine him for the role of Japan's knight of the horseshoe table.

Matsuoka's English was impeccable. (He had been graduated from the University of Oregon.) He had been Japan's delegate to the Versailles Conference and had signed that pact for his country. He had been a consul-general in Mukden and a vice-president of the South Manchuria Railway Company. He had participated skillfully in the negotiations aboard the *Kent* at the Battle of Shanghai. He was fifty-two, ambitious, and a rising star in Japanese politics.

The right-wing groups, however, who were already calling for withdrawal from the League, voiced some doubts about Matsuoka's reliability. Actually, Matsuoka's instructions from moderates such as Prince Saionji and Baron Makino were to find a way to save the League's face and allow friends in London and Paris to arrive at a compromise that would avoid a Japanese walkout.

In preparation for his mission, Matsuoka went into seclusion at a spa in the Hakone Mountains and studied all of the relevant documents, including a copy of the Lytton Report.

That document was harsh, in some respects at least. It bluntly declared that Manchukuo was a Japanese puppet state, condemned Japanese military action, and undercut all of the Japanese claims of "self-defense" and Chinese "aggression." But, on the other hand, it acknowledged Japan's "legitimate" interests in China, as it did those of other powers. It granted Japanese claims that China was weak, divided, and incompetent to handle its own affairs, although it pointed out that this was additional reason why no undue advantage should be taken. (It pointedly did not consider the commercial exploitation by the Powers as any undue advantage.) Although it ruled out any outright carving of Manchuria from the body of China, it recommended a certain "autonomy" for the province on the grounds that the central government was not yet in a position to administer it. Finally, it had some complimentary things to say about Japan's administrative efficiency and recommended a "closer rapprochement" between China and Japan, with international cooperation in the reconstruction of China. It stressed the point that Japan must be represented by an "adequate number" of advisers.

To Matsuoka the report offered room for maneuver, and he was successful in talking the military into a tactic of agreeing to discuss the report at Geneva. Earlier they had favored a blunt refusal even to consider it and a demand for direct negotiations with China without the interference of the League, Europe, or the United States.

In September 1932, Matsuoka took the Trans-Siberian Express for Geneva, stopping in Moscow on the way to turn down a Soviet bid for a nonaggression pact. He did, however, assure Foreign Commissar Maxim Litvinov that Japan would not violate any Soviet rights in China so long as the Soviet Union did not interfere with Japanese operations in Manchuria. This was not merely a sop to the Russians. It had long been

Matsuoka's conviction, shared by many of the anti-Communist military agrarians in Japan, that no regime could be solidly planted in Manchuria without the benevolent, but not too effusive, blessings of the Soviets.

Once in Geneva, Matsuoka lost no time in taking advantage of the gulf that yawned between the big and little powers. He went into private conferences with Britain's Prime Minister MacDonald and Foreign Secretary Simon, each of whom lent an attentive and understanding ear. He went to Paris to talk with Premier Herriot. He wooed Drummond directly and through his undersecretary, Yoturo Sugimura.

Arranging for a series of Japanese broadcasts to be beamed directly at the United States, he went out of his way to court American newsmen in Geneva. After November he realized that the election of Franklin D. Roosevelt made Stimson (and perhaps his "doctrine" as well) a lame duck. He thereupon opened conversations with Norman Davis, known as a confidant of the President-elect. Davis was in Geneva at the time as an American representative to the Disarmament Conference.

Matsuoka emphasized in his talks with Davis that nothing could divert Japan from carrying through its present policy in Manchuria, where it was motivated, in large part at least, by fear of the Soviet Union. This, he thought, would be quite understandable in the United States.

Matsuoka said that he was himself disturbed by the anti-American feeling in Japan, which he characterized as quite "dangerous." He said it was based largely on the popular view that the United States was attempting to block Japanese moves in Manchuria in order to gain possession of the railway system there. "In spite of the fact that thinking Japanese realize that American public opinion has no thought of war," Matsuoka told Davis, "the Japanese government may be forced to take sides with the already inflamed public opinion in the event of some incident."

Concerning the outlook in Geneva, Matsuoka warned that if there should be what he considered "a concerted derogation of Japanese dignity," Japan might have to leave the League.

Davis' rejoinder was mild but to the point. He stressed the fact that Stimson entertained no hostility toward Japan and that the situation in Geneva now offered a "constructive opportunity" for Japan to "work out a solution with the other nations of the world."

Matsuoka closed the interview by describing his countrymen as "a race which is patient for a long time, but a point is arrived at which, with suddenness and violence, the repressed irritation breaks bounds and releases itself."

On the eve of the climactic session in Geneva, the indefatigable Ambassador Debuchi came by the State Department, where Stimson advised him to inform his government that the new Roosevelt administration was not likely to modify a position which had been "taken deliberately as a matter of principle." A week later President-elect Roosevelt told a press conference: "American foreign policy must uphold the sanction of international treaties. That is the cornerstone on which all relations must rest."

In Geneva, Matsuoka listened, with considerable equanimity, as Ireland's Connolly declared: "If the League falters or hesitates, fearing lest by its action it may offend, then as an organization built up by the moral support of what is right, it will not survive and in my opinion, will not deserve to survive." Nor did Czechoslovakia's Beneš alarm the Japanese when he said, with what later seemed like a grim foreboding of his own fate: "The League will emerge from this test greater and stronger and will inspire confidence, if we succeed in finding a worthy solution to the problem. Otherwise it will wend its way towards a period of weakness, disillusionment and skepticism, and thus one of the greatest and boldest undertakings of the human mind will inevitably be stricken down."

Spain (having come down from its position of "dignified abstention"), Ireland, Sweden, and Czechoslovakia joined in filing their own tough resolution, emphasizing the point, which tended to be lost in the debate, that the Lytton Commission had found Japan guilty of seizing Chinese territory by military force. The resolution proposed by these little powers would have authorized the Assembly's Committee of Nineteen to approach the United States and the Soviet Union for assistance in settling the dispute.

Matsuoka objected: "I am afraid . . . that the handling of this resolution may, I even think will, entail consequences perhaps not intended or anticipated by the authors of the resolution." The resolution was quietly tabled and never came to a vote.

The speeches of Sir John Simon were more significant, as well as more heartening to Matsuoka. Sir John, carefully selecting those passages of the Lytton Report which described the utter chaos of China, so delighted Matsuoka that he committed the gaffe of thanking him on the floor and declaring that Sir John had said "precisely what I have been trying to say."

This expression of gratitude from a prisoner in the dock might have been expected to unsettle a statesman supposedly playing a judicial role. Actually Sir John compounded the offense when reporters gathered around him after the session. He threw up his hands and exclaimed: "After all, what is China? A geographic expression!"

Matsuoka, in fine fettle, told the Assembly: "Our distinguished colleague from the United Kingdom very aptly said yesterday that none of us can accept the report of the Commission of Inquiry *in toto*. I do not quote his words, but refer to the sense of them. May I be allowed to undertake to improve his statement just a bit." He did so by eliminating the Latin.

He went on to point out the cost of additional League efforts, to be borne principally by the Great Powers, and talked of Japan's role as a guardian of all foreign interests in China and its desire to help China outgrow the stage of tutelage. He also noted, for the ardent supporters of the League, that the institution had already "fulfilled the high object of its existence" by preventing war between China and Japan.

In seventeen months Japanese forces had occupied all of Manchuria, a territory far bigger than France and Germany combined, but would not call it war. The Chinese could not claim that a state of war existed because Generalissimo Chiang Kai-shek had never so much as severed diplomatic relations with the invaders.

Canada and Australia carried the Commonwealth banners into the fight, defending the Japanese even more blatantly than did Sir John.

Italy's Baron Pompeo Aloisi said that the crisis was "a test not of the efficacy but of the elasticity" of the League and called for "a solution based on realities."

Baron von Neurath of Germany deplored talk "on the basis of more or less absolute principles."

France seemed to have lost interest altogether.

A compromise was in the wind, in the form of a conciliation commission, which, like Lytton's group, would have very little power but would extend invitations to the United States and the Soviet Union to participate.

Quite pleased with himself and confident that he had preserved Japan's respected place in the League and its army's unshakable position in Manchuria, Matsuoka went off on a Christmas holiday to Vienna (he was very fond of Mozart), Istanbul, Rome, and Milan. When he returned to Geneva, Matsuoka found, as many League diplomats had before him, that the rug had been pulled from under him. The right wing in Tokyo, grown restless, had won the day. His instructions now were to reject any conciliation machinery that involved the United States and/or the U.S.S.R.

Drummond told Matsuoka privately that the Commission would include his friends, the big powers—the United Kingdom, France, Italy, and Germany—as well as Belgium. The participation of the United States was absolutely vital, he warned, if the smaller powers were to be appeased. The invitation to Moscow, he said, was a mere formality since there was no doubt that it would be rejected. (The Soviet press had been bitterly assailing the League as a collaborator with Japanese imperialist aggression.)

Matsuoka then engaged in a series of heated telegraphic exchanges with Tokyo and tried to light fires among Japanese newsmen. One day he gathered together the entire Japanese press corps in Geneva and said that, if he were forced to reject the commission idea, Japan would have to withdraw from the League of Nations. He meant this as a threat to the moderates at home and to the business interests, who had a considerable stake in international trade and good will. Unfortunately those were not the most influential forces in Tokyo, and Matsuoka's maneuver backfired.

Instead of taking alarm at the prospect of Japan's withdrawal from Geneva, the Japanese press began to clamor for it. Again and again Matsuoka put the alternatives to Tokyo in the form of an ultimatum and the answer was always: Withdraw.

In those days the diplomatic barometer could best be read in Geneva's Hôtel Métropole, where the Japanese delegation was headquartered. Matsuoka customarily signaled a deteriorating situation by emerging from his suite clad in a brown kimono and carrying a bottle of French cognac. In the closing days of February 1933 the brown kimono appeared frequently like a danger flag in a hurricane season.

On February 24, 1933, Matsuoka listened to the motion accepting the Lytton Report, then rose and walked out of the Assembly chamber. Members of his delegation, who were scattered throughout the hall, got up and followed him amid total silence.

On his return to Japan, Matsuoka broadcast a message to the nation in which he said: "If all our efforts have failed and we were forced to withdraw from the League, in that event I wanted to do my best to let the foreigners understand the spirit of our nation without equivocation . . . If I had to part company with others, I wanted to be like a cherry blossom in its graceful parting."

The West, even in the friendliest capitals, did not think of cherry blossoms when they thought of the Manchurian crisis. Matsuoka for his part became disenchanted with all of the Occident—with the possible exception of Mozart. He took to reading Buddhist sutras and declared that he preferred a Japanese tearoom to Vienna's Schönbrunn Castle. "Only in the tearoom can one find the soul of Japan," he said. Finally he concluded, "There is no such thing as one humanity."

Late in March came Japan's anticlimactic notice of its intention to withdraw from the League. (Under the Covenant two years' notice was required, but this was a technicality; when Matsuoka walked out Japan went with him.)

The delegates at Geneva tried to tidy up the disorder after Japan's withdrawal. A report based on the Lytton findings had been accepted with one abstention, that of Siam, and a commission was pieced together. Predictably the Soviet Union declined the invitation to join, but this time with unaccustomed friendliness, signifying the new winds from that quarter and the rising influence of Maxim Litvinov. The Soviet rejection noted that "a certain concordance may be observed between the starting points of the decisions taken by the League and the views of the Soviet Union." The Soviet Union at the same time promised to associate itself with any League action calculated to settle the conflict.

The United States fully endorsed the action of the League and agreed to be represented on the Commission, as always reserving its traditional right to remain "unentangled." Once formed, however, the Commission proceeded to hibernate in a slumber that was to last unbroken for four years until the onset of a new war in China.

The British, with evenhanded injustice, clamped an arms embargo on both mighty Japan and powerless China. The Foreign Office explained that this was an interim move until other powers—principally the United States—might join in a genuine anti-Japanese embargo. Cordell Hull, shortly after taking over the State Department from Stimson, sent a message to the Senate Committee on Foreign Relations, then considering just such an embargo. Hull argued that the move would do little good since Japan would only seize arms addressed to China, and that in any case it was quite capable of supplying its armies. The bill died in committee.

Japanese forces went on to capture Jehol in North China while Chiang Kai-shek made an uneasy peace, ending the war that never was.

The departure of the Japanese from Geneva, where they had long served as some of the League's most conscientious advocates and earnest negotiators, was followed within a few months by the farewell of Sir Eric Drummond. He summoned the Secretariat staff in the Palais Wilson for a ceremonial leave-taking. This was one public appearance Drummond could not avoid. He dreaded it, but it was a gesture that could not be made behind closed doors.

"I notice," he said, "that there is, even among us perhaps, a certain feeling of pessimism as to the future of the League. Before I go, I want to say that I am convinced that that pessimism is neither justified nor well-founded.

"It is true that the political outlook may be a little black today but I feel—and M. de Madariaga [Spain's philosopher-diplomat] once told me that if an Englishman feels, he is probably right; it is only when he begins to reason that he goes wrong—that the League is really in an unassailable international position, that it has come to stay and that we need have no fears on that score."

Drummond was whistling in the dark. There were, however, some grounds for cheerfulness even in the shambles left by the Samurai. Thanks largely to Drummond's astute back-room negotiating, the United States had been wooed closer to the League than it had been since Wilson's time. The Soviet Union, also, was clearly on its way into the League.

Drummond went off to Rome as Britain's ambassador, charged with the task of keeping Mussolini away from Hitler. His friends and associates at the League tried to dissuade him from accepting the assignment. It set a dangerous precedent for League executives, who might henceforth trim their sails in office with the prospect of a diplomatic plum on retirement. Further, Drummond had received confidential information on Italy, and statesmen in the future might think twice before revealing their minds to a Secretary-General who might one day use the information in a different capacity.

Drummond's successor had been picked in the course of a strenuous ten-day meeting of an Assembly subcommittee in September 1932, shortly after Drummond had given notice of his intended retirement. It had been assumed all along that Sir Eric would be succeeded by Sir Alexander Cadogan, a man very much in the Drummond mold. But at about the time the matter came up, Albert Thomas, the French head of the International Labor Organization, dropped dead at a table in a Paris café. The I.L.O. post was then filled by a British Laborite, Harold Beresford Butler. It would not do to have Englishmen at the top of both the League and the I.L.O., and Cadogan thus had to be passed over.

The likeliest candidate then seemed to be Joseph Avenol, the most highly placed Frenchman in the League and Drummond's unloved deputy. At fifty-three Avenol was a frustrated banker and looked it. He dressed in formal black suits, imported from England, wore his collars starched stiff, and peered through rimless spectacles, humorlessly and with considerable distaste, at the diplomatic scene.

He had been persuaded into this alien world of international politics in 1922 by Poincaré to replace Jean Monnet, who was retiring from the financial apparatus of the Secretariat. Avenol had made clear his preference for a job in the Bank of France, for which his entire past, his interests, and his predilections seemed to qualify him. In 1905, as a highly conservative young man with only the most impeccable right-wing associations, Joseph Avenol had come out of the School of Political Science at the University of Paris and scored first place in the qualifying examinations for a post in the French Treasury Department. He had risen steadily since then. During the war he organized the finances of military zones and later went to London as financial attaché in the French Embassy. He was an inspector-general in Paris when Poincaré thought of him as France's man in League finances.

Avenol reluctantly took up his post in Geneva and proved himself an able administrator when no political issues were at stake. He devised financial solutions for Hungary, Greece, Bulgaria, Estonia, and China. In 1929 Drummond sent him to China, a trip which, Avenol felt, entitled him to some recognition in the handling of the Manchurian crisis. In actual fact, however, he was not vitally interested in or particularly well-informed on political matters. Pablo de Azcarate, the ranking Spanish diplomat in the Secretariat, said Avenol's usefulness was limited to the administrative side and that "whenever he mixed into political questions there was a catastrophe." The American Arthur Sweetser, then in the Secretariat, described him as "distant" and "cynical."

Drummond sought every possible alternative to Avenol. He tried in vain to persuade Monnet to return to Geneva. He offered the name of a Dutch justice of the Permanent Court, but that dignitary preferred to stay at The Hague. Drummond turned to his undersecretary, Yoturo Sugimura, a mountain of a man with the face and build of a Sumo wrestler and the agile mind of a diplomatic tight-rope walker. However, the Japanese march through Manchuria made such a nomination unthinkable.

The proposal of the Americans Newton Baker or Norman Davis stirred a very cool reaction among the Powers, inasmuch as it would seem to confess a lack of talent in Europe. Why not the Scandinavians? Drummond suggested in desperation. Germany and Italy ended that line of pursuit by indicating their preference for the national of a Great Power. A representative of a small power, they said, would in the end be dominated by the English or the French and they preferred to confront such influence openly.

Prentiss Gilbert, in a memo to Stimson, explained the preference for Avenol: "Avenol is much less industrious than Sir Eric, and it is felt that under his direction there would be more decentralization of authority which the representatives of a number of powers have long been anxious to bring about."

Accordingly, when Drummond paid his farewells and left the Secretary-General's mansion, La Pelouse, Joseph Avenol moved in, installing his English mistress, Vera Lever, as his hostess. She made up in wit and affability for the somewhat pedestrian style of the new Secretary General. (Mme Avenol, who had introduced Miss Lever to her husband, stayed on in Paris, refusing to consent to a divorce.)

Avenol and Miss Lever tended the gardens at La Pelouse with devotion. They gathered paintings for the mansion, since art was one of their major interests and their term of occupancy stretched ahead for ten years, a semipermanent lease. It might have seemed that at last the League was getting its low-key, nonpolitical administrator, a role for which Drummond had been miscast and which he declined to play. The difficulty was that Avenol inherited an office which Sir Eric had made into a key political post. Furthermore, he was taking it over at a time of the organization's most formidable crises.

From the start Avenol exhibited an extraordinary sensitivity to the Japanese point of view in the Manchurian crisis. Commenting on the new approach, Prentiss Gilbert wrote: "I cannot express too strongly my impression of a decided intent to denude this League endeavor . . . of any political connotations which might be offensive to the Japanese or embarrassing to any important government, notably perhaps the British."

Eleven

DISARMING
ILLUSION

At nine o'clock in the morning of February 7, 1932, a procession of
women wound through the Old Town of Geneva. The women wore
white armbands bearing the word "Pax," and sported green sashes on
which were inscribed their country of origin. Many of them carried
bundles—"like presents for a Christmas tree," as the *Journal de Genève*
described the scene. The packages contained petitions bearing the signatures of over eight million persons from all parts of the world appealing
for an end to the arms race and an assurance of peace. The women were
bringing them ceremonially to the opening of the World Disarmament
Conference, seven years in wordy preparation, the fulfillment of a League
of Nations promise made in the halcyon days of the Protocol.

There were a few men as well, in that parade of women. Viscount
Cecil of Chelwood slouched along in a greatcoat that reached to his
ankles. He was a member of the British delegation, but he marched that
day as the representative of the League of Nations Associations. Tall and
fierce with jutting goatee, Léon Jouhaux was also in the ranks, representing officially some fourteen million French trade-unionists. And the
Belgian socialist and delegate Emile Vandervelde, wearing his usual wide-
brimmed floppy fedora, called out from the line of march: "We do not
ask—we demand."

They trooped into the dreary hall that had been set aside for the
Conference by the city of Geneva and piled up the petitions in front of

the podium until the stacks threatened to topple off the edge of the stage. Delegates themselves brought up more millions of signatures, so that Mary Dingman, representing some forty-five million women in a variety of organizations, had to speak to the delegates over a barrier of paper. She flung at them the statistic that every twenty-four hours some sixty-five million gold francs were being spent on preparations for war. And an American student, James Green, suggesting that the ten million who died in the late war "were victims of an illusion when they fell to earth only a few years ago," presented what he termed "not a petition but an ultimatum."

The idea of permitting the emphatic and uncomplicated affirmations of plain people to be heard for at least one morning came from the President of the Conference, Arthur Henderson, who beamed from the dais throughout the two-and-a-half-hour plenary session, reading scores of telegrams, all voicing an almost universal clamor for peace. This was one of those rare mornings when the issue appeared neat and simple: peace or war. Henderson would have liked it to remain that way.

"Arthur Henderson always kept a clean desk," wrote his biographer, Mary Agnes Hamilton. It would be hard to find a more apt characterization of him. A stolid Scot socialist and ardent Wesleyan Methodist, Henderson cut the figure of a *bon bourgeois* in Geneva. In his walks along the Rhône he wore a bowler hat and carried a rolled umbrella. When he played tennis with the Drummonds or with Beneš, he exchanged his bowler for a cloth cap, which gave him as jaunty a look as he could carry off.

His biographer noted that "some Socialists are positively alarmed by Switzerland, seeing it as Exhibit A of the flattening of values by general comfortable diffusion." But not Henderson. He was at home in Calvinist Geneva, in the prim rectitude of his hotel, the Beau Rivage, with its potted plants and antimacassars, its view of the lake that gave an air of Brighton-by-the-Sea. Arthur Henderson touched neither liquor nor tobacco ever since as a young man he determined to "follow Christ." His Christianity led to the trade-union movement and to socialism. He had gone to work as an apprentice to an iron molder at the age of twelve. Like MacDonald, he had learned his socialism under Keir Hardie in the 1890's. When the war broke out, Henderson suspended his pacifism although MacDonald did not. Since that time, however, MacDonald had come to water the purity of his convictions more than had Henderson, and by the opening of the Disarmament Conference the two had reached a definite break. MacDonald was the Prime Minister of a coalition government and Henderson was a leader of the opposition. The Prime Minister was reputedly less than pleased when the League Council chose his erstwhile counselor to preside over the Disarmament Conference. For Henderson, broken in party politics, the assignment was a new lease on life. Bolstered by his aides, Philip Noel-Baker and Konni Zilliacus, he recovered his spirit for what was to be a final effort.

This humorless, conscientious Wesleyan Methodist socialist was given a task which Arnold Toynbee compared with that of Alice in her heroic croquet game, during which she had to contrive mallets out of reluctant flamingos and balls out of hedgehogs that would not stay nicely curled into shape. Throughout the years of laborious preparation, agreements kept coming undone as fast—or faster—than they were made.

Disarmament had been enshrined as Point Four of the Fourteen Points; it was included in the Covenant of the League; and the Germans were persuaded to accept their own disarming as the "first steps towards that general reduction and limitation of armaments which . . . will be one of the first duties of the League of Nations to promote."

In 1925 the United States, Germany, and the Soviet Union were invited to join with League members in preparations for a world disarmament conference. Germany and the United States agreed, but the Soviet Union demurred. A Russian observer had been murdered in Lausanne and the Swiss courts had promptly acquitted his anti-Bolshevik assassin. No relations with Switzerland would be tolerated by Moscow until reparations were made. A token payment to the victim's family was eventually conceded, however, and in 1927 a delegation of eighteen Bolsheviks showed up in a hostile Geneva to take their seats for the first time at an international assemblage. The debut was not auspicious. All the hotels in Geneva declined to accept them until the Swiss government obliged one of them—the Angleterre—to admit the dread guests under heavy guard.

This was not Maxim Litvinov's first entrance on the diplomatic stage. He had appeared—as a voice from the wings—at Genoa in 1922 and had successfully lured the Germans into friendly gestures toward a rapprochement. In 1927 in Geneva, only the Germans and the Turks dared break the icy cordon of the anti-Bolshevik powers to have an occasional friendly chat. A stout, bespectacled, twinkling-eyed Pickwick of a revolutionary, Litvinov had served his apprenticeship by working as an editor with Lenin. He went to jail repeatedly and repeatedly escaped.

Years before the war he could no longer do his work in Czarist Russia and took the road to exile in London, where he found a job as a clerk in a bookseller's firm, lived in Whitechapel, and taught Russian to a handful of students (including, ironically, Rex Leeper of the British Foreign Office). He married Ivy Lee, the daughter of a British professor at the University of London.

Litvinov came to public notice in England in 1918, when the Soviet government formally named him ambassador to the Court of St. James's. Inasmuch as his Czarist predecessors refused to relinquish their building, he set up his embassy in a two-room flat on Victoria Street. It was there that he was arrested in reprisal for the jailing in Moscow of Bruce Lockhart, for whom he was subsequently exchanged, to the satisfaction of all concerned.

With the warm and good-humored Litvinov came Anatole Lunacharsky, the Commissar for Education, who had tried in vain to re-create the Russian Orthodox Church in a Bolshevist image. A lean and sharp-featured man, with pince-nez and reddish beard, he was often in the shadow of his wife, who sported an array of jewelry that raised the eyebrows of bourgeois Geneva.

Lord Cushendun, who had taken the place of Lord Cecil as head of the British delegation that year, recalled having dandled Mme Ivy Litvinov on his knee when she was a child. The connection helped to thaw the Anglo-Russian chill. In his youth Cushendun had once made a stir by tossing a book at the head of Winston Churchill during a stormy debate on home rule for Ireland. Now a venerable white-haired diplomat, he told the delegates that "war would no longer be a gallant adventure but a national dishonor."

The Americans produced for the occasion a diplomat of the most consummate polish. Hugh Gibson's iron-gray hair, his clothes of the most elegant cut, and his suave smile lent a gloss of high professionalism. He was the American ambassador in Brussels; he was known to be a personal friend of President Hoover; and he had endeared himself to many Europeans by his fight for the life of Edith Cavell, the British nurse who was shot as a spy by the Germans when they occupied Belgium.

Somewhat marring the smooth Gibson style, however, was the persistent presence of lobbyists representing American armaments manufacturers, who were perhaps the only ones who credited the Conference with sufficient vigor to impair their future. One such arms promoter, a man named Shearer, was said to have attempted to bribe American newsmen and, according to Major General A. C. Temperley, the British military adviser, was "in touch with minor members of the American delegation and received useful information from them."

In 1927 and in the five years of preparatory conferences that followed, the delegates did a curious dance. Most would state a very firm position only to retract it later for the sake of harmony, so that at times the sessions seemed, as General Temperley called them, "an orgy of conciliation." So it went with proposals to abolish conscription or limit the armed reserves or set a ceiling to arms budgets. One after another the schemes would be launched, and then sadly withdrawn. Every such sacrifice was made mournfully and heroically and greeted with the warmest sympathy as the hallmark of a truly conciliatory spirit. When the French surrendered the hope of limiting the nations' military budgets, Temperley reported, the development was "rapturously welcomed by the U.S. delegate, who was again driven into ecstasies of enthusiasm when the French made the further sacrifice of giving up investigation on the spot by an international commission."

Only Litvinov continued to plug for total, unconditional disarmament down to rifles.

There were a few close shaves. At one point, in 1929, there was an attempt to assuage French demands for security before disarmament by sharpening Article XVI of the Covenant, which dealt with the application of economic sanctions against an aggressor. Temperley summed up the reactions of the British delegation on rewriting the article: "Our chief refuge in this respect had always been its vagueness and any more precise definition of its language was contrary to our interests. Various formulae were hawked around and I thought at one time that we should be committed. Fortunately we withdrew in time."

(Actually the League Assembly on three separate occasions between 1924 and 1932 voted to stiffen the sanctions article, but none of the proposed amendments received the necessary ratifications to bring them into force.)

When Arthur Henderson called the long-delayed Disarmament Conference to order in 1932, the seven years of backing and filling had resulted in no preliminary agreements whatever. Henderson had a draft resolution which in fact met the requirements of few of the Powers and was expected to be largely ignored. It was precise on the limits of German armaments and vague on that of other Powers.

Still, the bare fact that the Conference was being held was a victory over the cynics. The Republic and Canton of Geneva had thrown up two new hotels for the delegates of the sixty nations, had established a temporary conference hall near the Secretariat, had hung all the bridges over the Rhône with bunting, and, most hospitably of all, had fixed firm ceilings on prices in cafés, stores, and restaurants.

The mood on February 2, 1932, was nonetheless grim. The opening session was set for three-thirty in the afternoon, but it had to be post-

poned an hour to allow the disarmament delegates to attend an emergency meeting of the League Assembly on the Japanese invasion of
Manchuria. Even aside from that melancholy opening chord, there were
gloomy rumblings. Only a month earlier President Hoover had chilled
the ardor of the disarmers by declaring that the Conference "would be of
something less than primary interest to the United States." The American
delegation would be instructed, he said, to make no promises about reducing United States land forces, it was to offer no security guarantees and to
stay clear of the much dreaded "entanglements." Still, the dapper Gibson
arrived with what he called "an open mind," which did something to
dissipate the fog of despair over Geneva. And Henderson firmly announced: "I refuse to contemplate even the possibility of failure."

To maintain that stoic optimism, Henderson had to grit his teeth in the
gales that blew from Manchuria and from Germany, where Hitler stood
on the threshold of power. Confronted by such inclement weather,
Henderson held to the legalities of the situation as to a mast. The German
demand for "equality" in disarmament had an undeniable basis in the 1919
commitments. How to achieve that without endangering the security of
Europe was the challenge.

Henderson's opening speech was an earnest if uninspired statement.
The French response was prompt and sharp. *Le Petit Parisien* noted that
"in eight large printed pages" Henderson had avoided "uttering even
once the words of sanctions or mutual guarantees." While the Conference took time off to receive the parade of petitions and attended to the
process of dividing into committees of the whole and specialized commissions, the French delegate, André Tardieu, performed a deft flanking
maneuver. It had been understood that the Anglo-Americans would open
the general debate on February 8, offering a scheme for limited disarmament, drawing the distinction between offensive and defensive weapons,
and favoring a general recognition of the German claim to equality.

Three days before, in the afternoon of February 5, the French circulated their own plan. It embodied France's traditional preoccupation with
strengthening the League as the one rock of security on which all
disarmament schemes must rest. It would place under League command
all tanks, bombers, and heavy artillery of the world. Though these would
be stockpiled in the countries that produced them, they could be used
only in defense of national territory or with the approval of the League.
The League was to be given its own police force, very much as had been
proposed repeatedly and without effect by Léon Bourgeois back in 1919.
Arbitration would be compulsory and nations which rejected such peaceful solutions would face severe sanctions.

Tardieu closed his presentation of the new-old plan with a proper French flourish: "Finally the present conference offers the greatest opportunity which has ever occurred for a definite choice between a League of Nations disposing of an executive authority, and a League of Nations paralyzed by the intransigency of national sovereignty. France has made her decision; she asks that other nations make theirs."

They had, in fact, made their decisions long ago. Delegates of the major powers treated the restatement of the French position as the tiresome plowing of a well-worn rut. Most speakers ignored the plan in debate. Litvinov poured scorn on the proposals, recalling that not long ago many of the leading powers in the League were invading his country and he could not see security in entrusting them with the world's heavy armament. He called again for total disarmament, and when the delegates laughed at what they conceived to be yet another rut, the jovial Russian joined in, sensing perhaps the total unacceptability of simple solutions.

The Persians and the Turks were the only ones to rally to Litvinov's position. The Japanese took a diametrically opposite view, insisting that the Disarmament Conference firmly oppose any measures to disarm.

Sir John Simon looked neither to Paris nor to Moscow but plunged straight ahead along the Anglo-American line favoring a "qualitative disarmament," which tried to distinguish between "offensive" deadly weapons and "defensive" deadly weapons.

The German Chancellor, Dr. Heinrich Brüning, approached the matter gingerly. All of the diplomats knew that he was performing a most difficult and daring balancing act. With the Nazis howling for his scalp, it was clear that his political life depended upon his bringing back from Geneva at least some hope for German "equality" in armaments. He made his pitch moderately but firmly.

The Italians supported his claim. So did Sir John. After the first round of opening speeches it was clear that the French had lost again, and that there was an Anglo-American disposition to at least compromise with the Germans. The Manchester *Guardian* summed up the view from London this way: "After the opening bravura of the French 'what might be' theme, the Conference got down to business with the staid British enunciation of 'what could be.'" Dr. Brüning's willingness to accept some control over bombers, of which Germany had none, and his resistance to any limitation on civilian planes, of which it had many, prompted the *Guardian* to remark that his proposals "could hardly escape a slightly academic air—as of the lamb lecturing the wolves on the advantages of vegetarianism."

Still another parable of the animals came from Spain's Salvador de

Madariaga, who summed up the opening gambits of the Powers this way: "The lion, looking sideways at the eagle, said, 'Wings must be abolished.' The eagle, looking at the bull, declared: 'Horns must be abolished.' The bull, looking at the tiger, said, 'Paws, and especially claws, must be abolished.' The bear, in his turn, said, 'All arms must be abolished; all that is necessary is a universal embrace.' "

When the speeches were over, Beneš and his committee went off and developed an agenda of 104 items. The Conference approved that formidable schedule of labor and then adjourned, on March 3, for a week to discuss the Manchurian crisis.

They reconvened on the eleventh and adjourned again for Easter on the nineteenth. The London *Daily Herald* commented: "It is now five weeks since the Disarmament Conference first met, and people are beginning to wonder when it is likely to finish. It is more urgent to ask when it is going to begin."

Although the desultory progress within the conference hall made the *Herald*'s question pertinent, events were moving elsewhere that would have an impact on Geneva. Before the Easter recess General von Hindenburg was re-elected to the presidency of the Reich, polling 18.6 million votes to Adolf Hitler's 11.3 million, and Dr. Brüning was reprieved from extinction. He had swung the country behind Hindenburg and felt that presidential gratitude would strengthen his hand. Still, the German mood was impatient and Brüning would have difficulty living with it.

The *Deutsche Allgemeine Zeitung* commented: "Six weeks of the Conference and we realize that twelve years of work have prepared nothing at all . . . it is an unsuccessful Conference which only awaits the final blow which is to finish it and with it our hopes of equality of armaments . . . Unless we at last abandon our reserve . . . unless we try either to revive the Conference after its breakdown and to divert it towards general disarmament, or, if already too late for that, we ourselves resolve to give the final blow to the Conference. Our gun is the Preamble to Part V of the Treaty; our shell: If not equality then liberty!" The liberty to which the newspaper referred was, of course, the liberty to rearm with or without consent of the Powers who had won a bitter war twelve years earlier.

If, however, Germany was to rearm in defiance of the Powers, the diplomacy at Geneva would have to be declared a failure. Chancellor Brüning was painfully aware that he could not survive the demise of his diplomacy, and that not even Hindenburg's gratitude—an undependable commodity at best—could save him from his Nazi opponents. He proceeded to walk the high wire without a safety net.

Brüning accordingly proposed to the Disarmament Conference that Germany be permitted an army of 200,000 men, to be composed of 150,000 regulars on a six-year enlistment and a militia of 50,000 serving actively for three months and thereafter in the reserves. He asked that Germany be allowed to have all of the types of heavy weapons in the arsenals of other powers, but only in small "sample" quantities—mere tokens of equality. Actually, the proposal, although presented as a reasonable compromise, fitted precisely into the plans of General Hans von Seeckt, the man assigned the task of rebuilding the German army out of the ashes of defeat. He had set as his objective not a mighty mass army but a small, professional, highly mechanized striking force backed by a large reserve of draftees and a tightly organized industrial machine.

Brüning was encouraged by the news that United States Secretary of State Stimson was coming over to take a personal hand and that the British Prime Minister, not to be outdone, would be in Geneva as well. The American Secretary of State arrived on April 15 and moved into the Château de Bessinges across the lake, from which he could have a clear view of the hall in which the Conference was supposed to be deliberating. Actually, the major business was being conducted in the château, where Stimson engaged in a round of conferences with Brüning, MacDonald, and Dino Grandi separately and together. They agreed that Brüning's proposals could be accepted at least as a basis for discussion. The accord of the Four, however, was ineffective without the Fifth, France, and Tardieu was not in Geneva. He had gone to Paris to engage in a fight for the life of his government. They sent urgent messages to Tardieu urging his speedy return, but at that moment he developed a timely and stubborn laryngitis that seemingly would yield neither to medical skill in Paris nor to blandishments from Geneva.

There were a number of complications that may have prolonged Tardieu's laryngitis. The French had a dossier showing very convincingly that the Germans had already rearmed far past the levels ordained by the Treaty of Versailles. As early as March 12, 1932, the French had reported this confidentially to the British, to whom it came as no surprise at all. Temperley later admitted that he had his own dossier amounting to "an indictment of German good faith, backed up by unimpeachable evidence, but, after all, the past was past and we saw no point in raking it up."

Tardieu had therefore little heart for trusting even the liberal Brüning with "samples" of heavy weapons and agreeing to new levels of German troop strength with no guarantees that these would be adhered to any more than had the Versailles clauses. Also, the wily General Kurt von Schleicher, maneuvering to assure the Chancellor's downfall, had delicately hinted to the French ambassador in the course of a Berlin party that Brüning's political doom was sealed and that the French might do better with his successor.

These factors, combined with a dimming prospect for his own government, complicated Tardieu's laryngitis. Stimson and MacDonald thereupon threw up their hands and went home. Brüning also went off to Berlin, sadly declining to talk to the newsmen who saw him off for the last time at the railway station in Geneva.

Brüning had hoped to combat the Nazis by inviting them to share cabinet responsibilities with him, but it was too late for such maneuvers. On May 4, 1932, Paul Joseph Goebbels noted in his diary: "Hitler's mines are beginning to go off. . . . Brüning must go." Four days later Goebbels recorded that Hitler had a "decisive conference with General Schleicher and with some gentlemen close to the President. Everything goes well. Brüning will fall in a few days. The President will withdraw his confidence in him."

Von Hindenburg had indeed found reasons to overcome his gratitude for Brüning's help in the elections. The unlucky Chancellor had suggested that the Reich take over some vast bankrupt estates in East Prussia, compensate their Junker owners, and distribute them to the landless peasantry, which earned for him the indignation of his President and the epithet of "an agrarian Bolshevist." On May 18, Goebbels noted wryly that, despite the balmy season in Berlin, "for Brüning alone winter seems to have set in. . . . He can't find men for his Cabinet. The rats are leaving the sinking ship." On May 29, von Hindenburg asked for Brüning's resignation.

The cast of characters in Geneva was now changed once more. Tardieu was out and a left coalition in France had installed Herriot. His prime antagonist was no longer the seemingly reasonable Brüning but a newcomer to the stage, a Chancellor hand-picked by General von Schleicher after a back-door agreement with Hitler. He was Franz von Papen, whose prime qualifications for public honor up to that point rested on his wife's relations among the industrialists of Germany; his own ability as a horseman; and his war record as German military attaché in Washington, where he was expelled for allegedly plotting to blow up bridges before the United States entered the war.

On June 10, 1932, the Conference on Reparations met at Lausanne, up the lake from Geneva, to effectively cancel the German burden of payment. This was a bitter blow for the French, and Herriot balked at signing the final document until Walter Runciman of the British delegation walked over to him and whispered: "Remember, you fought with *us* against *them*." What was doubly galling to Herriot as he signed was the knowledge that while Germany was to be let off the hook of the alleged "Carthaginian peace," the United States showed no inclination whatever to relax its demands for payment of the war debts owed by France and Britain.

Hugh Gibson had established an American base of operations at the quiet lakeside town of Morges, midway between Lausanne and Geneva, to waylay selected statesmen as they shuttled between the cities. It was there one afternoon that the suave Gibson joined the question of war debts to an arms policy in a forceful effort to persuade Herriot to modify his demands for security. The United States, Gibson said, would not consider reducing the debt without a reduction in the French arms budget.

Back-room diplomacy at Morges had little effect on France and ended by rousing the fury of the little powers, whose delegates were left to while away the time at Geneva like children waiting for their indecisive elders to lay down the law. Led by Spain's Madariaga, they formed what was called the "Straight Eight"—composed of Spain, Sweden, Norway, Belgium, the Netherlands, Switzerland, Czechoslovakia, and Denmark— to oppose the presumably less-than-straight Five—Britain, France, Italy, Japan, and the United States. The revolt met the fate of all such efforts of the little powers to assert their rights. The equality of the ballot flew in the face of a manifest inequality of power.

Major General Temperley expressed the irritation of the mighty at the "unmitigated nuisance" occasioned by protests from the meek. "The most vociferous representatives of the Small Powers," he wrote, "were always nagging at and bullying the Great Powers and telling them to 'play the game.' . . . I have some sympathy with the complaint of Herr Hitler and Signor Mussolini against the Constitution of the League that confers equality as between, say, Germany and El Salvador."

On or off stage made no matter; the negotiations dragged fruitlessly until June 20, when with dramatic abruptness a plenary session of the Disarmament Conference was called on forty-eight hours' notice to hear a bold new plan from the Americans. The affair was stage-managed with the flair of an electoral maneuver. Indeed, observers noted that the event came in the midst of a hard-fought presidential election in the United States, in which President Hoover, dogged by a depression which would not turn the promised corner, was groping for a victory in international affairs. On June 22, the Americans unveiled their plan simultaneously in Washington and Geneva.

The time had come, President Hoover said, "when we should cut through the brush and adopt some broad and definite method of reducing the overwhelming burden of armament which now lies upon the toilers of the world. This would be the most important world step that could be taken to expedite economic recovery. We can add to the assurances of peace and yet save the people of the world from ten to fifteen billions of wasted dollars during the next ten years."

The plan called for a slash of one-third of all existing land forces, a third of naval tonnage, and a third of the number of battleships. It would dismantle a fourth of all existing aircraft carriers and cruisers. It would totally abolish all tanks, heavy guns, and heavy bombers. If it had been adopted, the United States itself would have had to scrap 30,000 tons of war vessels, more than 1,000 mobile guns, 900 tanks, and 300 bombers, thereby easing the hard-pressed American taxpayer's burdens.

Hoover's scheme drew instant support from the small powers and from the Soviet Union. Litvinov accurately pointed out that Herbert Hoover had moved into a position the Soviets had taken as far back as 1928. The Germans gave it cautious encouragement, hoping to tag on their long-demanded equality clause. Dino Grandi telephoned Rome and dramatically announced that Il Duce had given the proposal his blessings.

The British reply was polite but cool. It had reservations about the reduction of the Royal Navy and heavy bombers. The Japanese found the whole scheme unthinkable, since the non-war in Manchuria was calling upon the Empire's full military resources.

The basic problem, as expected, was the French, and their problem was the Americans. Paul-Boncour tactfully called the Hoover plan "attractively simple" but added that it was "too simple." It ignored the French demand for security against aggression, a demand which the Americans had it in their power to grant if they could shake loose from the stern isolationism which still gripped them. To the French, the Americans, from their citadel across the seas, were again preaching high-mindedness to people who felt threatened by a juggernaut. It was a familiar argument that had gone on since 1919. The *Journal de Genève* summed it up: "Mr. Stimson knows that in diplomacy what matters is not to be right, not to have good arguments; it is to have something to give in return for what one asks. America can have disarmament; but she must pay the price. And that price is security. Not security through selective disarmament as M. Gibson proposes; France wants bread not a brioche. The security that Europe asks is the promise that in no case will the United States ever assist an aggression. That is the price of disarmament. Is M. Stimson in a position to pay it?"

Clearly neither Stimson nor Hoover, in an election year, would offer any pledge that could be construed as a loathsome "entangling alliance." In the year 1932, with the illicit German rearmament an open diplomatic secret, with the Nazis on the verge of power, France was not likely to come down on its price. The right-wing press in Paris attacked the plan; the left-wing expressed a certain sympathy for its spirit. All factions deplored what seemed an American attempt to take the Conference by storm. In the end the Hoover plan, although it would have indeed disarmed the nations, seemed little more than a grandstand play.

Throughout the summer the debate dragged on amid increasing acrimony. Litvinov tried repeatedly to save the Hoover plan by amendment and each time went down to crushing defeat. The genial Dino Grandi was replaced by the tougher Italo Balbo. Germany's Rudolf Nadolny took on a new and threatening tone which did nothing to diminish French fears. "The German government," he said, "must point out at once that it cannot undertake to continue its collaboration if a satisfactory solution on this point [equality], which for Germany is a decisive one, is not reached . . ."

On July 26, General von Schleicher broadcast a speech ridiculing the Disarmament Conference and declaring that Germany would not "put up with being treated as a second-class nation any longer" and would rearm "in any case."

L'Echo de Paris retorted: "Germany wishes to do in the full light of day that which she has been doing in secret for the past ten years." *Le Journal* in Paris said it preferred "this frankness to Stresemann's deceitfulness; at least we know where we stand."

In Rome, too, the mood had grown nasty by midsummer. Admiral Balbo called the League "a limited liability company under the control of England, France and indirectly America." He described the Disarmament Conference as "that monstrous factory of delusions and traps for the ingenuous." On that note Henderson moved that the Conference sum up what he called its "progress" and adjourn to allow for private peacemaking. In a vain attack on the adjournment resolution, Litvinov declared: "I vote for disarmament but against the resolution." He went down to a predictable defeat.

At the summer's end Geneva seemed more than ever to be apart from the real world. The delegates were engaged in scholastic disputes as to whether a battleship is offensive or defensive while Manchuria was falling to the Japanese. In Berlin, seventy-five-year-old Communist leader Clara Zetkin was being helped into the presidential chair in the Reichstag, an honor that was hers by seniority. "The President and Government ought to be impeached before the Supreme Court of the Reich," said the frail first lady of German Communism, "only this would be like impeaching the Devil before his grandmother."

The Reichstag then proceeded to elect Captain Hermann Göring as its President, and he in turn moved quickly with the help of von Hindenburg to dissolve that quarrelsome parliament to make way for new elections. Hitler was indeed moving, as he put it, "with the certainty of a somnambulist."

When the Disarmament Conference reconvened in September 1932, the German delegation had officially withdrawn, although Foreign Minister von Neurath remained handily available in Geneva for the League Council and Assembly meetings. A Big Four meeting was set for October 4 in London, but Herriot insisted that if they were going to talk disarmament they ought at least to meet in Geneva so as not to flagrantly bypass the Conference. Baron von Neurath opposed the Geneva site for the same reason that Herriot wanted it—it would have meant Germany's re-entry into the Conference through the back door.

In November the French tried again. Paul-Boncour unveiled a variation on the defeated Tardieu plan. The new elements were presented in an intricate model of a cosmos made up of three concentric spheres: in the outer heavens were the signatories of the Kellogg-Briand Pact, chief among them the United States, which would at last be brought into the scheme of things. The American obligations would be minimal; little more than a promise to "consult" with the victims of aggression.

The second sphere would be composed of League members, who would be subject to the strict interpretation of the Covenant on the application of economic and diplomatic sanctions against an aggressor.

The innermost circle would be the countries of the European continent, who would pledge outright military assistance to any victim of aggression.

Then, if the internationalization of heavy weapons and all civil aviation à la Tardieu were accepted, Germany could have full equality of armaments.

The proposal was ingenious, logical, and precise. It was doomed to failure in an arena dominated by an unshakable Anglo-American commitment to a diplomacy of ambiguity. On the American exemption from hard-and-fast commitments under the Tardieu plan, Anthony Eden commented: "However tolerable such a division of responsibility might have been in practice to all concerned, the British did not want to enshrine it in a treaty." The Americans were noncommittal, clearly unwilling to fit themselves into even the topmost sphere of an international structure. The little powers rallied to the plan as they had to every plan, from whatever source, that promised a hope for peace and disarmament. They watched the balloon go up, as had others before it, hover in the air over Geneva, and in short order sag and fall.

On December 2, the brisk, efficient, cheerful, and ardently pro-League Norman Davis, a confidant of President-elect Roosevelt, proposed "a Christmas present for the world" in the form of a resolution summing up the progress of the disarmament talks and pledging to continue the deliberations until 1936. MacDonald and Sir John Simon came down from London and went into a five-day conference with Davis, von Neurath, and Italy's Pompeo Aloisi in Geneva's lakeside hotel, the Beau Rivage. Von Neurath, however, scorned the proposal as a device to postpone for three years Germany's demand for equality.

However, out of the back-room conference at the Beau Rivage came a face-saving formula that nicely balanced French and German points of view by asserting as the universal objective: "equality of rights within a system which offers security to all nations." Their ruffled feathers thus soothed by mention of the sacred word "equality," the Germans agreed to return to the Disarmament Conference. It was the best the statesmen could afford on that cheerless Christmas of 1932.

Early in the following year Sir Alexander Cadogan, the chief adviser to the British delegation at the Disarmament Conference, outlined his views to Anthony Eden, then in Yorkshire preparing to take over as the government's principal spokesman at Geneva. "This blessed Conference will fail," the elder statesman warned the fledgling diplomat, "unless it is taken properly in hand. We are the people who ought to do that. The French won't; if the Italians did the French wouldn't follow; the Germans would wreck everything; the Americans talk very big when there is nothing doing, but old Norman Davis is a direct descendant of the Duke of Plaza-Toro. We are the only people who could make it a success . . ."

The British up to that point had played the role of the politic naysayer, the skillful evader of unresolvable issues. Sir John Simon, who as Foreign Minister nominally headed the delegation at the Disarmament Conference, offered Parliament a solution that typified his approach: grant the Germans full right to equality in armaments provided they give private assurances that they would not exercise that right. He had been looking about for a bright young diplomat who could carry on in that spirit in Geneva without demanding too much authority.

His choice fell on Anthony Eden, the son of a baronet of venerable lineage, a young man of impeccable good looks who had served gallantly in the King's Royal Rifles during the war, had a charming smile and excellent manners, and wore the proper clothes with distinction. Eden had his odd quirks for a politician: he was well-read, could quote yards of Shakespeare, was an expert on Sanskrit, and spoke Arabic and Persian with considerable fluency, as well as French. An even greater political handicap than his erudition was his pronounced dislike for gentlemen's clubs and his lack of interest in any sport but lawn tennis.

His scholarly tastes, however, scarcely ever intruded upon his conversation. Randolph Churchill wrote of Eden: "No epigram or witticism has ever been attributed to him and he has never made a speech which showed any originality or distinction of thought. Nor has he ever employed any memorable phrases." That seems a bit unfair to him, inasmuch as he once did pronounce a verdict on his century: "Modern communications corrupt good manners."

Though he looked like an elegant thoroughbred, Eden had the talents of a work horse. Following Cadogan's advice, he proceeded at once to prod and drag his government into taking a stand. To do so he drafted a convention on disarmament and then, with Cadogan's help, persuaded MacDonald and Simon to give it an appropriate send-off with a personal appearance of the Prime Minister at Geneva. His plan was a variation of the French proposals, their keenness dulled to make them practical. It provided for a 200,000-man ceiling on continental European armies but allowed France an additional 200,000 troops overseas. It would have limited naval strengths and tanks. (Eden wanted to outlaw bombers, but the Air Ministry insisted that they might come in handy in those parts of the world vaguely designated as "outlying areas.") The United States would be involved in a consultative role and the British navy would be left intact. Germany would be henceforth relieved of all Versailles restrictions, but there would be a five-year trial of international controls before full equality would be achieved.

The details were worked out for each country by General Temperley, who, however, committed the gigantic gaffe of totally omitting Turkey from his list. The Turks raised an enormous furor, asking ironically whether the Bosporus, like the English Channel, was to be considered the boundary of continental Europe. After registering formal protests with the British ambassador at Ankara and in Whitehall, the Turks "were gravely assured," as Temperley reported, "that no slight upon Turkey was intended and reasons were given for the omission that I had never even thought of." He himself had only one, too simple explanation: he forgot.

On the evening of March 15, MacDonald, Cadogan, Simon, Eden, and Temperley wrangled over the plan's details until one in the morning.

Then MacDonald went before the Conference and delivered an address which so heavily interlarded the plan with irrelevancies and preachments that it verged on incoherence. "At one moment," Temperley noted, "I saw him reel backwards and start exhorting the audience to be 'men not mannequins.'" The Prime Minister admitted afterward that for a moment he had come close to losing not only the thread of his discourse but even any consciousness of what he was saying.

The Prime Minister and Simon did not wait for reactions to the proposal, which became known as "the MacDonald plan," but took off at once in a plane, piloted by Admiral Balbo himself, for Ostia. At the airport Mussolini met them, handed them carbon copies of a projected four-power agreement, and asked them to read it while he himself drove them in a limousine at top speed to Rome. The proposed pact left all changes in the Versailles Treaty to the four signatories, promised equality to the Germans if the Conference broke down, and paved the way for unspecified colonial adjustments. MacDonald, greatly impressed by the neatness and discipline of Mussolini's Italy, allowed himself to be photographed giving the Fascist salute, and accepted the pact as a great step forward.

The pact, which was never ratified, stirred alarm in most of Europe. In the House of Commons, MacDonald had trouble defending both the pact and the Disarmament Conference against attacks from all sides of the House. Churchill called the Conference "a solemn and prolonged farce."

In Geneva, German delegate Nadolny took to banging the table as a reflection of the new mood in Berlin, where Adolf Hitler was now Reichschancellor. Germany would not wait five years for equality; Germany would not count as its military effectives the S.A. troops or the Stahlhelm (now enrolled as auxiliary police) or the uniformed crews of its "sport" planes, who had been training in Russia; Germany would rearm, come what may.

On May 1, 1933, Eden wrote to Stanley Baldwin: "One feels it is rather like a 1917 campaign in Flanders; we can only make such progress as we may in the mud between pillboxes . . . and as in Flanders the pillboxes are occupied by Germans."

In the House of Lords, Lord Hailsham declared that the Allies must rally to prevent German rearmament by force if necessary, and his sentiment was echoed the next day by Paul-Boncour in Paris. Franz von Papen, now Hitler's Vice-Chancellor, broadcast a blood-curdling cry to battle. Germany had "struck the word pacifism from its vocabulary," he said. "There is in the world no better death than to be slain by the foe . . . Mothers must exhaust themselves in order to give life to children. Fathers must fight on the battlefield in order to secure a future for their sons."

In Danzig, still under the protection of the League, storm troopers and police broke down the doors of the trade-union headquarters, took over the files and funds, and raised the swastika banner. Later, at the insistence of the League High Commissioner, the swastika was lowered, but the headquarters remained in Nazi hands. From Silesia complaints poured in to the League on the hounding of Jews. The Nazis were threatening to reconquer northern Schleswig from Denmark and march through Switzerland, if need be, to get at France. They were organizing the 25,000 German miners in the Netherlands province of Limburg, until the Dutch dissolved all Nazi organizations and expelled their leader.

Both the Germans and the Italians were attempting to allay Soviet fears, but to little avail. Karl Radek, although he admitted that the terms of the Versailles Treaty had been "predatory," nonetheless declared in *Izvestia* that "discussion of revision is the smoke screen behind which Imperialism prepares the most terrible and ruthless war that the human brain can conceive, a war by comparison with which all the horrors of the Imperialist War of 1914–1918 will pale."

In the House of Commons anti-Nazi revulsion crossed all party lines. Churchill thundered: "What is this new spirit of German nationalism? The worst of the old Prussian Imperialism with an added savagery, a racial pride, an exclusiveness which cannot allow to any fellow-subject not of pure Nordic birth equality of rights and citizenship, within the nation to which he belongs. Are you going to discuss [treaty] revision with a government like that?"

When Nazi lieutenant Alfred Rosenberg arrived in London on a good-will tour, British hostility in government circles and in the street forced him to cut his visit abruptly. At a press conference at Claridge's he was asked how many Jews had been tortured and beaten that week. "In January last year there were twelve National Socialists killed by Communists," he responded.

On May 16, President Roosevelt took a hand in the crisis and, in a message to "the Emperors, Kings and Presidents" of the fifty-four states represented at the Disarmament Conference, declared: "If any strong nation refuses to join with genuine sincerity in these concerted efforts for political and economic peace . . . the civilized world will know where the responsibility for failure lies." He supported the British plan and called for abolition of bombers, tanks, and big guns.

The message, which was widely hailed as an American step toward joining in the security of Europe, made the mood less grim in Geneva, where the delegates and much of the world stood still, awaiting a momentous and widely billed foreign-policy address by Chancellor Adolf Hitler to the Reichstag.

After all the drumbeats of that uneasy spring, Hitler surprised the world by sounding like an airy flute. "The proposal made by President Roosevelt, of which I learned last night," said the Führer, "has earned the warm thanks of the German government . . . The President's proposal is a ray of comfort for all who wish to cooperate in the maintenance of peace . . . Germany is entirely ready to renounce all offensive weapons if the armed nations, on their side, will destroy their offensive weapons . . . Germany is prepared to agree to any solemn pact of non-aggression, because she does not think of attacking but only of acquiring security . . . The mentality of the last century, which led people to think that they would make Germans out of Poles and Frenchmen, is alien to us." He called war "unlimited madness."

The world heaved an enormous sigh of relief. The *Times* of London applauded Hitler for his departure from the "turgid rhetoric which has swayed millions of Germans," said the speech would have to be read in the light of *Mein Kampf* and other statements, but still Britain "would prefer to regard Herr Hitler as sincere in his desire to collaborate with the rest of the world in building a common prosperity and peace on an agreed basis of equal rights."

President Roosevelt was reported eminently pleased, and at the Disarmament Conference Norman Davis was empowered to take still another step toward cooperation in collective security. "We are willing to consult with other states in case of a threat to peace," Davis said, "with a view to averting a conflict. Further than that, in the event that the States, in conference, determine that a State has been guilty of a breach of the peace and take measures against the violator, then, if we concur in that judgment, we will refrain from any action tending to defeat such collective effort which these States may thus make to restore peace."

The words were far from any promise that the Yanks would be coming over once again; it held out no hope of an American presence in the League. Still, Europe was grateful and read exciting promises between the lines of the message.

The French, however, remained stubbornly uneasy. Unconvinced by Hitler's sweet song before the Reichstag and the Americans' timid promise to refrain from contributing to France's troubles if it were attacked, Herriot turned to Litvinov and stirred talk of a revived Franco-Russian alliance. He responded warmly to the Russians' new approach, which would seek to define and condemn aggression rather than distinguish between aggressive and defensive weapons.

The violent spring thus ended somewhere short of total despair, and when the Conference adjourned for the summer Arthur Henderson was determined to come up with a workable draft convention by the autumn. The chief delegates were expected to change their hats from disarmament specialists to economists and attend the World Economic Conference scheduled to open in London on June 10, in an effort to solve the problems of the Great Depression.

Henderson and his chief aide, Thanassis Aghnides, went along. The experience was depressing. They could not persuade MacDonald to let them use a room in the geological museum which housed the Conference, and the delegates were impervious to being buttonholed in the lobby. On July 10, Henderson and the faithful Aghnides pursued their pilgrimage in Rome, Prague, Berlin, Paris. Hitler was not on hand in his capital and they had to catch up with him in Munich. The meeting of Henderson and Hitler did not go well. The dialogue was singularly uninspired. Recalling the event years later, Aghnides said that Hitler began by expressing his "great admiration for the British people" but indicated a deep distress at the way the British press was treating him. To which Henderson replied in effect: "How do you expect my countrymen to behave if you treat the Jews this way?"

Hitler then flew into a rage, according to Aghnides, and hurled a timeworn irrelevancy at Henderson's head: "Why don't you hold elections in India?"

The best that Henderson could do was to suggest that Hitler meet with French Premier Edouard Daladier to prevent all Europe from being dragged into a war based on German-French hostility. Hitler was cool and the French were cooler. When Henderson broached the possibility of such a meeting in Paris, Paul-Boncour told him: "M. Daladier cannot grasp those blood-soaked hands." The French Foreign Minister went on to remark acidly on the newsreel shots he had seen of the crowds in Munich cheering Henderson on his arrival. To which Henderson replied sharply that peacemakers used to get such welcomes in Paris but that was when Briand was Foreign Minister.

Instead of talking with Hitler, Daladier chose to confer with the British and Americans in Paris concerning a two-stage approach to German arms parity that would in effect put Germany and the system of international controls on a four-year probation. If all went well in those trial years, Germany would have its equality with France under strict international supervision. Eden thought the French "justified in their mistrust of the

Nazis," and the British went along with the idea, but few had hopes that the Germans would find it acceptable.

What the Germans would or would not find acceptable was a major preoccupation of the world in the middle of 1933, as it had been ever since the Kaiser's gray legions returned home and crowned their helmets with victory's laurels in the midst of defeat. Then the world had been tired of war. Now defeated Germany could extol the military virtues once again while the victorious powers still sickened at the thought. In September 1933, four huge men strode down the aisles of the Salle de la Réformation in Geneva, completely concealing in their midst a thin wisp of a man with a limp, Dr. Paul Joseph Goebbels. By alphabetical chance—Autriche following Allemagne—he was seated next to another diminutive doctor, the Austrian Chancellor Engelbert Dollfuss.

Dollfuss was not popular, but when he stood at the podium, the delegates rose to their feet in an unprecedented ovation while Goebbels watched in silence. Dollfuss and others had read the future in the first paragraph of *Mein Kampf*. Hitler, like Stresemann before him, had written there that the sacred union of Germany and Austria was a task "to be furthered with every means our lives long."

With prophetic gallows humor Dollfuss in that Assembly session turned to a man who represented another roadblock to Hitler, Geoffrey Knox, president of the League's Governing Commission in charge of the Saar. Dollfuss told him that their lives probably commanded the highest life-insurance premiums in Europe.

The Disarmament Conference returned to its deliberations on October 14. The Germans, now quite ostracized in the salons of Geneva, were holding out for their right to "sample" quantities of all the arms in the arsenals of the world powers. Mussolini quietly urged the French and English to give them to Hitler on the grounds that he probably had them already in any case.

On the morning of October 12, Sir John Simon chatted with the German delegate, Nadolny, who had to go to Berlin for a cabinet meeting the following day. President von Hindenburg was reported returning from East Prussia for the occasion. There was nothing in that conversation to alarm Sir John, and he was inclined to believe the American newsmen who were sedulously spreading the word they had picked up that the Germans, if pressed, would compromise.

Sir John thereupon opened the debate on October 14 by presenting the plan agreed upon with the French, allowing a very limited increase in the German armaments, proposing a trial period after which there would be full parity. Baron von Rheinbaben, filling in for Nadolny, put forth the usual demand for immediate parity in familiar phrases. It seemed a routine, uneventful morning in Geneva, and the delegates broke for lunch at twelve-thirty.

Before they returned to the Salle de la Réformation, they read in the morning newspapers that had come down from Berlin the astonishing news that Germany had decided to withdraw from the Disarmament Conference and to resign from the League. Delegates tried desperately to check the story amid whirling rumors. At three o'clock Arthur Henderson was handed a telegram from Reich Foreign Minister von Neurath: ". . . it is now clear that the Disarmament Conference will not fulfill what is its sole object, namely general disarmament . . . due solely to unwillingness on the part of the highly armed states to carry out their contractual obligation to disarm . . . The German Government is accordingly compelled to leave the Disarmament Conference."

Later Hitler spoke, and again all the wheels of international diplomacy stood still for his broadcast. He made it clear that Germany would rearm, but he skillfully avoided any suggestion of belligerence. He complained that Germany had been "profoundly humiliated" and was compelled for this reason to leave the League. He beguilingly offered "to destroy even the last German machine gun and to discharge the last man from the army if other nations decide to do the same." To France he said: "As a National Socialist, I, with all my followers, refuse by reason of our national principle to acquire by conquest the members of other nations who will never love us." Although he declared there were "no grounds for territorial conflict," he paved the way for his next demand: "When the Saar Territory [the fate of which was to be decided by plebiscite] has been restored to Germany only a madman would consider the possibility of war."

The alarm that swept Geneva and all Europe was felt in Berlin as well. On Hitler's orders, General Werner von Blomberg issued secret directives to the German forces to hold, "as long as possible," limited defense lines against possible attack from France, Poland, and Czechoslovakia. It was clear to the generals that such defenses could not hold for long. It was equally clear to Hitler that no such defense would be necessary. The Allies had not marched on Berlin in 1918, when the United States was with them; they would not march in 1933, when the United States was withdrawn beyond the Atlantic wall seemingly forever.

Daladier fired off a salvo of elegant phrases, declaring that France would be "deaf to no appeal but blind to no act. If one sincerely wishes for understanding, why begin with ruptures?"

Henderson wrote to Hitler in the name of the Conference: "I regret

. . . that this grave decision should have been taken by your government for reasons which I am unable to accept as valid."

Having said all that could be said, the delegates proved Hitler's guess was accurate: they continued to talk. The United States and Italy saw little point in going on with the Conference, but the French, the little powers, and Arthur Henderson would not give up. Litvinov suggested turning the Disarmament Conference into a Peace Conference and, as usual, was voted down. Notes flew back and forth between Berlin and the capitals of Western Europe, rehashing old arguments and devising variations on the formula for computing Germany's military establishment. Hitler ridiculed the notion that his storm troopers, Labor Corps, and Stahlhelm could be considered part of the German armed forces. He called them bulwarks against Bolshevism, even as Stresemann had, and compared them to the Salvation Army.

Hitler had called upon the German people to demonstrate to the world that they were solidly behind him in his withdrawal from Geneva. The German people were asked to give Hitler a vote of confidence in an election and plebiscite on November 12, 1933. Forecasting the result, Hitler told his people: "On an eleventh of November the German people formally lost its honor; fifteen years later came a twelfth of November and then the German people restored its honor to itself." On the eve of the election, Hindenburg broadcast to the voters: "Show tomorrow your firm national unity and your solidarity with the government. Support with me and the Reichschancellor the principle of equal rights and of peace with honor . . ."

After a year of murders, beatings, purges, and concentration camps, 95 percent of the German electorate, in an unprecedentedly high turnout, gave their full support to Hitler. At the concentration camp in Dachau, 2,242 prisoners were given the right to vote. Of these, 2,154 were recorded as voting to back Hitler and to return the Nazis to complete control of the Reichstag and the Reich. Unbiased observers testified that the vote and the tally were in the main honest.

For the League of Nations, 1933 was the year when discourse, however witty or dull, reasoned or absurd, seemed powerless to inhibit unmannerly men who could shout, as Alice does in Wonderland, "You're nothing but a pack of cards."

Twelve

MURDER BREAKS
THE PAPER RING

On January 8, 1934, in the French Alpine resort of Chamonix, while police pounded on his door, Alexandre Stavisky shot himself. His death seemed remarkably well timed to save the reputations of certain friends in high places, and the police were generally suspected of helping Stavisky to his end. At least they did nothing to retard it throughout the hour that he lay dying, according to a parliamentary report on the affair.

The forty-seven-year-old Stavisky had reached a climax in a career of richly diversified corruption. However, it was not his activities in prostitution, stock swindles, narcotics traffic, and shady night-club operations that made his death a political event of prime importance. It was the apparent immunity he enjoyed from serious prosecution. He had been jailed in 1926 after charges by outraged stockholders in one of his enterprises, but he was released the following year. His trial was postponed nineteen times in the seven years that followed, while he continued to enjoy an enterprising and lucrative liberty. When he fell into trouble after passing a worthless check for seven and a half million francs, four deputies—one of them a Vice-President of the French Chamber of Deputies—intervened to spring him from jail. His friends included not only deputies but police commissioners and cabinet ministers.

Stavisky's death touched off riots, toppled the government, threatened to consume France in bloody revolution, and led indirectly to dramatic changes at Geneva.

Caught up in the tempest that broke over Paris were plain citizens outraged by the spectacle of corruption in high places, rightists and royalists who saw in the affair an opportunity to destroy the Third Republic, and leftists who hoped to destroy the political right, even at the cost of the Republic. The government of Camille Chautemps gave way to that of Edouard Daladier. He vowed to get to the bottom of the matter but ineptly disposed of one tarnished police chief by transferring him to Morocco and another by making him head of that venerable temple of French drama, the Comédie Française. The latter act scandalized even those elements of the populace which had hitherto remained aloof.

On the evening of February 6, 1934, mobs swirled through the Place de la Concorde and the Left Bank up to the gates of the Chamber. The deputies vanished one by one as the sound of firing grew more ominous, so that by eight-thirty in the evening, when the session was adjourned, only a handful were left. Reporters stayed at their posts and scrawled on the door of the press gallery: "Notice to the demonstrators: No Deputies in here!"

Edouard Herriot also stayed to the end, then walked calmly through the mob toward his home. When his familiar face and figure were recognized, an angry crowd surrounded him, shouting: "Throw him into the Seine." Calmly he told his captors: "At least have the decency to take me to the Rhône"—the river which runs by his native Lyons.

He was narrowly rescued—as was the Republic ultimately—by the disorganization of the royalists, rightists, Communists, and outraged citizens. Daladier refused to call out the tanks and the army. Instead he resigned. He was followed by the venerable conservative Gaston Doumergue, who put together a government to the right of center, though it was far from meeting the demands of the royalists and the Fascists. The seventy-one-year-old Doumergue, it was said, was persuaded to come back from retirement by Pierre Laval, who further convinced him to appoint Marshal Pétain to the post of Minister of War. For Foreign Minister, Doumergue chose another apparently ageless diplomat, the nimble, seventy-two-year-old Louis Barthou. The choice of that elfin minister with the fierce rhetoric was not only to change the policy of France but to revise the strategies of peace and greatly enliven the arena at Geneva. The return of Barthou was perhaps the most significant by-product of the death in Chamonix of that fantastic swindler Stavisky.

At seventy-two, Louis Barthou had already had several careers. He had been noted for his agile footwork in the tangled French politics of Clemenceau's day and earlier. He had also been the author of distinguished biographies of Danton and Mirabeau, and had written essays on feminism, Baudelaire, and the love affairs of Victor Hugo. His interests and his conversation ranged sparklingly over rare editions, engravings, bawdy stories, politics, scandal, and food, all of which he enjoyed mightily. He much resembled a mischievous and voracious little owl as he peered amusedly through his spectacles at the world in disarray around him.

His impishness once led him to introduce a renowned Parisian attorney as an after-dinner speaker with a tribute that unsettled the poor man. "Monsieur," said the unpredictable Barthou, "your name may be illegitimate, but you have made it immortal."

Even in his seventies Barthou persevered in a rigorous life style. He would rise at five, take an ice-cold bath and a quick stroll, breakfast at seven-thirty, and be shaved by a barber at eight, during which operation he would receive the first visitor of his day. He was fiercely French, though more in the Clemenceau than in the Briand manner. In private conversation he would refer to the League as a *fumisterie*—a cloud of smoke that was both obfuscating and ephemeral. He was to do much in that year of 1934 to change the quality of the *fumisterie* and to provide a fresh alternative to the grim prospects confronting the diplomats of Europe.

It was a year when liberals, having stripped the 1914–18 bloodshed of all delusory heroics, echoed Benjamin Franklin's dictum that there never could be a good war or a bad peace. The sins of Versailles had made German intransigence "understandable." Though Nazism seemed loathsome, it was still an "internal" phenomenon of Germany. "Appeasement" had not yet taken on a villainous connotation. To the alternatives of an unthinkable preventive war and an equally unthinkable resignation to the rebuilding of a German military juggernaut, Barthou added a third way. It involved a ring of paper which Barthou would twine around renascent Germany. France would depend not exclusively on England, so chary of commitments, or on the United States, entrenched in righteous, if not so splendid, isolation. It would build its security on the lesser powers along Germany's borders. It would recruit into the block Italy and above all the Colossus of the East, the Soviet Union, that fire-eating dragon of revolution, rendered more homey and reasonable by the genial Litvinov.

Accordingly, in April, Louis Barthou alighted at a suburban station of Warsaw. At first the reception seemed chill, for Colonel Józef Beck, the proud and touchy Foreign Minister of Poland, was not on hand to meet him—an ominous breach of protocol. Poland had been by tradition and expediency the firmest ally of France in Eastern Europe, but Pilsudski had been edging closer to Germany. Beck's absence, however, had more to do with pique than with politics, it developed. It was in reprisal for the fact that, on Beck's last visit to Paris, the French Foreign Minister had been prevented by cabinet crises from meeting him at the Gare du Nord.

In any case, Barthou's misgivings were quickly dissipated by the Warsaw crowds which broke through police lines and swept the astonished and delighted French minister into their arms. Obviously, popular feeling was still running pro-French, whatever policy the aging Marshal Pilsudski and Colonel Beck might be pursuing in their passionate mistrust of all things Russian.

The demonstrations at the station served to cool still further the attitude of Colonel Beck, and the state dinner that night started in icy formality. According to the French ambassador, Jules LaRoche, Barthou warmed to the challenge and was soon delighting Mme Beck with a flow of anecdotes. Mme Beck responded and the cheer radiated around the table, for she not only was a charming hostess but exercised a significant influence on her husband. (She had been the wife of his friend and fellow army officer when the Colonel fell in love with her. She now controlled his consumption of champagne at banquets and added her charm to his political expertise in the management of Poland.)

Pilsudski, who granted Barthou an audience in the gemlike Belvedere Palace, managed to charm Barthou. He and Beck repeatedly asserted their devotion to the French alliance and their insistence that Poland had no secret agreements with Germany affecting France, Russia, or Austria. Beck admitted that he preferred the "heroic and cavalier" Hungarians to the Czechs, but added that this was a matter of romantic temperament having little to do with the current German pressures on Czechoslovakia.

The Marshal outlined the problem: Poland had two powerful neighbors; one of them had never been in the League, and the other had just left it. That was why Poland had to conduct a foreign policy outside the League. Moreover, the aging Marshal told Barthou, the League tends to distract itself too much with arguments about opium and the white-slave traffic.

On German rearmament, Pilsudski warned that France was not really firm enough. At this Barthou protested vehemently. Pilsudski chuckled, reached over, and tapped Barthou's knee like a wise uncle. "No, no," he said, "believe me, you will give in, you will give in, and then what could I do?"

By the visit's end, the ordinarily forbidding Beck had dropped his reserve. He wore his hat at an uncommonly jaunty angle when he saw Barthou off at the station and assured him: "I see nothing that can separate us." Barthou murmured to Ambassador LaRoche a characterization of

Beck that was not usually offered in that officer's career. "Deep down," said Barthou, "he's a good lad." In the months that followed, Beck was to recover his chilling reserve, and Barthou would refer to Warsaw as a "wasps' nest."

But now it seemed a fitting place to start a diplomatic idyll. The pixie-like Minister floated down the Danube on a barge while saber-wielding Serbian cavalrymen raced along the embankments to offer their salutes and girls stood waiting at the village piers to toss their flowers. In Belgrade he met the sad-eyed, slender King Alexander I, broached the subject of a Mediterranean Locarno that would reconcile Yugoslavia with Italy, and made a date to continue their talks in France in the autumn.

Barthou toured Czechoslovakia and saw Dollfuss in Vienna. Everywhere his efforts to enclose Hitler in a ring of Locarno Pacts which, indeed, the Führer would be asked to join, was promising to be fruitful. It even had the cautious blessings of the British. It was, thus, a particularly buoyant Barthou who turned up at Geneva in mid-May for the last climactic session of the Disarmament Conference.

In the time that had elapsed since Germany's walkout from Geneva and while France was convulsed in the Stavisky affair, British diplomacy had been vacillating between outrage and alarm, at times taking fright from the fury of its own words. At the end of January the British ambassador in Berlin, Sir Eric Phipps, warned London that Hitler "believes neither in the League nor in negotiations" and listed German objectives as: *Anschluss*, the modification of Germany's eastern frontiers, the opening up of German outlets to the south and the east, and the recovery of some of Germany's former colonies. These aims could have come as no surprise whatever; they had been voiced, although in softer tones, by Stresemann. Phipps ventured his guess, however, that Hitler would not be prepared to risk a war for these objectives for at least a decade.

Hitler showed a singular lack of interest in the latest proposals from Britain for a gradual approach to German arms parity with the other European powers. In February, Anthony Eden, serving as Lord Privy Seal, embarked on his own travels, which, on the whole, turned out less spectacularly than Barthou's tour. Eden's itinerary took him to Paris, Berlin, Rome, and back to Paris. The British proposal scarcely aroused any more enthusiasm in Paris than it did in Berlin. Barthou noted ironically that it postponed parity in the air and on the sea, where British interests lay, but envisioned a much swifter timetable for land forces, in which the security of France was precariously placed.

Hitler made efforts to be cordial and seemed to Eden in a mood for compromise. Mussolini behaved rather like an enthusiastic reporter, pumping Eden and Sir Eric Drummond (who was then Britain's ambassador in Rome) on their impressions of the new Chancellor of the Reich, whom he had not yet met. When Eden remarked that the Nazis insisted that they wanted peace while speaking obsessively of their war exploits, Mussolini commented jokingly, "Yes, like all Germans." He told Eden that there was only one way to stop German rearmament (which, he noted, was obviously far advanced) and that was by preventive war. Short of that, he urged that some agreement be put on paper at least to forestall an increase in Hitler's demands, which seemed to worry him.

The French were too engrossed in their private crises to offer a detailed comment on the British proposals but held to the original price of cooperation: a measure of security in the form of a commitment from either Britain or the United States. Without such a commitment the approaching climactic session of the Disarmament Conference would be a shambles. The British Cabinet wavered, and Eden, disappointed, had to go off to Geneva with the customary vague directives amounting to little more than a cheery "Carry on." Eden told his diary: "The timidity is almost terrible."

On the eve of the reassembling of the Disarmament Conference in the spring of 1934, all sides seemed determined to cling to previously prepared positions. Hitler, with what seemed like monumental tactlessness, had announced, in routine fashion, a greatly increased military budget in all fields, including a 160 percent boost in the air force, which under Versailles was not supposed to exist. Mussolini responded by putting into print in *Popolo d'Italia* the warning he had privately handed Eden: that the only way to prevent German rearmament was by preventive war. Failing that, and he did not advocate it certainly, an effort might be made to limit the rearmament.

Arthur Henderson's dogged optimism took on a desperate tone when he opened the session by calling the situation "really critical." Norman Davis voiced the customary American loathing for "foreign entanglements" in terms which seemed to rule out any possible crumb of security for France. The United States, said Davis, "would not make any commitment whatever to use its armed forces for the settlement of any dispute anywhere."

Having lost all hope for the Disarmament Conference and having substituted for it his strategy of the paper cordon, Barthou made his first entrance on the disarmament stage as a destroying angel, hurling brickbats in all directions. Before the session began he confided to Norman Davis that he could not trust Foreign Minister Simon, who had come down with Eden. Preliminary huddles with Barthou left Sir John gloomy and

nettled as if he had been too close to a playful porcupine. This was merely
a foretaste of Barthou's opening statement to the Conference, a performance which Eden characterized as "appallingly witty."

Barthou followed Sir John to the podium, referred to him as "*mon cher
collègue et presque ami*" (my dear colleague and almost my friend), and
proceeded to tear him apart for talking as if only the British had offered a
plan of disarmament. "Paternity has its illusions," Barthou said. He
granted the importance of the British offspring, but added: "Signor
Mussolini, who is certainly not incapable of paternity, also had a child
. . . The French Government also . . . had a child . . . and M. Paul-
Boncour had been its godfather."

He teased the delegates for having truckled to Germany. The minutes
of that session reported Barthou's speech this way: "Germany had left
the League. Were the principles laid down on October 14 no longer valid
on that account? After prolonged efforts certain Great Powers had agreed
upon a reasonable, impartial and acceptable system. Germany had refused
to accept it, and because Germany had rejected it, was this system to be
declared unacceptable? Had matters come to such a pass that there was
one power which was both invisible and present—present, if they would
excuse the metaphor, by its very absence—which was not participating in
the Conference, had left the League, was thus faced with no responsibility and which had all the rights without any of the corresponding
duties?"

Barthou said that the new German military budget was Germany's way
of declaring: "We care nothing for all your conversations . . . Since
October 14, 1933, when we abruptly left the League, we have assumed
our full freedom, and we are making use of it; so much the worse for you
who go on discussing and negotiating; we rely on our own strength, on
the strength of our rearmament."

He lightly rapped the wrist of the Conference President by noting that
though Henderson "still had a remnant of platonic veneration for the
attitude which hoped that peace would come from disarmament . . . his
good sense immediately resumed its sway," obliging him to espouse the
axiom of "no disarmament without security."

Barthou kept a kind, if guarded, word for Litvinov, who had stressed
the need for security. "A practical man," Barthou noted, ". . . not a man
who tries to please everybody." He closed by warning of false prophets:
"the confirmed optimists who denied the cruel evidence of the most
urgent peril . . . and the pessimists who refused to admit that there was
any hope."

There was little more to be said after Barthou's exuberant performance.

Sir John packed up and went home, convinced that no formula could be found that would satisfy German demands for rearmament, French demands for security, and the Anglo-American aversion to commitments. The Conference lingered on amid desultory talk, and Barthou continued his playful way leaving his barbs in the hides of his sensitive colleagues.

Belgium's distinguished veteran of diplomacy, Paul Hymans, brought him and Eden together at a luncheon to repair the fragile Anglo-French unity, in which Belgium saw its only security. Barthou listened sympathetically but could not repress a prickly comment on Belgium's position. "It's quite simple," Barthou said at the lunch. "Belgium has a wife, France, and a mistress, England. That is why Belgium pays more attention to the mistress than to the wife."

Even Colonel Beck, whose benevolent neutrality, if not friendship, he had so adroitly pursued earlier in the spring, became a target for Barthou's irrepressible urge to wither with a word. The Colonel, who carried his country's honor on his sleeve, bristled noticeably when Barthou concluded an informal speech at a luncheon for the Council members by remarking: "There are the Great Powers . . ." Here he paused. "And Poland, Poland, we all know because we have been told so, is a Great Power." He paused again. ". . . A very Great Power."

In a more serious vein he confided to Eden the negotiations then under way for a Franco-Soviet pact, which, he wished to assure Britain, was not to be a pact against Germany but part of the celebrated Eastern Locarno which might include Germany. He saw as a prerequisite to that pact the entry of the Soviet Union into the League.

The Soviet Union had come a long way from the pariah status conferred upon it at birth. The conscientious, adroit, and cheerful conduct of Maxim Litvinov at the Disarmament Conference had shown that dealing with the Bolsheviks was not only possible but even, on occasion, pleasant. It was beginning to seem vitally necessary in view of the Nazi threat. Beneath the rhetoric of ideologies the old imperatives of geography and power balances could be seen, unchanged from the days of 1914, when Russia was a natural target for an expansionist Germany and a natural ally of Western Europe. The principal powers of Europe were sending ambassadors to Moscow. In November 1933 the United States had recognized the regime, signaling belatedly the end of a policy which began with intervention and proceeded to anathema and excommunication, all to no avail.

The French had debated the problem of consorting with the devil in 1933, and the deputies had to be persuaded by the citation of distinguished precedents, such as Francis I, who joined with the Turks despite the rallying calls of Christendom; and Richelieu, who dickered with German Protestants for the greater glory and the security of France. Now that the fiery Bolsheviks had decided to concentrate on the internal construction of the Soviet state, the world no longer needed to tremble. As Arnold Toynbee wrote at the time, "A man who has settled down to cultivate his own garden is a man who has a stake in the status quo."

Britain, though it had recognized the Soviet government back in 1924, now followed labyrinthine reasoning, full of doubts, to end by endorsing Russia's entrance into the League. The thought process was exemplified by a tortuous editorial in the *News-Chronicle* of July 12, 1934: "Unless Russia enters the League, France cannot carry through her policy [of a Franco-Soviet pact] . . . A section of the British Cabinet, on the other hand, is opposing the entry of Russia into the League for fear of offending Japan. Yet an attempt to renew a Japanese alliance means abandoning all hope of closer relations with America, and the support of the immense power of Russia is the one immediate hope of restoring the prestige of the League . . . The only direct contribution to the peace of Europe possible at the moment is a policy which will bring Russia into the League."

In July 1934, Barthou journeyed to London and successfully resolved the remaining British doubts. Though Sir John and Parliament were convinced, the fierce socialist Harold Laski called Barthou a "Frenchman with a load of mischief" and declared: "Great Britain does not like the Franco-Russian rapprochement. She dislikes still more the idea of a League in which Russia plays a vital part."

From the point of view of Moscow, it was the League that had changed in ways acceptable to a revolutionary state. It was no longer to be denounced as a coterie of capitalists seeking to hold back a historic tide; nor was it any longer an alliance of victorious powers imposing the unjust terms of Versailles. In Moscow, as in Paris, the League seemed a useful tool for collective security in a time of trouble. For the Soviet Union, the dread encirclement was no longer the Anglo-French-American *cordon sanitaire*. The links now were Japanese in the East and German in the West. Accordingly, at Christmastime 1933, Josef Stalin told *The New York Times:* "If the League is only the tiniest bumper to slow down the drift towards war and help peace, then we are not against the League. In that event I would not say that we would not support the League." In maneuvering the Soviet Union into the League of Nations, Barthou was thus officiating, like a midwife, at a natural event.

In the spring, with the impending event widely heralded, France's allies—Czechoslovakia, Rumania, Yugoslavia, and Bulgaria—hurriedly recognized the Soviet regime. (King Alexander of Yugoslavia gave his royal consent to the act but could not bring himself to sign because he had grown up in the Imperial Russian Court of the last Czar.)

There were die-hard anti-Sovieteers, however, who would not be persuaded by political exigencies. They were few but they could be troublesome. Even a single dissenting vote in the Assembly could block an invitation to the Soviet Union. (The Soviets could scarcely be expected to knock on the door uninvited when, in the preceding three years, lesser powers such as Mexico and Turkey had been granted the dignity of a formal bid.)

Switzerland, the Netherlands, and Portugal were the only ones determined to oppose the invitation. Mussolini had given his blessings in the spring, and Marshal Pilsudski, for whom ineffective gestures were wasted motion, resigned himself to the entrance of the Russians. He took one precaution, however. Fearful lest the Soviets raise the embarrassing matter of Poland's treatment of Russians within its borders, he instructed Colonel Beck to denounce unilaterally all existing Polish commitments on the care of minorities. The Colonel did so emphatically and phrased it as a matter of national pride. Poland was demanding equality, he said in accents reminiscent of the German claim for arms parity. Unless all nations in the League undertook similar commitments, Poland would no longer entertain inquiries or offer reports on such matters of internal policy. The League, absorbed in other concerns, passed over in silence this precedent-setting open disavowal of a solemn treaty.

An ingenious way was found around the little threesome of resisters in the Assembly. Maxim Litvinov, waiting in his hotel, was asked whether an invitation would be acceptable if it came not from the Assembly but from a large group of League members. If the number were adequate, he said, it would do. There was no difficulty in rounding up thirty-four signatories to the bid, representing far more than the two-thirds Assembly vote needed for ultimate acceptance. Barthou thereupon suggested that, since approval was a foregone conclusion, the Assembly might dispense with the debate, which was certain to be useless and could be acrimonious. Eamon de Valera of Ireland, however, insisted on the parliamentary niceties. The Assembly had never and, he trusted, would never let anything pass without discussion. Though he himself would vote for the Soviets' admission, he would have a sermon on Godlessness to deliver.

Knowing that these formalities would be tiresome but not decisive, Barthou was cheerful on the eve of the Assembly session. He had been reassured that, once admitted to the League, the Soviet Union would be accorded a permanent seat at the Council table. Argentina would abstain

on that question because it was opposed on principle to the whole institution of permanent Council membership. (It had walked out over the same
issue at the time of Germany's stormy entrance into the League.) Panama
and Portugal, also on the Council, would offer no more than token
opposition.

Barthou's exuberance at the fruition of his plan to involve the Russians
in collective security did not render him starry-eyed concerning the
impending alliance. At lunch one day in the midst of his strenuous
maneuvers, Rumania's Nicolae Titulescu, observing Barthou's new wrist-
watch, remarked acidly: "No doubt Litvinov gave it to you for getting
him into the League." Barthou answered with an undiplomatic quip:
"No, no, if ever Litvinov gives me a watch there will be a chain attached."

The Assembly met on September 17, 1934, and the matter of the
admission of the Soviet Union was in the hands of the Sixth Committee
by four-thirty that afternoon.

Caeiro da Mata of Portugal led off for the opposition in terms which, in
other years, would have gladdened the heart of a Soviet satirist caricatur-
ing the decadence of empire. He prefaced his assault by saying: "Portugal's vote will be an affirmation of principle on the part of a power which
is proud of its age-long existence, its vast colonial empire, and its
economic and financial situation, which has attained the equilibrium almost
universally lacking elsewhere."

Giuseppe Motta, Switzerland's veteran diplomat, recalled that at the
League's first Assembly on November 20, 1920, he had voiced the hope
that Russia would one day be "cured of her madness" and "delivered
from her misery" and so made fit for League membership. That day had
not arrived, he continued, and now the League was "attempting to wed
water and fire." De Valera hoped, without much conviction, that League
membership might attenuate the Godlessness of Soviet Russia.

Teufik Rustu Bey of Turkey gave the friendliest support. He spoke
glowingly of the joys of being the neighbor of the Soviet Union, praised
the adroitness of its diplomats, and the depth of its devotion to peace.

Barthou tried to steer the opposition away from its preoccupation with
the religious issue and onto the political plane, hoping to substitute fear
for self-righteousness as a motivating force. "From the point of view of
religious beliefs, my own views are, I think, widely dissimilar to those of
M. de Valera or M. Motta. But I belong to a class of freethinkers who
respect the freedom of thought of others . . . If we now reject Russia,
will she not turn against Europe? I need say no more."

In the tally, Portugal, the Netherlands, and Switzerland were the only naysayers. Argentina, Belgium, Cuba, Luxembourg, Nicaragua, Peru, and Venezuela abstained.

At the plenary meeting the following night, September 18, 1934, Salvador de Madariaga of Spain brought in the Committee's report and added his hope that "the great American republic" would follow suit and so give the League the universality "without which it cannot succeed or, indeed, exist at all."

The formal welcome of the Soviet Union into "the great world family of states cooperating for the safeguarding of peace" was delivered enthusiastically by the Assembly President, Rickard Sandler of Sweden, a veteran socialist. "The Second International is welcoming the Third," Colonel Beck was heard to comment at that moment.

Litvinov then rose to make his first address from the League podium. It was a quiet, statesmanlike speech. He pledged full adherence to the League statutes, making reservations only in connection with the mandates system, the absence of a racial-equality clause, and those sections of the Covenant which could be interpreted as sanctioning war under certain circumstances. He issued one of the earliest calls for "the peaceful coexistence of different social systems." In a gentle plea for toleration of his country, Litvinov asked for "the liberty to preserve what I might call its State personality and the social and economic system chosen by it."

The discovery of aims held in common by the Soviet Union and the League were "greatly facilitated by the events of the last two or three years," Litvinov said. A decade earlier, he observed, "war seemed to be a remote theoretical danger, and there seemed to be no hurry as to its prevention. Now war must appear to all as the threatening danger of tomorrow . . . Now the organization of peace, for which so far very little has been done, must be set against the extremely active organizing of war . . . Now everybody knows that the exponents of the idea of war, the open promulgators of the refashioning of the map of Europe and Asia by the sword, are not to be intimidated by paper obstacles."

That maiden speech of Litvinov's sketched the line he was to take before the League in the years to come. At the time, however, it was treated as the merest verbiage. The London *Times* reported on September 19, 1934: "There were no demonstrations of any kind and not the slightest glimmer of enthusiasm."

The *Daily Express* lead editorial of September 15, 1934, voiced an outrage that ran considerably beyond the general British sentiment. "Every member of the League of Nations Union, who is a Christian earnestly concerned in defending the faith, should resign from that body forthwith," said the paper. Few did.

The reactions of the world to Russia or to the League were of relatively small importance, however, to Louis Barthou, who was achieving his grand design. The Polish link in the chain of Locarnos, however, showed alarming flaws within ten days after the Soviet Union entered the League. Poland announced that it would have no part of an Eastern Locarno unless Germany were a full-fledged member, that it felt no responsibility whatever to Czechoslovakia and wanted no involvement in the Balkans.

The Italian connection was also weakening. Mussolini frowned on any agreement with Yugoslavia, rendering dubious Barthou's idea of a Mediterranean Locarno. The key to that front was Alexander of Yugoslavia, who had sound reasons for the melancholy look he customarily put on. His neighbors Hungary and Italy were forever looking at his kingdom with undisguised appetites. And within his realm there were great and historic centrifugal forces. Of these the Croats were the most fiercely separatist. The Ustachi—a Croatian movement given to terrorism—were accorded comfort and sometimes more tangible assistance when they fled into either Hungary or Italy. Indeed, the refugee camps in those countries were frequently charged with being the schools and bases of the Croat terrorists. Further indicating their widespread support was the fact that much of the Ustachi propaganda was printed in Germany.

Earlier in the year Barthou had made a date with King Alexander to come to France for a conference and for a state display of French-Yugoslav friendship. The King set sail on a Yugoslav warship from the port of Shibenik on October 6, 1934, and reached Marseilles three days later. Barthou was waiting at the dock when the King walked down the gangplank at four o'clock in the afternoon of October 9. Together they entered an open touring car, from which the King and his host could wave to the enthusiastic crowds in the street or at their windows. The Garde Mobile was out but in a relaxed ceremonial formation with some five yards between each pair of guards. This was odd because rumors of plots against the King had circulated through Marseilles the week before. On the other hand, there were always plots against Alexander. Because the rumor was routine, it was discounted.

As they passed the Stock Exchange a man shouted, *"Vive le Roi,"* and leaped from the sidewalk. He darted around the horse of a colonel in command of the guard, mounted the running board of the slowly moving car, and fired point-blank at the King. The colonel of the guard wheeled his horse and cut the assassin down with his sword, but the man continued to fire as he lay on the pavement, wounding police and bystanders until he was killed.

Amid the pandemonium that raged on that Marseilles street corner, the King of Yugoslavia lay dead in the car and Louis Barthou, wounded, was quietly bleeding. When at last it occurred to some that the life blood of the Foreign Minister of France was flowing out into the street, he was taken to a hospital, but it was too late to save him.

To die almost unnoticed, as an incidental casualty in another's assassination, might have seemed ironic to Barthou, who set considerable store upon the manner of one's going. He once said: "No one ever utterly dies, least of all when he dies well."

With Alexander and Barthou both dead, diplomacy in the Balkans rushed in to fill a vacuum. Amid the universal show of grief diplomats whirled like sea gulls snatching at happy accidents in the wake of a ship. For three days after the shooting Italian radio broadcasts predicted that this was the preface to the timely dissolution of Yugoslavia and acclaimed the assassins. When the Yugoslav chargé d'affaires at Rome protested on October 12, his reception at the Foreign Affairs Ministry came close to being a rebuff. The climate called to mind the shooting of another Balkan royal personage at Sarajevo twenty years before. The following day, however, the Italian mood changed abruptly. The Undersecretary of State for Foreign Affairs summoned the Yugoslav representative and, with elaborate courtesy and every sign of sympathy, promised an immediate halt to the broadcasts. Throughout Italy flags were flown at half-staff, and Mussolini sent earnest messages of condolence and dispatched a naval escort for the Yugoslav vessel that was bearing home the body of the fallen King through Italian waters.

Mussolini was probably moved to reconsider his attitude by an uncertainty as to the intentions of Adolf Hitler. Germany in 1934 was not yet prepared to launch a war, but it already loomed so menacingly over Europe that other nations walked on tiptoe. Although the death of the King had been plainly desired, if not encouraged, in Rome and Budapest, and Barthou's disappearance was greeted with considerable satisfaction in Berlin, grief was decorously displayed by all at the state funeral in Belgrade. In between ceremonies, however, Hermann Göring took time to woo the Prince Regent, who would henceforward rule Yugoslavia. Few doubted that whatever Germany was promising would ultimately be at the expense of Italian policy or ambitions.

Also in Belgrade for the funeral, the ministers of the Little Entente— Rumania, Czechoslovakia, and Yugoslavia—met, along with their Turkish and Greek counterparts, to speak out boldly, as only little powers can do. They ascribed the assassination to "forces beyond the frontiers" and declared that not only was it a plot against the life of the late King

Alexander and against the union of Yugoslavia, but it was in fact an
"outrage against the present international order in Europe." They would
not be content with a condemnation of the man who pulled the trigger,
or even of his comrades in Italy or Hungary, but called for the disclosure
of the "real organizers of the plot in all its extensive scope."

Then followed a month of jockeying at Geneva, for the League Council was the chosen battleground of all sides. The police disclosures were
not calculated to ease tensions. The assassin had carried a Hungarian
passport. He had come to Marseilles directly from Turin, where he left
two associates—members of the Ustachi—whom Italy declined to extradite. (Eden noted, long after the event, that in a general way he thought
Mussolini was at least aware of the plot before it was carried out.)

Yugoslavia and its allies had decided, even before the King was buried,
that Hungary, not Italy, must bear the brunt of the charges; it would be
safer that way. Dino Grandi let it be known that Italy would nevertheless
stand by her Hungarian ally. Beneš told Eden that though he "wanted to
handle the matter as quietly and tactfully as possible," the Council had
better take some action to satisfy the outraged Yugoslavs. France would,
of course, support Yugoslavia, but there would be a difference, now that
Barthou was gone.

When Pierre Laval appeared at Geneva in Barthou's place, Titulescu
commented: "France is a superb thoroughbred, accustomed to be
mounted by jockeys trained in a great tradition. Under Laval, France is
being ridden by a third-rate groom." Laval, at the age of fifty-one, was
master of the Château de Châteldon in the village of Puy-Guillaume in
the Auvergne, where his father had been innkeeper, butcher, and postmaster and where he himself as a boy had worked at all three trades. The
road from postman-butcher to chatelain ran by way of a career in law,
and subsequently in Parliament, with exceedingly profitable excursions
into business investments. Laval's path also ran from left to right. He was
a Marxist socialist when he was twenty, although in later years he explained that his was "a socialism of the heart" and that he was not really
interested in "the digressions of the great German pontiff."

He won his fame as a lawyer—in the manner of many French politicians—by defending strikers and leftists. He once told a meeting of trade-
unionists: "I am a lawyer in the service of manual laborers, who are my
comrades; a worker like them. I am their brother. Comrades, I am a
manual lawyer." His style was exceedingly plain and frank and it
charmed such diverse people as Henry Stimson, Sir John Simon, and
Marshal Pétain, that hero of Verdun whom Laval had seized upon years
earlier as a valuable political property. Laval had one abiding idea in

foreign policy: a Franco-German rapprochement. He had held stubbornly to it from the days of the Kaiser, through the Weimar Republic, to the ascendancy of Adolf Hitler. He once explained his point of view to his private secretary: "Regimes follow one another and revolutions take place but geography remains unchanged. We will be neighbors of Germany forever." As corollaries to the German policy were a fierce anti-Communism at home and a hope that Russia might one day be "thrust back into Asia." Now this man with the trim mustache and the white tie (it was his hallmark and he wore no other) came to Geneva in November 1934 with the proclaimed purpose of cooling the Yugoslavs, while comforting them.

All sides in the controversy turned to Britain as the one disinterested party who could restrain everybody, find a formula to save their faces, and keep them from a war that nobody wanted. Anthony Eden, on whom the burden fell, noted: "With all this tinder around the less public discussion we had the better."

Before the Council opened on December 7, 1934, the ground rules had been generally agreed upon: Yugoslavia was not to accuse Italy of anything and was to charge only secondary-echelon Hungarian officials, not the actual government. Eden would ultimately be elected the *rapporteur* charged with handling the delicate matter.

On the eve of the Council meeting, however, Yugoslavia began a mass expulsion of Hungarians, numbering many thousands, who had been living in its territory. The action was not calculated to reduce the temperature in the glass-enclosed Council Chamber at Geneva. To make matters more difficult, Eden started badly with a speech that was so bland it pleased nobody. He could not comment on the responsibility for the Marseilles assassinations, he said, because the matter was still *sub judice*. (France had not yet tried the assassin.) He added veiled warnings against extending the debate too far afield. He aimed that point at the Hungarians, who were threatening to open the matter of treaty revisions. On the other side, he offered a gentle admonitory tap to Yugoslavia by expressing the hope that no one would allow "local conditions"—meaning the expulsions—to exacerbate the question. The Council members had wanted him as a peacemaker, but he was being far "too neutral," Beneš told him afterward. And Titulescu suggested that the election of the *rapporteur* be put off over the weekend. The Paris papers were already referring to Eden as a Pontius Pilate.

On Sunday, Eden and a party of friends went off walking in the Jura Mountains, where, as he later recalled the episode, he sat on a hillside and resolved that he would not take the difficult chore of *rapporteur* unless he were given "a free hand." While he was thus meditating on his historic role, his diplomatic colleagues were looking for him everywhere in Geneva. When he returned that evening he talked with Laval, who suggested that inasmuch as war was quite possible this was not the time for Sunday excursions. The Yugoslav Foreign Minister, Boguljub Yevtitch, was gloomily predicting that, if he had to leave Geneva empty-handed, his government would fall and he would be replaced by a far less moderate man. Beneš, too, was nervous.

While the delegates made speeches on Monday, December 10, Eden shuttled back and forth between conferences with the nervous little Yevtitch and the smooth and suave Hungarian diplomat Kálmán de Kánya. A diplomatic formula was arrived at: all explicit references—and there would be few of them—would be put into the mouth of the *rapporteur*, Eden, so that neither side would be committed in fact to anything at all, but everybody could find satisfaction in one or another delicate nuance. De Kánya said he could not give his approval without communicating with Budapest. A Council session was set for the evening, while discussions went on over dinner and in repeated recesses. At eleven-thirty word came from Budapest that Admiral Horthy, the Regent and absolute ruler of Hungary, had given his approval to Eden's draft.

The resolution, a brilliant example of moderation carried to an extreme, declared that the Council, "being of the opinion, as a result of these discussions and documents, that certain Hungarian authorities may have assumed, at any rate through negligence, certain responsibilities relative to acts having a connection with the preparation of the crime of Marseilles:

"Considering, on the other hand, that it is incumbent on the Hungarian Government, conscious of its international responsibilities, to take at once appropriate punitive action in the case of any of its authorities whose culpability may be established;

"Convinced of the goodwill of the Hungarian Government to perform its duty,

"Requests it to communicate to the Council the measures it takes to this effect."

This resolution, expertly devised to resolve nothing, was hailed everywhere as a great victory for peace, the League of Nations, and Anthony Eden. The London *Times* on December 12, 1934, reported "sighs of relief" from Hungary and "acclamation" in the Yugoslav press. Italy foresaw a rapprochement with France. Prince Paul, the Regent of Yugoslavia, halted all deportations of Hungarians.

In Geneva the Hungarians formally offered "sincere thanks" to Eden. The Yugoslav delegate rose to express his gratitude "on behalf of the Royal Yugoslav Government." The Italians, the French, the Rumanians, followed suit in warm tribute. The President of the Council, Maxim Litvinov, said he, too, viewed the happy denouement "with the greatest satisfaction."

Eden modestly thanked his admirers. The world, it seemed, had been saved by the dexterous use of British fog to obscure the harsh contours of a political murder. In due course the Hungarians reported to the Council that two police officers had been dismissed from the force and that a commandant of the gendarmerie and two junior members of his staff had been transferred. The incident was closed.

The diplomatic consequences of Alexander's death had been neatly circumscribed, but the abrupt removal of Louis Barthou left an edifice half built. Parts of it would have to remain. The presence of Maxim Litvinov in the League Council was irreversible, but there were other sections of the building Barthou had planned that could be modified or dismantled. The mission of Pierre Laval, as he conceived it, was to do precisely that.

The Franco-Soviet pact would have to be completed, but it could be rendered no more than a façade. The Franco-Italian accord, which Barthou saw as a solid rampart against Germany, could and in time would be transformed into a gateway looking north to Berlin. In February 1935, Laval conferred with Mussolini, and completed an agreement the terms of which were not fully revealed at the time. He brought a partial report of the Rome conversations to London, where they received British approval and where he helped put together yet another plan for peace.

This new Anglo-French effort would hold out to Germany the bait of a revision of the Versailles disarmament provisions if it would return to the League, and sign Locarno-type treaties with all its neighbors to the east and an "air Locarno" in the west pledging united retaliation against the first power to use its bombers. The plan was to be presented to Hitler in Berlin on March 8, and afterward Eden was to sell the idea to Moscow, Warsaw, and Prague.

Just four days before the scheduled meeting in Berlin, British diplomacy torpedoed itself. While the left hand of Prime Minister Ramsay MacDonald was bestowing his blessing on a new approach to Berlin, his right hand was signing a White Paper announcing a vigorous British rearmament and placing the blame squarely on the Germans. It was German rearming, said the paper issued on March 4, 1935, that was imperiling the peace. It assailed the military training of German youth and concluded that "the international machinery of peace cannot be relied on as a protection against an aggressor."

Labour's member for Limehouse, Clement Attlee, attacked the White Paper as a blow against the League. On the far right Lord Lothian denounced it as unfair to Germany. And Adolf Hitler came down with an indignant diplomatic cold which required an indefinite postponement of the visit.

Strenuous and humble wheedling produced some improvement in Hitler's health, so that the visit could be rescheduled for March 25. On March 9, however, Göring publicly revealed the existence of the Luft-waffe, which was far more embarrassing as an acknowledged fact to be confronted than it had been as an open secret. Then, on March 16, 1935, Hitler publicly tore up the Versailles Treaty and, in the politest terms, defied the signers of that document to do anything at all about it. It was a proclamation to the German people of considerable dexterity in which Hitler appeared as a disillusioned champion of the purest internationalism, whose patron saint he invoked.

"When in November 1918," the proclamation read, "the German people, trusting in the promises given in President Wilson's Fourteen Points, grounded arms after four and a half years' honorable resistance in a war whose outbreak they had never desired, they believed they had rendered a service not only to tormented humanity, but also to a great idea per se . . . The idea of the League of Nations has perhaps in no nation awakened more fervent acclaim than in Germany, stripped as she was of all earthly happiness. Only thus was it conceivable that the German people not only accepted but also fulfilled the conditions, verily senseless in many respects, for the destruction of every condition and possibility of defense."

Hitler itemized Germany's dismantling of its armed forces, cited the failure of other nations to disarm, and declared that his government desired nothing more than "the power to safeguard peace for the Reich and thereby, really also, for all Europe." He then declared in effect a draft law that would raise an army of thirty-six divisions (about 600,000 men).

It was a plausibly worded, persuasive statement, although Hitler did not name the enemy that was necessitating armed defense of the Reich. Indeed, it would have been hard to do so, for all of Europe had watched Germany rearm in plain violation of the Treaty and permitted it although at any point its fledgling forces could have been overwhelmed. Even now, having provided the legal justification for military action by unilaterally renouncing a treaty, he knew there was little likelihood of any such reprisal.

There were expressions of shock in the press of England and France, where a sense of panic was in the air. France was now entering its lean years when its military effectives would be drawn from the diminished baby crop of 1914–18. For the next five years France could scarcely hope to raise an army of more than 350,000 men, and Hitler had just projected a force of almost twice that number, an army stronger than any in Western Europe.

The French, Russians, and Italians (Mussolini was exhibiting an unmistakable fright) confidently expected that Sir John Simon would retaliate with some diplomatic malaise, like Hitler's convenient cold, requiring cancellation or postponement of his voyage to Berlin. He remained in stubborn good health, however. The British Cabinet met on March 18, dispatched a protest to Hitler without any effort to concert the action with Britain's allies, and sent a rather self-abasing message by diplomatic channels hoping that Hitler's invitation still stood. Defending this policy against a stormy House of Commons on March 22, Sir John said: "To refuse to go, to cancel your engagement, why, sir, it leads you nowhere."

Laval, Litvinov, and Mussolini sent off their own heated protests to Berlin, but it was clear that there was no common front. The German note assuring the British that the Führer would still be glad to give them an audience was couched in the most cheery and cordial terms. On his way to join Simon in Berlin, Eden stopped by to soothe Laval and Mussolini, promising that the talks with Hitler would be no more than exploratory and that he would report fully to his friends. Mussolini suggested that the three powers meet at Stresa as soon as Eden's tour was over, in order, as he put it, "to take steps immediately to stop the rot."

Laval, who had already asked Avenol to summon the Council into extraordinary session, quickly agreed to put off the date for the meeting until after the Stresa conference. It was yet another humiliation for the League to have the Council wait on the private deliberations of the Great Powers at Stresa. This rankled with the lesser powers.

The Anglo-German talks in Berlin lasted for two days and rambled widely and indecisively. Hitler moved Eden to laughter when he compared the Officer Training Course at Eton to the militarization of German youth, but on other counts the Führer was more grim: Germany would return to the League only if it were rewarded with some of its former colonies, and it wanted an air force equal to France's. How big is the Luftwaffe now? asked Simon. As big as England's, said Hitler. (There are grounds to believe that Hitler was bragging at the time but the comment produced a shock.)

Eden seems to have differed from Simon and the Cabinet in his view of the gravity of the German preoccupation with the East. He wrote in his diary after an afternoon of listening to Hitler expounding on the Russian peril that he was opposed to permitting any German expansion eastward. "Apart from its dishonesty," Eden noted, "it would be our turn next." In a telegraphed report sent after leaving Berlin, Eden offered his opinion that an agreement with Germany was unlikely and that there might be only one course left for Britain: ". . . to join with those powers who are members of the League of Nations in reaffirming our faith in that institution and our determination to uphold the principles of the Covenant."

Eden took off from Berlin for Moscow confused by the fact that, though Hitler and the Nazi politicians inveighed against Russia in the most warlike tones and referred to the "leprous journey" he was now undertaking, the German military showed no such hostility. General Werner von Blomberg in particular asked him to carry greetings to his friend Marshal Voroshilov.

In Moscow a deeply worried Litvinov listened to Eden talk about Hitler's ambitions in the East. If this is so, said Litvinov, it is only "because [Hitler] thinks his policy is acceptable to Great Britain and other powers . . . he obviously considers that hatred of the Soviet Union in the world at large is so great as to excuse any venture on his part."

Litvinov also confirmed Eden's impression of the divergent views of the German General Staff. "The Reichswehr is much less hostile to the Eastern Pact and is always ready to make a bargain with the Soviet Union," Litvinov told Eden. "I have evidence of this from secret sources. The plan of the Reichswehr is always to dispose of France first, rather than to waste valuable time and energy on Russia. What is absolutely certain is that Germany intends to attack somewhere."

Stalin was calmer than Litvinov, though he thought the situation more alarming than that of 1913, because there were two "potential aggressors —Germany and Japan." Both Russians stressed the need for convincing Hitler that an attack anywhere would meet united resistance. When Litvinov came to the train to say his farewells, he grasped Eden's hand and said: "I wish you success. Your success will be our success—now."

Poland and the Poles charmed Eden but his interviews with Colonel Beck and the dying Pilsudski were chilly. Poland, blithely unworried about Germany, freely indulged its historic antagonism to Russia. In Prague, Eden relished Pilsener and ham while he listened to Beneš's warning that if the West isolated Russia it would come to terms with Berlin at the expense of the West. This was the view of Mussolini as well, Beneš assured Eden.

Seeking to avoid a stopover in Berlin, inevitable if he took the train from Prague, Eden chose to fly instead, and was caught in a violent storm north of Leipzig. Airsick, exhausted, with a racing pulse and a badly affected heart, he was taken off at Cologne, where the plane was forced down. A German officer was on hand to offer "the Führer's compliments." A German doctor who examined Eden pronounced the verdict: *"sehr schlecht"* (very bad), and ordered the dashing young diplomat humiliatingly to bed. When he was well enough to go on he took the boat-train to Dover and realized that he was in no shape to go to Stresa. Prime Minister MacDonald himself would go with Simon to confer with Laval and Mussolini on the crisis of German rearmament.

Whatever was in Mussolini's mind when he proposed the Stresa meeting, he proceeded to downgrade it before it convened. As his guests arrived he assured his people, through *Popolo d'Italia*, that the only purpose of the conference was consultation and that consultation implied no action whatever. Consultation was indeed the perfect solution in a situation where the alternatives of forthright resistance and forthright acquiescence seemed equally unbearable.

Frank Walters wrote: "The Stresa Conference was a meeting of powers which did not propose to do anything, and its results were in exact proportion to this fact." The statesmen met for three days in April in that pleasant resort on the shores of Lake Maggiore and wrapped up their deliberations in a resolution so vaporous that only one specific feature could be discerned by the naked eye—an accord on the independence of Austria. This was a particular preoccupation of Mussolini.

The Great Powers of Western Europe brought this shapeless package to Geneva and presented it to the League Council on the afternoon of April 16. It was offered for acceptance in terms which seemed to leave no room for amendment. It proclaimed the sanctity of treaties, condemned Germany for violating that sanctity, and would establish a committee to consider measures "which might be applied, should in the future a State . . . endanger peace by the unilateral repudiation of its international obligations."

In introducing the resolution, Laval said that it was designed "to provide a conclusion to this debate."

Salvador de Madariaga gently reproved the Great Powers for inventing a procedure which put a conclusion first and debate afterward: "I need not remind you," he said, "that it is the Council's custom first to hold a discussion and then to embody the results of that discussion in a resolution. . . . I presume that the text submitted to us will not remain unchanged; that has never happened at the Council, and it is unlikely to happen this time."

He was wrong. Whenever a Council member ventured a criticism, however oblique, he was steamrollered into impotent silence. Litvinov tried by homespun analogy to portray the menace of German rearmament: "Let us suppose that in a certain town private citizens are allowed to carry arms. Theoretically this right should be extended to all the inhabitants of such a town. Should, however, any citizen publicly threaten his fellow-townsmen, near or far, with attack or with the destruction of their houses, the municipality is scarcely likely to hasten to issue to such a citizen a license to carry firearms or quietly to tolerate his furnishing himself with such arms by illegal means. The promises of such an aggressive individual to spare certain quarters and only to give free play to his arms in other quarters can hardly be taken very seriously . . . it would scarcely be reasonable to expect them to defend the illegal acquisition by him of arms on the ground of the abstract principle of equality."

Sir John heatedly defended the resolution and warned Litvinov against trying to push things too far so that "our efforts may be lost in shallows and miseries."

De Madariaga also tried to impress upon the Powers that they were dealing not only with a treaty violation but with a potential aggressor. He too resorted to a simple illustration so that the case would be crystal clear: "The important thing when a man in the street carries a revolver is not to know what is its calibre or even if he has other weapons in his pocket, but to know whether he is a policeman or a criminal."

At the end of the second day the resolution, precisely as drafted at Stresa, was put to a vote. There was no opposition, and only Peter Munch of Denmark abstained. Even the milk-and-water of the Stresa resolution was too strong for him, he said, and he declined to sit in judgment on Germany.

Laval concluded the session on a note of self-congratulation. "It is by acts such as those of which France has already given proof at Rome, London and Stresa, that we shall continue to serve the ideal of peace."

His words rang incongruously, like the playing of the "Marseillaise" at the launching of a paper boat in a bathtub.

Thirteen

PARAGUAY, PALESTINE, AND
THE LAST DAYS OF DANZIG

Throughout the uneasy peace and informal, though bloody, hostilities that preoccupied the world since 1918, there was no declaration of war anywhere until May 10, 1933. On that day Paraguay declared war on Bolivia. At issue was a vast and largely uninhabited jungle of uncertain value—the Gran Chaco. In an inhospitable terrain, which alternated according to season between drought-parched soil and rain-soaked marsh, some 100,000 lives were lost in eighteen months. Yet despite the appalling loss of life, the war was treated as a side show; it was far from the main arena in Europe.

The League proceeded to its peacemaking calmly and with none of the excitement attendant upon European crises. The Chaco war was not without interest to European and North American states, however. Bolivia's transport system had been organized by a German general, Hans Kundt, and its army had been trained by Ernst Röhm, the man invited by Hitler to come home and head the storm troopers in 1930 before the Nazi accession to power. (The promotion proved a disaster for Röhm, who was killed in Hitler's purge of June 30, 1934.)

The Paraguayan army, on the other hand, was under the command of Colonel José Estigarribia, who had been trained at St. Cyr, France's military academy. The result, as Toynbee noted, was that both sides adopted the 1914–18 strategies of their respective military traditions, neither of which was at all applicable to the jungle. The dispute arose from conflicting interpretations of ancient Spanish land grants and vague mediation rulings by United States Presidents in the nineteenth century and more recent Pan-American Commissions.

Both sides brought the matter to the League's attention in July 1932, before war had been declared, though sporadic fighting had been going on for years. In July 1933, two months after the war was formally declared by Paraguay, the League Council appointed a fact-finding commission composed of Argentines, Brazilians, Chileans, and Peruvians. Later a young Spanish diplomat was sent out to head the mission. He was Julio Alvarez del Vayo, a jaunty, outspoken, and buoyantly optimistic man of boundless energy and left-wing convictions. He reached the Chaco shortly before Christmas of 1933, during a time of truce. He stayed in the battle zone until the middle of March and returned to Geneva in May 1934 to report on the war, which he termed "singularly pitiless and horrible."

In a statement broadcast from Geneva, he declared that the essential motive behind this apparently senseless war was "the lure of oil." Standard Oil of New Jersey admitted that it had invested heavily in Bolivian oil fields but insisted that these were not in the Chaco and that it had followed a policy of "neutrality" in the war. It was clear, however, that a Paraguayan victory would jeopardize the company's holdings.

The League commission drew up a peace treaty which both sides promptly rejected. Now Del Vayo urged that Latin American nations join with the League to impose a rigid arms embargo on both sides. Neither side could fight a day without imported weapons.

The Council delegates, their minds occupied with the crucial 1934 meeting of the Disarmament Conference, had little time for intervention in a South American jungle war. They were on the point of postponing the matter when Anthony Eden seized on Del Vayo's report and demanded that it be discussed within forty-eight hours. Britain had advocated an arms embargo earlier and, though the Council had accepted the principle, the consensus was that action would be utterly useless unless it was coordinated with the United States. Congress, however, had made no move. With Barthou rallying vigorously to his support, Eden succeeded in enrolling twenty-eight arms-producing League member states in a pledge to cease all sales to the belligerents.

Within days after the Eden-Barthou action at Geneva, President Roosevelt asked Congress for the power to impose an embargo. Congress complied this time. The ban was not quite airtight because the presidential decree allowed for the fulfillment of existing contracts, and that provided the fuel for several months' more useless slaughter. Some critics pointed out that the action was nicely timed to save Standard Oil fields in Bolivia from Paraguayan attack, and indeed Congress took pains in its bill to demand protection for those fields.

In January 1935, the embargo was lifted on arms sales to Bolivia but not to Paraguay, because that country had proven uncompromising. Paraguay was thus obliged to yield, and the war came to an end on June 14, 1935. Eden in his memoirs said that the League decision "was the first effective move in strangling a war which was bleeding two countries to death." But whether the victory, such as it was, properly belonged to the League, Bolivia, or Standard Oil of New Jersey was not quite clear.

At about the same time another South American war came to the attention of the League and proved more amenable to diplomatic handling. The prize for which this war was being fought was Leticia, a village of some three hundred people on the upper Amazon. There was no oil in the area to involve the Great Powers, but in earlier years the rubber in the region had been exploited with an enterprise so savage that it had shocked the world. Leticia was also a possibly strategic river port, should the cotton, tobacco, timber, and minerals nearby ever be rendered commercially important.

The town lay in a hazy border area where boundaries of four nations met: Colombia, Peru, Brazil, and Ecuador. A 1922 treaty had given the town to Colombia, which nettled Peru though it had received territory elsewhere in compensation. On the night of August 31, 1932, a band of Peruvians from the village of Iquitos, some two hundred and fifty miles upstream, swept down on Leticia. There were reports that the expedition was led by a disappointed Peruvian rancher who had tried in vain to sell his land to the Colombians. On the morning of September 1, the irregulars hoisted the Peruvian flag over Leticia and expelled all Colombian officials. (There was no garrison.)

At first the Peruvian government was the soul of diplomatic rectitude; it joined in condemning the raid, and offered full cooperation in the restoration of order and the return of the village to Colombia. Then, as popular feeling mounted in the frontier area, President Sánchez Cerro changed his mind. His military government was unsteady and he would not risk further disaffection. He therefore recalled that the original treaty assigning Leticia to Colombia had been negotiated by a dictator and was hence invalid. He offered to invoke the Pan-American arbitration machinery, but Colombia refused on the grounds that the border was not really in dispute and that the whole thing must be treated as a rebellion.

As the situation worsened the Council took time off from worrying about the meaning of Hitler's rise to power to dispatch a telegram to both sides urging them to avoid war. The Colombians had meanwhile sent a flotilla by way of the Panama Canal and the lower Amazon to Leticia. Whereupon the Peruvians shelled the vessels and took over not only Leticia but the surrounding area as well, which became known in diplomatic references as the Leticia Trapezium. Peru cited the precedent of Vilna.

In March 1933, the Council, having listened to Colombia's impassioned protests, voted to condemn Peru for aggression—an action which had no effect whatever in Leticia. The assassination of Peru's President did, however, achieve the desired results. Under terms of a treaty signed in May of that year, the Trapezium was to be administered for a year by a League commission with Colombian military backing. The commission sat out its year on the Amazon, at the end of which time Peru formally apologized to Colombia and renewed the original treaty. Perhaps the most significant aspect of the whole affair was that the League had to devise some banner to fly over the village. It chose a blue-bordered white flag on which was printed in simple large letters: "Leticia Commission, League of Nations." Aside from the banner contrived for the League pavilion at the 1939 World's Fair, it was to be the only flag ever made for the League. (Although the League tried to avoid exacerbating fears of a superstate, its American supporters continuously bombarded the Secretariat with designs for banners, emblems, pins, and anthems.)

The impotence of the League in the face of the Monroe Doctrine, and the determination of the United States to avoid any public links to the organization, led to a steady erosion of Latin American interest. It was a process the United States did nothing to discourage. By 1938, Chile, Brazil, Paraguay, Costa Rica, Nicaragua, Guatemala, and Honduras had all walked out of the League, never to return.

An area more open to the winds of European diplomacy and League intervention was the Middle East which had been carved at the bargaining table in Paris in 1919. The old Ottoman Empire had been chopped into mandates, and the League intervened mainly to solemnize accords arrived at between the mandatory power and its wards or to set the stage for compromise.

One such case was the uproar over the Sanjak of Alexandretta—the northwestern part of Syria, a French mandate. Less than half of the Sanjak's population of 220,000 was Turkish, but by special arrangement to appease Kemal Atatürk, the official language was Turkish and Turkish vessels were granted extraordinary privileges in the port of Alexandretta. The mandate was to end in 1939; unless events intervened, Syria would be independent and would include the Sanjak, which, it was agreed, would continue to operate along the same lines. This was not quite enough for Turkey. Accordingly, in 1936, Turks were seized with a sudden concern for their "brothers" over the border. Turkish troops were massed at the frontier, and Kemal himself set up his command post there. The French, to whom it would matter not at all whether the Sanjak residents spoke Turkish or Arabic and who were preoccupied as never before with the German threat, turned to the League Council to settle the matter.

The Syrian Arabs were irritated but unwilling to antagonize the Turks, on whom they counted for support when independence came. The only people gravely worried about out-and-out Turkish rule in the region were the Alawi-Armenians, who had barely survived the massacre by the Turks at Musa Dagh in 1915.

At Geneva, French and Turkish views were nicely harmonized by Eden and Rickard Sandler of Sweden. To seal the effectiveness of the understanding and calm Turkish fears, a permanent League delegate was dispatched to the Sanjak. As the time for local elections drew near at the end of 1937, the League sent a commission to assure the absolute freedom of the ballot. Kemal, however, did not find such assurance reassuring. An internationally supervised election in a region where Turks were in a minority would scarcely achieve the results he wanted. The French mandate authorities, under the guidance of Pierre Laval, desired nothing but to be rid of the problem and to retain Turkish friendship. They therefore collaborated with the Turks in rendering the League commission's task impossible. Opposition leaders, whether Arab or Alawi, were tossed into jail. Ultimately the League commission gave up and disbanded in a forthright burst of indignation. Non-Turkish elements were invited to leave for other parts of Syria, and the Sanjak was for all practical purposes turned over to Turkey. Thus Turkey and France, two of the most loyal pro-League nations, had conspired to defeat the League's machinery. To be defeated in the Sanjak of Alexandretta, however, was not regarded as a grave humiliation in Geneva. The injury was in too remote a part, like a stubbed toe that can be awkward but is rarely fatal.

No complication in the Middle East, however, compared with the collection of dilemmas, passions, hopes, and fears let loose by a straightforward letter which James Balfour had written to Lord Rothschild on November 2, 1917.

"His Majesty's Government," wrote Balfour, "view with favor the establishment in Palestine of a national home for the Jewish people, and will use their best endeavors to facilitate the achievement of this object, it being clearly understood that nothing shall be done which may prejudice the civil and religious rights of existing non-Jewish communities in Palestine or the rights and political status enjoyed by Jews in any other country."

In that year of world-wide convulsions no one could foresee the consequences of that sentence, which was subsequently converted into a formal pledge by the House of Commons. President Wilson gave it his blessing and read into it far more than Balfour had written: "The foundation of a Jewish Commonwealth." General Smuts had the same vision of "a great Jewish state rising . . . once more" in Palestine.

The Balfour Declaration had the happy British characteristic of combining high-mindedness with incidental advantages of a practical nature—all wrapped in convenient ambiguity. Stephen King-Hall wrote that it "seemed a great act of international justice, of idealistic Liberalism towards the chosen people, made by a race which in its heart of hearts also feels it is 'chosen' to play a peculiar part in world history." It also seemed a clever way of endearing the Allied cause to Jews, whether in Central Europe or in America. And it gave a moral justification to the British presence near Suez. Arab doubts were appeased by suggestions of a great unified Arab Empire rising out of the debris of Ottoman rule, and a promise that the return of the Jews to Palestine would not in any way infringe upon the political and civil rights of the Arabs there or elsewhere.

The writing of the check was easy; making it good proved enormously painful, bloody, and almost impossible despite heroic efforts. Events in Palestine followed a wild zigzag course, marked by high irony. The League's part in that history, rarely noted, was among the most ironic. The tremendous issues which were to wrack the area for half a century were all probed in the League, and the lines were drawn for a battle that might have altered the tragic pattern in the Near East.

Britain, as the power mandated by the League to bring Palestine to viable independence, tried desperately and vainly to reconcile the conflicting promises of the Balfour Declaration. It would veer from plan to plan, favoring the Arabs one year, the Jews another, seeking peace and being shot at, trapped in the contradiction of trying to facilitate the construction of a national home for one hard-driven people within the home of another people without infringing upon anybody's national aspirations.

In November 1936, Lord Peel, dying of a stomach cancer, listened to Jews and Arabs tell of their frustrations. As head of a Royal Commission he concluded that the Mandate, so proudly undertaken, was impossible to fulfill. In July 1937 he recommended that the Mandate be confined to the

Holy Places and that the rest of Palestine be divided into an Arab state and a Jewish state, both to be given immediate independence.

The Jews, though disappointed in the size of the projected state, endorsed the plan because it would carry the long-sought recognition of their nationhood. The League Mandates Commission, which had often been critical of previous British proposals, gave its approval. The Arabs, however, would have no part of it, emphasizing their dissatisfaction by means of a general strike and a wave of violence against the British and the Jews that took on the proportions of an uprising. Mussolini's growing ambitions in the Mediterranean inspired a stream of pro-Arab, anti-British, anti-Zionist propaganda in Arabic from the radio transmitters at Bari, and the official German news agency sent reams of copy to the Arab press, which used the material, often uncritically.

In 1938, another British commission found the Peel plan unworkable, and Prime Minister Neville Chamberlain summoned Arab and Jewish spokesmen to meet in St. James's Palace, London, on February 7, 1939. The Arabs refused to recognize the Jewish Agency and therefore there could not be a sensible round-table meeting. Arabs and Jews entered the Palace by separate gates so as to avoid incidents. At ten-thirty in the morning of February 7, Chamberlain gave his speech of welcome to the Arabs in their room, and at noon had to do the job over again for the Jews in their chamber. Colonial Secretary Malcolm MacDonald, the son of the former Prime Minister, and R. A. Butler shuttled back and forth between the two rooms in a vain effort to bring about some minimal agreement. The representatives of Egypt, Saudi Arabia, and Iraq did meet informally with the Jews, but all negotiations were wrecked on the issue of Jewish immigration. The Jews could not see the doors of Palestine closed at a time when thousands of their people were fleeing for their lives from Germany. The Arabs would not consent to opening the door for fear that they would be submerged.

After a month of these rancorous discussions, the Chamberlain government disbanded the conference and shortly thereafter produced the celebrated White Paper containing a new plan: A maximum of 75,000 Jews would be allowed into Palestine over the next five years, limiting the Jewish proportion in the country to one-third of the total population. Thereafter, additional Jewish immigration would depend on Arab consent. Jewish rights to buy land would also be restricted. Palestine would be neither a Jewish state nor an Arab state. Although it would have a built-in two-thirds Arab majority, the Jewish minority would be "safeguarded." The plan envisaged independence in about ten years.

Both sides opposed the White Paper, although the Arabs were somewhat less vehement about it than the Jews. In Britain popular reaction was also running against it. It was then that Malcolm MacDonald took the Chamberlain plan to the League of Nations Permanent Mandates Commission at Geneva. This was a body of experts holding no decisive power but wielding an enormous influence. Their recommendations to the League Council had never been disregarded. Commission members, chosen by the Council, were individuals holding no governmental posts, presumably representing no special interests.

On the afternoon of June 15, 1939, Malcolm MacDonald explained the dilemmas involved in "this most difficult of all mandates" to the six men and one woman comprising the Commission. When the Balfour Declaration was first drafted, with its promise to the Jews and its guarantees to the Arabs, there were in Palestine 80,000 Jews and 600,000 Arabs. Now, he said, there were 450,000 Jews, and even with the natural and immigrant Arab increase, the Jews accounted for a third of the population.

"The Jews have responded magnificently to their opportunity," said MacDonald. "They have achieved a creative work which can only be accounted for by the fact that, for many of them, the mandate was an inspired summons back to their historic homeland." Furthermore, he went on, the strength of the Jewish community cannot be reckoned in numbers alone. "It is skillful and self-confident, it is well disciplined; it has an economic power which makes its position in the country decisive."

On the other hand, the Arabs were in revolt against any further immigration of the Jews, he pointed out. Although well aware of the material prosperity the Jews have brought to the region, MacDonald said, "they are thinking of something more precious to them than any material advantage. They are thinking of their freedom. They recognize the industry and the skill and the wealth of the Jews, which are superior to those of most peoples, and they fear that the time is soon coming when the Jewish population will dominate them in their native country not only economically, but socially, politically and in every way."

MacDonald granted that the Arab revolt had been "disgraced by many acts of murder by bandits of the worst type," but added that nonetheless "it has also borne the undeniable stamp of a wide, patriotic, national protest." The White Paper, he said, embodied a plan to reconcile the hitherto irreconcilable.

William Rappard was not favorably impressed. A Swiss member of the Commission, Rappard had been for five years the director of the League Secretariat's Section on Mandates and knew the history of the question from its infancy. He had also been a professor of history and economics at the University of Geneva and at Harvard. He brought to the discussion a grasp of the situation and a schoolmaster's flair for withering irony. "The Commission had always done its best to approve the efforts of the Mandatory Power," the minutes quoted him as saying, "and had been almost acrobatic in its attempts to agree with the fluctuations of the latter's policy." If one were to interpret the Balfour Declaration as the British had, giving equal weight to both sides, it was an absurdity, Rappard pointed out. "How could there simultaneously be two entirely free peoples within the boundaries of the same country?"

The defects of the Balfour Declaration were harshly summed up by the Count José Capelo Franco Frazano de Penha Garcia, a former Portuguese Colonial Secretary who had been a delegate to the 1919 Peace Conference. The idea of creating a Jewish National Home in Palestine was a political error and possibly an economic one as well, he said. It was "a political error because the project of the creation of the Home was carried through without seeking the assent of the population already inhabiting Palestine, and an economic error because the great economic success of the Jews, which had been the cause of the economic solidity of the country, had not greatly impressed the Arabs or altered their attitude." The original error was impossible to correct, the Count declared, but what would become of the Jewish National Home if the Jews could not buy more land? he asked. Would it not be a "dead home"?

Lord Hankey, who had guided much of the British delegation's day-to-day task in Paris during the 1919 Conference and who had been a senior member of the British Cabinet, tried to justify the fatal omission of consulting the Palestinian Arabs before the Declaration was made. They were still under Turkish rule at the time, he pointed out. They were "a backward primitive sort of people without political consciousness." However, "as soon as they became aware that a wealthy and alien people was crowding their shores, they very naturally became alarmed." Later in the debate Lord Hankey recalled that the Declaration had been made "at a critical stage of the Great War" and that it was impossible to imagine that the British government meant to neglect the rights of the Arabs, "its actual allies, for the benefit of the Jews, the extent and power of whose assistance was as yet uncertain, notwithstanding the brilliant work of Dr. Weizmann in a technical field." (Weizmann was a distinguished chemist as well as diplomat.)

Lord Hankey offered the only shred of comfort to MacDonald in those June days of debate. All of the Commission seemed to deplore the Balfour Declaration, but six out of the seven regarded it as an ineradicable fact of history. The Jewish National Home was "the essential part" of the Declaration and the Mandate, as Valentine Dannevig, a leading educator and feminist of Norway, put it. The Home was "clearly against the will of the Arabs," she said, "but they had to submit to it. It was a Peace Agreement, and such agreements were often unjust to somebody—in this case, to the Arabs in Palestine—but it must be remembered that by the same Peace Agreement, the Arabs as a people had received full compensation elsewhere." They had been freed from Turkish rule, she said, and given sovereign rights over five extensive territories.

The chairman, Pierre Orts of Belgium, still another ex-delegate of the Paris Peace Conference and a former Red Cross president, agreed with Mlle Dannevig. He saw in the deal a bargain for the Arabs, though he declined to distinguish between those in Palestine and those outside it. "Was not consent to the establishment of a Jewish National Home in Palestine the price—and a relatively small one—which the Arabs had paid for the liberation of lands extending from the Red Sea to the border of Cilicia on the one hand, Iran and the Mediterranean on the other, for the independence they were now winning or had already won, none of which they would ever have gained by their own efforts and for all of which they had to thank the Allied Powers, and particularly the British forces in the Near East?"

Baron Frederick Mari van Asbeck, a Dutch jurist and former colonial official in the East Indies, also held that the essence of the Mandate lay in its promise that "the Jews would cease to be a minority in one part of the world." If it had been anticipated that the Arabs would have a constant two-to-one majority in Palestine, why would it have been necessary to guarantee their rights? he asked. And why would the Jews have come to Palestine if it were anticipated that the promise would be "whittled down" to the point where they might again feel they were "living in a ghetto"?

"The Jews were fighting for their lives," said Mlle Dannevig, "whereas the Arabs were fighting only for their political rights and national prestige."

MacDonald presented the grim picture of attempting to police the Mandate. He could not believe, he said, "that the Mandate was intended to provide that if the national feeling of the Arabs were so strong that they were ready to sacrifice their lives in defense of what they regarded as their liberty in their own country, those Arabs must be crushed by force." MacDonald tried to explain the intricacies of the governmental formula under the White Paper plan, how a two-thirds majority of Arabs would somehow share equal representation with the Jewish minority, how "executives" would really be "advisers," and how "advisers" would hold executive power.

Rappard said at that point that he "would not pursue further a verbal quibble" and that "it was a part of the great administrative experience and wisdom of the Government of the British Commonwealth of Nations to use words intended to give satisfaction to those who misunderstood them—a course often justified by results."

The verdict was plain before the vote. Chairman Orts had already declared that the plan was "contrary to the Mandate," and that any scheme which nullified the Jewish National Home would be unacceptable. The British should continue to exercise the Mandate and reconsider the possibilities of the Peel partition, he said.

In the end the Commission unanimously held that the Chamberlain White Paper was not consistent with the Mandate, and declared, by a four-to-three vote, that the Mandate could not possibly be "reinterpreted" to make the plan acceptable. The Commission report, greeted enthusiastically by the British public and press, was to be debated at the League Assembly scheduled for September 1939.

It may be doubted that the League Assembly—or any Assembly—could have solved the puzzle of Palestine, but it is equally doubtful, on the basis of past behavior, that the League would have scorned the advice of its Permanent Mandates Commission and approved the White Paper. In that crucial June a solemn League Commission had heard issues and arguments that perplexed and would continue to perplex the world for decades to come; it had arrived at tentative conclusions that might have changed the course of events in the Near East. Then, at the very moment of decision, the curtain fell.

On September 3, 1939, Britain was at war with Germany. When the Permanent Mandates Commission met again, on December 12 of that year, after an inevitable postponement, Chairman Orts reported: "As my colleagues are aware, circumstances have not yet made it possible for the Council or Assembly to proceed with the consideration of our last report."

Far simpler than persuading Jews and Arabs into peaceful cohabitation was the League assignment to adjudicate between French and German ambitions in at least one bit of Europe—the Saar. There, in 1934, a bill that had been incurred fifteen years earlier came due. According to the Treaty of Versailles, the coal mines of the Saar, a small but profitable region on the Franco-German border, were to be worked for the benefit of the French, as reparations for German destruction in northern France. A League commission was to administer the area for fifteen years, at the end of which time a plebiscite would determine the Saar's future.

What might have been a most ticklish crisis was made much more easily soluble by a series of unanticipated developments. In 1920, when the arrangement was decided upon, to the anguish of Germany and those who saw in it the imposition of harsh terms by a victor over the helpless vanquished, the Saar did indeed seem a rare prize of war. That was a time of acute scarcity, and reparation claims against Germany looked oppressive on paper. By 1932, however, reparations were a dead letter and the world was suffering from an acute depression, burdened everywhere with overproduction. Moreover, economically the cartels of Europe had learned to work together quite smoothly, undeterred by national considerations. The mines had been operated with reasonable efficiency and at a modest profit throughout most of the fifteen years, but in the 1930's they no longer looked like a prize worth fighting for. The government of the Saar under the League Commission had been free of grave crises. There had never been any real doubt as to the ultimate decision of the plebiscite, because the population was overwhelmingly German. A peaceful change-over might have seemed assured, but the accession of Adolf Hitler to power in Germany and the tactics of his followers began to pose problems.

In 1934 those tactics had been exhibited in Austria, where the pressure for forcible *Anschluss* was being applied by Nazis, both German and Austrian, in a drumfire pattern of back-to-the-Fatherland propaganda, intimidation of all opposition, threats, and riots. It was said at the time in Geneva small talk that the diminutive Chancellor Engelbert Dollfuss (barely five feet tall) was plainly worried and that he was seen pacing up and down—under his bed.

The jokes ceased abruptly, however, on July 25, 1934, when Dollfuss was brutally murdered and allowed to die without benefit of doctor or priest. Mussolini, alarmed at the prospect of Hitler absorbing Austria and camping on his Tyrolean borders, moved three army corps to the Brenner Pass. (It was only a month earlier that Hitler had promised him at Venice that he would not move in on Austria.) The Nazi coup of 1934 failed inside Austria, and Hitler called off the campaign. Yet now there were ominous echoes of that same style of persuasion on the borders of the Saar.

The motives were different, however. There was no doubt that the League plebiscite would return the Saar to Germany but the question was by what margin. It had been universally accepted that in the days of the Weimar Republic the vote, if it had been taken, would have been 90 percent for a return to Germany. Any sizable falling off from that figure would now appear as a defeat for Hitler. And there was the possibility of such a drop because, although Nazis were sent to infiltrate the Saar and political organizing was strenuous, anti-Nazis had fled there as well.

The five-man Governing Commission of the League was headed at that moment by an Englishman, Geoffrey Knox. He had at his disposal a police force of twelve officers and twenty-four men. (Originally the Governing Commission had the backing of four thousand French troops, but these had been withdrawn in 1927 to ease German resentment.) Furthermore, Knox was hemmed in on all sides by German spies. In desperation he ordered the arrest of both his chauffeur and his butler.

In November 1933 and again in January 1934, Hitler had tried to avoid the vote altogether in a deal with France. If the Saar would be quietly turned over to Germany—an action which would set a pretty precedent for nullifying the Treaty of Versailles—Hitler said he "would be prepared and determined not only to accept the letter, but also the spirit of Locarno." In August 1934, he held out the bait of lasting peace: "The question of the Saar is the only territorial question which separates us from France today. Once it has been solved there remains no visible ground why two great nations should continue to quarrel to all eternity."

The French declined the offer, choosing to preserve the framework of the League. However, the French, whether policy was made by Barthou or Laval, were not going to put up much of an electoral battle for the Saar. At a League Council meeting on January 20, 1934, Paul-Boncour proudly announced that France would abide by the freely expressed will of the Saarlanders. Their propaganda, directed mainly to promising a democratic government in return for a pro-French vote, was modestly financed, soft-spoken, and largely ineffective.

The Nazi point of view was expressed more emphatically. Deputy Party Leader Anton Scherer promised: "After the plebiscite in 1935, the National Socialist party of the Saar will be granted twenty-four hours for the day of reckoning and the night of the long knives. During those twenty-four hours the houses of the Jews and Marxists will be burned."

Göring let it be known that his eye was on the tiniest sparrow in the Saar: "Over there in the Saar they have the same agitators we used to have. There rules the Jew, as in Prague and Paris . . . When the time comes, I will see to it that the red rats do not creep into the holes of the black mice. There will then be no more question of 'assimilation' from one day to the next. I shall take care to mark my men."

Aside from the customary rallies and marches close to the border (Knox had banned such electioneering within the territory), the German political campaign was enlivened by repeated kidnappings of opposition spokesmen. Someone shot at the Police Commissioner and the local Nazis regularly assailed Knox as a "tyrant."

In May 1934, the League Council approved the plebiscite arrangements worked out by a committee of three, representing Italy, Spain, and Argentina. Sunday, January 13, 1935, was the day chosen for the vote. Baron Pompeo Aloisi of Italy addressed a strong appeal to both Germany and France to refrain from any attempts to influence the vote from outside: a vain plea inasmuch as France had scarcely raised its voice and Germany was simply channeling its support through the Deutsche Front in the Saar.

In the fall Eden conferred not only with Knox but with General Temperley, who, later recalling his own reactions to the emergency, commented: "We could not abandon an Englishman to his fate merely because he was temporarily a League official."

In November, Eden had a talk with Laval in Geneva which left him deeply troubled. Barthou had made a standing commitment that French troops would always be available to back up Knox should he need them. Now Laval, bemused by his policy of a Franco-German rapprochement, would do nothing to antagonize Hitler. If trouble came, Laval said, he would send no troops unless the League Council asked Britain and Italy to supply contingents as well.

On November 23, the embattled Knox came to Geneva. He voiced doubts that he could control the situation up to the plebiscite and the night of the long knives he feared would follow. He had hoped for a force of two thousand, but the Council's Saar Committee of Three had already told him that was impossible because no nation would be prepared to send in troops. The fate of Dollfuss was much in his mind. He wondered whether it was possible to give him a modest force of twenty-five officers and a hundred and forty men.

Eden wrote a memorandum outlining the dangers and proposing that Britain take the initiative of offering a military force to police the plebiscite. Then he hurried to London to press the matter. He met with a coolness verging on disinterest from his cabinet colleagues: Neville Chamberlain, Chancellor of the Exchequer, Lord Hailsham, Secretary of State for War, and Sir John Simon, that ever-cautious fixture of the Foreign Office. The Prime Minister, Stanley Baldwin, however, shocked the conservatism of his Cabinet by seconding Eden's proposal and declaring that "the country wants us to display more decision in international affairs and this is an occasion to do so." Eden's instructions, however, were very vague.

The objective was to leave French troops out of the picture altogether. Britain would merely offer to join an international force representing nations having no stake in the plebiscite's outcome. Italy would have to be persuaded in advance to follow Britain's lead. The whole move would have to be approved by both France and Germany.

The Council was due to meet on the Saar question at three-thirty in the afternoon of December 5. Eden arrived in Geneva on the evening of the fourth and gave the good news to Geoffrey Knox. On the morning of December 5, he saw Laval, who was much relieved at being let off the hook and gave the plan his fervent blessing. However, no sooner had Eden left Laval after the most explicit conversation than he received a telegram from Sir John instructing him to make no definite commitment to the French. Then came another message from London: The Cabinet was meeting at three-forty; could the Council be postponed?

It was too late for Eden to cover his tracks in fog and difficult to ask for a postponement without creating more doubt and confusion, which already existed in abundance. With only a few hours left for diplomacy, Eden hurried over to Baron Aloisi. The move would be an Anglo-Italian operation, he said, a prospect that he knew would delight Mussolini, who was feeling uneasy over the possibility of facing Hitler alone at the Brenner Pass. Aloisi went off to telephone Rome and came back in a few minutes with the promise of a brigade. It was one hour before the time set for the Council meeting when Eden dropped by his hotel and found still another message from London. The Italians would not be enough, the Cabinet felt. There must be at least a third contingent and, if possible, a fourth. He could choose from among the Netherlands, Belgium, and Switzerland. None of these nations were then represented on the Council and it was too late to enter into long-range negotiations. Eden decided he would have to go out on a limb and press his plan with no firm supporters other than the Italians.

Baron Aloisi was late for the Council meeting, a circumstance that gave Eden some bad moments, but he turned up smiling and the plan was quickly presented and quickly approved. Sweden and the Netherlands offered to support the force shortly thereafter and Germany gave its consent, so long as neither Russian nor Czech troops would be included.

The problem of getting the international force to the Saar by December 22 at the latest was left to General Temperley. There were to be 3,500 troops in all: 1,500 each from Britain and Italy, 250 each from Sweden and the Netherlands. The Italian military representative bridled at the suggestion that the force be commanded by an Englishman and offered a bargain: 1,500 troops if an Italian commands, otherwise no more than 1,300. General Temperley cheerfully accepted the 1,300 and turned the command over to a British major general.

As election day approached, special trains—all arranged by the Nazis—carried voters with a claim of Saar residency rights from all parts of Germany and some from the United States. On the day itself the Saarland voter was courteously called for by a representative of the Deutsche Front, saluted in the Nazi manner, and escorted to the polling booth, where a uniformed member of the Ordnungsdienst by his very presence symbolized the inevitable shape of things to come. Still, there was no blood flowing. The presence of the international force had been a sufficient deterrent and in fact there was little for the soldiers to do.

The vote went as expected: Of 528,105 ballots cast, 477,119 were for a return to the Reich; 46,613 for the *status quo* under League rule; 2,214 for incorporation into France. Hitler had topped the 90 percent mark, but only by a hair. The pro-German tally was 90.35 percent. The Council of the League met and formally recommended the return of the Saar to Germany. The French military insisted that the League assure the demilitarization of the Saar, the abolition of all fortifications in the zone, and a ban on military movements there, whether by the regular army or by storm troopers. However, Laval would not let such unpleasant considerations mar the burgeoning harmony with the Reich and forcefully overruled his General Staff. He declared that the vote had been free and France would prove its fidelity to the Treaty.

The Governing Commission filed its last report to the League Council. It had started operations in debt and after fifteen years was turning over to Germany a relatively prosperous industrial community, in which public works had been built, communications extended, and the budget balanced. The Third Reich paid France the agreed-upon price of nine hundred million francs for the mines, railroads, and improvements. By the end of February the international force had gone, and on March 1 the Saar returned to the Fatherland.

The League had certainly proved its usefulness in the Saar, and Anthony Eden proclaimed that the orderly conduct of the plebiscite was "a glimpse of a supra-national salvation." The salvation, of course, was procedural and careless of political consequence, which in this case was an aggrandizement of Nazi territory and prestige.

The victory at the polls in the Saar gave encouragement to German political leaders in another zone which had also been detached from the Reich by Versailles and where another League commissioner was kept dancing on a griddle heated by Nazi claims and by the protests of their apparently helpless opponents.

The status of the Free City of Danzig, situated where the Vistula empties into the Baltic, had been the result of some desperate map drafting at Versailles in 1919 designed to give the newly independent state of Poland access to the sea without doing too much violence to the Wilsonian notions of equity for the conquered and ethnic self-determination. The port and a backup area of some 750 square miles was to be a self-governing, democratic province under a constitution safeguarded by the League of Nations in the person of a resident High Commissioner. The League was also empowered to handle the port's relations with Poland.

Poland was given access to Danzig through a "corridor" about one hundred miles long and fifty miles wide carved out of Prussia. The corridor was an ever-rankling grievance for Germans, to be sedulously preserved for use as tinder. Facing the corridor on the East Prussian side stood a simple monument inscribed: "Never forget, Germans, of what blind hatred robbed you."

The Senate ruled the port and the High Commissioner of the League smoothed over the occasional arguments with Poland, all quite uneventfully until Hitler came to power in Germany and stirred echoes in the Free City. In May 1933, the Danzig Nazis won a majority in the city's Senate, and Hermann Rauschning became the President. An elderly man, he proved to lack the proper Nazi vigor. He did not hate the Jews quite as much as he hated the Poles, and his conservative ideas about the management of the port's economics made inevitable either his surrender or a clash with Albert Forster, Gauleiter of Danzig and personal friend of Adolf Hitler, who fondly called him "Bobby." Forster was a young Hitlerian in mind and soul, and expressed himself fully in the newspapers he controlled.

On October 31, 1933, Arthur Greiser, Forster's lieutenant, a weak man who could smile up at his superiors and look harshly down on all others, laid down the line: There were to be no more political parties; anti-Nazis were to be eliminated from civil service posts; and only certified Nazis could be in the police force. Two Danzig newspapers that commented unfavorably on Herr Greiser's speech were shut down. When their editors complained to the League, they were jailed, charged with imperiling the state by involving the League before seeking recourse through Danzig law.

The matter came before the Council of the League on January 18, 1934. In preparation for the discussion Forster and Greiser had released the editors and lifted the ban on the papers. Sir John Simon was given the job of *rapporteur*, in which capacity he followed a familiar formula for obscuring the issue by diluting every statement with some countervailing condition that rendered the whole thing innocuous.

He granted that in the interest of public safety newspapers might have to be suspended, although he would not go so far as to say that in this case such action was justified. Nor would he go so far as to say that it was not justified. Certainly, penalizing the editors was unconstitutional. On the other hand, the question was: Had the editors exhausted all legal remedies within the framework of the Free City's laws? The High Commissioner would have to consider that question while taking no action that would tend to discourage those Danzigers who wished to bring complaints to the League.

The resulting Council resolution hit the Danzig Nazis with the force of a feather. Still, it served to remind them that the Constitution and the League were potential obstacles. The Saar vote inspired in them a hope of accomplishing reforms by "constitutional" means, reinforced by the Nazi manner of forceful electioneering. The objective was to win two-thirds of the Senate, which would give them power to rewrite the Constitution of the Free City and thoroughly Nazify it by way of preparation for its return to the Reich.

Accordingly, on February 21, 1935, they dissolved the Senate and called for new elections. Rauschning had been denounced as a traitor and had been replaced by the cooperative Greiser in the office of President of the Senate.

The rules of the election campaign were laid down. Only Nazis were permitted to broadcast. Opposition papers were allowed to publish, but frequently entire issues would be confiscated. From Germany came a string of campaigners to bring to Danzig the razzle-dazzle of Nazi spectaculars. Göring, Goebbels, Julius Streicher, and Rudolf Hess addressed mammoth rallies. Still, when the votes were counted the Nazis had gained only two seats in the Senate, giving them forty-three out of a total of seventy-two, five short of the necessary two-thirds. They had a bare 57 percent of the popular vote.

Frustrated but nonetheless determined, Greiser and Forster began to run the city as if they had won their objective. Into the offices of the High Commissioner of the League, the quiet but courageous Irish diplomat Sean Lester, came a stream of anguished petitions from Catholics whose schools were being invaded, from Jews whose shops were boycotted or wrecked, from old-line constitutionalists whose organizations and liberties were being stomped on. Lester intervened where he could and thereby made himself a target. The new High Commissioner, who had come fresh from the comparatively genteel Latin American sector of League diplomacy, found himself in a world of street brawls and terror.

The family walks of the Lesters through the woods were occasionally interrupted by the furtive appearance of a victim of the Nazis who would leap from the shrubbery to seize the opportunity of bringing a complaint to the High Commissioner without running the risk of being seen going into his office.

Lester asked the Council to intervene, and in May 1935 he presented a torrent of petitions at Geneva. Greiser and Lester were both on hand. The President of the Danzig Senate answered all attacks by declaring that the boycotts of Jews, the suppression of Catholics, and the humiliation of the moderates were merely spontaneous expressions of the people's will, which the government, being responsive to that will, could scarcely control. He followed that defense up with a blistering attack on Lester.

Anthony Eden, not Simon, was the *rapporteur* this time. His reaction was so unexpectedly tough that Greiser backed down, and apologized for his outburst against Lester as one that was meant not personally but only as indicative of "popular opinion." At Eden's suggestion, the Council named a committee of eminent jurists to investigate the constitutional violations, and, at the end, a somewhat humbled Greiser promised to abide by the Committee's findings.

Still, the Nazi momentum could scarcely be halted or slowed. The Committee of Jurists issued their report in the summer of 1935, declaring illegal and unconstitutional the entire set of Nazi regulations restricting associations to those approved by the Senate, banning newspapers, and authorizing repressive measures against the Jews. The situation of the Jews, the Committee warned, was very grave. Forty-eight hours after the Committee closed its books, trucks of storm troopers drove into Danzig to give the locals "a lesson in Jew baiting."

Lester, in line with the High Commissioner's role as watchdog of the Constitution, then challenged the legality of new amendments to the Criminal Code making it possible to punish Danzigers "in accordance with healthy [that is, Nazi] public opinion" even if they violated no laws. As a result he came under increasing attack. On November 13, 1935, Lester noted in his diary: "A trench is being dug in the garden—ostensibly to repair drains. It is symptomatic of conditions here that I take note of any operations of this kind. I heard from ex-President Rauschning some time ago that a cable had actually been laid from the Senate to my garden wall with the intention of installing dictaphones during his period of office as the first National Socialist President. It came to his knowledge and he stopped it . . . The telephones are, of course, tapped. My butler is a spy."

Lester's visitors were photographed on his doorstep. Once, when he went to dine with a distinguished political figure who had presided over the Senate in pre-Forster days, he felt the ubiquitous Nazi presence. "As we alighted from the car," he noted, "four young men converged, examined us and withdrew. Police or Nazi."

He went to Berlin to complain and was given soothing but unconvincing reassurances that Gauleiter Forster's behavior did not have German backing. In Danzig protocol required the maintenance of friendly relations with Greiser, in his official capacity, if not with Forster. This meant bridge games and hunting trips interspersed with occasional confidences. Lester came, as he confessed, to have "a sneaking sympathy" with Greiser because he seemed to be a reluctant if still pliant tool of the Gauleiter. The clash between them was nonetheless inevitable.

On January 22, 1936, Lester came before the League Council and declared: "There must be a complete change in the attitude of the local government or a change in the machinery through which the League's guarantee is made effective." Eden, as the Council's *rapporteur*, entered into private talks with Greiser and with Poland's Colonel Beck. It is not known precisely what was said, but Eden had a trump to play: the possible pull-out of the League from Danzig. At the time this was a threat of some significance because if that occurred the Germans and Poles would face each other with no buffer between them. Poland would not yield Danzig and the Germans were not yet ready to fight a war for that port. The time for that was still three and a half years away.

When the Council on January 24, 1936, itemized the steps which the Danzig Senate must take to bring its administration into line with the Constitution, Greiser gave in. For four months after that there was relative calm in the Free City, and Greiser's family even cultivated seemingly cordial relations with the Lesters. In June, however, the wind from Berlin veered again, and now the League was denounced for its comfort to Jews and "traitors." When the German cruiser *Leipzig* scheduled Danzig as a port of call, Lester followed diplomatic protocol by inviting the ship's officers and high Danzig notables to an official reception. The High Commissioner was waiting for his guests when word came from the cruiser that under orders from Berlin the officers were not to call on him.

On June 13, 1936, Lester was faced with brutal confirmation of the end of the truce. He came home that evening from a ceremonial attendance at a display of horsemanship to be told that people had been clamoring at the door with stories of a "massacre" only a hundred yards up the street. Storm troopers had broken up a conservative but non-Nazi political meeting. Ambulances had been coming and going all evening, carting off the injured, including many elderly people. For days afterward witnesses streamed to the High Commissioner's house carrying the still-bloody weapons snatched from the storm troopers. "We all served in the war and we won't be killed in cold blood," some of them told Lester. The law, he reminded them, was their only strength, and in Danzig the only reliable guardian of the law was Lester.

His report to Geneva brought an invitation to Greiser to appear before the Council of the League on July 4, 1936. Greiser complied but traveled by a roundabout route to allow for a stopover in Berlin.

The mood in the Council chamber was somber. Only the day before Greiser was due to appear, a Czech photographer and journalist, Stefan Lux, walked to the Council table and, in full view of the Council members and the press, raised a pistol and shot himself. Anthony Eden, presiding, suspended the session. Lux died in a Geneva hospital later that night. He left letters addressed to King Edward VIII, to Eden, and to several colleagues and friends to explain that his death was designed as a protest against the treatment of Jews in Germany.

Arthur Greiser came into the Secretariat building on the morning following the tragedy. His voice, never soft at the most relaxed of times, now fairly boomed in the corridors, where he announced that the time had come to deal with the League as it deserved, by means of heavy bombers.

When he spoke from his seat at the Council table his voice filled the chamber, and, though he was careful to flatter the Poles, he assailed the League and all its works. He declared at the outset that he spoke "as the governor of 400,000 Germans who did not wish their destinies to be eternally linked with the League of Nations; who . . . did not understand the ideals of that institution; and whose hearts, united to the German people by ties of blood and racial affinity, spoke a different language from that which it was sought to impose upon them by a Constitution that remained alien to them." He complained that twice in a single year his "peaceful work" had been interrupted by a summons to Geneva, a mission which, he implied, was a total waste of his time.

He blamed the League and Lester for failing to solve the problem of unemployment, for exacting contributions to afford the High Commissioner a way of life in "flagrant contrast with the poverty of the mass of the population." Above all, he denounced Lester for violating "democratic principles" by assisting a minority that was "arrogating to itself the right to terrorize a constitutional majority." If anyone doubted that he had the support of the majority and hence a democratic legitimacy, he was ready to organize still another plebiscite. Danzig owed its security not to the League but to the "greatness" of two men: Adolf Hitler and Marshal Pilsudski. Eden, in the President's chair, noted that Colonel Beck squirmed in visible uneasiness at this.

Greiser offered two alternatives to the Council: Send a new High Commissioner to Danzig with instructions to refrain from "interference in internal politics" or else dispense with the High Commissioner altogether, in which case he, as President of the Danzig Senate, would be responsible to the League of Nations. "In this way, order and peace would be assured forever in Danzig . . ."

When he concluded his speech Greiser rose from his seat, walked around the table to where Eden sat, shook his hand, and then gave the Hitler salute. From the press gallery which rose in tiers facing the head of the table came mocking laughter. Solemnly he walked behind the chair of Colonel Beck, where he again offered the Nazi gesture. Again the press laughed. He continued on, then passed in front of the press gallery. He raised his arm a third time, then bent it at the elbow and defiantly and ridiculously thumbed his nose and stuck out his tongue—"cocked a snook," as the British press reported it.

Eden was at that moment in a huddle with Avenol about arrangements for a closed Council meeting to consider the situation. He looked up as Greiser exited amid pandemonium. Robert Dell, correspondent for the Manchester *Guardian* and dean of the Geneva press corps, called out in a shrill voice, unaccountably using French in his excitement: "Monsieur le Président, la presse du monde insultée." ("The press of the world has been insulted.") Eden insisted he had not seen what had happened and could therefore take no action, but he told the press that "whatever it was, he thought it best became their dignity to take no notice."

The Council formally voted its confidence in Lester, but that was its last gesture of resistance. Within two months Lester was appointed a deputy to Secretary-General Avenol and thus removed from the scene. A new Committee of Three (composed of representatives of Britain, France, and Sweden) investigated and filed yet another report on the terror imposed by the Senate of the Free City. It asked the Polish government to intervene. Colonel Beck made efforts to protect the Polish inhabitants of Danzig but showed a marked lack of interest in other minorities. In January 1937, he suggested that the new High Commissioner chosen to replace Lester be instructed to refrain from "hampering the internal administration of Danzig." (Poland by then was seeking its security in a pact with Germany.)

In February, the Council stripped the High Commissioner's post of almost all its powers. Henceforth that functionary could receive complaints, but he could not place them on the Council's agenda. Such action could be taken only by the Committee of Three. By that time the Nazis had achieved their two-thirds majority in the Senate, and the Constitution was abolished, so that terror would be legal, just as the dominance of the Nazis was now "democratic."

The man chosen to exercise the impotence of the High Commissioner's office was Carl Burckhardt, a Swiss professor, who thought that, rather than defy the Nazis, it would be better to palliate the evils of the regime, cajole or manipulate the Gauleiter, and thus perhaps save a few individuals. Hitler conferred his blessing on this policy by expressing his "appreciation and respect" for the new League representative.

Burckhardt handled Forster with irony that may have missed its mark and with flattery that didn't. He practiced a similar brand of diplomacy on Göring, whom Hitler had put in charge of Danzig affairs. As Burckhardt later told the story to Lester, he found the General "lying on a large canapé [couch] covered with bright velour. He wore a gay uniform, his breast covered with decorations, knee breeches and pink silk stockings. He could not rise as he was having applications of ice to his leg where he had received a kick from a horse." Burckhardt won Göring's admission that the handling of the Free City seemed to be "maladroit." He admitted to Burckhardt that it was German policy "to keep the wound open in Danzig" but said that he wanted no more excitement than was absolutely necessary.

Burckhardt tried to prevent the imposition of the Nuremberg Laws in Danzig, but they were slyly imported from Germany while he was on a trip to Berlin. For a while he refused to go back to his post in protest, but finally he was persuaded by the Council's Committee of Three to resume his "palliation."

He was still at his post on August 31, 1939, though he knew the end was coming. That afternoon Gauleiter Forster had come by to tell him that the Führer wanted things to go smoothly in Danzig. Burckhardt, knowing that it was too late for palliating diplomacy, brushed him off by asking why he should come with absurd jokes when he knew perfectly well that they were about to launch the war.

Burckhardt had sent his family away to safety and had only the British consul-general with him that evening for dinner. With a kind of gallows humor they persuaded the butler to wear a gas mask while he served the coffee. After the consul-general had left, three Gestapo men came to the door to warn the High Commissioner not to go to bed because the Gauleiter would want to see him later. Coolly Burckhardt said he would see Gauleiter Forster in the morning and went to his bedroom while the Gestapo men busied themselves cutting the telephone wires and occupying the lower floor of the house.

At four-thirty in the morning the windows in Burckhardt's bedroom were shattered, as the German battleship *Schleswig-Holstein* began shelling the tiny garrison on the Westerplatte.

At eight o'clock Forster arrived with his aides and told the High Commissioner of the League: "You represent the Treaty of Versailles; the Treaty of Versailles no longer exists. In two hours the Swastika will be hoisted above this house. You will be escorted to the frontier or, if you wish to stay, you will stay as a private individual."

Burckhardt said he preferred to leave. At this Forster stepped slightly out of his role and said: "I hope this will not interfere with our private relations."

"Sir," said Burckhardt, "I never had any private relations with you and never wish to have."

The last League High Commissioner of Danzig packed under the eyes of the Gestapo and departed.

Fourteen
"GOD AND HISTORY WILL REMEMBER . . ."

"Throughout their history the people of Ethiopia have seldom met with foreigners who did not desire to possess themselves of Ethiopian territory and to destroy their independence. With God's help and thanks to the courage of our soldiers, we have always, come what might, stood proud and free upon our native mountains."

This serene reflection on a salient fact of his country's life was made by Regent Ras Tafari Makonnen, who, after his coronation as Emperor Haile Selassie I, was to embody the epitaph of an age. He made this wry and gallant observation in a circular letter to the member states of the League on June 19, 1926, at a time when England and Italy were agreeing upon a list of concessions each wanted from the two-thousand-year-old empire. Britain wanted a dam on Lake Tsana to control the Blue Nile and a road running from the lake across seventy miles of Ethiopian territory to the Sudan. Italy wanted to build a railroad linking its two colonies in Eritrea and Somaliland, which embraced a portion of Ethiopia like the arms of pincers. Only after the newspapers leaked the Anglo-Italian secret compact to promote each other's interests did the two powers inform the Ethiopians. When Ras Tafari formally protested to the League, both Italy and Britain promptly renounced their campaign of pressure, and in 1928 Ethiopia signed a treaty of friendship with Italy.

Friendly relations with Italy were not surprising in that year. In 1923 Italy had been among the most ardent champions of the admission of

Ethiopia to the League, over objections by the British, who stressed the feudal character of Ethiopian society, the uneven control of the central government, and the continuing institution of slavery.

In 1930, when Ras Tafari assumed the crown, he resolved upon a gradual but determined effort to bring Ethiopia into the modern world without diminishing its ancient dignity. He was an autocrat but did not treat his country as his private property. He "lived like a gentleman within his bounds and spent the state's money on the state," according to the London *Times* correspondent George Steer. He indulged a taste for good wines, books, music, and horses, and he had a private cinema. His most extravagant desire, never actually realized, was to import a couple of motorboats.

To "modernize" his country he hired an array of experts in various fields. These included Swiss, Belgians, English, Germans, Swedes, one Italian, and an American. It was the American, Everett Colson, who became the Emperor's financial adviser and one of his closest political mentors. Everett Colson was a large, quiet, cool man given to high irony. Washington had suggested him for the job because he had served successfully to untangle the finances of the Philippines, China, and Haiti. He combined a stockbroker's canniness with a lofty idealism and a profound distrust of European—particularly Italian—encroachments. The tall American, with his shaggy gray mustache and his floppy-brimmed hat, became an important figure in the colorful court of the Emperor. Much of Ethiopian diplomacy was hatched in his little six-room house, where he would meet reporters and interpret the Emperor's policy.

Colson's wariness of Italian ambitions was soundly based, for the Roman Empire in the 1920's consisted of some pathetically profitless strips of African real estate, and there was vigorous Italian hunger for a real empire. In the 1920 Assembly of the League it was the Italian representative, Tommaso Tittoni, who bridled at a Canadian suggestion that economics had no place on the League agenda. "Henceforth, it must be frankly admitted that the existence of nations depends on the solution of economic questions," said Signor Tittoni. "To those privileged states which enjoy a monopoly with regard to raw materials, and to those whose wealth has permitted them to acquire a monopoly of these materials outside their boundaries, I say, 'Do not wait to be appealed to by the poorer states which are at the mercy of your economic policy, but come forward spontaneously and declare to this Assembly that you renounce all selfish aims, and before the bar of the League of Nations declare yourselves ready to support the cause of international solidarity.' " The appeal was largely lost upon the Powers of the League, and by the early 1930's this economic grievance was intensified by Benito Mussolini's infatuation with his image as a latter-day Caesar.

On January 3, 1933, Mussolini was dispatching Count Vinci, his ambassador, to Ethiopia. Baron Pompeo Aloisi, the Italian representative at the League, who was present at the time, noted in his diary that the Duce "gives his instructions for a policy of friendship designed by all means to conceal our plans and the peripheral policies which will be followed by Rome. Mussolini believes, without sharing the view held in military circles, that a war operation in Ethiopia on our part would succeed on the condition that we are completely free in Europe. He says that the military committee, headed by De Bono, has already studied all the plans. In the course of his mission Vinci must allay all suspicions."

A free hand in Europe was thenceforth to be the aim of Italian diplomacy at Geneva and elsewhere. It was not in sight, however, when a ready-made pretext for war presented itself. In December 1934, an Anglo-Egyptian boundary commission was trying to determine the border between Ethiopia and Italian Somaliland. The commission's Ethiopian escort of about six hundred men reached a group of wells at Walwal in the disputed zone. The wells had always been used in peace by the local inhabitants. A small Italian army post had been set up a few miles south of Walwal without major protest from Addis Ababa. Now, however, with the arrival of Ethiopian escort troops in some strength, trouble broke out between them and the Somali soldiers under the Italian flag. Reinforcements rushed up from both sides. Italian planes buzzed the Ethiopians and the British colonel in charge of the boundary mission withdrew, complaining that he had been "constantly thwarted" by the Italians.

On December 5, 1934, the fighting began on a larger scale, and in the weeks that followed, Italian tanks and bombers forced the Ethiopians to withdraw, leaving some one hundred dead behind. The Somali troops of the Italians lost about thirty. Haile Selassie promptly invoked the 1928 Treaty of Friendship with its machinery for arbitration. Rome, however, would have no part of it, insisting that there was no matter of doubt to be decided by an arbiter. Walwal was Italian; the Ethiopians had attacked; therefore the governor of the province must appear at Walwal and, in the presence of Italian and Ethiopian troops, salute the Italian flag, apologize, and pay reparations for Italian losses. The Ethiopians, who not long before had undergone a similar ritual of abasement in connection with an incident at an Italian consulate, were in no mood to repeat the ceremony. The Emperor thereupon addressed a series of telegrams to League Secretary-General Avenol calling the attention of the Council to the breach of peace and to the ominous massing of Italian troops.

Still, the Duce was not yet prepared in Europe. He was encouraged, however, by the advent on the scene of Pierre Laval, who had assumed the French Ministry of Foreign Affairs following the murder of Barthou.

On Christmas Day 1934, Mussolini summoned Baron Aloisi and told him that the Ethiopian affair would not be "ripe" for action until a pact with France was achieved and that he, Aloisi, had better speed up his diplomacy. Laval, who saw a pact with Italy as a prerequisite to his ultimate ambition of a Franco-German rapprochement, was no less eager. Accordingly, on January 4, 1935, the French party arrived at the seedy provincial station of Roma Termini. Mussolini, striking the pose of a stern Roman Emperor, confronted the unprepossessing Laval, wearing his customary white tie and soft beige hat, exhibiting in his smile a set of blackened teeth. With him was his daughter, Josée Laval, and a string of diplomatic advisers.

Plumed carabinieri and Blackshirts were everywhere, as assassination threats had been reported. The crowds along the way to the Hotel Excelsior were unenthusiastic, dutifully shouting, *"Viva il Duce,"* but murmuring, *"Vive Laval."*

A few days before his arrival, the French Premier had sent ahead an offer of parts of French Somaliland, which he thought might appease Mussolini's African ambitions. The gesture was not appreciated, and Mussolini was grim when the talks opened at the Palazzo Venezia. "I am not a collector of deserts," he said, pointing out that he already had too much African sand for his taste. "I have sent Marshal Balbo to take photographs of the zones you have suggested you might grant me," he told Laval. "I have them here for you. They are lunar landscapes."

"All the same," said Laval, "there are two towns." (Actually they were bases where the French had kept some camel-corps troops but had to withdraw them because of the mosquitoes.)

"Two towns!" Mussolini exclaimed.

"Obviously," Laval said smilingly, "I don't mean that they are Rome or Aubervilliers," Laval's home town, where he still held the title of Mayor. Mussolini then burst out laughing and the chill was taken off the talks.

At the French Embassy in the Farnese Palace, the diplomats and the glittering lights of Roman society gathered for a banquet to celebrate the signing of a Franco-Italian pact of peace and friendship. After the dinner (at which the Duce was confined to boiled vegetables out of consideration for his ulcer) the two principals retired to an office upstairs to tie up the loose ends. The diplomatic experts of France and Italy confronted each other in yet another room. Jean-Paul Garnier of the French staff ran messages back and forth.

It was after midnight, Garnier later recalled, when Mussolini suddenly sent word to his negotiating team to yield completely to the French on outstanding technical points. The Italian negotiators felt "betrayed," Garnier reported. Plainly something had been resolved in private between Laval and Mussolini, though what it was did not appear on the record and was to be a matter of violent controversy.

In subsequent correspondence between the two, Mussolini contended that he had been given a "free hand" in Ethiopia. Laval insisted that he had meant a "free hand" in economic matters only. When Anthony Eden later told Mussolini that Laval had so confined that free Italian hand, the Duce "flung himself back in his chair with a gesture of incredulous astonishment."

Whether Pierre Laval assured Mussolini that he would in fact be free to ravish Ethiopia, or inadvertently allowed himself to be misunderstood, or purposely enshrouded his words in diplomatic ambiguity, it is impossible to determine. In any case, to Laval, bent on salvation through an understanding with Germany, and to Mussolini, with his eye on the glories of a new Roman Empire, the Franco-Italian pact was a matter for self-congratulation. To lesser diplomats, unblinded by such visions, the agreement seemed badly flawed even at the moment of its signing. The Italian Secretary for Africa, Guarnaschelli, when asked to comment the night after the conclusion of negotiations at the Farnese Palace, said cryptically: "When a cat is hurried, she gives birth to blind kittens."

Meanwhile, the Ethiopian delegate to the League, Tecle Hawariate, was proceeding according to the rules as if everything that happened outside of Geneva were irrelevant. He had formally asked that the question of Italian aggression be placed on the Council's agenda. Pompeo Aloisi, who had hurried back to his post after bidding Laval farewell in Rome, conferred with Avenol and Eden on ways to circumvent this awkward item of Ethiopia vs. Italy. Avenol tried but failed to persuade Hawariate to retract his letter. It was then thought that the matter would be allowed to come up but only after an agreement among the Powers that there would be no discussion. (Even Litvinov, preoccupied with the German threat and unwilling to antagonize Italy, saw some merit in silence.) Hawariate was obstinate until he was granted what he regarded as a "victory": a letter from the Italian government to the Council expressing willingness to arbitrate the Walwal dispute under the Italo-Ethiopian Treaty of Friendship of 1928. The letter indeed marked an Italian diplomatic retreat. Gone were the demands for the formal salute to the Italian flag and the bluster about reparations. The whole question, the note reassured the Council, was unlikely to affect the peaceful relations between Italy and Ethiopia.

Then ensued a respite for the League while the Italians delayed further proceedings by lengthy deliberation concerning their nominees for the Board of Arbitration. (Each side was to name two arbiters and agree on a neutral chairman to adjudicate the matter.) Meanwhile military preparations, accompanied by oratorical drumbeats, went ahead in Rome and on the borders of Ethiopia.

The actual decision for war was taken "irrevocably" but secretly by Mussolini on January 23, 1935. On February 1, Mussolini declared: "I wish to create a nation of workers and soldiers. Relations between nations are founded on force, the force of arms." And on February 6, as the first of a series of troop transports left Italy, Baron Aloisi noted in his diary: "Il Duce is of the opinion that for a nation to keep healthy it must make war every twenty-five years."

In Geneva throughout that spring, the ingratiating and aristocratic Baron Aloisi was busy mending fences to assure Mussolini that his European allies would offer no obstacles to his imperial ambitions. It was important, however, that no offense be given to the League, which was still considered by France, England, and the Soviet Union to be a useful piece of machinery in the containment of Hitler. Litvinov made that clear when he lunched with Aloisi at the Hôtel des Bergues on May 23. Afterward, Aloisi noted the Soviet ambassador's assurances that his country "sought only to be agreeable with Italy, provided, of course, that the Covenant was respected."

Only the Ethiopians, eyeing the massive build-up of forces in Eritrea and Italian Somaliland, grew impatient. When the Council convened on May 20, 1935, it had before it two fresh appeals from Addis Ababa: that the arbitration proceedings be hurried and that something be done about the unmistakable Italian preparations for war. Resourceful Italian diplomacy then hit upon still another pretext for delay by objecting that the Ethiopians had named not their own countrymen but two foreigners to the Board of Arbitration: Gaston Jèze, a professor of international law at the Sorbonne, and the Emperor's American adviser, Everett Colson. This argument was a little too thin for Eden or Laval to defend, and it was decided that if the arbitration machinery was not in motion by July 25, the Council would consider the matter again. Furthermore, if the question was not fully resolved by August 25, the Council would have to step into the affair.

Again Italy agreed but raised new obstacles. Aloisi questioned whether the Board of Arbitration, when it was finally constituted, should be allowed to consider the question whether Walwal was Ethiopian or Italian. If that question was ruled out, it was difficult to see what else might be arbitrated. Clearly, time played for the Italians and the League played for time.

At first Mussolini seemed to listen only to imperial trumpets and had no patience for Aloisi's caution. In a tempestuous interview he warned his ambassador to Geneva that he was considering a break with the League, that he cared nothing for public opinion, and that "he would not hesitate to set Europe on fire." But in the end he agreed to wait. He mobilized gradually and maintained an apparent loyalty to the League, though he scarcely controlled the fire-eating pronunciamentos of his staff. When the Soviet ambassador to Italy, Boris Stein, asked why Mussolini and others insisted on tactlessly proclaiming to all the world that Italy wanted to devour Ethiopia, the Baron had no answer but confided to his diary that Stein's criticism was well taken.

England's policy remained a vaporous question in Mussolini's mind. In January 1935, he had asked both Paris and London for a frank statement of what each country regarded as its interests in Ethiopia. Laval answered promptly that France's interests were minimal and the reply seemed to confirm the offer of a free hand. The British agreed to submit such a statement but dragged their heels throughout the spring. A British interdepartmental committee had, in fact, prepared a report on Ethiopia, which might have been buried forever if the Italian Secret Service had not penetrated Drummond's embassy in Rome and efficiently photographed the entire document. In it Mussolini read that, aside from assurances regarding Lake Tsana and the waters of the Blue Nile and some grazing rights, it was a matter "of indifference" to Britain's national interests whether Ethiopia was independent or Italian.

Moreover, when MacDonald and Simon went to Stresa in April, they did not avail themselves of the opportunity to discuss the Ethiopian affair with Mussolini although it was then a raging issue. Mussolini had been prepared for such talks, and conversations at a lower-echelon level did touch on the question, but obviously it was considered by the British leaders as of less than major importance.

In Geneva, though, Eden blew alternately hot and cold, and the British press was in general vehemently hostile to Italian ambitions. Mussolini summed up his frustration with the inscrutable British in a speech to the Blackshirts of Cagliari, Sardinia, on June 8, 1935: "We will imitate to the letter those who are lecturing us. They have shown that when it was a question of creating an empire, or of defending it, they never took any account at all of the opinion of the world."

In England itself, a governmental reshuffle was in progress. Stanley Baldwin replaced MacDonald as Prime Minister, and Sir John Simon, that master in the use of fog as a diplomatic weapon, was sent to the Home Office. It had been assumed by most political observers that Eden would now step into Simon's shoes. Certainly Eden assumed it. Instead, Baldwin offered him a new title—Minister for League of Nations Affairs—with full cabinet rank and an undersecretary all his own. When Eden seemed crestfallen at being denied the coveted Foreign Office by the man who had been his political sponsor and mentor, Baldwin said: "After all, it isn't everyone who has the chance to be in the Cabinet before he is thirty-eight."

The man for whom Eden was thus passed over was Sir Samuel Hoare—a veteran of the India Office. He was vastly popular with Parliament. He enjoyed a reputation for intelligence, imagination, and tact, but he was of uncertain physical health. Eden ascribes the appointment of Hoare—without personal rancor—to the influence of Neville Chamberlain.

The new management of Britain's foreign policy began with a review of Europe as Sir Samuel saw it: The rising dangers of Germany and Japan made Italy's friendship absolutely essential. Happily, Mussolini seemed to be on very bad terms with Hitler. The Dollfuss assassination did not sit well with the Duce. Compounding the political menace implicit in the event was the personal relationship between the families. (The Austrian Chancellor's family was being entertained by Mussolini's at the time of the assassination.) Italian troops were now holding the line against Hitler on the Brenner Pass. Moreover, the massacre of Ernst Röhm and his forces, reportedly caught in the midst of a pederastic orgy the previous year, had offended the Duce's emphatically heterosexual *machismo*, and he was known to have called Hitler "a horrible sexual degenerate, a dangerous fool . . ."

Hoare fancied himself in a position to woo this all-important Roman Emperor who could safeguard the Mediterranean for the Allies. He had made contact with him years before at a time when Mussolini was a young man "uncertain about which side of the barricades he preferred." It was during the rout of Caporetto when war-sick Italian deserters and refugees clogged the roads from Udine to Naples. Hoare, who was then a lieutenant colonel in British Military Intelligence, had heard of a fierce socialist editor in Milan named Benito Mussolini, to whom he sent an intermediary. "Leave it to me," Mussolini told the envoy, "I will mobilize the *mutilati* in Milan and they will break the heads of any pacifists who try to hold antiwar meetings in the streets." To facilitate the head breaking that might keep Italy in the war, Hoare arranged for a discreet British subsidy to this "resistance movement." He thought that Mussolini would remember that helping hand of almost twenty years earlier and be grateful.

It was clear, however, that it would take more than grateful nostalgia to keep Mussolini in line. Accordingly, Hoare, Eden, and Robert Vansittart, a permanent undersecretary at the Foreign Office, unshakably convinced of the importance of keeping Mussolini happy, groped for something more tangible to appease him and still keep intact the League of Nations. What they came up with, however, was a pathetic offer of yet another desert for the Duce, this one carved from the Ogaden Province of Ethiopia along with a bit of British Somaliland. To sweeten the arrangement for Haile Selassie, Ethiopia would be given the British-owned port of Zeila, offering the Emperor a much-valued access to the sea. They tried the scheme out on Drummond in Rome, and, to their surprise, he said it had a fifty-fifty chance of success. In any case, Drummond suggested, it would provide an opportunity for Anglo-Italian talks, for which Mussolini seemed eager.

Unfortunately, the whole plan was splashed across the front pages of the British Sunday papers due to an indiscretion by a parliamentary undersecretary of one of the cabinet ministers. This robbed the scheme of any lingering hopes for success.

Eden found the Duce in a somber, angry mood. He told Eden in effect that, if the Emperor Haile Selassie could be prevailed upon to settle peacefully, he would be left with sovereignty, however nominal, over a tightly circumscribed central area of his country. If it came to war, the Emperor would be left with nothing. Mussolini dismissed the Zeila plan because it would give Ethiopia a port and a corridor through which it could bring in arms, a favor for which she would be grateful to England, not to Italy. Baron Aloisi summed up the Italian reaction: "The English offer was a trap, for if it were accepted it would have given England a dominant position in Ethiopia to our detriment, and we would be left with a desert in our hands."

Over lunch at Castelfusano on June 25, Baron Aloisi proposed to a thoroughly depressed Eden a subtle strategy to preserve the prestige of the League while allowing Italy to fulfill its destiny at Ethiopia's expense: "At a suitable moment," Aloisi suggested, "I would open an attack on Ethiopia at Geneva. . . . After this attack, if France and England agree, the Council, as it has already done in the Chaco affair, would be persuaded to refer the question to the parties directly concerned, that is: France and England. Thus, by the intervention of the League, the question would be left to the Western states, France and England, to resolve. And public opinion, particularly in England, would see that the prestige of the League of Nations is safe and would not hesitate to judge the facts which I would point out."

Aloisi said he would base his attack on Ethiopia's unworthiness to belong to the League because of the continuing practice of slavery—no more than an echo of earlier British objections. "Eden was not opposed to this plan and later came to ask me if he could send Strang [William Strang, a member of his staff] to go into the details," Aloisi noted in his diary. Aloisi and Strang conferred the following day.

Eden himself makes no mention of the proposal in his memoirs and describes his final meeting with Mussolini as fruitless, his conferences with Drummond and Strang as steeped in unremitting gloom. Nothing more was mentioned of the Aloisi plan, and yet, although all the events of that troubled summer and autumn seemed to occur in a deepening muddle of improvisation, they followed in general the course outlined by Aloisi over lunch at Castelfusano on June 25.

On July 31 the League Council met in special session, as had been promised in May. By then the Arbitration Commission had been organized at last under the chairmanship of Nikolaos Politis of Greece, but it ran into the stone wall of Italy's insistence that on no account must it concern itself with the question of who owned Walwal. Eden attended, with the ill-fated and much-publicized Zeila scheme still hanging around his neck. "Mr. Eden is off again on his travels to Geneva today," commented the *Daily Express* on July 31, 1935, recalling his last effort to bribe Mussolini with a piece of the British Empire. "He is the Minister without Portfolio. . . . Better if our Foreign Ministers were appointed with portfolio but without passport."

The Council thereupon decided to reopen the entire matter of Italo-Ethiopian relations but postponed the debate to September 4. The Ethiopians took this as yet another victory, apparently failing to grasp the Italian strategy of delay, which had just secured a five-week reprieve. Moreover, the Council decided, England, France, and Italy should seek to resolve the issues under the terms of a 1906 treaty of mutual interests in the area. Eden went along with the plan but insisted that the conference carry League authority. He repeatedly promised that any settlement reached would be in tune with the Covenant and that he would report on the matter to the Council. There was no opposition, for the big powers needed Italy and the little powers in Central and Eastern Europe feared it.

J. L. Garvin in the *Observer* of August 4, 1935, summed up that Council session: "An illusory respite of one month has been gained. . . . The League, further, has asserted its indefeasible right to continue talking until war breaks out."

As the summer wore on, Mussolini made his strategy crystal clear. He sent word to Aloisi on August 9: "I do not want any agreement unless it concedes me everything including the Emperor's head. I must prepare for war, even a general conflict. Therefore let's gain time." Two days later, even the Emperor's head was inadequate. "Even if they give me everything I prefer to avenge Adowa [the rankling defeat of Italian forces by Menelik II of Ethiopia in 1896]. I am ready."

In mid-August the three powers met in Paris. Aloisi had no plan to offer. Laval came up with a proposal to reform the national life of Ethiopia to bring it into line with the Covenant. The League would entrust this delicate task to England, France, and Italy. England and France would in turn entrust it to Italy. Italy would get its railroad to link Eritrea with Italian Somaliland and other economic bonuses. Britain and France would cede parts of their territory to Ethiopia in exchange.

Privately Aloisi thought the plan was "not bad," but publicly he told newsmen that he thought the League should give Italy a mandate over Ethiopia, disarm all Ethiopian troops, and leave the preservation of law and order to Italy.

Mussolini would have none of the Paris plan. He sent a long telegram of rejection, which Aloisi read to Laval by telephone. And to General De Bono, at invasion headquarters in Asmara, Mussolini cabled: "Conference came to no conclusions. Geneva will do the same. Make an end." To which De Bono replied: "I have never believed in conferences." September 10 was set down tentatively as the invasion date, for which some 300,000 men and 250 planes were waiting on Ethiopia's borders.

In Ethiopia meanwhile, the Emperor, in what the *Times* of August 1, 1935, termed a "calm of almost Chinese dimensions," called in the American chargé d'affaires and handed him a note suggesting that Washington might wish to interest itself in the Italian war preparations as a violation of the Kellogg-Briand Pact to outlaw war. Cordell Hull's reply was stiff, formal, and unhelpful. The United States government, he said, "would be loath to believe that either [side] would resort to other than pacific means as a method of dealing with this controversy or would permit any situation to arise which would be inconsistent with the commitments of the Pact." And in London, Sir Ronald Lindsay, British ambassador to Washington, was quietly telling Hoare that any action taken against Italy might meet with near-unanimous approval by the American public but would bring no governmental action.

August was a time for intensive lobbying. Avenol was openly pressing for giving all of Ethiopia to Italy as a mandate. Up to that moment Avenol had been a most quiescent Secretary-General, in marked contrast to his predecessor, Drummond. He had tended to his flower gardens and only occasionally turned up with Miss Lever at Geneva's political salons. Now, however, he took a very firm hand. He went so far as to advise the Italians on the preparation of an enormous dossier to be presented at the September Council. It was Avenol's suggestion, Aloisi noted, that the "memorandum" be drafted to "develop the theory of continuous aggression on the part of Ethiopia against all European powers." This, said the Secretary-General, "would permit the League to resolve the Ethiopian question according to Italian desiderata."

Nicolae Titulescu of Rumania journeyed to London to convey the alarm of the little powers. He had stopped off to talk with Laval and now warned Hoare that the French Premier was following an open and ominously persistent policy of total collaboration with Mussolini. Titulescu, who treasured his own gems of wit, told Hoare of his parting shot in Paris. "You are not a statesman," he had told Laval. "You are a tendency."

Mussolini had warned that any arms trade with Ethiopia would be regarded as an unfriendly act, and France, Belgium, Czechoslovakia, and Denmark promptly complied with Italian wishes. In July, Britain embargoed arms to Italy as well as Ethiopia, which had the effect noted in laws forbidding rich and poor alike to sleep in the street.

Hoare heard advice from all sides. Lloyd George favored lifting the embargo but warned against other unilateral action. Lord Cecil urged scrupulous defense of the Covenant. Chancellor of the Exchequer Neville Chamberlain said: "The real danger is Germany and nothing must be done to weaken the anti-German front." He also insisted, however, that the League must be maintained as a rampart against German aggression.

As the fateful Council and Assembly meetings neared, "secret" reports hinted at possible "mad dog acts" by Mussolini against Malta and the British Mediterranean fleet, which took to sea during the summer so as not to be caught in port. Still, Prime Minister Baldwin would not be deterred from his annual holiday in Aix, and Chamberlain went summering in Switzerland. Hoare stayed in bed in his Norfolk home, suffering from arthritis in his foot and preparing his maiden speech before the League of Nations.

In a petulant letter to Chamberlain in Switzerland, Hoare summed up his painful thoughts:

"As you may imagine I have received little or no help from other quarters. Stanley [Baldwin] would think of nothing but his holiday and the necessity of keeping out of the whole business almost at any cost. Ramsay [MacDonald] has written me a curious and almost unintelligible letter warning me of all the dangers that surround us, generally taking the side of the Italians and making the amazing suggestion that the Italians are likely to be our great Empire rivals in the future and will almost certainly be stronger than ourselves.

"Outside the Cabinet, public opposition has been greatly hardening against Italy. . . . I see, myself, the making of a first-class crisis in which the Government will lose heavily if we appear to be repudiating the Covenant. When I say this I do not mean that I have changed my views since we both discussed the question in London. What, however, I do mean is that if we adopt Stanley's attitude of indifference or Ramsay's alarmist and pusillanimous surrender to the Italians, we shall get the worst of every conceivable world. Our line, I am sure, is to keep in step with the French . . ."

Hoare could think of no fresh approach to a presentation of British policy but reached for a warmed-over offer of a freer access to raw materials, a long-standing Italian plea. He had slaved over his speech, and when he went down to Chequers to show it to Baldwin, who had come back from his holiday in Aix, he was disappointed at the Prime Minister's bland reaction. Baldwin scanned it and said only, "It must have taken you a long time to make it up."

When the Council convened in Geneva on September 4, arbitration efforts had already collapsed. Chief arbiter Nikolaos Politis, after being warned by Aloisi that a misstep could bring on war, declined to place the blame on either side. Eden and Laval also reported the failure of their mission of reconciliation. Although the two agreed in substance, there was a discernible difference in emphasis, with Eden stressing loyalty to the Covenant, and Laval, the need for conciliation. Aloisi proceeded along the lines he had forecast in his June lunch with Eden. He blasted Ethiopia as unfit for League membership and declared it should have "equality neither of rights nor of duties with civilized states." As he spoke, copies of the memorandum, prepared at Avenol's suggestion, were distributed to the members. This consisted of two printed volumes and a file of maps and photographs showing barbarous practices, border incursions, and sabotage of the boundary adjudications, allegedly committed by the Ethiopians.

Professor Jèze, the Sorbonne scholar chosen to represent Ethiopia, then noted that apparently the Italians no longer regarded the Walwal incident as crucial and were preparing instead a sweeping attack on Ethiopia. "The Italian government," he said, "having resolved to conquer and destroy Ethiopia, begins by giving Ethiopia a bad name."

During the professor's somewhat scholarly rejoinder (he went so far as to include a French expert's appraisal of Ethiopian civilization), Baron Aloisi and his second-in-command ostentatiously rose from their seats and left the chamber.

The following day was consumed with private huddles, and the Council did not convene until seven in the evening. The prime objective of the conversations was to agree on the timeworn device of referring the matter to a committee. Aloisi at first demanded that Italy be represented on such a committee, and when the absurdity of such a move was pointed out to him, declared that in that case neither England nor France should serve on it. Litvinov declined to have any part of the proposed committee because he saw it as a dodge to let the Council off the hook of its responsibilities. It was a fruitless day, and the Council session in the evening did nothing to cheer Aloisi's spirits.

Jèze spoke again for Ethiopia, and Litvinov declared that the Italians seemed to be asking the members of the Council to "repudiate their international obligations, to disregard the Covenant of the League of Nations on which, in no little degree, depends the whole edifice of international peace and the security of nations." Granting the possible validity of some Italian accusations against Ethiopia, Litvinov proceeded to deliver the toughest condemnation of Italy yet voiced at the Council: "Nothing in the Covenant of the League entitles us, however, to discriminate between members of the League as to their internal regime, the color of their skin, their racial distinctions or the stage of their civilization, nor accordingly to deprive some of them of privileges which they enjoy in virtue of membership in the League, and, in the first place, of their inalienable right to integrity and independence. I venture to say that, for the development of backward peoples, for influencing their internal life, for raising them to higher civilization, other means than military may be found."

The Russian delegate's statement seems to have surprised Aloisi, who gloomily noted: "The opposition to us increases; even Litvinov delivered a speech clearly against us." Laval felt so concerned that he telephoned Aloisi to urge calm. The Italian delegate felt bedeviled not only by his Geneva opposition but by Mussolini himself. Sure that he could win a total victory by diplomacy and still keep Italy in the League, Aloisi bewailed the fact that the decision was not up to him. On the following day, September 6, he yielded, contenting himself with an abstention instead of a veto, and allowed the Council to designate a committee "to make a general examination of Italo-Ethiopian relations and to seek for a peaceful settlement." Spain, Poland, and Turkey were to serve on it in addition to England and France. The astute and urbane De Madariaga was to be the chairman.

The group convened hastily and asked each side in the dispute to sit tight. The Emperor indicated his wholehearted willingness to do just that, adding only the wistful admonition that "the question of political expediency must not predominate over justice."

Mussolini, whose invasion troops were waiting at Ethiopia's borders, not for a break in Geneva negotiations but for an end to the rains, declined to let Aloisi make even the slightest commitment. In Asmara, Count Ciano, the Duce's son-in-law, thundered, in an English-language broadcast beamed to the American people, that whatever Geneva might do, Italy had decided "to consider as closed forever the period of attempts at pacific collaboration with Ethiopia."

Still, the Committee of Conciliation went about its work. In the midst of these seemingly vain negotiations, Sir Samuel Hoare arrived in Geneva on September 10. He had a warning fresh from Drummond in Rome to the effect that "in their present mood both Mussolini and the Italian people are capable of committing suicide if this seems the only alternative to climbing down." He also had his first face-to-face encounter with Laval, who impressed him with his "versatile mind," his "dirty white tie," and his "shifty look." Laval reinforced Drummond's warning against driving Mussolini into the waiting arms of Hitler. He cautioned against any steps that would lead to war with Italy, and he drew an alarming picture of Mussolini bombing Malta, attacking the British fleet, and letting Hitler loose upon Europe. Hoare agreed that war must be avoided but that if Italy invaded Ethiopia the least the League could do would be to recommend a ban on Italian imports. Laval thought the League could well do less.

On September 12, the third day of the Assembly session, Sir Samuel Hoare, still suffering from an arthritic foot, limped up the steps of the speaker's dais and proceeded to read his painstakingly drafted declaration.

The effect of his address was noticeable even during its delivery, so that years later Sir Samuel recalled, as if it were a rare occurrence, that "I became conscious of the fact that I was interesting my hearers." Not only was he interesting them; he was in fact electrifying them, for not since the crusading Wilson, the doggedly loyal Cecil, the impassioned Briand, had one heard the spokesman for a major power utter such a fierce, unqualified pledge of devotion to the League of Nations.

"It would be a grievous error," he warned, "for any member of the League, still more for the League as a whole, to be lost in generalities, and not to consider with care, candor and courage the best and most practical methods for exerting our collective influence and for achieving our peaceful objective."

He spoke of "the obligation to take collective action to bring war to an end in the event of any resort to war in disregard of the Covenant obligations." And he closed with what seemed a British warning to Mussolini on the brink of war: ". . . the League stands, and my country stands with it, for the collective maintenance of the Covenant in its entirety, and particularly for steady and collective resistance to all acts of unprovoked aggression."

When Hoare stepped down from the podium after his speech, which took three-quarters of an hour to deliver, he was surrounded by delegates who had flocked to congratulate him. He confessed later that he was "amazed at the universal acclamation." It seemed to him that almost everything he had said had been said before. He reread his text to see whether he had unwittingly uttered something new and could find no such novelty except perhaps his suggestion to look into the matter of a monopoly of raw materials and seek to promote a fairer access to them.

"Was there ever a better example of the fact that in nine cases out of ten it is the occasion that makes the speech and not the speech the occasion?" he wrote modestly in his memoirs.

Thus working in a British muddle, without premeditation, almost without preparation of any sort, Sir Samuel Hoare gave the League its greatest moment of glory in fifteen years. British prestige and League prestige mounted majestically. Belgium's Paul Hymans summed up the universal interpretation of Hoare's statement: "The British have decided to stop Mussolini, even if that means using force."

As if to confirm that interpretation came word the day after Hoare's speech that the British battle cruisers *Hood* and *Renown* had arrived at Gibraltar to strengthen the fleet in the Mediterranean.

Mussolini answered on September 10 by causing all the church bells in Italy to ring, the drums to roll, and sirens to shriek by way of marking the gathering of the Fascist forces. (The patriotic noises had to substitute for the invasion jump-off originally set for that day but called off because of continued rain in Ethiopia.)

The Assembly debate that followed Hoare's rallying was marked by certain nuances that distinguished the statements of African powers. Armindo Monteiro, the youthful Portuguese Foreign Minister, for example, warned the Assembly of the dangers of parliamentary maneuvering: "I must say that there is one thing I loathe more than war, and that is plundering by procedure." Privately, however, he told Eden that what worried him was the effect of a war on the latent national feelings of Africans, a matter of some concern to a nation with a long-standing empire on that continent.

The same specter haunted Charles Theodore Te Water of South Africa and made him one of the most vigorous opponents of Italy. He was concerned about any European power stirring "the still thinly overlaid war-mindedness, the savage and warlike instincts of Black Africa." If Africans were "conscripted by Europe for its own purposes and designs," he said, "armed Africa will, we profoundly believe, in its due and patient time rise . . . and revert to that Black barbarism which it has been our difficult destiny in the South to penetrate and enlighten. . . . Let it never be forgotten: the long memory of Black Africa never forgets an injury or an injustice."

Within the Committee of Conciliation, Laval worked out a variation on an earlier theme, not unlike that developed during the Anglo-French-Italian talks in Paris. Aloisi was delighted when Laval told him that Eden would go along with the scheme. It would have given Italy much of what it wanted, but under cover of a League-sponsored reform of Ethiopia. It was crystal clear now that, for England and most of Europe, the issue was not the independence of Ethiopia but the preservation of the League. For Mussolini, however, the question was whether a proper Roman Emperor should receive his empire as a handout from the League of Nations or win it on the battlefield. Even though the odds given Italian tanks and planes against Ethiopian rifles robbed the adventure of some of its glory, he chose the latter, against all of Aloisi's hopes. It took the Duce only twenty-four hours to consider and reject the proposal of the Committee of Conciliation.

Aloisi suggested to Laval on September 18 that, if only "inoffensive" sanctions were imposed, Mussolini could embark upon his war "and then we could come to an understanding with England." Following Aloisi's suggestion, Laval asked Eden to give him private assurances that under no circumstances would England support military sanctions, close the Suez Canal, or impose a blockade on Italy. Eden, who seems to have mistaken Hoare's oratory for a policy statement, refused to make any such commitments and on September 20 reported the matter to Hoare.

Hoare's reply baffled Eden because it suggested vaguely that he should follow Laval's lead. He telegraphed his superior again on September 25: "I submit that it would be fatal in any way to reduce pressure on Signor Mussolini . . . to relax pressure upon him could only restore his confidence and undo the good work that has been done . . ."

Hoare's reply was in violent contrast with his brave speech of two weeks earlier: "I trust that you will not allow any haste in the Council in regard to the discussion of sanctions. The feeling of the Government is that, though the efforts of the Committee of Five [on Conciliation] have proved unavailing and they have rightly remitted the matter to the Council, the latter should make a further effort to find a solution, and that it might not yet prove hopeless in view of the somewhat altered atmosphere produced at Rome by the combination of pressure and friendly message." The hand was the hand of Hoare, but the "friendly message" was certainly that of Laval.

In Ethiopia the Emperor showed signs at last of abandoning his serenity. In the face of massing Italian troops, he had withdrawn his own army some twenty miles from the border to avoid incident. He had urged the League Council to send observers to the scene, but that body had merely appointed a committee to investigate whether League observers could in fact observe. This discouraged the patient monarch, and on September 28 the Ethiopian minister informed Eden that at last and reluctantly the Emperor had ordered mobilization.

On October 2, 1935, while the forces of Marshal De Bono were pouring across the frontiers of Ethiopia, Benito Mussolini issued a manifesto which candidly gave the lie to the pious Wilsonian pretensions of 1919 concerning a peace without plunder. He recalled the unpaid bribe of the Secret Treaties of London of 1915:

"Blackshirts of the Revolution, men and women of all Italy, Italians scattered throughout the world, across the mountains and across the oceans, listen . . . Not only is an army marching toward its objectives, but 40,000,000 Italians are marching in unison with this army, all united because there is an attempt to commit against them the blackest of all injustices, to rob them of a place in the sun. When in 1915 Italy united its lot with those of the Allies, how many shouts of admiration and how many promises: But after the common victory . . . when it came to sitting around the table of the mean peace, to us were left only the crumbs from the sumptuous colonial booty of others . . . At the League of Nations, instead of recognizing the just rights of Italy, they dared to speak of sanctions . . . it is against this people, to which humanity owes the greatest of its conquests, it is against this people of heroes, poets, artists, navigators and administrators, that they dare to speak of sanctions. Italy, proletarian and Fascist Italy . . . to your feet!"

The official excuse for hostilities, contained in a telegram to Avenol, was the general mobilization ordered by Haile Selassie on September 28.

Now at last the League seemed to act quickly as it moved for the first time to penalize the aggression of a Great Power. The Council gathered on October 5 and appointed a committee, which on the evening of the sixth reported "that the Italian Government has resorted to war in disregard of its obligations under Article 12 of the League of Nations." Under a strict interpretation of the Covenant, Italy, by making war on Ethiopia, was to be considered as having committed an act of war against all League members. Aloisi's was the only voice in the Council to be raised against the finding, and the Assembly was to meet within forty-eight hours to consider the Council's report.

On the afternoon of October 7, Laval insisted on a serious talk with Eden, but the solemnity of the occasion was vitiated by trivia. They headed out of Geneva toward an inn in the Savoy for a quiet lunch, but the French guard at the border soured Laval by acknowledging his Premier with a salute so lukewarm it was almost an insult. "Sale [Dirty] communiste," Laval muttered. Then the innkeeper's wife took the opportunity to complain about taxes and could only be appeased by having the Premier visit with her pet fox. In the end Laval unveiled merely another plan to reopen negotiations with Mussolini, which Eden side-stepped by pointing out that the Council was now seized with the problem.

The Assembly posed a difficulty: a single adverse vote could obstruct a formal commitment to sanctions, and indeed this might have been an excuse for impotence that could have buried the League. The nimble parliamentary footwork of Beneš in the President's chair saved the day, however. He ruled that the imposition of sanctions was not a matter for an Assembly vote but for each country to decide on its own. The individual nations so inclined could, however, set up a Coordinating Committee. Fifty nations did exactly that. The Committee of Fifty then entrusted its decisions to a more manageable Committee of Eighteen, which proceeded to impose the collective judgment of the League.

None stood for the full penalty prescribed by the Covenant, amounting to a virtual excommunication. They clamped an arms embargo on Italy and banned the extension of loans and credits and the import of Italian goods. Austria, Hungary, and Albania, Italy's client states, would have no part of any of the sanctions. And Switzerland found the strain on its neutrality too severe.

A far more serious sanction was the proposed ban on exports to Italy, which could indeed impair the war effort. Britain, France, and Russia were agreed that it would make no sense to refuse to sell Italy supplies which it could obtain quite easily from their competitors in the United States and Germany, beyond the reach of League persuasion. A list of commodities potentially available in non-League countries was therefore drawn up and put aside. Another list of commodities more or less exclusively obtainable among the sanctionist states was prepared for embargo. This included tin, aluminum, nickel, and rubber.

Other sanctions which might have been instantaneously effective were not considered at all in any official proceedings. South Africa had advocated a rupture of diplomatic relations with Italy on the part of the sanctionist states but did not press the matter. Sir Austen Chamberlain was among those who privately urged the closing of the Suez Canal, Italy's only supply line to the front, a step which would have brought Mussolini to his knees, but no official notice was taken of it.

That any sanctions were voted at all is remarkable, considering that throughout 1935, as Toynbee pointed out, "the Italian military campaign in East Africa could be described in economic terms as a world-wide business transaction." And 1935 was a lean depression year that needed business. The Italian army marched in boots made in Northamptonshire, England; coal, oil, and cereals came from the Soviet Union; army blankets from Poland; gasoline, beer, and soap from Kenya; drinking water from Aden; and wheat from all corners of the world.

The United States tripled its export of scrap iron to Italy in 1935 and continued merrily to trade with the belligerents, being under no compulsion to do otherwise, although popular opinion in the United States was distinctly pro-League, pro-Ethiopia, and militantly anti-Italian. The American neutrality policy did require an arms embargo, but it was imposed on the Ethiopians as well.

That policy put Ethiopia at a crippling disadvantage. Italy could forge its own weapons and use American scrap metal in the process. President Roosevelt tried to discourage private firms from profiting from the war boom by warning that they traded with belligerents at their own risk, but American suppliers continued to be available to the lure of Italian money.

In a seeming paradox, Germany, though it remained hostile to the League, declined to boost its exports to Italy, whose role in Europe seemed undependable and whose power was therefore to be discouraged.

Labor throughout the world was virtually unanimous on the side of the League and Ethiopia. Dockers were refusing to load Italy-bound cargoes in San Diego, Capetown, Marseilles, Alexandria. Unions, women's organizations, church groups, joined in support for the League, which was no longer regarded as a visionary dream but as a vital force in world affairs.

Italy, cast as the villain in the drama, was not doing well, although sanctions had not yet begun to hurt it seriously. Actually, their threat was proving useful as fuel for oratory, enabling Mussolini to charge that England was seeking to starve Italian women and children. (In fact, they were eating better than ever because Italy's food exports had dropped and consequently prices on the domestic market fell.) However, the lira had taken a terrible beating, money was drying up, and Marshal De Bono's invasion army was unaccountably stalled after a short initial advance.

In England, meanwhile, the Ethiopian crisis had produced not only a spurt of business but a positive boom in national pride. To those who did not read the private communications of diplomats, Great Britain seemed the repository of the world's honor, the chivalric champion of the under-dog, and the firmest supporter of world order and justice as embodied in the Covenant of the League of Nations. The Baldwin government found itself unexpectedly popular not only abroad but at home. Nobody had planned or foreseen such an eventuality any more than Sir Samuel Hoare had expected to be a hero. Baldwin, shrewd enough to seize upon the happy accidents of history, moved up the time of the elections to take his fortunes at flood tide. He set the vote for November and campaigned on his government's record in the League.

That record seemed to correspond to the British mood of militancy. It was in the previous June that some half a million volunteers had canvassed the country distributing a peace ballot, to which twelve million people responded. The overwhelming majority had staunchly supported the League, a straw vote that no politician dared ignore. The Laborites, who had always been pro-League, found themselves outflanked. They could only echo the government's strong line while protesting its increased arms budget, a seeming contradiction not lost upon government cam-paigners. Rarely had the British electorate been more united and never had loyalty to the League been such a password to political success. On November 17, the Baldwin government was returned with a handsome majority.

While England was in the midst of its rally-behind-the-League cam-paign, the Sanctions Committee met on November 2 and provided an opportunity for Hoare quietly to pursue a line somewhat at variance with his party's euphoric electioneering. He conferred at length with Aloisi, who noted that Hoare was now quite amenable to the idea of a "gentle-men's agreement," though reluctant to make any commitments toward the Italian objective: a withdrawal of the British fleet and an Italian mandate over Ethiopia. Aloisi understandingly observed in his diary: "It is obvious that the English government wishes to present itself at the elections on the basis of the existing situation without modifying its policy in any respect."

Hoare also conferred with Laval and agreed to delay the imposition of any sanctions to November 18, a maneuver which irritated the smaller powers. When the Committee reluctantly assented, Hoare and Laval suggested that while they were prepared to carry out the sanctions they were at the same time eager to continue their search for a settlement with Italy. The Belgian Prime Minister, Paul van Zeeland, promptly moved, as if on cue, that the representatives of England and France be formally empowered by the Committee to conduct these negotiations. The Committee went along with that as well because to do otherwise would be to vote no confidence in the two dominant powers of the League. But the proposal had punctured the belief in a renascent League, and doubts began to creep back.

Whether oblivious to this change of mood or undaunted by it, Dr. Walter Riddell of Canada took a daring step by proposing to extend the embargo to iron, steel, coke, and, most significant of all, oil. This move to make sanctions decisive caused a near-panic among the Great Powers. (It was apparently the work of an innocent rather than the calculated maneuver of a government; Canada thereafter disowned the scheme, censured Riddell, and recalled him from Geneva.)

The oil embargo was set for consideration at the next meeting of the Sanctions Committee on November 29. This left almost four weeks to devise a formula for evading Riddell's challenge. Although the suggestion of an oil embargo was unwelcome to Rome, Aloisi found encouragement in private talks. In his diary he listed November 2 as "quite favorable after so many gloomy days." Belgium's Van Zeeland and Spain's De Madariaga expressed "great friendship for our country even while they are applying sanctions!!!" (The three exclamation marks are Aloisi's.)

The first objective was to play for time, and accordingly Laval, citing "personal" reasons, asked the Sanction Committee's chairman, Vasconcellos, for a postponement to December 11. The chairman could not allow the exigencies of Ethiopia's life-and-death struggle to interfere with normal courtesies and obligingly set the meeting date for December 12, 1935.

At this point Sir Samuel Hoare's health fell into a decline, and doctors prescribed a holiday in Switzerland, where he could indulge his favorite recreation of ice skating. Cheerfully, Hoare persuaded a resort at Zuoz in the Engadine to open up the rink ahead of the season for him. At the last moment, however, Laval said he wished to come to London for a conference. Fearing that this would delay his holiday, the Foreign Secretary offered instead to stop off for a chat in Paris on his way to the Swiss Alps. A British team, including the Foreign Office Ethiopian expert Maurice Peterson and Vansittart, was already in Paris working with Laval's staff to spin new variations on old formulas in order to bribe Mussolini into stopping the war.

Hoare set off from London on Saturday, December 7, with no instructions whatever but only a cheery word from Baldwin: "Have a good leave and get your health back. That is the most important thing. By all means stop in Paris and push Laval as far as you can, but on no account get this country into war."

At the top of the staircase in the Foreign Office, Eden ran into Hoare just before he left and offered a parting caution: "Don't forget that Van [Vansittart] can be more French than the French."

"Don't worry," said Hoare, "I shall not commit you to anything. It wouldn't be fair on my way through to my holiday."

Hoare's conversations at the Quai d'Orsay began at five-thirty that evening. Within easy reach of Laval as he presided was a private telephone, which he would use frequently, sometimes to call his staff and sometimes to call Mussolini, with whom, Hoare noted, "he seemed to have a direct and secret line."

Laval hammered away at the threatened oil embargo as the sure precursor of a wider war and hinted that in case of Anglo-Italian hostilities the French might not leap to Britain's aid.

By six-thirty Sunday evening, December 8, the two teams had reached agreement on a program that would have tied Ethiopia in League ribbons and turned it over to Italy. There were only two points: The first, an "exchange" of territory much like earlier ones proposed, would give Italy some 60,000 square miles of Ethiopia. In return, Ethiopia would get a corridor to the sea to be carved from Italian territory or, if that would be too much for the Duce, then from British and French colonies.

The second point was new and far more devastating: It would make the entire southern half of Ethiopia—some 160,000 square miles—a "zone of economic expansion and settlement reserved for Italy." The administration of the entire plan would be left to Italy acting in the name of the League of Nations.

Hoare initialed the pact pending approval by his government, the League, and Mussolini, then wired the British ambassador in Addis Ababa to press the Emperor to agree. The Foreign Minister then went off to skate in Switzerland.

Extraordinary precautions had been taken in Paris to prevent press leaks, which had dogged all negotiations up to that point. The French Foreign Office had ordered reporters to refrain from even a hint of speculation on what was transpiring at the Quai d'Orsay. This served only to alert the press. While reporters surrounded the principals as they left the Foreign Office, two of the most influential of the diplomatic press corps—Geneviève Tabouis of *L'Oeuvre* and André Géraud (Pertinax) of *L'Echo de Paris*—were in London, out of harm's reach and in touch by telephone with their sources in Paris. On Monday both papers carried the terms of the Hoare-Laval plan before any government but Italy's had seen them.

The reaction was swift and explosive. In the Commons a Laborite, K. Griffith, declared that, if reports of the plan were accurate, "over the door of the League of Nations should be written: 'Abandon half, all ye who enter here—half your territory, half your prestige.'" An Independent, Miss Rathbone, brought cheers when she asked: "Had the Government been forced into this disgraceful surrender because it was thought that the oil embargo was likely to fail, or was it because that embargo was likely to be only too successful?"

When it was revealed that the one consolation left to Ethiopia—the corridor to the sea—was to be rendered useless by a secret understanding that no railroad would be allowed to run there, the *Times* of London on December 16 commented: "[The corridor] was apparently to remain no more than a strip of scrub, restricted to the sort of traffic which has entered Ethiopia from the days of King Solomon, a corridor for camels."

The Manchester *Guardian* of December 13 asked: "Why wrap up Abyssinia in a diplomatic parcel and send it to Mussolini for a Christmas present?" And the *News-Chronicle* of December 12 declared: "It was not for this that Mr. Baldwin asked for and obtained his mandate from the British electorate just a month ago."

Harold Macmillan, then an M.P., in a letter to the *Times* neatly nailed the coffin of the Hoare-Laval proposal: "It may be true that we must face the failure or collapse of the League in its present form. That is no reason that we should help to undermine the very structure which a few weeks ago the nation authorized us to underpin. I have never attended the funeral of a murdered man; but I take it that at such a ceremony some distinction is made between the mourners and the assassins."

Baldwin's defense was a flight into mystery. "My lips are not yet unsealed," he said. "Were the troubles over I would make my case and I guarantee that not a man would go into the lobby against me." Who sealed Baldwin's lips and why remained a mystery that was never satisfactorily resolved.

A glimpse of what was happening inside the Cabinet is revealed in the memoirs of Duff Cooper, who had just been made Secretary of State for War. He favored a much stronger line against Italian aggression, but, as he put it, "I was a newcomer and as such it behooved me to voice my views with becoming modesty." Even his timid objections were stamped on heavily. He recalled one colleague, whom he declined to name, as challenging him: "Are all your preparations for war completed? Is your expeditionary force ready to sail?" The hapless Duff Cooper noted: "So far as I knew, the War Office might still be preparing for war against Russia in Afghanistan . . ."

Hoare was out of the battle. He had met his wife at Zuoz in the Engadine on Tuesday morning, December 10. He thought he should return, but Baldwin urged him to go on resting. There was "blue sky, white snow and black ice," he recalled later. He skated onto the rink and promptly blacked out. When he regained consciousness, his nose was broken in two places and he was ordered to rest.

After three days he flew back to Croydon and was whisked off to his home and put to bed. Neville Chamberlain came by and confided to him that the Cabinet originally decided to back his plan but had to give up after the uproar in the press. Baldwin murmured soothingly: "We must all stand together." Hoare told Eden: "I wish I were dead."

In the end Hoare stood alone and was not allowed to make his planned defense: that he and Laval were only acting to preserve the League of Nations. Baldwin insisted that he publicly recant and admit that it had been a mistake.

"I emerged into a world that had turned against me," Hoare recalled. He thereupon resigned, to the immense relief of the government, which could use him henceforth as a scapegoat. It was as a simple M.P., therefore, that he rose in the Commons, with his nose still bandaged as if he were a war casualty, and gave his apologia:

"It seemed clear that, supposing an oil embargo were to be imposed and that the non-member States took an effective part in it, the oil embargo might have such an effect upon the hostilities as to force their termination." Although that might have been regarded as the essential aim of the sanctions, Sir Samuel hurried on to explain that if sanctions achieved their objective they would in fact be fatal. Italy would make war on Britain and, although "judging from our past history we should retaliate with success (Cheers)," it would "almost inevitably lead to the dissolution of the League." It was a curious argument—that the League could survive only if it were ineffective, like the King who may reign but dares not rule. Sir Samuel sat down to loud cheers. Reporters wrote that he broke down and wept, but Hoare insisted that he was reaching to wipe not his eyes but his injured nose. He went with his wife back to the Engadine in temporary political eclipse.

The Hoare-Laval plan seemed thoroughly dead, murdered by the press and an aroused British electorate. Baldwin said it would not be revived. Haile Selassie, who had been belatedly informed of its proposals, protested vehemently. Mussolini kicked the corpse and said he wouldn't have accepted the plan anyway. Eden announced its burial in Geneva. Laval, still clinging to the wreckage, insisted that actually the proposal had not been officially rejected by Italy and used that technicality to delay any fresh moves by the League.

In Geneva delegates from the little powers of Europe and from the Commonwealth vented their outrage on Eden. Vasconcellos, chairman of the Sanctions Committee, asked him: "Why have our countries been asked to put on sanctions, to suffer loss of trade and other inconvenience, if the only result is that Italy should be offered by France and Great Britain more, probably, than she would ever have achieved by herself alone, even if sanctions had not been put on?"

Disconsolate, without answers, Anthony Eden took the train to be home for Christmas. At Calais there was a message asking him to hurry to 10 Downing Street. There an irascible Baldwin was going down the list of possible Foreign Secretaries to replace Hoare and wanted Eden's suggestions. Eden offered a few, to which Baldwin had objections. Then, the supply of names exhausted, the Prime Minister told Eden: "I guess it will have to be you." When Eden paid the ceremonial visit to King George, his Majesty was in chipper holiday mood and repeated the doubtful witticism to which he had succumbed on receiving Hoare's resignation: "You know what they're all saying—no more coals to Newcastle, no more Hoares to Paris."

In Italy the war situation hung in a precarious balance. The Italian armies were making very slow and difficult headway despite the thunderous oratory. The sanctions thus far imposed by the League had hurt but not stopped the war effort and came in handy as a rallying cry and alibi. An oil cutoff was the only real threat, as Mussolini made clear to Aloisi in a conversation on January 17, 1936. "As for the other sanctions," Aloisi noted, "he wants them to go on because they please us." The diplomat added his own comment: "That must be a joke." Concerning the ban on credit and loans, Mussolini had quoted Napoleon: "Without money one does not wage war," then topped it by adding: "But for war one always finds money."

The accession of Eden to the Ministry of Foreign Affairs was dismal news to Italy, but even more of a jolt was the parliamentary upset that displaced Pierre Laval. Laval adjusted to his momentary defeat with a wry humor, scribbling a parting memo to Eden during a meeting of the Sanctions Committee: "Baron Aloisi needs petrol for his lighter."

The Council had turned down Emperor Haile Selassie's plea for loans, although only six years earlier the Assembly had unanimously supported a resolution pledging all members to give financial aid to the victim of aggression. (Few nations had ratified that resolution, however.) The Sanctions Committee had decided that it would be useless to withhold coal, iron, and steel from the Italian army because the United States, among other nations, would not cease its trade despite the Roosevelt administration's disapproval.

Oil, however, could not so lightly be dismissed, and a committee of experts was set up to study the effectiveness of such a move. In February the experts reported that indeed a clamp-down on oil from the sanctionist states, even if the United States continued its supplies, would be extremely effective. With such reassurance the governments represented in the Council said they still must have time to consider such a move, although it had been in the very center of world attention ever since the hapless Canadian, Dr. Walter Riddell, had brought the matter up the previous September.

By the time the Council convened again in early March, General Pietro Badoglio, who had replaced the dilatory De Bono, was sweeping through Ethiopia and spraying mustard gas on the roads and fields where the barefoot soldiers, women, and children of Ethiopia were bravely fighting a rear-guard action.

Pierre Etienne Flandin, who had replaced Laval with a change of style but not of content, asked for yet another postponement to allow for possible conciliation. Eden now took the lead in pressing for an oil embargo and asserted that Britain would impose one unilaterally if necessary. The Council, nevertheless, continued in its weary performance and asked conquering Italy and dying Ethiopia whether they would now negotiate "in the framework of the League and the Spirit of the Covenant." It sounded rather like the administration of last rites, but the Emperor quickly agreed. After a five-day wait Mussolini agreed as well.

It was March 8. At dawn the day before Adolf Hitler—who, throughout the Ethiopian crisis, had been an interested observer of the rewards and penalties meted out to aggressors by the League—had embarked on a gamble. The step had long been planned and was in flagrant contradiction to the advice of his military advisers.

He sent a small detachment of the Reichswehr to march into the Rhineland, demilitarized by the terms of Locarno. Only a year earlier Hitler had reaffirmed that pact as one freely entered into and strictly to be maintained.

Across the border were 200,000 French troops. If they moved, the German troops were to withdraw, under contingency plans of General Werner von Blomberg. The General thought they would move. Hitler thought they wouldn't. Though for twenty-four hours there was talk in France of mobilization, in the end the buck was passed to the League.

By ten o'clock in the morning of March 7, Hitler's emissaries were announcing the Rhineland news in diplomatic notes to the embassies of France, Britain, and Italy. Hitler's excuse: the recent ratification of the Franco-Soviet Pact so laboriously negotiated by Barthou and concluded by Laval. This, he said, violated the spirit of Locarno and left Germany free of any obligations. Along with the announcement came abundant promises of nonaggression pacts in all directions. Hitler also offered a demilitarization scheme that would apply to both sides of the border—a suggestion which sounded reasonable until one looked at the map and found that this would entail a major breach in the Maginot Line of French fortifications. Lastly, Hitler offered to return to the League. The French ambassador in Berlin, André François-Poncet, commented: "Hitler struck his adversary in the face and as he did so declared: 'I bring you proposals for peace!' "

Throughout the Ethiopian crisis, it had been repeatedly emphasized that if there seemed some reluctance to stop Mussolini it was only because the major danger was Hitler. Now the major danger had edged closer, but there was even greater reluctance to do anything about it. Everywhere in England and France, from the government to the opposition, in the press as in Parliament, there was a profound readiness to "understand" Hitler's move into the Rhineland. True, he had violated solemn treaty obligations, but, after all, the Rhineland was undisputedly German territory and it was difficult to say to a sovereign government, whatever one might feel about that government, that it could not move its own troops into its own territory. Certainly this could not be allowed to become a cause of war, despite all the legal justification in Locarno.

The *Times* called it "A Chance to Rebuild." *Le Matin* thought the move might be helpful in restraining the Communist menace. And the Socialist *Populaire* considered it absurd to imagine that any country would be barred from militarizing its own frontier. "Hitler has torn up a treaty . . ." the paper admitted, "but at the same time he speaks of peace and of Geneva. We must take him at his word."

Flandin put up a somewhat leisurely show of resistance. Thirty-two hours after German troops took up positions in the Rhineland, he telegraphed Avenol in Geneva to ask for a Council meeting. He then journeyed to London to rub British noses into the fact that now it was they who were balking at stopping aggression. Eden himself stood for a firm line, but the Cabinet restrained him. Harold Nicolson recalls a party at the Belgian Embassy at which Eden, "his lovely eyes rimmed with red and puffy with sleeplessness," laid down a brave line that moved Churchill to exclaim: "Now here we are, elder statesmen plus heads of Opposition. We could sign a manifesto this very minute pledging ourselves to an agreed policy. Yet the world outside imagines that the House of Commons and the Government are torn by dissension."

"And so they are," Eden answered in a low, sad voice.

Baldwin admitted to Flandin that he was not an expert on foreign policy but claimed that he knew the British people and that they wanted peace. The French Premier blustered about throwing the Germans out of the Rhineland, but not a soldier stirred beyond the Maginot Line. The League Council was called into session not in Geneva but in St. James's Palace, London. The change of scene was the idea of Belgium's Prime Minister, Paul van Zeeland, who argued that in London lay the key to the Rhineland dilemma. He suggested that Britain might state categorically that the movement of one German soldier across the border into France or Belgium would bring war, which sounded brave and would leave the Rhineland alone.

Paul-Boncour and Flandin denounced the Van Zeeland approach and called for sanctions but did not press the matter. The prime business was to bring Germany before the Council. After a suitable delay for purposes of face, Joachim von Ribbentrop arrived at St. James's Palace on March 19. Von Ribbentrop had boasted to Hitler of his connection with influential Britons and to the British of his intimate relationship with the Führer. He was apparently right on both counts.

He was a vain and humorless man of "good stock," by which was meant he could boast of an old Rhenish family line, a military career as staff officer with the Twelfth Hussars, and a father-in-law who was one of the liquor barons of Germany. He sat stiffly in his chair as he read a long prepared speech echoing Hitler's proclamation that Germany's humiliations were now ended, and he closed with a routine pledge of friendship for France. Then he sat back grimly, with arms folded, and took very little part in the debate.

The Council formally came to the inescapable conclusion that a treaty had been violated. Only Chile, sensing perhaps the turn of the tide, voted against the resolution. Ecuador, which already had lifted its sanctions against Italy, was conveniently absent. Dino Grandi, representing Italy for all the world as if it were a loyal League member, spoke ritualistically of his country's devotion to peace and deplored the League's position on Ethiopia. Peter Munch of Denmark voted for the resolution but characteristically avoided all apportionment of blame.

Eden went on pursuing new formulas: A German promise not to increase its troop strength in the Rhineland if France would do likewise across the border; Anglo-French staff talks to bolster French morale (which drew a curt but vigorous protest from Von Ribbentrop in private); a token international force to patrol the border.

In the end Germany offered a four-month standstill, during which time no fortifications would be built in the Rhineland, because, as Ribbentrop pointed out, it would take that long to plan them. Eden drew up a lengthy questionnaire on German intentions which Hitler agreed to consider but did not answer. And so Locarno died.

Hitler, refreshed by the returns of a plebiscite showing the usual overwhelming support of the German people and relishing the vindication of his own judgment over that of his generals, proceeded to fortify the Rhineland and to watch the progress of Mussolini. The latter had proved a remarkable mine sweeper, demonstrating that the road of aggression was quite safe.

In Ethiopia Italy's army was storming its way toward Addis Ababa with planes and tanks and mustard gas while its representative kept his place at the Council table as a member in good standing. Against the aggressor the League still had its two commissions: one for conciliation under De Madariaga, the other for sanctions under Vasconcellos. In both, the diplomats talked in grave tones. On April 8, De Madariaga spoke urgently of Italian mustard gas. But did not the Ethiopians use dumdum bullets? Flandin inquired, and thus sidetracked the debate. De Madariaga shuttled between Geneva and Rome and got nowhere. Finally, on April 17, he admitted that conciliation was impossible. Eden tried to persuade the Italians not to bomb Addis Ababa. Baldwin privately called Mussolini a "savage." And still the armies of Italy drew nearer the Ethiopian capital.

On April 20, with Italian victory sweeping to its inevitable climax, the Ethiopian delegate, Wolde Mariam, was appealing to the Council for oil sanctions, still under slow deliberation in the Sanctions Committee. Eden said he was ready to accept them, but no one made a formal proposal, mindful perhaps of Aloisi's comments that Italy's future role in Europe would depend upon the attitude of the Council members. Paul-Boncour offered the hope that Italy, once this troublesome matter was disposed of, would take its rightful place at the side of France and Britain. The alternative hung over the Council: that at last Mussolini would embrace Hitler.

Avenol lunched with Eden and, according to the latter, "surpassed the French Ministers in excuses for Mussolini's attitude." Eden made the standard pro-League pronouncements, for which Wolde Mariam thanked him profusely, and said that Britain had been Ethiopia's only friend. But Pompeo Aloisi that night entered a curious note in his diary:

"During today's closed session and after, Eden twice looked me up to talk with me, and everybody noticed it. In substance, he told me that it was he who had asked Baldwin, in his speech the day before yesterday, to declare that the British government had no hostility toward the Italian government and would act only within the collective framework. He could swear it. He added that he knew he was supposed to be anti-Italian but that 'God knows' he was the opposite." Although this seems to belie Eden's proclaimed convictions, it is consistent with the ambiguous instructions handed to that errant knight. In effect: "Rescue the damsel if you can but don't annoy the dragon."

On April 27, Princess Tsahai, the seventeen-year-old daughter of Emperor Haile Selassie, called the press to the headquarters of the Ethiopian Women's Work Association in Addis Ababa, where she and other women were making gas masks. She sat in her white overalls and read a statement:

"For God's sake help us. Get something done that will really harm the Italian armies and not merely the Italian people . . . We are only a small race but I am seventeen and its leading daughter, and I know, as you know, that if mankind lets armies and gas destroy my country and people, civilization will be destroyed. We have common cause, you and I . . . Italian aggression and gas have set humanity a test. If you fail to help us now, we shall all die . . . We, though we have few modern arms to help us, still do our best to be strong, but if you do not help quickly with all your strength, gas and aggression will be found to pay and will take such root in 'civilized' human conduct that you too will be overshadowed with us by death. We thank most of you for sanctions. They may help but plainly they are not enough. For God's sake join together and get something done that will really help us before it is too late."

As she spoke Italian planes were buzzing Addis Ababa and dropping leaflets demanding surrender.

From Eden and Vasconcellos came unavailing denunciations of the use of mustard gas. The Emperor, on May 2, took a surer way to save his people from the poisonous sprays. He left the capital and took refuge in Jerusalem. After four days of chaos, terror, and looting, the victor of Ethiopia, General Badoglio, entered devastated Addis Ababa. And on May 9, Benito Mussolini, standing on the balcony of the Palazzo Venezia, bestowed upon the diminutive King Victor Emmanuel the title of Emperor of Ethiopia.

The new empire builder spelled out his views to Ward Price, correspondent of the *Daily Mail.* To a question concerning his imperial designs, Mussolini answered as Hitler did on similar occasions. "I give you my word," he said, "that they are wrong about Italy having any further colonial ambitions. Believe me, this victory in East Africa puts Italy into the group of 'satisfied' Powers. Britain and France should realize the importance of that. It brings us on to the other side of the barricades. In colonial questions we Italians shall henceforth belong no more to the dissatisfied proletariat. We shall become sound conservatives instead."

When Mussolini promised to keep an open door in Ethiopia for the "economic enterprise of friendly countries," Ward Price asked whether that favored category would include Britain and France. "They are certainly included," replied the generous victor.

The Council convened on May 11, determined to be firm, now that the battle was safely lost. Before them was Haile Selassie's appeal from Jerusalem, declaring that he had fled only to spare his people annihilation by gas. Wolde Mariam was on hand ready with evidence that resistance was still continuing, thereby rendering the retention of sanctions meaningful. Aloisi asked for congratulations on the triumph of civilization and suggested that, since Ethiopia no longer existed as a state, at last the agenda could be freed of the vexing item: "Dispute between Ethiopia and Italy."

The irrepressible Titulescu of Rumania, whom Aloisi occasionally referred to in his diary as "the pig," was quoted as saying: "The Italians want us to eat shit. All right. We will eat it. But they also want us to declare that it is rose jam. That is a bit much."

When the Council sternly voted to preserve the Ethiopian question on its agenda and to seat Wolde Mariam at the table, Aloisi, on orders from Mussolini, withdrew from Geneva. Back in Rome, he reported encouragingly to the Duce that Litvinov had expressed a friendly willingness to recognize the realities and to lift the sanctions but that England and France, the controlling factors in the situation, were still reluctant. The Baron also talked with Soviet ambassador Boris Stein in Rome and side-stepped Russian demands for an Italian policy commitment in Europe that would make possible a swift resolution of the sanctions question.

The Council adjourned meanwhile, having decided to leave the whole question to a special session of the Assembly convened for June 30. In the month that followed it was plain that the sanctions front was wavering. Several countries reportedly were trading under the table. Only the Scandinavian countries and some of the neutrals held firm. Léon Blum had come to power in France at the head of a Popular Front government that was staunchly pro-League. Yet when Blum and Eden met (they liked each other instantly), both felt they were in a dilemma. Eden still worried about a Mediterranean war with Italy if sanctions were kept on but was reluctant to sacrifice League prestige. Blum, more concerned about Hitler, cautioned Eden not to fall into the trap of appeasing Hitler to woo him away from Mussolini. A marriage of the two was inevitable in any case, he thought.

In London, Eden found that Hoare and MacDonald were both back in the Cabinet and could be counted on to favor the lifting of sanctions. Before Parliament, Eden urged that the question be left to the Assembly, but he was himself beginning to regard the continuance of sanctions as quixotic. The decision was taken out of his hands, however, by Chancellor of the Exchequer Neville Chamberlain, who in an address to the conservative 1900 Club on June 11 assailed the proposal of the League of Nations Union to continue and intensify sanctions against the aggressor and force him to disgorge at least a part of his conquest.

"This," said Chamberlain, "seems to me the very midsummer of madness . . . if we have retained any vestige of common sense, surely we must admit that we have tried to impose upon the League a task which it was beyond its powers to fulfill . . . Is it not apparent that the policy of sanctions involves, I do not say war, but a risk of war?"

Baldwin issued his customary disclaimer of official backing for the Chamberlain line, but there can be little doubt that Chamberlain accurately sensed the drift of official thinking. In his diary on June 17, he noted: "I did it deliberately because I felt that the party and the country needed a lead, and an indication that the Government was not wavering and drifting without a policy. . . . I did not consult Anthony Eden, because he would have been bound to beg me not to say what I proposed."

The Chamberlain speech toppled the sanctions front. Poland and Haiti jumped the gun and officially removed all controls on Italian trade. Eden, abandoning the pretense of waiting for an Assembly debate and without any consultation with the French, declared that Britain would favor the lifting of sanctions.

On June 30, the Assembly delegates gathered in a doleful mood. It was as if they had been invited to witness an execution which, the smaller powers felt, might well turn out to be their own. Van Zeeland, presiding, first read the gracious words of the conqueror—a note from Count Ciano, son-in-law of the Duce and the new Foreign Minister:

"Italy views the work she has undertaken in Ethiopia as a sacred mission of civilization, and proposes to carry it out according to the principles of the Covenant of the League of Nations . . . Italy will consider it an honor to inform the League of Nations of the progress achieved in her work of civilizing Ethiopia. . . ." If the League would view the situation "in a spirit of fair understanding," Ciano continued, as if dangling bait at the end of his line, his government would be "ready to give once more their willing and practical cooperation to the League of Nations in order to achieve a settlement of the grave problems on which rests the future of Europe and the world." The Italian government would also be willing to lend a hand in appropriate reform of the League.

The Argentine delegate spoke briefly and inconsequentially, and then Van Zeeland called upon Emperor Haile Selassie I. The Emperor, whose small figure, dark face, and black beard had become familiar to the world as the picturesque sacrificial victim, walked to the lectern.

He had barely opened his speech, talking in French, when an uproar broke out in the press and public galleries. Italian newsmen were on their feet whistling and hooting. From other parts of the chamber came cheers for the Emperor by way of answer. Titulescu leaped to his feet and asked the President of the Assembly to shut up "this *canaille*" and "throw the savages out." Police hustled the jeering, yelling Italian reporters from the chamber. Throughout the commotion the Emperor had stood motionless and silent at the lectern. When it was over he began calmly to read his text in Amharic:

"I, Haile Selassie I, Emperor of Ethiopia, am here today to claim that justice which is due to my people and the assistance promised to it eight months ago when fifty nations asserted that an aggression had been committed. It is my duty to inform the Governments assembled in Geneva of the deadly peril which threatens them by describing to them the fate which has been suffered by Ethiopia."

He pictured the effects of mustard gas, which, in that comparatively innocent year of 1936, seemed an ultimate in horror: "The deadly rain that fell from the aircraft made all those whom it touched fly shrieking with pain."

In tracing the failure of the League to halt the destruction, he put the onus on Laval, though he would not be so indecorous as to pronounce his name: "Unhappily for Ethiopia this was the time when a certain Government considered that the European situation made it imperative at all costs to obtain the friendship of Italy."

The Emperor revealed that he "personally refused all proposals to my personal advantage made to me by the Italian Government if only I would betray my people and the Covenant of the League of Nations. I was defending the cause of all small peoples who are threatened with aggression."

The problem, he said, went far beyond Ethiopia. "It is the very existence of the League of Nations . . . It is the principle of the equality of States on the one hand, or otherwise, the application laid down upon small Powers to accept the bonds of vassalship."

To an Assembly that had already conceived its verdict but could not utter it, the defeated Emperor closed by saying: "God and history will remember your judgment . . . Representatives of the world, I have come to Geneva to discharge in your midst the most painful duties of a Head of State. What reply shall I have to take back to my people?"

The reply came slowly, falteringly, amid acute embarrassment, but the apologies of the executioner made the ax no less deadly. "Not one of those here present can contemplate with any measure of satisfaction the circumstances in which the Assembly meets," Eden began. He went on to call the sanctions imposed by fifty nations a gallant effort but one that had failed. To maintain sanctions now "could serve no useful purpose." However, he said firmly, the Assembly should not recognize the conquest.

Léon Blum offered his maiden speech, which looked away from Ethiopia to broader horizons of closer relevance to France. His country, he said, would incur any risk in a European conflict to preserve an "indivisible peace." He welcomed Italy's kindly references to cooperation with the League and only hoped that Hitler would answer Eden's questionnaire in a similar vein looking forward to a "peaceful reconstruction of Europe."

Litvinov was sterner and called on League members to examine their own responsibility for the failure. He had harsh words for those who would reform the League by weakening it and thus say in effect: "Let us make the League safe for aggressors." He, too, however, looked beyond Ethiopia to a brighter future. The decision by the overwhelming majority of League members to impose sanctions had been "a tremendous step forward," he thought. It was surely better than referring the dispute to an endless succession of committees. Next time, perhaps, the victim might be saved.

Te Water of South Africa was one of the few who spoke that day for the continuation of sanctions. To abandon them would be a surrender of the League, he said, and would "shatter for generations all international confidence and all hope of realizing world peace." Only maintenance of the collective action begun in October 1935 could preserve the League. He proposed that course of action "even at the eleventh hour as the only way which would ensure salvation to the nations."

The delegates sought salvation elsewhere. While Van Zeeland privately discussed vague formulas with the Italian delegates in their hotels, the Assembly in short order turned down proposals that would oblige member states to refuse to recognize the conquest, or even those which would suggest that lifting of the sanctions implied no modification of the previously uttered condemnation of Italy. It was plain that Italy would have nothing less than unalloyed surrender.

It was too much for the Mexican delegate, Narciso Bassols, who walked out of the meeting, predicting that Ethiopia would survive "as Banquo's ghost called to disturb the tranquility of Geneva's conscience."

The formal vote on the lifting of sanctions was taken on July 4 in an atmosphere of funereal gloom. Only Ethiopia voted against it. South Africa, despite the heroic speeches of Te Water, abstained. When the Ethiopian delegation moved a resolution declaring that the Assembly of the League of Nations would not recognize any annexation of territory by force, Van Zeeland refused to put it to a vote. The Ethiopians then filed a motion asking the Assembly to facilitate a loan of ten million pounds to purchase only defensive arms. That too went down to defeat: 23 against, 23 abstentions, one vote in favor—Ethiopia's.

The Council then adjourned, and the same delegates reconvened as the Sanctions Committee to vote the formal end of all sanctions against Italy by July 15, 1936.

The Swiss applied the final turn of the screw. The Emperor was informed that he could not continue to live in his château at Vevey unless he undertook to refrain from all political activity. It was a needless offense because, in any case, the Emperor could no longer maintain his château. He had mortgaged it to an armaments firm to get weapons for his country and all that he had by way of personal fortune was a £25,000 trust fund for the education of his children. On July 5, clad in a long black cloak, he went to the railroad station at Geneva to take a train that would bring him ultimately to the refuge offered by the British government. A few reporters were on hand, and as he mounted the steps of the train, they called out, *"Vive l'Empereur."*

Another cry was heard from the balcony of the Palazzo Venezia ten days later. Mussolini crowed his triumph and the pathetic defeat of the League of Nations: "On this day, the fifteenth of July in the fourteenth year of the Fascist Era, the white flag has been hoisted on the bastions of world sanctionism. It is only a sign of surrender, but one would wish it were a symptom of a return to common sense."

The League, always so adroit in temporizing, could not decide to die swiftly and the result was a slow agony. The next regular session of the Assembly was set for September 21, which would give Avenol time to tidy up the place and remove the debris of the Ethiopian affair.

The difficulty was the persistent ghost of the victim, who, Italians indicated, would certainly keep them from the feast. The League had no provisions for canceling the membership of a state simply because it had been conquered by another League member. To resolve the problem, Avenol went to Rome on September 8 and 9 and conferred with Ciano on the best ways to exorcise troublesome specters. He came back to Geneva and reported to the Council that the problem could be resolved simply by challenging the credentials of the Ethiopian delegates.

When the Assembly met on September 21, the routine business of establishing a credentials committee ran into obstacles. The delegates of small nations, usually chosen for this minor honor, all declined to serve as hatchet men. The situation was awkward because the Italian delegates were waiting in Rome for the signal that all was clear. In the end, the luminaries Eden, Yvon Delbos of France, and Litvinov had to volunteer for the chore. Even then, the mood of the Assembly was so hostile to this final graceless maneuver of Avenol's that the big powers felt they could not exclude the Ethiopians without precipitating an unseemly row.

As it was, the Ethiopian delegation had been thinned considerably. The Blum government had threatened to deprive Dr. Jèze of his chair at the Sorbonne if he continued to act as an Ethiopian delegate. That left only one Ethiopian, Dr. Martin-Toazaz, and the faithful American adviser to the Emperor, the shaggy, unflappable Everett Colson.

The distinguished and embarrassed members of the Credentials Committee brought in a milk-and-water report expressing doubts about the validity of the Ethiopian credentials but declaring that they nevertheless should have the benefit of those doubts.

Ever since 1920 the League Assembly had yearned to see an American seated in their midst. Now there was one, and his presence, behind an

Ethiopian name plate, seemed to mock the vanished hopes of the League. He and Dr. Martin-Toazaz did nothing at the session, but their presence kept the Italians out and thus for a brief space reminded the delegates of what had been and what might have been.

For the League the failure in Ethiopia was fatal; the rest would be epilogue.

Fifteen

LESTER'S
LAST STAND

In the 1920's the League of Nations planned a palace in Geneva that would be the heart of world diplomacy and a monument to peace. When at length the site was chosen—Ariana Park, with its ancient cedars, its green lawns and modest zoo—few thought the optimism totally misplaced. The Council had its choice of plans submitted by 377 architects from all over the world. With its customary eye for political niceties and dubious compromise, it chose two designs—one by a Swiss, the other by a Frenchman. The project was blessed with an American touch—a two-million-dollar donation from John D. Rockefeller earmarked for a library.

Yet by the time the workmen topped the roof of the structural shell with the traditional sapling hung with multicolored streamers, it was November 1933 and a frost was on the League, for Adolf Hitler was in power and Japan was rampaging through China despite the disapproval of Geneva. When Avenol moved the Secretariat into the still-unfinished palace in 1936, the League was already confessing its impotence in Ethiopia. In that year the Council met in the multitiered green-and-gold chamber, surrounded by gigantic murals celebrating the banishment of war. These, painted in stark monochromatic style by José María Sert, had been the gift of the Spanish Republic. But when the delegates gathered beneath its heroic message, Generalissimo Franco was marching on

Madrid under an umbrella of Italian and German aircraft, and Sert himself had turned his back on the legal government of Spain.

In 1938 the palace was completed, covering an area as vast as Versailles, with squared-off buildings done in the epic style of the 1930's, clean, uncluttered, but graceless. By then the bright new palace had become a mausoleum of hopes, and its marble corridors and spacious Assembly Hall were haunted by three ghosts: Ethiopia, China, and Spain.

Spain's agony, unlike that of Ethiopia and China, was endured for the most part outside the League. Shortly after the rebellion began on July 18, 1936, Léon Blum, then heading the Popular Front government in France, banned the shipment of war material to either side, and invited other countries to do likewise. The resulting Nonintervention Committee was established in London, with the principal interveners, Germany and Italy, as members in good standing. The dreary, futile deliberations of that body were carried on with the blessings of the League, though not under its auspices.

The Spanish government did not oppose the theory of nonintervention and clamored only for its strict enforcement, confident that if the rebels were denied German and Italian support they could easily be defeated. When the diplomats of the Nonintervention Committee met in London, they gave equal weight to the Spanish government and to the rebels. But when the same delegations journeyed to Geneva for the meetings of the League, they treated the Spanish Republican government as the only representatives of a proper, dues-paying state member. Officially, at least, the rebels had no standing in Geneva; their spokesmen were not heard, and their communications were not circulated.

The pity of it, however—from the standpoint of the Spanish Republic—was that the possibilities of collective action lay with the Nonintervention Committee, not the League. The League had been bypassed and could serve only as a sounding board for the orations of Foreign Minister Julio Alvarez del Vayo and Premier Juan Negrín. (De Madariaga took a dim view of both sides in the civil war and withdrew from active politics.) At virtually every Council and Assembly meeting from 1936 to 1938, the League delegates would dutifully listen to the pleadings of the Spanish government, to the documentation of the agony of Guernica perpetrated by German aircraft or the sinking of Spanish freighters with all hands aboard by Italian submarines. And after each such revelation the League would pass resolutions, always to the same effect: the intervention of foreign powers was to be deplored and the Nonintervention Committee was urged yet again to do something.

When in the autumn of 1937 Italian destroyers and submarines swept the Mediterranean from the Dardanelles to Gibraltar and sank not only Spanish ships but British and Russian vessels that were bringing supplies to Spanish ports, the Powers decided that something should be done about the "pirates."

The euphemistic term "pirate"—which saved the Nonintervention Committee from the embarrassment of incriminating one of its own members—was joyously taken up by the Italians themselves. Count Ciano, the Italian Foreign Minister, for example, records in his diary: "Dinner with the 'pirates'—the Duce gathered at the table the staff officers of the ships which have unleashed piracy against the Reds. He speaks to them briefly, acclaiming the work of the Navy in the Spanish War."

It was after a British destroyer was attacked by a "pirate" that a Conference of European Powers was called. The League Assembly was about to meet in September 1937, and it seemed sensible to hold the Conference in Geneva. But Germany and Italy served notice that they would not attend if there was even the most tenuous geographical connection with the League.

Accordingly, the site was moved to Nyon, some twelve miles up the lake, a pleasant town notable for its château, its walks, and its Roman ruins. Neither Germany nor Italy would be seduced into attending, however. The Conference was held nevertheless, and it was decided that at least sixty British and French destroyers would henceforth patrol the Mediterranean and would counterattack all "pirates" making war on merchant ships of any nation—except those of Spain, which were in effect termed fair game for piracy.

To the enormous relief of the British, Litvinov made no objections to the arrangement and was content with the promise that the patrols would call on the Russian fleet for help if needed. Entry of Soviet warships into the Mediterranean was perhaps the last thing any of the Powers wanted. The Tyrrhenian Sea was to be left for Italy to patrol, and Mussolini accepted the offer graciously.

After the agreement was signed at Nyon, newsmen asked Eden whether he thought this would mean an end to piracy. "If there's another attack, I'll eat my hat," he replied gaily, seeing in the show of Anglo-French naval strength a rallying of resistance. Indeed, the unidentified Italian submarines lay low and Eden preserved his homburg.

Whatever comfort Paris and London might take from the suppression of the piracy, there was very little to feed Alvarez del Vayo's customarily buoyant optimism. He now called for an end to the Nonintervention Committee that seemed powerless to stop a land, sea, and air invasion of his country. Eden admitted the Committee's weakness but said, "Even a leaky dam is better than none," and pointed out that at least the Spanish war had not yet spread to engulf all Europe.

In September 1937, while Mussolini was proclaiming to great crowds in Berlin that Italians were dying by the thousands in Spain, it became difficult to defend nonintervention. Yvon Delbos of France and Eden jointly offered a resolution at the League Assembly that month recommending the ending of the Nonintervention Committee if foreign troops were not withdrawn "in the near future."

The resolution drew the support of thirty-two countries, including almost every European state represented on the Nonintervention Committee. Others abstained, but the only negative votes came from Portugal and Albania. Under the unanimity rule, one vote was enough to defeat the resolution, but it made no matter. Britain and France had apparently announced their intention to break with the policy of nonintervention.

Jubilantly Alvarez del Vayo telephoned the "victory" news to Valencia, where the government had been forced to move. Over the phone he heard the bombs exploding in the new capital. The "victory" was premature, however. Bombs continued to fall while a commission studied future procedures should the invaders be withdrawn.

In England, Neville Chamberlain had become Prime Minister and was following a Laval-like course of seeking to mollify the aggressor with kind words, an understanding approach, and, if necessary, the supreme sacrifice of other people's territory. The Prime Minister worked around and behind his Foreign Minister, Anthony Eden. He desperately wanted a pact with Italy, which had at last dropped all pretenses and left the League in December 1937. To woo Mussolini, Chamberlain was prepared to recognize the Roman Empire in Ethiopia and to ignore the Italian invasion of Spain.

The courtship of Mussolini was abetted by Chamberlain's sister-in-law, the widow of Sir Austen, who had died shortly after Neville took over 10 Downing Street. Lady Chamberlain, who politically leaned more to Neville than to Austen, had taken up residence in Rome and was accustomed to share her brother-in-law's correspondence with Count Ciano and with the Duce.

In February, Lady Chamberlain sent a message to the Prime Minister: "Count Ciano lunched with me today and asked me whether I had any further message from you. I said, 'no.' He then begged me to let you know time is everything. Today an agreement will be easy but things are happening in Europe which will make it impossible tomorrow." (Among the "things" that were happening was Hitler's seizure of Austria, a matter which was not even called to the attention of the League, although it meant the quiet expunging of a member state from the roster.)

The short-circuiting of Sir Anthony, who was objecting to the high price of a pact with Rome, was accomplished with the deft assistance of Dino Grandi, the Italian ambassador to England. Grandi, in his dispatches home, told of his curious relations with the British Prime Minister; how he would meet Chamberlain's secret agent in a London taxicab; how he witnessed a celebrated verbal duel between Eden and Chamberlain at 10 Downing Street; and how he earned the thanks of the Prime Minister for feeding him ammunition to discomfit the Foreign Secretary.

British sources have suggested that perhaps the self-dramatizing Grandi was exaggerating his role, but in any case Sir Anthony in February 1938 found himself obliged to resign. The way was then cleared for an Anglo-Italian understanding, assisted once again in Rome not only by Lady Chamberlain but also by Sir Eric Drummond, that stalwart of the League's early days, who had now become Lord Perth. Despite his shyness and initial distaste for Fascist ways, Perth seemed to have endeared himself to Count Ciano. (In his diary Ciano came to call him "a man who, at the cost of great effort, has come to understand fascism and even to love it. He has an affection for me and I reciprocate it.")

A first installment on the price of the Anglo-Italian pact was to be paid at the League Council meeting of May 1938, when Britain was set to recognize the conquest of Ethiopia. Haile Selassie accurately read the signs in the diplomatic weather and sought an interview with Eden's successor, Lord Halifax. The new Foreign Minister could scarcely refuse the courtesy but first cleared it with Rome. On March 2, 1938, Ciano recorded in his diary: "In the evening I received . . . a phone call informing me that Lord Halifax had to receive the Negus and that he asked me to attach no importance to the thing and not to begin a press campaign." On the following day, Ciano observed: "The visit of the former Negus seems to be void of substance."

Throughout the early weeks of April, Ciano saw Perth almost daily and received word that Halifax would esteem it a personal favor if the Anglo-Italian accord was signed on his birthday. "All this is very romantic," observed Ciano.

As the Council meeting drew near, Perth timidly warned Mussolini that Lord Halifax could not disavow the policy of sanctions but that he would call for adapting it realistically to the new conditions. Mussolini assured Perth that this would not trouble him, that practical results were what counted. "It would not be elegant," he said, "to insist that England cover her head with ashes." He even suggested that it would not be out of place to "perfume Eden's memory with a little incense."

The 101st meeting of the Council that convened in that balmy May of 1938 was described by the *Times* Geneva correspondent as "particularly cheerless." He added: "The best that can be said is what some of the delegates already are saying in private: that at any rate they are clearing the air, they are facing the problem in a realistic if limited way, and they are trying to bridge the gap between *de jure* and *de facto*."

The first haunting presence to be exorcised by the realists was China, whose dossier had been closed in 1933 after the Manchurian crisis. Since then the Japanese had pushed on south and west, and Generalissimo Chiang Kai-shek had been fighting the Chinese Communists and acquiring from Germany a Hitlerian expertise for his officer corps. None of this, however, was considered a matter for the League.

Though *de facto* there was bloody fighting, *de jure* there was no war. If China had declared war, the American Neutrality Act would have cut off a vital flow of war matériel. For while the United States was shipping to Japan massive quantities of scrap metal and other necessities for a war machine, it was supplying China as well. A declaration of war by either side in that conflict would have deprived both of valuable matériel, but China, more dependent on outside sources, would have been at a greater disadvantage.

What reopened the Chinese affair in Geneva was the new offensive that began in the summer of 1937 with a minor clash on the Marco Polo Bridge near Peiping. Japan used the incident as a pretext for demanding whole provinces by way of reparations. It then poured troops into Shantung, took Nanking, and bombed Canton and Hangchow. The League in the fall of 1937 referred the matter to the Far East Committee, a non-League body on which the United States was represented. China at that point was decidedly more hopeful about salvation from Washington than from Geneva. What it got, however, was the customary condemnation of Japan, seconded by the League and endorsed by Washington. It was difficult to translate such words into military terms. A Nine-Power Conference at Brussels offered only sympathy.

The League had asked its members to do nothing that would hinder China's defense. A Chinese suggestion that its fellow members of the League might also promise not to help Japan was a bit strong for the enfeebled organization. The proposal roused the painful memory of sanctions as in the Ethiopian debacle. It had been difficult for the League to backtrack from those brave resolutions. A similar dance with the imperial Japanese would be exhausting.

Now, in May 1938, the dapper Wellington Koo appeared again in the Council Chamber to remind his colleagues of their failure in a restrained but urgent appeal:

"While European democracies are still trying to gain time with the resources of diplomacy in the hope of avoiding war at any cost," he told the Council, "China, in the face of aggression, has been fighting for the cause of peace by sacrifice of flesh and blood . . . Just now a wave of so-called realism is sweeping over the West, and emphasis is placed on facts instead of principles. Let me again call attention to the continuation of armed aggression in the Far East, the daily slaughter of thousands of men engaged in the conflict, the indiscriminate bombing by Japanese aircraft of open and undefended towns in China with its heavy toll of death upon innocent civilians, the unprecedented violence done to Chinese women by the Japanese troops, the plunder and destruction of Chinese property, and the appalling loss of human life inflicted upon the Chinese people. Let me recall to you the scrapping of solemn treaties by Japan and her trampling down of the rules of international law and morality."

The President of the Council, Vilhelms Munters of Latvia, said only: "The Members of the Council will probably desire to examine more closely the statement made by the representative of China and discuss it at a later meeting." Yet again the Council shelved China, promising that the Assembly would consider the matter in September.

Some voices clamored for action by the League. Winston Churchill, for example, declared that "if the League has been broken, it must be rebuilt, if the Covenant has been derided, we must reinforce it." He spoke of China resisting with the aid of the Soviet Union, of Italy's conquest in Ethiopia that was proving "a curse," of the hope of Anglo-French solidarity in the face of aggressive dictators. But Churchill spoke at Manchester, England, and Lord Halifax spoke at Geneva.

Lord Halifax—who, the previous November at Berchtesgaden, had told Hitler that England could accept the German absorption of Austria—now confronted the second ghost at the feast: Spain, in the person of Alvarez del Vayo. That Spanish diplomat of eternal hope had been encouraged, shortly before the Council assembled, by the rumor that the Roosevelt administration had decided to back a congressional resolution calling for suspension of the Neutrality Act, which was so effectively strangling the supply line to Spain. (The rumor proved untrue.)

On May 11, Alvarez del Vayo took his place at the Council table and, as Wellington Koo had done, brought into the chamber the blood and horror of war and the exquisite patience, dignity, and courage of its victims. And again he called for the withdrawal of foreign troops from both sides under rigid international inspection:

"However great the provocation to which the Spanish Government has been exposed—and it would be difficult to imagine anything more provocative and exasperating than the international treatment that has been accorded to us—and notwithstanding the scandalous manner in which the invaders of its territory have been encouraged in certain circles, where loyalty to the principles of the League of Nations is confined to high-sounding public pronouncements on international affairs, the Government of the Republic has not used the obvious possibilities open to it for causing disturbances . . . Both from the trenches and from the seat of Government, we have watched day by day the incomprehensible desertion of certain democracies; we have watched them conspire with the aggressor; they have tolerated bombardments of open towns, and the mass murder of women and children with no more than a superficial protest; and finally they have signed agreements with the aggressors which legalize this intervention."

Then Alvarez del Vayo spoke his prophecy: ". . . it is sad to contemplate that these democracies, by reason of their failure to react in time, have brought much nearer than they think the day when their own cities will fall victims to the same atrocities as have filled my country with horror and death."

Lord Halifax responded by pointing out that unfortunately "the terms of the Covenant were not drawn with an eye to civil war," that foreign intervention was occurring on both sides, and he offered yet another defense of the "leaky dam" of nonintervention. Georges Bonnet of France cited the "deep and powerful sympathy of France for the Spanish people."

William Joseph Jordan of New Zealand cut through the soupy sentiment that habitually drowned debate on Spain. "My only comment," he said, "is that, in the face of facts which seem so tragically plain, the request for an examination of the situation and of the Spanish arguments and statements, so that the operation of international law may be considered, is so amazingly moderate that surely we cannot hesitate for a moment in acceding to it."

Actually the Council did hesitate and was about to close the discussion when Alvarez del Vayo pleaded for the right to speak again at a later session. At that time he offered a resolution which would have fulfilled the brave words of the previous autumn that promised an end to the

Nonintervention Committee unless foreign troops were withdrawn in "the near future."

The resolution was formally moved shortly before six o'clock in the evening of May 13. Acting with unaccustomed speed, the Council adjourned and reconvened at seven-thirty as if impressed at last with the urgency of the situation. The delegates met, however, only to vote down the Spanish resolution and maintain the fiction of nonintervention. Only the Soviet Union voted with Spain. France, England, Poland, and Rumania voted against it. Wellington Koo and William Jordan explained that the timing of the vote had unfortunately given them no opportunity to communicate with their respective governments. They therefore had to abstain along with the delegates of Belgium, Bolivia, Ecuador, Iran, Latvia, Peru, and Sweden.

The preponderant number of abstentions was chalked up by the Spaniards as yet another "moral victory" for their cause, but it was not certain how many more such victories the Spanish government could survive.

The Ethiopian ghost came trailing clouds of glory. First came a message from the Emperor Haile Selassie to the Secretary-General, and even the salutation was an ironic reproach, like that of a King to a group of regicides: "The Conquering Lion of the Tribe of Judah, Haile Selassie I, Elect of the Lord, Emperor of Ethiopia. Peace be with you!"

It listed the members of his delegation that would attend the Council meeting. In addition to the permanent delegate of Ethiopia, Dr. M. L. Toazaz, and the first secretary, Dr. M. E. Medhen, there were to be some formidable British intellectuals who might be expected to embarrass Lord Halifax. These were Sir Norman Angell, that apostle of international morality; Oxford professor of international law J. L. Brierly; and professor of political science Stanley Jevons. The Council wrangled for three hours in bitter debate behind closed doors before agreeing that the Emperor's distinguished delegation would be seated without challenge but without formal acknowledgment as a precedent.

On the evening of May 11, the Emperor himself arrived, looking frail and tired. A crowd was on hand at the station to greet him. There were cheers and a few mocking whistles that were quickly hushed. The first objective of the Ethiopians was to prove to the League—twenty of whose members had already recognized the Italian Empire—that the Ethiopian cause was not yet lost.

"Ethiopia is far from having been conquered," began a statement signed by the Emperor and issued the night of his arrival. ". . . The resistance of a population of different races and religions is more intense, united and effective than at any time since the autumn of 1936. There is every reason to believe that armed resistance will be intensified during the coming rainy season, when the Italian Air Force cannot be effectively employed."

On the morning of May 12, the elegant, restrained Lord Halifax rose to refute the Emperor's statement that Ethiopia was still alive. It was dead, he said, and unless it was buried it would be troublesome. He seemed also to be saying as much for the League of Nations. His sentiments followed unwaveringly the line approved in advance by the Duce. "I do not over-look the fact that there are many in my own country, as perhaps in others," he said, "who feel . . . that any action designed to facilitate the recognition of the Italian conquest does impinge on principle, and would, therefore, deplore the adoption of such a course. I regret that I cannot share their view."

He staked out the course of realism as opposed to principle, peace as opposed to the League of Nations: "It is the considered opinion of his Majesty's Government that for practical purposes Italian control over virtually the whole of Ethiopia has become an established fact and that sooner or later, unless we are prepared by force to alter it, or unless we are to live in an unreal world, that fact, whatever may be our judgment on it, will have to be acknowledged . . ." His parting shot was for the League, which he identified as an obstacle to peace. "Great as is the League of Nations," he said, "the ends that it exists to serve are greater than itself, and the greatest of those ends is peace."

As Halifax spoke, the Emperor Haile Selassie had seemed to be staring at Sert's murals, depicting among other things the spectacle of European soldiers driving black men in front of them. Now, in his royal cloak of slate gray, the tiny Emperor spoke: "Though only just recovered from an illness I decided, in spite of the state of my health, to come myself to the Council of the League of Nations to defend the cause of my people. The Council will, I hope, spare me the fatigue of reading my statement in person and allow Ato Toazaz, permanent delegate of Ethiopia to the League of Nations, to do so in my place."

Then the tall Amharic Toazaz began to read: "Denied all succor, the Ethiopian people mounts its Calvary alone.

"The victim of aggression has been spared no humiliation. All the resources of procedure have been tried in order to exclude Ethiopia from the League of Nations at the aggressor's behest . . . Since 1935, Ethiopia has observed with sorrow how, one after another, the signatures affixed to the Covenant have been denied. A number of Powers, themselves threat-ened by aggression and realizing their own weakness, have abandoned

Ethiopia. Their cry has been 'Everyone for himself—sauve qui peut,' the cry of the panic-stricken and the demoralized. In the vain hope of currying favor with the aggressor, they have thrown over the undertakings which they had assumed for their common security and, in so doing, have made havoc of the very principles on which their existence depended. They have torn up the treaties which ensured their independence —Non-Aggression Treaties, the Covenant of the League of Nations, the Pact of Paris. By what right can they ever invoke such undertakings if they treat the agreements they have signed as mere scraps of paper?

"Aggressions have multiplied. The contagion has spread . . . The reign of fear dominates the world . . . International morality has disappeared. The excuse of the weak is their very weakness, their certainty that they will be left to their fate, as Ethiopia has been. Of the two evils they choose that which, in their fear of the aggressor, seems the less. May God forgive them!"

The Emperor's statement cited the Anglo-Italian Treaty, which had just been concluded in Rome on April 16, and the note annexed to it, in which the British promised to work in the Council for the removal of "such obstacles as might at present be held to impede the freedom of Member States as regards recognition of Italian sovereignty over Ethiopia." He contrasted the bargain sealed at Rome with the declarations in 1932 and 1936 pledging League members to withhold recognition from any situation brought about by means contrary to the Covenant.

Gallantly the Emperor acknowledged his debts: "It is with the keenest regret that I find myself in opposition to a Government for which I feel genuine admiration and profound gratitude. It is that Government which, in my distress, has granted me its generous hospitality. I forget nothing of what I owe to Great Britain." And he summed up British motives this way: "I am, of course, aware that to justify its actions the United Kingdom Government claims that it is moved by lofty preoccupations: nothing less than the promotion of general appeasement by the sacrifice of a people." ("Appeasement" still had the virtuous ring of peacemaking without the odious connotations that within a year would change the meaning of the word.)

To Halifax's posing of the question of Peace vs. the League, Haile Selassie answered: "True, the essential object of the League is to maintain peace. But there are two ways of maintaining peace: there is the maintenance of peace through right, and there is peace at any price. Ethiopia is profoundly convinced that the League of Nations has no freedom of choice. It would be committing suicide if, after having been created to maintain peace through right, it deserted that principle for the principle of peace at any price, even by the immolation of a State Member at the feet of its aggressor."

Unfortunately for Ethiopia, the pulse of the League in 1938 was too feeble to be stirred by eloquent calls to honor. Only Litvinov, Koo, and Jordan spoke up for the sanctity of the Covenant. No vote was taken and none was needed. Each government would search its own conscience. On May 12, 1938, Count Ciano jotted down a one-line entry in his diary: "At Geneva the Ethiopian question was buried."

That was the net accomplishment of the Council that spring.

When the delegates next came to Geneva for the Assembly meeting in September, the city was scheduling blackout drills; frontier guards were at their posts along the Rhine and atop the Jura; artillery lined the railroad tracks; and, as elsewhere in Europe, churches were filled on "Days of Prayer in Times of Crisis."

The First Committee of the Assembly, dealing with financial matters, struck Austria off the list of dues-paying member states. The Spanish delegate, Rey y Arrojo, remarked on the sad irony that the disappearance of a state should be noted by the League only in connection with a bookkeeping procedure. Official word of Austria's demise as a state had come to the League from Germany in the course of disposing of the effects of the deceased.

In the Sixth Committee (Political), Juan Negrín and Alvarez del Vayo were still trying forlornly to get a resolution passed that would pinpoint a time limit for the withdrawal of foreign troops from Spain more closely than the "near future." The British delegate read a draft composed of the familiar milk and water, but this time Del Vayo would have no part of it and refused to attend what he called "those private conferences so dear to the heart of the Secretary-General, and responsible for the incessant concessions and settlements which brought the League of Nations to its ruin."

Thereafter, Del Vayo noted, Avenol glared at him as if "the imperiling of a draft resolution was a crime more deserving of sanctions than the rudest act of aggression." Spain did not appear on the formal agenda of that Assembly.

The Sixth Committee was also seized with the various projects for reforming the League—some to water down the Covenant, others to strengthen it. The British paved the way for a compromise formula that would leave the shell of the League as a noble monument while removing the guts from the glorious ruin. "It should be recognized that the principles of the Covenant remain unaltered. But those Governments which felt it necessary, in present circumstances, to define the manner in which they would interpret their obligations under Article 16 [dealing with sanctions against an aggressor] would do so in declarations which would be formally recorded in the proceedings of the Sixth Committee."

It was as if the solemn obligations of a treaty could be modified by the addition of the words "if convenient." In effect the British formula embodied an existing reality. So many member states had already declared themselves unbound by the enforcement provisions of the Covenant that, when the Council formally declared that any state was henceforth free to apply sanctions against Japan, it stirred no hope in China, no alarm in Japan, and scarcely more than a paragraph in the press. Article XVI was in effect a dead letter.

The war that seemed about to break in that September was occasioned by Adolf Hitler's passionate desire to liberate the Germans in the Sudetenland of Czechoslovakia. In earlier years the slightest hint of a border clash in Europe was the matter for an emergency session of the Council and/or the Assembly. Now, when all the world trembled in the face of catastrophe, the question of Czechoslovakia was not even raised in the Secretary-General's report. It was widely rumored that the Great Powers had tacitly agreed that it would be best to pretend that nothing whatever was happening. The Spaniards and the Russians broke the rule in the general discussion of the plenary session of the Assembly, but this lapse in taste was passed over in silence.

Del Vayo told the Assembly: "The Chinese people who, like the Spanish people, preferred death rather than that their country should cease to exist as a nation, had been abandoned to their fate. They had seen a Member of the League [Austria] disappear, as it were, overnight, without a single word of condolence or farewell being devoted to it in the Secretary-General's report. The aggressors, therefore, thought that the disappearance of a Member of the League could take place with absolute impunity, and that such a disappearance would not even be recorded in the list of international crimes. It was therefore only to be expected that the effects of the so-called realist policy should result in fresh attempts at aggression, this time against Czechoslovakia."

Maxim Litvinov, who was called by some members of the Seretariat "the last loyal member of the League" and "a latter-day Lord Cecil," in this, his last appearance at the League, also mentioned the unmentionable. "In the case of Czechoslovakia," he said, "the U.S.S.R. Government had abstained from all advice to the Czechoslovak Government, considering it quite inadmissible that [Czechoslovakia] should be asked to make concessions to the detriment of its interests as a State, in order that the U.S.S.R. should be set free from the necessity of fulfilling its obligations under the Treaty bearing its signature."

He revealed in part the Soviet version of the diplomatic maneuvers that were then nearing a portentous climax: "When consulted by the French and Czechoslovak Governments as to its attitude in the event of an attack on Czechoslovakia, the U.S.S.R. Government had given the perfectly clear and unambiguous reply that in accordance with the Soviet-Czech Pact, it was prepared to render Czechoslovakia immediate and effective aid if France, loyal to its obligations, would render similar assistance and had proposed that the question be raised at the League of Nations, if only as yet under Article 11 [acknowledging a threat to the peace], with the object of mobilizing public opinion and ascertaining the position of certain other States, whose passive aid might be extremely valuable."

As Litvinov spoke in Geneva, Polish troops were taking up their positions along the frontier with Czechoslovakia, thus underscoring a demand for a plebiscite among the Poles in Czechoslovakia as Hitler had been doing for the Germans. On the following morning, while Hungary imitated the Polish imitation, Neville Chamberlain left London to meet Hitler at the Hotel Dreesen in Godesberg on the Rhine. He came to offer Hitler those areas of the Sudetenland with a German majority and to guarantee that what would be left of Czechoslovakia would be neutral— and defenseless. It was precisely what Hitler had demanded and what Chamberlain had induced France and bludgeoned Czechoslovakia into accepting.

Hitler, however, like the Kaiser's generals and admirals before 1914, scorned to accept as a gift what he could take by force of arms. He therefore discomfited Chamberlain by delivering an ultimatum requiring the Czechs to leave all of the Sudetenland before October 1, or be invaded.

"Is the position hopeless, sir?" a reporter asked Chamberlain.

"I would not like to say that," Chamberlain replied. "It is up to the Czechs now."

Chamberlain's blithe disclaimer of responsibility was typical of the antics performed on the edge of the abyss in that September of 1938.

The Assembly of the League of Nations in that historic hour took time, in its committees, to consider the standardization of signals at road crossings; international legislation on automobile insurance; and the protection of monuments in time of war.

While the League was thus engaged, Hitler shrieked with fury at the Sportspalast; the British dug air-raid trenches in their gardens; Harold

Nicolson, walking through Trafalgar Square amid children playing and pigeons swirling, heard a companion moodily urge: "Those children should be evacuated at once, and so should the pigeons." In Rome, Lord Perth pleaded for Mussolini to intervene with Hitler for even a twenty-four-hour reprieve. The Führer granted the world another day, and Mussolini traveled with Ciano to Munich, there to meet with Hitler and Daladier. On the way the Duce confided to Ciano the fundamental reason why Britain was doomed. "When a nation adores animals," Mussolini explained, "to the point of building cemeteries for them, hospitals, houses; when in any country they create foundations for parakeets, this is an obvious sign of decadence."

Decadent or not, England and France proceeded to negotiate the total surrender of Czechoslovakia to Hitler's demands. Chamberlain brought out of the conference a brief note which he had drafted and Hitler had signed, promising that Germany and Britain would henceforth consult each other to "remove possible sources of difference, and thus to contribute to assure the peace of Europe."

It was one o'clock in the morning of September 30 when the pact was signed, and everyone shook hands all around. Daladier told his colleagues that even the Czechs, who had been kept waiting in the anteroom, were pleased at their country's peaceful dismemberment. Only André François-Poncet, the French ambassador to Berlin, permitted himself the luxury of spoken bitterness. According to Ciano, the veteran French diplomat blushed and burst out: "This is the way France treats the only allies who remained loyal to her." It is unknown whether François-Poncet did in fact give way at that moment or Ciano used an apocryphal quotation to spice his diary and dramatize France's humiliation. In any case, the humiliation of France, as of England, was real, the triumph of Hitler was real, and real also was the general rejoicing that the world—with some exceptions, of course—was still not at war on October 1, 1938.

"No conqueror returning from a victory on the battlefield has come adorned with nobler laurels," said the *Times* of London in hailing Chamberlain. In Geneva, too, the peace of Munich seemed infinitely preferable to a war over the seizure of a German-inhabited part of Czechoslovakia, which, after all, was only in line with the Wilsonian call for the adjustment of boundaries according to ethnic composition. Hitler had said there would be no more demands, and even if the Czechoslovak state was now to lose any real vestiges of independence, it seemed not too great a price for a world at peace.

García Calderón, Peruvian minister to Paris and a member of the delegation in Geneva, voiced what much of the world felt on that first day of the Munich peace, though few perhaps would paint their relief in such purple colors. He said of Chamberlain: "This knight of peace, who possesses neither hatred, envy nor fierceness, has attained the highest summit of human grandeur and acquired honor greater than that of all conquerors. His name is blessed today in all the homes of the Earth."

There were dissenters, of course. Sean Lester, Deputy Secretary-General of the League, wrote in his diary: "What Chamberlain has done is a logical sequence of the policy pursued by Britain and France during the past two years; they paralysed the League of Nations; they gave no help to the weak attacked by the strong; they ran away every time a threat was uttered; now they have given Germany, for nothing but a temporary peace, the fruits of a great campaign . . . Democracy, in a way, does not matter, but the other makes decent life for civilized man entirely impossible. There is still the garden and the river."

During the panic that preceded the calm of Munich, few people gave much thought to how the League might stagger on in the midst of world-wide hostilities. Avenol had pushed through a plan that gave the Secretary-General full power to take any administrative decision on consultation with a Supervisory Commission composed of five members, headed by Carl Hambro of Norway. This Commission would in effect replace the Assembly in time of war. The replacement of a cipher by a zero was not considered a matter worthy of extensive debate.

The League was already in limbo in the first half of 1939 while the glow of Munich was turning to ashes. The Italian seizure of Albania and the German grab at Memel did not disturb the even routine of the Secretary-General. The paintings of the Prado received shelter and devoted care at the League, which had provided such scant comfort for the rest of Spain. The Council and the Assembly were due to meet in Geneva in September, but those sessions, necessarily confined to the barest rituals, had to be canceled. On September 1, Hitler had marched into Poland. France and Great Britain, in their extremity, did not completely forget the League. They duly informed Geneva that they were at war with Germany. They cited, as legal bases for their action, the German violations of the Kellogg-Briand Pact and the treaties with Poland. Significantly, they did not mention the Covenant of the League of Nations.

The document upon which Woodrow Wilson and Colonel House and Lord Cecil and Clemenceau and Léon Bourgeois and all the specialists of the Allied and Associated Powers had labored with the ardor of lawyers rewriting the Ten Commandments had been removed from the international shrines. If the still-functioning Secretariat, commissions, and bureaus of the League attempted to seriously consider the war that had come to Europe, Switzerland was prepared to expel the entire organization. The League Secretariat could stay only if it would not violate Swiss neutrality. As Switzerland had told the Emperor of Ethiopia only a year earlier, it could stay if it pledged to undertake no political activity. The League, too, had become in effect a prisoner of war.

There was, however, one last political fling reserved for the League. The Soviet Union, battening down its hatches for the storm, had moved to bolster the defenses of Leningrad. In the view of Soviet military circles, this required the long-term lease or outright concession of territory by the Baltic republics. Latvia, Lithuania, and Estonia yielded, but Finland refused to grant the Soviets' demand of a naval base; the Soviet Union, in the name of national security, proceeded to take what it needed.

No war was declared because the Soviets had found a convenient Finn-in-exile, Otto Wilhelm Kuusinen, who formed a government of the Democratic Republic of Finland which the Soviets recognized as legitimate. The new Finnish regime was cooperative in giving the Russians the facilities needed for the defense of Leningrad, and in return the Soviet Union obliged by helping it to power. To the rest of the world, however, the affair looked very like an invasion, and the bombing of Helsinki very like a war.

The Swiss, who had always considered quite regrettable the admission of the Soviet Union to the League, saw no violation of their neutrality in League consideration of this Baltic war, although the war that had engulfed the rest of Europe was far too sensitive a matter to be even mentioned. The Russians were far away from Geneva while the Germans were thundering over the border.

The Russians, in fear, had made a Munich of their own after the Anglo-French fiasco. This allowed the frustrated ex-partners of Hitler to adopt a tone of high moral superiority to the partner who had succeeded them in Hitler's capricious favor. It was a time for the pot to call the kettle black.

Thus, when Finland appealed to the League of Nations on December 2, 1939, Secretary-General Avenol was free to respond with unaccustomed efficiency. The Council was called into session on December 9, and a special Assembly was summoned for December 11. Not Manchuria or Spain or China or Ethiopia—to say nothing of Austria or Czechoslovakia or Albania or Poland or Memel—had provoked such swift emergency measures. There was only one item on the agenda of the League in December 1939: Finland vs. the Soviet Union.

On December 5, Vyacheslav Molotov had sent a telegram to Avenol conveying the Soviet Union's refusal to appear at its own beheading. "The U.S.S.R. is not at war with Finland and does not threaten the Finnish nation with war," the message said. "The Soviet Union maintains peaceful relations with the Democratic Republic of Finland, whose Government signed with the U.S.S.R. on December 2nd a pact of assistance and friendship. This pact settled all the questions which the Soviet Government had fruitlessly discussed with delegates from the Finnish Government now divested of its power."

The hostilities then raging in Finland were explained this way: "By its declaration of December 1st the Government of the Democratic Republic of Finland requested the Soviet Government to lend assistance to that Republic by armed forces with a view to the joint liquidation at the earliest possible moment of the very dangerous seat of war created in Finland by its former rulers."

Germany took a dim view of the League's unexpected manifestation of life. A leading Nazi political commentator, in line with the friendly relations between the Soviet Union and Germany at the time, leveled this warning at the Swiss and the neutrals gathering at Geneva: "Every State which has sent a representative to the Council meeting at Geneva must realize that it is participating in an Anglo-French plot to make trouble for Russia and Germany, and thus taking its stand in one of the two belligerent camps. It is incompatible with neutrality that such a meeting, which merely aims either at provoking the neutrals to a quarrel or at suppressing their independent action, should be taking place at all on neutral territory."

The Assembly met and reveled in the recollection of the words of Maxim Litvinov, who had vanished from the management of his country's foreign policy. Almost every speaker quoted from the speeches of the Russian exponent of collective security as ammunition to be hurled at his country. Rudolf Holsti, the Finnish delegate, chose Litvinov's text on the device of recognizing a rebel government in Spain: ". . . the recognition of the rebels as the lawful Government was in itself a form of intervention." The curious thing was that when Litvinov made such statements they were generally ignored. Now they were cited as the veriest Gospel of the League. It was as if a saint had been found with his hand in the cashbox, a sight always pleasing to sinners.

The neutrals were assigned to carry the ball, with only seconding assists from Britain and France. It was left to Argentina's delegate, Rodolfo Freyre, to make the final motion. "The League has no doubt lost all coercive force," he said, "but there is still one gesture that it has to make, one gesture that it cannot refuse to make, unless it is prepared to resign its functions in a spirit of truly suicidal defeat. The gesture consists in excluding from its midst those who, after having proclaimed themselves the defenders of the essential principles for whose establishment this institution was founded, have repudiated those same principles without exhibiting the slightest scruple, without giving their reasons, thus placing themselves outside what still remains of the League's heritage—the honor we hold dear."

On the morning of December 14, the Assembly, by a standing vote, declared that the Soviet Union "has by its own action placed itself outside the Covenant," and having thus passed its sentence of excommunication, referred the matter to the Council for execution. (The vote was recorded as unanimous, but Bulgaria, Sweden, Norway, Denmark, Latvia, Lithuania, and Estonia all abstained.)

The Council, again with unprecedented speed, met at five o'clock that same afternoon. Again Paul-Boncour recalled Litvinov's championing of collective security and noted the "somewhat tardy awakening of the universal conscience." One hour of debate was all that was needed. At six in the evening the President of the Council, Costa du Rels of Bolivia, read the Soviet Union out of the League of Nations. Finland abstained, as befitted its role as a party in the dispute. She was joined by China, Yugoslavia, and Greece.

A dead silence hung over the Council Room in the Palais after the vote, reporters noted. There had been a triple irony in the proceedings. The Soviet Union had been expelled from the deathbed of a moribund as if from some majestic throne room; the most potent arguments for its conviction were its own words; the League had singled out the Soviet Union as the sole member ever to be expelled after having spent years in attempting to woo back into the fold other aggressors who had defied and scorned it.

The Soviet Union took its excommunication calmly. Tass, the official news service, said it greeted the "absurd decision" with "an ironic smile." After the Russians were dealt with, the delegates hurried away from Geneva and left the League to Joseph Avenol. The Secretary-General used his office to rally all possible aid for embattled Finland. His enthusiasm occasionally produced ridiculous effects, as when the appeal for Finnish relief was sent to the Emperor of Ethiopia. Haile Selassie, in exile, responded with a telegram of elaborate and possibly ironic courtesy expressing his unfailing support for "the victims of aggression."

When news of this was published gleefully in *Popolo d'Italia*, Thanassis Aghnides, still with the Secretariat, explained the gaffe to his superiors by

pointing out that technically Ethiopia was still a League member and as
such automatically received all documents issued by the League. Sean
Lester scribbled a memo on Aghnides' explanation saying, "It is clear that
some discretion is required in such cases . . . Papers requiring action
should not go to the Emperor." He approved Aghnides' suggestion for a
study "of non-existing governments of member States."

Aside from raising support for Finland, Avenol's preoccupation was to
spin a cocoon in which to wrap the League for the duration of the war.
Before the end of 1939, some 140 members of the Secretariat had been
dismissed and all wages slashed by 20 percent. The pay cut not only
would save funds for the League, now for the most part financially
dependent upon Britain, but, it was hoped, would encourage other
employees to leave. In any case, the exodus was on as increasing numbers
of League staff members responded to their countries' mobilization. In
the winter three hundred more were fired or resigned. In the spring of
1940, Avenol sent a circular letter to all the staff calling for resignations.

Sean Lester knew that his departure from the post of Deputy Secretary-
General would be enthusiastically welcomed by Avenol, who hoped to
offer the bones of the League to those he was convinced would be the
masters of Europe. But Lester was an obstacle that would not go away.
He stayed and watched with anguish the progress of the war and the
dismantling of the League.

"The dearth of leadership and inspiration was unbelievable," he wrote
to Arthur Sweetser in May 1940. "The office seemed without soul. One
who had known the Secretariat in the old days of its glory would not
have thought it could have sunk so low."

Lester was a Protestant from Northern Ireland who went south,
worked as a Dublin newspaperman, and became an ardent Sinn Feiner.
He fell into diplomacy when the government of the Irish Free State,
groping desperately to replace an ailing delegate to Geneva, settled for a
knowledgeable journalist who had worked in the Ministry of Information. Lester stayed on and found himself at the head of League committees on crises in South America, and later as the occupant of the hot seat
in Danzig. When he became *persona non grata* to the Nazis in that
beleaguered city, he was brought to Geneva to become the Deputy
Secretary-General. Anthony Eden told him then that the move might
mean he would be the next Secretary-General of the League. "If I
thought so, you wouldn't see my heels for dust," Lester replied.

Lester was not an ambitious man, though Avenol charged him with a
most unlikely lust for power, but he was a very dogged man. Avenol
confined him to the most peripheral aspects of League affairs and would

not talk to him for months at a time. Nevertheless, though all that he believed in seemed about to be swept away in the Nazi storm, Lester quixotically clung to the fragments of the shipwrecked League, resigned to glorious defeats in the approved Irish manner. When a friend of his left for England in June of that year, Lester told him: "I would like to go, too, but I began my life politically in one 'lost cause' and it seems likely I shall finish it in another."

To Sweetser he wrote in that fearful June: "The German troops are marching along the Jura and may be in Bellegarde today . . . The world is crashing round our ears but [we] are keeping our heads up if our hearts are broken . . . At the moment I have only two principles, or at any rate, two immediate objectives: the first is that we should endeavor to keep a little bit of personal dignity whatever comes (an ideal, as I have no confidence in my own physical courage); and the other is [that] we should try to look after our staff who have been standing by us here, and especially those who are isolated, either from an invaded country or otherwise."

Avenol whirled about in those months while Western Europe was falling. He fended off offers from Rockefeller and other American sources to assist the survival of the League's technical committees and tried in vain to persuade Aghnides to approach the German consul. It was his idea that Hitler might find the League machinery useful in the New Order or that Mussolini might wish to utilize it as a balance against Hitler. Then he tried to approach Laval for adoption of the League by Vichy.

The Secretary-General did his best to speed the resignations of all British staff members from the Secretariat. He tried unsuccessfully to play Aghnides against Lester, who, for two months, was banned from communication with his chief, then suddenly "let out of the dog house" and asked whether he would carry on in Geneva, "as it was most important the Secretary-General should not fall into German hands." "Of course," answered the unflappable Lester, who, with exquisite patience, had resisted all pressures to resign or even to accept Avenol's lure of an indefinite holiday with pay.

When the danger of a German invasion hung over Switzerland, Avenol thought it best that he spend his nights in France to prevent capture by a Swiss Fifth Column. And Lester buried his fragmented diary under a stone in the garden of La Pelouse. Other papers he burned. Avenol would frequently threaten to resign, only to reverse himself and assert his determination to stay on, because (as he liked to say) he had been appointed to his high office by fifty states "including Germany and Italy."

At last, the Vichy government decided the matter for him. A French Secretary-General of the League of Nations would smack of subversion to the German conquerors, it was thought. Accordingly, in a circular letter to League member states, dated July 25, Avenol gave up his office though he declined to set an effective date for his resignation. The summer slipped by in graceless maneuvers to wipe out the League. Avenol declared a League budget to be impossible and noted that without a budget no organization could exist.

In despair Aghnides wrote to Lester on August 7, 1940: "I understand the work of destruction continues unabated and with more method and vigor than ever." Aghnides had submitted his resignation on June 25, but Avenol had refused to accept it, preferring to play him against Lester. Aghnides went on: "Indeed I feel heartbroken to realize that I was displaying useless efforts for the last twenty-one years . . . Could you not as Acting S.G. [Secretary-General] facilitate my exit? I wish the initiative now to come from him [Avenol]. It is only fair as my letter is in his hands for now six weeks. I hope you won't misunderstand me or think I am trying to desert you. You know *such is not my intention.* [Emphasis is Aghnides'.] But honestly what use would I now be anyhow if nothing is left of our activities?" In the end Aghnides stayed on.

At the end of the summer Avenol negotiated with the Treasurer, Seymour Jacklin, for sixty francs a day and the salaries of two League secretaries, to complete some "technical work." Then, on August 30, the Secretary-General left the Palais without a word of farewell to his deputy and successor, Sean Lester. He declined to be present at the small ceremony inaugurating the new regime on September 2, and Lester noted that "his empty chair was a reproach to his manners."

On September 4, Lester summed up for Sweetser the agonies he had lived through with Avenol: ". . . my main offense was in refusing tempting opportunities to go away. I should have many good marks somewhere for the restraint and forbearance I exercised, but I felt my personal interest, my inclinations having been sacrificed, I had to add an almost infinite tolerance . . . He [Avenol] has gone, undignified, indecent, and has done everything, literally everything he could to render survival impossible."

Sean Lester was now the Acting Secretary-General, as Eden had predicted. After Avenol and the faithful Miss Lever had left, he moved into a small upstairs apartment in the mansion of La Pelouse and closed off the rest of the house to save fuel. He had sent his wife and three daughters home to Ireland and was alone. His staff was down to thirty professional members and a grand total of one hundred, counting the cleaners, guards, clerks, and typists. They clustered around the Secretary-General's office and the library, abandoning the rest of the Palais to cold and silence. For political guidance, Lester had the faithful League stand-by, Aghnides, and a Frenchman who did not heed the call from Vichy, Henri Vigier.

Although the League's political work had long since ceased, the quiet commissions that had been designing improved machinery for international communications, trade, education, and health worked on. Lester's little band, holed up in the empty Palais, resembled the monks who illuminated ancient texts during the Dark Ages, oblivious of the barbarism that raged around them. Even the library was painstakingly maintained, though few readers called on its services.

Geneva, however, offered poor sanctuary with only the Swiss army to guard a little island of nervous neutrality. As the war went on, Switzerland grew more nervous than neutral and added somewhat to Lester's troubles. Survival of the headquarters in Geneva, which Lester valued as a brave symbol of continuity, required the suppression of the League wireless station. The Swiss then canceled their minimal financial contribution, although, as Lester pointed out, the League was paying out three times that amount to Swiss citizens. Switzerland went so far as to suppress all postage stamps bearing pictures of the Palais or the I.L.O. headquarters, lest it irritate German sensitivities.

Even before Avenol left, and over his opposition, the cordial beckoning of American philanthropy became too insistent to be denied. Accordingly, Alexander Loveday, the most professorial and philosophical member of the embattled Secretariat, was dispatched to carry the files of all the League's work on economics, finances, and international transit to the United States.

He left with seven of his staff and their wives and children aboard a bus that was to cross France and Spain to Portugal and the coast. Near Grenoble a tram ran into them at a crossroads and the bus landed in a ditch. Three of the party, including one of Loveday's sons, were sent to a hospital. But the group got another bus and pushed on. At roadside inns the women and children were given what beds there were; the men slept on the floor. They navigated bombed-out, washed-out roads but made it to Lisbon, thence to New York, and finally to Princeton University, which had opened its doors to the nonpolitical agencies of the League.

Now at last the League had come full circle. It was home in the United States, where the ideas that prefigured its genesis were first espoused with American missionary zeal and where it met its first humiliating rejection at the hands of American provincialism. It was home in the very university where Woodrow Wilson once presided as president. But it was a shadow that mocked the Wilsonian vision.

Lester, working at long distance with his associates, kept the nonpolitical work of the League going, turning out bulletins and surveys and sending representatives to study groups that were looking ahead to still another postwar era of hope.

The League agencies on the opium trade were given house room in Washington. No isolationists saw subversion in such hospitality. Edward Phelan, then Director of the International Labor Organization, set up shop in Montreal. Seymour Jacklin, the League Treasurer, was dispatched to open offices in London, close to the main financial source. He had to travel circuitously, by way of Casablanca and New York, and arrived at his destination only to be greeted by the first heavy air raid of the war.

Sometimes in Lisbon and at other times across the Atlantic, Carl Hambro convened his Supervisory Commission at intervals to lend legitimacy to Lester's administration and provide the budget Avenol had declared impossible. While the bulk of the money came from Britain, tokens arrived from neutrals and governments-in-exile. On one occasion Lester tried to get to Lisbon for a Commission meeting but was turned back at the Spanish border, and so returned to La Pelouse, which he still used in spring and summer, though the house had grown too cold to live in during the winter.

In 1942 one of his daughters, eighteen-year-old Ann, using her Irish passport, which carried the protection of her country's neutrality, zigzagged across Europe to Geneva, delegated by the family to keep her father company in his forlorn wartime outpost. Together, the two of them walked the gardens of La Pelouse, studied the cultivation of mushrooms, and maintained a meager social life within the shrunken circle of Geneva's international set.

Lester took only one clear-cut political action during the war. On April 19, 1941, Vichy's Admiral Jean François Darlan cabled him notice of France's intention to leave the League. As in all such withdrawals, two years had to elapse before it could be effective. Lester waited until March 20, 1943—barely a month before France was to be struck from the League rolls. Then he took up the matter with Leland Harrison, the United States minister to Switzerland; Harrison passed the word along to Robert Murphy, then acting for the State Department in North Africa; Murphy conferred with one of the co-leaders of the Free French forces, General Henri Giraud, in Algiers.

That conversation resulted in two telegrams to Lester—one from Giraud and another from his partner in leadership, General de Gaulle, then operating out of London. In effect the messages declared that the withdrawal notification of April 1941 had been made "when the French people were deprived of their sovereignty" and was therefore invalid. Giraud said: "France continues to be Member of the League of Nations." De Gaulle added that France would retain all its "engagements and prerogatives" and would continue to report to the League on the execution of its mandates.

The French gesture was encouraging in a year when the League was all but forgotten. Lester dashed off a notice to all the far-flung offices of the League reporting the De Gaulle–Giraud messages "with lively satisfaction."

Lester was liberated along with France at the end of 1944. In January 1945, he traveled to London for a family reunion and a taste of free air after his "long vigil," as he put it. Everywhere there was talk of "a new League." In the spring Lester returned once more to La Pelouse to draft a report on his wartime administration of the League, which he thought would be required of him in preparation for the San Francisco Conference, then being planned to launch the United Nations Organization.

Lester was invited to San Francisco along with other ghosts of the League-between-the-wars. It was plain, however, that he evoked unpleasant memories. For example, had not the League, in its dying gasp, spewed out the Soviet Union, which had turned into one of the principal victors of the war? It took considerable persuasion from Washington to cajole Moscow into even admitting Lester and his colleagues as "unofficial representatives" at San Francisco. The invitation had to come from the "host country," not the Conference itself. And it was further specified that the League people would be on hand only for "informal discussion."

In San Francisco, after trying throughout the war to keep the League idea alive for the great peace that was to come, Lester, Loveday, and Jacklin found themselves barely tolerated. They who had been at least partly responsible for the League's slender virtues found themselves an embarrassment at the oratorical feast of the Powers who had been responsible for the League's manifold absurdities and its ultimate ruin.

State Department spokesmen privately indicated to Lester that his presence would be troublesome. The League delegation was assigned a second-rate hotel and for the first month of the Conference no seats could be found for them on the main floor of the Opera House, where the United Nations Organization was being discussed. They sat instead in the last row of the gallery. Lester was never invited to appear before a single commission, nor did any official care to draw on his fund of experience in international organization. Loveday was allowed to discuss only the most mechanical aspects of organizational structure before the Economic and Social Committee. And Jacklin was given fifteen minutes to talk about financing.

After a month, Lester, disappointed but uncomplaining, journeyed back to Geneva to prepare for the final Assembly of the League, which would turn over its properties and its heritage of hope and folly to the new management of the world. Even that last rite was almost denied the League. United Nations officials favored a fast, unpublicized meeting in London to wind up the business, as if it concerned a bawdyhouse going into receivership. The British, however, insisted that the League be allowed the dignity of burial with full honors in its own marble tomb above the Lake of Geneva.

At noon on April 8, 1946, the Assembly of the League of Nations met again at the Palais. They performed the customary parliamentary rituals of organization, received Sean Lester's report of his wartime stewardship, and rewarded him with the title of Secretary-General, making it retroactive to 1940. It was the least and the most that the League, in its weakened state, could do for the long-suffering Lester, who henceforth would resist all political assignments and devote himself to fishing in Galway.

Carl Hambro, after being elected to preside over the Assembly, addressed the delegates as if they were the honored dead, liberated at last from passionate strife: "For us there are no longer any questions of political discussion, and we are no longer divided by considerations of individual and national prestige . . ."

He invited the Assembly "to decide to dissolve the League of Nations as such and to dissolve the Permanent Court of International Justice and to declare this twenty-first session of the Assembly of the League of Nations to be its last one."

The eulogies were intoned with due solemnity. Lord Cecil, who had attended the first session of the League in 1920 as the representative of South Africa, now spoke for England. Leaner and more stooped, he looked beyond the sad occasion, as do the devoutly optimistic at all funerals. And he invoked the departed members of the congregation. He recalled the early days in the Salle de la Réformation and the flush of excitement in the campaign to rescue the Armenians. He called up names redolent of oratory, wit, the gay flourishes and the gray routine of diplomatic history: Balfour, Briand, Hymans, Nansen, Beneš, Henderson.

Despite all the attempts to disclaim the connection with the United Nations, the stubborn Cecil insisted upon the League's paternity. "The fundamental principles of the Charter [of the United Nations] and the Covenant are the same and it is gratifying to some of us that, after the violent controversies that have raged for the last quarter of a century, it is now generally accepted that peace can be secured only by international cooperation, broadly along the lines agreed to in 1920."

"The League is dead! Long live the United Nations!" he cried with a fervor undiminished by twenty-five years of frustrated hopes.

Paul-Boncour, that venerable theatrical orator of the earlier days, arose to point out the difference between the League and the United Nations. The new United Nations would not be powerless as was the League. It would have armed forces at its disposal to impose its decisions, just as the French had repeatedly called for in 1919. It would tackle the economic causes of international conflict and rectify the "unequal distribution of raw materials." Paul-Boncour could not, however, refrain from a warning: ". . . the strength and weakness—I repeat the strength and weakness—of the new institution is that it depends on agreement between the five permanent Great Powers."

On April 18, Carl Hambro spoke the final farewell: "So, we may look back without compunction but with some sadness—a longing and wistful sadness such as we may feel when we look back on days gone by when our hopes were younger and brighter, when our ambitions soared higher and when our eyes held no shadows caused by memories of lost horizons."

He spoke bravely of his hopes that the United Nations would fulfill the promise of the League, but he also uttered a mournful prophecy.

"Should a time ever come," Hambro warned, "when the Palais of the League of Nations is left as a derelict monument to the faded ideals of an age more unsophisticated than ours, any visitor to this place, and any person of any of our nations reflecting on the history of the present and the past, would certainly feel that at night the empty corridors were full of forms of fear, that this place was haunted by the ghosts of forlorn hopes and unfulfilled aspirations."

On the following day, April 19, 1946, the League of Nations ceased to exist.

The League's epitaph had been written while it was still struggling to be born, and it was fittingly composed by one who did much to hasten its end, Benito Mussolini. In the *Popolo d'Italia* of March 7, 1920, he wrote: ". . . brotherhood is a fable which men listen to during the bivouac and the truce."

The League's birth arose out of a series of political fantasies: that the cease-fire of 1919 was a peace and not merely a truce; that national interests could be subordinated to world interests; that a government can espouse a cause other than its own; and that, if it did, it could survive the wrath of the people it was designed to serve.

The League idea withered and died when each nation remembered that its holy mission was to serve itself, and that all agreements, oaths, treaties, and compacts are invalid when they conflict with that sacred cause. Where patriotism is a virtue it is hard to espouse a brotherhood that laughs at boundaries.

NOTES

CHAPTER I

Page 3
"*I am going . . .*" Charles Seymour, *The Intimate Papers of Colonel House* (hereafter referred to as *IPCH*), IV, 88.

Page 4
"*England and France . . .*" Ibid., III, 54.

Page 4
"*Never had a philosopher . . .*" John Maynard Keynes, *The Economic Consequences of Peace*, 38.

Page 5
"*. . . my second personality.*" *IPCH*, I, 118.

Page 5
"*I have been thought . . .*" George Sylvester Viereck, *The Strangest Friendship in History*, 24.

Page 8
"*I never go . . .*" *IPCH*, I, 246.

Page 8
"*the Great Adventure . . .*" Ibid., I, 253, 254.

Page 10
"*I found no . . .*" Ibid., I, 262.

Page 14
"*virtually the same . . .*" Kenneth Young, *Arthur James Balfour*, 376.

Page 14
"*. . . angry as hell.*" Ibid., 377.

Page 14
"*You do not need to be told . . .*" Ibid., 378.

Page 15
"*I thought he was . . .*" IPCH, II, 468.

Page 15
"*the most extraordinary . . .*" Young, op. cit., 413.

Page 16
"*Everything is now . . .*" Ibid., xi.

Page 16
"*I hope you will . . .*" IPCH, III, 40.

Page 16
"*My conversation . . .*" Ibid., III, 42.

Page 17
"*dividing the bearskin . . .*" Ibid., III, 47.

Page 17
Balfour's letter to Wilson Ibid., III, 52, 53.

Page 18
"*Mr. Wilson's denial . . .*" Viereck, op. cit., 214.

Page 18
"*I can see more and more . . .*" IPCH, III, 56.

Page 19
"*the least vocal . . .*" Richard M. Watt, *The Kings Depart*, 29, and U. S. Department of State, *Papers Relating to the Foreign Relations of the United States—The Paris Peace Conference, 1919*, III, 583.

Page 20
"*We cannot take . . .*" IPCH, III, 166.

Page 20
"*Wasn't it horrible? . . .*" Sigmund Freud and William C. Bullitt, *Thomas Woodrow Wilson*, 200, 201.

Page 21
"*It is better . . .*" Geneviève Tabouis, *Perfidious Albion*, 12.

Page 21
"*their disclosure . . .*" *The Nation*, August 3, 1918.

Page 22
"*The Supreme War Council . . .*" IPCH, III, 310.

Page 24
Balfour's cablegram Ibid., III, 349.

Page 26
"In a very deep sense . . ." Ibid., III, 353, and New York *Tribune*, 1/9/1918.

Page 26
"Our chief criticism . . ." Ibid., III, 355, and London *Times*, 1/9/1918.

Page 27
"deceive Russia . . ." Ibid., III, 356.

Page 27
"cynical brutality"; "a draconic . . ." *Fremdenblatt*, as cited in the London *Times*, 1/12/1918.

Page 27
"a scheme . . ." *Neue Freie Presse*, as cited in the London *Times*, 10/17/1918.

Page 27
"demands which are . . ." *Neues Wiener Tageblatt*, as cited in the London *Times*, 10/17/1918.

Page 28
"I hope . . ." Karl Friedrich Nowak, *The Collapse of Central Europe*, 45.

Page 28
"He is putting . . ." Ibid., 19.

Page 29
"Their knees . . ." H. W. V. Temperley, *A History of the Peace Conference of Paris*, I, 231.

Page 29
"We must not . . ." Ibid., I, 232.

Page 29
"My own conviction . . ." IPCH, IV, 16.

Page 30
"The trouble that I see . . ." Ibid., IV, 20.

Page 30
"I remember one afternoon . . ." Ibid., IV, 50, 51.

Page 31
"an absolute end . . ." H. W. V. Temperley, op. cit., I, 83.

Page 31
"To that I answer . . ." Ibid., I, 85.

Page 31
"I am not a wizard." Karl Graf von Hertling, *Ein Jahr in der Reichskanzlei*, 183, and George Slocombe, *A Mirror to Geneva, 1938*, 83.

Page 32
"I cannot even . . ." Prince Max von Baden, *The Memoirs of Prince Max von Baden*, II, 3.

Page 32
"You have not . . ."; "The Supreme Command . . ." Ibid., II, 19.

Page 32
"In a sleepless hour . . ." Ibid., II, 85.

Page 33
"*What impertinence!*" Sir Henry Wilson, *Journal du Maréchal Sir Henry Wilson*, 434.

Page 33
"*the temptations . . .*" General Erich von Ludendorff, *My War Memories, 1914–1918*, II, 749.

Page 33
"*We have laid down one condition . . .*" New York *Tribune*, 10/7/1918.

Page 34
"*dangerous consequences*"; "*League of democratic governments . . .*" Foreign Office Archives, Political Intelligence Department, 10/30/1918.

Page 35
"*it might also be taken . . .*" Ibid.

Page 35
"*had himself put forward demands . . .*" Ibid.

Page 35
"*If once the enemy . . .*" Baden, op. cit., II, 92, 93.

Page 36
"*We should not exaggerate . . .*" Ibid., II, 110.

Page 36
"*Only a minute*"; "*I sail . . .*" Lincoln Steffens, *The Letters of Lincoln Steffens*, I, 433.

Page 36
"*I'd rather have you there . . .*" Ibid., I, 433.

CHAPTER 2

Page 37
"*total usurpation . . . super-Gladstone . . .*" Sir Henry Wilson, op. cit., 439.

Page 38
"*unrestricted selfishness . . .*" "Through German Eyes," London *Times*, 10/12/18.

Page 38
"*For God's sake . . . easily be able . . .*" Baden, op. cit., II, 233, 234, 235.

Page 38
"*In the name of . . .*"; "*Because you treat . . .*" Watt, op. cit., 155.

Page 39
"*There I had . . .*"; "*chaos, Bolshevism . . .*"; "*national self-discipline . . .*" Ludendorff, op. cit., II, 764.

Page 39
"*It is my duty . . .*" Baden, op. cit., II, 205.

Page 40
"*I have no illusions . . .*" Paul Mantoux, *Les Délibérations du Conseil des Quatres—24 Mars–28 Juin, 1919*.

Page 47
"*As soon as . . .*" IPCH, IV, 99.

Page 47
"*whole kennelry of . . .*" Watt, op. cit., 24, citing Frank Owen, *Tempestuous Journey: Lloyd George, His Life and Times,* 22. London, 1954.

Page 47
"*He speaks the same language . . .*" Slocombe, op. cit., 41.

Page 48
"*Surely . . .*" Ibid., 40.

Page 48
"*He was never able . . .*" Harold Nicolson, *Peacemaking, 1919,* 65.

Page 48
"*If the British . . .*"; "*our people, if challenged . . .*" IPCH, IV, 164.

Page 49
"*Have you ever been asked . . .*"; "*Yes, and the five . . .*" Ibid., IV, 168.

Page 50
"*That would amount . . .*" Ibid., IV, 168, 169.

Page 50
"*My statement had a very . . .*" Ibid., IV, 171.

Page 50
"*I have rarely . . .*" General Jean-Henri Mordacq, *L'Armistice du 11 Novembre, 1918,* 165.

Page 50
"*I fell to thinking . . .*" IPCH, IV, 174.

Page 51
"*would not let them . . .*" Mordacq, op. cit., 166.

Page 51
"*I feel it . . .*" IPCH, IV, 173.

Page 52
"*You draw up . . .*"; "*Whenever the Prime Ministers . . .*" Ibid., IV, 99, 100.

Page 52
"*I do not see any reason . . .*" Ibid., IV, 189.

Page 53
"*Will he like . . .?*" Ibid., IV, 179.

Page 53
"*Are we agreed . . . ?*"; "*Yes*" Ibid., IV, 179.

Page 54
"*I consider that . . .*"; "*Frankly, I did not . . .*" Ibid., IV, 194, 195.

Page 55
"*Here an example . . .*" Baden, op. cit., II, 297.

Page 55
"*Unless the Kaiser . . .*" Watt, op. cit., 183, from Owen, op. cit., 22.

Page 56
"[*The Germans*] *also objected* . . ." IPCH, IV, 141, 142.

Page 56
"*He who has* . . ." Mordacq, op. cit., 27, 28.

Page 57
"*save the Reich* . . ." Ibid., 51.

Page 57
"*Have you forgotten* . . . ?" Watt, op. cit., 198, 199.

Page 57
"*You have a right* . . ." Cablegram from House to Wilson, 11/10/1918, *IPCH*, IV, 144.

Page 57
"*Not fair!*" Mordacq, op. cit., 29, citing Matthias Erzberger, *Souvenirs de Guerre*, 382. Paris, 1920.

Page 58
"*A people of seventy million* . . ." Ibid., 30.

Page 58
"*Our dead on* . . ." Ibid., 80, 81.

Page 58
"*Autocracy is dead* . . ." IPCH, IV, 145.

Page 58
After receiving the news . . . Mordacq, op. cit., 184.

Page 58
"*Yes, the Eternal Father* . . ." Ibid., 105.

Page 60
"*in the face of* . . ." H. W. V. Temperley, op. cit., I, 103.

Page 61
"*Our Allies and our enemies* . . ." IPCH, IV, 155.

CHAPTER 3

Page 62
"*cozy dining room* . . ." Edith Bolling Wilson, *My Memoir*, 172, 173.

Page 63
"*You are leaving* . . ." Ray Stannard Baker, *Woodrow Wilson and World Settlement*, I, 5.

Page 63
"*We come therefore* . . ." Ibid., I, 7.

Page 63
"*As I see it* . . ." Steffens, op. cit., 422.

Page 63
"*It is to America* . . ." Baker, op. cit., I, 8.

Page 65
Bowman report IPCH, IV, 291, et. seq.

Page 65
"Tell me what's right . . ." Baker, op. cit., I, 113.

Page 66
"dangerous and academic . . ." James Thomson Shotwell, *At the Paris Peace Conference,* 74, 75.

Page 66
General Confederation of Labor proclamation Ibid., 84.

Page 67
"I assume also . . ." IPCH, IV, 218, 219.

Page 67
"shocked" Nicolson, op. cit., 74.

Page 67
"one of the greatest mistakes . . ." Ibid., 73.

Page 67
"In Washington . . ."; *"I infer that . . ."* IPCH, 220–23.

Page 68
"stepped from his lofty pedestal . . ." Nicolson, op. cit., 74.

Page 68
"My judgment is . . ." IPCH, IV, 223.

Page 68
"My God . . ." Edith Bolling Wilson, op. cit., 184.

Page 69
"making the League . . ."; *"They simply did not . . ."* IPCH, IV, 263.

Page 69
"it might be because . . ." Ibid., IV, 226.

Page 69
"noble candeur" Watt, op. cit., 47.

Page 69
"The French want . . ." IPCH, IV, 252 n.

Page 70
Labour meeting at Albert Hall London *Times,* 1/5/1919.

Page 71
Woodrow Wilson in Italy *The New York Times,* 1/7/1919.

Page 72
"Ah, but I do not . . ." Edith Bolling Wilson, op. cit., 215.

Page 72
"that Italy went into . . ." *The New York Times,* 1/6/1919.

Page 72
"We cannot but show . . ." *L'Humanité,* reported in *The New York Times,* 1/3/1919.

Page 73
"Don't be wangled . . ." London *Herald,* 12/21/1918.

Page 73
"No peace must be . . ." *The New York Times,* 1/5/1919.

Page 73
Senator Lawrence Y. Sherman's speech *The New York Times,* 1/4/1919.

Page 74
"la volonté générale" Nicolson, op. cit., 53.

Page 74
"The French Republic . . ." Tabouis, op. cit., 28.

Page 75
". . . the great majority . . ." Henry Wickham Steed, *Through Thirty Years —1892–1922,* 71.

Page 75
"The time has come . . ." Tabouis, op. cit., 158, 159.

Page 75
"We must have . . ." Ibid., 157.

Page 76
"You are right . . ." IPCH, IV, 281.

CHAPTER 4

Page 78
"If snow comes . . ." *Le Temps,* 1/9/1919.

Page 79
"Oh, it was a time . . ." Baker, op. cit., I, 102.

Page 80
"America, the daughter . . ." London *Times,* 1/20/1919.

Page 81
"Grand Young Man . . ." Ibid.

Page 81
"Is it not a startling circumstance . . . ?" Ibid.

Page 83
Benes's negotiations Steed, op. cit., 231 et seq.

Page 85
Massey and Hughes Secretary's notes of a conversation held at M. Pichon's room at Quai d'Orsay, Paris, Thursday, Jan. 30, 1919, as recorded in David Hunter Miller, *The Drafting of the Covenant,* II, 206, 207.

Page 85
"The spectacle of New Zealand . . ." *The New York Times,* 2/9/1919.

Page 86
Hughes and Lloyd George on Japan British Foreign Office Archives.

Page 86
Lloyd George and Clemenceau   Miller, op. cit., I, 116.

Page 87
First Commission meeting   Ibid., I, 135.

Page 90
Third Commission meeting   Ibid., I, 162.

Page 93
"Practically everything . . ."   IPCH, IV, 323.

Page 94
"the backs of the British . . ."   Ibid., IV, 324.

Page 94
"Viscount Chinda . . ."   Ibid., IV, 323.

Page 95
Baron Makino's press conference   Charles H. Grasty in *The New York Times*,
    2/17/1919.

Page 97
"I am glad you asked me . . ."   London *Times*, 2/17/1919.

Page 98
"When this dawns . . ."   IPCH, IV, 322, 323.

Page 99
"he did not wish . . ."   Ibid., IV, 328.

Page 99
"Those who thought . . ."   London *Times*, 2/15/1919.

Page 99
"The Commission on the . . ."   Le Figaro, 2/15/1919.

Page 99
"a sublime act . . ."   Giornale d'Italia, 2/18/1919.

Page 99
"It is clear to the . . ."   L'Humanité, 2/16/1919.

Page 99
"There is no safeguarding . . ."   New York *Tribune*, 2/15/1919.

Page 100
"lose its national identity"   Philadelphia *Inquirer*, 2/15/1919.

Page 100
Comments on Covenant   Ibid., 2/16/1919.

Page 100
"take it that . . ."   IPCH, IV, 326, 327.

Page 101
"I'm all right so far."   The New York Times, 2/17/1919.

Page 101
Reception in Boston   Ibid., 2/25/1919.

Page 101
"off the record"   London *Times*, 2/18/1919.

Page 101
White House dinner   Ibid., 2/27/1919.

Page 102
"yielding up our . . ."   New York *Sun*, 3/18/1919.

Page 103
"the missionaries of eternal smash."   *The New York Times* editorial, 2/6/1919.

Page 103
"those leaders who were instrumental . . ."   Ibid., 1/27/1919.

CHAPTER 5

Page 106
"I'm glad I'm not . . ."   Stephen Bonsal, *Unfinished Business*, 68.

Page 107
"I must make a peace . . ."   Ibid., 69.

Page 107
"I would have clipped . . ."   Ibid., 72.

Page 107
"a turbulent collision . . ."   Nicolson, op. cit., 186.

Page 108
"The feeling that the whole business . . ."   London *Times*, 3/4/1919.

Page 109
"by the endorsement . . ."   Miller, op. cit., Document 19, II, 389.

Page 109
"One of two things . . ."   Ibid., II, 389.

Page 110
"Nevertheless, I should be . . ."   Ibid., II, 391.

Page 111
"It will show these Dagos . . ."   Roger Butterfield, *The American Past*, 327.
    New York, 1957.

Page 112
"Nothing in the Covenant . . ."   Miller, op. cit., 14th meeting, League Committee, 4/10/1919.

Page 112
"A hundred years ago . . ."   Ibid., March 1919 meeting, League Committee.

Page 113
"If the people of France . . ."   Ibid., 13th meeting, League Commitee, II, 359.

Page 115
"You speak as if . . ."; *"And so . . ."*   Nicolson, op. cit., 160.

Page 115
"Our hands were tied . . ."; *"We longed for . . ."*   Ibid., 177.

Page 115
"Balfour hates . . ."   Steed, op. cit., 268.

Page 117
"*although it obtained* . . ." Ibid., II, 703.

Page 118
"*The only hope* . . ." IPCH, IV, 455.

Page 118
"*In the past, international relations* . . ." Paul Mantoux, op. cit., I, 325.

Page 118
"*The concessions the Germans obtained* . . ." IPCH, IV, 452.

Page 119
Bliss on Bolshevism Paul Mantoux, op. cit., I, 54–55.

Page 120
Wilson on Bolshevism Ibid., I, 55–56.

Page 120
Orlando on Bolshevism Ibid., I, 56–57.

Page 120
Lloyd George on Bolshevism Ibid., I, 57.

Page 121
"*We must have a Government* . . ."; "*By the end of March* . . ." André
Tardieu, *The Truth About the Treaty*, 116.

Page 124
"*Gentlemen, I am drunk.* . . ." Alma Luckau, *The German Delegation at the
Peace Conference*, 124.

Page 125
"*The Treaty, which our* . . ." Ibid., 120.

Page 126
"*Italy is waiting for* . . ." Ibid., 133.

Page 126
"*black troops*" Ibid., 133–34.

Page 131
"*It was not so much a duel* . . ." IPCH, IV, 392.

CHAPTER 6

Page 134
"*When they found* . . ." Arthur W. Rovine, *The First Fifty Years: The
Secretary-General in World Politics, 1920–1970*, 24, citing Stephen W.
Schwebel, *The Secretary-General of the United Nations*, 4.

Page 134
"*perfect private secretary* . . ."; "*Behind the scenes* . . ." Ibid., 25; Schwebel,
87.

Page 135
"*The offices are* . . ." From a letter from P. Denis to Paul Mantoux, 9/19/
1919, League of Nations Archives.

Page 136
"it was more important . . ."   Minutes of staff meeting, 8/27/1919, League of
Nations Archives.

Page 136
Swiss opinion   Ibid.

Page 137
"a mass of . . . an integral factor . . ."   Letter and memo from J. A. Salter
to Eric Drummond dated 5/15/1919, ibid.

Page 138
". . . neither the action . . ."   IPCH, IV, 508.

Page 138
"It indicates . . ."   Ibid., IV, 506, 507.

Page 139
"Our annual falling-out . . ."   Ibid., IV, 530.

Page 139
"is trusted by all . . ."   Ibid., IV, 531.

Page 139
"Ninety per cent of . . ."   Congressional Record, 5/26/1919, quoted in Alan
Cranston, *The Killing of the Peace*, 113.

Page 139
"The Covenant of the League . . ."   Ibid., 6/20/1919, quoted in Cranston, op.
cit., 118, 119.

Page 140
"If there were twenty nations . . ."   Lewis P. Showalter, *League of Nation*
[sic] *Joe—The Backwoods Farmer from the Ohio Hills*, 4.

Page 140
"the only concrete . . ."   The New Republic, May 31, 1919.

Page 140
"It amounts to . . ."   Steffens, op. cit., II, 478.

Page 140
"Hear ye our petition . . ."   Senate Documents, 66th Congress, 1st Session,
X, 691.

Page 141
"the whole thing guaranteed . . ."   Walter Lippmann, *The Political Scene*,
69, 70. New York, 1919.

Page 142
"poor little minds . . ."   Gene Smith, *When the Cheering Stopped*, 56, citing
Arthur Walworth, *Woodrow Wilson, American Prophet*, 348. New York,
1958.

Page 142
Senate Foreign Relations Committee meeting with Wilson   Senate Documents,
66th Congress, 1st Session, X, 518 et seq.

Page 147
". . . *if you had made your fight* . . ." Letter from William C. Bullitt to Woodrow Wilson dated 5/17/1919, reprinted as "Bullitt Exhibit No. 28," ibid., 1273.

Page 147
"*Mr. Lansing then said* . . ." Ibid., 1276–77.

Page 147
"*This from a man* . . ." Joseph P. Tumulty, *Woodrow Wilson, As I Knew Him*, 442.

Page 148
"*At a moment* . . ." Bonsal, op. cit., 246.

Page 148
"*The President is absolutely* . . ." Ibid.

Page 148
"*The record is made up* . . ." IPCH, IV, 521.

Page 150
"*were more concerned with verbiage* . . ." Bonsal, op. cit., 248 et seq.

Page 151
"*I think he would like* . . ." Ibid., 251.

Page 152
"*We do not know* . . ." Ibid., 252, 253.

Page 152
"*it will probably* . . ."; "*On the one hand your* . . ." IPCH, IV, 524–26.

Page 153
"*You have performed* . . ." Ibid., IV, 505.

Page 154
"*Wilson's Last Mad Act*" Smith, op. cit., 144.

Page 155
"*I hold the doctrine* . . ." *Current History*, April 1920, 27, 28, as cited in Denna Frank Fleming, *The United States and the League of Nations, 1918–1920*, 437.

Page 155
"*He told me that he was* . . ." At meeting of Foreign Policy Association, New York City, 1/4/1930, quoted in Fleming, op. cit., 475.

Page 155
"*I was at the door* . . ." Fleming, op. cit., 476.

Page 156
"*emasculate* . . ." Ibid., 476, cited from letter to the New York *Herald Tribune*, 3/7/1930.

Page 156
"*I want the United States* . . ." Fleming, op. cit., 469.

Page 156
"*You need not worry . . .*" Ibid., 499, citing David F. Houston, *Eight Years with Wilson's Cabinet,* II, 94, 95. New York, 1926.

Page 157
"*The Republican majority . . .*" Fleming, op. cit., 472, citing Walter Lippmann, *Public Opinion,* 195, 196. New York, 1922.

Page 157
"*Department has practically . . .*" U. S. Department of State, *Papers Relating to the Foreign Relations of the United States,* 1921, I, 1.

Page 157
"*Any method of withdrawal . . .*" Ibid., 2, 3.

Page 158
"*it is impossible . . .*" Ibid., 5.

Page 159
"*Anybody could see . . .*" Address, dinner of welcome, Society of Pilgrims, May 19, 1921.

CHAPTER 7

Page 161
"*I still have my teeth.*" Tabouis, *Tribune de Genève,* 2/16/73.

Page 162
"*Threats of war . . .*" League of Nations Archives, Mantoux Papers.

Page 163
"*Eighteen months ago . . .*" London *Daily Herald,* 11/13/1920.

Page 163
"*If the Assembly does not . . .*" *Die Züricher Post,* 11/16/1920.

Page 164
"*Nothing serious . . .*" *L'Avanti,* 11/16/1920.

Page 164
"*The defeat suffered . . .*" *L'Humanité,* 11/16/1920.

Page 164
"*All great enterprises . . .*" *L'Indépendance Belge,* 11/23/1920.

Page 164
"*The Liberal Party was shattered . . .*" Lord Cecil, *A Great Experiment: An Autobiography,* 101.

Page 165
"*We have had a speech . . .*" Drummond Papers, League of Nations Archives.

Page 165
"*To keep peace . . .*" Ibid.

Page 166
"*it is not in the lifetime . . .*" Stephen King-Hall, *Our Own Times—1913–1938,* 256.

Page 166
"bears the impress of . . ." London *Daily News*, 11/20/1920.

Page 167
high-powered pressures Cecil, op. cit., 109.

Page 167
"The reason for the change . . ." Ibid., 117.

Page 169
"The Republican Party . . ." Sweetser to Drummond, Drummond Letters, League of Nations Archives.

Page 169
United States against the League Paul S. Mowrer, Chicago *Daily News*, 9/7/1921.

Page 170
Harding's aloofness toward the League Ibid.

Page 171
"He transforms the guttural tongue . . ." *L'Oeuvre*, 9/21/1921.

Page 172
"In my opinion . . ." Mowrer, Chicago *Daily News*, 9/5/1921.

Page 173
"Our fears that a foreign race . . ." League of Nations Archives.

Page 175
"Danzig has now . . ." Ibid.

Page 177
"He was entirely . . ." Rom Landau, *Pilsudski: Hero of Poland*, 184.

Page 178
"a swashbuckler . . ." Ibid., 186.

Page 179
"I had a great deal of trouble . . ." Slocombe, op. cit., 276, quoting Francesco Tommasini, Italian ambassador to Warsaw, in his book *Risurrezione della Polonia* (Milan, 1921).

Page 180
"looked like a peasant . . ." Slocombe, op. cit., 264.

Page 180
"After the Armistice . . ." Tabouis, op. cit., 191.

Page 181
"showed himself willing . . ." Ibid., 193.

Page 181
"Peace with Russia . . ." Drummond Papers, League of Nations Archives.

Page 182
"I think D was right . . ." Frances Stevenson, *Lloyd George: A Diary*, 216.

Page 182
"*In Paris they had . . .*" Letter to P. H. Kerr, British diplomat, 11/17/21, Drummond Papers, op. cit.

Page 183
"*These people who came . . .*" Drummond Papers, op. cit.

Page 184
"*The situation is peculiar . . .*" Mantoux Papers, op. cit.

CHAPTER 8

Page 187
"*Righteousness and impossible desires . . .*" Steffens, op. cit., I, 464.

Page 188
"*I remember that we had . . .*" Liv Nansen Høyer, *Nansen: A Family Portrait by His Daughter*, 223.

Page 188
"*The League of Nations asked me . . .*" Emil Ludwig, *Leaders of Europe*, 42.

Page 189
"*. . . produced a particularly . . .*" *Politiken*, 9/10/21.

Page 192
"*The world's most eminent . . .*" *Politiken*, 11/24/20.

Page 195
"*Responsibility for protection . . .*" Nansen Papers, League of Nations Archives.

Page 195
"*Would it not therefore . . .?*" Drummond Papers, League of Nations Archives.

Page 195
"*The high hopes . . .*" Nansen Papers, League of Nations Archives.

Page 196
"*I saw one myself . . .*" Ibid.

Page 197
"*We had hoped . . .*" Ludwig, op. cit., 48.

Page 197
"*Annexations*" Lockhart, op. cit., 185.

Page 197
"*The only phrase . . .*" Slocombe, op. cit., 320.

Page 198
Mrs. Wilson "ordered" H. B. Butler Papers, League of Nations Archives.

Page 200
"*It is understood that there can be . . .*" Letter from Albert Thomas 10/21/24 to Drummond, Drummond Papers, op. cit.

CHAPTER 9

Page 202
"This symbolizes . . ." Tabouis, *Tribune de Genève*, 2/17–18/1973, weekend edition.

Page 203
"Your regicides were . . ." Georges Suarez, *Briand*, VI, 49.

Page 203
"Why did Joan of Arc . . . ?" Ibid., VI, 5.

Page 205
"I shall go to Switzerland . . ." Slocombe, op. cit., 117.

Page 205
"Gentlemen, be logical . . ." Ibid., 122.

Page 208
"Yes, it will take . . ." Nicolson, op. cit., 39.

Page 208
"It is my task . . ." Slocombe, op. cit., 115.

Page 208
"His wisdom . . ." Suarez, op. cit., VI, 115.

Page 210
"the economic uses . . ." Slocombe, op. cit., 206.

Page 210
"It is the policy . . ." Gustav Stresemann, *Les Papiers de Stresemann*, I, 349.

Page 211
Chamberlain-Herriot meeting Suarez, op. cit., VI, 64.

Page 212
"the pens which write . . ." Cecil, op. cit., 171.

Page 213
"I remember whispering . . ." Ibid., 167.

Page 213
"A nation, however great . . ." Le Quotidien, 9/11/1925.

Page 214
"It was then that . . ." Suarez, op. cit., VI, 117.

Page 214
"Briand almost fell off the sofa . . ." Stresemann, op. cit., II, 141.

Page 215
"Barkis is willin' " Suarez, op. cit., VI, 125.

Page 215
"the barbarians of the North . . ." Ibid., VI, 125.

Page 215
"No, don't speak to me . . ." Ibid., VI, 127.

Page 215
"In my view . . ." Ibid., VI, 99.

Page 217
"If the Imperial Cabinet . . ." Antonina Vallentin, *Stresemann*, 192.

Page 217
"You can't call it . . ." Vallentin, op. cit., 193.

Page 218
". . . in the case of a territory . . ." Mantoux Papers, League of Nations Archives.

Page 221
"For us Locarno . . ." Suarez, op. cit., VI, 180.

Page 222
"an important discovery" Kurjer Porauny, 9/3/26.

Page 222
"that Russia . . ." Deutsche Allgemeine Zeitung, 9/9/26.

Page 223
"A League of Nations is . . ." Vallentin, op. cit., 199.

Page 223
"So long as the members . . ." Izvestia, 9/11/26.

Page 223
". . . a sizeable section of the leaders . . ." Drummond Papers, op. cit.

Page 224
"follow the work of the League . . ." Ibid.

Page 225
". . . a great army does not . . ." Suarez, op. cit., VI, 224.

Page 225
"If we do not combine . . ." Slocombe, op. cit., 223.

Page 228
"Germany had to choose . . ." Mantoux Papers, op. cit.

Page 228
"It is one of those questions . . ." Vallentin, op. cit., 290.

Page 228
". . . Mozart and Schubert . . ." Stresemann, op. cit., III, 268, 269.

Page 229
"I agree with you . . ." Ibid., III, 269, 271.

Page 230
"I am an old man . . ." Duff Cooper, *Old Men Forget: An Autobiography*, 146.

CHAPTER 10

Page 232
"If the United States . . ." Mantoux Papers, League of Nations Archives.

Page 232
"In spite of the assurances . . ." Ibid.

Page 232
"*How much would the League* . . . ?" Ibid.

Page 235
"*It would be bitter bread* . . ." Cablegram received by Chinese delegation from Nanking, 9/ 23/ 31, Council of the League of Nations proceedings, 2461.

Page 238
"*Donald stated that the Marshal* . . ." Telegram from Johnson to Stimson dated Peking, 9/ 19/ 31, received in Washington, 9/ 18/ 31, *Foreign Relations of the U.S., Japan, 1931–1941 (FRUS),* I, 1.

Page 238
"*Guests in hotels* . . ." *FRUS,* I, 2–4.

Page 238
"*It is my conviction* . . ." Johnson telegram to Stimson, 9/ 22/ 31, *FRUS,* I, 5.

Page 239
"*a sharp cleavage between Shidehara* . . ." Stimson memo to Katsuji Debuchi, 9/ 22/ 31, *FRUS,* I, 6, 7.

Page 239
"*they will cause their military* . . ." Stimson message to China and Japan, 9/ 24/ 31, *FRUS,* I, 9.

Page 240
"*feel free to communicate* . . ." *FRUS,* I, 17.

Page 240
"*desirable that the League* . . ." *FRUS,* I, 17.

Page 240
"*In regard to this valuable information* . . ." Drummond Papers, League of Nations Archives.

Page 244
"*The Japanese aims are now* . . ." Avenol Papers, League of Nations Archives.

Page 245
". . . *there is one thing* . . ." Ibid.

Page 246
"*After the first surprise* . . ." Ibid.

Page 246
"*Japan has been goaded* . . ." Robert Dell, "Is France Backing Japan?" *The Nation,* Feb. 24, 1932.

Page 247
"*You should be in Paris* . . ." *FRUS,* I, 41.

Page 247
"*I have no use* . . ." Lester diary, 4.

Page 249
"*I cannot tell you of the harm* . . ." Drummond Papers, League of Nations Archives.

Page 249
"*Unhappily I agree with you . . .*" Ibid.

Page 250
"*I quoted the words of an observer . . .*" Forbes to Stimson, 12/24/31, *FRUS*, I, 65.

Page 251
"*Marshal Chang Hsueh-liang at 9:30 this evening . . .*" Johnson to Stimson, 12/29/31, *FRUS*, I, 75.

Page 251
"*hot headed . . .*" 12/24/31, *FRUS*, I, 67.

Page 251
"*He laid great stress upon the open door . . .*" 1/16/32, *FRUS*, I, 79.

Page 254
"*the Japanese people . . .*" 1/28/32, *FRUS*, I, 164.

Page 260
"*two of the most leisurely weeks . . .*" L. T. Chen, "What a Chinese Member of the Lytton Commission Observed in Manchukuo," *China Weekly Review*, April, 1932.

Page 261
"*a festering sore . . .*"; "*Apropos of this . . .*" 7/16/32, *FRUS*, I, 93–95.

Page 261
"*is built for war . . .*" 8/13/32, *FRUS*, I, 99, 100.

Page 263
"*In spite of the fact . . .*" Stimson telegram to Joseph C. Grew, 11/21/32, *FRUS*, I, 104, 105.

Page 264
Stimson-Debuchi meeting Stimson memo, 1/12/33, *FRUS*, I, 108, 109.

Page 266
"*If all our efforts have failed . . .*" et seq. Unpublished Ph.D. thesis, delivered at 1969 annual meeting of the Association for Asian Studies, Boston, by David J. Lu of the Center for Japanese Studies, Bucknell University.

Page 269
"*Avenol is much less industrious . . .*" Rovine, op. cit., 109, 110, citing National Archives, 500, C113/71, p. 10.

CHAPTER II

Page 271
"*like presents for a Christmas tree*" Procession described in *Journal de Genève*, 2/7/32.

Page 272
"*some socialists are positively alarmed . . .*" Mary Agnes Hamilton, *Arthur Henderson: A Biography*, 321, 322.

Page 273
This humorless, conscientious Wesleyan . . .   Arnold J. Toynbee, *The Survey of International Affairs*, 1932, 177.

Page 273
"first steps towards . . ." Note from the Allied and Associated Powers to Count Brockdorff-Rantzau, 6/16/1919.

Page 274
"in touch with minor members . . ." A. C. Temperley, *The Whispering Gallery of Europe*, 70.

Page 275
"Our chief refuge . . ." Ibid., 124.

Page 276
"would be of something less . . ." et seq.   London *Times*, 2/3/32.

Page 276
"in eight large printed pages . . ." Le Petit Parisien, 2/3/32.

Page 277
"After the opening bravura . . ." Manchester *Guardian*, 2/10/32.

Page 278
"It is now five weeks . . ." London *Daily Herald*, 3/11/32.

Page 278
"Six weeks of the Conference . . ." Deutsche *Allgemeine Zeitung*, 3/23/32.

Page 279
"an indictment of German good faith . . ." A. C. Temperley, op. cit., 221.

Page 280
"Hitler's mines are beginning . . ." et seq.   William L. Shirer, *The Collapse of the Third Republic*, 161.

Page 281
The United States would not consider . . .   Journal de Genève, 6/21/32.

Page 281
"unmitigated . . ." et seq.   A. C. Temperley, op. cit., 256.

Page 282
"Mr. Stimson knows that . . ." Journal de Genève, 4/17/32.

Page 283
"The German Government . . ." Toynbee, op. cit., 256.

Page 284
"However tolerable such a division . . ." Anthony Eden, *The Eden Memoirs*, 26.

Page 285
The Duke of Plaza-Toro   Gilbert and Sullivan, *The Gondoliers*, Act I:

> In enterprise of martial kind,
>   When there was any fighting,
> He led his regiment from behind—
>   He found it less exciting.
> But when away his regiment ran,

His place was at the fore, O—
That celebrated,
Uncultivated,
Underrated
Nobleman,
The Duke of Plaza-Toro!

Page 286
"*No epigram or witticism* . . ." Randolph Spencer Churchill, *The Rise and Fall of Sir Anthony Eden*, 18.

Page 286
"*Modern communications corrupt* . . ." Geoffrey McDermott, *The Eden Legacy and the Decline of British Diplomacy*, 14.

Page 286
"*were gravely assured* . . ." A. C. Temperley, op. cit., 237.

Page 287
"*At one moment* . . ." Ibid., 240.

Page 289
"*turgid rhetoric* . . ." London *Times*, 5/18/33.

Page 290
"*great admiration for the British* . . ." *et seq.* Thanassis Aghnides on Hitler, in a personal interview with the author.

Page 291
Dollfuss told him that their lives . . . A. C. Temperley, op. cit., 256.

CHAPTER 12

Page 295
"*Notice to the demonstrators* . . ." Shirer, op. cit., 196.

Page 296
"*Monsieur, your name may be illegitimate* . . ." Geneviève Tabouis, *They Called Me Cassandra*, 197.

Page 297
In any case, Barthou's misgivings Jules LaRoche, *La Pologne de Pilsudski: Souvenirs d'une Ambassade, 1926–1935*, 155.

Page 297
The Marshal outlined the problem Ibid., 159.

Page 298
"*believes neither in the League* . . ." Eden, op. cit., 54, 55.

Page 299
"*Yes, like all Germans.*" Ibid., 76.

Page 299
"*The timidity* . . ." Ibid., 88.

Page 301
"Belgium has a wife . . ." Ibid., 94.

Page 301
"There are the Great Powers . . ." Ibid., 95.

Page 302
"A man who has settled down . . ." Toynbee, op. cit., 374.

Page 302
"Frenchman with a load . . ." London *Daily Herald*, 7/7/34.

Page 302
"If the League is only . . ." The New York Times, 12/25/33.

Page 304
"No doubt Litvinov . . ." Eden, op. cit., 98.

Page 307
"No one ever utterly dies . . ." Frederick Lewis Schuman, *Europe on the Eve*, citing Octave Aubert, *Louis Barthou*, 210.

Page 308
Mussolini was at least aware . . . Eden, op. cit., 110.

Page 308
"a socialism of the heart" Yves-Frédéric Jaffré, *Les Derniers Propos de Pierre Laval*, 141.

Page 309
"Regimes follow one another . . ." Geoffrey Warner, *Pierre Laval and the Eclipse of France*, 23, 24, citing Walter E. Edge, *Jerseyman's Journal*, 207.

Page 314
"Apart from its dishonesty . . ." Eden, op. cit., 141.

Page 314
". . . to join with those powers . . ." Ibid., 142, 143.

Page 314
Greetings to Voroshilov . . . Ibid., 141.

Page 314
"I wish you success . . ." Ibid., 162.

Page 315
"The Stresa Conference . . ." F. P. Walters, *A History of the League of Nations*, II, 609.

CHAPTER 13

Page 319
"was the first effective move . . ." Eden, op. cit., 91.

Page 319
Disappointed rancher Toynbee, op. cit., 440 n.

Page 322
" . . . a great act of international justice . . ." King-Hall, op. cit., 605.

Page 329
"*The question of the Saar . . .*" Hitler's speech at Ehrenbreitstein, 8/26/34, reported in *Völkischer Beobachter*, 8/28/34, in Stephen Heald and John Wheeler-Bennett, *Documents on International Affairs*, 1934, 28–30.

Page 329
"*After the plebiscite . . .*" *League of Nations Journal*, March 1934, 325.

Page 329
"*Over there in the Saar . . .*" Ibid., 325 et seq., speech at Treves.

Page 330
"*We could not abandon . . .*" A. C. Temperley, op. cit., 288.

Page 332
". . . *supra-national . . .*" Eden, op. cit., 106.

Page 333
Danzig Much of the material on the final Danzig crisis, including not only the Lester administration but that of Burckhardt as well, comes from Sean Lester's unpublished diary of notes, and from conversations with his daughter, Mrs. Ann Lester Gorski, and Mr. Christophe Gorski.

Page 337
Greiser in Geneva Heald and Wheeler-Bennett, op. cit., 1936, 433; *League of Nations Journal*, 1936, 124, 92nd Session of Council, July 4, 1936.

CHAPTER 14

Page 343
"*gives his instructions . . .*" Baron Pompeo Aloisi, *Journal*, 45.

Page 344
Mussolini on French pact Ibid., 245.

Page 344
Mussolini and Laval Jean-Paul Garnier, "Autour d'un Accord," *La Revue de Paris*, September 1961, 109.

Page 345
The Duce's "incredulous astonishment" Eden, op. cit., 224.

Page 345
"*When a cat is hurried . . .*" Garnier, op. cit., 114.

Page 346
Decision for war Aloisi, op. cit., 253.

Page 346
"*sought only to be agreeable . . .*" Ibid., 274.

Page 347
". . . *set Europe on fire.*" Ibid., 276.

Page 347
Report photographed Samuel John Gurney Hoare, *Nine Troubled Years*, 156, 157.

Page 347
"We will imitate to the letter . . ." Toynbee, op. cit., 1935, 159.

Page 348
"After all, it isn't everyone . . ." Eden, op. cit., 218.

Page 348
"a horrible sexual degenerate . . ." Hoare, op. cit., 153.

Page 348
"uncertain about which side . . ." Ibid., 154.

Page 349
"The English offer . . ." Aloisi, op. cit., 282.

Page 350
"Eden was not opposed . . ." Ibid., 283.

Page 351
"I do not want any agreement . . ." Ibid., 294.

Page 352
Avenol's suggestion Ibid., preface by Mario Toscano of the University of Rome, xiv in Aloisi, op. cit.

Page 352
"You are not a statesman . . ." Hoare, op. cit., 158.

Page 352
"The real danger is Germany . . ." Ibid., 160.

Page 353
Letter to Chamberlain 8/18/35, ibid., 164, 165.

Page 353
"It must have taken you . . ." Ibid., 167.

Page 354
". . . even Litvinov . . ." Aloisi, op. cit., 300.

Page 355
"in their present mood . . ." Hoare, op. cit., 167.

Page 355
"versatile mind" Ibid., 168.

Page 355
". . . I was interesting . . ." Ibid., 169.

Page 356
"amazed . . ." Ibid., 170.

Page 356
"The British have decided . . ." Eden, op. cit., 262.

Page 357
Eden would go along Aloisi, op. cit., 304.

Page 358
Laval's lead Eden, op. cit., 266.

Page 358
"I submit that it would be fatal . . ."　Ibid., 268.

Page 358
"Blackshirts of the Revolution . . ."　Heald and Wheeler-Bennett, op. cit., 1935, II, 170–172.

Page 359
Laval and Eden　Eden, op. cit., 278, 279.

Page 360
"the Italian military campaign . . ."　Toynbee, op. cit., 1935, II, 221 n.

Page 362
"quite favorable . . ."　Aloisi, op. cit., 320.

Page 363
"Have a good leave . . ."　Hoare, op. cit., 178.

Page 363
"Don't worry, I shall not commit you . . ."　Eden, op. cit., 298.

Page 363
"he seemed to have . . ."　Hoare, op. cit., 179.

Page 364
"It may be true that . . ."　London *Times*, 12/18/35.

Page 365
"I was a newcomer . . ."　Duff Cooper, op. cit., 193.

Page 365
"Are all your preparations for war . . . ?"　Ibid., 194.

Page 365
"I wish I were dead."　Eden, op. cit., 309.

Page 366
"I guess it will have to be you." et seq.　Ibid., 316, 317.

Page 366
"As for the other sanctions . . ."　Aloisi, op. cit., 343.

Page 367
"Baron Aloisi needs petrol . . ."　Ibid., 344.

Page 368
"Hitler struck his adversary . . ."　André François-Poncet, *The Fateful Years*, 193, quoted in Shirer, *The Collapse of the Third Republic*, 261.

Page 368
"Hitler has torn . . ."　Shirer, *The Collapse of the Third Republic*, 265.

Page 369
"And so they are"　Harold Nicolson, *Diaries and Letters, 1930–1939*, 245.

Page 371
"surpassed the French Ministers . . ."　Eden, op. cit., 379.

Page 372
Open door　London *Daily Mail*, 5/6/36, in Heald and Wheeler-Bennett, op. cit., 1935, II, 464.

Page 372
"*The Italians want us to eat* . . ." Aloisi, op. cit., 384.

Page 373
"*I did it deliberately* . . ." Eden, op. cit., 385, citing Keith Feiling, *The Life of Neville Chamberlain*. London, 1945.

Page 376
". . . *Banquo's ghost* . . ." Schuman, op. cit., 238.

CHAPTER 15

Page 381
"*Dinner with the 'pirates'* . . ." Count Galeazzo Ciano, *Ciano's Diplomatic Papers*, March 12, 1938, 145.

Page 381
"*If there's another attack* . . ." Eden, op. cit., 469.

Page 382
"*Count Ciano lunched with me* . . ." Ibid., 579.

Page 383
". . . *understand fascism* . . ." Ciano, op. cit., 323.

Page 383
"*In the evening* . . ." Ibid., 137, 138.

Page 383
"*All this is very romantic*" Ibid., 165.

Page 384
"*It would not be elegant* . . ." Ibid., 168.

Page 384
"*The best that can be said* . . ." London *Times*, 5/8/38.

Page 385
"*if the League has been broken* . . ." Ibid., 5/10/38.

Page 387
". . . *far from having been conquered* . . ." Ibid., 5/12/38.

Page 390
". . . *Ethiopian question was buried.*" Ciano, op. cit., 184.

Page 390
"*those private conferences* . . ." Julio Alvarez del Vayo, *Freedom's Battle*, 42.

Page 390
"*the imperiling of a draft* . . ." Ibid., 43.

Page 392
"*Is the position hopeless* . . . ?" Schuman, op. cit., 396, citing London *Times*, 9/24/38.

Page 393
"*Those children* . . ." Nicolson, *Diaries and Letters, 1930–1939*, 362.

Page 393
"*When a nation adores animals* . . ." Ciano, op. cit., 264.

Page 393
"*This is the way* . . ." Ibid., 267.

Page 394
"*This knight of peace* . . ." London *Times*, 10/1/38.

Page 394
"*What Chamberlain has done* . . ." Sean Lester's diary, 10/8/38, 259, 260.

Page 396
"*Every State which has sent* . . ." London *Times*, 12/12/39.

Page 397
"*absurd decision* . . ." Ibid., 12/16/39.

Page 398
"*It is clear that some discretion* . . ." Avenol Papers, League of Nations Archives.

Page 398
"*The dearth of leadership* . . ." Rovine, op. cit., 176, citing Sweetser Papers.

Page 398
". . . *my heels for dust*" Letter from Sean Lester to Christophe Gorski (son-in-law), dated Recess, Connemara, Ireland, June 25, 1958.

Page 399
"*I would like to go, too* . . ." Ibid.

Page 399
"*The German troops are marching* . . ." Sean Lester diary, 436.

Page 399
"*including Germany and Italy*" Sean Lester diary, June 25, 1940, 469.

Page 400
Letter from Thanassis Aghnides to Sean Lester Dated Crans (Switzerland), August 7, 1940, Lester diary, 527, 528.

Page 400
"*his empty chair* . . ." Lester diary, 569.

Page 400
". . . *my main offense* . . ." Letter from Lester to Sweetser, Rovine, op. cit., 179, from Sweetser Papers.

Page 401
Alexander Loveday's trip to the United States Letter from Loveday to Lester, dated Lisbon, August 12, 1940, Lester diary, 540 et seq.

Page 405
". . . *brotherhood is a fable* . . ." Schuman, op. cit., 153, citing *Popolo d'Italia*, March 7, 1920.

A BIBLIOGRAPHY

On the third floor of the library of the Palais des Nations in Geneva are to be found the public records of the League of Nations: the proceedings, journals, summaries, verbatim reports of the Assembly, of its committees, of the Council, of the various commissions, and of related agencies. Therein lies one part of the story of the League of Nations.

On another level (the ground floor, to be exact) are the private papers of the League: the letters, memoranda (many still bearing in faded ink the stamp of secrecy), notes, minutes, complaints, petitions from refugees, questions from school children, expense accounts, budgets, and luminous projects for lasting peace. Here are mines yielding both historical insights and footnotes of trivia; diplomacy, gossip, and memorabilia. Here also are file drawers of cartoons, photographs, caricatures, conveying the flavor of the times.

This book, as must any work on the League, drew heavily on both floors of the Library as well as on that compact and well-organized little museum on the second floor, where the trophies of the League's victories are enshrined.

Additional material comes from the archives of the Quai d'Orsay, the Public Records Office in London, and the documents at the Library of Congress in Washington. An exhaustive history—to which title this book makes no claim—might have drawn on similar files in Rome, Tokyo, Berlin, Madrid, and Moscow, but of these the author cannot speak with any personal knowledge.

Volumes of published diplomatic documents were indispensable to the writing of this work: for example, the U.S. State Department's *Papers Relating to the Foreign Relations of the United States* and its *Documents on German Foreign Policy;* the annuals such as *U.S. and World Affairs,* edited by Walter Lippmann with the aid of the research staff of the Council on Foreign Relations; and *The Survey of International Affairs,* written in some years by

Arnold J. Toynbee and in others by H. Beeley for the Royal Institute of Foreign Affairs. Also important were the *Documents on International Affairs*, collected by Stephen Heald and John Wheeler-Bennett; and the *Documents on British Foreign Policy*. *Le Livre Jaune Français* provided some information on the latter years.

The running chronicle of the period in the newspapers and magazines of the world offered clues to the world's hopes and fears in each crisis and often gave a sense of life to the bare bones of the official record. Publications of the League of Nations Societies also lent a fresh aspect to the story, as did pamphlets, pro and con, on the League—for example, the folksy diatribe *League of Nation Joe—The Backwoods Farmer from the Ohio Hills*, by Lewis P. Showalter.

The writer was fortunate also to be able to draw on such unpublished works as Sean Lester's revealing and sensitive diary and the valuable paper by David J. Lu of the Center for Japanese Studies at Bucknell University, delivered at the 1969 annual meeting of the Association for Asian Studies.

Personal interviews with some of those who participated in League affairs yielded invaluable guidance and insight.

The following is a partial list of published memoirs, diaries, biographies, autobiographies, documentary collections, and secondary sources which the author found valuable, interesting, or, most often, both.

ALOISI, Baron Pompeo. *Journal (25 Juillet, 1932–14 Juin, 1936)*, translated from the Italian by Maurice Vaussard, Paris, 1957.

ALVAR, M. F. *La Gran Obra: Palabras de Salvador de Madariaga*, Madrid, 1936.

AMES, Sir H. B. *Seven Years with the League of Nations*, lectures at Amherst, 1927.

ANGELL, Norman. *The Great Illusion*, London, 1913.

Association for International Conciliation. *Taft, Root and U.S. Criticism: U.S. Attitudes to the Peace Conference*, Union League Club, 1919.

BADEN, Prince Max von. *The Memoirs of Prince Max von Baden*, authorized translation by W. M. Calder and C. W. H. Sutton, London, 1928.

BAKER, Ray Stannard. *Woodrow Wilson and World Settlement*, New York, 1922.

BARROS, James. *Betrayal from Within*, New Haven, 1969.

BEAVERBROOK, Lord. *The Decline and Fall of Lloyd George*, London, 1963.

BENEŠ, Edward. *L'Avenir de la Société des Nations*, Prague, 1925.

BIRDSALL, Paul. *Versailles Twenty Years After*, New York, 1941.

BONO, General Emilio de. *Anno XIV: The Conquest of an Empire*, London, 1937.

BONSAL, Stephen. *Suitors and Supplicants*, New York, 1946.

———. *Unfinished Business*, London, 1944.

BOURGEOIS, Léon. *Le Traité de Paix de Versailles*, Paris, 1919.

Breycha-Vauthier, Arthur Carl. *Sean Lester,* U.N. Special, Vol. 9, No. 21, July 1959.

Broué, Pierre. *Révolution en Allemagne: 1917–1923,* Paris, 1971.

Cecil, Lord Robert Edgar Algernon. *A Great Experiment: An Autobiography,* London, 1941.

Churchill, Randolph Spencer. *The Rise and Fall of Sir Anthony Eden,* London, 1959.

Ciano, Count Galeazzo. *Journal Politique, 1937–1938,* translated by Jean Imbert and André Mauge, Paris, 1949.

———. *Ciano's Diplomatic Papers,* edited by Malcolm Muggeridge, London, 1948.

Clemenceau, Georges. *Grandeurs et Misères d'une Victoire,* Paris, 1930.

———. *In the Evening of My Thought,* translated by Charles Miner Thompson and John Heard, Jr., New York and London, 1929.

Cooper, Duff (Viscount Norwich). *Old Men Forget: An Autobiography,* London, 1953.

Cranston, Alan. *The Killing of the Peace,* New York, 1945.

Creel, George. *The War, the World and Wilson,* New York, 1920.

Daniels, Josephus. *The Wilson Era: Years of War and After—1917–1923,* Chapel Hill, N.C., 1946.

———. *The Life of Woodrow Wilson,* Chicago and London, 1924.

Dell, Robert. *The Geneva Racket: 1920–1939,* London, 1941.

Del Vayo, Julio Alvarez. *Freedom's Battle,* translated by Eileen E. Brooks, New York, 1940.

Dillon, E. J. *The Inside Story of the Peace Conference,* New York, 1920.

Duroselle, J. B. *Histoire Diplomatique de 1919 à Nos Jours,* Paris, 1971.

Eden, Anthony. *The Eden Memoirs,* London, 1962.

Elian, George. *The International Court of Justice,* Leyden, 1971.

Ferrell, Robert H. *Peace in Their Time: The Origin of the Kellogg-Briand Pact,* New Haven, 1952.

Fleming, Denna Frank. *The United States and the League of Nations, 1918–1920,* New York, 1932.

Floto, Inga, *Colonel House in Paris,* translated by Pauline M. Katborg, Aarhus, 1973.

Foley, Hamilton, *Woodrow Wilson's Case for the League of Nations,* New York, 1969.

François-Poncet, André. *The Fateful Years: Memoirs of a French Ambassador in Berlin, 1931–1938,* New York, 1949.

Freud, Sigmund, and William C. Bullitt. *Thomas Woodrow Wilson: A Psychological Study,* Boston, 1966, and London, 1967.

Garnier, Jean-Paul. "Autour d'un Accord," *La Revue de Paris,* September 1961, 102 et seq.

————. *La Tragédie de Dantzig*, Paris, 1935.

GEORGE, Alexander L. and Juliette L. *Woodrow Wilson and Colonel House: A Personality Study*, New York, 1956.

GIBBONS, Herbert Adams. *Venizelos*, Boston, 1922.

GOEBBELS, Paul Joseph. *The Goebbels Diaries, 1942–1943*, edited by Louis P. Lochner, New York, 1948.

GOLDBERG, George, *The Peace to End Peace: The Paris Peace Conference of 1919*, New York, 1969.

GREW, Joseph C. *Ten Years in Japan, 1932–1942*, New York, 1944.

HAMILTON, Mary Agnes. *Arthur Henderson: A Biography*, London, 1938.

HEALD, Stephen, and John WHEELER-BENNETT. *Documents on International Affairs*, London, annual.

HENDRICK, Burton Jesse. *The Earlier Life and Letters of Walter H. Page: The Training of an American*, London, 1928.

————. *The Life and Letters of Walter H. Page*, New York, 1922–25.

HERTLING, Karl Graf von. *Ein Jahr in der Reichskanzlei*, Berlin, 1919.

HOARE, Samuel John Gurney (1st Viscount Templewood). *Nine Troubled Years*, London, 1954.

HOUSE, Edward Mandell. *Philip Dru, Administrator: A Story of Tomorrow, 1920–1935* (no by-line appears on the title page), New York, 1912, reprinted 1920.

————. *The Intimate Papers of Colonel House*, edited by Charles Seymour, London, 1926–28.

———— with Charles SEYMOUR, editors. *What Really Happened at Paris: The Story of the Peace Conference, 1918–1919*, New York, 1921.

HOWARD-ELLIS, Charles. *Origin, Structure and Workings of the League of Nations—1928*, New York and London, 1928.

HØYER, Liv Nansen. *Nansen: A Family Portrait by His Daughter*, New York, 1957.

HSIA, Chi-Feng. *China and the League and My Experiences in the Secretariat*, Shanghai, 1928.

International Labour Office. *International Labour Organization: The First Decade*, London, 1931.

JAFFRÉ, Yves-Frédéric. *Les Derniers Propos de Pierre Laval*, Paris, 1953.

KELEN, Emery. *Peace in Their Time: Men Who Led Us In and Out of War—1914–1945*, New York, 1963.

KENNAN, George F. *American Diplomacy, 1900–1950*, Charles R. Walgreen Foundation Lectures, Chicago, New York and Toronto, 1951.

KEYNES, John Maynard. *The Economic Consequences of Peace*, New York, 1920.

KING-HALL, Stephen. *Our Own Times—1913–1938: A Political and Economic Survey*, London, 1938.

LANDAU, Rom. *Pilsudski: Hero of Poland,* translated by Geoffrey Dunlop, London, 1930.

LANSING, Robert. *Lansing Papers—1914–1920: United States Department of State Papers Relating to Foreign Relations,* Vols. I, II.

LAROCHE, Jules. *La Pologne de Pilsudski: Souvenirs d'une Ambassade, 1926–1935,* Paris, 1953.

LAWRENCE, David. *The True Story of Woodrow Wilson,* London and New York, 1924.

LEONHARDT, Hans L. *The Nazi Conquest of Danzig,* Chicago, 1942.

LLOYD-GEORGE, David. *The Truth about the Peace Treaties,* London, 1938.

———. *War Memoirs,* London, 1933–36.

LOCKHART, R. H. Bruce. *Memoirs of a British Agent,* London, 1937.

LUCKAU, Alma. *The German Delegation at the Peace Conference,* New York, 1941.

LUDENDORFF, General Erich von. *My War Memories, 1914–1918,* London, 1919.

LUDWIG, Emil. *Leaders of Europe,* London, 1934.

MANTOUX, Etienne. *The Carthaginian Peace or the Economic Consequences of Mr. Keynes,* London, Toronto, and New York, 1946.

MANTOUX, Paul. *Les Délibérations du Conseil des Quatres—24 Mars–28 Juin, 1919,* Edition du Centre National de la Recherche Scientifique, Paris, 1955.

MARTIN, Georges-Henri. "En Souvenir de Sean Lester: La Vigile de la Paix," *Tribune de Genève,* 10/2/59.

MAURICE, Sir Frederick. *The Armistice of 1918,* London, 1943.

McADOO, Eleanor Randolph Wilson. *The Woodrow Wilsons,* New York, 1937.

McDERMOTT, Geoffrey. *The Eden Legacy and the Decline of British Diplomacy,* London, 1969.

MILLER, David Hunter. *The Geneva Protocol,* New York, 1925.

———. *The Drafting of the Covenant,* New York, 1928.

MORDACQ, General Jean-Henri. *L'Armistice du 11 Novembre, 1918,* Paris, 1937.

MORLEY, Felix. *Society of Nations: Its Organization and Constitutional Development,* Washington, 1932.

MURRAY, Dr. Gilbert. *Annual Memorial Lecture, April, 1955: The League of Nations Movement; Some Recollections of the Early Days,* London, 1955.

———. *From the League to UN,* London, 1948.

NICOLSON, Harold. *Diaries and Letters, 1930–1939,* London, 1966.

———. *Peacemaking, 1919,* London, 1933.

NOEL-BAKER, Philip. *Recovery,* published by Economics and Disarmament Information Committee, Vol. I, No. 11, November 10, 1973.

NOWAK, Karl Friedrich. *The Collapse of Central Europe,* New York, 1924.

PHELAN, E. J. *"Yes and Albert Thomas,"* London, 1936.

REYNOLDS, E. E. *Nansen,* London, 1932.

ROVINE, Arthur W. *The First Fifty Years: The Secretary-General in World Politics, 1920–1970*, Leyden, 1970.

SCHUMAN, Frederick Lewis. *Europe on the Eve: The Crisis of Diplomacy, 1933–1939*, New York, 1939.

SCHWEBEL, Stephen W. *The Secretary-General of the United Nations*, Cambridge, Mass., 1932.

SELBY, Sir Walford, *Diplomatic Twilight, 1940*, London, 1953.

SEYMOUR, Charles. *The Intimate Papers of Colonel House*, London and New York, 1926–28.

SHARTLE, Samuel G. *Spa, Versailles, Munich: An Account of the Armistice Committee*, Philadelphia, 1941.

SHIRER, William L. *The Collapse of the Third Republic: An Inquiry into the Fall of France in 1940*, New York, 1969.

———. *The Rise and Fall of the Third Reich*, New York, 1960.

SHOTWELL, James Thomson. *At the Paris Peace Conference*, New York, 1937.

SLOCOMBE, George. *A Mirror to Geneva*, Toronto and London, 1937.

SMITH, Gene. *When the Cheering Stopped*, London, 1964.

STEED, H. W. *Through Thirty Years—1892–1922: A Personal Narrative*, London, 1924.

STEER, George. *Caesar in Abyssinia*, Boston, 1937.

STEFFENS, Lincoln. *The Letters of Lincoln Steffens*, New York, 1938.

STEVENSON, Frances. *Lloyd George: A Diary*, London, 1971.

STIMSON, Henry B. *The Far East Crisis*, New York, 1936.

STRESEMANN, Gustav. *Les Papiers de Stresemann*, Paris, 1932.

SUAREZ, Georges. *Briand*, Paris, 1952.

———. *Les Hommes Malades de la Paix*, Paris, 1933.

SZEMBEK, Jean. *Journal—1933–1939*, Paris, 1952.

TABOUIS, Geneviève. *They Called Me Cassandra*, New York, 1942.

———. *Perfidious Albion: Entente Cordiale*, London, 1938.

TARDIEU, André. *Devant l'Obstacle: L'Amérique et Nous*, Paris, 1927.

———. *The Truth About the Treaty*, London and Indianapolis, 1921.

TAYLOR, A. J. P. *Europe: Grandeur and Decline*, London, 1969.

———. *The Origins of the Second World War*, London, 1961, and New York, 1964.

TEMPERLEY, A. C. *The Whispering Gallery of Europe*, London, 1938.

TEMPERLEY, H. W. V. *A History of the Peace Conference of Paris*, London, 1920.

THORNE, Christopher. *The Limits of Foreign Policy: The West, the League and the Far Eastern Crisis, 1931–1933*, London, 1972.

TUMULTY, Joseph P. *Woodrow Wilson, As I Knew Him*, New York, 1921.

VALLENTIN, Antonina. *Stresemann*, London, 1931.

VIERECK, George Sylvester. *The Strangest Friendship in History: Woodrow Wilson and Colonel House*, New York, 1932.

WALTERS, F. P. *A History of the League of Nations*, London, 1952.

WARNER, Geoffrey. *Pierre Laval and the Eclipse of France*, London, 1968.

WATT, Richard M. *The Kings Depart: The Tragedy of Germany; Versailles and the German Revolution*, New York, 1968.

WHEELER-BENNETT, John W. *The Disarmament Deadlock*, London, 1934.

WHELAN, Frederick Leman. *Geneva, 1932: An Account of the 13th Assembly of the League of Nations*, London, 1932.

WHITAKER, John T. *And Fear Came*, New York, 1936.

WHITE, Freda. *Geneva, 1933*, London, 1933.

WHITE, William Allan. *Woodrow Wilson: The Man, His Times and His Task*, Boston and New York, 1924.

WILLOUGHBY, W. W. *The Sino-Japanese Controversy and the League of Nations*, London, 1968.

WILSON, Edith Bolling. *My Memoir*, New York, 1939.

WILSON, Sir Henry. *Journal du Maréchal Sir Henry Wilson*, Paris, 1929.

WILSON, Hugh R. *Diplomat Between Wars*, New York and Toronto, 1941.

YOUNG, Kenneth. *Arthur James Balfour*, London, 1963.

ZILLIACUS, Konni. *Why the League Has Failed*, by Vigilantes (pseudonym of Zilliacus), London, 1938.

———. *The Origin, Structure and Workings of the League of Nations*, London, 1928.

The following abbreviations have been used: L. of N. (League of Nations), WW I (World War I), WW II (World War II).

A NOTE ABOUT THE AUTHOR

Elmer Bendiner was born in Pittsburgh in 1916 and was educated at the City College of New York. After three years as a newspaper reporter he joined the United States Air Force at the onset of World War Two, becoming a navigator; he received the Distinguished Flying Cross, the Air Medal, and a Purple Heart. An experienced journalist, he has contributed to many publications, including *Esquire, The New York Times Magazine,* and *The Nation,* as well as a number of medical and scientific journals. His first book, *The Bowery Man,* was published in 1962. Mr. Bendiner is married, has two daughters, and lives in Woodstock, New York.

A NOTE ON THE TYPE

This book was set on the Linotype in Janson, a recutting made direct from type cast from matrices long thought to have been made by the Dutchman Anton Janson, who was a practicing type founder in Leipzig during the years 1668–87. However, it has been conclusively demonstrated that these types are actually the work of Nicholas Kis (1650–1702), a Hungarian, who most probably learned his trade from the master Dutch type founder Dirk Voskens. The type is an excellent example of the influential and sturdy Dutch types that prevailed in England up to the time William Caslon developed his own incomparable designs from them.

The book was composed, printed, and bound by American Book–Stratford Press, Inc., New York, New York. Typography and binding design by Margaret Wagner.